Exploring Artificial Intelligence
in the
New Millennium

Exploring Artificial Intelligence

in the

New Millennium

Edited by

Gerhard Lakemeyer

Reinisch-Wesfälische Technische Hochscule Aachen

Bernhard Nebel

Albert-Ludwigs-Universität

MORGAN KAUFMANN PUBLISHERS

AN IMPRINT OF ELSEVIER SCIENCE

AMSTERDAM   BOSTON   LONDON   NEW YORK
OXFORD   PARIS   SAN DIEGO   SAN FRANCISCO
SINGAPORE   SYDNEY   TOKYO

Senior Editor   Denise E. M. Penrose
Assistant Publishing Services Manager   Edward Wade
Senior Production Editor   Cheri Palmer
Production Coordinator   Mei Levenson
Editorial Coordinator   Emilia Thiuri
Cover Design   Yvo Riezebos Design
Cover Image   ©Istvan Orosz/Represented by the Marlena Agency
Pasteup/Additional Composition   Susan M. Sheldrake
Copyeditor   Sharilyn Hovind
Proofreader   Ann Wood
Printer   Edwards Brothers, Inc.

This book was author typeset using LaTeX.

Designations used by companies to distinguish their products are often claimed as trademarks or registered trademarks. In all instances in which Morgan Kaufmann Publishers is aware of a claim, the product names appear in initial capital or all capital letters. Readers, however, should contact the appropriate companies for more complete information regarding trademarks and registration.

Morgan Kaufmann Publishers
An Imprint of Elsevier Science
340 Pine Street, Sixth Floor
San Francisco, CA 94104-3205, USA
www.mkp.com

Library of Congress Control Number: 2002104301

ISBN: 1-55860-811-7

This book is printed on acid-free paper.

Contents

vi   Contents

Preface

If you want to get an idea of where artificial intelligence (AI) stands at the beginning of the new millennium, you might have a hard time finding it. There are so many subareas in AI—with their own conferences and journals—that it is hard to keep track of what is going on. For the International Joint Conference on Artificial Intelligence 2001 (IJCAI-01), it was decided to counter this fragmentation of the field by bringing together excellent research from different subareas. Thirteen distinguished recent papers from international conferences on robotics, vision, knowledge representation, machine learning, planning, and other areas were selected to be presented again at IJCAI-01. These papers either received "best paper" awards at the respective conferences or were nominated as outstanding work by the respective program chairs, committee members, or the IJCAI program committee members.

In addition to the presentation at the conference, the authors were asked to revise and extend their papers for this book. In order to make the book as accessible as possible to a wide range of people interested in AI, the authors broadened the scope of their presentations so that they not only focus on particular results, but also introduce the individual research area, its history, milestones, open issues, and so on. To ensure the highest standards, each paper was reviewed by an eminent scholar in the respective subarea, as well as by two researchers not familiar with the field.

This book does not provide a comprehensive overview of AI. Instead, it presents highlights of some of the best AI has to offer at the start of the new millennium. As such, the book is intended for researchers who would like to get a sense of where AI research stands today. It is also intended for graduate students in AI who are looking for inspiration as to which area to pursue their research. Moreover, the papers provide enough background material and pointers to related work to make them suitable for a seminar course. The reader is expected to have basic knowledge of AI at the level of an introductory course to the field. To access some of the papers, it will be helpful to know the basics of probability theory, and for others, some familiarity with mathematical logic is necessary. However, even without a mathematical background, the reader should find much of this volume accessible and, hopefully, inspiring.

The chapters themselves are puposefully not ordered in any particular way, in recognition of the fact that each of the represented areas stands on its own. However, this is not to say that there are no connections between the chapters—far from it. Here we mention but a few and invite the reader to discover more connections on their journey through this volume. From a methodological point of view, it is interesting to note that seven chapters (1, 3, 5, 8, 9, 12, and 13) and hence a majority use a statistical approach, in contrast to just four (4, 6, 10, and 11) that are logic based. To be fair, at least two of the seven (3 and 12) also include symbolic components. (Given the editors' logicist backgrounds, you should trust that this seeming imbalance is not due to any bias on our part!) Four chapters are concerned with machine learning, from theoretical concerns (9) to applications in natural language understanding (3) and multi-agent systems (2), to practical applications in chip manufacturing. Chapters 6 and 11 address issues regarding the complexity of reasoning, an important subarea of knowledge representation. Lastly, Chapters 2 and 7 both deal with multi-agent systems, which perhaps reflects the current growing interest in this field of AI.

Let us now briefly highlight the topics covered in this book, in the order in which they appear:

Robotics: In Chapter 1, Sebastian Thrun gives an overview of how mobile robots acquire a spatial representation of their environment, with a focus on indoor scenarios. It turns out that virtually all state-of-the-art approaches to robotic mapping are probabilistic in nature.

Multi-Agent Systems: In Chapter 2, Bruce Blumberg considers the problem of building synthetic characters that are able to learn useful skills. The work is directly inspired by the way dogs learn and are trained, and the insights gained are combined with state-of-the-art machine learning techniques.

Natural Language Understanding: In Chapter 3, Daniel Gildea and Daniel Jurafsky propose a statistical method to identifying the semantic roles of the constituents of a sentence, like speaker or topic. By using a frame-based representation, the system is able to assign such roles with remarkable accuracy.

Planning: In Chapter 4, Derek Long and Maria Fox consider the problem of automatically extracting domain constraints for planning purposes. The motivation is that domain constraints can drastically reduce the search space of a planner, yet it is often difficult to generate them manually.

Vision: In Chapter 5, David J. Fleet et al. consider the problem of visual motion analysis, in particular with respect to occlusion boundaries. The authors apply probabilistic techniques like Bayesian inference and particle filtering, which have been found very useful in quite different areas, such as robotics (see also Chapter 1).

Knowledge Representation: In Chapter 6, Frank Wolter and Michael Zakharyaschev are concerned with reasoning effectively about both time and space, which so far had been studied only separately. They explore a number of different ways of creating qualitative spatiotemporal calculi, making use of results achieved in the area of modal logics.

AI and Education: In Chapter 7, Jeff Rickel and W. Lewis Johnson consider the use of virtual humans in team training scenarios, where, for example, not all members of a team can be present at the same time. The system allows students to learn their roles in a team as well as how to coordinate with other teammates.

Reasoning under Uncertainty: In Chapter 8, Jonathan Yedidia et al. look at foundational issues of reasoning under uncertainty. In particular, they introduce a form of belief propagation, which can be viewed as a generalization of many existing probabilistic inference methods from AI, but also from other areas, like statistical physics.

Computational Learning Theory: In Chapter 9, David McAllester and Robert E. Schapire provide new insights into the basic problem of learning a language model. They introduce so-called *leave-one-out estimators* to help explain why existing statistical language models like those used in speech recognition work so well.

Theorem Proving: In Chapter 10, Peter Baumgartner generalizes a theorem-proving technique, which has been used very successfully in propositional logic, to the first-order case. Among other things, the new method outperforms other techniques on an important class of first-order formulas.

Constraint Satisfaction: In Chapter 11, David Cohen et al. consider complexity issues in constraint satisfaction, a popular problem-solving paradigm. The authors show how to take tractable classes of constraint solvers and synthesize new classes from them that are both tractable and more expressive.

Information Retrieval: In Chapter 12, Jaana Kekäläinen and Kalervo Järvelin address the question of finding the most relevant documents for a given query in text-based retrieval. They propose two new measures of relevance and demonstrate the payoff of expanding user queries based on a conceptual model of the domain.

Data Mining: In Chapter 13, Tony Fountain et al. apply machine learning techniques to reduce the cost of functional testing of integrated circuits during manufacturing. With the help of a probabilistic model of failure patterns learned from existing data, a decision-theoretic policy is generated that guides and optimizes the testing process.

We believe all of the authors did a remarkable job in presenting their research areas and their particular results. We thank them, and also thank the reviewers for their invaluable feedback, which helped improve the papers significantly. Gerhard Lakemeyer would like to thank Alexander Ferrein for his help with LaTeX. Finally, we thank the Morgan Kaufmann team, who made this book possible. In particular, Denise Penrose deserves special mention. Without her, it would have been impossible to create this book.

Gerhard Lakemeyer and Bernhard Nebel
Aachen and Freiburg, Germany, February 2002

Robotic Mapping: A Survey

Sebastian Thrun
School of Computer Science
Carnegie Mellon University
www.cs.cmu.edu/~thrun

Abstract

This article provides a comprehensive introduction into the field of robotic mapping, with a focus on indoor mapping. It describes and compares various probabilistic techniques, as they are presently being applied to a vast array of mobile robot mapping problems. The history of robotic mapping is also detailed, along with an extensive list of open research problems.

1   INTRODUCTION

Robotic mapping has been a highly active research area in robotics and AI for at least two decades. Robotic mapping addresses the problem of acquiring spatial models of physical environments through mobile robots. The mapping problem is generally regarded as one of the most important problems in the pursuit of building truly autonomous mobile robots. Despite significant progress in this area, it still poses great challenges. At present, we have robust methods for mapping environments that are static, structured, and of limited size. Mapping unstructured, dynamic, or large-scale environments remains largely an open research problem.

This article attempts to provide a comprehensive overview of the state of the art in robotic mapping, with a focus on indoor environments. Virtually all state-of-the-art robotic mapping algorithms are probabilistic. Some algorithms are incremental, and hence can be run in real time, whereas others require multiple passes through the data. Some algorithms require exact pose information to build a map, whereas others can do so using odometry measurements. Some algorithms are equipped to handle correspondence problems between data recorded at different points in time, whereas others require features to carry signatures that make them uniquely identifiable.

When writing this article, I tried to keep the level of mathematics at a minimum, focusing instead on the intuition behind the different techniques. However, some mathematical notation was deemed necessary to communicate the basic concepts in a crisp way. The serious reader is invited to read some of the articles referenced in this chapter, which discuss many of the ideas presented here in more depth.

2 HISTORICAL OVERVIEW

In the 1980s and early 1990s, the field of mapping was widely divided into metric and topological approaches: metric maps capture the geometric properties of the environment, whereas topological maps describe the connectivity of different places. An early representative of the former approach was Elfes and Moravec's important *occupancy grid-mapping algorithm* (Elfes 1987; Elfes 1989; Moravec 1988), which represents maps by fine-grained grids that model the occupied and free space of an environment. This approach has been used in a great number of robotic systems, such as (Borenstein and Koren. 1991; Buhmann et al. 1995; Burgard et al. 1999; Guzzoni et al. 1997; Schneider 1994; Thrun et al. 2000; Yamauchi and Langley 1997; Yamauchi et al. 1998). An alternative metric mapping algorithm was proposed by Chatila and Laumond (Chatila and Laumond 1985), using sets of polyhedra to describe the geometry of environments. Examples of topological approaches include the work by Matarić (Matarić 1990), Kuipers (Kuipers and Byun 1991), and many others (Choset 1996; Choset and Burdick 1996; Engelson and McDermott 1992; Kortenkamp and Weymouth 1994; Pierce and Kuipers 1994; Shatkay 1998; Shatkay and Kaelbling 1997; Torrance 1994; Yamauchi and Beer 1996; Zimmer 1996). Topological maps represent environments as a list of significant places that are connected via arcs. Arcs are usually annotated with information on how to navigate from one place to another. However, the distinction between metric and topological approaches has always been fuzzy, since virtually all working topological approaches rely on geometric information. In practice, metric maps are finer grained than topological ones. Higher resolution comes at a computational price, but it helps to solve various hard problems, such as the correspondence problem discussed further below.

Historically, a second taxonomy of mapping algorithms is *world-centric* versus robot-centric. World-centric maps are represented in a global coordinate space. The entities in the map do not carry information about the sensor measurements that led to their discovery. Robot-centric maps, in contrast, are described in measurement space. They describe the sensor measurements a robot would receive at different locations. At first glance, robot-centric maps might appear easier to build, since no "translation" of robot measurements into world coordinates is needed. However, robot-centric maps suffer two disadvantages. First, it is often difficult to extrapolate from individual measurements to measurements at nearby, unexplored places—an extrapolation that is typically straightforward in world-centric approaches. Put differently, there is usually no obvious geometry in measurement space that would allow for such extrapolation. Second, if different places look alike, robot-centric approaches often face difficulties to disambiguate them, again due to the lack of an obvious geometry in measurement space. For these reasons, the dominant approaches to date generate world-centric maps.

Since the 1990s, the field of robotic mapping has been dominated by probabilistic techniques. A series of seminal papers by Smith, Self, and Cheeseman (Smith and Cheeseman 1985; Smith, Self, and Cheeseman 1990) introduced a powerful statistical framework for simultaneously solving the mapping problem and the induced problem of localizing the robot relative to its growing map. Since then, robotic mapping has commonly been referred to as *simultaneous localization and mapping*, or *SLAM* (Dissanayake et al. 2000; Durrant-Whyte et al. 2001), and *concurrent mapping and localization*, or *CML* (Leonard and Feder 1999; Thrun, Fox, and Burgard 1998), respectively.

One family of probabilistic approaches employ Kalman filters to estimate the map and the robot location (Castellanos and Tardós 2000; Csorba 1997; Dissanayake et al. 2001; Guivant and Nebot 2001; Leonard et al. 1992; Newman 2000; Williams et al. 2001). The resulting maps usually describe the location of landmarks, or significant features in the environment, although recent extensions exist that represent environments by large numbers of raw range measurements (Lu and Milios 1997). An alternative family of algorithms (Dellaert et al. 2000; Shatkay 1998; Shatkay and Kaelbling 1997; Thrun 2001c; Thrun et al. 1998) is based on Dempster's *expectation maximization* algorithm (Dempster, Laird, and Rubin 1977; McLachlan and Krishnan 1997). These approaches specifically address the *correspondence problem* in mapping, which is the problem of determining whether sensor measurements recorded at different points in time correspond to the same physical entity in the real world. A third family of probabilistic techniques seek to identify *objects* in the environment, which may correspond to ceilings, walls (Iocchi et al. 2000; Liu et al. 2001; Martin and Thrun 2002), doors that might be open or closed (Avots et al. 2002), or furniture and objects that move (Biswas et al. 2002; Schneider 1994). Many of these techniques have counterparts in the computer vision and photogrammetry literature—a connection that is still somewhat underexploited (Allen and Stamos 2000; Bajcsy et al. 2000; Becker and Bove 1995; Cheng et al. 2000; Debevec et al. 1996; Hakim and Boulanger 1997; Shum et al. 1998).

Robot exploration in the context of mapping has also been studied extensively. Today's approaches are usually greedy—that is, they chose control by greedily maximizing information gain (Burgard et al. 2000; Choset 1996; Simmons et al. 2000; Yamauchi and Beer 1996), sometimes under consideration of safety constraints (Gonzalez-Banos and Latombe 2002). However, the topic of robot exploration is beyond the scope of this article, and hence will not be addressed further.

3   THE ROBOTIC MAPPING PROBLEM

The problem of robotic mapping is that of acquiring a spatial model of a robot's environment. Maps are commonly used for robot navigation (e.g., localization) (Borenstein, Everett, and Feng 1996; Kortenkamp, Bonasso, and Murphy 1998). To acquire a map, a robot must possess sensors that enable it to perceive the outside world. Sensors commonly brought to bear for this task include cameras, range finders using sonar, laser, and infrared technology, radar, tactile sensors, compasses, and GPS. However, all of these sensors are subject to errors, often referred to as *measurement noise*. More important, most robot sensors are subject to strict range limitations. For example, light and sound cannot penetrate walls. These range limitations make it necessary for a robot to navigate through its environment when building a map. The motion commands (controls) issued during environment exploration carry important information for building maps, namely, the locations at which different sensor measurements were taken. Robot motion is also subject to errors, and the controls alone are therefore insufficient to determine a robot's pose (location and orientation) relative to its environment.

A key challenge in robotic mapping arises from the nature of the measurement noise. Modeling problems, such as robotic mapping, are usually relatively easy to solve if the noise in different measurements is statistically *independent*. If this were the case, a robot could simply take more and more measurements to cancel out the effects of the noise. Unfortunately, in robotic mapping, the measurement errors are statistically dependent. This is because errors in control accumulate over time, and they affect the way future sensor measurements are interpreted. This is illustrated in Figure 1(a), which shows a sample path of a mobile robot in a given map of the environment. As

(a)   (b)

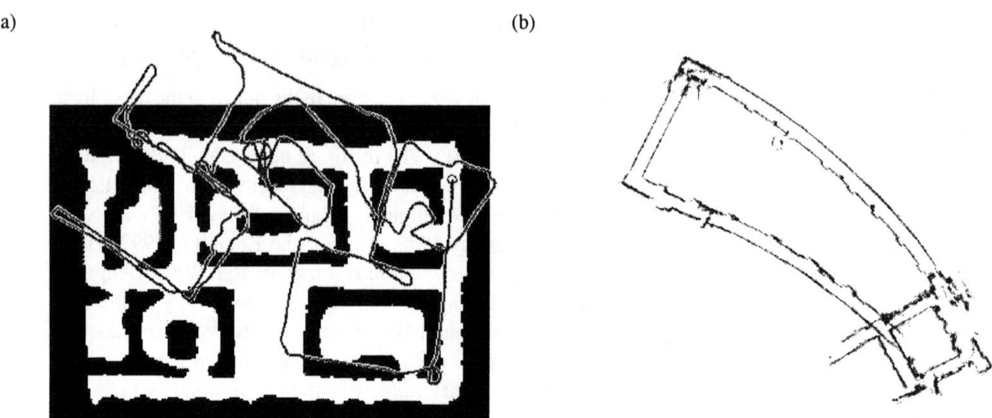

Figure 1   **(a)** Example of odometry error: Shown here is a robot's path as obtained by its odometry, relative to a given map. Small odometry (or control) errors can have large effects on later position estimates. **(b)** One of the many faces of the correspondence problem: Shown here is a robot traversing a cyclic environment, simultaneously accruing a significant odometry error.

this example shows, a small rotational error on one end of a long corridor can lead to many meters of error on the other. As a result, whatever a robot infers about its environment is plagued by systematic, correlated errors. Accommodating such systematic errors is a key to building maps successfully, and it is also a key complicating factor in robotic mapping. Many existing mapping algorithms are therefore surprisingly complex, both from a mathematical and from an implementation point of view.

The second complicating aspect of the robotic mapping problem arises from the high dimensionality of the entities that are being mapped. To understand the dimensionality of the problem, consider how many numbers it may take to describe an environment such as your own home. If you confine yourself to the description of major topological entities, such as corridors, intersections, rooms, and doors, a few dozen numbers might suffice. A detailed 2D floor plan, which is an equally common representation of robotic maps, often requires thousands of numbers. But a detailed 3D visual map of a building (or of an ocean floor) may easily require millions of numbers. From a statistical point of view, each such number is a dimension of the underlying estimation problem. Thus, the mapping problem can be extremely highdimensional.

A third and possibly the hardest problem in robotic mapping is the *correspondence problem*, also known as the *data association problem*. The correspondence problem is the problem of determining if sensor measurements taken at different points in time correspond to the same physical object in the world. Figure 1(b) shows an instance of this problem, in which a robot attempts to map a large cyclic environment. When closing the cycle, the robot has to find out where it is relative to its previously built map. This problem is complicated by the fact that, at the time of cycle closing, the robot's accumulated pose error might be unboundedly large. The correspondence problem is difficult, since the number of possible hypotheses can grow exponentially over time. Most scientific progress on the correspondence problem has emerged in the past five years, after a long period in which the problem was basically ignored in the robotic mapping community.

Fourth, environments change over time. Some changes may be relatively slow, such as the varying appearance of a tree across different seasons, or the structural changes that most office buildings are subjected to over time. Others are faster, such as the change of door status or the location of furniture items, such as chairs. Even faster may be the change of location of other agents in the environment, such as cars or people. The dynamism of robotic environments creates a big challenge, since it adds yet another way in which seemingly inconsistent sensor measurements can be explained. Imagine a robot facing a closed door that previously was modeled as open. Such an observation may be explained by two hypotheses, namely, that the door status changed, or that the robot is not where it believes itself to be. Unfortunately, there are almost no mapping algorithms that can learn meaningful maps of dynamic environments. Instead, the predominant paradigm relies on a static world assumption, in which the robot is the only time-variant quantity (and everything else that moves is just noise). Consequently, most techniques are only applied in relatively short time windows, during which the respective environments are static.

A fifth and final challenge arises from the fact that robots must choose their way during mapping. The task of generating robotic motion in the pursuit of building a map is commonly referred to as *robotic exploration*. While optimal robotic motion is relatively well understood in fully modeled environments, exploring robots have to cope with partial and incomplete models. Hence, any viable exploration strategy has to be able to accommodate contingencies and surprises that might arise during map acquisition. For this reason, exploration is a challenging planning problem, which is often solved suboptimally via simple heuristics. When choosing where to move, various quantities have to be traded off: the expected gain in map information, the time and energy it takes to gain this information, the possible loss of pose information along the way, and so on. Furthermore, the underlying map-estimation technique must be able to generate maps in real time, which is an important restriction that rules out many existing approaches.

As noted above, the literature refers to the mapping problem often in conjunction with the localization problem, which is the problem of determining a robot's pose. The reason for suggesting that both problems—the problem of estimating where things are in the environment and the problem of determining where a robot is—have to be solved in conjunction will become a bit more obvious below, when I state the basic statistical estimators that underlie all state-of-the-art techniques. In essence, both the robot localization and the map are uncertain, and focusing just on causes the other to introduce *systematic noise*. Thus, estimating both at the same time has the pleasing property that both the measurement and the control noise are independent with regard to the properties that are being estimated (the state). Postponing further detail on this issue to further below, we notice that the robotic mapping problem is like a chicken-and-egg problem: If the robot's pose was known all along, building a map would be quite simple. Conversely, if we already had a map of the environment, there exist computationally elegant and efficient algorithms for determining the robot's pose at any point in time (Borenstein, Everett, and Feng 1996; Fox, Burgard, and Thrun 1999). In combination, however, the problem is much harder.

Today, mapping is largely considered the most difficult perceptual problem in robotics. Progress in robotic mapping is bound to impact a much broader range of related perceptual problems, such as sensor-based manipulation and interaction with people.

4   WHY PROBABILITIES?

Virtually all state-of-the-art algorithms for robotic mapping in the literature have one common feature: They are probabilistic. They all employ probabilistic models of the robot and its environment, and they all rely on probabilistic inference for turning sensor measurements into maps. Some authors make the probabilistic thinking very explicit—for example, by providing mathematical derivations of their algorithms from first probabilistic principles. Others use techniques that on the surface do not look specifically probabilistic, but that in fact can be interpreted as probabilistic inference under appropriate assumptions.

The reason for the popularity of probabilistic techniques stems from the fact that robotic mapping is characterized by uncertainty and sensor noise. As discussed above, perceptual noise is complex and not trivial to accommodate. Probabilistic algorithms approach the problem by explicitly modeling different sources of noise and their effects on the measurements. In the evolution of mapping algorithms, probabilistic algorithms have emerged as the sole winner for this difficult problem. It is probably the complexity of this problem—mapping is arguably the hardest perceptual inference problem in mobile robotics, that has forced the community to adopt a singular view and use a single mathematical methodology for solving it.

The basic principle underlying virtually every single successful mapping algorithm is Bayes' rule:

$$p(x \mid d) \quad = \quad \eta \, p(d \mid x) \, p(x) \tag{1}$$

Bayes' rule is the archetype of probabilistic inference. Suppose we want to learn about a quantity x (e.g., a map) based on measurement data d (e.g., range scans, odometry). Then Bayes' rule tells us that the problem can be solved by multiplying two terms: $p(d \mid x)$ and $p(x)$. The term $p(d \mid x)$ specifies the probability of observing the measurement d under the hypothesis x. Thus, $p(d \mid x)$ is a *generative* model, in that it describes the process of generating sensor measurements under different worlds x. The term $p(x)$ is called the *prior*. It specifies our willingness to assume that x is the case in the world *before* the arrival of any data. Finally, η is a normalizer that is necessary to ensure that the left side of Bayes' rule is indeed a valid probability distribution.

In robotic mapping, data arrives over time. Already in this chapter, I distinguished two different types of data: sensor measurements and controls. Let us denote sensor measurements (e.g., camera images) by the variable z, and controls (e.g., motion commands) by u. For convenience, let us assume that the data is collected in alternation:

$$z_1, u_1, z_2, u_2, \ldots, \tag{2}$$

Here, subscripts are used as time index. In particular, z_t is the sensor measurement taken at time t, and u_t specifies the robotic motion command asserted in the time interval $[t - 1, t)$. Sometimes, odometry measurements or measurements from inertial navigation units (INUs) are used for u instead of controls, since they may more accurately reflect the actual robotic motion.

In the field of robotic mapping, the single dominating scheme for integrating such temporal data is known as *Bayes' filter* (Jazwinsky 1970), which is highly related to Kalman filters (Kalman 1960; Maybeck 1979), hidden Markov models (Rabiner 1989), dynamic Bayes networks (Russell and Norvig 1995), and partially observable Markov decision processes (Kaelbling, Littman, and Cassandra 1998; Lovejoy 1991; Monahan 1982; Sondik 1971). The Bayes filter extends Bayes' rule to temporal estimation problems. It is a recursive estimator for computing a sequence of posterior probability distributions over quantities that cannot be observed directly—such as a map. Let us call this unknown quantity the *state* and refer to it as x_t, where t is the time index. The generic Bayes filter calculates a posterior probability over the state x_t via the following recursive equation:

$$p(x_t \mid z^t, u^t) \quad = \quad \eta \, p(z_t \mid x_t) \int p(x_t \mid u_t, x_{t-1}) \, p(x_{t-1} \mid z^{t-1}, u^{t-1}) \, dx_{t-1} \tag{3}$$

Here we follow common notation by using a superscript ^{t} to refer to *all* data leading up to time t—that is:

$$z^t = \{z_1, z_2, \ldots, z_t\} \tag{4}$$

$$u^t = \{u_1, u_2, \ldots, u_t\} \tag{5}$$

Equation 3 might look complex, but in fact it embodies the most simple approach of probabilistic inference from temporal data. We notice that Bayes filters are recursive—that is, the posterior probability $p(x_t \mid z^t, u^t)$ is calculated from the same probability one time step earlier. The initial probability at time $t = 0$ is $p(x_0 \mid z^0, u^0) = p(x_0)$. The recursiveness suggests that the time per update is constant, enabling Bayes filters to integrate information indefinitely.

A crucial requirement of Bayes filters is that the state x_t contain all unknown quantities that may influence sensor measurements at multiple points in time. In the context of robotic mapping, there are typically two such quantities: the map and the robot's pose in the environment. Hence, when using probabilistic techniques, the mapping problem is truly one where both the map and the robot's pose have to be estimated together. If we use m to denote the map and s for the robot's pose, we obtain the following Bayes filter:

$$p(s_t, m_t \mid z^t, u^t) \tag{6}$$

$$= \eta \, p(z_t \mid s_t, m_t) \int \int p(s_t, m_t \mid u_t, s_{t-1}, m_{t-1}) \, p(s_{t-1}, m_{t-1} \mid z^{t-1}, u^{t-1}) \, ds_{t-1} \, dm_{t-1}$$

Most mapping algorithms assume that the world is static, which implies that the time index can be omitted when referring to the map m. Also, most approaches assume that the robotic motion is independent of the map. This leads to the convenient form of the Bayes filter in the robotic mapping problem:

$$p(s_t, m \mid z^t, u^t) = \eta \, p(z_t \mid s_t, m) \int p(s_t \mid u_t, s_{t-1}) \, p(s_{t-1}, m \mid z^{t-1}, u^{t-1}) \, ds_{t-1} \tag{7}$$

Notice that this estimator does not require an integration over maps m, as was the case for the previous one (6). Such an integration is difficult, due to the high dimensionality of the space of all maps. Thus, the static-world assumption has great practical importance.

To put the estimator (7) into action, two generative probabilities have to be specified: $p(s_t \mid u_t, s_{t-1})$ and $p(z_t \mid s_t, m)$. These distributions are usually assumed to be time invariant—that is, they do not depend on the time t. Thus, they are commonly written as $p(s \mid u, s')$ and $p(z \mid s, m)$. Both of them are generative models of the robot and its environment. The probability $p(z \mid s, m)$ is often referred to as *perceptual model* in robotics, since it describes in probabilistic terms how sensor measurements z are generated for different poses s and maps m. The perceptual model is a generative model that describes the workings of a robot's sensors. The probability $p(s \mid u, s')$ specifies the effect of the control u on the state s. It describes the probability that the control u, if executed at the world state s', leads to the state s. For moving robots, this probability is usually referred to as a *motion model*.

We also notice that the mapping equation (7) cannot be implemented on a digital computer in its general form, stated above. This is because the posterior over the space of all maps and robotic poses is a probability distribution over a continuous space, hence possessing infinitely many dimensions. Therefore, any working mapping algorithm has to resort to additional assumptions. These assumptions and their implications on the resulting algorithms and maps constitute the primary differences between the various solutions to the robotic mapping problem.

The remainder of this chapter describes specific mapping algorithms that can be directly derived from Bayes filters and relates them to each other. Table 1 summarizes key properties of some of the most important algorithms. Such a comparison has to be taken with a grain of salt, since it is necessarily inaccurate given the flood of publications on this topic. Our goal is to instead report current strengths and limitations of proven algorithms in a way that enables novices in the field to understand the advantages and shortcomings of individual approaches.

The map representation is summarized in the *Representation* field, which will be defined in more detail when discussing the individual algorithms in depth. The field labeled *Uncertainty* refers to the way uncertainty is represented in the resulting map. A Bayesian posterior characterizes the map along with its uncertainty, whereas a maximum likelihood estimate generates only a single map, and hence is less informative. The *Convergence* field states what is known about the convergence properties of an algorithm, under appropriate assumptions. Different mapping paradigms come with different convergence properties. In particular, the notion of convergence in *expectation maximization*, or *EM* (see Section 6), is a local one, where the resulting solution might characterize a locally optimal map. In the table, we call such convergence *weak*, to distinguish it from stronger results concerning the optimality of the estimate. Whether or not an algorithm is subject to local minima is specified in the next row. The *Incremental* field tells us whether maps can be build incrementally (and possibly in real time) or whether multiple passes through the data are necessary. In general, incrementality is a desirable property, especially for robots that explore autonomously while building a map. The *Requires Poses* field is an important one: Only a subset of mapping algorithms attacks the full mapping problem above, where the robotic poses are unknown. Other algorithms require exact pose information. The latter ones are usually used in conjunction with the former ones, to postprocess the data. The nature of sensor noise is listed in the next field, followed by the dimensionality of the maps that can be generated in practical implementations. The *Correspondence* item specifies whether an algorithm can cope with unknown correspondence problems—that is, accommodate features in the environment that look alike, a property that is highly desirable. The next item, *Raw Data*, tells us whether in practical implementations data preprocessing and filtering is necessary or, alternatively, an algorithm can build maps from raw sensor data. Maps computed from raw sensor data often possess more detail. Finally, the *Dynamic Environments* item states whether the approach is tailored toward dynamic environments. Certain approaches can accommodate limited types of dynamics, as indicated by the term "limited." From the range of algorithms discussed here, only one addresses environment change at its core.

5   KALMAN FILTER APPROACHES

A classic approach to generating maps is based on Kalman filters (Kalman 1960; Maybeck 1979). This approach can be traced back to a highly influential series of papers by Smith, Self, and Cheeseman (Smith and Cheeseman 1985; Smith, Self, and Cheeseman 1990), who in 1985 through 1990 proposed a mathematical formulation of the approach that is still in widespread use today. In the following years, a number of researchers developed this approach further (Castellanos et al. 1999; Castellanos and Tardós 2000; Dissanayake et al. 2000; Dissanayake et al. 2001; Durrant-Whyte et al. 2001; Leonard and Feder 1999; Newman 2000), most notably a group of researchers located at the University of Sydney. In the literature, Kalman filter–based mapping algorithms are often referred to as *SLAM algorithms*, where SLAM stands for simultaneous localization and mapping, as noted above. Technically speaking, SLAM is a problem and not a solution, but the term is now closely affiliated with a family of algorithms that uses Kalman filters for jointly estimating the map and the robot pose.

	Kalman	Lu/Milios	EM	Incremental ML	Hybrid	Occupancy Grids	Multi-planar Maps	Dogma
Representation	Landmark locations	Point obstacles	Point obstacles	Landmark locations or grid maps	Point obstacles	Occupancy grids	Objects and polygons	Occupancy grids
Uncertainty	Posterior poses and map	Posterior poses and map	Maximum likelihood map	(Local) maximum likelihood map	Maximum likelihood map	Posterior map	Maximum likelihood map	Posterior map
Convergence	Strong	No	Weak?	No	No	Strong	Weak	Weak
Local Minima	No	Yes	Yes	Yes	Yes	No	Yes	Yes
Incremental	Yes	No	No	Yes	Yes	Yes	No	No
Requires Poses	No	No	No	No	No	Yes	Yes	Yes
Sensor Noise	Gaussian	Gaussian	Any	Any	Any	Any	Gaussian	Any
Can Map Cycles	Yes	No	Yes	No	Yes, but not nested	N/A	N/A	N/A
Map Dimensionality	$\sim 10^3$	Unlimited	Unlimited	Unlimited	Unlimited	Unlimited	Unlimited	Unlimited
Correspondence	No	Yes	Yes	Yes	Yes	Yes	Yes	Yes
Handles Raw Data	No	Yes	Yes	Yes	Yes	Yes	Yes	Yes
Dynamic Env's	Limited	No	No	No	No	Limited	No	Yes

Table 1   An attempt to compare the major mapping algorithms described in this chapter.

Kalman filters are Bayes filters that represent posteriors $p(s_t, m \mid z^t, u^t)$ with Gaussians. Gaussians are unimodal distributions that can be represented compactly by a small number of parameters. In the context of the robotic mapping problem, the Gaussian model is the full state vector x, which comprises the robot's pose s and the map m:

$$x_t \;=\; (s_t, m)^T \tag{8}$$

Here and in the following, ^{T} refers to the transpose of a vector or matrix. For robots operating on a planar surface, the robot pose s is usually modeled by three variables: the Cartesian coordinates in the plane and the heading direction. Let us denote those coordinates by s_x, s_y, and s_θ, respectively. Maps in the Kalman filter approach are commonly represented by the Cartesian coordinates of sets of features. Appropriate feature may be landmarks, distinctive objects, or shapes in the environment. Denoting the number in the map by K, the corresponding state vector is given by the following $2K + 3D$ vector:

$$x_t \;=\; (s_{x,t}, s_{y,t}, s_{\theta,t}, m_{1,x,t}, m_{1,y,t}, m_{2,x,t}, m_{2,y,t}, \ldots, m_{K,x,t}, m_{K,y,t})^T \tag{9}$$

Here $m_{k,x,t}, m_{k,y,t}$ are the Cartesian coordinates of the kth feature in the map. As is commonly the case in Kalman filtering, the Gaussian representing the posterior over the joint pose and map estimate $p(s_t, m \mid z^t, u^t)$ is given by a mean μ_t and a covariance matrix Σ_t. The mean vector possesses $2K + 3$ dimensions, and the covariance $(2K + 3)^2$ dimensions.

Before discussing the Kalman filter–based mapping algorithm, let us inspect an example. Figure 2 is an image of a map obtained using the Kalman filter approach. The image shows the path of an underwater vehicle, along with range measurements obtained using a pencil sonar. The map itself consists of 14 point features, extracted from the sonar data. Five of those features correspond to thin, vertical artificial landmarks; the others correspond to other reflective objects in the environment. The ellipses around these landmarks illustrate the residual uncertainty that remains after mapping, as specified by the covariance matrix Σ. Similarly, the robot's path itself is uncertain, as indicated by the ellipses that can be found in regular intervals along the path. All of these ellipses are 2D projections of a single Gaussian $\langle \mu, \Sigma \rangle$ that represents the joint posterior over all landmark locations and the robot pose. Additional dots in Figure 2 depict hypotheses for the location of additional landmarks whose evidence is too weak for inclusion in the map. Figure 3 illustrates the result after successful mapping, using a simulation example. Of importance is the matrix shown in Figure 3(b), which depicts the correlation (normalized covariance matrix Σ) between the robot's 3D pose and all 20 landmarks' 2D locations. The checkerboard appearance suggests that there are strong correlations between all location estimates in the x and y dimensions. This makes sense, since measurements convey only information about the *relative* location of the robot to landmarks (and, by induction, between the landmarks themselves), not about their absolute coordinates. Consequently, the final map in Figure 3(a) is still somewhat uncertain.

Kalman filter mapping relies on three basic assumptions: First, the next state function (motion model) must be linear with added Gaussian noise. Second, the same characteristics must also apply to the perceptual model. And third, the initial uncertainty must be Gaussian. I will now elaborate on these three assumptions.

A linear next state function is one where the robot pose s_t and the map m_t at time t depend *linearly* on the previous pose s_{t-1} and map m_{t-1}, and also linearly on the control u_t. For the map, this is trivially the case since, by assumption, the map does not change. However, the pose s_t is usually governed by a nonlinear trigonometric function that depends nonlinearly on the previous pose s_{t-1} and the control

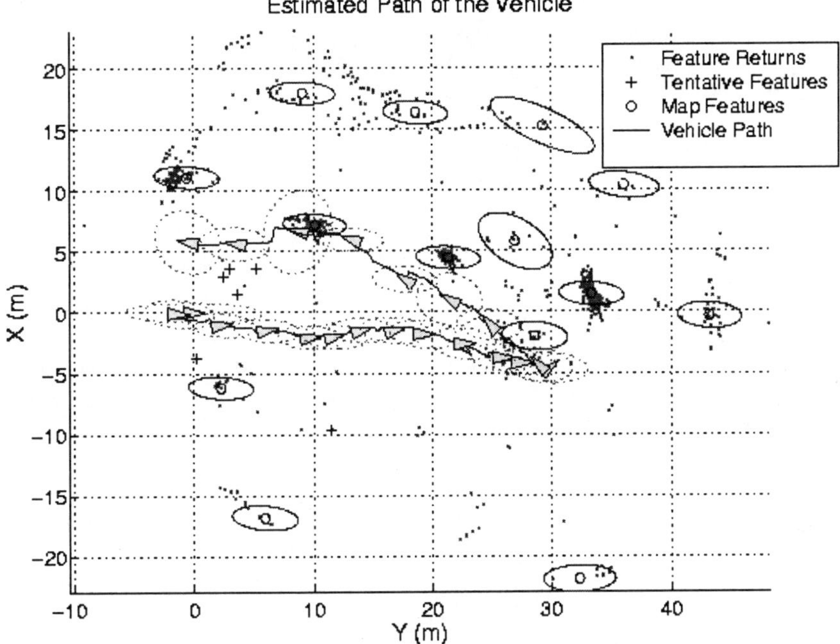

Figure 2   Example of Kalman filter estimation of the map and the vehicle pose. (Courtesy of Stefan Williams and Hugh Durrant-Whyte of the Australian Centre for Field Robotics at the University of Sydney (Williams, Dissanayake, and Durrant-Whyte 2001).)

u_t. To accommodate such nonlinearities, Kalman filters approximate the robotic motion model using a linear function obtained via Taylor series expansion. The resulting Kalman filter is known as an *extended Kalman filter* (Maybeck 1979; Julier and Uhlmann 1997), and single motion commands are often approximated by a series of much smaller motion segments, to account for nonlinearities. For most robotic vehicles, such an approximation works well. The result of the linearization is that the state transition function can be written as a linear function with added Gaussian noise:

$$p(x \mid u, x') \quad = \quad Ax' + Bu + \varepsilon_{\text{control}} \tag{10}$$

Here, A and B are matrices that implement linear mappings from states x' and the motion command u to the next state variable x, respectively. Noise in perception is modeled via the variable $\varepsilon_{\text{control}}$, which is assumed to be normal distributed with zero mean and the covariance Σ_{control}.

As with robotic motion, sensor measurements in robotics are usually nonlinear, with non-Gaussian noise. Thus, they are also approximated through a first-degree Taylor series expansion. Put into equations, Kalman filter methods require that $p(z \mid x)$ with $x = \langle s, m \rangle$ is of the following form:

$$p(z \mid x) \quad = \quad Cx + \varepsilon_{\text{measure}} \tag{11}$$

Here, C is a matrix (a linear mapping) and $\varepsilon_{\text{measure}}$ is normal distributed measurement noise with zero mean and covariance Σ_{measure}. Such approximations are known to work well for robots

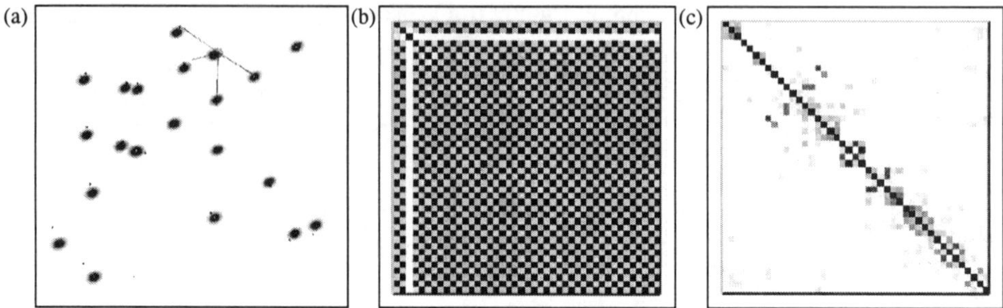

Figure 3   (a) A map of landmarks obtained in simulation. **(b)** A correlation matrix after 278 iterations of Kalman filter mapping. The checkerboard appearance verifies the theoretical finding that in the limit, all landmark location estimates are fully correlated. **(c)** The normalized inverse covariance matrix of the same estimate shows that dependencies are local, an effect that is exploited by some algorithms that build local maps.

that can measure the ranges and bearings to landmarks. Under the linearity and Gaussian noise approximation, the Bayes filter in Equation 7 can be calculated conveniently using the standard Kalman filter equations (Kalman 1960; Maybeck 1979; Welch and Bishop 1995):

$$
\begin{aligned}
\mu'_{t-1} &= \mu_{t-1} + Bu_t \\
\Sigma'_{t-1} &= \Sigma_{t-1} + \Sigma_{\text{control}} \\
K_t &= \Sigma'_{t-1}C^T(C\Sigma'_{t-1}C^T + \Sigma_{\text{measure}})^{-1} \\
\mu_t &= \mu'_{t-1} + K_t(o - C\mu'_{t-1}) \\
\Sigma_t &= (I - K_tC)\Sigma'_{t-1}
\end{aligned}
\tag{12}
$$

As the reader may verify, these equations are equivalent to the standard Kalman filter update equations (Maybeck 1979). Their mathematical derivation from the Bayes filter is mathematically straightforward.

In practical implementations, the number of features in the map lies usually between a dozen and a few hundred. Sensor measurements are usually sparse (e.g., the robot observes one landmark at a time). The most costly operations in updating the Kalman filter are matrix multiplications (and not matrix inversions), which can be implemented in $O(K^2)$ time, where K is the number of features in the map—not to be confused with the matrix K_t in Equation 12. Recent research has led to a range of extensions that can handle larger number of features, by breaking the problem into multiple smaller ones (Guivant and Nebot 2001; Leonard and Feder 1999). Some techniques, such as the FastSLAM algorithm described in (Montemerlo et al. 2002), promise a reduction to $O(\log K)$ complexity for certain situations, by using nonclassical statistical sampling techniques for robot path estimation (Doucet et al. 2000; Murphy and Russell 2001), along with efficient tree representations.

In practice, the number of features is not known a priori. State-of-the-art implementations often increase this list dynamically. To do so, they maintain a list of candidate features, using a separate Kalman filter for these candidates. If a feature is observed sufficiently often, it is permanently added to the list of features in the map. Outliers—that is, measurements that do not correspond to any known feature with sufficient likelihood, are usually ignored. These techniques work particularly well when features in the environment are scarce.

Some of the key characteristics of the Kalman filter approach to robot mapping are summarized in Table 1. The primary advantage of the Kalman filter approach is the fact that it estimates the full posterior over maps m in an online fashion. To date, the only algorithms that are capable of estimating the full posterior are based on Kalman filters or extensions thereof, such as a mixture of Gaussian methods (Durrant-Whyte et al. 2001), or a Rao-Blackwellized particle filter (Doucet et al. 2000; Montemerlo et al. 2002; Murphy and Russell 2001). There are many advantages to estimating the full posterior: In addition to the most likely map and robotic poses, Kalman filters maintain the full uncertainty in the map, which can be highly beneficial when using the map for navigation. Additionally, the approach can be shown to converge with probability one to the true map and robotic position, up to a residual uncertainty distribution that largely stems from an initial random drift (Newman 2000; Dissanayake et al. 2000; Dissanayake et al. 2001). As is commonly the case with theoretical results, they only hold under the specific conditions discussed above. They also require that the robot encounters each landmark infinitely often. Nevertheless, this result is the strongest convergence result that presently exists in the context of robotic mapping.

Probably the most important limitation of the Kalman filter approach lies in the Gaussian noise assumption. In particular, the assumption that the measurement noise $\varepsilon_{\mathrm{measure}}$ must be independent and Gaussian poses a key limitation, with important implications for practical implementations. Consider—for example, an environment with two indistinguishable landmarks. Measuring such a landmark will induce a multimodal distribution over possible robot poses, which is at odds with the (unimodal) Gaussian noise assumption. More generally, Kalman filter approaches are unable to cope with the *correspondence problem*, which is the problem of associating individual sensor measurements with features in the map.

This limitation has important practical ramifications. Implementations of the Kalman filter approach usually require a sparse set of features that are sufficiently distinctive—either by their sensor characteristics or by their location—that they can be identified reliably. Errors in the identification of environment features usually imply failure of the mapping algorithm. For this reason, Kalman filter approaches are usually forced to ignore large portions of the sensor data and work with only a small number of landmark-type features. The resulting maps contain the locations of these landmarks but usually lack detailed geometric descriptions of the environment.

A recent extension of the basic paradigm is known as the Lu/Milios algorithm (Lu and Milios 1997). This algorithm was successfully implemented by Gutmann (Gutmann 2000; Gutmann and Nebel 1997). The Lu/Milios algorithm is somewhat specific to laser range data. It combines two basic estimation phases: A phase where Kalman filters are used to calculate posteriors over maps, and another where the range measurements in multiple range scans are associated with each other. The correspondence is obtained via *maximum likelihood*, or *ML*, data association—that is, the algorithm simply pairs up nearby measurements. However, by iterating both phases, the correspondence is calculated repeatedly, enabling the approach to recover from wrong correspondences. In practice, this approach is able to build maps from raw data with unknown correspondences. However, the fact that it uses maximum likelihood to "guess" the correspondences—instead of calculating the full posterior over correspondences and maps—imposes important limitations.

In practice, the algorithm works amazingly well when the errors in the initial pose estimates are small (e.g., smaller than 2 meters). Larger pose errors, such as those typically encountered when mapping a cyclic environment, cannot be accommodated. Moreover, this approach requires multiple passes through the data, and hence is not a real-time algorithm. Figure 4(c) depicts a map generated using this algorithm from the range data shown in Figure 4(b). The final map is highly accurate and exhibits detailed structure. Notice, however, that the data fed into this algorithm is prealigned.

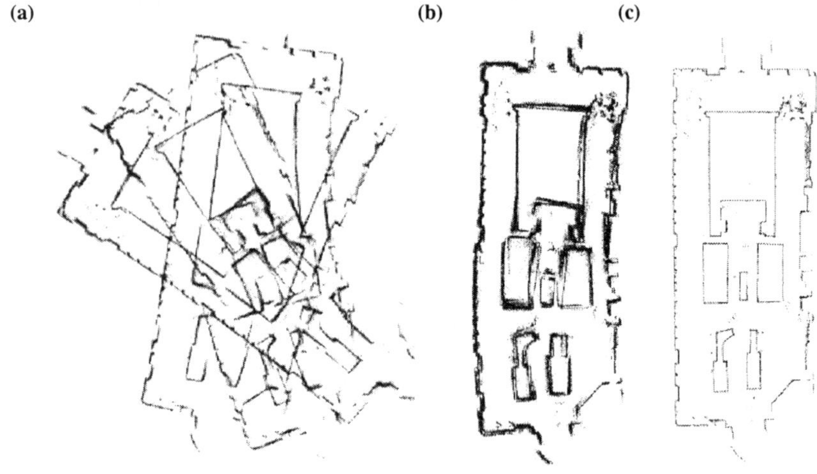

Figure 4   **(a)** Raw range data of a large hall in a museum. **(b)** Data aligned with EM using artificial but indistinguishable landmarks. **(c)** Result of applying the Lu/Milios algorithm to the prealigned data.

The raw data using the robot's odometry for pose estimation, shown in Figure 4(a), is too erroneous for the Lu/Milios algorithm. The problem with such erroneous data is the failure of the maximum likelihood correspondence step, which in turn leads to wrong maps when using Kalman filtering. This result illustrates the strength and weakness of the basic approach. (Note that the prealignment from Figure 4(a) to Figure 4(b) was performed using an algorithm described in the next section.)

The discussion of Kalman filter approaches raises the more general question as to whether it is principally possible to perform full posterior estimation in the face of unknown correspondences. The basic Kalman filter algorithm cannot cope with ambiguous features, and even extensions such as the Lu/Milios algorithm resort to (brittle) maximum likelihood techniques to guess the best correspondence during mapping. Unfortunately, calculating the full posterior under unknown correspondences is hard. If there exist n ambiguous features in the world, each measurement of such a feature will in the worst case multiply the modes of the posterior by a factor of n. Thus, the number of modes in the posterior may grow exponentially over time. This suggests that no incremental algorithm exists that can calculate the full posterior under unknown correspondences. However, recent research suggests that it may suffice to maintain a small number of those modes, using a mixture of Gaussian representation (Durrant-Whyte et al. 2001) or a—highly related—particle filter representation (Montemerlo et al. 2002; Murphy and Russell 2001). Such representations have been applied with great success in lower dimensional robot localization problems (Cox and Leonard 1994; Jensfelt and Kristensen 1999; Reuter 2000; Roumeliotis and Bekey 2000), commonly under the name *multihypothesis Kalman filters*. The development of techniques for posterior estimation with unknown correspondence is currently the subject of ongoing research, with enormous potential for practical applications.

6 EXPECTATION MAXIMIZATION ALGORITHMS

A recent alternative to the Kalman filter paradigm is known as the *expectation maximization* family of algorithms or, in short, *EM*. EM is a statistical algorithm that was developed in the context of maximum likelihood (ML) estimation with latent variables, in an influential paper by Dempster, Laird and Rubin (1977). A recent book by McLachlan and Krishnan (1997) on this topic illustrates the wealth of research that presently exists on the EM algorithm.

Applied to the robotic mapping problem, the EM algorithm has quite orthogonal characteristics. EM algorithms constitute today's best solutions to the correspondence problem in mapping (Burgard et al. 1999; Thrun et al. 1998). In particular, EM algorithms have been found to generate consistent maps of large-scale cyclic environments even if all features look alike and cannot be distinguished perceptually. However, EM algorithms do not retain a full notion of uncertainty. Instead, they perform hill climbing in the space of all maps, in an attempt to find the most likely map. To do so, they have to process the data multiple times. Hence, EM algorithms cannot generate maps incrementally, as is the case for many Kalman filter approaches.

The EM algorithm exploits the chicken-and-egg nature of the mapping problem. In particular, it builds on the insight that determining a map when the robot's path is known (in expectation) is relatively simple, as is the determination of a probabilistic estimate of the robot's location for a given map. To exploit this insight, EM iterates two steps: An *expectation step*, or *E-step*, where the posterior over robot poses is calculated for a given map, and a *maximization step*, or *M-step*, in which EM calculates the most likely map given these pose expectations. The result is a series of increasingly accurate maps, $m^{[0]}, m^{[1]}, m^{[2]}, \ldots$. The initial map, $m^{[0]}$, is an empty map.

Formally, the function that is being maximized is the expectation over the joint logarithmic likelihood of the data d^t and the robot's path $s^t = \{s_1, \ldots, s_t\}$:

$$m^{[i+1]} \quad = \quad \underset{m}{\operatorname{argmax}} \, E_{s^t} [\log p(d^t, s^t \mid m) \mid m^{[i]}, d^t] \tag{13}$$

This equation follows from the Bayes filter under several mild assumptions. The $(i+1)$th map is obtained from the ith map by maximization of a logarithmic likelihood function. The logarithm is a monotonic function; hence, maximizing the logarithm is equivalent to likelihood maximization. Part of the likelihood that is being maximized is the robot's path s^t. However, in mapping, the path is unknown. Equation 13, thus, computes the expectation of this likelihood over all possible paths the robot may have taken. Under mild assumptions, this equation can be reexpressed as the following integral:

$$m^{[i+1]} \quad = \quad \underset{m}{\operatorname{argmax}} \sum_{\tau} \int p(s_\tau \mid m^{[i]}, d^t) \log p(z_\tau \mid s_\tau, m) \, ds_\tau \tag{14}$$

Here, the right side contains the term $p(s_\tau \mid m^{[i]}, d^t)$, which is the posterior for the pose s_τ conditioned on the data d^t and the ith map $m^{[i]}$. Further above, we have already encountered various such estimation problems, and I have shown how to use Bayes filters to solve them. The specific problem here is a low-dimensional robot localization problem, since we are given the ith map and only need to compute the posterior over the robot pose. The key difference to standard localization is that in our case, data in the entire time interval $\{1, \ldots, t\}$ is used to estimate the posterior pose at time τ, even for $\tau < t$. Thus, we need to incorporate past and future data relative to the time step τ. Luckily, under further mild assumptions this can be achieved by running Bayes filters twice: once forward in time, and once backward in time. The forward run provides us with a posterior $p(s_\tau \mid m^{[i]}, d^\tau)$ conditioned on all data leading up to time τ. The backward pass gives us the posterior $p(s_\tau \mid m^{[i]}, d^{\tau+1}, \ldots, d^t)$ conditioned on all data collected after time step τ. Multiplication of these two estimates and subsequent normalization gives us indeed the desired probability $p(s_\tau \mid m^{[i]}, d^t)$. This calculation is known as the *E-step in EM*, since it calculates expectations (probabilities) for different poses at all points in time.

The final step, the M-step, is the maximization in (14). Here the expectations $p(s_\tau \mid m^{[i]}, d^t)$ are fixed, as obtained in the E-step. The goal of the M-step is to find a new map m that maximizes the log likelihood of the sensor measurements $\log p(z_\tau \mid s_\tau, m)$, for all τ and all poses s^t and under the expectation calculated in the E-step. Unfortunately, there exist no known closed-form solutions to this high-dimensional maximization problem. A common approach is to solve the problem for each map location $\langle x, y \rangle$ independently (Burgard et al. 1999; Thrun et al. 1998). This assumes that the map is represented by a finite number of locations—for example, by a fine-grained grid. The component-wise maximization is then relatively straightforward. Existing implementations of the EM paradigm rely on grid representations for all densities involved in the estimation process. They also rely on probabilistic maps instead of zero-one maps, which has a smoothing effect on the maximization and avoids getting trapped in local maxima during the optimization.

Key characteristics of the EM algorithm are summarized in Table 1. A key advantage of the EM algorithm over Kalman filtering lies in the fact that it solves the correspondence problem. It does so by repeatedly relocalizing the robot relative to the present map in the E-step. The pose posteriors calculated in the E-step correspond to different hypotheses as to where the robot might have been, and hence imply different correspondences. By building maps in the M-step, these correspondences are translated into features in the map, which then either get reinforced in the next E-step or gradually disappear.

Figure 5(a) shows an example of a data set mapped using EM. In this specific example, the robot measures 28 landmarks that are perceptually indistinguishable. These landmarks correspond to corners, intersections, and distinctive places; however, for the exercise of mapping with unknown correspondence, the robot is not given any perceptual information that would help disambiguate them. When traversing the large loop in the environment for the first time, the error in the pose estimate using odometry is too large to use it to resolve the correspondence problem. Such large loops are known to be challenging to map (Gutmann and Konolige 2000). Figure 5(c) shows the result of applying EM to this data set. The resulting map and path is topologically correct. To illustrate the accuracy of the map, Figures 5(b) and 5(d) show occupancy grid maps built from sonar range measurements using the raw range data without and with the poses estimated by EM, respectively.

Such results cannot be obtained using present-day Kalman filtering techniques, since those techniques do not address the correspondence problem in ways that would scale to environments of this complexity. However, we notice that EM is inferior to Kalman filter algorithms in that it is an offline algorithm that is subject to local maxima. Generating maps like the one shown here may take several hours on a low-end PC.

7   HYBRID APPROACHES

The literature on robotic mapping provides ample examples of hybrid solutions that integrate probabilistic posteriors with computationally more efficient maximum likelihood estimates. One of the most common approaches, which from a mathematical point of view is inferior to both Kalman

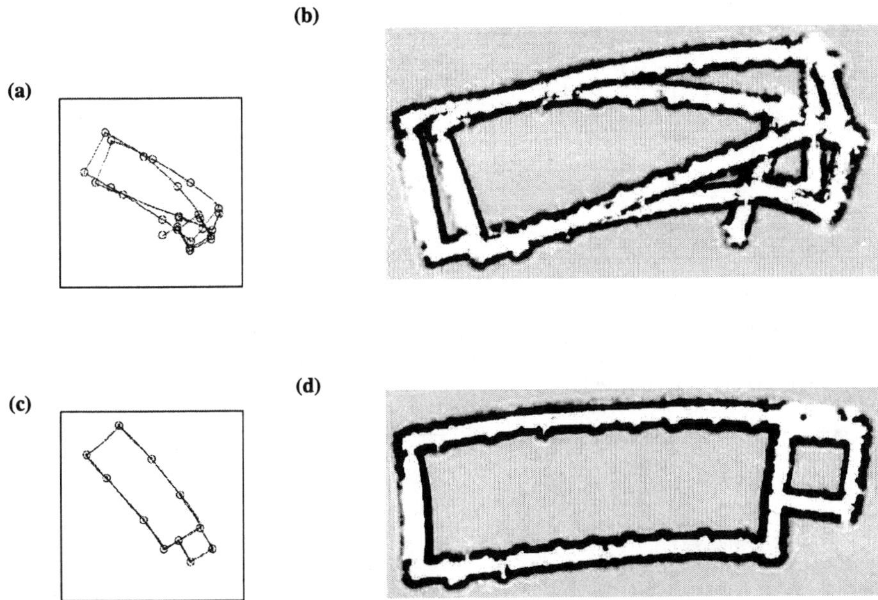

Figure 5 (**a**) Raw data of a large-scale cyclic environment with indistinguishable landmarks. (**b**) Occupancy grid map built from raw data using sonar sensors. (**c**) Map and robot path aligned by EM, demonstrating EM's ability to solve hard correspondence problems. (**d**) Occupancy grid map built on top of the outcome of the EM mapping algorithm.

filters and EM, is the *incremental maximum likelihood method* (Elfes 1989; Moravec 1988; Thrun 1993; Yamauchi and Beer 1996; Yamauchi et al. 1998). The basic idea is to incrementally build a single map as the sensor data arrives, but without keeping track of any residual uncertainty. Such a methodology can be viewed as an M-step in EM, without an E-step. The advantage of this paradigm lies in its simplicity, which accounts for its popularity.

Mathematically, the basic idea is to maintain a series of maximum likelihood maps, $m_1^*, m_2^*, \ldots,$ along with a series of maximum likelihood poses $s_1^*, s_2^*, \ldots.$ The tth map and pose are constructed from the $(t-1)$th map and pose via maximization of the marginal likelihood:

$$\langle m_t^*, s_t^* \rangle \;\; = \;\; \operatorname*{argmax}_{m_t, s_t} p(z_t \mid s_t, m_t)\, p(s_t, m_t \mid u_t, s_{t-1}^*, m_{t-1}^*) \tag{15}$$

This equation directly follows from the Bayes filter (6) under the assumption that the $(t-1)$th map and robot pose are known. In practice, it usually suffices to search in the space of poses s_t, since the map m_t is usually uniquely determined once the pose s_t is known. Thus, the incremental ML method simply requires a search in the space of all poses s_t when a new data item arrives, to determine the pose s_t^* that maximizes the marginal posterior likelihood. Like Kalman filters, this approach can build maps in real time, but without maintaining a notion of uncertainty. Like EM, it maximizes likelihood. However, the incremental one-step likelihood maximization differs from the likelihood maximization over an entire data set d^t. In particular, once a pose s_t^* and a map m_t^* have

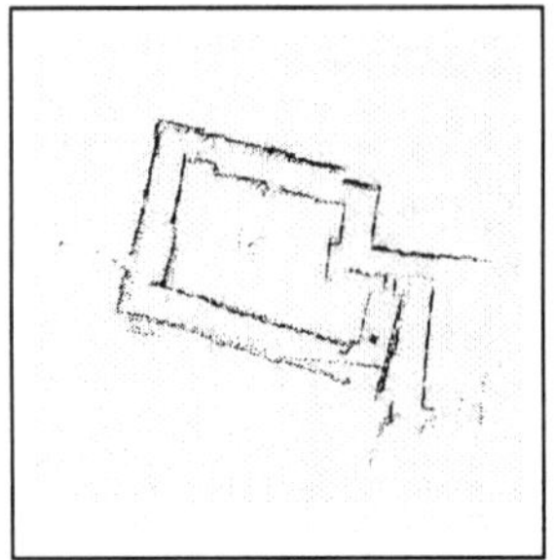 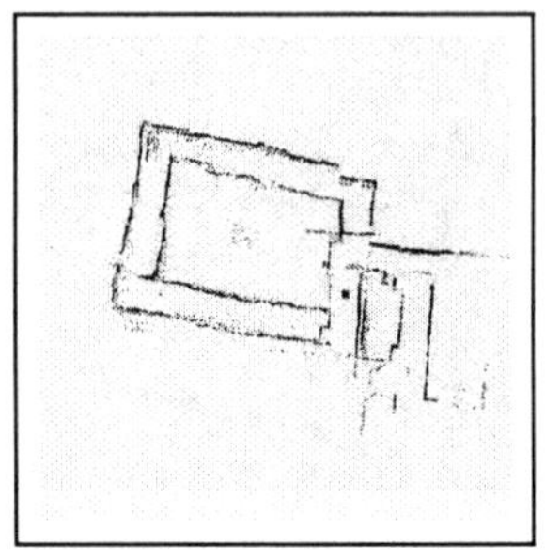 

Figure 6 Incremental maximum likelihood mapping: at every time step, the map is expanded by finding the most likely continuation. This nonprobabilistic approach works well in a noncyclic environment but is generally unable to handle cycles.

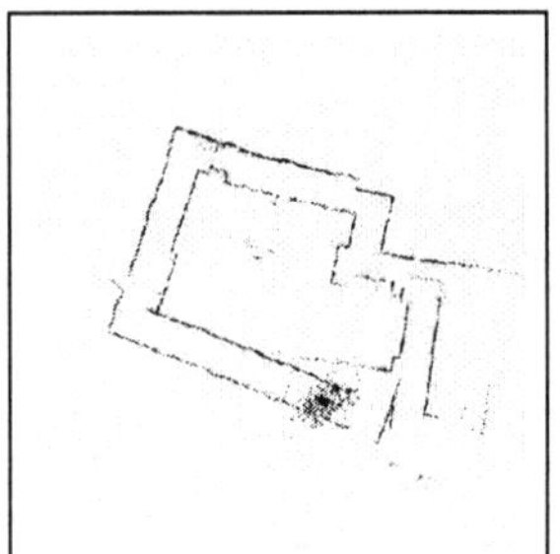 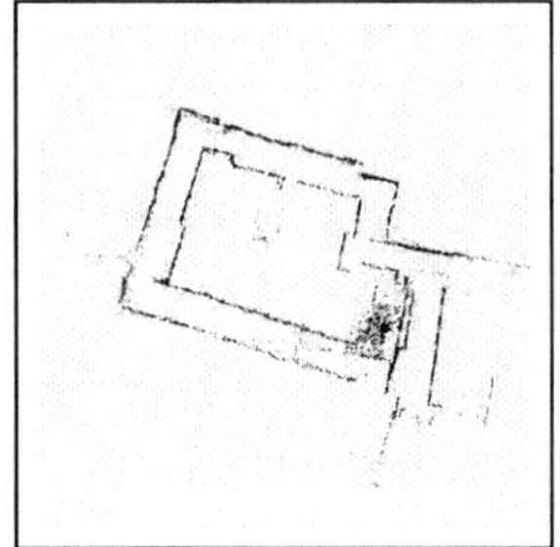 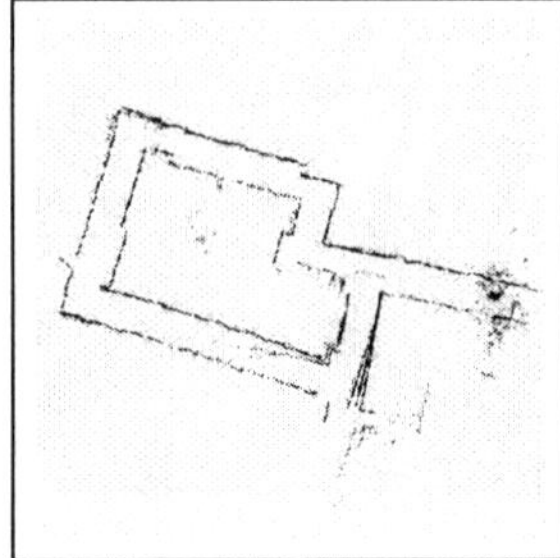

Figure 7   Hybrid approach, which maintains a posterior estimate over the robot poses, represented by a set of particles. When closing the loop, these samples are used to relocalize the robot in the map and correct the map accordingly.

been determined, they are frozen once and forever and cannot be revised based on future data—a key feature of both the Kalman filter and the EM approach.

This weakness manifests itself in the inability to map cyclic environments, where the error in the poses s_t^* may grow without bounds. Figure 6 shows an example where the incremental maximum likelihood approach is used to map a cyclic environment, with a robot equipped with a 2D laser range finder. While the map is reasonably consistent before closing the loop, the large residual error leads to inconsistencies that cannot be resolved by the incremental maximum likelihood approach. This is a general limitation of algorithms that do not consider uncertainty when building maps and that possess no mechanism to use future data to adjust past decisions.

Hybrid approaches overcome this limitation by maintaining an explicit notion of uncertainty during mapping, short of the full posterior over maps and poses maintained by Kalman filters. A good example are the algorithms described in (Gutmann and Konolige 2000; Thrun 2001c; Thrun, Burgard, and Fox 2000). Both of these algorithms use the incremental maximum likelihood approach to build maps, but in addition maintain a posterior distribution over robot poses s_t. This distribution is calculated using the standard Bayes filter (3) applied to robot poses s_t (but not maps):

$$p(s_t \mid z^t, u^t) \quad = \quad \eta \, p(z_t \mid s_t) \int p(s_t \mid u_t, s_{t-1}) \, p(s_{t-1} \mid z^{t-1}, u^{t-1}) \, ds_{t-1} \qquad (16)$$

The idea is that by retaining a notion of the robot's pose uncertainty, conflicts like the one faced by the incremental maximum likelihood method can be identified and the appropriate corrective action can be taken. Figure 7 shows a sequence of map estimation steps using this approach, for the same data used to generate Figure 6. The pose posterior estimate $p(s_t \mid z^t, u^t)$ is implemented using *particle filters* (Dellaert et al. 1999; Doucet et al. 2001; Liu and Chen 1998; Pitt and Shephard 1999), which is a version of the Bayes filter that represents posteriors by samples. The samples can be seen in all three diagrams in Figure 7. When the robot traverses a cyclic environment, it uses the samples to localize itself relative to the previously built map. When it has determined its pose with high likelihood, it uniformly spreads the resulting error along the cycle in the map. Consequently, the approach still maintains just a single map, which is computationally advantageous. But unlike the incremental maximum likelihood methods, it also has the ability to correct its map backward in time whenever an inconsistency is detected. Mathematically, this hybrid algorithm can be derived as a rather crude approximation to the EM algorithm, which performs the E-step and the M-step selectively, as discrepancies are detected.

However, the hybrid approach suffers many deficiencies. First and foremost, the decision to change the map backward in time is a discrete one that, if wrong, can lead to catastrophic failure. Moreover, the approach cannot cope with complex ambiguities, such as the uncertainty that arises when the robot traverses multiple nested cycles. Finally, the hybrid approach is—strictly speaking—not a real-time algorithm, since the time it takes to correct a loop depends on the size of the loop. However, practical implementations appear to work well in real time when used in office-building-type environments.

The hybrid mapping algorithm has been extended to handle multiple robots that jointly acquire a single map (Konolige et al. 1999; Thrun 2001c). Figure 8 plots a map acquired by three autonomous robots, which coordinated their exploration efforts while the map was being built (Burgard et al. 2000; Simmons et al. 2000). Such results exploit the approximate real-time property of the hybrid algorithm.

8   OCCUPANCY GRID MAPS

The mapping algorithms described above all address the mapping problem with unknown robot poses, which, as pointed out above, is known as the simultaneous localization and mapping (SLAM) problem. The simpler case—mapping with *known* poses—has also received attention in the literature. One mapping algorithm known as *occupancy grid maps*, developed by Elfes and Moravec in the mid-1980s (Elfes 1989; Moravec 1988), has enjoyed enormous popularity. This algorithm is used by a number of autonomous robots, typically in combination with one of the algorithms described above.

The central problem addressed by occupancy grid mapping and related algorithms is the problem of generating a consistent metric map from noisy or incomplete sensor data. Even if the robot poses are known, it is sometimes difficult to say whether a place in the environment is occupied or not, due to ambiguities in the sensor data. The best-explored applications of occupancy grid maps require robots with range sensors, such as sonar sensors or laser range finders. Both sensors are characterized by noise. Sonars, in addition, cover an entire cone in space, and from a single sonar measurement it is impossible to say *where* in the cone the object is. Both sensors are also sensitive to the angle of an object surface relative to the sensor and the reflective properties of the surface (absorption and dispersion).

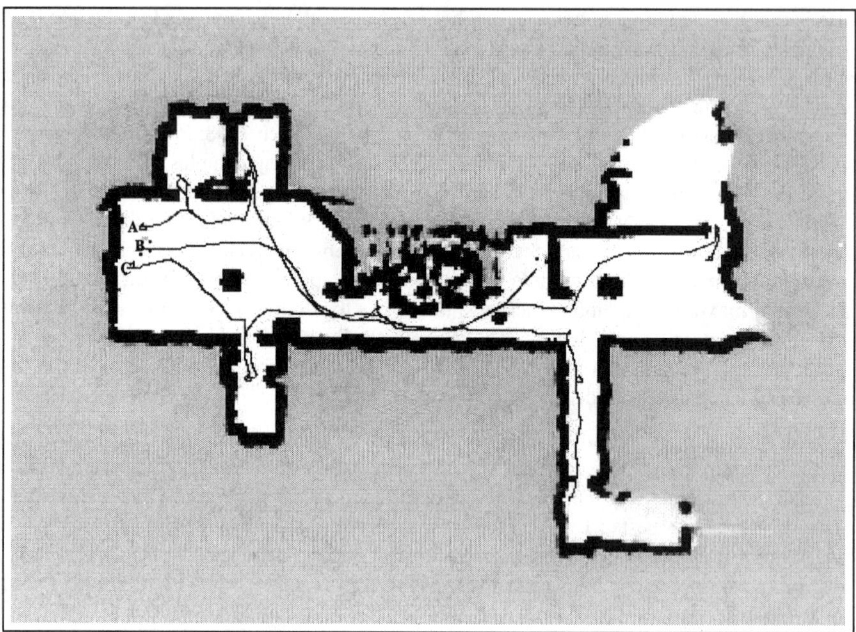

Figure 8   Map built by three autonomously exploring robots. The initial robot poses are on the left, as marked by the letters A, B, and C.

Occupancy grid maps resolve such problems by generating probabilistic maps. As the name suggests, occupancy grid maps are represented by grids, which are usually 2D (Moravec 1988) but may also cover all three spatial dimensions (Moravec and Martin 1994). The standard occupancy grid mapping algorithm is a version of Bayes filters, just like any other major mapping algorithm. In particular, Bayes filters are used to calculate the posterior over the occupancy of each grid cell. Let $\langle x, y \rangle$ be the coordinates of a grid cell and $m_{x,y}$ its occupancy. Occupancy is a binary variable: either the cell is occupied or it is free. The problem, thus, is to calculate a posterior over a set of binary variables, each of which is a single numerical probability $p(m_{x,y} \mid z^t, x^t)$. Again, Bayes filters provide the framework for calculating these posteriors.

The binary Bayes filter is often written using *odds*. The odds of an event x with probability $p(x)$ is defined as $\frac{p(x)}{1-p(x)}$. In odds notation, the binary Bayes filter for a static map with known poses s^t works as follows:

$$\frac{p(m_{x,y} \mid z^t, s^t)}{1 - p(m_{x,y} \mid z^t, s^t)} = \frac{p(m_{x,y} \mid z_t, s_t)}{1 - p(m_{x,y} \mid z_t, s_t)} \frac{1 - p(m_{x,y})}{p(m_{x,y})} \frac{p(m_{x,y} \mid z^{t-1}, s^{t-1})}{1 - p(m_{x,y} \mid z^{t-1}, s^{t-1})} \tag{17}$$

The basic update equation is often implemented in logarithmic form, which is computationally advantageous (additions are faster than multiplications) and also avoids numeric instabilities that arise when probabilities are close to zero:

$$\log \frac{p(m_{x,y} \mid z^t, s^t)}{1 - p(m_{x,y} \mid z^t, s^t)}$$

(a)   (b)

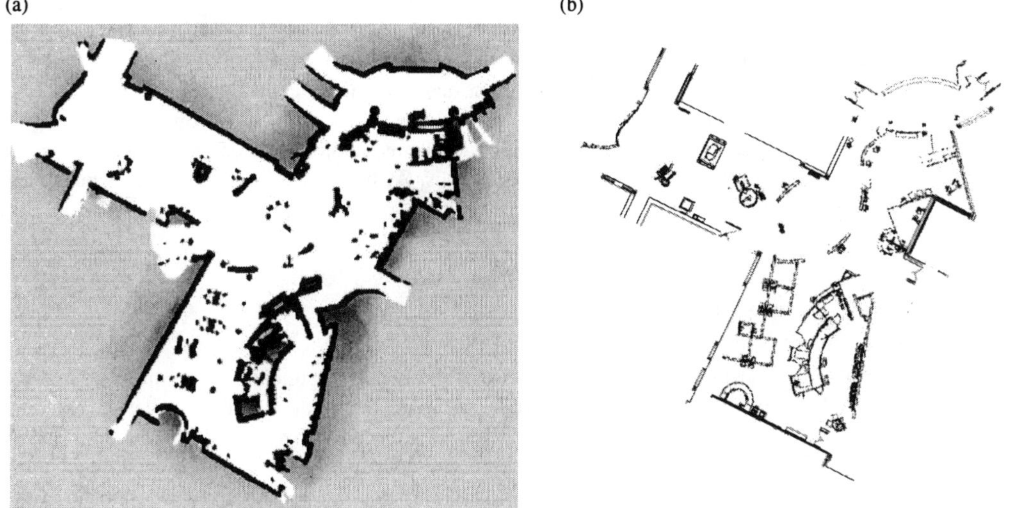

Figure 9   (a) Occupancy grid map. (b) Architectural blueprint of a recently constructed building. The blueprint is less accurate than the map in several locations.

$$= \quad \log \frac{p(m_{x,y} \mid z_t, s_t)}{1 - p(m_{x,y} \mid z_t, s_t)} + \log \frac{1 - p(m_{x,y})}{p(m_{x,y})} + \log \frac{p(m_{x,y} \mid z^{t-1}, s^{t-1})}{1 - p(m_{x,y} \mid z^{t-1}, s^{t-1})} \quad (18)$$

It is easy to see that the desired probability of occupancy, $p(m_{x,y} \mid z^t, s^t)$, can be recovered from the log-odds representation. Moreover, we notice that the occupancy grid mapping algorithm is recursive, allowing for incrementally updating the individual grid cells as new sensor data arrives. Finally, occupancy grid maps require two probability densities, $p(m_{x,y} \mid z_t, s_t)$ and $p(m_{x,y})$. The latter probability, $p(m_{x,y})$, is the *prior* for occupancy that, if set to 0.5, makes an entire term disappear in Equation 17.

The remaining probability, $p(m_{x,y} \mid z_t, s_t)$, is called an *inverse sensor model*. It specifies the probability that a grid cell $m_{x,y}$ is occupied based on a single sensor measurement z_t taken at location s_t. The literature has devised numerous versions of this probability, for sensors such as sonars, lasers, cameras (mono and stereo), and infrared sensors (Murray and Little 2001; Thrun et al. 1998). Inverse models for range sensors usually attribute high probability of occupancy for grid cells that overlap with a detected range, and low probability for grid cells in between this range and the sensor. These functions can be crafted by hand (Moravec 1988) or learned from sensor data (Thrun et al. 1998).

We already encountered examples of occupancy grid maps in Figures 1(a) and 5. The maps shown there were built using sonar sensors. Figure 9 gives another example, constructed from laser range finders. In this example, the pose information s^t was obtained using the hybrid mapping algorithm described in the previous section. The resulting occupancy grid map exhibits a great level of accuracy when compared with a CAD map of the building, shown on the right.

The occupancy grid mapping algorithm enjoys the reputation of being extremely robust and easy to implement, which has contributed to its popularity. Its major shortcoming is the lack of a method for accommodating pose uncertainty. A second deficiency is inherited from the Bayes filter, which assumes independent noise. When sensor noise is strongly correlated, the resulting maps can be erroneous. This is particularly the case when sonar measurements are integrated while the robot stands still. Most implementations remedy this problem by simply discarding all sensor measurements, unless the robot is in motion. A final, more subtle deficiency stems from the independence assumption between multiple grid cells. Such an assumption, while convenient, can lead to inferior maps. See (Thrun 2001b) for more details.

9   OBJECT MAPS

Another family of mapping algorithms addresses the problem of building maps composed of basic geometric shapes or objects, such as lines, walls, and so on. In mobile robotics, the idea of representing maps by simple geometric shapes can be traced back to a paper by Chatila and Laumond (1985), who proposed to represent 2D maps by collection of lines rather than grids. However, they did not provide a practical algorithmic solution. Since then, researchers have devised a few practical algorithms that can use object information in the process of mapping (Biswas et al. 2002; Liu et al. 2001; Martin and Thrun 2002).

There are four basic advantages of object maps over grid maps: First, object maps can be more compact than occupancy grid maps, especially if the environment is structured. Second, they can also be more accurate, assuming that the basic objects in the approach are adequate to describe the actual objects found in the environment at hand. Third, object representations appear to be necessary for describing dynamic environments where objects might change their location over time. And fourth, object maps are often closer to people's perception of environments than grid maps, thereby facilitating the interaction between humans and robots.

However, object maps also suffer a major disadvantage. In particular, they are usually confined to environments that can be expressed through simple geometric shapes and objects. Real environments are complex, and any list of shapes and objects will typically be incomplete. One way to overcome this limitation is to allow for hybrid maps, which represent some parts of the environment via objects and others using gridmap–style representations. Another is to broaden the notion of objects and learn models of object concurrently to learning the map.

A good example of learning with parametric object models is described in (Liu et al. 2001; Martin and Thrun 2002). The specific problem addressed in both of these papers is that of constructing 3D maps. The data used for the mapping task is collected by the robot equipped with two 2D laser range finders. One of those 2D sensors is pointed forward to accomplish localization during mapping. A second sensor is pointed upward, perpendicular to the robot's motion direction, enabling the robot to scan the 3D structure of the environment as it moves about. Figure 10 shows a slightly preprocessed raw data set of a 3D structure, represented by small polygons that connect adjacent range measurements. This structure was constructed with the help of the hybrid 2D mapping algorithm described in Section 7, to obtain accurate localization. The surface structure in Figure 10 is extremely rugged, reflecting the noise in the sensor measurements. One might be tempted to apply occupancy grid–style techniques for reducing the noise, as in (Moravec and Martin 1994). However, in this specific data set, each feature in the environment is sensed at most once, whereas techniques like occupancy grids require that a grid cell can be measured many times, so that information can be integrated using Bayes filters.

 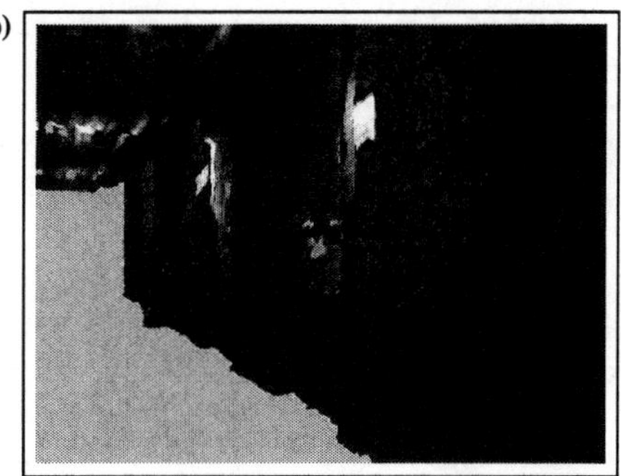

Figure 10   (a) Polygonal model generated from raw data, not using any geometric shape information. (b) Texture superimposed onto this model.

The object mapping approach in (Liu et al. 2001; Martin and Thrun 2002) remedies this problem by assuming that parts of the environment consist of large flat surfaces—which is the one and only type of object that is accommodated in this approach. This assumption is certainly valid for a corridorlike environment with flat walls and ceiling. The technical problem, thus, is how to determine the number, sizes, and locations of these surfaces.

Interestingly enough, this problem can be solved with a variant of the expectation maximization algorithm that we already encountered. EM generates a sequence of object maps that explain the data with increasing accuracy: $m^{[0]}, m^{[1]}, m^{[2]}, \ldots$. Above, the EM algorithm was used to generate maps, where the latent variables were robot poses. Here, the poses are known. Instead, the latent variables are correspondence variables that specify which of the measurements were caused by which of the flat surfaces—or whether a measurement was caused by a surface at all. For simplicity, let us assume that each measurement z_t is a single range measurement that, by virtue of knowing the robot pose s_t, can be mapped into 3D coordinates using the standard geometric laws. Let us assume the world contains J flat surfaces, called $m_1, m_2, \ldots, m_J$. For now, let us assume J is given, although the work in (Liu et al. 2001; Martin and Thrun 2002) provides techniques for estimating J along the way (see below). The correspondence variables will be written as c_{tj} and c_{t*}, where c_{tj} is 1 if and only if a measurement z_t was caused by surface j, and c_{t*} is 1 if and only if this measurement was not caused by any of the surfaces. The set of all correspondence variables at time t will be denoted by c_t, and the correspondences leading up to time t by c^t. Clearly, these variables are not observable. However, it turns out that calculating expectations for these correspondence variables for any given map m is relatively straightforward, as is generating a new improved map under knowledge of these expectations. Thus, the problem lends itself nicely to the EM algorithm.

Applied to this mapping problem, the EM algorithm generates a sequence of maps by maximizing the following expected log likelihood function:

$$m^{[i+1]} \quad = \quad \underset{m}{\operatorname{argmax}} E_{c^t}[\log p(z^t, c^t \mid m, s^t) \mid m^{[i]}, z^t] \tag{19}$$

Notice the similarity to Equation 13. In both cases, EM maximizes a log likelihood function over the data z^t and some hidden variables. In both cases, the hidden variables are integrated out by calculating the expectation over them. However, in the present mapping problem, the poses s^t are known. Instead, the correspondences c^t are not.

Under the familiar conditional independence assumptions and further mild assumptions on the nature of sensor noise, this expression unfolds to the following one:

$$m^{[i+1]} \quad = \quad \operatorname*{argmin}_{m} \sum_{t} \sum_{j} p(c_{tj} \mid m^{[i]}, z_t, s_t) \, \mathrm{dist}(z_t, m_j) \qquad (20)$$

Here, "dist" is the Euclidean distance function, which is obtained by taking the logarithm of a Gaussian noise model. EM maximizes Equation 20 in two steps: (1) The E-step calculates the expectation of the correspondence variables $p(c_{ij} \mid m^{[i]}, z_t, s_t)$ and $p(c_{i*} \mid m^{[i]}, z_t, s_t)$ for a fixed, given map $m^{[i]}$. Put differently, the E-step calculates the probability that a measurement z_t was caused by any of the surfaces in the present model. (2) The M-step generates a new map $m^{[i+1]}$ by maximizing the data log likelihood under these fixed expectations. Both steps are mathematically straightforward and can be implemented in closed form (Liu et al. 2001). The result, as stated above, is a sequence of maps that successively maximizes the expected log likelihood of the data or, put differently, generates maps that are increasingly accurate.

The basic algorithm in (Liu et al. 2001) contains two additional ideas. First, while the EM map itself consists exclusively of flat surfaces, the underlying mathematical framework allows for the possibility that measurements are not caused by such surfaces. This makes it possible to include such "unexplained" measurements into the final map, effectively devising a hybrid approach that integrates flat surfaces with raw polygonal models. This property is important when applying any object-based mapping algorithm in practice.

Second, the EM algorithm provides no answer as to how many surfaces are contained in the world. This is not a trivial question, as it is unclear how small a surface we are willing to accept. The approach in (Liu et al. 2001) solves this through a Bayesian model selection algorithm, which varies the number of surfaces J in the model concurrently while running EM. The specific approach realizes a Bayesian prior that effectively requires the presence of a certain number of measurements in a certain spatial density to warrant the creation of a surface. The algorithm itself is stochastic, seed starting surfaces at random locations and terminating others whose posterior probabilities, after running EM for a few iterations, do not warrant their existence under the Bayesian prior. The resulting algorithm is a strict maximum likelihood algorithm that generates a single map, which combines large flat surfaces and many small polygons. In a recent paper (Martin and Thrun 2002), the approach was extended as an online algorithm.

Figure 11 compares sample views, generated without (top row) and with (bottom row) EM and the flat surface model. The object model is 20 times as compact as the original one. In fact, 95% of all original measurements are easily explained by $J = 7$ flat surfaces. It is also visually much more accurate, due to the fact that the texture is mapped onto a flat surface, instead of a rugged surface like the one shown in Figure 10. The online algorithm described in (Martin and Thrun 2002) requires less than two minutes to construct maps of comparable sizes. Clearly, these results are encouraging, though they only hold in cases where the basic geometric object templates describe significant portions of the environment. The remaining challenge is to find richer models that can describe more complex environments than the relatively simple corridor environment.

10   MAPPING DYNAMIC ENVIRONMENTS

Physical environments change over time. As noted in Section 3, the vast majority of published algorithms make a static world assumption, and hence are principally unable to cope with dynamic

(a) Polygonal models generated from raw data

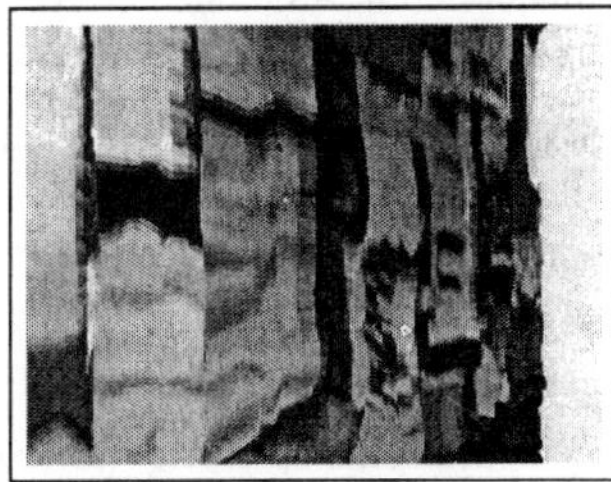

(b) Low-complexity multi-surface model

Figure 11   3D models generated **(a)** from raw sensor data and **(b)** using our algorithm, in which 94.6% of all measurements are explained by seven surfaces. Notice that the model in **(b)** is much smoother and appears to be more accurate.

environments. Some of these algorithms, however, can be modified to cope with *certain* types of changes. For example, the Kalman filter approach is easily adapted to one in which landmarks move slowly over time, on trajectories that resemble—for example—Brownian motion. Technically, this is achieved by adding a Gaussian motion variable into the landmark's location. The effect is an increase in the location uncertainty of each landmark over time, which subsequently may be counteracted by sensing. Such algorithms are popular in the target tracking literature (Bar-Shalom and Fortmann 1998; Montemerlo et al. 2002; Schulz et al. 2001). Similarly, occupancy grid maps may accommodate certain types of motions by decaying occupancy over time, as discussed in (Yamauchi and Langley 1997). Extensions of occupancy grids exist that can detect frequently changing locations such as doors (Schneider 1994) and, once detected, quickly estimate their present status during everyday navigation (Avots et al. 2002). Nevertheless, the issue of the robotic mapping of dynamic environments remains poorly explored, and the approaches outlined above cover only a narrow set of cases.

A final algorithm addresses environment change at its very core. The assumption here is that the environment possesses objects whose locations are static in the short run, but that change over longer periods in time. The static world assumption, thus, may be sufficient to develop snapshots at individual points in time, but it is insufficient to capture the changes that might occur. A motivating example of such a situation is the typical office environment, where the location of furniture and other larger items (e.g., boxes) may change frequently over time.

Biswas and colleagues recently proposed an algorithm called *Dogma*, short for *dynamic occupancy grid mapping algorithm* (Biswas et al. 2002). As the name suggests, the algorithm is based on the occupancy grid mapping algorithm described in Section 8. On top of that, Dogma learns the models of dynamic objects, represented by local, object-specific occupancy grid maps. For example, Dogma may learn the characteristic shape of a chair as represented in occupancy grid maps and use this as a model of a new object. As the environment is inspected, the algorithm assumes that this object may have moved, and as a result the global occupancy grid map may have changed.

The key challenge for learning the models of objects is again a correspondence problem. Figure 12(a) illustrates this problem. Shown there are nine conventional occupancy grid maps, acquired in the same environment but at different points in time. Clearly, some of the objects move, and not all of the objects are present in all maps. To learn the models of the moving objects, the robot has to establish correspondence between the individual footprints found in the occupancy grid maps.

It should come as little surprise that Dogma's method for solving this problem is a variant of the EM algorithm. Similar to the multiplanar object modeling technique, the Dogma algorithm constructs a sequence of object models, denoted $\theta^{[0]}, \theta^{[1]}, \theta^{[2]}, \ldots$. Each such model $\theta^{[i]}$ is a collection of local occupancy grid maps, each describing individual objects in the environment. From the locally built occupancy grid maps m_t, Dogma extracts local object footprints using standard image differencing techniques known from the computer vision literature (Zucker 1976). The correspondence variables c_t associate sets of object footprints with sets of objects in the model θ. This is again done via maximizing an expected log likelihood function of the form

$$\theta^{[i+1]} \quad = \quad \underset{\theta}{\operatorname{argmax}} \, E_{c^t}[\log p(m^t, c^t \mid \theta) \mid \theta^{[i]}, m^t] \tag{21}$$

The exact optimization is subject to a *mutual exclusivity constraint* (Dellaert et al. 2000; Pasula et al. 1999), which specifies that the same object cannot be seen twice in the same map. This constraint is important—as otherwise there may be a tendency to map multiple similar-looking objects to the same object in the model θ. The mutual exclusivity constraint is easily incorporated into the E-step of the EM estimation.

A typical trace of Dogma's EM is shown in Figure 12(c), starting with a random set of object models on the top, and a final set at the bottom. The number of objects is obtained using a Bayesian model selection criterion similar to the one applied for learning multiplanar maps. Once such an object model is learned, dynamic objects can quickly be identified and their locations updated.

The Dogma algorithm is among the first to address dynamic environments. The idea of learning object models is particularly appealing in environments that change, since local object characteristics are independent of the location of a particular object. However, Dogma is far from being a general solution to this important problem. In particular, this algorithm is unable to accommodate fast-moving objects such as people, it is limited to objects that can easily be segmented in a preprocessing step, and it cannot handle noncontiguous objects or objects that may change shape. Further research is warranted on more powerful algorithms that can cope with a wider variety of dynamic environments.

11   SUMMARY AND OPEN PROBLEMS

The goal of this chapter was to survey major algorithms in the field of robotic mapping. The major paradigms surveyed here include Kalman filter techniques, approaches based on Dempster's expectation maximization algorithm, occupancy grid techniques, and techniques for learning object models. Emphasis is placed on relating these techniques to each other, to point out their relative strengths and weaknesses.

I believe that the algorithms described here are representative examples of the state of the art in robotic mapping, specifically in the area of indoor navigation. It is quite remarkable that virtually all state-of-the-art algorithms in robotic mapping share the same mathematical foundation: they

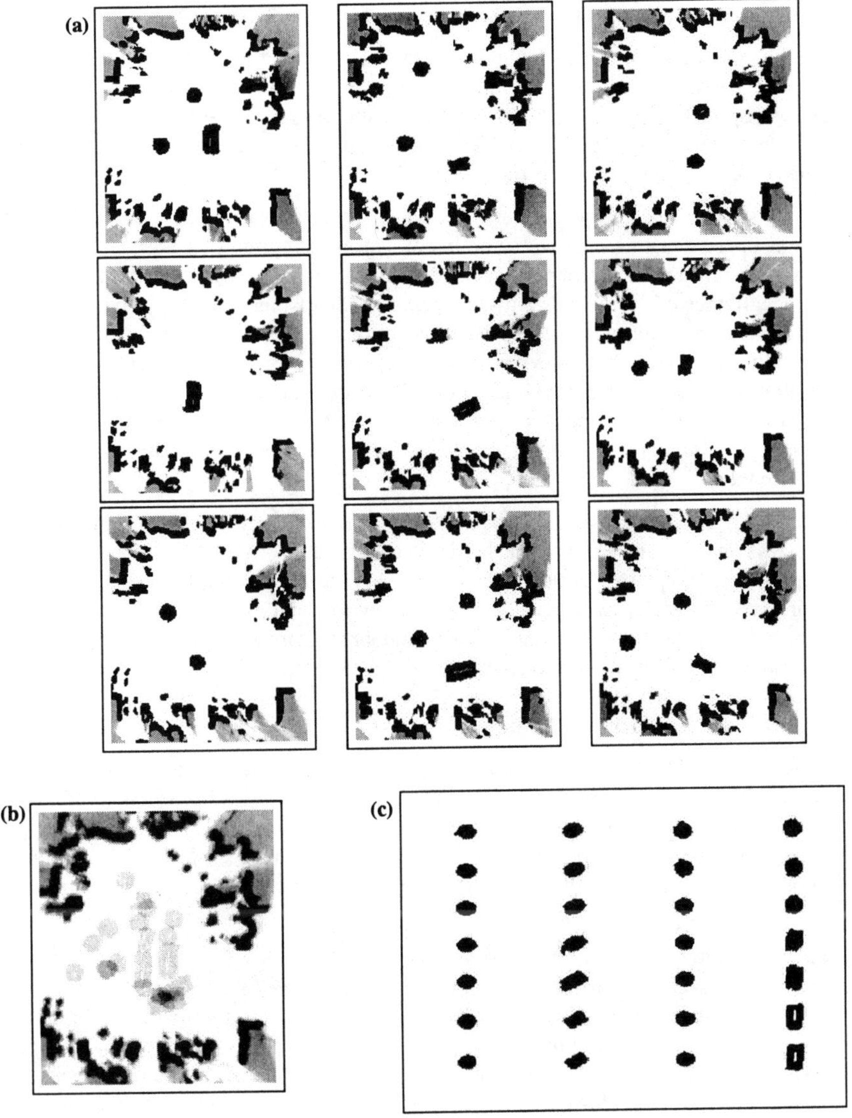

Figure 12   (a) Nine occupancy grid maps maps of a changing indoor environment recorded at different points in time. (b) Map generated by the standard occupancy grid mapping algorithm with static world assumption. (c) Four different objects identified by the Dogma algorithm in seven iterations of EM.

are all probabilistic. Moreover, they are all versions of Bayes filters and an underlying generative probabilistic description of robot motion and perception. This development parallels a much broader trend in mobile robotics, where probabilistic techniques are commonly the method of choice over more ad hoc approaches, such as behavior-based techniques (Thrun 2001a).

Overall, the situation in robotic mapping is encouraging. After approximately two decades of research, the field has matured to a point where detailed maps of complex environments can be built in real time, specifically indoors. Many existing techniques are robust to noise and can cope with a large range of environments. Nevertheless, there still exists a large number of challenging open problems worth many more decades of research.

In particular, most published methods assume that the world does not change during mapping. Real environments are dynamic. Despite some initial successes—some of which is discussed in Section 10—we are still far away from practical algorithms for mapping dynamic environments, and from a theoretical framework accompanying such methods. Clearly, the issue has to be addressed if robots shall operate in environments over long periods of time, such as the long-envisioned personal service robots (Engelberger 1999; Lacey and Dawson-Howe 1998; Roy et al. 2000; Schraft and Schmierer 1998). A viable research goal, thus, would be to develop a lifelong mapping robot, one that is capable of continually updating its map (and its object models) over its lifetime. We also need technologies for *understanding* environment dynamics, rather than just adapting to changes, so that we can anticipate them.

A second shortcoming of current technology arises from the vast amount of knowledge that we, as people, possess about environments, but that is presently not brought to bear for the mapping problem. The 3D-object mapping algorithm exploits one very basic piece of information, namely, the frequent occurrence of large flat surfaces in corridor-type environments. Clearly, we have tremendous knowledge about the objects that surround us in typical indoor environments, the vegetation objects in outdoor environments, the objects found on the sea bed, and so on. In many cases, we have additional information about a specific environment, such as satellite imagery or architectural blueprints. Methods are needed that can make use of such information during mapping.

From a statistical point of view, the holy grail of mapping is to calculate full posteriors over maps, robot poses, and object models, under hard problems such as unknown correspondences. While this problem is hard and effectively unsolved even for static environments, it is even more challenging for dynamic environments. At present, it is unclear if calculating posteriors is feasible for reasonably complex problems at all, or if we will have to resort to solutions such as the EM algorithm, which maximize likelihood and are subject to local maxima.

This chapter places little emphasis on multi-robot collaboration during mapping. Clearly, many envisioned operational scenarios involve teams of robots (Matarić 1997; Parker 1996; Simmons et al. 2000), and using multiple collaborative robots for building maps is clearly a worthwhile research goal. Existing techniques work well if the relative starting positions of all robots are known (Burgard et al. 2000; Simmons et al. 2000), as the existence of multiple robots simply adds a few dimension to the statistical mapping problem. However, building reasonable maps if the relative initial position of the robots is unknown is largely an open problem. A complicating factor in multi-robot mapping is that the overlap of the maps acquired locally by the robots may be unknown. This makes it challenging to estimate the relative location of the robots as they acquire local map information. Moreover, if robots can detect each other (Fox et al. 2000), complex correspondence problems may arise related to the identification of individual robots.

Another dimension worth exploring is the topic of unstructured environments. Most examples in this survey focus on indoor environments, which possess a lot of structure. Outdoor, underwater, and planetary environments also possess some structure, but come in a much larger variety. In the extreme, the environment may be entirely unstructured, such as piles of rubble that a robot might want to explore after a natural disaster or a terrorist attack. Many of the techniques described in this chapter are inapplicable. Extending existing mapping techniques to such environments is therefore an important goal of ongoing research.

Finally, none of the approaches reviewed here addresses the issue of robot control. The ultimate goal of robotics is to make robots do the right thing. During map acquisition, this might mean controlling the exploration of the robot(s) acquiring the data. In a broader context, this issue involves the question of what elements of the environment have to be modeled to successfully enable a robot to perform its task therein. While these issues have been addressed for decades in ad hoc ways, little is known about the general interplay between mapping and control under uncertainty.

In summary, it is difficult to imagine a truly autonomous robot that would not be able to acquire a model of its environment. This list provides only a sample of important open problems. I hope that this chapter documents why I believe that robot mapping will continue to be a highly active and viable research area, with significant relevance to the goal of building truly autonomous robots.

ACKNOWLEDGMENTS

This research is sponsored by DARPA's MARS Program (contract number N66001-01-C-6018) and the National Science Foundation (CAREER grant number IIS-9876136 and regular grant number IIS-9877033), all of which is gratefully acknowledged. The views and conclusions contained in this document are those of the author and should not be interpreted as necessarily representing official policies or endorsements, either expressed or implied, of the United States government or any of the sponsoring institutions.

References

Allen, P., and I. Stamos (2000). Integration of range and image sensing for photorealistic 3D modeling. In *Proceedings of the IEEE International Conference on Robotics and Automation (ICRA)*, pp. 1435–1440.

Avots, D., E. Lim, R. Thibaux, and S. Thrun (2002). A probabilistic technique for simultaneous localization and door state estimation with mobile robots in dynamic environments. Unpublished.

Bajcsy, R., G. Kamberova, and L. Nocera (2000). 3D reconstruction of environments for virtual reconstruction. In *Proceedings of the Fourth IEEE Workshop on Applications of Computer Vision*.

Bar-Shalom, Y., and T. E. Fortmann (1998). *Tracking and Data Association*. Academic Press.

Becker, S., and M. Bove (1995). Semiautomatic 3-D model extraction from uncalibrated 2-D camera views. In *Proceedings of the SPIE Symposium on Electronic Imaging,* San Jose.

Biswas, R., B. Limketkai, S. Sanner, and S. Thrun (2002). Towards object mapping in dynamic environments with mobile robots. Unpublished.

Borenstein, J., B. Everett, and L. Feng (1996). *Navigating Mobile Robots: Systems and Techniques*. Wellesley, MA: A. K. Peters, Ltd.

Borenstein, J., and Y. Koren. (1991). The vector field histogram—fast obstacle avoidance for mobile robots. *IEEE Journal of Robotics and Automation 7*(3), 278–288.

Buhmann, J., W. Burgard, A. Cremers, D. Fox, T. Hofmann, F. Schneider, J. Strikos, and S. Thrun (1995). The mobile robot Rhino. *AI Magazine 16*(1).

Burgard, W., A. Cremers, D. Fox, D. Hähnel, G. Lakemeyer, D. Schulz, W. Steiner, and S. Thrun (1999). Experiences with an interactive museum tour-guide robot. *Artificial Intelligence 114*(1-2), 3–55.

Burgard, W., D. Fox, H. Jans, C. Matenar, and S. Thrun (1999). Sonar-based mapping of large-scale mobile robot environments using EM. In *Proceedings of the International Conference on Machine Learning*, Bled, Slovenia.

Burgard, W., D. Fox, M. Moors, R. Simmons, and S. Thrun (2000). Collaborative multi-robot exploration. In *Proceedings of the IEEE International Conference on Robotics and Automation (ICRA)*, San Francisco.

Castellanos, J., J. Montiel, J. Neira, and J. Tardós (1999). The SPmap: A probabilistic framework for simultaneous localization and map building. *IEEE Transactions on Robotics and Automation 15*(5), 948–953.

Castellanos, J., and J. Tardós (2000). *Mobile Robot Localization and Map Building: A Multisensor Fusion Approach*. Boston, MA: Kluwer Academic Publishers.

Chatila, R., and J.-P. Laumond (1985). Position referencing and consistent world modeling for mobile robots. In *Proceedings of the 1985 IEEE International Conference on Robotics and Automation*.

Cheng, Y.-Q., E. Riseman, X. Wang, R. Collins, and A. Hanson (2000). Three-dimensional reconstruction of points and lines with unknown correspondence across images. *International Journal of Computer Vision*.

Choset, H. (1996). *Sensor Based Motion Planning: The Hierarchical Generalized Voronoi Graph*. Ph.D. thesis, California Institute of Technology.

Choset, H., and J. Burdick (1996). Sensor based planning: the hierarhical generalized voronoi graph. In *Proceedings Workshop on Algorithmic Foundations of Robotics*, Toulouse, France.

Cox, I. and J. Leonard (1994). Modeling a dynamic environment using a Bayesian multiple hypothesis approach. *Artificial Intelligence 66*, 311–344.

Csorba, M. (1997). *Simultaneous Localisation and Map Building*. Ph.D. thesis, University of Oxford.

Debevec, P., C. Taylor, and J. Malik (1996). Modeling and rendering architecture from photographs. In *Proceedings of the 23rd International Conference on Computer Graphics and Interactive Techniques (SIGGRAPH)*.

Dellaert, F., D. Fox, W. Burgard, and S. Thrun (1999). Monte Carlo localization for mobile robots. In *Proceedings of the IEEE International Conference on Robotics and Automation (ICRA)*.

Dellaert, F., S. Seitz, C. Thorpe, and S. Thrun (2000). EM, MCMC, and chain flipping for structure from motion with unknown correspondence. *Machine Learning*. To appear.

Dempster, A., A. Laird, and D. Rubin (1977). Maximum likelihood from incomplete data via the EM algorithm. *Journal of the Royal Statistical Society, Series B 39*(1), 1–38.

Dissanayake, G., H. Durrant-Whyte, and T. Bailey (2000). A computationally efficient solution to the simultaneous localisation and map building (SLAM) problem. Working notes of ICRA 2000 Workshop W4: Mobile Robot Navigation and Mapping.

Dissanayake, G., P. Newman, S. Clark, H. Durrant-Whyte, and M. Csorba (2000). An experimental and theoretical investigation into simultaneous localisation and map building (SLAM). In P. Corke and J. Trevelyan (Eds.), *Lecture Notes in Control and Information Sciences: Experimental Robotics VI*, London: Springer-Verlag, pp. 265–274.

Dissanayake, G., P. Newman, S. Clark, H. Durrant-Whyte, and M. Csorba (2001). A solution to the simultaneous localisation and map building (SLAM) problem. *IEEE Transactions of Robotics and Automation.*

Doucet, A., N. de Freitas, and N. Gordon (Eds.) (2001). *Sequential Monte Carlo Methods in Practice.* New York: Springer-Verlag.

Doucet, A., N. de Freitas, K. Murphy, and S. Russell (2000). Rao-Blackwellised particle filtering for dynamic Bayesian networks. In *Proceedings of the 16th Conference on Uncertainty in Artificial Intelligence*, Stanford, pp. 176–183.

Durrant-Whyte, H., S. Majumder, S. Thrun, M. de Battista, and S. Scheding (2001). A Bayesian algorithm for simultaneous localization and map building. In *Proceedings of the 10th International Symposium of Robotics Research (ISRR'01)*, Lorne, Australia.

Elfes, A. (1987). Sonar-based real-world mapping and navigation. *IEEE Journal of Robotics and Automation RA-3(3)*, 249–265.

Elfes, A. (1989). *Occupancy Grids: A Probabilistic Framework for Robot Perception and Navigation.* Ph.D. thesis, Department of Electrical and Computer Engineering, Carnegie Mellon University.

Engelberger, G. (1999). Services. In S. Y. Nof (Ed.), *Handbook of Industrial Robotics* (2nd ed.)., Chapter 64., pp. 1201–1212. John Wiley and Sons.

Engelson, S., and D. McDermott (1992). Error correction in mobile robot map learning. In *Proceedings of the 1992 IEEE International Conference on Robotics and Automation*, Nice, France, pp. 2555–2560.

Fox, D., W. Burgard, H. Kruppa, and S. Thrun (2000). A probabilistic approach to collaborative multi-robot localization. *Autonomous Robots 8(3)*.

Fox, D., W. Burgard, and S. Thrun (1999). Markov localization for mobile robots in dynamic environments. *Journal of Artificial Intelligence Research 11*, 391–427.

Gonzalez-Banos, H. H., and J. C. Latombe (2002). Navigation strategies for exploring indoor environments. *International Journal of Robotics Research.* To appear.

Guivant, J., and E. Nebot (2001). Optimization of the simultaneous localization and map building algorithm for real time implementation. *IEEE Transaction of Robotic and Automation.*

Gutmann, J.-S. (2000). *Robuste Navigation Autonomer Mobiler Systeme.* Berlin: Akademische Verlagsgesellschaft Aka. In German.

Gutmann, J.-S., and B. Nebel (1997). Navigation mobiler roboter mit laserscans. In *Autonome Mobile Systeme.* Berlin: Springer-Verlag.

Gutmann, J.-S., and K. Konolige (2000). Incremental mapping of large cyclic environments. In *Proceedings of the IEEE International Symposium on Computational Intelligence in Robotics and Automation (CIRA).*

Guzzoni, D., A. Cheyer, L. Julia, and K. Konolige (1997). Many robots make short work. *AI Magazine 18(1)*, 55–64.

Hakim, S., and P. Boulanger (1997). Sensor based creation of indoor virtual environment models. In *Proceedings of the Fourth Internetional Conference on Virtual Systems and Multimedia (VSMM).*

Iocchi, L., K. Konolige, and M. Bajracharya (2000). Visually realistic mapping of a planar environment with stereo. In *Proceedings of the 2000 International Symposium on Experimental Robotics*, Waikiki, Hawaii.

Jazwinsky, A. (1970). *Stochastic Processes and Filtering Theory.* New York: Academic.

Jensfelt, P., and S. Kristensen (1999). Active global localisation for a mobile robot using multiple hypothesis tracking. In *Proceedings of the IJCAI Workshop on Reasoning with Uncertainty in Robot Navigation*, Stockholm, pp. 13–22.

Julier, S. J., and J. K. Uhlmann (1997). A new extension of the Kalman filter to nonlinear systems. In *In Proceedings of AeroSense: The 11th International Symposium on Aerospace/Defence Sensing, Simulation and Controls*.

Kaelbling, L., M. Littman, and A. Cassandra (1998). Planning and acting in partially observable stochastic domains. *Artificial Intelligence 101*(1-2), 99–134.

Kalman, R. E. (1960). A new approach to linear filtering and prediction problems. *Trans. ASME, Journal of Basic Engineering 82*, 35–45.

Konolige, K., J.-S. Gutmann, D. Guzzoni, R. Ficklin, and K. Nicewarner (1999). A mobile robot sense net. In *Proceedings of SPIE 3839 Sensor Fusion and Decentralized Control in Robotic Systmes II*, Boston.

Kortenkamp, D., R. Bonasso, and R. Murphy (Eds.) (1998). *AI-based Mobile Robots: Case studies of successful robot systems*, Cambridge, MA: MIT Press.

Kortenkamp, D., and T. Weymouth (1994). Topological mapping for mobile robots using a combination of sonar and vision sensing. In *Proceedings of the Twelfth National Conference on Artificial Intelligence*, Menlo Park, CA, pp. 979–984. AAAI Press/MIT Press.

Kuipers, B., and Y.-T. Byun (1991). A robot exploration and mapping strategy based on a semantic hierarchy of spatial representations. *Journal of Robotics and Autonomous Systems 8*, 47–63.

Lacey, G., and K. Dawson-Howe (1998). The application of robotics to a mobility aid for the elderly blind. *Robotics and Autonomous Systems 23*, 245–252.

Leonard, J., H. Durrant-Whyte, and I. Cox (1992). Dynamic map building for an autonomous mobile robot. *International Journal of Robotics Research 11*(4), 89–96.

Leonard, J., and H. Feder (1999). A computationally efficient method for large-scale concurrent mapping and localization. In J. Hollerbach and D. Koditschek (Eds.), *Proceedings of the Ninth International Symposium on Robotics Research*, Salt Lake City, Utah.

Liu, J., and R. Chen (1998). Sequential Monte Carlo methods for dynamic systems. *Journal of the American Statistical Association 93*, 1032–1044.

Liu, Y., R. Emery, D. Chakrabarti, W. Burgard, and S. Thrun (2001). Using EM to learn 3D models with mobile robots. In *Proceedings of the International Conference on Machine Learning (ICML)*.

Lovejoy, W. (1991). A survey of algorithmic methods for partially observable markov decision processes. *Annals of Operatons Research 28*(1), 47–65.

Lu, F., and E. Milios (1997). Globally consistent range scan alignment for environment mapping. *Autonomous Robots 4*, 333–349.

Martin, C., and S. Thrun (2002). Online acquisition of compact volumetric maps with mobile robots. In *IEEE International Conference on Robotics and Automation (ICRA)*, Washington, DC.

Matarić, M. J. (1990). A distributed model for mobile robot environment-learning and navigation. Master's thesis, MIT, Cambridge, MA. Also available as MIT AI Lab Tech Report AITR-1228.

Matarić, M. J. (1997). Reinforcement learning in the multi-robot domain. *Autonomous Robots 4*(1), 73–83.

Maybeck, P. (1979). *Stochastic Models, Estimation, and Control, Volume 1*. Academic Press, Inc.

McLachlan, G., and T. Krishnan (1997). *The EM Algorithm and Extensions*. New York: Wiley Series in Probability and Statistics.

Monahan, G. E. (1982). A survey of partially observable Markov decision processes: Theory, models, and algorithms. *Management Science 28*(1), 1–16.

Montemerlo, M., S. Thrun, D. Koller, and B. Wegbreit (2002). FastSLAM: A factored solution to the simultaneous localization and mapping problem. Unpublished.

Montemerlo, M., W. Whittaker, and S. Thrun (2002). Conditional particle filters for simultaneous mobile robot localization and people-tracking. In *IEEE International Conference on Robotics and Automation (ICRA)*, Washington, DC.

Moravec, H. P. (1988). Sensor fusion in certainty grids for mobile robots. *AI Magazine 9*(2), 61–74.

Moravec, H., and M. Martin (1994). Robot navigation by 3D spatial evidence grids. Mobile Robot Laboratory, Robotics Institute, Carnegie Mellon University.

Murphy, K., and S. Russell (2001). Rao-Blackwellized particle filtering for dynamic Bayesian networks. In A. Doucet, N. de Freitas, and N. Gordon (Eds.), *Sequential Monte Carlo Methods in Practice*, pp. 499–516. Springer-Verlag.

Murray, D., and J. Little (2001). Interpreting stereo vision for a mobile robot. *Autonomous Robots*. Forthcoming.

Newman, P. (2000). *On the Structure and Solution of the Simultaneous Localisation and Map Building Problem*. Ph.D. thesis, Australian Centre for Field Robotics, University of Sydney, Sydney.

Parker, L. E. (1996). On the design of behavior-based multi-robot teams. *Journal of Advanced Robotics 10*(6).

Pasula, H., S. Russell, M. Ostland, and Y. Ritov (1999). Tracking many objects with many sensors. In *Proceedings of the 16th International Joint Conference on Artificial Intelligence (IJCAI)*, Stockholm.

Pierce, D., and B. Kuipers (1994). Learning to explore and build maps. In *Proceedings of the 12th National Conference on Artificial Intelligence*, Menlo Park, CA, pp. 1264–1271. AAAI Press/MIT Press.

Pitt, M., and N. Shephard (1999). Filtering via simulation: auxiliary particle filter. *Journal of the American Statistical Association 94*, 590–599.

Rabiner, L. R. (1989). A tutorial on hidden Markov models and selected applications in speech recognition. In *Proceedings of the IEEE*. IEEE Log Number 8825949.

Reuter, J. (2000). Mobile robot self-localization using PDAB. In *Proceedings of the IEEE International Conference on Robotics and Automation (ICRA)*, San Francisco.

Roumeliotis, S., and G. Bekey (2000). Bayesian estimation and Kalman filtering: A unified framework for mobile robot localization. In *Proceedings of the IEEE International Conference on Robotics and Automation (ICRA)*, San Francisco, pp. 2985–2992.

Roy, N., G. Baltus, D. Fox, F. Gemperle, J. Goetz, T. Hirsch, D. Magaritis, M. Montemerlo, J. Pineau, J. Schulte, and S. Thrun (2000). Towards personal service robots for the elderly. In *Proceedings of the Workshop on Interactive Robotics and Entertainment (WIRE)*, Pittsburgh, PA. Carnegie Mellon University.

Russell, S., and P. Norvig (1995). *Artificial Intelligence: A Modern Approach*. Englewood Cliffs, NJ: Prentice Hall.

Schneider, F. E. (1994). Sensorinterpretation und Kartenerstellung für mobile Roboter. Master's thesis, Department of Computer Science III, University of Bonn, Bonn, Germany. In German.

Schraft, R., and G. Schmierer (1998). *Serviceroboter*. Springer-Verlag. In German.

Schulz, D., W. Burgard, D. Fox, and A. Cremers (2001). Tracking multiple moving targets with a mobile robot using particles filters and statistical data association. In *Proceedings of the IEEE International Conference on Robotics and Automation*, Seoul, Korea.

Shatkay, H. (1998). *Learning Models for Robot Navigation*. Ph.D. thesis, Computer Science Department, Brown University, Providence, RI.

Shatkay, H., and L. Kaelbling (1997). Learning topological maps with weak local odometric information. In *Proceedings of IJCAI-97*.

Shum, H., M. Han, and R. Szeliski (1998). Interactive construction of 3D models from panoramic mosaics. In *Proceedings of the International Conference on Computer Vision and Pattern Recognition (CVPR)*.

Simmons, R., D. Apfelbaum, W. Burgard, M. Fox, D. an Moors, S. Thrun, and H. Younes (2000). Coordination for multi-robot exploration and mapping. In *Proceedings of the AAAI National Conference on Artificial Intelligence*, Austin, TX. AAAI.

Simmons, R., D. Apfelbaum, D. Fox, R. Goldmann, K. Haigh, D. Musliner, M. Pelican, and S. Thrun (2000). Coordinated deployment of multiple heterogeneous robots. In *Proceedings of the IEEE/RSJ International Conference on Intelligent Robots and Systems (IROS)*.

Smith, R., M. Self, and P. Cheeseman (1990). Estimating uncertain spatial relationships in robotics. In I. Cox and G. Wilfong (Eds.), *Autonomous Robot Vehnicles*, pp. 167–193. Springer-Verlag.

Smith, R. C., and P. Cheeseman (1985). On the representation and estimation of spatial uncertainty. Technical Report TR 4760 and 7239, SRI.

Sondik, E. (1971). *The Optimal Control of Partially Observable Markov Processes*. Ph.D. thesis, Stanford University.

Thrun, S. (1993). Exploration and model building in mobile robot domains. In E. Ruspini (Ed.), *Proceedings of the IEEE International Conference on Neural Networks*, San Francisco, pp. 175–180. IEEE Neural Network Council.

Thrun, S. (2001a). Is robotics going statistics? The field of probabilistic robotics. *Communications of the ACM*. Forthcoming.

Thrun, S. (2001b). Learning occupancy grids with forward models. In *Proceedings of the Conference on Intelligent Robots and Systems (IROS'2001)*, Hawaii.

Thrun, S. (2001c). A probabilistic online mapping algorithm for teams of mobile robots. *International Journal of Robotics Research 20*(5), 335–363.

Thrun, S., M. Beetz, M. Bennewitz, W. Burgard, A. Cremers, F. Dellaert, D. Fox, D. Hähnel, C. Rosenberg, N. Roy, J. Schulte, and D. Schulz (2000). Probabilistic algorithms and the interactive museum tour-guide robot Minerva. *International Journal of Robotics Research 19*(11), 972–999.

Thrun, S., A. Bücken, W. Burgard, D. Fox, T. Fröhlinghaus, D. Henning, T. Hofmann, M. Krell, and T. Schmidt (1998). Map learning and high-speed navigation in RHINO. In D. Kortenkamp, R. Bonasso, and R. Murphy (Eds.), *AI-based Mobile Robots: Case Studies of Successful Robot Systems*. MIT Press.

Thrun, S., W. Burgard, and D. Fox (2000). A real-time algorithm for mobile robot mapping with applications to multi-robot and 3D mapping. In *Proceedings of the IEEE International Conference on Robotics and Automation (ICRA)*, San Francisco.

Thrun, S., D. Fox, and W. Burgard (1998). A probabilistic approach to concurrent mapping and localization for mobile robots. *Machine Learning 31*, 29–53. Also appeared in *Autonomous Robots 5*, 253–271 (joint issue).

Torrance, M. C. (1994). Natural communication with robots. Master's thesis, MIT Department of Electrical Engineering and Computer Science, Cambridge, MA.

Welch, G., and G. Bishop (1995). An introduction to the Kalman filter. Technical Report TR 95-041, University of North Carolina, Department of Computer Science.

Williams, S., G. Dissanayake, and H. Durrant-Whyte (2001). Towards terrain-aided navigation for underwater robotics. *Advanced Robotics 15*(5).

Yamauchi, B., and R. Beer (1996). Spatial learning for navigation in dynamic environments. *IEEE Transactions on Systems, Man, and Cybernetics—Part B: Cybernetics Special Issue on Learning Autonomous Robots*. Also located at *www.aic.nrl.navy.mil/~yamauchi/*.

Yamauchi, B., and P. Langley (1997). Place recognition in dynamic environments. *Journal of Robotic Systems 14*(2), 107–120.

Yamauchi, B., P. Langley, A. Schultz, J. Grefenstette, and W. Adams (1998). Magellan: An integrated adaptive architecture for mobile robots. Technical Report 98-2, Institute for the Study of Learning and Expertise (ISLE), Palo Alto, CA.

Zimmer, U. (1996). Robust world-modeling and navigation in a real world. *Neurocomputing 13*(2–4).

Zucker, S. (1976). Region growing: Childhood and adolescence. *Comput. Graphics Image Processing 5*, 382–399.

Chapter 2

Multi-Agent Systems

D-Learning: What Learning in Dogs Tells Us About Building Characters That Learn What They Ought to Learn

Bruce M. Blumberg
The Media Lab, MIT
77 Massachusetts Avenue, N18-5FL
Cambridge, MA 02139
bruce@media.mit.edu

Abstract

A fundamental capability of compelling autonomous animated characters is the ability to learn from experience and to alter their observable behavior accordingly. In this chapter, I highlight important lessons from animal learning and training, from machine learning, and from the incorporation of learning into digital pets. I then briefly present an approach, informed by the lessons above, toward building characters that learn. Finally, I discuss a number of installations we have built that feature characters that learn what they ought to learn.

1 Introduction

If presented with an autonomous virtual character such as a virtual dog, people expect the character to be able to learn the kinds of things a real dog can and to alter its behavior accordingly. The reason, simply put, is that people expect a level of common sense from any animate system such that it will behave so as to "get the good" and "avoid the bad," given its desires, repertoire of actions, and beliefs about how the world works. Part of the common sense expected from an intelligent system is that it will learn from experience. Indeed, the ability to learn from experience is one measure of what people often label as intelligence—that is, more intelligent creatures are better able to learn than less intelligent ones.[1] When a character doesn't learn from experience, we are left wondering, "Is it stupid, or is it simply broken?"

The goal of the Synthetic Characters Group at the Media Lab of MIT is to understand how to build autonomous animated characters that possess the everyday common sense, ability to learn, and apparent sense of empathy that one finds in animals such as dogs. That is, we take our fundamental inspiration from animal learning and training. Our belief is that by paying close attention to how animals learn and to successful techniques by which they are trained, we can not only improve on existing models for machine learning, but also develop robust techniques for real-time learning in autonomous animated characters.

Our choice of dogs as a subject is far from accidental. Dogs represent a fascinating model of a computational system. While perhaps not possessing the full cognitive richness that we associate with humans, nonetheless dogs do a remarkable job of learning what they ought to learn and doing what they ought to do so as to exploit the hugely successful adaptive niche of "man's best friend." Not only do dogs exploit this niche, but they do so in such a way that we often find ourselves seeing the very best of human qualities in their behavior. And they do this despite virtually no understanding of human language beyond the use of words as cues, little apparent ability to learn more than proximate causality, and our own limited ability to understand their internal state.

To put their success in perspective, consider that there are perhaps 400 million dogs in the world (Coppinger and Coppinger 2001), whereas there are only 400 thousand wolves, despite their having a 20% greater brain to-body-weight ratio. While many of these 400 million dogs undoubtedly fend for themselves, the fact remains that humans devote considerable resources to their welfare. Americans alone spend over $30 billion a year on pet food, supplies, veterinary care, and other services. Yet, for all of the cost, a third of dog owners consider themselves closer to their dog than to any family member, and the most popular place for a pet dog to sleep is on its master's bed. While these statistics may say as much about us as they do about dogs, the fact remains that dogs have hit on a highly successful evolutionary strategy.

One element of dogs' success is their ability to fit into the social structure of a human household and use it to their advantage. The social learning of which dogs are capable may not be as sophisticated as that observed in wolf packs, but it is sufficient for their needs. Through their interactions with members of their human family, they appear to learn their relative place in the social order with respect to access to resources. Implicit here is the seeming ability to associate relevant qualities with different individuals (e.g., this person feeds me, this person doesn't). They also act as if they learn contexts that signal an important interaction with their human companions (e.g., supper time, getting ready to go for a walk, the human arriving home at the end of the day, etc.) Similarly, they act as if they pick up on cues that signal our internal state and respond appropriately. Stories abound of the dog that knows when its master is sad, and comes over and lies down at the master's feet as if to provide comfort.

Much of this social learning rests on dogs' ability to learn apparent proximate causality, especially when the immediate consequences of their actions are motivationally significant

---

[1] Note that, while we speak of "learning from experience," our measure of this learning is the extent to which the creature alters its actions in a manner that we believe makes sense given our understanding of its goals and its experience.

to them. Indeed, this is the basis of our ability to train dogs with comparative ease (although we may be overstating the ease given the fact that there are almost 600 books available from Amazon.com on dog training). To put this in perspective: a dog can be taught to roll over on command in less than 100 repetitions (Pryor 1999; Wilkes 1995). This is no mean feat given that this requires them to perform some level of motor learning, to associate the action of rolling over with the subsequent appearance of a treat, and to learn that the association is only valid in the context of a unique acoustic or gestural pattern. In the case of aversive stimuli, dogs are sometimes capable of learning from a single example.

Finally, part of dogs' success in fitting into our social structure is undoubtedly due to their tendency to provide consistent and seemingly easy-to-interpret cues (e.g., ear position, posture, tail movement and position, and vocalizations such as whines and growls) that help us to explain and predict their behavior. Not only do such cues suggest an internal state that is explicable in human terms, but they also have the effect of eliciting strong and perhaps innate responses in us.

The ability of dogs to fit into the social structure of another species, to adapt to all of its oddities, and even to manipulate that species into amply meeting their needs is both an awe-inspiring accomplishment in itself and a grand challenge for our research. Can we create a computational system that does even half as well? How hard would it be? What lessons would we learn in the process?

As we build systems that learn what they ought to learn, we must also consider training techniques for these systems. Once again, there is no better place to look for inspiration than animal training in general and dog training in particular. The practice of dog training is fascinating not only for what it reveals about the heuristics that dogs may employ when learning but also for understanding how they and their trainers effectively work together to make it easy for the dog to learn.

This chapter explores one aspect of this problem, namely, how to build an autonomous animated creature that can learn the same kinds of apparent proximate causality as real dogs can. Its purpose is fourfold:

- First, to argue that intentional beings, such as autonomous characters, need, at a minimum, to be able to learn the kinds of things that dogs can learn.

- Second, to show how robust techniques for real-time learning and training in autonomous animated characters can be informed by paying close attention to how dogs learn, and to the successful techniques by which they are trained.

- Third, to suggest strategies, directly inspired by dog learning and training, for guiding state and action space discovery, thereby addressing an important area of difficulty for traditional reinforcement learning.

- Fourth, to lead to a greater understanding of how real dogs learn.

I begin by presenting the case that an autonomous character's ability to modify its beliefs based on experience is a fundamental requirement for any character whose actions are intended to seem intelligent. Using dogs as a model of a system that does just that, the question then becomes, What scaffolding needs to be in place in order for an autonomous character to be able to learn the kinds of things a dog can learn? To answer this question, I begin by discussing two approaches to learning in autonomous creatures: namely, the kind of learning embedded in the current generation of digital pets, and a popular technique of machine learning called *reinforcement learning.* Having examined the core ideas of reinforcement learning, and in particular having identified some of the thorny issues associated with its use in practice, I will turn to a discussion of how dogs learn and are trained. I then turn to a number of insights, drawn from our understanding of dog learning and training, that suggest strategies for addressing some of the issues associated with machine learning. I follow this with a brief discussion of our computational approach, and, finally, discuss our experiences to date building creatures that embody some level of dog learning.

2   Why Characters Need to Learn: Learning and the Intentional Stance

We expect intelligent beings, be they people, dogs, or animated characters, to behave in a way that is easy to explain given our understanding of their desires, their beliefs about how the world works, and their available repertoire of actions: that is, in a way that makes it easy for us to take what philosopher Daniel Dennett calls the *Intentional Stance* (Dennett 1987). The Intentional Stance, in Dennett's view, is the fundamental strategy we use to predict and explain the actions of animate systems. It is simple: First, one decides what goals or desires the character ought to have and what set of actions it can perform. Then, one decides what set of beliefs the character ought to have about the effect of its actions on the world and ultimately on its desires. Finally, one assumes that it will always act in a commonsensical way (given its character) so as to satisfy those desires given its beliefs. Seen in this way, we can use the Intentional Stance to predict a character's actions based on our knowledge of its presumed desires and beliefs. Conversely, we can also use it to infer a character's desires and beliefs based on the character's motion and the quality of that motion. In the context of Dennett's work, one sees that the techniques put forth in the animation classic *Illusion of Life* (Thomas and Johnson 1981) are essentially a recipe for making it easy for the viewer to take the Intentional Stance relative to a character.

The philosopher Daniel Plotkin views learning (which he calls the "second heuristic," the first heuristic being evolution) as a mechanism for tracking aspects of an animal's environment that cannot be encoded in the genes, either because they can't be specified a priori (e.g., who is my mother?) or because they change too rapidly (e.g., "location of a good feeding site; who one can rely on for support; who is dangerous...") (Plotkin 1994). The best that evolution can do in these situations is to provide mechanisms that make it easier for the animal to learn these kinds of predictable regularities, or, as Plotkin (1994) puts it, "to prime and direct the activities of the second heuristic."

Within the context of the Intentional Stance, learning implies the revision of existing beliefs and possibly the creation of new beliefs that reflect the system's actual experience with the world. Specifically, the character needs be able to learn predictable and relevant regularities of the world in which it finds itself, and which cannot be encoded a priori— that is, what Plotkin calls the "spatial and temporal relationship of events and objects" relevant to satisfying the creature's underlying desires. Otherwise, its beliefs may not reflect the reality of the world, and it may not be able to act in a way that makes sense to an observer.

Thus, if at its simplest the Intentional Stance can be interpreted as expecting intentional systems to act in the same way we would act if we had the same set of desires, beliefs, and actions, then we also expect those systems to learn what we would learn given the same set of experiences. For example, suppose we observe a character that repeatedly answers the door after it hears a knock and who each time gets blasted by a fire hose when the door is opened. We expect that after a few such experiences, the character should be very nervous when it hears the knock on the door and increasingly reluctant and fearful about actually opening the door. After all, that is how we would behave; it doesn't seem like rocket science to learn the connection. Indeed, the more obvious the connection, or the more significant the consequences, the greater our expectation that the character will modify its beliefs based on its experience. Of course, there are limits to what we expect a system to be capable of learning. For example, we don't expect a thermostat to learn at all and we don't expect a dog to learn how to drive to the supermarket, no matter how hungry it is. However, we might expect the dog to learn that begging at the table is a reliable strategy for getting food.

2.1   What Characters Should be Able to Learn

We believe that intentional characters should be able to learn at least three different kinds of things about how the world works:

- *Correlations between events that are independent of the character's actions, but potentially relevant to satisfying its desires.* For example, learning that event A reliably predicts event B may allow the character to respond proactively once it observes A, knowing that B is likely to follow. This may make the difference between catching and eating a mouse and watching someone else have that mouse instead. The better able a character is at doing this kind of learning, the cleverer it will seem.

- *The effects of their actions.* Essentially, this requires learning that given a motivationally significant goal, certain actions are more reliable and relevant to achieving that goal than others, particularly if performed in specific contexts. This type of learning is necessary in order to behave in a goal-directed manner.

- *The best form of an action.* Indeed, for all but the simplest characters, the form of the action is almost as important as the action itself. For example, there are many ways that a predator can stalk its prey, and some work better than others.

Dogs, of course, are very good at the kinds of learning tasks described above, especially if the events, actions, and consequences are proximate in space and time and as long as the consequences are motivationally significant. After all, classical conditioning is nothing more than learning the first type of prediction, operant conditioning is essentially the same as learning the second type, and much of animal training involves the third type of learning. My belief is that by embedding the kind of learning of which dogs are capable into the control systems of autonomous characters, we can provide them with a robust mechanism for adapting their actions and beliefs so as to be seen as behaving in a commonsensical way in a dynamic and unpredictable world.

The question before us then is, What scaffolding needs to be in place in order for an autonomous character to be able to learn the kinds of things that a dog can learn?

Figure 1 Sydney doing a jump in an agility trial. In this sport, the dog and its handler must work together as a team to negotiate a course of obstacles within a prescribed time period. In order to be successful, the dog must carefully attend to the verbal cues and body language of its handler, and the handler must carefully manage the information and motivation that they provide to the dog. To be good at agility requires a high degree of training and teamwork.

3 Lessons

In this section we will look at three sources of inspiration to guide our thinking about how to build characters that can learn the kinds of things that dogs seem to learn with ease. These sources include the current generation of digital pets, the domain of machine learning, and finally animal learning and training.

3.1 Lessons from Digital Pets

Simple learning has been integrated into several members of the current generation of digital pets, most notably AIBO and Dogz (Resner, Stern, and Frank 1997). Typically, learning is limited to biasing choice of action based on reward or punishment. Actions that appear to lead to reward increase in frequency, whereas actions that appear to lead to punishment decrease in frequency. Despite the relatively limited amount of learning that these virtual pets can actually perform, the learning is believable and compelling. There are a number of reasons why the learning is so effective. In the case of Dogz, one pats the dog as a reward or squirts him with a spray bottle as punishment. Thus, the feedback signal is both simple and visible. The dog reacts to the feedback immediately and expressively, suggesting that the consequences really matter. An immediate and observable change in the frequency of the behavior that precedes the feedback signal suggests that the dog associates the behavior with the good or bad consequences. This change in frequency together with the observed emotional response makes it appear that the dog learned from the experience. The entire model is very simple and intuitive. Finally, the creators of these digital pets can rely on our apparent innate tendency to read more into the behavior of autonomous creatures than may actually be warranted (this is the power of the Intentional Stance).

One moral from digital pets is that learning doesn't have to be complex to work. Even the simplest and most limited form of learning, when done well, can be extremely compelling. Indeed, people tend to assume that digital pets learn a great deal more than they actually do.

3.2   Lessons from Machine Learning

Machine learning is an extremely active field with impressive results in a number of domains. As we will see, however, traditional approaches need to be augmented if they are to be used for autonomous characters. For our purposes, I will limit this discussion to one type of machine learning, *reinforcement learning*, or *RL*. Excellent introductions to machine learning can be found in (Ballard 1997; Kaelbling 1990; Mitchell 1997; Sutton and Barto 1998).

RL is often used by autonomous systems that must learn from experience. In RL, the world in which the creature lives is assumed to be in one of a set of perceivable states. The goal of RL is to learn an optimal sequence of actions that will take the creature from an arbitrary state to a goal state in which it receives a reward. The main approach is to probabilistically explore states, actions, and their outcomes to learn how to act in any given situation. Before describing how this is done, I will define some pertinent terms:

State refers to a specific, hopefully useful, configuration of the world as sensed by the creature's entire sensory system. As such, state can be thought of as a label that is assigned to a sensed configuration. The space of all represented configurations of the world is known as the *state space*.

Performing an *action* is how a creature can affect the state of its world. Typically, the creature is assumed to have a set of finite actions from which it can perform exactly one at any given instant (e.g., walk or eat). The set of all possible actions is referred to as the *action space*.

A *state-action* pair, denoted as $[S/A]$, is a relationship between a state S and an action A. It is typically accompanied by some numeric value (e.g., *future expected reward*) that indicates how much benefit there is in taking the action A when the creature senses state S. Based on this relationship, a *policy* is built, which represents a probability with which the creature selects an action given a specific state.

The creature receives *reinforcement*, or *reward*, when it reaches a state in which it can satisfy a goal. For example, if a dog sits and gets a treat for doing so, the reward or reinforcement is the resulting decrease in hunger or pleasure in eating the treat.

Credit assignment is the process of updating the associated value of a state-action pair to reflect its apparent utility for ultimately receiving a reward.

While there are a number of variants of reinforcement learning, *Q-learning* is a simple and popular representative that can be used to illustrate some key concepts. In Q-learning, introduced by Watkins, the state-action space is discretized if necessary and stored in a lookup table (Watkins and Dayan 1992). In the table, each row represents a state and each column represents an action. An entry in the table represents the "utility," or *Q-value,* of a given state-action pair with respect to getting a reward. Watkins showed that the optimal value for each state-action pair could be learned by incrementally (and exhaustively) exploring the space of state-action pairs and by using a local update rule to reflect the consequences of taking a given action in a given state with respect to achieving the goal state (Sutton and Barto 1998).

It is important to note that techniques such as Q-learning that focus on learning an optimal sequence of actions to get to a goal state solve a much harder problem than either animals solve or that we need to solve for synthetic characters. As we will see, animals are biased to learn proximate causality. Even in the case of sequences, the noted ethologist Leyhausen suggests that the individual actions may be largely self-reinforcing, rather than being reinforced via back propagation (Lorenz and Leyhausen 1973). In addition, Nature places a premium on learning adequate solutions quickly.

Thus, while reinforcement learning provides a theoretically sound basis for building systems that learn, there are a number of issues that make it problematic in the context of autonomous animated creatures. None of these issues is insurmountable but they do need to be considered. The more important of these issues include:

- *Representation of state.* For any but the most trivial problem, the state space can quickly become huge, even though most of it is irrelevant. Consider a dog that is to be taught to respond to arbitrary acoustic patterns. The space of all possible acoustic patterns is (1) continuous and (2) far too big to permit an exhaustive search even if it were discretized. Of course, the fact that most acoustic patterns are irrelevant to most dogs suggests that it isn't necessary to represent all possible acoustic patterns a priori. Rather, it is sufficient to discover, based on experience, those acoustic patterns that seem to matter and add them dynamically to the *state space.* This process is known as *state space discovery* and is an essential component to successful learning in the real world.

- *Representation of action.* Q-learning assumes that the form of the action remains constant and discrete. However, for an animal or animated character, the form of the action matters almost as much as the choice of action. To get around this problem, one could "discretize" the action space—for example, have 10 different actions, each of which corresponds to a specific style of walking. This, however, would cause the search space to grow substantially. Indeed, for a creature that can recognize 100 individual states of the world, each action adds 100 state-action pairs that must be visited repeatedly in order to learn their optimal Q-value. In addition, if the creature needs to learn actions that weren't programmed in, such as novel motor trajectories, it needs to perform the equivalent of state-space discovery in action space, that is, *action space discovery.*

- *Representation of time.* Q-learning makes the assumption that all actions take one unit of time to complete and that credit assignment occurs every time step. Typically, though, actions of an animal or autonomous character take variable amounts of time to complete. A "sit" may take a second, whereas a "fetch ball" may take 10 to 15 seconds. Even the same action may take a variable amount of time. For example, the time taken to complete "fetch ball" depends on the distance the ball is thrown.

- *Multiple goals.* Creatures and characters have multiple goals that they attempt to satisfy. Most work on learning assumes a single goal. For example, to use Q-learning for a character with multiple goals, one would need a separate table of state-action pairs for each goal and a way of choosing which goals to attend to at any given time.

- *Learning versus behaving.* Learning is just one thing a character needs to do. For animals and characters alike, learning augments existing behavior. Most approaches to machine learning assume that (1) learning is the primary task of the system and (2) learning starts *tabula rasa*. Conversely, relatively little work has been done in developing behavior architectures in which learning can take place as part of the overall agenda of the character or creature.

- *Exploration.* As the size of the state-action space grows, it becomes critical to have strategies or heuristics in place to guide the creature's exploration of this space—that is, to experiment with those state-action pairs that are most likely to be ultimately valuable. In most approaches to machine learning, this is left as "an exercise for the reader" since researchers are more concerned with asymptotic performance than with initial performance. By contrast, animals and characters are probably more concerned with quickly learning "acceptable" solutions than "optimal" solutions (Gould and Gould 1999; Lorenz 1981; Shettleworth 1998).

Conceptually, animals face the same problems as those faced by machine learning systems but appear to have no problem learning what they ought to learn. How do they do this? While we don't know for sure, a possible answer may lie in the use of heuristics and built-in structure that has the effect of simplifying the learning task. Indeed, the process of training is really one of guiding the animal's exploration of its state and action space toward the performance of specific actions in specific contexts. The implications of this are discussed more fully below.

3.3   Lessons from Nature

Here I will review some of the key lessons to be gained from animal learning and training (Gould and Gould 1999; Lindsay 2000; Lorenz 1981; Plotkin 1994; Pryor 1999; Ramirez 1999; Shettleworth 1998).

3.3.1   Learning

In nature, learning is a mechanism for adapting to significant spatial and temporal aspects of an animal's environment that vary predictably, but at a rate faster than that to which evolution can adjust, or that simply cannot be encoded in the genes. Indeed, the most adaptive course in this case is to evolve mechanisms that facilitate learning these rapidly varying features (Plotkin 1994). Thus, evolution determines much of what can be learned and the manner in which it is learned. Often this takes the form of innate structures and heuristics that have the effect of dramatically simplifying the task of learning specific things (Gould and Gould 1999; Plotkin 1994). Some of these important heuristics include the following:

- *Variability.* Variability of action and context is essential to learning. Variability of action allows the animal to discover new causal associations and, by varying how an action is performed, to find the most reliable form of the action. Variability of context allows the animal to identify relevant cues to apparent causality, and in particular to identify those cues that increase the reliability of the association between an action and an outcome. Animals appear to be sensitive to the variability of the expected outcome. Indeed, the more variable the outcome, the more variable the choice and form of action (Wilkes 2001). Trainers often make use of these phenomena by varying the reward associated with the performance of a desired trick. The computational implication is that the choice and style of action should be variable but biased toward those choices and styles of action that lead to good consequences or avoid bad consequences.

- *Motivation.* In general, the more motivationally significant the consequences, the more rapidly the animal will learn the context and actions that seem to lead to those consequences. In some cases, the motivation is an end result such as a treat. In other cases, the action itself is rewarding (Lorenz and Leyhausen 1973). The point, however, is that learning and motivation are closely linked. I will return to this point shortly.

- *Frequency of action is proportional to its perceived consequences.* Actions that seem to lead to good things tend to be expressed more often than those that don't (this is known as *Thorndike's Law of Effect*)(Lindsay 2000). This behavior makes sense for two reasons: First, it increases the chances of a desired outcome. Second, by increasing the frequency of a "promising" action, but varying how it is performed, the animal is exploring a potentially promising neighborhood. This, in turn, has three important implications for our computational model: First, there needs to be some representation of consequences, both good and bad. Second, the probability of a given action should reflect the value of the expected consequences given the state of the world. Third, the focus of learning should first be on learning the likely consequences of an action, and then on learning the contexts in which the action is especially reliable in producing the desired consequence.

- *Animals constrain their search for apparent proximate causality to a small temporal window around the performance of an action.* The rule of thumb in dog training is that unless the consequences of an action are signaled within two seconds of the performance of the action, a dog won't learn the connection (Lindsay 2000; Pryor 1999; Wilkes 1995). Similarly, events that occur within a small temporal window preceding and perhaps overlapping the performance of the action appear to represent the candidate set of stimuli relevant for increasing the reliability of the action. The computational implication is that our system needs to maintain memory sufficient to be able to answer questions such as, What stimuli were active within a given temporal window of an action becoming active? The good news is that the temporal window can be relatively short. Similarly, the relevant consequences are those that immediately follow the completion of the action.

- *Time and rate are fundamental building blocks.* Animals act as if they have internal representations of time, quantity, and rate and are capable of using these representations to make commonsensical decisions about how to organize their behavior (Gallistel and Gibbon 2000). Time, rate, and quantity should be explicitly represented in the system and used to guide not only choice of action, but exploration as well.

As we will see in the next section, the difference between a great trainer and a mediocre one is the degree to which the trainer takes advantage of the heuristics that seem to guide learning in animals.

3.3.2   Training

It is useful to examine training techniques not only because they provide insights into how animals learn but also because they may be useful for training autonomous characters. Below, I describe a popular and easy technique for animal training called *clicker training* and what it seems to imply about how animals learn.

Clicker training unfolds in three basic steps. The first step is to create an association between the sound of a toy clicker and a food reward. A dog conditioned to the clicker will expectantly look for a treat upon hearing the click sound. Once the association between clicks and treats is made, trainers use the click sound to "mark" behaviors that they wish to encourage. By clicking when the dog performs a desired behavior, and subsequently treating, the dog begins to perform the behavior more frequently.

Since clicker training relies on the dog to produce some approximation of a desired behavior before it can be rewarded (and producing a high level of reinforcement keeps the dog interested in the process), trainers utilize a variety of techniques to encourage the dog to perform behaviors it might otherwise perform infrequently, or not at all. A useful and popular technique is to train the dog to touch an object such as the trainer's hand or a target stick. By subsequently manipulating the position of the target, the trainer can, in effect, lure the dog through a trajectory or into a pose as it follows its nose. For example, by moving the target over the dog's head, a dog may be lured into sitting down.

Since the dog is unlikely to perform the desired final form of the behavior immediately, especially if it is an unusual behavior (e.g., dancing on the two rear feet), the trainer will often guide the dog toward the desired behavior by rewarding ever-closer approximations, in a process known as *shaping*.

The third and final step in clicker training is to add a discriminative stimulus such as a gesture or vocal cue and eventually extinguish the behavior in the absence of the cue. For example, a trainer would first reward a dog for sitting, and then only reward the dog for sitting when the sit is accompanied by the trainer uttering "Sit."

Thus, in using a process such as clicker training, the trainer is helping the animal answer five questions:

- *Why do it?* The trainer must ensure that the consequences are motivationally significant to the animal; otherwise, it is unlikely that the animal will be motivated to learn. That is, the consequences must be clearly significant relative to the inferred desires of the animal.

- *What to do?* The trainer must signal the animal when it has performed the action that is causal to the appearance of a subsequent reward. Reflecting the narrow window that animals appear to use for inferring causality, trainers typically use a short, clear event marker such as a click or a whistle. As we saw, the click acts both as an event marker as well as a bridge between the end of the desired behavior and the delivery of the reward (Pryor 1999; Wilkes 1995).

- *How to do it?* A good trainer is as sensitive to the form of a motion as is a good animator. Varying the level of reinforcement is one way a trainer can cause the animal to vary its performance of the behavior, since animals seem sensitive to variations in outcomes (Pryor 1999; Wilkes 1995). In addition, via shaping, the trainer effectively guides the exploration by rewarding ever-closer approximations to the desired final form of the behavior. Finally, through luring, the trainer may lure an animal into performing an approximation of a desired behavior. Indeed, virtually all animal tricks start with a naturally occurring action that is then shaped and perhaps expressed in a novel context (Lorenz 1981).

- *When to do it?* Typically, trainers will only begin associating a cue or context for a desired behavior once they are sure that the animal has learned it (Pryor 1999; Wilkes 1995). If rewarded for productions of the behavior when this cue is given and ignored for instances when it is not, the animal responds by decreasing the spontaneous production of the behavior and only performing it in response to the cue. This process typically takes between 20 and 50 repetitions (Wilkes 1995).

- *How long to do it?* Trainers rely on the seeming ability of animals to learn intervals— in particular, the expected interval and variance between the onset of the behavior and the subsequent reward.

In addition, the success of techniques such as clicker training, shaping, and luring may also provide clues as to the heuristics that animals use to simplify the learning process. For example, clicker training is a particularly effective training technique because animals appear to make an important simplifying assumption: An action or stimulus that immediately precedes a motivationally significant consequence is "as good as causal."

Similarly, the fact that animals learn from luring has an important implication. As mentioned above, if lured and rewarded repeatedly, the animal will begin to produce the action without being lured. This adaptation suggests that the animal is associating reward with its resulting body configuration or trajectory, and not for the action of simply following its nose.

Finally, several details of how clicker trainers teach an animal the association between a cue and an action are especially illuminating. For example, unlike other training techniques, they teach the action first, and then the cue. The superiority of this decomposition suggests that animals make associations more easily if they already "know" a particular action is valuable. Trainers also typically introduce the cue by presenting it as the animal is just beginning to perform the action, and then subsequently rewarding the action. That is, the animal has already decided what to do before the trainer issues a cue but is still able to learn to associate the action (and its subsequent reward) with a cue occurring in a temporal window proximate to the action onset.

The key point here is that the combination of the trainer and the use of these heuristics by the animal have the effect of simplifying the learning task for the animal by guiding its exploration of its state and action space. As we will see, by doing so, animals and their trainers effectively address one of the major problems faced by machine learning systems, namely, how to search the state and action spaces intelligently. These ideas take a central role in the discussion to follow.

4 Approach

The discussion above suggests that learning is fundamentally a process of goal-directed exploration. As we saw in our discussion of machine learning, there are three spaces that need to be explored: state space, action space, and state-action space. The bad news is that the sizes of these spaces make it impossible to learn much of anything unless this exploration is done in a clever and integrated manner. The good news is that animals such as dogs must face the same problem, yet they are able to learn what they need to learn pretty quickly by using heuristics that simplify and guide the exploration process. This section describes an integrated approach to state space, action space, and state-action space discovery that incorporates heuristics directly inspired by our understanding of dog learning and training.

4.1 Behavior-Driven State Space Discovery

In our earlier discussion, we took as a given that the creature's perceptual mechanism was able to assign unique labels to configurations of sensory data that in turn identified unique and potentially significant configurations of its world. These labels were referred to as *state*. While every possible configuration of sensor readings could be assigned a unique label, this is neither practical nor advisable. For example, due to noisy sensors, the same world configuration might produce sensor readings that vary around a mean. In this case, it makes sense to map all sensor readings within some distance of that mean to the same label. In this light, state is a label that identifies a cluster of sensor readings that arise from the same world configuration. Or, for example, suppose a sensor can take on a continuous range of values. In this case, it would make sense to partition the possible range of sensor readings into discrete bins and assign a label to each bin. Here, state is used to compress the space of possible observations. As we saw earlier, this is important because the smaller the state space, the easier the learning task.

In some cases, the partitioning of the sensor space can be done a priori based on the designer's understanding of the world and of the creature's sensory apparatus. Alternatively, the creature could learn useful partitions of the sensor space online as a result of its interaction with the world. Ideally, the partitioning would reflect not only any natural clustering of the data that was observed, but also the distinctions that were useful because they identified configurations of the world that were significant with respect to achieving the creature's goals. In both cases, this may not be something that can, or should, be done a priori. This online process is known as *state space discovery* (Ballard 1997; Ivanov 2001).

For example, assume a creature is to be taught to perform tricks in response to arbitrary acoustic patterns (utterances, whistles, etc.). The a priori approach would partition the space of acoustic patterns into all possible acoustic patterns and give each a label. This would, of course, result in an absolutely huge state space. The online approach is rather different. It assumes that the only acoustic patterns that need be considered are (1) those that are actually experienced, and (2) those for which there is some evidence that they matter with respect to the creature's goals.

An unsupervised technique such as *k-means clustering* can be employed to partition the observed patterns into distinct clusters, or classes (Therrien 1989). In the context here, k-means clustering provides a technique for partitioning a continuous space into k states.

However, k-means implies the use of a distance metric that reflects the relative similarity of two patterns. Given this metric, patterns that are similar should be closer than patterns that are less similar. With this metric in hand, k-means clustering partitions the observed patterns into k clusters, or classes, such that the distance between the center of a cluster and all of the observations that compose that cluster is minimized across all clusters and patterns. Once this is done, it is a simple matter to classify an incoming pattern as belonging to one of the clusters: simply choose the cluster whose center is closest to the incoming pattern or, if it is too far away from any of them, assume that it is an example of something new. This is an example of unsupervised learning, since the clusters emerge from the data without any supervisory signal providing feedback. Of course, this technique does not answer the question of whether the state represented by a cluster is relevant with respect to satisfying the creature's goals. Thus, it may create states for which there is zero evidence that the state will in fact be useful.

Our experience with dog learning suggests a simpler approach: only build models (i.e., clusters) of acoustic patterns that occur contemporaneously with an action that directly leads to a significant outcome, be it a cookie or a reprimand. The consequence essentially acts as a supervisory signal, suggesting that it may be worthwhile to pay attention to the pattern. Given differential experience of performing the action in the presence of the pattern and in its absence, the dog has even more evidence from which to assess the pattern's relevance. Note that even if k-means clustering were subsequently employed to build the clusters, the number of patterns that need be considered would be substantially less. However, an even simpler approach comes to mind: treat all patterns that occur contemporaneously with an action that directly leads to a significant outcome as belonging to the same cluster. In a sense, the action itself becomes the label for the cluster. This suggests a simple algorithm for state space discovery, and the one we use in our system.

1. When an acoustic pattern is detected, attempt to classify it, but do not update the model. If a match is found, make the associated state active and choose the most relevant action given that state.

2. In any event, store the pattern in short-term memory.

3. During the next credit assignment phase (when the current action completes), retrieve the pattern, if any, that occurred in a window overlapping the start of the action.

   (a) If the action was rewarded and the pattern was classified, add the pattern to the appropriate cluster (i.e., update the model). If the action was not rewarded, skip this step.

   (b) Otherwise, if the action was rewarded and an associated cluster doesn't already exist, create a new cluster and add the pattern to the cluster as its first example. In effect, this step creates a new state. Once again, skip this step if the action was not rewarded.

   (c) In either case, update reliability statistics associated with the cluster. Use these statistics to identify clusters/states that seem correlated with increased reliability versus those clusters/states that do not.

While dead simple, this algorithm captures, albeit at a cartoon level, what is necessary to learn the kinds of acoustic cues that dogs seem capable of learning. By limiting the set of candidate patterns to those that occur within a small temporal window, we dramatically reduce the number of patterns that need to be considered. The reward acts as a natural supervisory signal that indicates if the pattern is a good example either of the cluster in which it was classified (and so should be included in the cluster) or as a seed for a new cluster. Performing the action in the presence of the pattern and in its absence provides a measure of the relevance of the associated cluster in signaling a context in which performance of the action will directly lead to a reward. Finally, the action itself acts as a natural label[2] and by doing so dramatically simplifies the creation of the clusters by avoiding the work associated with k-means that must "discover the clusters" on its own.

Ivanov (Ivanov 2001; Ivanov, Blumberg, and Pentland 2001) has explored these ideas more formally and in fact has shown how this simple idea can be incorporated into the well-known expectation-maximization learning algorithm to result in superior performance. (Also see (Ivanov, Blumberg, and Pentland 2001) for a detailed discussion of the algorithm used to perform clustering and classification.)

4.2   Action Space Discovery

As we saw in our discussion of dog training, much of training involves manipulating the dog into performing an action for which it can be subsequently rewarded. In shaping, the trainer rewards successive approximations to a final form of the behavior. Shaping relies on the fact that for a variety of reasons, animals continuously vary the form of an action, and that this variation is sensitive to the pattern of subsequent rewards. Indeed, there is evidence that the variance of how an action is performed is tied to the variance in the expected reward. By contrast, in luring, the trainer lures the dog into performing an action by using some sort of target such as a treat. Luring relies on the animal's seeming ability to "recognize" that while it is essentially following its nose into a configuration (e.g., a "down") or into a trajectory (e.g., a "figure-eight"), it is rewarded for the resulting configuration or trajectory and not for the action of following its nose. In both cases, the trainer is guiding the dog's exploration of its action space. Here, we discuss the computational implications of supporting these techniques.

In order to support shaping, it must be possible to vary the form of an action. As mentioned earlier, one way of accomplishing this is to discretize the action space—for example, rather than having 1 action that corresponds to "sit," have 10 actions, each of which represents a different form of a "sit." However, there is a problem and a lost opportunity associated with this approach. The problem is that it complicates the action-selection problem by potentially increasing the policy space (i.e., the space of state-action pairs) rather dramatically. The lost opportunity is that by treating all variants of the action as independent, there is nothing to tell the system that because one form of the action is rewarded it may be worth exploring other variants of the action as well.

A simple hierarchical approach can be employed to avoid these problems. This can be done in one of two ways. If the action can be parameterized, the parameters can be drawn from a local probability distribution that reflects the pattern of rewards. When an action

---

[2]This approach, as described, suffers from the limitation that only one acoustic pattern can be associated with a given action. In order to remove this restriction, the classifier would need to be able to recognize that a pattern was far enough away from its model that it should construct an additional model. Subsequently, it would need to decide which model to update with a successful example.

is about to be performed, a value for the parameter is chosen probabilistically. If the action is subsequently rewarded, the probability distribution is adjusted to make it more likely in the future that a value near the chosen value will be selected. If the action is not rewarded, the probability distribution is left unchanged or adjusted to make it less likely that a similar value will be chosen in the future. The other way is to create a two-level hierarchy in which the discrete forms of the action are represented by a "virtual" parent in the main policy space. If done in the context of Q-learning, the parent's Q-value should reflect the maximum of its children's Q-values. When the action is chosen, a secondary process chooses which child action to perform, and correspondingly it is the child's Q-value that is updated during credit assignment. See (Humphreys 1996; Kaelbling 1993) for other examples of hierarchical Q-learning. Both of these approaches provide an elegant way to support the kind of local search necessary for shaping.

In order to address luring, it will be necessary to add a richer representation of action as well as to modify the process of credit assignment. If we consider an animal as having a *pose space* that contains all of its possible body configurations, then an action can be thought of as a specific path through pose space.[3] Indeed, just as state is a label for a class of observations, action can be thought of as a label associated with a path or class of paths in pose space. Given this model, luring can be viewed as the process of leading a creature along a path in its pose space and the creature subsequently "recognizing" that the path is similar to one that it already "knows" about. This, of course, requires the existence of a distance metric that evaluates the similarity of two paths.

Luring also requires the existence of an action such as "follow-your-nose" that both allows the dog to track a target and records the path through pose space that is taken while the action is active. Finally, luring requires a modification to the credit-assignment process so that the "follow-your-nose" action can delegate its credit to an action that, if active, would have produced a similar path to that followed during the time "follow-your-nose" was active. This follows from the observation that dogs act as if they assign credit to the action that would have resulted in the configuration or trajectory performed as a result of following their noses.

Once the appropriate representation, metric, and luring actions are all in place, the algorithm for supporting luring is straightforward:

1. When "follow-your-nose" is activated, clear the path buffer.
2. While "follow-your-nose" is active, record the path through pose-space.
3. During credit assignment (i.e., when the action ends)
   (a) If no reward is received, ignore the path.
   (b) Otherwise:
       i. If the path is similar to an existing path, reward the action associated with that path (i.e., give it the credit), and update the model of the rewarded path using the path just taken as a new example.
       ii. If the path is novel, then create a new action, assign the path just taken to it, and add the action to the system's list of actions.

---

[3]Downie (2000) has shown that pose space (or as he calls it *pose graphs*) is an extremely powerful representation for action in synthetic characters, in part because it allows us to model luring. The pose graph is the representation of motion used in our system.

This algorithm incorporates a number of generally useful heuristics. First, by treating action as a label that is associated with a path or class of paths in pose space, we allow the system not only to perform action space discovery but also to do so in a manner very similar to state space discovery. For example, reward is used as a natural feedback signal to guide both action space and state space discovery. In both cases, its presence or absence is used to decide whether a new model (i.e., state or action) should be created or an existing model updated. The practical effect in both cases is that fewer models are built, and those that are built tend to be more relevant and robust. Second, we modify the credit assignment rule in the case of an exploratory action. As we saw, even though "follow-your-nose" may directly precede a reward, the algorithm gives the credit to the action whose associated path is closest to that just taken. Certain actions are valuable not only for what they do, but also for what they allow the system to discover about the value of other actions. This information in turn should be reflected in the credit assignment rules. Luring works because we explicitly include an exploratory action (i.e., "follow-your-nose"), but also because credit assignment is handled differently in the case of that action than in others.

The cumulative effect of these heuristics is that the policy space grows in a hierarchical fashion as evidence of potentially valuable states and actions grows, but in such a way that local search can occur without greatly affecting the size and complexity of the policy space.

4.3   State-Action Space Discovery

The previous two sections suggested techniques for efficiently performing state and action space discovery that I believe are widely applicable regardless of the underlying learning technique. Here, I turn to learning the value of state-action pairs, the ultimate task of reinforcement learning. As with state and action space discovery, this approach, while grounded in the ideas of reinforcement learning, is influenced by a number of observations about the realities of animal training and learning.

4.3.1   Hierarchical Search

In a traditional reinforcement learning algorithm, the system observes the world and identifies the state, chooses an action to perform in response and performs it, then observes the new state and reward (if any), and finally performs credit assignment by updating the value of the state-action pair just performed. However, there are a few observations from dog training that suggest small but significant changes to this approach. For example, as mentioned earlier, when trainers teach an association between a cue (i.e., a state) and an action, they typically do this by giving the cue *as the animal is beginning to perform* the action. That is, the animal has *already decided* what to do before the trainer issues the cue. In effect, the animal is performing one state-action pair while the trainer is rewarding a related state-action pair, one whose action is the same but whose state is likely different. This suggests that dogs act as if they are attending to a temporal window that overlaps some portion of the time the action is active, and additionally that they are capable of forming an association between an active stimulus that occurs in this window (even if after the start of the action), the action, and a significant outcome. In the language of reinforcement learning, there are two important implications: First, they act as if they form new state-action pairs based on evidence acquired while performing an existing state-action pair that shares the same action. Second, they act as if the "worthy" candidate gets credit, even if it wasn't the state-action pair that was performed.[4]

Conventionally, the set of state-action pairs are represented as a 2D table in which each row corresponds to a particular state and each column corresponds to a particular action. What gets lost in this representation is the naturally hierarchical organization of certain state spaces—for example, the space of utterances, and individual utterances such as "sit," "down," "roll over," and so on. By organizing the state space in a hierarchical fashion, the system can "notice" that a given action is more reliable when a class of states is active (e.g., the space of utterances). This can then be used as evidence to justify exploring to see if the action is even more reliable in the presence of a particular instance of that class. Our intuition is that during training, dogs, with the help of their trainers, perform an analogous hierarchical search. Thus, by taking advantage of the often hierarchical nature of state, the search for promising state-action pairs can be made more efficient, and more closely mirror how animals seem to do it.

To describe how we address this problem in our work, I need to briefly introduce how we represent state and state-action pairs, and how they are organized in this system.

As illustrated in Figure 2, we use a hierarchical mechanism called a *percept tree* to extract state information from the world. Each node in the tree is called a *percept*, with more specific percepts nearer to the leaves. Percepts are atomic perception units, with arbitrarily complex logic, whose job it is to recognize and extract features from raw sensory data. For example, one percept may recognize the presence of the utterance "sit" in an auditory stream, and another might recognize the performance of a particular motor trajectory. Similarly, an "utterance" percept might recognize the presence of "utterances" in an auditory field, and its children might recognize the presence of specific utterances such as

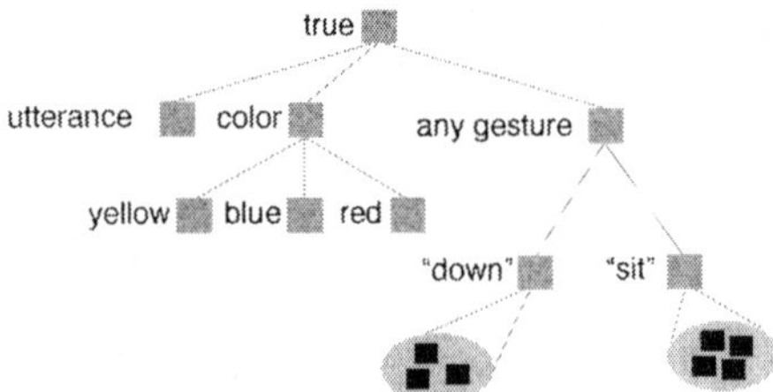

Figure 2   In my work, the state space is represented by a percept tree. The percept tree maintains a hierarchical representation of the sensory input, where leaf nodes represent the highest degree of specialization and the root node matches any sensory input. The structure of the tree is sequentially "discovered" and refined with time, as indicated by its utility with respect to getting the reward.

---

[4]There is another pragmatic reason for pursuing this idea with respect to training synthetic creatures: Typically, trainers have no visibility into the system when they reward a creature for performing an action. They hope, of course, that the creature performed the action in response to the cue. But, in fact, it is only a hope. They may be rewarding a different state-action pair from the one that was actually active. To the extent that the system makes the "right guess" about what the trainer was in fact rewarding, it will facilitate the training process.

"sit," "down," "roll over," and so on. The root of the tree is the most general percept, which I call "true" since it is always active.

Percepts are typically model-based recognizers, meaning that on each simulation cycle, they compare raw sensory data to an internal model and become *active* if they match within some threshold. If a percept is active, the sensory data is passed recursively to the percept's children for more specific classification. If not, all its children can be pruned from the update cycle. This culling is important, since percept models can vary in complexity. For symbolic data, the model is trivial: it is a string. In the case of an utterance percept, however, the model may be a collection of vectors of cepstral coefficients (Rabiner and Juang 1993) that represent the mean of a set of previously learned examples (Ivanov 2001). Motion percepts use a model that represents a path through the space of possible motions. Also associated with each percept is a short-term-memory mechanism that keeps track of its activation history over some period of time.

In the language of RL, a percept represents a subset of the entire state space—that is, it looks for a specific feature in the state space. In RL, state refers to the *entire* sensed configuration of the world; a percept is focused on only *one* aspect of that configuration. As we will see, percept decomposition of state allows for a heuristic search through potentially intractable state and state-action spaces. The downside is that it makes learning conjunctions of features harder.

The representation of a particular state-action pair in our system is called an *action tuple*. An action tuple is composed of five elements that specify what to do, when, to what, for how long, and why. This structure is larger than those typically found in RL systems, but you can think of an action tuple as an augmented state-action pair in which the state information is provided by an associated percept (when), and the action (what) is the label for a given path through pose space. Action tuples are organized into groups and compete probabilistically for activation based on their value and applicability (i.e., if their associated percept is active). The discussion below uses action tuple and percept-action pair interchangeably. I use *percept-action pair* rather than *state-action pair* to reinforce the idea that an action tuple makes its "when decision" based on a subset of the entire state of the world as indicated by its "when" percept.

Each action tuple keeps reliability and novelty statistics for its associated percept and any children of that percept. Reliability models the correlation between an action tuple being rewarded and a percept being active in an overlapping temporal window. The novelty statistic reflects the relative frequency of the event of the percept being active; a novel percept is one that is rarely active. While the novelty statistic is a measure of the overall likelihood of the percept being active, the reliability statistic is associated with the action. It is used to identify more-specific percepts that seem correlated with an increased reliability of the action in producing a reward. As we will see, these statistics are used by the system to guide the exploration of potentially useful states.

Mirroring our hierarchical representation of state, action tuples that invoke the same action but that depend on different percepts are organized hierarchically according to the specificity of the percept. During action selection, each action gets to choose its "best" action tuple to compete with the "best" action tuples associated with other actions. When a transition between active actions occurs, we perform credit assignment and the outgoing action chooses its "best" action tuple to receive credit.

For this approach to work, we need a metric to determine the "best" candidate for credit assignment and a temporal window over which to search. We use a search window that overlaps with the action by some specified amount chosen as a parameter. With respect to "best," we use the percept-action pair with the same action as the one that was active, but with a percept that was both active during the temporal window and that best meets reliability, novelty, and specificity criteria.

For example, suppose we have the following three percept-action pairs in order of specificity: [true/sit], [any-gesture/sit], and [sit-gesture/sit]. Now suppose the dog chose [true/sit], but the trainer gave the "sit-gesture" within the attention window associated with sitting. At credit-assignment time, the "best" percept-action pair would be [sit-gesture/sit], since its percept became active in the window and is the most specific percept. In addition, the "sit-gesture" is both novel and a highly reliable predictor of reward if the creature sits in response. Thus, novelty, reliability, and specificity go into the determination of "best." Finally, as we saw in the section on action space discovery, by allowing the credit assignment phase to choose the entity to be credited, we can dramatically simplify the learning and training process.

More details about this system can be found in (Burke et al. 2001; Isla et al. 2001). However, for the purposes of the discussion here, we can now turn to how we use the structure to model dog training. Specifically, this structure allows the credit-assignment process to choose the "best" percept-action pair for credit assignment from among relevant percept-action pairs, and guides the creation of new percept-action pairs as evidence is acquired that suggests they might be valuable.

In short, this system creates new percept-action pairs when it has evidence that suggests that by paying attention to a more specific element of state, an action can increase its reliability. As mentioned earlier, each percept-action pair (i.e., an action tuple) maintains reliability and novelty statistics for its associated percept, and its percept's children. Together, these statistics are used to guide the creation of new percept-action pairs, a process referred to as *innovation*. While inspired by dog training, this approach is similar to that proposed by Gary Drescher several years ago to model infant development (Drescher 1991).

During the credit-assignment phase, the percept-action pair selected for credit assignment has the option of innovating—that is, spawning a child percept-action pair whose percept is more specific than its own. Two conditions must be met to be eligible for innovation: First, the value of the percept-action pair must be over some threshold—that is, there needs to be some evidence that the percept-action pair or a variant is potentially valuable. Second, there needs to be a child of the percept whose reliability and novelty is above a certain threshold. These statistics essentially provide evidence that a new percept-action pair utilizing that child percept could be more reliable than a percept-action pair relying on the parent percept. If these conditions are met, then a new child percept-action pair is created with the same action as the parent but with the child percept, and the new pair is made a child of the original percept-action pair. As such, it becomes eligible to be selected as the most appropriate representative of all of the percept-action pairs that share its action.

By way of an example, assume that our virtual dog has a [true/sit] percept-action pair, but no more specific variants of that percept-action pair. The trainer begins by rewarding the performance of [true/sit], with the effect being that the reliability and value of [true/sit] increases. Of course, what the trainer observes is only the increased frequency of the dog performing a sit. Once the dog is sitting frequently, the trainer starts saying "Sit" as the sit action is performed and continues to reward the sit. After a few repetitions, the [any-utterance/sit] percept-action pair is spawned as the dog notices that the reliability of being rewarded is high when the "any-utterance" percept is active, and that the "any-utterance" percept is relatively novel. Through more training, the system will discover that the reliability seems particularly high when the sit-utterance percept is active and will spawn a new child [sit-utterance/sit]. Indeed, once the trainer "thinks" the dog knows the cue, in this case the sit-utterance, the trainer typically stops rewarding spontaneous sits or sits in response to other utterances (i.e., [true/sit] or [any-utterance/sit]). The effect is that their reliability (and value) drops in comparison with that of [sit-utterance/sit]. This is shown in Figure 3.

The mechanism described above provides a simple hierarchical search of the percept-action space, focusing on those areas that seem most promising and exploring variants of percept-action pairs for which there is evidence that a variant may prove more valuable than its parent.

4.3.2   The Problem of Sequences

Reinforcement learning techniques such as Q-learning work by propagating value back from a goal. A consequence of this approach is that the system learns backward from the goal. That is, the state-action pair that leads directly to the goal must be discovered first, and only then can the penultimate state-action pair be discovered, and so on. An implication of this approach is that state-action pairs that occur early in a sequence can be performed many times without receiving any useful information with respect to their relevance to achieving the ultimate goal. This is a particularly insidious problem if an action early in the sequence needs to be performed in a certain way in order for the goal ever to be achieved. Not only won't there be useful feedback to guide the subject's choice of how to perform the action until it has learned the remaining elements of the sequence, but the chances of learning those elements are greatly diminished, since it will rarely achieve the goal because it is not performing this critical step correctly.[5] The bottom line is that while Q-learning can find an optimal solution, it may do so very, very slowly. Even simple sequences may require thousands of trials. Here I sketch out a possible solution, once again guided by how animals seem to address this problem.

On the surface, the idea of propagating value back from a goal state seems both intuitive and easy to apply to animal behavior. For example, one can easily imagine how it might be applied to learn the sequence of actions that make up the predatory repertoire of mammals: orient, stalk, chase, grab, bite to kill, dissect, and eat. That is, the animal would first learn that eating prey reduced hunger, then that tearing apart the dead carcass made it possible to eat it, then that a particular type of bite was especially reliable at killing the prey so it could be dissected, and so on. Each action's value (more correctly, each state-action pair's value) would reflect its distance from the ultimate goal of reducing hunger.

---

[5]See (Sutton 1991) for a discussion of some model-based approaches that learn the state-transition matrix associated with the state-action pairs and then use this information to propagate value back.

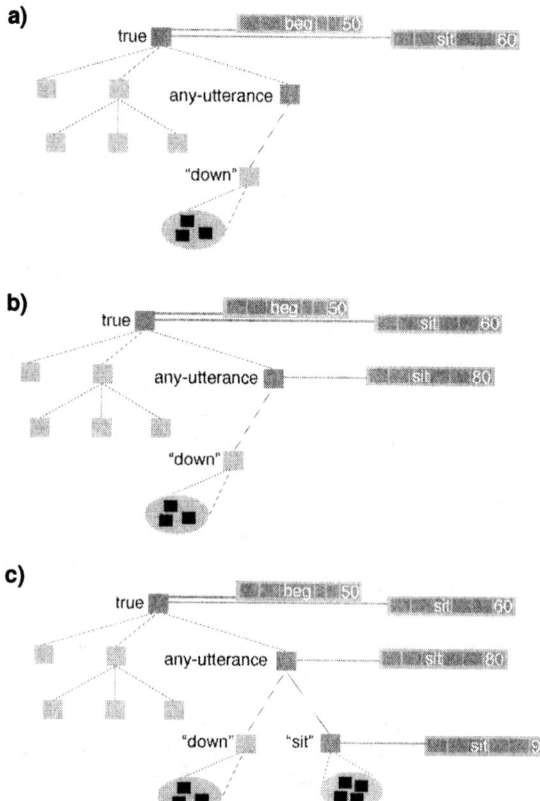

Figure 3 Here is an example of innovation in state and state-action space. Initially in (a), the dog chooses between sitting and begging, but the trainer preferentially rewards sitting, so its value goes up. In (b) a new percept-action pair is created as the dog notices that the reliability of sitting is higher when performed in the presence of an utterance. In (c) an even more specific percept-action is created as the dog learns that sitting in response to a specific utterance (i.e., "sit") is maximally reliable.

Indeed, animal trainers use a technique known as *backward-chaining* (Ramirez 1999) to train sequences that on the surface appear to work by propagating value back from a goal. In backward-chaining, the last action in the sequence is trained first, together with a cue that signals that if the animal performs the action in response to the cue, it will get a reward. The next-to-last action is trained next, but with the consequence being the cue previously associated with the last action. This cue acts as secondary reinforcer since it signals a known strategy for getting the actual reward.

If on the surface backward-chaining appears to be propagating value back from a goal, a closer look suggests otherwise. Typically, each action in the chain is individually trained with a separate cue prior to training the sequence. This is important because as the trainer teaches the sequence they give the cue for the next action in the sequence as the animal is finishing the previous action in the sequence. Thus, the animal may be learning a very local lesson, namely that a given action leads to either a treat or a change in state (i.e., the appearance of the cue), which in turn may result in a treat if the animal responds with the appropriate action. This interpretation is consistent with the advice of a trainer who suggests: "It will be essential that you occasionally interrupt the chain and reinforce a particular behavior with something other than the next behavior in the chain" (Ramirez 1999). Indeed, the ratio suggested is one out of four times. In other words, it is not clear if the animal is learning a "sequence" leading to a motivationally significant event, or rather learning (1) a variable ratio of reward associated with the components of the sequence, and (2) associating the performance of a behavior with the subsequent appearance of a cue that signals a context in which the performance of another action may lead to a reward. This is very different than back propagation of value from a distant goal.

Paul Leyhausen extensively studied the development and organization of predatory behaviors in cats and concluded: "As far as I have been able to establish, cats have action-specific energies for lying in wait, stalking, chasing, seizing, killing, eating, and a whole series of other instinctive movements within the functional system of catching and consuming prey. *What they certainly do not have is one unitary prey-catching drive to which these are subordinate*" (Lorenz and Leyhausen 1973). In other words, he doesn't believe back propagation of value from a distant motivational goal is the main mechanism for sequence learning.

Leyhausen makes several important points in his analysis of predatory behavior in cats that are worth noting here. First, he argues that the actions that make up the predatory sequence, while at root instinctual, are expressed and perfected long before the cat actually kills and eats prey. That is, cats perfect their stalking skills—for example, on their ever-present littermates—rather than just learning from successful, but relatively rare sequences of predatory actions leading to the consumption of prey. In other words, they are exploring the space of actions that will eventually be useful in predatory behavior in a context that provides greater opportunity for expression and feedback.

Second, he argues that each action in the sequence has its own drive or motivation; as he puts it, "Therefore, a mouse is an object to ambush or chase, to kill, to eat, to fish after, or throw around, i.e. the stimulus quality of the mouse changes according to the hierarchal order of appetences" (Lorenz and Leyhausen 1973). Thus, a cat may "throw around" a mouse, not because it is hungry and eventually wants to eat it, but rather to satisfy its "throw around" drive. Indeed, if an action has not been performed for some period of time, the animal may act so as to bring itself into a state in which the action may be performed. Leyhausen suggests that this tendency is particularly strong for early actions in the sequence and argues that they "must develop strong appetences of their own so that even frequent lack of success can not put the animal off ('extinguish') them" (Lorenz and Leyhausen 1973). That is, he uses action-specific drives to explain why actions that have a low chance of success even under the best of circumstances are not extinguished. There is an interesting parallel to the earlier discussion of backward-chaining in which the importance of placing the individual behaviors on a variable ratio was stressed. By putting the action, which may have no intrinsic drive, on a variable reward ratio, the trainer makes the action resistant to extinction.

Third, Leyhausen argues that when cats make the connection between killing prey and eating prey, the sequence of predatory actions comes online very quickly, but in their innate (i.e., unpracticed) form. Subsequently, the innate forms are replaced by the learned forms that they "in a certain sense, already learned before killing for the first time" (Lorenz and Leyhausen 1973). He emphasizes that the learned forms coexist with innate forms; as he puts it, "Cats ... have a complete set of pure instinctive movements for prey-catching, and at the same time they have a more or less rich store of learned motor patterns, varying according to the individual, which can serve the same goal" (Lorenz and Leyhausen 1973).

The argument is that back-propagation of value from a distant motivational event is slow under the best of circumstances. This is especially true if there is a specific level of skill required before there is any chance of ultimately reaching a distal goal. An alternative approach is to bias the expression of important actions in the chain, especially those that require some degree of skill, so that the creature gains experience using them apart from their use in leading to a given goal. Following Leyhausen, there may be an intrinsic drive to perform the action, in which case the very performance of the action is the reward. Alternatively, the action may be expressed in a context in which the performance of the action leads to another, but more immediate goal. In either case, two things are necessary: First, there needs to be an immediate and accurate feedback signal indicating, in effect, the quality of the performance in order for the performance of the action to improve.[6] Second, there needs to be a mechanism to generalize from the performance of the action in pursuit of one goal to its use in the pursuit of another. As a thought experiment, let us see how one would implement this using a Q-learning formulation.

In Q-learning, as you will remember, there needs to be a separate Q-table for each goal. Here we will assume two tables: one that we will call "play," whose goal is to learn the best form of a given action A (e.g., "stalk"), and another, called "hunt and eat," whose goal is achieved only through a sequence of actions, one of which is action A. Thus, the first Q-table only contains various forms of the given action A, and associated with that table is a reward that is only reachable by performing a particular form of A. The second table contains the actions and states that are relevant to the second goal, including action A, its variations (organized as described in the earlier section on shaping), and of course the other actions. Finally, there is some mechanism that decides which goal to pursue at any given time. Initially, the system should be biased to pursue "play," but over time switch the bias to the "hunt and eat" goal. Given this structure, a simple, but very useful, heuristic would be to bias the choice of which form of A to perform in the second table

---

[6]In the case of an action that leads to a more immediate goal, the feedback signal is clear—namely, achievement of the immediate goal. However, if the performance of the action is in fact the reward, it is much less clear what feedback signal could be used to improve the performance.

based on the form of A that had the highest Q-value in the first table. The advantage of this approach is that it allows the system to explore the action space associated with A in a context in which there is immediate feedback, and then be able to use that knowledge in a more difficult context (or one in which there is less immediate guidance).

We still have the problem of how sequences are formed. The approach above only addresses the question of how to learn the best form of an action within a sequence of actions; it assumes that the sequence itself will be learned via the back propagation of value that is inherent in Q-learning. It should be noted that in the presence of cues, the problem is easy because it is the sequence of cues that produces the sequence of actions. In a trained sequence, the trainer is giving the cues and so is controlling the sequence. In a sequence such as a predatory sequence, the world itself is providing the cues that trigger the various actions. The actions themselves are either innately rewarding or have some probability of being directly rewarding (the result of being put on a variable ratio of reward schedule). As such there need not be any representation of a distant reward in order for an apparent sequence to form.

Coppinger notes that while all breeds of dogs display the same general predatory sequence, the details of the sequence vary greatly. In some breeds, certain actions are extremely prominent, while in others they are rarely observed. Similarly, in some breeds, the actions of the sequence are strongly linked, meaning that if one action in the pattern is expressed it is very likely that the next action in the pattern will be as well, whereas in other breeds, the actions are very loosely connected. Indeed, some breeds can jump into the sequence at any point, whereas others must start from the beginning each time (Coppinger and Coppinger 2001). All of which suggests that, to a varying extent, the performance of an action in a sequence biases the subsequent choice of action. While this may be due in part to the action setting up the relevant context for the subsequent action, it may also be due in part to the performance of the action *itself* being the context for the next action. This latter explanation is consistent with the phenomenon of *cue fading*. Cue fading occurs when a trainer gradually reduces the magnitude of a cue (be it a sound or gesture), but the animal continues to respond as if the magnitude of the cue remained unchanged. When training sequences, the cue associated with an intermediate action may be faded altogether.[7] The fact that the sequence remains intact suggests that the performance of an action can itself be the context for a subsequent action. Once again, we can have the appearance of a sequence without a representation of a distal goal.

4.4 Summary

We have incorporated many of the lessons discussed above into a toolkit developed by the Synthetic Characters Group for modeling adaptive autonomous animated characters. Space does not permit a detailed discussion of the specific learning mechanism (see (Burke et al. 2001; Isla et al. 2001) for a detailed description of the toolkit and the actual learning mechanism), but the key lessons incorporated into the architecture are summarized below.

- We exploit aspects of the world that effectively limit the search space. For example, temporal proximity is used to infer apparent causality. That is, we utilize a temporal attention window that overlaps the beginning of an action to identify a potentially

---

[7]It is worth noting though that the animal may be using subtle cues that the handler is giving without even being aware of it (Gould and Gould 1999).

relevant state. Similarly, we assign credit to the action that immediately precedes a motivationally significant event in a manner similar to Q-learning, although, as suggested earlier, percept-actions pairs have the option of choosing a more appropriate pair to participate in credit assignment.

- As discussed above, we utilize loosely hierarchical representations of state, action, and state-action space and rely on simple statistics to identify potentially promising areas of the respective spaces for exploration. Through a process known as *innovation* we grow the hierarchy downward toward ever more fine-grained representations of state and more specific (and hopefully more reliable) percept-action pairs. Thus, the process is one of starting with rather generic percept-action pairs and generating more specific instances of pairs for which there is some evidence that they are both potentially valuable and more reliable. Measures of novelty and reliability, as well as temporal proximity are used to guide this process.

- We use natural feedback signals such as a significant change in a motivational variable to guide state, action, and state-action space discovery. For example, if a model-based recognizer is being built from examples to identify a particular state of the world (e.g., an acoustic pattern that signals when a dog should beg), We use the reward signal to disambiguate between good and bad examples. As the state and action space trees grow downward, we are then able to make use of the new states and actions in our percept-action tree, as described above.

- We utilize biases that affect the frequency and timing of actions. These biases take two forms: One bias is to perform actions that have led to reinforcement in the past. This not only allows the creature to exploit what it knows but also more opportunities to discover more reliable variations. There is also an innate bias to perform a given pattern at a given time, thereby providing an opportunity to incorporate the pattern into the behavioral repertoire should it prove useful.

- We tie variability of action to variability of outcome. That is, the variability in expected outcome is treated as a signal indicating the degree to which the creature is successful in controlling its environment through its actions. When the outcome is highly variable, the choice and form of action is highly variable as well.

The learning mechanism in my toolkit is still a work in progress, but it is already at a level at which we can train a virtual dog using techniques borrowed from real dog training.

5 Our Experience So Far

In this section, I review a number of the characters that have been built to date using this approach.

5.1 Duncan and Terrence

Duncan the Highland Terrier (Burke et al. 2001; Isla et al. 2001; Ivanov 2001) and his cousin Terrence are part of an ongoing research effort to build an autonomous animated dog whose ability to learn, behavioral complexity, and apparent sense of empathy rivals that of a real dog. Duncan is shown in Figure 4, and Terrence is shown in Figures 5 and 6. Duncan was featured in *sheep|dog,* an interactive installation piece in which a

Figure 4   Duncan the Highland Terrier herding sheep in sheep|dog: Trial by Eire

Figure 5   Terrence is an autonomous animated pup that can be trained using clicker training. The trainer's interface is a microphone and a pair of virtual hands controlled by a gamepad. The left hand holds a clicker that makes a sound when pressed. The right hand serves as a target for luring and can also give an extra reward by scratching the dog's head.

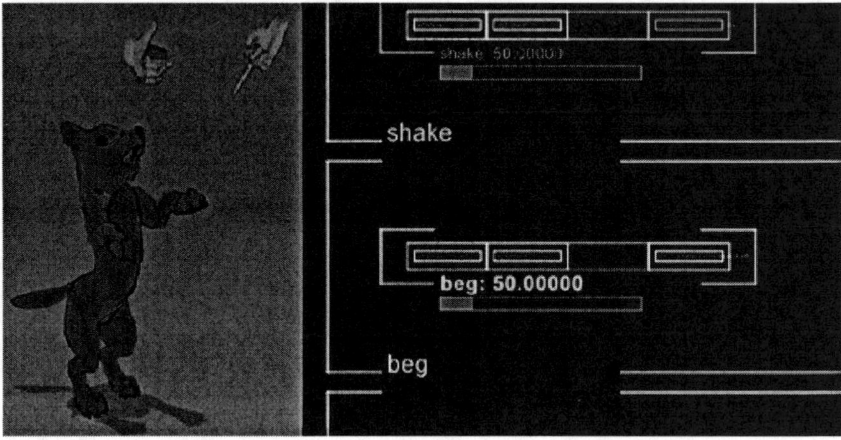

Figure 6   On the left, Terrence is performing a beg. On the right, our action tuple visualizer is shown.

user plays the role of a shepherd who must interact through a series of vocal commands with Duncan to herd a flock of sheep. This system demonstrated some of Duncan's basic reactive, perceptual, and spatial abilities, as well as his ability to classify user utterances as one of six possible commands. This classification could be trained through a one-shot learning interface so that a new user could achieve a high recognition rate after a very short (about one minute) training routine. Indeed, one user trained Duncan to respond to commands in Gha, the language of Ghana. While tangential to the discussion here, Isla (2001) has done very exiting work incorporating spatial learning and rudimentary object permanence into Duncan as well.

Terrence is an autonomous animated pup that can be trained using clicker training, shaping, and luring in an application called *Clicker*. The trainer's interface is a microphone and pair of virtual hands controlled by a gamepad (see Figure 5.) The left hand holds a clicker that makes a sound when pressed. The right hand serves as a target for luring and can also give an extra reward by scratching the dog's head. Given an initial repertoire of a dozen basic behaviors (e.g., "sit," "shake," "lie down," "beg," "jump," "go out"), together with basic navigational and behavioral competencies we have been able to train him to respond to both symbolic gestures (i.e., gamepad button presses) and, more significantly, to arbitrary acoustic patterns. A dozen such tricks can be trained in real time within the space of 15 minutes. We have also demonstrated simple shaping and luring.

A typical training session is described below, and Figure 7 shows the frequency of the expressed behaviors over time in response to the trainer's actions. Initially, the pup experiments among its known actions. This is shown to the left of time A in the figure. Starting at time A, as the trainer preferentially rewards sitting, the frequency of sitting increases as shown in the interval between A and B. Starting at time B, when sitting is being performed reliably, the trainer starts giving the verbal cue "sit" as the pup begins to sit, while also reducing the rate of reinforcement if the pup sits in the absence of the cue. The system, through state space discovery, creates a new percept that contains a model of

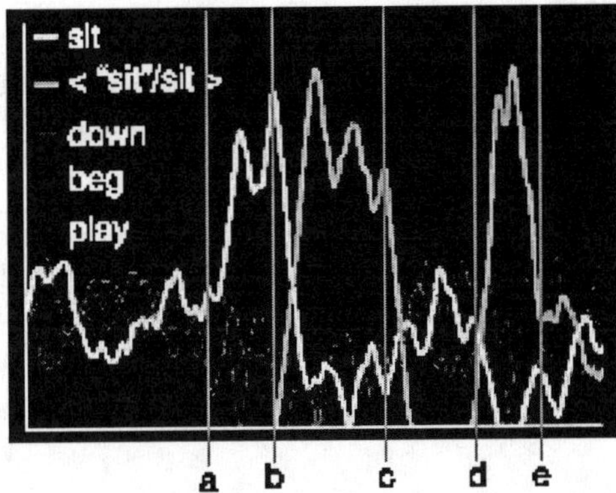

Figure 7   Graph showing a typical training session.

the (arbitrary) acoustic pattern associated with the rewarded sit and adds it to the pup's percept tree. Eventually, a new percept-action pair is created that represents ["sit"/sit]. At the same time, we see that the frequency of spontaneous sitting decreases. At time C, the trainer stops rewarding sitting in response to "sit," and the frequency of sitting in response to "sit" drops significantly, while the frequency of sitting spontaneously increases. At time D, the trainer resumes rewarding sit in response to "sit" and its frequency returns to its previous level.

To lure the dog into a sit, for example, the trainer simply moves the target hand over the dog's head and clicks as he gets into the sit pose. Terrence can also be lured through a novel trajectory—for example, walking in an S pattern on the ground. When rewarded, this lured trajectory is added to the action space as a new action (through action space discovery) and can be selected randomly by the pup in the future just like any of the previously known actions and ultimately associated with a cue.

Some of Terrence's actions (e.g., shake paw) are parameterized and thus can be shaped by the trainer. As the pup experiments with different forms of his parameterized "shake paw" action, the trainer can reward ever-higher versions of the shake action until the pup shakes his paw with high reliability.

6   Conclusion

The computational model underlying all of this work focuses on the kind of learning that dogs do. It must be said that not only do dogs learn many more things than are addressed in this model at present, but also that people can learn a great deal more than dogs. Nonetheless, I believe that this kind of everyday learning underlies much of our everyday common sense and our expectations about what a sentient creature is minimally capable of learning. As people interact with synthetic characters over extended periods of time, they expect them to learn from experience in the same commonsensical way. In the long run, only Wile E. Coyote can get away with not learning from experience.

Acknowledgments

The work reported in this paper represents the collective work of the Synthetic Characters Group at the Media Lab of MIT. Members of the group whose ideas are reflected here include Matt Berlin, Robert Burke, Jennie Cochran, Marc Downie, Scott Eaton, Jesse Gray, Michel Halvac, Damian Isla, Yuri Ivanov, Michael Patrick Johnson, Christopher Kline, Derek Lyons, Dolphin Nain, Ben Resner, Ken Russell, Bill Tomlinson, and Song-Yee Yoon. Thanks also to Professor Gerald Schneider. We are indebted to Gary Wilkes for his insights into dog training and behavior. The Digital Life Consortium of the Media Lab sponsors this work.

References

Ballard, D. (1997). *An Introduction to Natural Computation*. Cambridge, MA: MIT Press.

Burke, R., D. Isla, M. Downie, Y. Ivanov, and B. Blumberg (2001). Creature smarts: The art and architecture of a virtual brain. In *Computer Game Developers Conference*, San Jose, CA.

Coppinger, R., and L. Coppinger (2001). *Dogs: A Startling New Understanding of Canine Origin, Behavior, and Evolution*. New York: Charles Scribner.

Dennett, D. (1987). *The Intentional Stance*. Cambridge, MA: MIT Press.

Downie, M. (2000). *Behavior, animation, music: The music and movement of synthetic characters*. Thesis, MIT.

Drescher, G. (1991). *Made-up Minds: A Constructivist Approach to Artificial Intelligence*. Cambridge, MA: MIT Press.

Gallistel, C. R., and J. Gibbon (2000). Time, rate and conditioning. *Psychological Review 107*.

Gould, J., and C. Gould (1999). *The Animal Mind*. New York: W.H. Freeman.

Humphreys, M. (1996). Action selection methods using reinforcement learning. In *The Fourth International Conference on Simulation of Adaptive Behavior*, Cape Cod, MA.

Isla, D. (2001). *The Virtual Hippocampus: Spatial Common Sense for Synthetic Creatures*. M.eng. thesis, Department of Electrical Engineering and Computer Science, MIT.

Isla, D., R. Burke, M. Downie, and B. Blumberg (2001). A layered brain architecture for synthetic creatures. In *The International Joint Conference on Artificial Intelligence*, Seattle.

Ivanov, Y. (2001). *State Discovery for Autonomous Creatures*. Ph.D. thesis, MIT.

Ivanov, Y., B. Blumberg, and A. Pentland (2001). Expectation maximization for weakly labeled data. In *The International Conference on Machine Learning*, Williamstown MA.

Kaelbling, L. (1990). *Learning in embedded systems*. Ph. D. thesis, Stanford University.

Kaelbling, L. (1993). Hierarchical reinforcement learning: Preliminary results. In *The 10th International Conference on Machine Learning*.

Lindsay, S. (2000). *Applied Dog Behavior and Training*. Ames: Iowa State University Press.

Lorenz, K. (1981). *The Foundations of Ethology*. New York: Springer-Verlag.

Lorenz, K., and P. Leyhausen (1973). *Motivation of Human and Animal Behavior: An Ethological View*. New York: Van Nostrand Reinhold.

Mitchell, K. (1997). *Machine Learning*. New York: McGraw-Hill.

Plotkin, H. (1994). *Darwin Machines and the Nature of Knowledge*. Cambridge, MA: Harvard University Press.

Pryor, K. (1999). *Clicker Training for Dogs*. Waltham, MA: Sunshine Books.

Rabiner, L., and B.-H. Juang (1993). *Fundamentals of Speech Recognition*. Englewood Cliffs, NJ: Prentice Hall.

Ramirez, K. (1999). *Animal Training: Successful Animal Management through Positive Reinforcement*. Chicago: Shedd Aquarium.

Resner, B., A. Stern, and A. Frank (1997). The truth about catz and dogz. In *The Computer Games Developer Conference*, San Jose, CA.

Shettleworth, S. J. (1998). *Cognition, Evolution and Behavior*. New York: Oxford University Press.

Sutton, R. (1991). Reinforcement learning architectures for animats. In *The First International Conference on Simulation of Adaptive Behavior*. Cambridge, MA. MIT Press.

Sutton, R., and A. Barto (1998). *Reinforcement Learning: An Introduction*. Cambridge, MA: MIT Press.

Therrien, C. (1989). *Decision Estimation and Classification: An Introduction to Pattern Recognition and Related Topics*. New York: John Wiley & Sons.

Thomas, F., and O. Johnson (1981). *The Illusion of Life: Disney Animation*. New York: Hyperion.

Watkins, C. J., and P. Dayan (1992). Q-learning. *Machine Learning 8*.

Wilkes, G. (1995). *Click and Treat Training Kit*. Mesa, AZ: Click and Treat Inc.

Wilkes, G. (2001). Role of variability. Personal communication.

Chapter 3

Natural Language Understanding

Identifying Semantic Relations in Text

Daniel Gildea
University of California, Berkeley, and
International Computer Science Institute
gildea@icsi.berkeley.edu

Daniel Jurafsky
University of Colorado, Boulder
jurafsky@colorado.edu

Abstract

Over the past decade, natural language processing has been transformed by the adoption of statistical methods. The statistical approach began with shallow problems such as part-of-speech tagging, progressed to syntactic parsing, and is now being applied to higher-level semantic tasks. We present a statistical system for identifying the semantic relationships, or *semantic roles*, filled by constituents of a sentence. The system operates at the level of *frame semantics*, which provide us with an intermediate representation between the detail of complete theories of semantics and simpler domain-specific slot-filler representations. Given an input sentence, the system labels constituents with roles such as SPEAKER, MESSAGE, and TOPIC, identifying participants in various types of actions or states.

The system is based on statistical classifiers that were trained on roughly 50,000 sentences hand labeled with semantic roles in the FrameNet semantic labeling project. We then parsed each training sentence and extracted various lexical and syntactic features, including the syntactic category of the constituent, its grammatical function, and position in the sentence. These features were combined with knowledge of the target verb, noun, or adjective, as well as information such as the prior probabilities of various combinations of semantic roles. We also used various methods of lexical clustering to generalize across possible fillers of roles. Test sentences were parsed, annotated with these features, and then passed through the classifiers.

Our system achieves 80% accuracy in identifying the semantic role of pre-segmented constituents. At the harder task of simultaneously segmenting constituents and identifying their semantic role, the system achieved 65% precision and 61% recall.

1   Introduction

Recent years have been exhilarating ones for natural language understanding. The excitement and rapid advances that had characterized other language-processing tasks like speech recognition, part-of-speech tagging, and parsing have finally begun to appear in tasks in which understanding and semantics play a greater role. For example, there has been widespread commercial deployment of simple speech-based, natural language–understanding systems that answer questions about flight arrival times, give directions, report on bank balances, or perform simple financial transactions. More sophisticated research systems can generate concise summaries of news articles, answer fact-based questions, and recognize complex semantic and dialogue structure.

But the challenges that lie ahead are still similar to the challenge that the field has faced since Winograd (1972): moving away from carefully hand-crafted, domain-dependent systems toward robustness and domain-independence. This goal is not as far away as it once was, thanks to the development of large semantic databases like WordNet (Fellbaum 1998) and of general-purpose domain-independent algorithms like named entity recognition.

Current information-extraction and dialogue-understanding systems, however, are still based on domain-specific frame-and-slot templates. Systems for booking airplane information are based on domain-specific frames with slots like FROM_AIRPORT, TO_AIRPORT, or DEPART_TIME. Systems for studying mergers and acquisitions are based on slots like JOINT_VENTURE_COMPANY, PRODUCTS, RELATIONSHIP, and AMOUNT. In order for natural language–understanding tasks to proceed beyond these specific domains, we need semantic frames and semantic-understanding systems that do not require a new set of slots for each new application domain.

In this chapter, we describe a shallow semantic interpreter based on semantic roles that are less domain-specific than TO_AIRPORT or JOINT_VENTURE_COMPANY. These roles are defined at the level of semantic frames (see (Fillmore 1976) for a description of frame-based semantics), which describe abstract actions or relationships along their participants. The interpreter itself is a statistical classifier that is trained on sentences annotated with role labels. We first parse sentences with the Collins parser (Collins 1999) and then train a statistical classifier based on the output parse to label the semantic roles (e.g., AGENT, PATIENT, INSTRUMENT, PROPOSITION) in the input sentence. The semantic classifier is trained on 50,000 sentences that were hand labeled with semantic roles and uses features computed from the parse, such as the grammatical function and lexical heads of each constituent, lexical dependency information, and clause mood, as well as statistical features derived from the training set (e.g., the probability for each verb, noun, and adjective taking a particular complement type).

1.1   Approaches to Natural Language Understanding

Modern approaches to natural language understanding may be grouped into two classes: domain-independent, logic-based systems, and domain-dependent, statistical systems. In the first class, logic-based, or symbolic, systems have the goal of producing a deep and rich semantic and pragmatic interpretation of a text. They generally use representations based on predicate logic and include hand-built knowledge structures and inference patterns necessary to understand the meaning of connected texts. In the second class, statistical systems typically forgo such deep representations in favor of directly modeling the task to be performed. These systems tend to reformulate the task of understanding as a pattern-recognition problem. These tasks are then addressed by machine learning techniques, allowing systems to be trained directly from examples of input/output pairs.

An early paradigm of a deep and rich representation of meaning is exemplified by Schank (1972). The *conceptual dependency theory* provided a frame-based formal representation of the meaning of sentences and connected discourses. A prominent feature of the representation was the analysis of the meaning of individual words into semantic primitives, such as the predicate "TRANS" for transfer, together with case-grammar-like argument roles such as "recipient," and sortal restrictions on role fillers. Interpretation of even simple sentences included complex inference to fill in aspects of the semantics not explicitly stated.

A more modern, highly developed, and fairly complete language–understanding system of the symbolic variety is exemplified by the *core language engine* of Alshawi (1992). The system uses a unification-based grammar for syntactic parsing, generating a semantic representation based on a "Quasi-Logical Form," which includes models of semantic domains such as tense, aspect, modality and measure terms, and such difficult phenomena as quantifier scoping, co-reference resolution, and long-distance syntactic dependencies.

The logic-based approach was extended by the TACITUS system of (Hobbs et al. 1990), which interprets sentences by searching for the minimal set of assumptions and inferences necessary to prove the sentence from previous knowledge. As an example, from the sentence

(1)   The Boston office called.

Hobbs et al. (1990) are able to determine that "the Boston office" really refers to "a person working at the Boston office," as "call" requires an agent. The system also determines that the relation expressed by the noun compound "Boston office" is one of physical location, and resolves the referents of the office and the person calling to specific objects in the knowledge base. The system also makes syntactic parsing decisions in this manner—for example, by attaching prepositional phrases as necessary for the best logical explanation of the sentence. When interpreting the sentence fragment

(2)   Disengaged compressor after lube-oil alarm.

the system coerces "lube-oil alarm" to mean "the sounding of the lube-oil alarm" and as a by-product attaches the pronoun "after" to the verb "disengaged" rather than the noun "compressor." Hobbs et al. (1990) attached numeric weights to the inference steps stored in their knowledge base in order to make the system prefer certain more natural explanations over others. These weights are prescient of the probabilistic systems that followed; however, the weights are set by hand rather than being learned from training data.

Despite their impressive coverage of deep linguistic phenomena and rich representations, the logic-based understanding systems are often quite limited in the texts they are able to handle. Language "in the wild" is not well-behaved, and robustness to its variety has proven hard to achieve in any hand-built system. The more logical inferences a system performs, the more relevant world knowledge must be encoded by hand. Thus, these systems have generally been applied to very domain-specific tasks, such as the air travel or merger-and-acquisition domains described above.

For these and other reasons, the field of natural language processing has undergone a fundamental shift toward statistical methods in recent years. The availability of large and annotated corpora has made possible a methodology based on training systems on labeled data and quantitatively evaluating their performance on held-out test data. Statistical methods began with relatively shallow problems such as part-of-speech tagging, for which it is relatively easy both to agree on the desired output and to collect corpora. Statistical methods have been gradually extended to higher-level tasks, such as parsing. Statistical parsers trained on the Penn Treebank, for example, give the tree structure of syntactic attachment in a sentence, as well as labels for syntactic categories such as noun phrase and verb phrase. Despite the fact that in many cases such attachment decisions require a great deal of world knowledge, statistical systems using fairly simple lexical statistics, without any sort of semantic representation, inference, or even stemming of inflected word forms have achieved the best reported results on the parsing task. Thus, although statistical systems are limited in their scope, they have been extremely successful at the tasks for which they are designed.

Other relatively high-level applications at which statistical systems have been at least as successful as purely symbolic approaches include information retrieval and topic detection. Even for the extremely difficult problem of machine translation, statistical systems of the type pioneered by Brown et al. (1990), which forgo any internal representation of syntax or semantics and instead directly model probabilities of word correspondences and word reorderings between source and target language, appear to perform at least as well as much more elaborate symbolic approaches.

Such statistical or data-driven techniques are commonly applied to specific, domain-independent semantic interpretation problems where the demands on the semantic task are simpler than full AI-complete understanding: tasks such as extracting information about joint ventures from business news, understanding weather reports, or summarizing radio news. Such *information-extraction* tasks are characterized by two properties: (1) the desired knowledge can be described by a relatively simple and fixed *template*, or frame, with slots that need to be filled in with material from the text, and (2) only a small part of the information in the text is relevant for filling in this frame; the rest can be ignored.

For example, one of the tasks used in the fifth Message Understanding Conference (MUC-5) (Sundheim 1993), a U.S. government–organized information-extraction conference, was to extract information about international joint ventures from business news. Here are the first two sentences of a sample article from Grishman and Sundheim (1995):

> Bridgestone Sports Co. said Friday it has set up a joint venture in Taiwan with a local concern and a Japanese trading house to produce golf clubs to be shipped to Japan.
>
> The joint venture, Bridgestone Sports Taiwan Co., capitalized at 20 million new Taiwan dollars, will start production in January 1990 with production of 20,000 iron and "metal wood" clubs a month.

The output of an information-extraction system can be a single template with a certain number of slots filled in, or a more complex, hierarchically related set of objects. The MUC-5 task specified this latter, more complex output, requiring systems to produce hierarchically linked templates describing the participants in the joint venture, the resulting

TIE-UP-1:
Relationship:	TIE-UP
Entities:	"Bridgestone Sports Co."
	"a local concern"
	"a Japanese trading house"
Joint Venture Company:	"Bridgestone Sports Taiwan Co."
Activity:	ACTIVITY-1
Amount:	NT$20000000

ACTIVITY-1:
Company:	"Bridgestone Sports Taiwan Co."
Product:	"iron and "metal wood" clubs"
Start Date:	DURING: January 1990

Figure 1   The templates produced by the FASTUS information-extraction engine (Hobbs et al. 1997) given the input text from above.

company, and its intended activity, ownership, and capitalization. Figure 1 shows the resulting structure produced by the FASTUS system (Hobbs et al. 1997).

Many information-extraction systems are built around cascades of finite-state automata. The FASTUS system, for example, produces the template given above, based on a cascade in which each level of linguistic processing extracts some information from the text, which is passed on to the next higher level. Each level is based on handwritten regular expressions. After tokenizing, FASTUS has a level that recognizes multiwords like *set up* and *joint venture*, and names like *Bridgestone Sports Co.* The name recognizer is a transducer, composed of a large set of specific mappings designed to handle locations, personal names, and names of organizations, companies, unions, performing groups, and so on. Then words are grouped into Noun-Groups and Verb-Groups based on handwritten rules. Then larger semantic entities and events are recognized and inserted into templates by a set of higher-level regular expressions. For example, the first sentence of the news story above realizes the semantic patterns based on the following two regular expressions (where NG indicates Noun-Group and VG, Verb-Group):

- NG(Company/ies) VG(Set-up) NG(Joint-Venture) with NG(Company/ies)
- VG(Produce) NG(Product)

The second sentence realizes the second pattern above, as well as the following two patterns:

- NG(Company) VG-Passive(Capitalized) at NG(Currency)
- NG(Company) VG(Start) NG(Activity) in/on NG(Date)

This simple template- or frame-based architecture is also used by simple dialogue agents and speech-based question-answering systems, beginning with the influential *Graphic User Shell (GUS)* system for airline travel planning (Bobrow et al. 1977) and including more recent Air Traveler Information Systems (ATIS) and other travel and restaurant guides.

For example, a simple airline system, based on a semantic parser like PHOENIX (Ward 1991) might have the goal of helping a user find an appropriate flight. These systems take an input sentence like Sentence 3 and produce parsed output like Sentence 4.

(3)   I want to go from Denver to Boston on Tuesday.

(4)   [TRAVEL I want to go] [ORIGIN from Denver] [DESTINATION to Boston] on [DATE Tuesday].

Such dialogue systems have a frame, or template, with slots for various kinds of information the user might need to specify, perhaps linked to an optional question for the user:

Slot	Optional Question
Origin	"From what city are you leaving?"
Destination	"Where are you going?"
Date	"When would you like to leave?"
Fare_class	
Airline	
Oneway	

In PHOENIX, for example, actions and objects in a domain are represented by frames. The individual pieces of information relevant to the frame are represented as slots in the frame. Finite-state or context-free grammar rules associated with each slot specify the word strings that can fill the slot. A dialogue system based on Phoenix may just ask questions of the user, filling out the template with the answers, until it has enough information to perform a database query, and then return the result to the user.

Parsers like FASTUS, in the information-extraction domain, or Phoenix, in the dialogue agent domain, are well suited for these limited-domain applications because they are very efficient and produce exactly the representation that is needed by the application. This is because the representation is created specifically for each domain.

But the main strength of these approaches is is also their primary weakness. Whether based on regular expressions or more complex grammars, these systems require the patterns that recognize, for example, ORIGIN or JOINT_VENTURE_COMPANY to be written by hand or derived from data annotated with the desired structure. While many of the rules, like DATE and TIME, represent concepts useful in many domains, many other concepts, like ORIGIN, are specific to the domain of discourse. The size, complexity, and domain-specific nature of these rules makes these systems expensive to transfer to new domains.

To summarize, the strength of the symbolic, logic-based systems is the nature of their output; they produce rich representations that deal with complex semantic phenomena such as negation and quantification. Their corresponding weakness is coverage; the entire system consists of extremely complex handwritten rules that are expensive to produce. Indeed, solving the general problem of deep semantic parser is presumably AI-complete.

By contrast, the strengths of the statistical, template-based approaches are their simplicity and effectiveness. By selecting a level of semantic representation that is adequate for solving some task, these systems are able to focus their attention on only necessary phenomena. Inside their narrow domains, such systems are also robust to ungrammatical sentences or misrecognized utterances. But such focus comes at the price of breadth; both the templates/frames themselves, and every one of the rules for filling the slots, must be handwritten.

In summary, current natural language–processing systems exhibit a trade-off between the robustness and broad coverage of statistical systems, and the complexity of representations necessary for more complete language understanding in more general domains. What is needed is a semantic parser that has the advantages of both types of systems, producing a level of semantic representation that is shallow enough not to require AI-complete processing of negation, quantification, and full inference, but that is broad enough to apply across domains. Finally, the parser needs to be statistically trainable, to avoid expensive handwriting of grammars and slot-recognition rules.

Inchoate versions of such a modern system can be seen in recent work. For example, in the context of ATIS for spoken dialogue, Miller et al. (1996) automatically trained Hidden Markov Models to compute the probability that a constituent such as "Atlanta" filled a semantic slot such as DESTINATION in a semantic frame for air travel. In a data-driven approach to information extraction, Riloff (1993) built a dictionary of patterns for filling slots in a specific domain such as terrorist attacks, and Riloff and Schmelzenbach (1998) extended this technique to automatically derive entire "case frames" for words in the domain. These last two systems make use of a limited amount of hand labor to accept or reject automatically generated hypotheses.

All three of these recent systems show promise for a more sophisticated approach to build semantic understanding systems that are domain-independent and statistically trained.

1.2   Our Proposal: Statistical Interpretations of Frame-Based Representations

Our goal, then, is to design a system that achieves at least some of the advantages of both statistical and logic-based systems. We propose that semantic frames (Fillmore 1976) are a good intermediate level of representation for closing the gap between the robustness and broad coverage of statistical systems and the rich representations of more complete theories of semantics. Frames represent abstract actions or states and can be thought of as evoking a particular common situation or scene. Frame descriptions include definitions of roles for the participants in the relationship or action described by the frame. In this work, we do not make use of any formal representation of the frame's meaning, considering the frame as simply a relation holding between the fillers of its roles. Thus, we avoid for now the well-known problems that accompany any attempt to reduce all of semantics into combinations of formal primitives, or of reducing all semantic roles to a small set such as that defined in Fillmore (1968). This will prevent us from making the complex inferences necessary to unravel the metonymy of Sentences 1 and 2. The resulting semantic representation is simple enough, however, that annotation of large amounts of data is possible and a statistical system capable of handling text from a variety of semantic domains can be effectively trained and evaluated.

Many current natural language techniques are based on statistical parsers. We believe that our system, by providing richer semantic information than is available from a syntactic parse, can play a useful role in machine translation, information retrieval, and many other natural language tasks. For example, an information-extraction system could determine that in the sentence "The first one crashed," the phrase "the first one" is the VEHICLE, but in the sentence "The first one crashed the car," the same phrase is the AGENT. A syntactic parse alone will not distinguish these cases, as the phrase appears as the syntactic subject in both cases.

Our shallow semantic level of interpretation can be used for many purposes besides generalizing information extraction and semantic dialogue systems. One such application is in word-sense disambiguation, where the roles associated with a word can be cues to its sense. For example, Lapata and Brew (1999) and others have shown that the different syntactic subcategorization frames of a verb like "serve" can be used to help disambiguate a particular instance of the word "serve" as belonging to one of the senses GIVE, FIT, MASQUERADE, or FULFILL. Analysis of the semantic roles present in a sentence should allow better sense disambiguation than purely syntactic information. Semantic roles could also act as an important intermediate representation in statistical machine translation or automatic text summarization and in the emerging field of *Text Data Mining (TDM)* (Hearst 1999). Finally, incorporating semantic roles into probabilistic models of language may yield more accurate parsers and better language models for speech recognition.

Future progress in natural language processing will require improvements both in the representation of semantic information and in methods for learning from annotated and unannotated corpora. Eventually, statistical and symbolic systems must grow together in order to combine robustness and ease of automatic training on the one hand and detailed representations and cross-domain generality on the other. We hope to contribute to this process by showing that statistical systems can be used for semantic representations. We have chosen an intermediate level of semantic representation in order to make this possible, but hold out hope for further progress as better representations are developed and as more training data for statistical systems are collected.

In this chapter, we present our system in stages, beginning in Section 2 with a more detailed description of the data and the set of frame elements or semantic roles used. We then introduce the statistical classification technique used and examine in turn the knowledge sources our system makes use of. Section 3 describes the basic syntactic and lexical features used by our system, which are derived from a Penn Treebank–style parse of individual sentences to be analyzed. We break our task into two subproblems, which are examined in turn: finding the relevant sentence constituents, and giving them the correct semantic labels. Section 4 adds higher-level semantic knowledge to the system, attempting to model the selectional restrictions on role fillers not directly captured by lexical statistics. We compare hand-built and automatically derived resources for providing this information. Section 5 examines a technique for adding knowledge about systematic alternations in verb argument structure with sentence-level features. Section 6 examines how the choice of the set of semantic roles affects results. Finally, we draw conclusions and discuss future directions.

2   Semantic Roles

Semantic roles are probably one of the oldest classes of constructs in linguistic theory, dating back thousands of years to Panini's *kāraka* theory. Longevity, in this case, begets variety, and the literature records scores of proposals for sets of semantic roles. These sets of roles range from the very specific to the very general, and many have been used in computational implementations of one type or another.

At the specific end of the spectrum are domain-specific roles such as the FROM_AIRPORT, TO_AIRPORT, or DEP_TIME discussed above, or verb-specific roles like EATER and EATEN for the verb *to eat*. The opposite end of the spectrum consists of theories with only 2 "proto-roles" or "macroroles": PROTO-AGENT and PROTO-PATIENT (Dowty 1991; Van Valin 1993). In between lie many theories with around approximately 10 roles, often refered as *thematic roles* such as Fillmore 1971's list of nine: AGENT, EXPERIENCER, INSTRUMENT, OBJECT, SOURCE, GOAL, LOCATION, TIME, and PATH.[1]

Many of these sets of roles have been proposed either by linguists as part of theories of *linking*, the part of grammatical theory that describes the relationship between semantic roles and their syntactic realization, or by computer scientists as part of implemented natural language–understanding systems. As a rule, the more abstract roles have been proposed by linguists, who are more concerned with explaining generalizations across verbs in the syntactic realization of their arguments, while the more specific roles are more often proposed by computer scientists, who are more concerned with the details of the realization of the arguments of single verbs.

The FrameNet project proposes roles that are neither as general as the 10 abstract thematic roles, nor as specific as the thousands of potential verb-specific roles. FrameNet roles are defined for each semantic frame. A frame is a schematic representation of situations involving various participants, props, and other conceptual roles (Fillmore 1976). For example, the frame CONVERSATION, shown in Figure 2, is invoked by the semantically related verbs "argue," "banter," "debate," "converse," and "gossip," as well as the nouns "argument," "dispute," "discussion" and "tiff," and is defined as follows:

(5)   Two (or more) people talk to one another. No person is construed as only a speaker or only an addressee. Rather, it is understood that both (or all) participants do some speaking and some listening—the process is understood to be symmetrical or reciprocal.

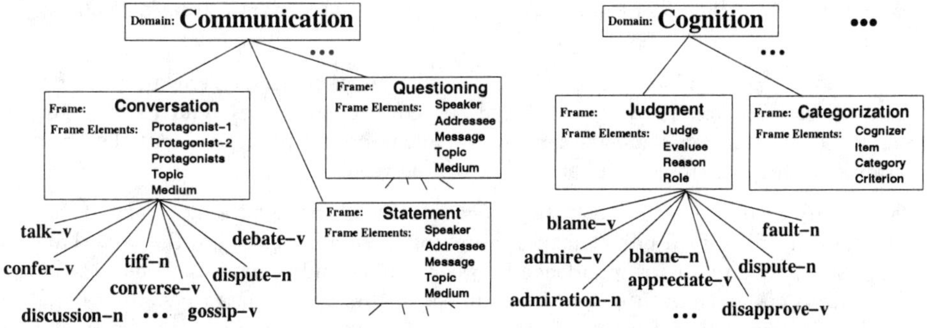

Figure 2   Sample domains and frames from the FrameNet lexicon.

---

[1]Theories with slightly different sets of roles include, among many others, (Fillmore 1968; Jackendoff 1972; Schank 1972); see (Somers 1987) for an excellent summary.

The roles defined for this frame, and shared by all its lexical entries, include PROTAGONIST1 and PROTAGONIST2 or simply PROTAGONISTS for the participants in the conversation, as well as MEDIUM and TOPIC. Similarly, the JUDGMENT frame mentioned above has the roles JUDGE, EVALUEE, and REASON and is invoked by verbs like "blame," "admire," and "praise," and nouns like "fault" and "admiration." A number of annotated examples from the JUDGMENT frame are included below to give a flavor of the FrameNet database:

(6) [$_{Judge}$ She] **blames** [$_{Evaluee}$ the Government] [$_{Reason}$ for failing to do enough to help] .

(7) Holman would characterize this as **blaming** [$_{Evaluee}$ the poor] .

(8) The letter quotes Black as saying that [$_{Judge}$ white and Navajo ranchers] misrepresent their livestock losses and **blame** [$_{Reason}$ everything] [$_{Evaluee}$ on coyotes] .

(9) The only dish she made that we could tolerate was [$_{Evaluee}$ syrup tart, which] [$_{Judge}$ we] **praised** extravagantly, with the result that it became our unhealthy staple diet.

(10) I 'm bound to say that I meet a lot of [$_{Judge}$ people who] **praise** [$_{Evaluee}$ me] [$_{Reason}$ for speaking up] but don't speak up themselves.

(11) Specimens of her verse translations of Tasso (*Jerusalem Delivered*) and Verri (*Roman Nights*) circulated to [$_{Manner}$ warm] [$_{Judge}$ critical] **praise**; but "unforeseen circumstance" prevented their publication.

(12) And if Sam Snort hails Doyler as monumental is he, perhaps, erring on the side of being excessive in [$_{Judge}$ his] **praise**?

Defining semantic roles at this intermediate frame level helps avoid some of the well-known difficulties of finding a unique small set of universal, abstract thematic roles, while also allowing some generalization across the roles of different verbs, nouns, and adjectives, each of which adds additional semantics to the general frame, or highlights a particular aspect of the frame. One way of thinking about abstract thematic roles in the context of FrameNet is as frame elements that are defined in very abstract frames such as "action" and "motion," at the top of an inheritance hierarchy of semantic frames (Fillmore and Baker 2000).

The examples above illustrate another difference between frame elements and thematic roles, at least as commonly implemented. Where thematic roles tend to be arguments mainly of verbs, frame elements can be arguments of any predicate, and the FrameNet database includes nouns and adjectives as well as verbs.

The examples above also illustrate a few of the phenomena that make it hard to automatically identify frame elements. Many of these are caused by the fact that there is not always a direct correspondence between syntax and semantics. While the subject of **blame** is often the JUDGE, the direct object of **blame** can be an EVALUEE (e.g., "the poor" in "blaming the poor") or a REASON (e.g., "everything" in "blame everything on coyotes"). The JUDGE can also be realized as a genitive pronoun (e.g., "his" in "his praise") or even an adjective (e.g., "critical" in "critical praise").

The preliminary version of the FrameNet corpus used for our experiments contained 67 frame types from 12 general semantic domains chosen for annotation. A complete list of

Domain	Sample frames	Sample predicates
Body	Action	flutter, wink
Cognition	Awareness	attention, obvious
	Judgment	blame, judge
	Invention	coin, contrive
Communication	Conversation	bicker, confer
	Manner	lisp, rant
Emotion	Directed	angry, pleased
	Experiencer	bewitch, rile
General	Imitation	bogus, forge
Health	Response	allergic, susceptible
Motion	Arriving	enter, visit
	Filling	anoint, pack
Perception	Active	glance, savor
	Noise	snort, whine
Society	Leadership	emperor, sultan
Space	Adornment	cloak, line
Time	Duration	chronic, short
	Iteration	daily, sporadic
Transaction	Basic	buy, spend
	Wealthiness	broke, well-off

Table 1   Semantic domains with sample frames and predicates from the FrameNet lexicon.

the domains is shown in Table 1, along with representative frames and predicates. Within these frames, examples of a total of 1462 distinct lexical predicates, or *target words*, were annotated: 927 verbs, 339 nouns, and 175 adjectives. There are a total of 49,013 annotated sentences, and 99,232 annotated frame elements (which do not include the target words themselves).

3   Probability Estimation for Roles

We divide the task of labeling frame elements into two subtasks: that of identifying the boundaries of the frame elements in the sentences, and that of labeling each frame element, given its boundaries, with the correct role. We first give results for a system that labels roles using human-annotated boundaries, returning to the question of automatically identifying the boundaries in Section 3.3.

3.1   Features Used in Assigning Semantic Roles

The system is a statistical one, based on training a classifier on a labeled training set, and testing on a held-out portion of the data. The system is trained by first using an automatic syntactic parser to analyze the 36,995 training sentences, matching annotated frame elements to parse constituents, and extracting various features from the string of words and the parse tree. During testing, the parser is run on the test sentences and the same features extracted. Probabilities for each possible semantic role r are then computed from the features. The probability computation is described in the next section; here, we discuss the features used.

The features used represent various aspects of the syntactic structure of the sentence as well as lexical information. The relationship between such surface manifestations and semantic roles is the subject of *linking theory,* ; see Levin and Rappaport Hovav (1996) for a synthesis of work in this area. In general, linking theory argues that the syntactic realization of arguments of a predicate is predictable from semantics—exactly how this relationship works is the subject of much debate. Regardless of the underlying mechanisms used to generate syntax from semantics, the relationship between the two suggests that it may be possible to learn to recognize semantic relationships from syntactic cues, given examples with both types of information.

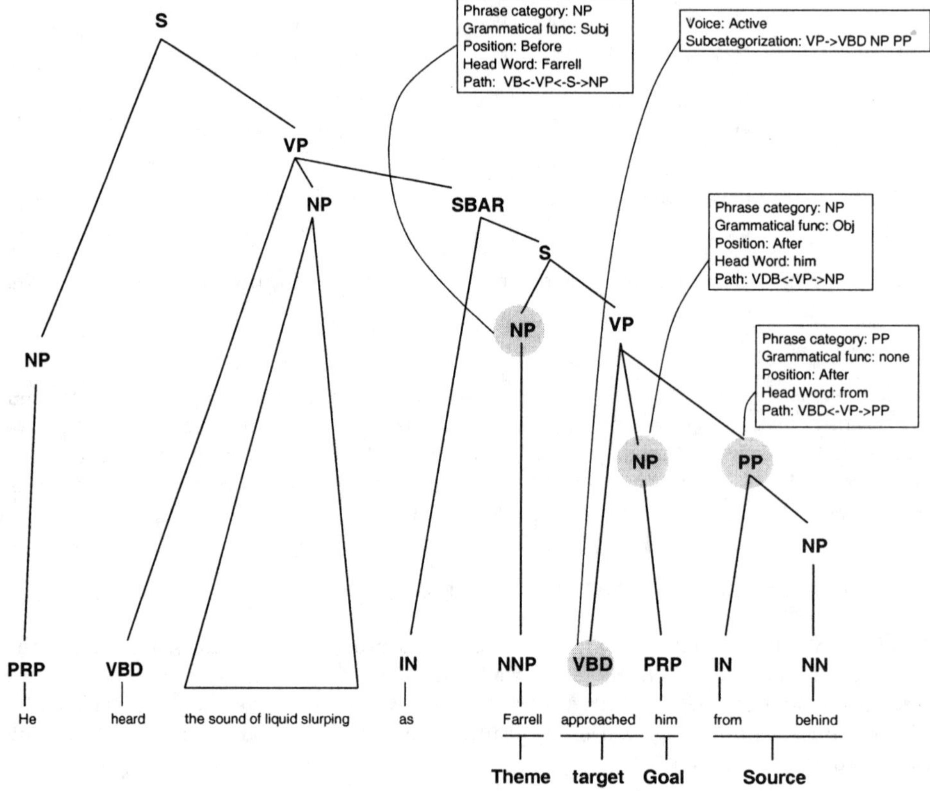

Figure 3 A sample sentence with parser output (above) and FrameNet annotation (below). Parse constituents corresponding to frame elements are highlighted, and the extracted features shown in boxes.

3.1.1 Phrase Type

Different roles tend to be realized by different syntactic categories. For example, in communication frames, the SPEAKER is likely to appear as a noun phrase, TOPIC as a prepositional phrase or noun phrase, and MEDIUM as a prepositional phrase, as in "We talked about the proposal over the phone."

The phrase-type feature we used indicates the syntactic category of the phrase expressing the semantic roles, using the set of syntactic categories of the Penn Treebank project, as described in Marcus, Santorini, and Marcinkiewicz (1993). In our data, frame elements are most commonly expressed as noun phrases (NP, 47% of frame elements in the training set) and prepositional phrases (PP, 22%). The next most common categories are adverbial phrases (ADVP, 4%), particles (e.g., "make something *up*," PRT, 2%), and sentential clauses (SBAR, 2%, and S, 2%).

We used the parser of Collins (1997), a statistical parser trained on examples from the Penn Treebank, to generate parses of the same format for the sentences in our data. Phrase types were derived automatically from parse trees generated by the parser, as shown in Figure 3. Given the automatically generated parse tree, the constituent spanning each set of words annotated as a frame element was found, and the constituent's nonterminal label was taken as the phrase type.

The matching was performed by calculating the starting and ending word positions for each constituent in the parse tree, as well as for each annotated frame element, and matching each frame element with the parse constituent having the same beginning and ending points. Punctuation was ignored in this computation. Due to parsing errors, or, less frequently, mismatches between the parse tree formalism and the FrameNet annotation standards, there was sometimes no parse constituent matching an annotated frame element. Thirteen percent of the frame elements in the training set had no matching parse constituent. These cases were discarded during training; during testing, the largest constituent beginning at the frame element's left boundary and lying entirely within the element was used to calculate the features. Doing this handles common parse errors such as a prepositional phrase being incorrectly attached to a noun phrase at the right edge, and it guarantees that some syntactic category will be returned: the part-of-speech tag of the frame element's first word in the limiting case.

3.1.2 Grammatical Function

The correlation between semantic roles and syntactic realization as subject or direct object is one of the primary facts that linking theory attempts to explain. It was a motivation for the case hierarchy of Fillmore (1968), which allowed such rules as "If there is an underlying AGENT, it becomes the syntactic subject." Similarly, in his theory of macroroles, Van Valin (1993) describes the ACTOR as being preferred in English for the subject. Functional grammarians consider syntactic subjects to have been historically "grammaticalized" agent markers. As an example of how this feature is useful, in the sentence "He drove the car over the cliff," the subject NP is more likely to fill the AGENT role than the other two NPs.

The grammatical function feature we used attempts to indicate a constituent's syntactic relation to the rest of the sentence—for example, as a subject or object of a verb. As with phrase type, this feature was read from parse trees returned by the parser. After experimentation with various versions of this feature, we restricted it to apply only to NPs, as it was found to have little effect on other phrase types. Only two values for this feature were used: *subject* and *object*. An NP node whose parent is an S node was assigned the function *subject,* and an NP whose parent is a VP was assigned the function *object.* In cases where the NP's immediate parent was neither an S nor a VP, the nearest S or VP ancestor was found and the value of the feature assigned accordingly.

3.1.3   Parse Tree Path

Like the grammatical function feature described above, this feature is designed to capture the syntactic relation of the constituent in question to the rest of the sentence. However, the path feature describes the syntactic relation between the target word and the constituent in question, whereas the previous feature is independent of where the target word appears in the sentence; that is, it identifies all subjects whether they are the subject of the target word or not.

This feature is defined as the *path* from the target word through the parse tree to the constituent in question, represented as a string of parse tree nonterminals linked by symbols indicating upward or downward movement through the tree, as in Figure 4.

For the purposes of choosing a frame element label for a constituent, this new feature will generally be equivalent to the previously grammatical function feature, though because it captures more information it may be more susceptible to parser errors and data sparseness. The path feature will, however, be important in identifying which constituents are frame elements for a given target word, as it gives us a way of navigating through the parse tree to find the frame elements.

3.1.4   Position

In order to overcome errors due to incorrect parses, as well as to see how much can be done without parse trees, we introduced position as a feature. This feature simply indicates whether the constituent to be labeled occurs before or after the predicate defining the semantic frame. We expected this feature to be highly correlated with grammatical function, since subjects will generally appear before a verb, and objects after.

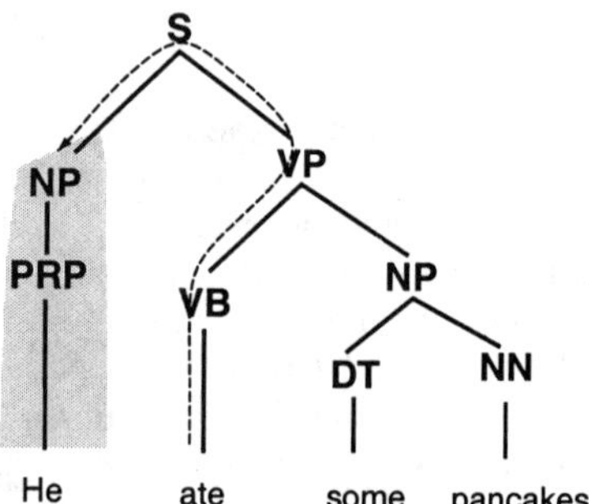

Figure 4   In this example, the *path* from the target word "ate" to the frame element "He" can be represented as VB↑VP↑S↓NP, with ↑ indicating upward movement in the parse tree and ↓, downward movement.

Although we do not have hand-checked parses against which to measure the performance of the automatic parser on our corpus, the result that 13% of frame elements have no matching parse constituent gives a rough idea of the parser's accuracy. Almost all of these cases are due to parser error. Other parser errors include cases where a constituent is found, but with the incorrect label or internal structure. This measure also considers only the individual constituent representing the frame element—the parse for the rest of the sentence may be incorrect, resulting in an incorrect value for the grammatical relation feature. Collins (1997) reports 88% labeled precision and recall on individual parse constituents on data from the Penn Treebank, roughly consistent with our finding of at least 13% error.

3.1.5   Voice

The distinction between active and passive verbs plays an important role in the connection between semantic role and grammatical function, since direct objects of active verbs correspond to subjects of passive verbs. From the parser output, verbs were classified as active or passive by building a set of 10 passive-identifying patterns. Each of the patterns requires both a passive auxiliary (some form of "to be" or "to get") and a past participle.

3.1.6   Head Word

As previously noted, we expected lexical dependencies to be extremely important in labeling semantic roles, as indicated by their importance in related tasks such as parsing. For example, in a communication frame, noun phrases headed by "Bill," "brother," or "he" are more likely to be the SPEAKER, while those headed by "proposal," "story," or "question" are more likely to be the TOPIC. (We did not attempt to resolve pronoun references.) Since the parser we used assigns each constituent a head word as an integral part of the parsing model, we were able to read the head words of the constituents from the parser output, using the same set of rules for identifying the head child of each constituent in the parse tree.

3.2   Probability Estimation

For our experiments, we divided the FrameNet corpus as follows: one-tenth of the annotated sentences for each target word were reserved as a test set, and another one-tenth were set aside as a tuning set for developing our system. A few target words with fewer than 10 examples were removed from the corpus. In our corpus, the average number of sentences per target word is only 34, and the number of sentences per frame is 732—both relatively small amounts of data on which to train frame element classifiers.

In order to automatically label the semantic role of a constituent, we wish to estimate a probability distribution telling us how likely the constituent is to fill each possible role given the features described above and the predicate, or target word, t:

$$P(r|h, pt, gf, position, voice, t)$$

It would be possible to calculate this distribution directly from the training data by counting the number of times each role is seen with a combination of features, and dividing by the total number of times the combination of features is seen:

Distribution	Coverage	Accuracy	Performance
$P(r\|t)$	100%	40.9%	40.9%
$P(r\|pt, t)$	92.5	60.1	55.6
$P(r\|pt, gf, t)$	92.0	66.6	61.3
$P(r\|pt, position, voice)$	98.8	57.1	56.4
$P(r\|pt, position, voice, t)$	90.8	70.1	63.7
$P(r\|h)$	80.3	73.6	59.1
$P(r\|h, t)$	56.0	86.6	48.5
$P(r\|h, pt, t)$	50.1	87.4	43.8

Table 2   Distributions calculated for semantic role identification: r indicates semantic role, pt, phrase type, gf, grammatical function, h, head word, and t, target word, or predicate.

$$P(r|h, pt, gf, position, voice, t) = \frac{\#(r, h, pt, gf, position, voice, t)}{\#(h, pt, gf, position, voice, t)}$$

However, in many cases, we will never have seen a particular combination of features in the training data, and in others we will have seen the combination only a small number of times, providing a poor estimate of the probability. The facts that there are only about 30 training sentences for each target word and that the head word feature in particular can take on a large number of values (any word in the language) contribute to the sparsity of the data. Although we expect our features to interact in various ways, we cannot train directly on the full feature set. For this reason, we built our classifier by combining probabilities from distributions conditioned on a variety of combinations of features.

Table 2 shows the probability distributions used in the final version of the system. *Coverage* indicates the percentage of the test data for which the conditioning event had been seen in training data. *Accuracy* is the proportion of covered test data for which the correct role is predicted, and *Performance*, which is the product of coverage and accuracy, is the overall percentage of test data for which the correct role is predicted. Accuracy is somewhat similar to the familiar metric of *precision* in that it is calculated over cases for which a decision is made, and performance is similar to *recall* in that it is calculated over all true frame elements. However, unlike a traditional precision/recall trade-off, these results have no threshold to adjust, and the task is a multiway classification rather than a binary decision. The distributions calculated were simply the empirical distributions from the training data. That is, occurrences of each role and each set of conditioning events were counted in a table, and probabilities calculated by dividing the counts for each role by the total number of observations for each conditioning event. For example, the distribution $P(r|pt, t)$ was calculated as follows:

$$P(r|pt, t) = \frac{\#(r, pt, t)}{\#(pt, t)}$$

Some sample probabilities calculated from the training are shown in Table 3.

$P(r|pt, gf, t)$	Count in training data
$P(r =\text{AGT}|pt =\text{NP}, gf =\text{Subj}, t =\text{abduct}) = .46$	6
$P(r =\text{THM}|pt =\text{NP}, gf =\text{Subj}, t =\text{abduct}) = .54$	7
$P(r =\text{THM}|pt =\text{NP}, gf =\text{Obj}, t =\text{abduct}) = 1$	9
$P(r =\text{AGT}|pt =\text{PP}, t =\text{abduct}) = .33$	1
$P(r =\text{THM}|pt =\text{PP}, t =\text{abduct}) = .33$	1
$P(r =\text{CoTHM}|pt =\text{PP}, t =\text{abduct}) = .33$	1
$P(r =\text{MANR}|pt =\text{ADVP}, t =\text{abduct}) = 1$	1

Table 3   Sample probabilities for $P(r|pt, gf, t)$ calculated from training data for the verb "abduct." The variable *gf* is only defined for noun phrases. The roles defined for the *removing* frame in the *motion* domain are: AGENT, THEME, CoTHEME ("...had been abducted *with him*"), and MANNER.

As can be seen from Table 2, there is a trade-off between more specific distributions, which have high accuracy but low coverage, and less specific distributions, which have low accuracy but high coverage. The lexical head word statistics, in particular, are valuable when data are available, but are particularly sparse due to the large number of possible head words. In order to combine the strengths of the various distributions, we combined them in various ways to obtain an estimate of the full distribution $P(r|h, pt, gf, position, voice, t)$.

In the *back-off* combination method, a lattice was constructed over the distributions in Table 2 from more specific conditioning events to less specific, as shown in Figure 5. The lattice is used to select a subset of the available distributions to combine. The less specific distributions were used only when no data was present for any more specific distribution. Thus, the distributions selected are arranged in a cut across the lattice representing the most specific distributions for which data is available. The selected probabilities were combined with both linear interpolation and a geometric mean.

The general technique of back-off is a common way of dealing with the data sparsity of natural language applications, in particular the sparsity of lexical features (Collins and Brooks 1995). Discounting (Katz 1987) and deleted interpolation (Jelinek and Mercer 1980) methods are used in language modeling for speech recognition to assign small, non-zero probability to a predicted variable unseen in the training data even when a specific

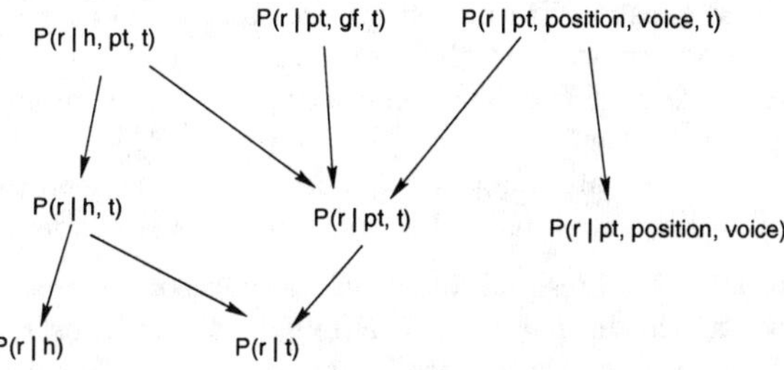

Figure 5   Lattice organization of the distributions from Table 2, with more specific distributions toward the top.

	Linear back-off	Baseline
Development set	80.4%	40.9%
Test set	76.9%	40.6%

Table 4   Results on test set, using back-off linear interpolation system. The test set consists of 7900 observations.

conditioning has been seen. Although this lattice is reminiscent of techniques of backing off to less specific distributions commonly used in n-gram language modeling, it differs in that we only use the lattice to select distributions for which the conditioning event has been seen in the training data. In our case, we are perfectly willing to assign zero probability to a specific role (the predicted variable), because we are only interested in finding the role with the highest probability.

The final system performed at 80.4% accuracy, which can be compared to the 40.9% achieved by always choosing the most probable role for each target word, essentially chance performance on this task. Results for this system on test data, held out during development of the system, are shown in Table 4.

3.3   Identification of Frame Element Boundaries

In this section we examine performance on the task of finding the correct frame elements in the sentence. Although our probability model considers the question of finding the boundaries of frame elements separately from the question of finding the correct label for a frame element, similar features are used to calculate both probability estimators. In the experiments below, the system is no longer given frame element boundaries, but is still given the human-annotated target word and the frame to which it belongs as inputs. We defer for now the task of identifying which frames come into play in a sentence, but envision that existing word sense–disambiguation techniques could be applied to the task.

As before, features are extracted from the sentence and its parse and used to calculate probability tables, with the predicted variable in this case being fe, a binary indicator of whether a given constituent in the parse tree is or is not a frame element.

The features used were the *path* feature of Section 3.1.3, the identity of the target word, and the identity of the constituent's head word. The probability distributions calculated from the training data were $P(fe|path)$, $P(fe|path, t)$, and $P(fe|h, t)$, where fe indicates an event where the parse constituent in question is a frame element, *path* the path through the parse tree from the target word to the parse constituent, t the identity of the target word, and h the head word of the parse constituent. Some sample values from these distributions are shown in Table 5. For example, the path VB↑VP↓NP, which corresponds to the direct object of a verbal target word, had a high probability of being a frame element. The table also illustrates cases of sparse data for various feature combinations.

By varying the probability threshold at which a decision is made, one can plot a precision/recall curve, as shown in Figure 6. $P(fe|path, t)$ performs relatively poorly due to fragmentation of the training data (recall that only about 30 sentences are available for each target word). While the lexical statistic $P(fe|h, t)$ alone is not useful as a classifier, using it in linear interpolation with the path statistics improves results. The

Distribution	Sample probability	Count in training data
$P(fe\|path)$	$P(fe\|path =\text{VBD}{\uparrow}\text{VP}{\downarrow}\text{ADJP}{\downarrow}\text{ADVP}) = 1$	1
	$P(fe\|path =\text{VBD}{\uparrow}\text{VP}{\downarrow}\text{NP}) = .73$	3963
	$P(fe\|path =\text{VBN}{\uparrow}\text{VP}{\downarrow}\text{NP}{\downarrow}\text{PP}{\downarrow}\text{S}) = 0$	22
$P(fe\|path, t)$	$P(fe\|path =\text{JJ}{\uparrow}\text{ADJP}{\downarrow}\text{PP}, t =\text{apparent}) = 1$	10
	$P(fe\|path =\text{NN}{\uparrow}\text{NP}{\uparrow}\text{PP}{\uparrow}\text{VP}{\downarrow}\text{PP}, t =\text{departure}) = .4$	5
$P(fe\|h, t)$	$P(fe\|h =\text{sudden}, t =\text{apparent}) = 0$	2
	$P(fe\|h =\text{to}, t =\text{apparent}) = .11$	93
	$P(fe\|h =\text{that}, t =\text{apparent}) = .21$	81

Table 5   Sample probabilities for a constituent being a frame element.

Type of Overlap	Identified Constituents	Number
Exactly matching boundaries	66%	5421
Identified constituent entirely within true frame element	8	663
True frame element entirely within identified constituent	7	599
Both partially within the other	0	26
No overlap with any true frame element	13	972

Table 6   Results on identifying frame elements (FEs), including partial matches. Results obtained using $P(fe\|path)$ with threshold at .5. A total of 7681 constituents were identified as FEs, and 8167 FEs were present in hand annotations, of which matching parse constituents were present for 7053 (86%).

"interpolation" curve in Figure 6 reflects a linear interpolation of the form

$$P(fe|p, h, t) = \lambda_1 P(fe|p) + \lambda_2 P(fe|p, t) + \lambda_3 P(fe|h, t) \tag{13}$$

Note that this method can identify only those frame elements that have a corresponding constituent in the automatically generated parse tree. For this reason, it is interesting to calculate how many true frame elements overlap with the results of the system, relaxing the criterion that the boundaries must match exactly. Results for partial matching are shown in Table 6. Three types of overlap are possible: the identified constituent entirely within the true frame element, the true frame element entirely within the identified constituent, and both sequences partially contained by the other. An example of the first case is shown in Figure 7, where the true MESSAGE frame element is "Mandarin by a head," but due to an error in the parser output, no constituent exactly matches the frame element's boundaries. In this case, the system identifies two frame elements, indicated by shading, which together span the true frame element.

When the automatically identified constituents were fed through the role-labeling system described above, 79.6% of the constituents that had been correctly identified in the first stage were assigned the correct role in the second, roughly equivalent to the performance when assigning roles to constituents identified by hand. A more sophisticated integrated system for identifying and labeling frame elements is described in Section 5.1.

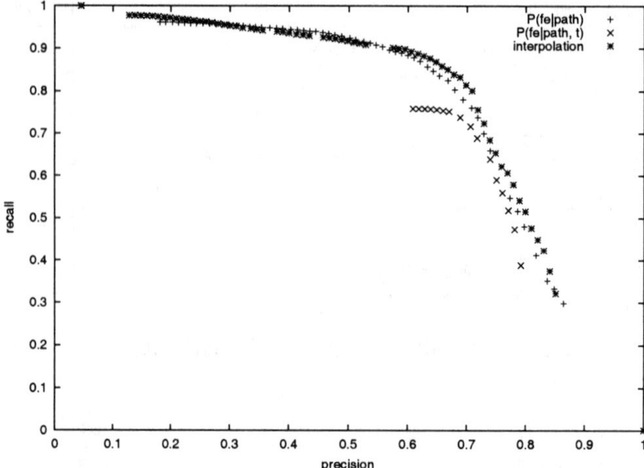

Figure 6   Precision/recall plot for various methods of identifying frame elements. Recall is calculated over only frame elements with matching parse constituents.

4   Generalizing Lexical Statistics

In this section, we examine ways of enriching features read directly from the syntactic parse tree with knowledge sources designed to incorporate information about the semantics of words in the sentence.

As can be seen from Table 2, information about the head word of a constituent is valuable in predicting the constituent's role. Of all the distributions presented, $P(r|h, pt, t)$ predicts the correct role most often (87.4% of the time) when training data for a particular head word has been seen. However, due to the large vocabulary of possible head words, it also has the smallest *coverage*, meaning it is likely that for a given case in the test data, no frame element with the same head word will have been seen in the set of training sentences for the target word in question. To capitalize on the information provided by the head word, we wish to find a way to generalize from head words seen in the training data to other head words. In this section we compare two different approaches to the task of generalizing over head words: *automatic clustering* of a large vocabulary of head words to identify words with similar semantics, and use of a hand-built *ontological resource*, WordNet, to organize head words in a semantic hierarchy. We will focus on frame elements filled by noun phrases, which compose roughly half the total.

4.1   Automatic Clustering

In order to find groups of nouns with similar semantic properties, an automatic clustering was performed using the general technique of Lin (1998). This technique is based on the expectation that words with similar semantics will tend to co-occur with the same other sets of words. For example, nouns describing foods will tend to occur as direct objects of verbs such "eat" as well as "devour," "savor," and so on. The clustering algorithm attempts to find such patterns of co-occurrence from the counts of grammatical relations

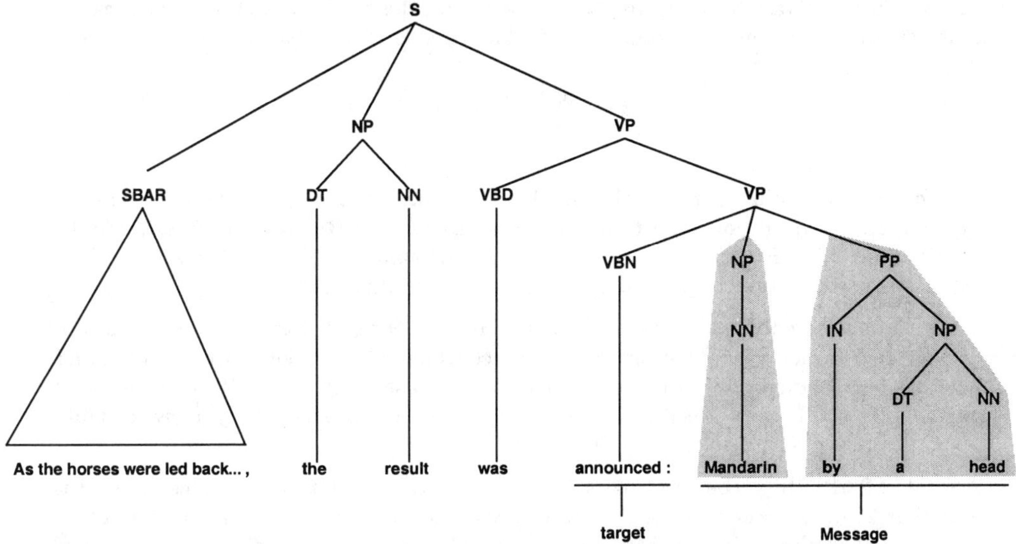

Figure 7   An example of overlap between identified frame elements and the true boundaries: the shaded areas represent frame elements identified by the classifier, with the human annotation below the sentence.

between specific words in the corpus, without the use of any external knowledge or semantic representation. The use of automatic clustering techniques to induce soft classes of related words was pioneered by Pereira, Tishby, and Lee (1993), who demonstrated that semantically related groupings could be found simply on the basis of verb–direct object pairs. Lin (1998) has used clustering over word pairs found in a wider variety of syntactic relationships to automatically produce a thesaurus from a large, syntactically parsed corpus. Rooth et al. (1999) looked more specifically at verb arguments to find the semantic classes of the various arguments of related verbs. Various mathematical clustering techniques have been used in the literature. As in (Rooth et al. 1999), we use the Expectation Maximization–based probabilistic co-occurrence model of Hofmann and Puzicha (1998), briefly described below.

In addition to being applied to word co-occurrences in syntactic relationships, similar clustering models have been applied to word co-occurrences at larger distances. Words co-occurring in the same set of documents can be identified as being related to the same topic, in a probabilistic version of Latent Semantic Analysis (Deerwester et al. 1991). Like Latent Semantic Analysis, probabilistic clustering models have been applied to information retrieval (Hofmann 1999), and language modeling for speech recognition (Gildea and Hofmann 1999).

For the purposes of frame element identification, we extracted verb–direct object relations from an automatically parsed version of the British National Corpus, using the parser of Carroll and Rooth (1998).[2] According the to probabilistic co-occurrence model used,

---

[2] We are indebted to Mats Rooth for providing us with the parsed corpus.

the two observed variables, in this case the verb and the head noun of its object, can be considered independent given the value of a hidden cluster variable c:

$$P(n, v) = \sum_c P(c)P(n|c)P(v|c)$$

One begins by setting a priori the number of values that c can take and using the expectation maximization algorithm (Dempster, Laird, and Rubin 1977) to estimate the distributions $P(c)$, $P(n|c)$, and $P(v|c)$. Deterministic annealing (Rose, Gurewitz, and Fox 1992) was used in order to prevent overfitting of the training data.

We are interested only in the clusters of nouns given by the distribution $P(n|c)$—the verbs and the distribution $P(v|c)$ are thrown away once training is complete. Other grammatical relations besides direct object could be used, as could a set of relations. We used the direct object, following Pereira, Tishby, and Lee (1993) because it is particularly likely to exhibit semantically significant selectional restrictions.

A total of 2,610,946 verb-object pairs were used as training data for the clustering, with a further 290,105 pairs used as a cross-validation set to control the parameters of the clustering algorithm. Direct objects were identified as noun phrases directly under a verb phrase node—not a perfect technique, since it also finds nominal adjuncts such as "I start *today*." Forms of the verb "to be" were excluded from the data, as its co-occurrence patterns are not semantically informative. The number of values possible for the latent cluster variable was set to 256. (Comparable results were found with 64 clusters; the use of deterministic annealing prevents a large number of clusters from resulting in overfitting.)

The soft clustering of nouns thus generated is used as follows: for each example in the frame-element-annotated training data, probabilities for values of the hidden cluster variable were calculated using Bayes' rule:

$$P(c|h) = \frac{P(h|c)P(c)}{\sum_i P(h|c_i)P(c_i)}$$

The clustering was applied only to noun phrase constituents; the distribution $P(n|c)$ from the clustering is used as a distribution $P(h|c)$ over noun head words.

Using the cluster probabilities, a new estimate of $P(r|c, nt, t)$ is calculated for cases where nt, the nonterminal or syntactic category of the constituent, is NP:

$$P(r|c, nt, t) = \frac{\sum_{j:nt_j=nt,t_j=t,r_j=r} P(c_j|h_j)}{\sum_{j:nt_j=nt,t_j=t} P(c_j|h_j)}$$

During testing, a smoothed estimate of $P(r|h, nt, t)$ is calculated as $\sum_c P(r|c, nt, t)P(c|h)$, again using $P(c|h) = \frac{P(h|c)P(c)}{\sum_i P(h|c_i)P(c_i)}$.

As with the other methods of generalization described in this section, automatic clustering was applied only to noun phrases, which represent 50% of the constituents in the test data. We would not expect the head word to be as valuable for other syntactic types.

Distribution	Coverage	Accuracy	Performance
$P(r|h, pt, t)$	41.6	87.0	36.1
$\sum_c P(r|c, pt, t) P(c|h)$	97.9	79.7	78.0
Interpolation of unclustered distributions	100.0	83.4	83.4
Unclustered distributions + clustering	100.0	85.0	85.0

Table 7 Clustering results on NP constituents only: 4086 instances.

Table 7 shows results for the use of automatic clustering on constituents identified by the parser as noun phrases. As can be seen, the vocabulary used for clustering includes almost all (97.9%) of the test data, and the decrease in accuracy from direct lexical statistics to clustered statistics is relatively small (from 87.0% to 79.7%). When combined with the full system described above, clustered statistics increase performance on NP constituents from 83.4% to 85.0% (statistically significant at $p = .05$). Over the entire test set, this translates into an improvement from 80.4% to 81.2%.

4.2 Using a Semantic Hierarchy: WordNet

The automatic clustering described above can be seen as an imperfect method of deriving semantic classes from the vocabulary, and we might expect a hand-developed set of classes to do better. We tested this hypothesis using WordNet (Fellbaum 1998), a freely available semantic hierarchy. The basic technique, when presented with a head word for which no training examples had been seen, was to ascend the type hierarchy until reaching a level for which training data is available. To do this, counts of training data were percolated up the semantic hierarchy in a technique similar to that of, for example, McCarthy (2000). For each training example, the count $\#(r, s, pt, t)$ was incremented in a table indexed by the semantic role r, WordNet sense s, phrase type pt, and target word t, for each WordNet sense s above the head word h in the hypernym hierarchy. In fact, the WordNet hierarchy is not a tree, but rather includes multiple inheritance. For example, "person" has as hypernyms both "life form" and "causal agent." In such cases, we simply took the first hypernym listed, effectively converting the structure into a tree. A further complication is that several WordNet senses are possible for a given head word. We simply used the first sense listed for each word; a word sense–disambiguation module capable of distinguishing WordNet senses might improve our results.

As with the clustering experiments reported above, the WordNet hierarchy was used only for noun phrases. The WordNet hierarchy does not include pronouns—in order to increase coverage, the words "I," "me," "you," "he," "she," "him," "her," "we," and "us" were added as hyponyms of "person." Pronouns that refer to inanimate, or both animate and inanimate, objects were not included. In addition, the CELEX English lexical database (Baayen, Piepenbrock, and Gulikers 1995) was used to convert plural nouns to their singular forms.

As can been seen from the results in Table 8, accuracy for the WordNet technique is roughly the same as the automatic clustering results in Table 7—84.3% on NPs, as opposed to 85.0% with automatic clustering. This indicates that the error introduced by the unsupervised clustering is roughly equivalent to the error caused by our arbitrary choice of the first WordNet sense for each word and the first hypernym for each WordNet

Distribution	Coverage	Accuracy	Performance
$P(r\|h, pt, t)$	41.6	87.0	36.1
$WordNet : P(r\|s, pt, t)$	80.8	79.5	64.1
Interpolation of unclustered distributions	100.0	83.4	83.4
Unclustered distributions + WordNet	100.0	84.3	84.3

Table 8   WordNet results on NP constituents only: 4086 instances.

sense. However, coverage for the WordNet technique is lower, largely due to the absence of proper nouns from WordNet, as well as the absence of nonanimate pronouns (in which we include both personal pronouns such as "it" and "they" and indefinite pronouns such as "something" and "anyone"). A proper noun dictionary would be likely to help improve coverage, and a module for anaphora resolution might help cases with pronouns, with or without the use of WordNet. The conversion of plural forms to singular base forms was an important part of the success of the WordNet system, increasing coverage from 71.0% to 80.8%. Of the remaining 19.2% of all noun phrases not covered by the combination of lexical and WordNet sense statistics, 22% consisted of head words defined in WordNet but for which no training data was available for any hypernym, and 78% consisted of head words not defined in WordNet.

4.3   Discussion

The three methods of generalizing lexical statistics each had roughly equivalent accuracy on cases for which they were able to derive with an estimate of the role probabilities for unseen head words. The differences between the three were primarily due to how much they could improve the *coverage* of the estimator—that is, how many new noun heads they were able to handle. The automatic clustering method performed by far the best on this metric; only 2.1% of test cases were unseen in the data used for the automatic clustering. This indicates how much can be achieved with unsupervised methods given very large training corpora. The WordNet experiment, on the other hand, indicates both the usefulness of hand-built resources when they apply and the difficulty of attaining broad coverage with such resources.

5   Verb Argument Structure

One of the primary difficulties in labeling semantic roles is that one predicate may be used with different argument structures. For example, in the sentences "He opened the door" and "The door opened," the verb "open" assigns different semantic roles to its syntactic subject. Such alternations in usage systematically affect all of the verb's arguments; they are not captured by the local syntactic features described in Section 3.1. In this section, we introduce a simple but effective way of handling such phenomena with a sentence-level feature for sets of frame elements.

Frame element group	Sample sentences
{ EVALUEE }	Holman would characterize this as **blaming** [$_{Evaluee}$ the poor] .
{ JUDGE, EVALUEE, REASON }	The letter quotes Black as saying that [$_{Judge}$ white and Navajo ranchers] misrepresent their livestock losses and **blame** [$_{Reason}$ everything] [$_{Evaluee}$ on coyotes] . [$_{Judge}$ She] **blames** [$_{Evaluee}$ the government] [$_{Reason}$ for failing to do enough to help] .
{ JUDGE, EVALUEE }	The only dish she made that we could tolerate was [$_{Evaluee}$ syrup tart, which] [$_{Judge}$ we] **praised** extravagantly with the result that it became our unhealthy staple diet.

Table 9   Sample frame element groups for the verb "to blame."

5.1   Priors on Frame Element Groups

The system described above for classifying frame elements makes an important simplifying assumption: it classifies each frame element independently of the decisions made for the other frame elements in the sentence. In this section, we relax this assumption and present a system that can make use of the information that, for example, a given target word requires that one role always be present, or that having two instances of the same role is extremely unlikely.

In order to capture this information, we introduce the notion of a *frame element group (FEG)*, which is the set of frame element roles present in a particular sentence (technically a multiset, as duplicates are possible, though quite rare). FEGs are *unordered*—examples are shown in Table 9.[3]

Our system for choosing the most likely overall assignment of roles for all the frame elements of a sentence uses an approximation that we derive beginning with the true probability of the optimal role assignment r^*:

$$r^* = argmax_{r_{1..n}} P(r_{1..n}|t, f_{1..n})$$

where $P(r_{1..n}|t, f_{1..n})$ represents the probability of an overall assignment of roles r_i to each of the n constituents of a sentence, given the target word t and the various features f_i of

---

[3]The FrameNet corpus recognized three types of "null instantiated" frame elements (Fillmore 1986), which are implied but do not appear in the sentence. An example of null instantiation is the sentence "Have you eaten?" in which "food" is understood. We did not attempt to identify such null elements, and any null instantiated roles are not included in the sentence's frame element group. This increases the variability of observed FEGs, as a predicate may require a certain role but allow it to be null instantiated.

Frame element group	Probability
{ EVAL, JUDGE, REAS }	0.549
{ EVAL, JUDGE }	0.160
{ EVAL, REAS }	0.167
{ EVAL }	0.097
{ EVAL, JUDGE, ROLE }	0.014
{ JUDGE }	0.007
{ JUDGE, REAS }	0.007

Table 10   Frame element groups for the verb "to blame" in the JUDGMENT frame.

each of the constituents. We can approximate this quantity as the following:

$$r^* = argmax_{r_{1..n}} P(\{r_{1..n}\}|t) \prod_i \frac{P(r_i|f_i, t)}{P(r_i|t)}$$

This leaves us with an expression in terms of the prior for FEGs of a particular target word $P(\{r_{1..n}\}|t)$, the local probability of a frame element given a constituent's features $P(r_i|f_i, t)$ on which our previous system was based, and the individual priors for the frame elements chosen $P(r_i|t)$. This formulation can be used either to assign roles where the frame element boundaries are known, or where they are not, as we will discuss later in this section.

Up to this point, we have considered separately the problems of labeling roles given that we know where the boundaries of the frame elements lie (Sections 3 and 4) and finding the constituents to label in the sentence (Section 3.3). We now turn to combining the two systems described above into a complete role-labeling system. We use equation 13 from Section 3.3 to estimate the probability that a constituent is a frame element:

$$P(fe|p, h, t) = \lambda_1 P(fe|p) + \lambda_2 P(fe|p, t)) + \lambda_3 P(fe|h, t)$$

where p is the path through the parse tree from the target word to the constituent, t is the target word, and h is the constituent's head word.

The first two rows of Table 11 show the results obtained by deciding which constituents are frame elements by setting the threshold on the probability $P(fe|p, h, t)$ to 0.5 and then running the labeling system of Section 3 on the resulting set of constituents. The first two columns of results show precision and recall for the task of identifying frame element boundaries correctly. The second pair of columns gives precision and recall for the combined task of boundary identification and role labeling; to be counted as correct, the frame element must have the correct boundary and be labeled with the correct role.

Contrary to our results using human-annotated boundaries, incorporating FEG priors into the system had a negative effect. No doubt this is due to introducing a dependency on other frame element decisions that may be incorrect—the use of FEG priors causes errors in boundary identification to be compounded.

One way around this problem is to integrate boundary identification with role-labeling, allowing the FEG priors and the role-labeling decisions to affect which constituents are frame elements. This was accomplished by extending the formulation

Method	FE prec.	FE recall	Labeled prec.	Lab. recall
Boundary id + baseline role labeler	72.6	63.1	67.0	46.8
Boundary id + labeler w. FEG priors	72.6	63.1	65.9	46.2
Integrated boundary id and labeling	74.0	70.1	64.6	61.2

Table 11 Combined results on boundary identification and role labeling.

$$argmax_{r_1..n} P(\{r_{1..n}\}|t) \prod_i \frac{P(r_i|f_i,t)}{P(r_i|t)}$$

to include FE identification decisions:

$$argmax_{r_1..n} P(\{r_{1..n}\}|t) \prod_i \frac{P(r_i|f_i,fe_i,t)P(fe_i|f_i)}{P(r_i|t)}$$

where fe_i is a binary variable indicating that a constituent is a frame element and $P(fe_i|f_i)$ is calculated as above. When fe_i is true, role probabilities are calculated as before; when fe_i is false, r_i assumes an empty role with probability 1, and is not included in the FEG represented by $\{r_{1..n}\}$.

One caveat in using this integrated approach is its exponential complexity: each combination of role assignments to constituents is considered, and the number of combinations is exponential in the number of constituents. While this did not pose a problem when only the annotated frame elements were under consideration, now we must include every parse constituent with a non-zero probability for $P(fe_i|f_i)$. In order to make the computation tractable, we implement a pruning scheme: hypotheses are extended by choosing assignments for one constituent at a time, and only the top m hypotheses are retained for extension by assignments to the next constituent. Here we set $m = 10$ after experimentation showed that increasing m yielded no significant improvement.

Results for the integrated approach are shown in the last row of Table 11. Allowing role assignments to influence boundary identification improves results on both the unlabeled boundary identification task, and the combined identification and labeling task. The integrated approach puts us in a different portion of the precision/recall curve from the results in the first two rows, as it returns a higher number of frame elements (7736 vs. 5719). A more direct comparison can be made by lowering the probability threshold for frame element identification from .5 to .35, in order to force the nonintegrated system to return the same number of frame elements as the integrated system. This yields a frame-element identification precision of 71.3% and recall of 67.6%, and labeled precision of 60.8% and recall of 57.6%, which is dominated by the result for the integrated system. The integrated system does not have a probability threshold to set; nonetheless it comes closer to identifying the correct number of frame elements (8167) than does the independent boundary identifier when the theoretically optimal threshold of .5 is used with the latter.

The FEG prior allows us to introduce a dependency between the classifications of the sentence's various constituents with a single parameter. Thus, it can handle the alternation of our example without, for example, introducing the role chosen for one constituent as an additional feature in the probability distribution for the next constituent's role. It appears that because introducing additional features can further fragment our already sparse data, it is preferable to have a single parameter for the FEG prior.

6 Thematic Roles

In this section, we return to the question of the representation of semantic information, examining the degree to which our results are influenced by the choice of the semantic frame as our level of representation.

In order to investigate the degree to which our system is dependent on the set of semantic roles used, we performed experiments using abstract, general semantic roles such as AGENT, PATIENT, and GOAL. Such roles were proposed in theories of linking such as Fillmore (1968) and Jackendoff (1972) to explain the syntactic realization of semantic arguments. This level of roles, often called *thematic roles*, was seen as useful for expressing generalizations such as "If a sentence has an AGENT, the AGENT will occupy the subject position." Such correlations might enable a statistical system to generalize from one semantic domain to another.

Recent work on linguistic theories of linking has attempted to explain syntactic realization in terms of the fundamentals of verbs' meaning—see Levin and Rappaport Hovav (1996) for a survey of a number of theories. While such an explanation is desirable, our goal is much more modest: an automatic procedure for identifying semantic roles in text. We aim to use abstract roles as a means of generalizing from limited training data in various semantic domains. We see this effort as consistent with various theoretical accounts of the underlying mechanisms of argument linking, since the various theories all admit some sort of generalization between the roles of specific predicates.

To this end, we developed a correspondence from frame-specific roles to a set of abstract thematic roles. Since there is no canonical set of abstract semantic roles, we decided upon the list shown in Table 12. We are interested in adjuncts as well as arguments, leading to roles such as DEGREE not found in many theories of verb-argument linking. The difficulty of fitting many relations into standard categories such as AGENT and PATIENT led us to include other roles such as TOPIC. In all, we used 18 roles, a somewhat richer set than often used, but still much more restricted than the frame-specific roles. Even with this enriched set, not all frame-specific roles fit neatly into one category.

An experiment was performed replacing each role tag in the training and test data with the corresponding thematic role, and training the system as described above on the new data set. Results were roughly comparable for the two types of semantic roles: overall performance was 82.1% for thematic roles, compared to 80.4% for frame-specific roles. This reflects the fact that most frames had a 1:1 mapping from frame-specific to abstract roles, so the tasks were largely equivalent. We expect abstract roles to be most useful when generalizing to predicates and frames not found in the training data, a future goal of our research.

One interesting consequence of using abstract roles is that they allow us to more easily compare the system's performance on different roles because of the smaller number of categories. This breakdown is shown in Table 13. Results are given for two systems: the first assumes that the frame element boundaries are known, and the second finds them

Role	Example
AGENT	**Henry** *pushed* the door open and went in.
CAUSE	Jeez, **that** *amazes* me as well as riles me.
DEGREE	I **rather** *deplore* the recent manifestation of Pop; it doesn't seem to me to have the intellectual force of the art of the Sixties.
EXPERIENCER	It may even have been that **John,** *anticipating* his imminent doom, ratified some such arrangement, perhaps in the ceremony at the Jordan.
FORCE	If this is the case, can it be *substantiated* **by evidence from the history of developed societies**?
GOAL	Distant across the river the towers of the castle rose against the sky, straddling the only land *approach* **into Shrewsbury**.
INSTRUMENT	In the children with colonic contractions, **fasting motility** did not *differentiate* children with and without constipation.
LOCATION	These fleshy appendages are used to detect and *taste* food **amongst the weed and debris on the bottom of a river**.
MANNER	His brow *arched* **delicately**.
NULL	Yet while she had no intention of surrendering her home, **it** would be *foolish* to let the atmosphere between them become too acrimonious.
PATH	The dung collector *ambled* slowly **over**, one eye on Sir John.
PATIENT	As soon as a character lays a hand on this item, the skeletal Cleric *grips* **it** more tightly.
PERCEPT	What is *apparent* is **that this manual is aimed at the nonspecialist technician, possibly an embalmer who has good knowledge of some medical procedures**.
PROPOSITION	It says that rotation of partners does not *demonstrate* **independence**.
RESULT	All the arrangements for stay-behind agents in northwestern Europe collapsed, but Dansey was able to *charm* most of the governments in exile in London **into recruiting spies**.
SOURCE	He heard the sound of liquid slurping in a metal container as Farrell *approached* him **from behind**.
STATE	Rex *spied* out Sam Maggott **hollering at all and sundry and making good use of his oversized red gingham handkerchief**.
TOPIC	He said, "We would urge people to be aware and be *alert* **with fireworks**, because your fun might be someone else's tragedy."

Table 12   Abstract semantic roles, with representative examples from the FrameNet corpus.

automatically. The second system, described in Section 5.1, corresponds to the rightmost two columns in Table 13. The labeled recall column shows how often the frame element is correctly identified, while the unlabeled recall column shows how often a constituent with the given role is correctly identified as being a frame element, even if it is incorrectly labeled as a different frame element.

EXPERIENCER and AGENT are the roles that are correctly identified most often—two similar roles generally found as the subject for complementary sets of verbs. The unlabeled recall column shows that these roles are easy to find in the sentence, as a predicate's subject is almost always a frame element, and the known boundaries column shows that they are also not often confused with other roles when it is known that they are frame elements. The two most difficult roles in terms of unlabeled recall, MANNER and DEGREE, are typically realized by adverbs or prepositional phrases and considered adjuncts. It is interesting to note that these are considered in FrameNet to be *general* frame elements that can be used in any frame.

		Known boundaries	Unknown boundaries	
Role	*Number*	*% correct*	*Labeled recall*	*Unlabeled recall*
Agent	2401	92.8	76.7	80.7
Experiencer	333	91.0	78.7	83.5
Source	503	87.3	67.4	74.1
Proposition	186	86.6	56.5	64.5
State	71	85.9	53.5	62.0
Patient	1161	83.3	63.1	69.1
Topic	244	82.4	64.3	72.1
Goal	694	82.1	60.2	69.6
Cause	424	76.2	61.6	73.8
Path	637	75.0	63.1	63.4
Manner	494	70.4	48.6	59.7
Percept	103	68.0	51.5	65.1
Degree	61	67.2	50.8	60.7
Null	55	65.5	70.9	85.4
Result	40	65.0	55.0	70.0
Location	275	63.3	47.6	63.6
Force	49	59.2	40.8	63.3
Instrument	30	43.3	30.0	73.3
Other	406	57.9	40.9	63.1
Total	8167	82.1	63.6	72.1

Table 13   Performance broken down by abstract role. The third column represents accuracy where frame element boundaries are given to the system, while the fourth and fifth columns reflect finding the boundaries automatically. Unlabeled recall includes cases that were identified as a frame element but given the wrong role.

7   Conclusion

Our preliminary system is able to automatically label semantic roles with fairly high accuracy, indicating promise for applications in various natural language tasks. Semantic roles turn out not to be simple functions of a sentence's syntactic tree structure, and lexical statistics were found to be extremely valuable, as has been the case in other natural language–processing applications. While lexical statistics are quite accurate on the data covered by observations in the training set, the sparsity of their coverage led us to introduce semantically motivated knowledge sources and allowed us to compare automatically derived and hand-built semantic resources. Various methods of extending the coverage of lexical statistics indicated that the broader coverage of an automatic clustering outweighed its imprecision. Finally, carefully choosing sentence-level features for representing alternations in verb-argument structure allowed us to introduce dependencies between frame element decisions within a sentence without adding too much complexity to the system.

We have attempted to address the tension between the robustness of statistical systems and the completeness of knowledge-based systems by choosing an intermediate level of representation. A similar direction toward statistical systems for higher-level, but narrowly constrained, semantic classification tasks has been taken by other recent research, including systems for classifying other types of parse tree annotations (Blaheta and Charniak 2000), verbal aspect (Siegel and McKeown 2000), and dialogue acts (Stolcke et al. 2000). Results have been encouraging on the individual tasks, and finding the appropriate language to combine the information provided by each is an important direction of research.

In our system, richer semantic representations would be helpful in addressing the current system's dependence on annotated training data for each predicate in each semantic frame. An interesting question for further investigation is what type of lexical information a human might be able to provide that will allow the system to generalize from its training data in order to identify the semantic roles of previously unseen predicates. Finding the right balance between representational power and data-driven simplicity for various applications, from summarization to machine translation to higher-level reasoning on and mining of textual information, is an exciting problem for the years to come.

References

Alshawi, H. (Ed.) (1992). *The Core Language Engine*. Cambridge, MA: MIT Press.

Baayen, R., R. Piepenbrock, and L. Gulikers (1995). *The CELEX Lexical Database (Release 2) [CD-ROM]*. Philadelphia, PA: Linguistic Data Consortium, University of Pennsylvania.

Blaheta, D., and E. Charniak (2000). Assigning function tags to parsed text. In *Proceedings of the First Annual Meeting of the North American Chapter of the ACL (NAACL)*, Seattle, Washington, pp. 234–240.

Bobrow, D. G., R. M. Kaplan, M. Kay, D. A. Norman, H. Thompson, and T. Winograd (1977). GUS, A frame driven dialog system. *Artificial Intelligence 8*, 155–173.

Brown, P. F., J. Cocke, S. A. Della Pietra, V. J. Della Pietra, F. Jelinek, J. D. Lafferty, R. L. Mercer, and P. S. Roossin (1990). A statistical approach to machine translation. *Computational Linguistics 16*(2), 79–85.

Carroll, G., and M. Rooth (1998). Valence induction with a head-lexicalized PCFG. In *Proceedings of the Third Conference on Empirical Methods in Natural Language Processing (EMNLP 3)*, Granada, Spain.

Collins, M. (1997). Three generative, lexicalised models for statistical parsing. In *Proceedings of the 35th Annual Meeting of the ACL*, Madrid, pp. 16–23.

Collins, M., and J. Brooks (1995). Prepositional phrase attachment through a backed-off model. In *Proceedings of the Third Workshop on Very Large Corpora*, pp. 27–38. ACL.

Collins, M. J. (1999). *Head-driven Statistical Models for Natural Language Parsing*. Ph. D. thesis, University of Pennsylvania, Philadelphia.

Deerwester, S., S. T. Dumais, T. K. Landauer, G. W. Furnas, and R. A. Harshman (1991). Indexing by latent semantics analysis. *Journal of the American Society for Information Science 41*(6), 391–407.

Dempster, A. P., N. M. Laird, and D. B. Rubin (1977). Maximum likelihood from incomplete data via the *EM* algorithm. *Journal of the Royal Statistical Society 39*(1), 1–21.

Dowty, D. R. (1991). Thematic proto-roles and argument selction. *Language 67*(3), 547–619.

Fellbaum, C. (Ed.) (1998). *WordNet: An Electronic Lexical Database*. Cambridge, MA: MIT Press.

Fillmore, C. J. (1968). The case for case. In E. W. Bach and R. T. Harms (Eds.), *Universals in Linguistic Theory*, pp. 1–88. New York: Holt, Rinehart & Winston.

Fillmore, C. J. (1971). Some problems for case grammar. In R. J. O'Brien (Ed.), *22nd Annual Round Table. Linguistics: Developments of the Sixties–Viewpoints of the Seventies*, Volume 24 of Monograph Series on Language and Linguistics, pp. 35–56. Washington, D.C.: Georgetown University Press.

Fillmore, C. J. (1976). Frame semantics and the nature of language. In *Annals of the New York Academy of Sciences: Conference on the Origin and Development of Language and Speech*, Volume 280, pp. 20–32.

Fillmore, C. J. (1986). Pragmatically controlled zero anaphora. In *BLS-86*, Berkeley, pp. 95–107.

Fillmore, C. J., and C. F. Baker (2000). FrameNet: Frame semantics meets the corpus. In *Proceedings of the Linguistic Society of America*.

Gildea, D., and T. Hofmann (1999). Probabilistic topic analysis for language modeling. In *Eurospeech-99*, Budapest, pp. 2167–2170.

Grishman, R., and B. Sundheim (1995). Design of the MUC-6 evaluation. In *Proceedings of the Sixth Message Understanding Conference (MUC-6)*, Morgan Kaufmann Publishers: San Francisco, pp. 1–11.

Hearst, M. (1999). Untangling text data mining. In *Proceedings of the 37th Annual Meeting of the ACL*, College Park, MD.

Hobbs, J. R., D. Appelt, J. Bear, D. Israel, M. Kameyama, M. E. Stickel, and M. Tyson (1997). FASTUS: A cascaded finite-state transducer for extracting information from natural-language text. In E. Roche and Y. Schabes (Eds.), *Finite-State Language Processing*, pp. 383–406. Cambridge, MA: MIT Press.

Hobbs, J. R., M. E. Stickel, D. Appelt, and P. Martin (1990). Interpretation as abduction. Technical Report 499, AI Center, SRI International, Menlo Park.

Hofmann, T. (1999). Probabilistic latent semantic indexing. In *22nd Annual International ACM SIGIR Conference on Research and Development in Information Retrieval*, Berkeley.

Hofmann, T., and J. Puzicha (1998). Statistical models for co-occurrence data. Memo, MIT Artificial Intelligence Laboratory.

Jackendoff, R. (1972). *Semantic Interpretation in Generative Grammar*. Cambridge, MA: MIT Press.

Jelinek, F., and R. L. Mercer (1980). Interpolated estimation of Markov source parameters from sparse data. In *Proceedings, Workshop on Pattern Recognition in Practice*, Amsterdam, pp. 381–397. North Holland.

Katz, S. M. (1987). Estimation of probabilities from sparse data for the language model component of speech recognition. *IEEE Transactions on Acoustics, Speech, and Signal Processing 35*, 400–401.

Lapata, M., and C. Brew (1999). Using subcategorization to resolve verb class ambiguity. In *Joint SIGDAT Conference on Empirical Methods in NLP and Very Large Corpora*, College Park, MD, pp. 266–274.

Levin, B., and M. Rappaport Hovav (1996). From lexical semantics to argument realization. Unpublished.

Lin, D. (1998). Automatic retrieval and clustering of similar words. In *Proceedings of the COLING-ACL*, Montreal, Canada.

Marcus, M. P., B. Santorini, and M. A. Marcinkiewicz (1993). Building a large annotated corpus of English: The Penn treebank. *Computational Linguistics 19*(2), 313–330.

McCarthy, D. (2000). Using semantic preferences to identify verbal participation in role switching alternations. In *Proceedings of the First Annual Meeting of the North American Chapter of the ACL (NAACL)*, Seattle, Washington, pp. 256–263.

Miller, S., D. Stallard, R. Bobrow, and R. Schwartz (1996). A fully statistical approach to natural language interfaces. In *Proceedings of the 34th Annual Meeting of the ACL*, Santa Cruz, CA, pp. 55–61.

Pereira, F., N. Tishby, and L. Lee (1993). Distributional clustering of English words. In *Proceedings of the 31st ACL*, Columbus, OH, pp. 183–190. ACL.

Riloff, E. (1993). Automatically constructing a dictionary for information extraction tasks. In *Proceedings of the Eleventh National Conference on Artificial Intelligence (AAAI)*, Washington, D.C., pp. 811–816.

Riloff, E., and M. Schmelzenbach (1998). An empirical approach to conceptual case frame acquisition. In *Proceedings of the Sixth Workshop on Very Large Corpora*, Montreal, pp. 49–56.

Rooth, M., S. Riezler, D. Prescher, G. Carroll, and F. Beil (1999). Inducing a semantically annotated lexicon via EM-based clustering. In *Proceedings of the 37th Annual Meeting of the ACL*, College Park, MD, pp. 104–111.

Rose, K., E. Gurewitz, and G. C. Fox (1992). Vector quantization by deterministic annealing. *IEEE Transactions on Information Theory 38*(4), 1249–1257.

Schank, R. C. (1972). Conceptual dependency: A theory of natural language understanding. *Cognitive Psychology 3*, 552–631.

Siegel, E. and K. McKeown (2000). Learning methods to combine linguistic indicators: Improving aspectual classification and revealing linguistic insights. *Computational Linguistics 26*, 595–628.

Somers, H. L. (1987). *Valency and Case in Computational Linguistics*. Edinburgh, Scotland: Edinburgh University Press.

Stolcke, A., K. Ries, N. Coccaro, E. Shriberg, R. Bates, D. Jurafsky, P. Taylor, R. Martina, M. Meteer, and C. V. Ess-Dykema (2000). Dialogue act modeling for automatic tagging and recognition of conversational speech. *Computational Linguistics 26*, 339–371.

Sundheim, B. (Ed.) (1993). *Proceedings, Fifth Message Understanding Conference (MUC-5), Baltimore, MD*. San Mateo, CA: Morgan Kaufmann.

Van Valin, R. D. (1993). A synopsis of role and reference grammar. In R. D. Van Valin (Ed.), *Advances in Role and Reference Grammar*, pp. 1–166. Amsterdam: John Benjamins Publishing Company.

Ward, W. H. (1991). Understanding spontaneous speech: The Phoenix system. In *Proceedings of the IEEE International Conference on Acoustics, Speech, & Signal Processing (IEEE ICASSP-91)*, pp. I.365–372. IEEE.

Winograd, T. (1972). Understanding natural language. *Cognitive Psychology 3*(1), 1–191. Reprinted as a book by Academic Press, 1972.

Chapter 4
Planning

Planning with Generic Types

Derek Long and Maria Fox
Department of Computer Science
University of Durham
United Kingdom
d.p.long@dur.ac.uk, maria.fox@dur.ac.uk

Abstract

Domain-independent, or knowledge-sparse, planning has limited practical application because of the failure of brute-force search to scale to address real problems. However, requiring a domain engineer to take responsibility for directing the search behavior of a planner entails a heavy burden of representation and leads to systems that have no general application. An interesting compromise is to use domain analysis techniques to extract features from a domain description that can exploited to good effect by a planner. In this chapter we discuss the process by which generic patterns of behavior can be recognized in a domain, by automatic techniques, and appropriate specialized technologies recruited to assist a planner in efficient problem solving in that domain. We describe the integrated architecture of STAN5 and present results to demonstrate its potential on a variety of planning domains, including two that are currently beyond the problem-solving power of existing knowledge-sparse approaches.

1   Introduction

Research in planning has been an active branch of AI since Newell and Simon's work on GPS (Newell and Simon 1963) and Green's work on QA3 (Green 1969) in the 1960s. Planning is a loaded term, carrying strong connotations for most people. In AI the most widely accepted usage of the term refers to the activity of selecting between alternative sequences of actions that can be executed from a given initial state of a modeled world in order to achieve some goal. The world is modeled in terms of the domain of objects, relations, and state transitions that capture its key problem-solving aspects. The planning

103

problem is simplified in classical planning by assuming that states are sets of propositional atoms drawn from a finite universe, that the goal is characterized by a finite set of propositions, and that actions are deterministic state-transition functions. Under these assumptions, the general planning problem is PSPACE-hard (Bylander 1992).

An important division in the planning field exists between *knowledge-rich* and *knowledge-sparse* planning. Knowledge-rich planning systems are able to exploit carefully crafted advice, in the form of expert domain knowledge, produced by a domain engineer. The underlying planning strategies they are based upon involve traversing the encoded knowledge with a minimum of search. Search is expensive and the knowledge-rich approach to avoiding it is to design *choice-points* out of the domain representation. In contrast, knowledge-sparse planning systems exploit weak general heuristic strategies to combat the combinatorial explosion inherent in a domain description that captures only the physical dynamics of the world being modeled. The decision making that supports the planning process is uninfluenced by advice from the domain engineer, and search is the means by which a potentially very large solution space is explored.

Experience has shown that, although we can learn many useful lessons about general problem-solving activity by the study of knowledge-sparse planning, it is knowledge-rich planning that leads most readily to application (Currie and Tate 1991; Jónsson, Morris, Muscettola, Rajan, and Smith 2000; Muscettola 1994; Nau, Gupta, and Regli 1995; Wilkins and desJardins 2000). This is unsurprising—planning in all but the most trivial of domains, even under the simplifying assumptions of classical planning, is too hard for exhaustive search to be a reasonable approach to take. Advice given by knowledgeable human problem solvers can sensibly prune the search space a planner must explore to a manageable size and can even allow a relaxation of some of the strong assumptions of classical planning. Unfortunately, it is hard to generalize from the experiences of problem solving with knowledge-rich systems, since the nature of the advice they exploit is typically strongly bound to the domain and does not easily transfer to new domains.

The work we describe in this chapter is motivated by the observation that many practical problems share common, or *generic*, features. For example, planning to achieve parcel deliveries between depots shares its underlying *transportation* nature with the apparently different problem of ensuring that building materials are available at the appropriate locations when needed on a building site. In these two domains, different predicates and object names are used to encode essentially the same underlying transportation behavior. The heart of the transportation problem, which arises in both cases, is to move objects (e.g., parcels or building materials) between locations (e.g., depots or building sites), identifying the best routes for traveling between locations independently of the roles the objects might play at their destinations. Planning technology can be made more powerful if it is able to recognize the generic structure of a domain behind the domain-specific language used to encode it and to exploit its presence by decomposing the planning problem around efficient handling of the associated subproblems.

If a knowledge-sparse planner can recognize generic structures of this kind and configure specialized technologies to handle these parts of a planning problem, it can compete, in performance terms, with a knowledge-rich planner equipped with domain-specific advice. An essential weakness of a knowledge-sparse planner lies in the application of weak search heuristics to hard problems, often embedded within planning problems, when specialized techniques for handling these problems already exist. An example is the planning of routes

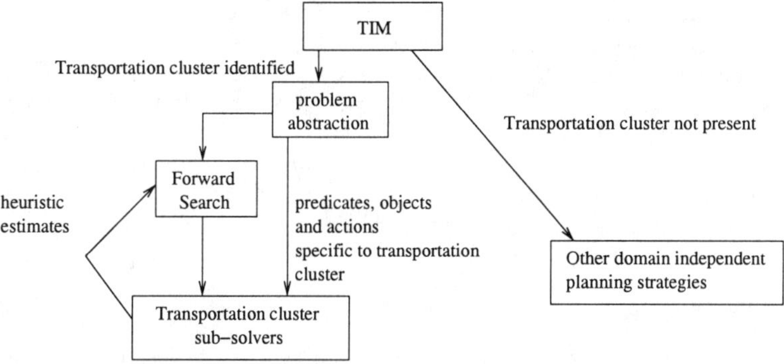

Figure 1 A hybrid planning architecture showing the main components of STAN5.

for vehicles that must visit several locations to fulfill tasks at each of them. This problem can appear as part of a planning problem, but there are already well-known techniques for finding efficient paths between locations and for deciding what order to visit locations so as to be efficient. A general planning strategy that uses the same weak heuristics to influence choices in solving this problem as to allocate tasks between different processors, or to schedule resources to activities, cannot be hoped to solve the problem as effectively as a specialized solver. A specialized solver can isolate the choices that are relevant to the subproblem from other decisions that the planner must make and can solve the subproblem with the benefit of richer and more specialized heuristics.

The successful integration of specialized solvers with a knowledge-sparse planning system presents many challenges. We have investigated these challenges in successive versions of STAN (STatic ANalysis planner), a planning system that exploits domain analysis techniques in order to bring domain-specific knowledge to bear on reducing search. The successive versions of STAN (indicated by version number) exploit increasingly sophisticated static analyses. STAN version 4 (Fox and Long 2001a) illustrates a first step towards using domain analysis to configure the integration of appropriate specialized techniques with a general-purpose planner. In (Fox and Long 2001b), we discuss how the architecture of the system can be made more robust and general, supporting the integration of a planner with multiple subsolvers through a uniform interface. Figure 1 shows the main components of STAN version 5 (STAN5). The integration of the system depends on the domain analysis techniques implemented in the *Type Inference Machinery* (TIM) system, discussed here (TIM is described in detail in Fox and Long 1998). Our work on STAN versions 4 and 5 has emphasized the automatic recognition of certain commonly occurring generic structures by analyzing the domain description prior to planning. In STAN5, this analysis constructs a profile of the domain in terms of its generic structure and enables the selection of appropriate subsolvers from a library. In Sections 4 and 5, we discuss the domain analysis techniques used to identify and isolate distinct subproblems within a planning domain.

In this chapter, we concentrate on describing the automatic recognition of a hierarchy of transportation-related generic types and behaviors. Transportation-related types occur in almost every planning problem, with varying degrees of centrality. Effective treatment of problems relating to transportation is therefore critical to achieving efficient plans in most domains. This treatment can only be achieved by application of appropriate problem-solving technology, for route-planning, load-scheduling, driver-allocation, and so on, which, in turn, demands that these elements of planning problems be recognized and passed to these appropriate subsolvers. The role of generic types extends beyond transportation-related types as we and others have shown elsewhere (Long and Fox 2001; Long et al. 2000; Fox and Long 2001b; Clark 2001), but the predominance of the transportation-related generic types in planning applications makes their exploitation particularly powerful, regardless of whether other generic types are identified and exploited.

1.1 Overview

The chapter continues with a brief overview of planning domain descriptions, the status of control knowledge in these descriptions, and the development of automatic domain analysis techniques, among which fits the work described here. The foundations of this work, implemented in the TIM system, are reviewed in Section 3 and illustrated in a running example. In Section 4, we introduce *generic types*: the abstract patterns of behavior found in the fundamental structures constructed by TIM, that recur across different domains. We concentrate on a key sample generic type—the *mobile type*—together with related components, such as the locations on which instances of a mobile type move and the map that links them. We illustrate these ideas with an example drawn from the running example, showing how a further stage of structural analysis helps to uncover important supporting structure in this case. In Section 5, we consider other generic types related to the mobile type and then, in Section 6, we extend the treatment of the mobile generic type to include a broader generalization. There is a brief discussion, in Section 7, of the architecture of our planner, STAN5, that is capable of exploiting the generic type analysis, and we review some of the results of doing so in Section 8, before concluding the chapter.

In the interests of focusing on domain analysis techniques, we do not provide the details of how the components of STAN5 are integrated. Although we briefly overview the structure of the hybrid system in Section 7, the technical details of the integration are omitted and can be found in (Fox and Long 2001b), a related paper that is dedicated to the description of how plan generation is achieved in STAN5.

2 Planning Domain Description and Domain Analysis

The first domain descriptions for planning were given in terms of first-order axiomatizations of the dynamics of the worlds being modeled (Green 1969; McCarthy 1968; Newell and Simon 1963). In order to express how the application of an action changes the state of the world, axioms prescribe how actions transform states into their successor states. This modeling approach is known as the *situation calculus* (McCarthy 1968), and it formed the foundation for the development of domain representation languages. However, axiomatizing behavior in this way leads to a serious practical problem known as the *frame problem*. This is the problem of correctly modeling what stays stable, after application of an action, as well as what changes. If inertia is not correctly modeled, then inconsistent world models can be constructed. Unfortunately, in all but the most trivial worlds, correct modeling of inertia requires too many axioms to be written for the situation calculus to be a feasible approach to domain description.

A solution to the frame problem was proposed by Fikes and Nilsson (1971) in the development of the Stanford Research Institute Planning System (STRIPS). This used a language that explicitly modeled only what changed when an action was applied. In maintaining a consistent view of the world state, as planning progresses, the planning system makes the assumption that every relation in the world state, not explicitly listed as affected by the action last applied, remains stable. This assumption became known as the STRIPS assumption, and remains a fundamental principle of domain modeling to this day. Indeed, the STRIPS language, which represents each (parameterized) action in terms of its *preconditions* (the facts that must be true in a state in order for the action to be applicable to that state), its *add-effects* (the new facts that become true after application of the action), and its *delete-effects* (the facts that are false after application of the action), continues to be a strong influence on the development of modern domain languages because of the convenient way in which it models parameterized state change.

Throughout the 1970s, 1980s, and early 1990s, planning researchers developed a large family of domain description languages, all sharing the STRIPS assumption and all restricted to the modeling of finite, deterministic worlds. This lack of standardization resulted in it being difficult to compare planning systems or to accumulate a suite of benchmark domains. In 1998, Drew McDermott released the PDDL language—the first attempt to standardize planning domain modeling (McDermott 1998). PDDL has a number of levels, the lowest of which supports the STRIPS-style modeling of simple domains. Other levels support the modeling of simple numeric computations, the modeling of conditional effects, quantified effects, and preconditions—called the *Action Description Language* (ADL) level of the language, after the work of Pednault (1989), who originally considered the modeling of such domain features)—and language extensions to support hierarchical modeling of a domain.

Domain descriptions expressed in the standard planning languages, both the STRIPS and ADL variants of PDDL, comprise unstructured collections of operators that give a restricted picture of the highly structured domain model in the mind of the domain designer. It has often been observed that PDDL (and other domain-description languages based on the STRIPS assumption) is similar to an assembly language in terms of the level of abstraction it offers in the representation of a domain. Not only is the language difficult for the nonspecialist to use, it also offers no search-control assistance to the planner. Indeed, a PDDL domain description is an implicit description of the search space, which the planner simply expands and then searches using a mixture of brute force and weak heuristics.

The advantage of this approach to modeling is that it captures what *can* be done in a domain, rather than what *should* be done. While this places a greater burden on the planner, which has to search to determine which choices to eliminate, there is more scope for original solutions to be identified by the planner than if the domain designer constrains choice by embedding search control information in the domain description. McDermott (2000) argues strongly for a distinction between the encoding of *physics* and the encoding of *advice*. A key reason for this is that the way that advice is used, its interpretation, and the impact it has on the completeness of the planning process is all very much planning-system dependent, and failure to separate the advice from the physics both obscures that dependence and makes the domain description far less reusable.

Of course, the domain designer often has knowledge of the domain that must be exploited to obtain reasonable problem-solving efficiency in that domain, and it can be argued that preventing the domain designer from expressing this important knowledge simply has

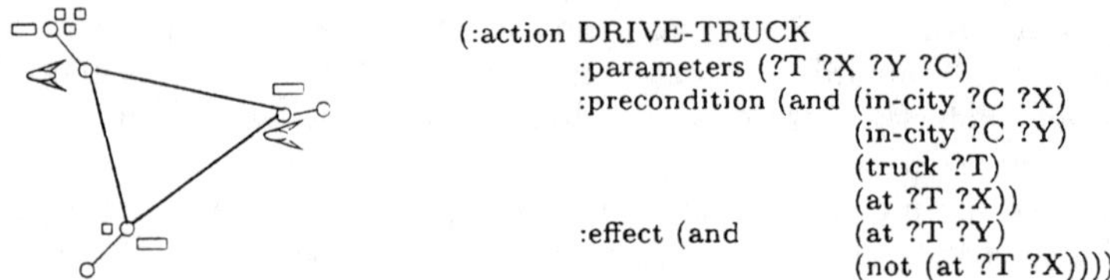

```
                        (:action DRIVE-TRUCK
                            :parameters (?T ?X ?Y ?C)
                            :precondition (and (in-city ?C ?X)
                                               (in-city ?C ?Y)
                                               (truck ?T)
                                               (at ?T ?X))
                            :effect (and    (at ?T ?Y)
                                            (not (at ?T ?X)))))
```

Figure 2 A simple logistics model and one operator from the domain. Thick lines are flight paths; thin lines are roads. The long rectangles are trucks, the squares are packages, and the other objects are planes. DRIVE-TRUCK is written in PDDL with parameterized pre- and postconditions: question marks annotate formal parameters. The operator is a schema that can be instantiated, using domain objects, giving rise to distinct *actions*.

the effect of artificially restricting the planner. Clearly there is a case for allowing such knowledge to be made available to a planner, but there are other interesting possibilities as well. In recent years, the field of automatic domain analysis has been developing as a subfield of planning (Fox and Long 1998; Fox and Long 1999; Gerevini and Schubert 1996a; Gerevini and Schubert 1996b; Gerevini and Schubert 1998; Kelleher and Cohn 1992; Morris and Feldman 1989; Nebel et al. 1997). This work has produced results that show that domain preprocessing can recover some of the structure that is lost in the representation process, and even identify additional structure not apparent to the domain designer. This information can be presented to the planner in a form that can be readily exploited.

The generic behaviors discussed in Section 4 are obtained by static analyses that depend on the underlying functionality of the TIM system. We refer to this underlying functionality as the *basic analysis* performed by TIM. The main features of the basic analysis are discussed in the following section.

3   The TIM System

A planning domain description is a model of the dynamics of a physical or software world. It comprises a concise representation of the states that objects can occupy and the actions, or operators, that cause them to change state. For planning to be decidable, there must be a finite collection of objects and hence a finite collection of states that they can occupy.

In most domains, objects are partitioned according to the states they can be in and the state transitions they can make. For example, in the logistics domain pictured in Figure 2, trucks and planes can be in states of location, and they make state transitions by driving or flying. Packages can also be in states of location, but they make state transitions by being loaded into, and unloaded from, trucks and planes. Since packages cannot drive or fly and vehicles cannot be loaded into or unloaded from anything, packages form a different partition from trucks and planes. This partitioning reflects functional differences between the package objects and the vehicle objects. We call these partitions *types*.

Given a partitioning of a finite domain according to the states objects can be in and the transforms that affect these states (called *transition rules*), it is possible to express the partitions as small finite state machines (FSMs) or automata. These automata tend to be small because there is generally quite a high degree of partitioning in any realistic problem domain. They provide a way of focusing attention on the capabilities of the distinct functional types in the domain and they make explicit many invariant properties of these types. For example, if a type is associated with a two-state *finite-state machine* (FSM), it can be concluded that these states are mutually exclusive and that objects of this type must be in one state or the other, but never both, at all times during planning. This is an invariant property of the objects of this type that can be extracted from the FSMs and can provide very useful search control information to a planner (Bacchus and Kabanza 2000; Bacchus and Kabanza 1996; Fox and Long 2000; Gerevini and Schubert 1998; Kautz and Selman 1998; Kvarnstrom and Doherty 2000; Nau et al. 1999).

The TIM system constructs this FSM view of the domain using automatic analysis techniques. It begins by identifying all of the state transitions that can be made by all of the objects in the domain. This is done by considering all of the parameterized actions in the domain description. For each parameter, TIM constructs a collection of transformation rules on the basis of what *properties* objects that can instantiate each parameter exchange on application of the action. A property is a projection of a proposition onto one of its arguments, denoted by the predicate name subscripted with the argument position being considered.[1] The FSMs constructed by TIM are also termed *property spaces*, because the states traversed are collections of properties, rather than of propositions.

For example, consider the *drive-truck* operator in Figure 2. Objects that can instantiate the variable T exchange an at_1 property for another at_1 property. In other words, that object changes location. The locations involved are irrelevant (they will be different for different applications of the action). This exchange is denoted

$$at_1 \rightarrow at_1$$

Similarly, objects that can instantiate the variable Y acquire the property at_2 without giving up anything in exchange. This is denoted

$$null \rightarrow at_2$$

and a rule of this form is called an *attribute-increasing rule*. Sometimes transitions are *enabled* by properties that are not part of the exchange. The object making the transition must have these enabling properties before the transition can be made. In the case of the drive operator, the transition on at_1, just shown, is enabled by $truck_1$. This is denoted

$$truck_1 \Rightarrow at_1 \rightarrow at_1$$

TIM groups together properties by forming closures of the properties on the left and right sides of the transition rules. The construction of these closures we call *uniting*. Each closure forms a disjoint set of properties governing which rules will be associated with those properties in a single property space. TIM then groups together all of the objects that can have any of the properties in each closure and builds an FSM indicating how these objects exchange these properties by means of the associated transitions. Property space construction is done in two stages: First, candidate property spaces are seeded from

---

[1]Where denoting an abstract property for which the argument position is not known, an unsubscripted identifier will be used.

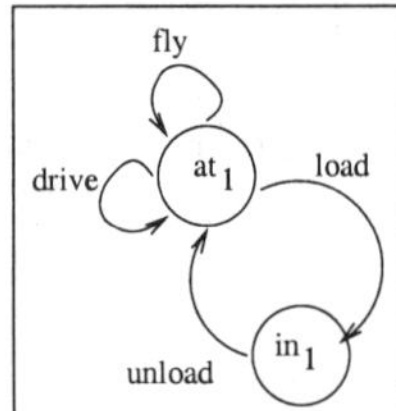 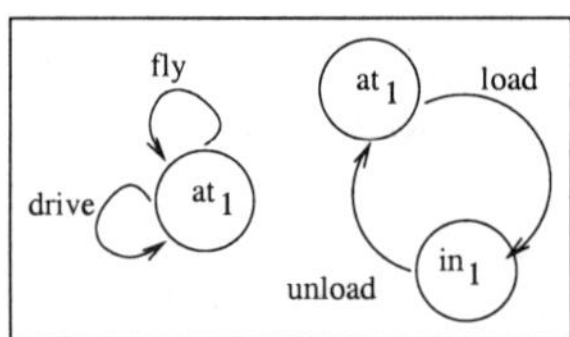

Figure 3 An FSM model of the behavior of vehicles and packages in Logistics, shown before (left) and after (right) splitting.

the objects, their initial states, and the inferred transition rules. Next, these seeds are grown into property spaces by a process called *extension*, in which the full set of states accessible to the objects, by applications of the transition rules, are inferred. Membership of the resulting property spaces is used to identify the partitions (types) to which each object in the domain belongs.

The initial phase of construction of property spaces can obscure the type distinctions that are present in the domain. In the Logistics domain, illustrated in Figure 2, it can be seen that packages can be at locations, just as vehicles can. If the domain description uses the same predicate to describe the location of packages as to describe the location of vehicles, packages and vehicles can appear to share the same behavior with respect to this property space. Figure 3 shows the property space that is constructed under this assignment. Of course, this is undesirable because packages and vehicles behave differently in this space, despite the fact that they share the at_1 property. This is because packages can exchange an at_1 property for an in_1 property, by means of a *load* transition, while vehicles cannot, and vehicles alone can perform $at_1 \rightarrow at_1$ transitions.

When a property space contains behaviors separated by a type distinction, as in Figure 3, the invariants that TIM infers, for the objects in that property space, are too weak to provide effective search control. For example, from the unsplit FSM in Figure 3, TIM can only infer that every object that can traverse this FSM must be either *at* somewhere or *in* something and this, while true, is weak because vehicles cannot have the in_1 property and therefore must always be *at* somewhere. The stronger invariant *is* available when the property space is separated into two—one for vehicles and one for packages. To separate these property spaces, TIM performs *subspace analysis* on the initial property space whenever it contains objects of different types, as in this case. Subspace analysis gives rise to the separated spaces shown on the right in Figure 3. In fact, the single-state property space can be split again, yielding two single-state automata, each with a single looping arc. One of these automata represents the type of truck, the other the type of plane. Trucks are distinct from planes because they can drive, but cannot fly.

As mentioned above, sometimes a property can be acquired without a concomitant exchange. In order to depict the acquisition and loss of such properties in a property space, it is necessary to know how many instances of the property are available in the world. For example, to know how many at_2 properties a location can acquire, it is necessary to know how many objects can instantiate the first argument of the *at* predicate. The size of the property space will be determined by that number, and the only useful invariants obtained will correspond to cardinality constraints on the number of such properties available in any consistent state during planning. Properties that can be freely acquired and lost are deemed to be *attributes*.

When transition rules on properties and on attributes occur in the same candidate property space, the size of that space is dominated by the number of times the attribute can occur in any state. This makes the subsequent processing of the property space, including the inference of invariants, potentially expensive. We have observed that when attribute rules and transition rules occur in the same candidate property space, it is usually possible to split the property space by subspace analysis. Therefore, TIM does not extend candidate property spaces that contain attribute rules. Such spaces are termed *attribute spaces*. TIM identifies which objects in the domain can acquire the attributes within the space, by application of the attribute rules, but does not further process an attribute space unless subspace analysis is possible and leads to the construction of a new property space. This might lead to the loss of some invariants, in rare cases, but we believe this possible loss is justified by the efficiency gains obtained.

The basic analysis performed by TIM consists of the construction of a collection of property spaces and the inference, during this process, of type partitions and invariant facts. In order to clarify how the basic analysis provides a foundation for the identification of generic structure in a domain, we now begin the presentation of a simple worked example. The Bulldozer domain[2] describes a simple world in which a bulldozer can be driven between locations connected by roads and bridges. Jack can *board* and *disembark* from a bulldozer, and can *drive* along roads or *cross* bridges. The domain operators, written in PDDL, are given in full in Figure 4, and an example of an initial state is illustrated in that figure.

3.1   Analyzing the Bulldozer Domain

Given the domain as described in Figure 4, the basic analysis performed by TIM produces the following attribute spaces. Note that the domain encoding uses the predicate *mobile*. This is not to be confused with the generic type "mobile" discussed in Section 4. The way TIM constructs these rules from the parameterized actions supplied in the domain description are described in detail in (Fox and Long 1998).

Attribute Space 1
Properties:
    driving2
Objects:

Rules:
    vehicle1,at1 $\Rightarrow$ null $\rightarrow$ driving2
    vehicle1,at1 $\Rightarrow$ driving2 $\rightarrow$ null

---

[2] This is a standard domain originally developed as part of the UCPOP release (Barret et al. 1996).

```
(:action Drive                              (:action Cross
    :parameters (?thing ?from ?to)              :parameters (?thing ?from ?to)
    :precondition (and (road ?from ?to)         :precondition (and (bridge ?from ?to)
                       (at ?thing ?from)                           (at ?thing ?from)
                       (mobile ?thing)                             (mobile ?thing)
                       (not (= ?from ?to)))                        (not (= ?from ?to)))
    :effect (and       (at ?thing ?to)         :effect (and       (at ?thing ?to)
                       (not (at ?thing ?from)))))                  (not (at ?thing ?from))))))


                       (:action Board
                           :parameters (?person ?place ?vehicle)
                           :precondition (and (at ?person ?place)
                                              (mobile ?person)
                                              (person ?person)
                                              (vehicle ?vehicle)
                                              (at ?vehicle ?place))
                           :effect (and       (driving ?person ?vehicle)
                                              (mobile ?vehicle)
                                              (not (at ?person ?place))
                                              (not (mobile ?person))))
                       (:action Disembark
                           :parameters (?person ?place ?vehicle)
                           :precondition (and (person ?person)
                                              (vehicle ?vehicle)
                                              (driving ?person ?vehicle)
                                              (at ?vehicle ?place)
                                              (mobile ?vehicle))
                           :effect (and       (at ?person ?place)
                                              (mobile ?person)
                                              (not (driving ?person ?vehicle))
                                              (not (mobile ?vehicle))))
```


Figure 4   The Bulldozer domain operators and a simple bulldozer world state.

<table>
<tr><td>

Attribute Space 2

Properties:

    at1, mobile1, driving1

Objects:

    Jack, bulldozer

Rules:

    mobile1 $\Rightarrow$ at1 $\rightarrow$ at1   [cross]

    mobile1 $\Rightarrow$ at1 $\rightarrow$ at1   [drive]

    person1 $\Rightarrow$ at1,mobile1 $\rightarrow$ driving1

    vehicle1,at1 $\Rightarrow$ null $\rightarrow$ mobile1

    vehicle1,at1,driving2 $\Rightarrow$ mobile1 $\rightarrow$ null

    person1 $\Rightarrow$ driving1 $\rightarrow$ at1,mobile1

</td><td>

Attribute Space 3

Properties:

    at2

Objects:

    a, e

Rules:

    road2 $\Rightarrow$ null $\rightarrow$ at2

    road1 $\Rightarrow$ at2 $\rightarrow$ null

    bridge1 $\Rightarrow$ at2 $\rightarrow$ null

    bridge2 $\Rightarrow$ null $\rightarrow$ at2

    at2 $\Rightarrow$ at2 $\rightarrow$ null

    at2 $\Rightarrow$ null $\rightarrow$ at2

</td></tr>
</table>

All three spaces are attribute spaces because they each contain at least one attribute rule. In the first space, the associated objects are those that have the at_1, $mobile_1$, or $driving_1$ properties in the initial state. Although the $person_1$ property is an enabling condition for some of the rules, that does not mean that it belongs to this space. Instead, it establishes a dependency between the (in this case, static) property and this attribute space. It is worth observing, at this point, that the first two rules in the space, which are apparently identical, are in fact distinguished by the operator that allows the $at_1 \rightarrow at_1$ transition. For one of the rules, *cross* is the operator, for the other, it is *drive*, as indicated in square brackets adjacent to the two rules. In the second space, the objects are those that have the at_2 property in the initial state. In the third space, the objects are those that start out with the $driving_2$ property, of which there are none, initially. Because all three spaces are attribute spaces, TIM does not perform extension to identify the states through which the associated objects can pass. However, TIM does go on to identify any further objects that belong with these spaces due to the ability to acquire the associated properties by application of the rules.

If a space contains attribute-increasing rules, any object that satisfies the enablers can acquire the property on the right side of the rule and should therefore be added to the space. In the first attribute space there is an increasing rule, $vehicle_1, at_1 \Rightarrow null \rightarrow mobile_1$, but no further objects satisfy the enabler in the initial state, so no further objects are added to the space. In the second attribute space there are two increasing rules: $road_2 \Rightarrow null \rightarrow at_2$ and $bridge_2 \Rightarrow null \rightarrow at_2$, and objects b, c, d, f, and g all satisfy either the $road_2$ or $bridge_2$ properties in the initial state. These objects could all, in principle, acquire the at_2 property, so they are added to the space. Similarly, the third attribute space starts off with an empty object collection, but the increasing rule $vehicle_1, at_1 \Rightarrow null \rightarrow driving_2$ reveals that the bulldozer can acquire the $driving_2$ property (because it has the properties at_1 and $vehicle_1$ in the initial state), so it is added to the space. This process yields the following attribute spaces by extension of Spaces 1 and 3 (Space 2 remains unchanged). The numbering of the spaces is intended to show their heritage (so Space $x.y$ is the yth space derived from Space x). The rules in the spaces shown below are the same as those in the spaces they are derived from, so are not repeated here.

<table>
<tr><td>

Attribute Space 1.1

Properties:

   driving2

Objects:

   bulldozer

Rules:

   . . .

</td><td>

Attribute Space 3.1

Properties:

   at2

Objects:

   a, e, b, c, d, f, g

Rules:

   . . .

</td></tr>
</table>

At this stage, the attribute spaces can be analyzed to reveal type distinctions in the domain. TIM can infer that Jack and the bulldozer are of different types because of their patterns of membership of the spaces. The locations form a third, distinct type.

3.2 Subspace Analysis

In order to gain access to domain structure that has been obscured by the attribute rules, TIM now refines the initial analysis to identify *subspaces*. The objective is to separate objects of different types into different spaces, in order to try to isolate the objects that are really affected by the attribute rules in the original space. Considering Attribute Space 2 above, it is easy to see that Jack cannot be affected by the attribute-increasing rule, since he does not satisfy the enablers, so it should be possible to isolate that rule with the bulldozer and gain a more precise picture of the state changes that Jack can make. The process by which this is done relies on the type inference having identified any type distinctions in the domain, because the attribute spaces are now subdivided around these type distinctions.

For example, Attribute Space 2 can be subdivided into two FSMs: one for the type including Jack, the other for the type including the bulldozer. Having split the space, TIM associates, with each subspace, the rules applicable to objects within them. The enablers of the rules are used to determine which subspace they are moved to. Any rule with no enablers appears in all subspaces obtained from the original attribute space. Initially this yields two spaces—a property space and an attribute space.

<table>
<tr><td>

Property Space 2.1

Properties:

   at1, mobile1, driving1

Objects:

   Jack

Rules:

   mobile1 $\Rightarrow$ at1 $\rightarrow$ at1

   mobile1 $\Rightarrow$ at1 $\rightarrow$ at1

   person1 $\Rightarrow$ at1,mobile1 $\rightarrow$ driving1

   person1 $\Rightarrow$ driving1 $\rightarrow$ at1,mobile1

</td><td>

Attribute Space 2.2

Properties:

   at1, mobile1, driving1

Objects:

   bulldozer

Rules:

   mobile1 $\Rightarrow$ at1 $\rightarrow$ at1

   mobile1 $\Rightarrow$ at1 $\rightarrow$ at1

   vehicle1,at1 $\Rightarrow$ null $\rightarrow$ mobile1

   vehicle1,at1,driving2 $\Rightarrow$ mobile1 $\rightarrow$ null

</td></tr>
</table>

The first of these is a property space, since it contains no attribute rules. For this space, TIM now identifies the legal states of the associated objects, first by finding the properties of the objects in the initial state, and then by using the extension process described in (Fox and Long 1998). Extension is used to identify any states that can be entered by the associated objects following applications of the rules in the property space, starting with the states inhabited in the initial planning state by the objects in the property space. It computes a reachability analysis from the perspective of the objects in the space. Extension completes the new property space as follows:

Property Space 2.1.1	
Properties:	at1, mobile1, driving1
Objects:	Jack
Rules:	mobile1 $\Rightarrow$ at1 $\rightarrow$ at1
	mobile1 $\Rightarrow$ at1 $\rightarrow$ at1
	person1 $\Rightarrow$ at1,mobile1 $\rightarrow$ driving1
	person1 $\Rightarrow$ driving1 $\rightarrow$ at1,mobile1
States:	[at1,mobile1], [driving1]

The example shows that the same properties can appear in more than one subspace. In the original analysis, used for type inference, it is important that no property belongs to more than one FSM. However, subspaces are not used for type inference, only for invariant extraction, and the duplication of properties does not affect this.

Having found a property space, TIM can now infer some invariants about its associated objects. Assuming that Jack has been determined to be of type T_0, the locations are of type T_1 and the bulldozer to be of type T_2, the invariants are reported as follows:

$$\forall x : T_0 \cdot (\exists y : T_1 \cdot (at(x,y) \wedge mobile(x)) \vee \exists z : T_2 \cdot driving(x,z))$$
$$\forall x : T_0 \cdot \forall y \cdot \forall z \cdot (at(x,y) \wedge at(x,z) \rightarrow y = z)$$
$$\forall x : T_0 \cdot \forall y : T_2 \cdot \forall z : T_2 \cdot (driving(x,y) \wedge driving(x,z) \rightarrow y = z)$$
$$\forall x : T_0 \cdot \neg(\exists y \cdot (at(x,y) \wedge mobile(x)) \wedge \exists z \cdot driving(x,z))$$

In (Fox and Long 1998), we prove two important results, which can be restated as follows:

Theorem 1 *Let P be a planning domain, I be an initial state containing an object o and S be a second state, S, reachable by application of actions from P to the state I. Then, in any property space, PS, constructed by* TIM *in analyzing P and I and containing o, the intersection of the properties in PS and the projection of S for o is a state in PS.*

Theorem 2 *All invariants generated from property spaces constructed by* TIM *are valid.*

The first result shows that TIM finds all the legal states that can be visited by objects in the structure of property spaces, while the second demonstrates that TIM is sound.

The processes by which these invariants are obtained might be considered to be somewhat involved given their rather obvious nature. Other researchers have inferred similar invariants by means of alternative preprocessing strategies (Gerevini and Schubert 1998; Gerevini and Schubert 1996b; Kelleher and Cohn 1992; Morris and Feldman 1989). However, an important feature of the TIM approach is that the data structures constructed during the basic analysis (the transition rules and property spaces) provide the foundations on which the recognition of generic types and behaviors is performed, as we will go on to demonstrate.

4   Generic Types and Behaviors

TIM is designed to construct an analysis of planning domains that is based on *behaviors*. The fundamental basis on which objects are collected into types is that of commonality of behavior. Behaviors are characterized by particular changes that objects can undergo as a consequence of being used in some role in an action. These changes can be changes of state, acquisition of new attributes, or the loss of existing attributes. Furthermore, we capture behaviors in which objects serve as catalysts of change in other objects. Where an object must be available, typically in some specific relation to objects undergoing change, to *enable* that change to take place, the object plays a role as a catalyst.

Although constructing types and associated behaviors within individual domains is fruitful—allowing us, for example, to infer invariants, symmetries, and other features of domains—it is potentially far more powerful to abstract from individual domains and explore common behaviors across multiple domains. In doing so, we find that certain common behaviors can be identified that correspond to intuitively familiar abstractions of well-understood problem structures. These abstractions of behaviors we refer to as *generic behaviors*, with the objects that play roles in the behaviors being of *generic types*. A generic type is therefore not simply a collection of objects that share a behavior within a single domain, but a collection of all possible collections of objects across all domains in which these collections share the same underlying behavior. Our types are hierarchical, so it is possible for a type in a specific domain to exhibit behavior that characterizes it as a particular generic type while, at the same time, exhibiting distinctive additional behaviors—perhaps even behaviors that characterize another generic type. The benefits that are offered from characterizing the behaviors of types with domains in terms of generic behaviors and generic types are the usual consequences of recognizing individuals as specializations of well-understood abstractions: all of the knowledge applying to the abstractions can be applied, in its specialized forms, to the individuals.

TIM identifies basic types in a domain by partitioning objects into equivalence classes according to functionality. Thus, basic types and their behaviors are defined and exist a posteriori. By contrast, generic types and behaviors are formed by abstraction of commonly occurring, and interdependent, functional equivalences across domains. Thus, generic types are defined in more general terms and exist a priori. The definition of a generic behavior is given in terms of a *fingerprint* that characterizes it in an abstract, domain-independent way. A fingerprint can be described in terms of required transition rules, FSM behaviors, predicate arities, relationships between variables appearing in operator schemas, invariants, and other features that can be identified in a domain description. Examples are given in Sections 4.1 and 5. Generic types are defined by the roles they play in generic behaviors—any basic type in a domain that fulfills a role described in a generic behavior can be ascribed the corresponding generic type. The presence of a generic type in a domain must be explicitly sought by identification of an appropriate fingerprint for a defining generic behavior. Any domain that features a fingerprint characterizing a specific generic behavior is deemed to contain that behavior and its associated generic types. Where a generic behavior depends on the roles of several types, it will determine correspondingly many generic types. It is typical for a generic behavior to determine several generic types, as we will see in the following sections. Moreover, it is common for generic behaviors themselves to form collections that, together, define a common subproblem. We call these collections *clusters*, and these clusters form the foundation for identifying an appropriate exploitation strategy, as discussed in Section 7.

A strong relationship exists between our notion of *fingerprint* and the software-engineering notion of *design pattern* (Gamma et al. 1995). Defining a design pattern in his seminal work, Christopher Alexander states:

> Each pattern describes a problem which occurs over and over again in our environment, and then describes the core of the solution to that problem in such a way that you can use this solution a million times over without ever doing it the same way twice.

This generality is exactly what generic types are intended to capture, and the fingerprints define, in a planning-domain pattern language, the necessary components, and relationships between them, that must be identified in the domain for the presence of the generic type to be inferred.

The fingerprint of a generic type and its associated cluster is a characterization in terms of abstract structures that must be identified by pattern matching within the domain structure identified by TIM. These structures are founded on the FSMs generated by TIM, but can include the arities of predicates, the types of relationships defined by predicates, and the linkages between the FSMs, the predicates, and the operator schemas that define the behaviors of the objects in a domain. These structures can be seen as design patterns specific to planning domains, defined by a pattern language for planning domains. The development of such a pattern language is a topic of our future work. The characterizations provided in Figures 5 and 10 have a similar status to the design patterns of programs and can play a similar role: to support the construction of planning domain descriptions using well-understood structural components that capture common behaviors. Seen in this light, the automatic recognition of generic types is an attempt to recognize and capture design patterns in use within a planning domain. The exploitation of generic types as planning domain design patterns is at an early stage, and we perceive there to be opportunities in domain engineering as well as in supporting efficient planning.

In the remainder of this section, we outline the generic types and behaviors associated with transportation clusters. We describe their fingerprints and the processes by which TIM identifies them in domain models.

4.1 The Generic Type of Mobile Objects

The most fundamental of the generic types recognized by TIM is that identified with one of the simplest fingerprints: a single state and an associated transition starting and ending at that state (Figure 5). This signature structure, when it is part of a property space, indicates that objects that belong to the space can make transitions between different associated values that are linked to the objects by the properties forming the state. For example, if the state contains the single property at_1, then the objects in the property space make transitions between values that they are at. Provided that the state is denoted by a single property, P_i, derived from the n-ary predicate P, then the values of the vector

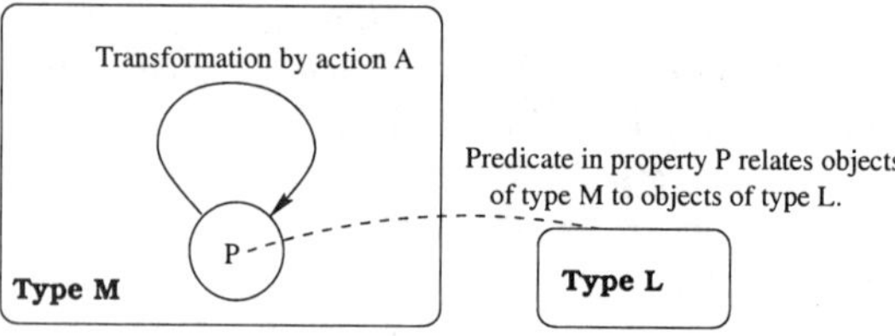

Figure 5 Simple structure characterizing a generic behavior.

x_i, which can occupy the $n - 1$ arguments excluding the ith argument of P, define the points between which the objects in the property space can, in principle, make transitions.

Consider the simplest case: Suppose that a property space contains a single state that is defined by a single property, P_i, derived from a binary predicate P, and that a single transition starts and ends at this state. In this case, the space encodes the fact that objects can make transitions between unique single-valued relations with objects, which can satisfy the $(2 - i)$th argument position of the predicate P. Execution of the operator from which the transition is derived causes an object in the property space to make a transition between an association with one of the related values to another. This can be seen as movement of the objects between locations. The operator causing the transitions is the "move" operation and the objects are *mobile*. The values with which the mobile objects are associated through P can be seen as *locations* and the predicate P as the *locatedness* condition linking the mobile objects and the locations.

The notion of a mobile object and the network of locations on which it moves is a powerful and common feature of planning problems. It is not surprising that mobile objects occur in problems that involve some sort of logistical element, where agents must be moved between the locations at which activities occur. It is less obvious that the same feature can arise in other domains. In particular, the locatedness condition can be a metaphor for any many-to-one relationship that must always hold between members of one collection of objects (the mobiles) and some subset of the members of a second collection (the locations). This metaphor is valuable, since the problem of navigating between locations in a map is equivalent to the problem of selecting an efficient sequence of values with which an object must be related in order to exchange a relationship with some initial value for a new relationship with some goal value. Thus, the same path-planning problem that solves the problem of efficiently crossing a map of locations will solve the metaphorically equivalent problem of efficiently traversing the range of a many-to-one relation, whatever that relation might actually be intended to represent in the planning problem. It is precisely this commonality of fundamental behavior that identifies these patterns as characteristic of generic types. In this case, the generic types involved are the mobile objects, or *mobiles*, and the *locations* between which they move.

In this basic case, identifying the signature structure and the consequent identification of the generic types and roles they play is relatively straightforward. It is a slightly more complex problem to identify the map that defines the legal transitions between locations available to mobiles. The process by which a map is derived is described in Section 4.3.

```
for each property space, P
    for each rule in P, r
        if r is of the form e ⇒ p → p
            and p corresponds to a binary predicate, pred
        then construct a new mobile collection, M;
            associate r with M;
            put the objects in P into M;
            mark the other argument of pred as a location type;
            record pred as the "at" relation of M;
        endif
    endfor
endfor


for each subspace, S
    for each rule in S, r
        if r is of the form e ⇒ p → p
            and p corresponds to a binary predicate, pred
        then if r is already associated with a mobile collection, M
            then if M is already refined
                then   contruct a related mobile collection, M';
                       associate M' with M;
                       put the objects in S into M';
                else   replace the objects in M with objects from S;
                       mark M as refined;
                endif
            else construct a new mobile collection, M;
                 put the objects in P into M;
                 mark the other argument of pred as a location type;
                 record pred as the "at" relation of M;
                 mark M as refined;
            endif
        endif
    endfor
endfor
```

Figure 6 Pseudo-code algorithm for detecting mobile objects in a planning domain description.

Figure 6 gives a pseudo-code description of the mobile-identification part of our analysis in property spaces and subspaces. The key observation regarding subspaces is that this analysis refines the analysis of the parent spaces, identifying subsets of mobile objects among a larger collection in the parent space. In situations in which TIM constructs a property space that contains a state transition rule, $p \to p$, implying the existence of a mobile, the objects in the space are proposed as members of a generic mobile type. However, it can happen that the members of the space cannot all exploit the rule that indicates movement. For example, if there is a collection of packages that can be either *at* a location or *in* a truck, while the trucks can only be *at* a location, the generic structure analysis carried out by TIM will place the *at* and *in* properties in the same property space, due to the *at* $\to$ *in* and *in* $\to$ *at* transition rules for packages, as we saw in Figure 3. This will cause the generic structure analysis to initially consider packages and trucks to both be part of the generic mobile collection, despite the fact that packages cannot exploit the *at* $\to$ *at* rule that makes the trucks mobile. However, as discussed, a more refined analysis performed by TIM will identify the separate types of trucks and packages and place them in separate subspaces. The analysis of these spaces will then allow TIM to determine that it is actually only trucks that are mobile. This more detailed analysis allows a *refinement* of the original mobile generic type and it replaces the collection of mobile objects in the original generic type. In the case where subspace analysis identifies more than one refinement of the original space containing mobile types, these subtypes will be said to be *related* mobile types, since they will use the same movement operator and network of locations.

It can be seen, in Figure 6, that the analysis looks for binary predicates encoding locatedness. As mentioned earlier, this restriction can be lifted by considering locations as vectors of objects that can fill the nonmobile arguments of a possible locatedness predicate. In fact, it is also possible to restructure a domain automatically to convert higher arity predicates that encode locatedness conditions into binary predicates. We discuss this further in Section 6. A further special case that can arise is that in which a domain contains only one mobile object. In this case, it is not uncommon for the domain engineer to leave the object implicit—essentially encoding the object directly in the predicate rather than as a named object of the domain. TIM can identify implicit mobiles and successfully extract them from the domain.

Returning to the analysis of the Bulldozer domain, it can be observed, from Property Space 2.1.1, that Jack is a mobile object because of the presence of the two $at_1 \rightarrow at_1$ rules. In fact, Jack is mobile by two different actions (*cross* and *drive*). At first glance, it seems strange that Jack can achieve mobility by these actions independently of the bulldozer. The reason is that Jack uses the same *at*-relation as the bulldozer, and has the property of being *mobile* in the initial state, so the two rules are available to both Jack and the bulldozer during subspace analysis. Indeed, Jack can satisfy the preconditions of the *cross* and *drive* actions, because of using the same *at*-relation, even though this may not have been intended by the domain designer.[3] Indeed, information of this kind, presented in an appropriate way, can be helpful in debugging domain descriptions as they are constructed.

We would now like to be able to infer invariants for the bulldozer, but it is still hidden in an attribute space (Attribute Space 2.2). The basic analysis is unable to identify the missing invariants and does not yet have access to the mobility of the bulldozer. This leads to the need for a further subspace analysis step. We cannot split further on the basis of the number of types inhabiting the space, as there is only one in Attribute Space 2.2. Instead, we observe that the initial subspace analysis can lead to some subspaces containing properties that are not linked by the behaviors described by the rules in those subspaces. This can occur when the original space contained rules that linked these properties, but those rules apply to only a subset of the types represented in the space.

For example, considering Attribute Space 1.2 for bulldozer, we see that the two $at_1 \rightarrow at_1$ rules would appear in a different space from the two attribute rules if we were to perform the uniting step at this stage. We therefore *reunite* the rules in the new space, yielding as many new subspaces as closures constructed by this process.

4.2 Refined and Generic Type Level Analysis of the Bulldozer Domain

In order to identify the hidden structure described above, TIM uses attribute spaces formed during subspace analysis to seed a collection of new FSMs. In each such attribute space TIM performs the uniting process on the rules. Any new closures that are produced result in

---

[3]Note that we have used the standard Bulldozer domain encoding available as part of the Blackbox release (Kautz and Selman 1995).

the construction of a new attribute or property space. This involves adding the appropriate rules, initial states, and objects to each of the new subspaces.

The following new property spaces are constructed by applying this process to the bulldozer attribute space (Attribute Space 2.2) built during subspace analysis.

<table>
<tr><td>

Property Space 2.2.1

Properties:
  at1

Objects:
  bulldozer

Rules:
  mobile1 $\Rightarrow$ at1 $\rightarrow$ at1
  mobile1 $\Rightarrow$ at1 $\rightarrow$ at1

</td><td>

Attribute Space 1.2.2

Properties:
  mobile1

Objects:
  bulldozer

Rules:
  vehicle1,at1 $\Rightarrow$ null $\rightarrow$ mobile1
  vehicle1,at1,driving2 $\Rightarrow$ mobile1 $\rightarrow$ null

</td></tr>
</table>

We note that the first of these two spaces contains the two, apparently identical, $at_1 \rightarrow at_1$ transitions, and recall that these transitions are actually distinguished by the actions that cause them (*cross* and *drive*). Both new spaces inherit all of the objects of the original attribute space. Now we find the initial state properties relevant to each property space. This yields

<table>
<tr><td>

Property Space 2.2.1.1

Properties: at1

Objects: bulldozer

Rules: mobile1 $\Rightarrow$ at1 $\rightarrow$ at1
               mobile1 $\Rightarrow$ at1 $\rightarrow$ at1

States: [at1]

</td></tr>
</table>

No additional states are accessible to the bulldozer via application of any of the rules in the property space. The process has successfully separated the attribute-valued properties of the bulldozer from its state-valued properties, allowing TIM access to the bulldozer invariants:

$$\forall x : T_2 \cdot \forall y \cdot \forall z \cdot (at(x,y) \wedge at(x,z) \rightarrow y = z)$$
$$\forall x : T_2 \cdot \exists y : T_1 \cdot at(x,y)$$

which tells us that no bulldozer can be in more than one place at a time and every bulldozer must be at some location at every point in time. Again, these facts are quite straightforward, but the property space that has been constructed during the analysis is critical for the identification and exploitation of the generic structure of the domain.

TIM is able to access the fact that the bulldozer is mobile by the *cross* and *drive* operators, so the current representation of mobility is extended to record the fact that the bulldozer is mobile. Because the mobility of the bulldozer is also given by the *cross* and *drive* actions, TIM records the mobility of the bulldozer as *related* to that of Jack. The next stage in the analysis of the Bulldozer domain is to determine the maps of locations that can be traversed by the mobile objects.

4.3 Inferring Maps for Mobiles

In order for mobile objects to move, there must be a network of locations through which they move. The definition of this network is found by identifying the parameters in the appropriate move action that correspond to the source and destination of the move. These are taken to be the nonmobile argument of the locatedness predicate affected by the move operator. The occurrence of the locatedness predicate in the preconditions of the move gives the source, and the occurrence in the effects of the move gives the destination. For example, in the Logistics domain, the action of driving from *city1-1* to *city1-2* specifies that the truck be at *city1-1*, and the effect specifies that the truck be at *city1-2* (see Figure 2). TIM is able to identify the nonmobile argument using the locatedness property of the mobile type, together with the assumption that the locatedness predicate is binary (possibly following transformation, as described in Section 6).

The move action might impose additional constraints on the circumstances under which a mobile might move between its source and destination. In the drive action described above, it is specified that *city1-1* and *city1-2* must be linked. Since links between cities in Logistics are static, this can be determined by examination of the initial state. The map that determines how the truck mobile type can move therefore connects two vertices only if they are linked in the domain description. In richer domains other constraints might be imposed—for example, it might be possible to travel to a specific location only with a pass, or visa. This would further constrain the connectedness of the network.

The preconditions that determine the constraints on access between the source and destination can be isolated and together form a predicate on the two parameters, with any additional parameters that are referred to in the appropriate precondition propositions being existentially quantified. This predicate is abstracted from the move operator and used to define the edge relationship between the location objects that form the vertices of the network on which the mobiles move. The process by which the predicate is abstracted from the preconditions of the movement action, and a network constructed governing the mobility of the corresponding mobile type, is described in detail in (Long and Fox 2000). For the Logistics DRIVE-TRUCK operator the edge predicate is

$$edge(from, to) \equiv \exists city \cdot in\text{-}city(city, to) \wedge in\text{-}city(city, from)$$

which demonstrates that locations in the same city will be linked by an edge in the inferred map. If the edge relationship includes dynamic propositions, then the map network, or map, is itself dynamic—perhaps having doors that can be used to grant or deny access to certain locations, or paths that close at certain points in the plan. The definition of the map structure can be used to plan routes for mobiles to move between locations. Where the map is static, this is a straightforward shortest-path problem, but when the map is dynamic, there is a more complex relationship between efficient paths and the achievement of access along the necessary edges of the paths.

There are many domains in which a mobile is able to use multiple forms of movement (referred to in Figure 13 as multimode movement). For example, amphibious vehicles can both drive and float. The presence of multiple-move actions indicates that in order to identify the most efficient route between two locations, it is necessary to combine the maps, produced by analysis of the move actions, into one (see Figure 7).

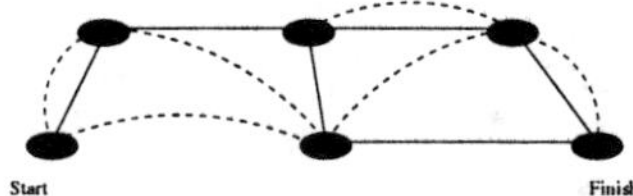

Figure 7   Moving on two maps: an example in which the route between two vertices is shorter on the combined map than on either map individually.

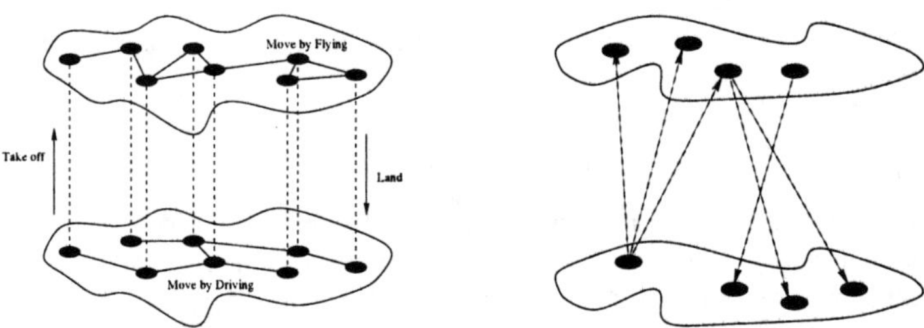

Figure 8   Moving between maps (left) and with multiple transit opportunities (right).

In the case where an object has more than one move action, as in the Bulldozer domain, the process is made more complex by the fact that the set of locations associated with each move action can appear disjoint even though all locations, in all of the sets, are accessible to the mobile object (because it can move by all of the move actions). In the Bulldozer domain, we see that the *drive* move action yields a map formed from all of the locations connected by the *road* map-link, while the *cross* mover yields a map formed from the locations connected by the *bridge* link. Since Jack and the bulldozer can use both of the move actions, they have access to all locations on both maps.

These two maps appear to be disjointed even though the bulldozer can actually travel between any two locations because it can traverse both road and bridge connections. No transit actions are required to gain access between the two maps because the locations in the two maps are shared. The situation can become more complex when mobiles can move between different maps, as discussed in Section 6. This situation is depicted in Figure 8. When multiple maps can be combined without *transit links* (special actions causing transition from one map to another), we call the mobile a *commuting* mobile.

5   Mobile-Related Generic Types: Portables, Passengers, and Drivers

Planning domains in which some collection of objects must be transported between locations are common, and, of course, such domains must include mobile objects to carry out the transportation tasks. The objects that are transported represent a further generic type—*portable* objects. We make the assumption that any carrier for portable objects must

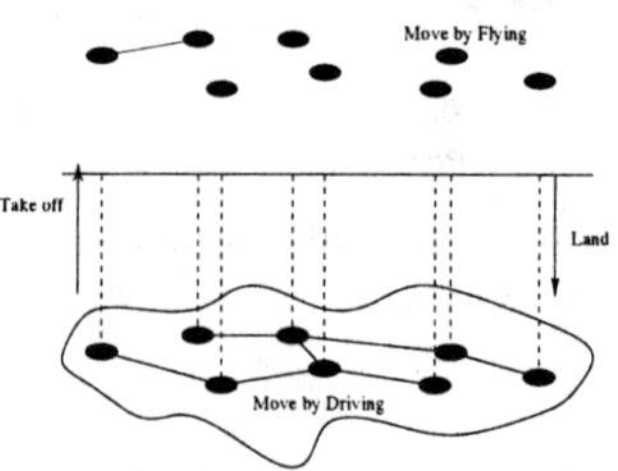

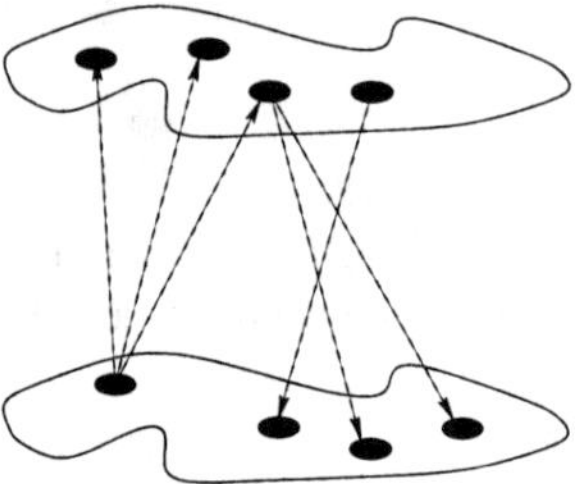

Figure 9   Moving between maps (left) and with multiple transit opportunities (right).

be mobile, so an object that is moved through space by the trajectory of a fixed robot arm would not currently be considered an example of the portable generic type. Objects can only be identified as portable if they participate in a specific kind of relationship with one or more mobile objects. Therefore, the presence of mobile objects must be inferred before TIM begins to look for portables.

Our algorithm for inferring the existence of portable objects begins by looking for FSM structures that indicate that any transition in the location of associated objects must pass through an intermediate state linking the potentially portable objects with a self-propelled (mobile) object. In Logistics, packages would be detected as portable because changes in their at_1 properties require them to pass through an *in-relation* with a mobile, indicating their transportation by a third party. Thus, the FSM for portable objects will always relate a *locatedness predicate,* used to describe the locatedness of portables that are not being carried, to a *portedness predicate,* used to describe the state of portables that are being carried. The locatedness predicate must place portable objects on locations within the map of some mobile that acts as carrier for that portable. The carrier will be the mobile referred to by the portedness predicate identified in the partner state in the FSM for the portable. Figure 10 shows the relevant FSM structure, inferred by TIM from the Logistics operator schemas, together with the relationships that must hold in order for the portable objects to be identified. Figure 11 shows the Logistics operator schemas that gave rise to this FSM: observe that the fact that the same variable is used to refer to the location at which the portable object and the carrier must be located for a load operation to be performed, and similarly for the location of the mobile for an unload operation and the final location of an unloaded portable.

It is important that the portable objects share the same location set as the carriers, since otherwise the movement of the supposed carrier will not be relevant to the location of the supposed portable. However, the portable objects might share the same location set indirectly. For example, if the locations that a carrier can visit all have pallets associated with them and some collection of portable objects moves from one pallet to another, carried by these carriers, then the portables will be linked to the locations used by the carrier, but indirectly through the relationship linking the pallets with the locations. An interesting variation on portable objects is the possibility for objects to be loaded into other objects that are themselves portable, such as loading fruit into boxes to be transported. We consider these *indirect* portable objects to be a specialization of portable objects.

The following components form the fingerprint for portability:

1. A previously identified mobile generic type, M, and its linked location generic type, L.

2. A new type, P, with an FSM containing two states linked by transitions in both directions.

3. One state of the FSM for P must include a property formed from a predicate linking the P type objects to the M type objects.

4. The *other* state of the FSM must contain a property formed from a predicate linking the P type objects to the L type objects.

5. The operators from which the two transitions in the P type FSM are derived must require an M object to be located at the same location as the P object is located at the appropriate end of the transition.

Note that the *names* of the operators and predicates are irrelevant and that the name of the predicate in Feature 4 need not be the same as the locatedness predicate for type M.

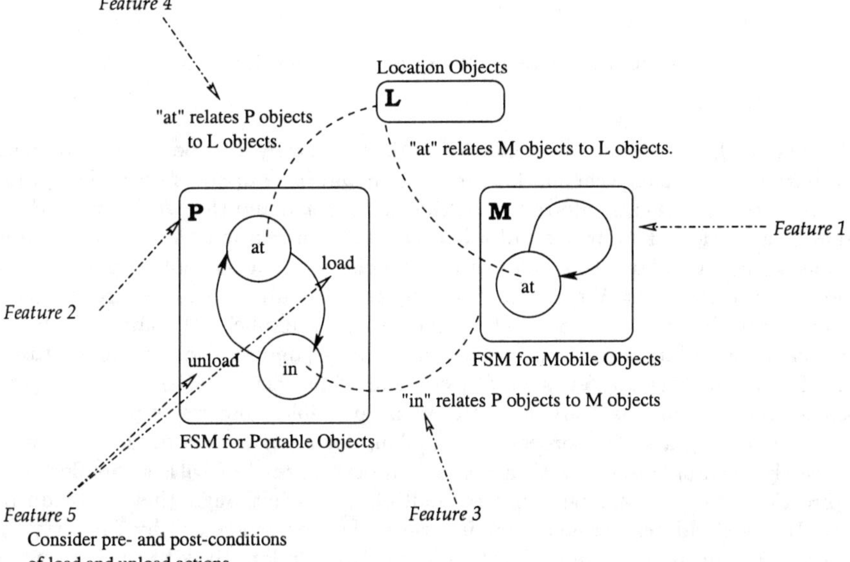

Figure 10   The features that identify portables and their associated behaviors.

```
(:action LOAD-TRUCK                      (:action UNLOAD-TRUCK
    :parameters (?T ?P ?X)                   :parameters (?T ?P ?X)
    :precondition (and (truck ?T)            :precondition (and (truck ?T)
                       (at ?T ?X)                               (at ?T ?X)
                       (package ?P)                             (package ?P)
                       (at ?P ?X))                              (in ?P ?T))
    :effect (and (in ?P ?T)              :effect (and (at ?P ?X)
                 (not (at ?P ?X))))                   (not (in ?P ?T))))
```

Figure 11   Logistics operators revealing presence of portables.

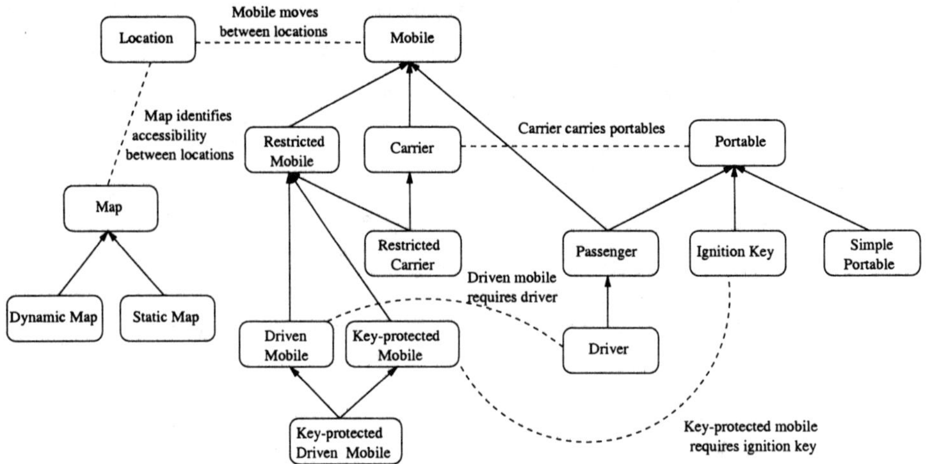

Figure 12 A hierarchy of generic types inferred by TIM.

The first task in finding portable objects is to identify the portedness predicate and establish the producing schemas for the $at \rightarrow in$ and $in \rightarrow at$ transitions. The producer for the $at \rightarrow in$ transition is inferred to be the *load schema* and the producer for the $in \rightarrow at$ transition is inferred to be the *unload schema*. The in-relation appears on the add-list of the *load* schema and on the delete-list of the *unload*, and it has both a portable argument and a carrier argument. We assume that portables are always explicit arguments, but our analysis can deal with the case where the carrier is implicit. Domain objects are made implicit by encoding them in predicates with corresponding dedicated operators. This is only feasible if there are few such objects, and while there is often only one mobile in a benchmark domain, there are generally many portables. Indirectly portable objects can be inferred using a similar process, but looking for a portedness predicate that links the indirectly portable objects with a portable object instead of with a mobile object. This indirection can, in principle, exist to multiple levels, although this is obviously rather rare. In the Bulldozer domain, Jack is a portable type, evidenced by Property Space 2.1 (Section 3) and the Board and Disembark operators, linking Jack to the carrier bulldozer.

A hierarchy of mobile-related types is recognized by TIM, as indicated in Figure 12. The figure illustrates some of the relationships among three hierarchies of generic types: location types, mobile types, and portable types. The figure also indicates a fourth structure, the map, formed from the relationships between locations. It can be seen that within the hierarchies of individual generic types, there can be rich and varied subtypes. For example, the mobile-type hierarchy includes carriers, which can carry portable objects. It also includes restricted mobile types, which are those that can only move when certain additional conditions are met, described in the preconditions of their move actions. Among the subtypes of restricted mobiles are those that require *drivers* and those that require *ignition keys*. The latter is a metaphor for any behavior in which a mobile is prevented from moving unless an object in a particular type (perhaps a type with only one object in it) is in the mobile. It can be seen that behaviors can be multiply inherited, so that, for example, a mobile can be both restricted and a carrier. The hierarchies for portable and mobile objects intersect in the generic type of *passengers*. This is the collection of types that are both mobile and portable, meaning that they can be carried between locations or move without a carrier. The maps on which they move in these two different contexts can be different, although the locations must be shared, just as with portable objects and their carriers. Jack exhibits this behavior in the Bulldozer domain. If a type is portable and mobile on two different collections of locations, then this implies a different behavior, since it must then be possible for the objects to be at a location in each of the two collections simultaneously.

A refinement of passengers appears when an object plays a special role in the mobility of its carrier. Jack has this property in the Bulldozer domain, causing the bulldozer to acquire the $mobile_1$ attribute when he climbs into it and to lose it again as he disembarks. We call this subclass of passengers, on which their carriers depend for mobility, *drivers*. Similarly, *ignition keys* are immobile portable objects on which mobile objects depend for mobility. The relationships that allow TIM to recognize these additional generic types are present in the preconditions of the move operator for mobiles (e.g., a move operator might specify that some third party be in place in order for the mobile to move) and are recognized in the effects of the operators responsible for allowing drivers to board and disembark from the mobiles.

In the case of drivers, recognition is based on identification of an enabling condition for the movement of the (driven) mobile that is achieved by application of a load operator. That is, if the driven mobile requires an enabling condition in order to move that is only achieved by the load operator that boards the driver into the mobile and is subsequently undone by the disembarkation of the driver from the mobile, then it is clear that the driver must be on board the driven mobile for it to actually move. The driver object itself might not be referred to directly in the move operator for the driven mobile—if the loading of the driver causes a state change in the driven mobile that enables the movement, then this will be a sufficient indication of the dependency between the driver and the driven mobile. A similar enabling condition on the movement of mobile objects involving the loading of a portable, but otherwise immobile, object indicates the need for an object of the generic type we have called ignition keys. In the Bulldozer domain, the fact that the $at_1 \rightarrow at_1$ transitions for the bulldozer each has an enabler, $mobile_1$, indicates that the ability of the bulldozer to move between locations depends upon it achieving mobility through the state transitions made by some other object. Mobility is achieved when Jack is in the bulldozer—the bulldozer cannot move without a driver. TIM can detect that Jack is of the driver generic type because Jack is both mobile and portable, and it is the *loading* of Jack (by means of the *board* action) into the bulldozer that achieves the enabler for the bulldozer's mobility rule. The additional feature that characterizes drivers and ignition keys and is not shown in Figure 10 is the enabling condition on the movement transition for M. This condition can only be achieved by the load action for P, which loads a P-type object into an M-type object. It is possible for a mobile to have multiple enabling conditions, implying the need for multiple drivers, ignition keys, or some combination of these objects.

The hierarchy in Figure 12 distinguishes static and dynamic maps: *Static maps* are those in which the accessibility relationships between locations, recorded in the accessibility predicate extracted from the preconditions of the appropriate movement operator, are entirely determined by the initial state. *Dynamic maps,* in contrast, are affected by actions, as indicated in Section 4.3. The figure also includes a subtype of portable objects that we call *simple portable objects.* This type includes those types of portables that play no role in a domain other than to be carried between locations. Objects of this kind are relatively common in benchmark planning domains (e.g., packages in the Logistics domain, balls in the Gripper domain (McDermott 1998), cars in the Ferry domain (McDermott 1998) and so on). It is worthwhile identifying this generic type since a useful heuristic can be applied to these objects: there is no point in putting these objects down in their starting locations or picking them up from their goal destinations. A further brief discussion of heuristics of this kind is included in Section 7.

Other dependencies between mobile types can exist, of course. For example, if a mobile can only move when an object, mobile on a different collection of locations, is present at an appropriate location, then, although we do not identify this as a driver-driven relationship, it clearly has much in common with it. This situation can arise when the enabling objects move directly between the mobiles they enable, so that the enabled mobiles are themselves locations for the movement of these enabling mobiles. We call this behavior *reallocation* of the enabling mobile between the dependent mobiles, the dependent mobiles being called *tasks* and the enabling mobiles *processors* (Long and Fox 2001).

It should be emphasized that although the names we use for the generic types are strongly suggestive of the roles they play, these roles might actually be metaphors for behaviors with quite different interpretations in the mind of the domain engineer. For example, if a domain allows walls to be painted with different-colored paints, perhaps specifying which paints can cover which other paints, then this can be interpreted, by TIM, as a situation in which the walls are mobile on a map of color locations. If there is a requirement for a decorator to be by the wall in order to paint it, and the decorators can move from wall to wall, then this is an example of the reallocation behavior of processors (decorators) between tasks (walls).

Generic types in the hierarchy of generic mobile and mobile-related types can occur in various combinations in a planning domain. These combinations form clusters (referred to in the introduction to this section), such as simple transportation clusters (carriers and simple portables moving on static maps), more complex logistical transportation clusters (driven carriers, drivers, and portables), driver scheduling clusters (driven mobiles and drivers), and so on. The cluster that involves the processors and tasks described above is called the *Multi-Processor Scheduling (MPS) cluster.* Strategies for exploitation of these clusters can apply to subsets of clusters or just to single clusters, as we will discuss in Section 7.

6 Generalizing Mobiles

The structure characterizing mobiles and their behavior can be generalized in several ways. These are summarized in Figure 13. In this figure, the entry in each row referring to n corresponds to the dimension of generalization. As discussed below, the fourth generalization can only occur in the context of the third generalization, so must contain more than one state. Otherwise the generalizations are broadly orthogonal to one another, and can appear in any combination in a domain.

Type of mobile	Arity	# S	# P	# M	FSM
Basic mobile	2	1	1	1	 at
Generalization 1: Mobile on $n-1$ dimensions	$n > 2$	1	1	1	 P
Generalization 2: Multi-mode moves	2	1	1	$n > 1$	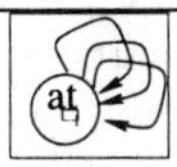 at
Generalization 3: Flying and hovering mobiles	2	$n > 1$	1	1	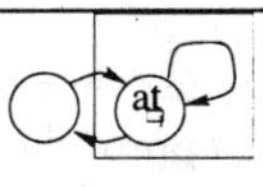 at
Generalization 4: Complex locatedness	2	> 1	$n > 1$	1	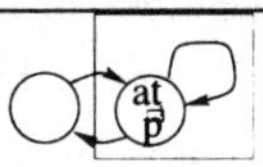 at / P

Figure 13 Table of generalizations of mobile structures. Arity is the number of arguments in the locatedness predicate. # S refers to the number of states in the state space containing the locatedness property; # P is the number of properties in the locatedness state; and # M is the number of movement actions.

In the first generalization, the predicate-defining locatedness can have more than two arguments. If the locatedness predicate is n-ary, then the mobiles move in space defined by $n-1$ coordinates. This does not imply that when n is 2 the mobiles move in 1D space—the connectedness of the locations can define the points of a (discretized) multidimensional space—but that the space is homogenous. Where n is greater than 2, the space in which the mobiles move is composed of the product of $n-1$ different homogenous spaces. These might represent, say, space, time, fuel availability, attitude, and so on. For example, a domain might be described using the predicate *configuration*, so that *configuration*(x, y, z) should be interpreted to mean that the object x is at location y, with current fuel-level z. In this case we might expect that movement would change the location and fuel-level values simultaneously. It is a straightforward transformation to convert higher-arity predicates into binary predicates, so this generalization can easily be converted into a standard mobile form and we can assume that all predicates are unary or binary for the purposes of the rest of this discussion. The transformation can be carried out in different ways, but the most effective converts mobility in the form of this first generalization into simultaneous mobility on a collection of maps (one for each dimension as indicated above).

The second possible generalization allows multiple transitions starting and ending at the locatedness state. This case arises when there are multiple ways that objects can move. These might correspond to different modes of movement. This case complicates the structure of the maps on which mobiles move, since they can move in different ways across the same map. The inference of maps and the composition of maps that arise from different movement modes is discussed in Section 4.3.

A third generalization is that the property space might include more than one state, with transitions linking the locatedness state to alternative states. This situation is more complex because it implies that the mobile objects can leave their locations and enter some different state. There are various interpretations of this behavior. It might be that the mobiles can be temporarily suspended from movement in order to play a role in some task so that, on conclusion of the task, the suspended mobile can return to movement from the location at which it was suspended. We call such mobiles *hovering mobiles*, since the mobile can be seen as hovering above its location before returning to it. A different possibility is that the mobiles can leave their original location and then make various transitions before returning to the first network at a different location to the one from which they left. Objects that exhibit an additional movement behavior in one or more of the states that they pass through in these transitions are called *flying mobiles* to reflect the idea that they can move on different networks ("flight paths" and "roads") using actions appropriate to each separate network ("flying" and "driving") and moving between the networks ("taking off" and "landing"—these are transit links referred to earlier in Section 4.3). These cases can all be identified by TIM and handled appropriately.

A final generalization is that the locatedness state might be characterized by more than one property. In fact, this situation cannot arise in the property spaces constructed by TIM unless there is at least one additional state in the property space, so that this generalization can only occur in the context of the third generalization described above. The reason for this is that TIM always *splits* properties that are common to the left and right sides of a rule from the rest of the rule, creating separate rules for the individual properties that appear on both sides of the original rule. Therefore, the only way that two properties can both appear in a single state with a rule of the appropriate form for movement is if the properties are forced into the same property space because of a transition to another state by another rule. The division of rules that refer to the same property on the left and right sides causes TIM to identify this generalization as a version of mobility without difficulty. In fact, the Bulldozer domain exhibits this generalization for Jack—the locatedness state for Jack contains both at_1 and $mobile_1$, although the transition rule responsible for moving Jack between locations is simply $mobile_1 \Rightarrow at_1 \to at_1$, indicating that the property $mobile_1$ is not affected by movement (either crossing or driving).

To summarize: Generalizations of the arity of the locatedness predicate and of the number of properties representing locatedness can both be transformed into the standard mobility case, but the other cases (Generalizations 2 and 3 in Figure 13) cannot be eliminated. These two generalizations can, of course, also appear together so that a *flying* mobile has multiple movement modes. However, TIM can recognize and manage these generalizations—the first form as more complex map structures and the second as various forms of generalized mobile types.

A final situation that should be noted arises when what might be considered as mobility of objects is encoded using a finer-grained encoding than that considered here. For example, consider the operators in Figure 14. In this case, the mobile objects make transitions between locations via intermediate states (a plane will be *at* a location, then take off to be *en route* on a flight path, then fly to arrive at the end of the path, where it will be *circling*, and finally land to be *at* its destination). To the domain designer it might appear obvious that the *at* predicate encodes locatedness, but syntactically the three states of the aircraft are equivalent. Our analysis will not currently identify this situation

```
(:action TAKE-OFF                        (:action FLY
      :parameters (?P ?X ?F)                   :parameters (?P ?F ?Y)
      :precondition (and (pathFrom ?X ?F)       :precondition (and (pathTo ?F ?Y)
                    (at ?P ?X))                               (enroute ?P ?F))
      :effect (and (enroute ?P ?F)             :effect (and (circling ?P ?Y)
                   (not (at ?P ?X))))                        (not (enroute ?P ?F))))

                          (:action LAND
                                :parameters (?P ?Y)
                                :precondition (circling ?P ?Y)
                                :effect (and (at ?P ?Y)
                                             (not (circling ?P ?Y))))
```

Figure 14 Finer-grained encoding of movement.

as one encoding mobility. This observation raises an important point about generic types and behaviors: the use of terms such as "mobile" is, intentionally, strongly suggestive of an intuitive interpretation of the structures in a domain. However, it should not be interpreted as a suggestion that the analysis will recognize all behaviors that a domain engineer might interpret as examples of a particular generic behavior. Instead, the analysis identifies a precisely characterized set of behaviors. The precision of the characterization is the strength of the approach, since it offers a guarantee, during exploitation, that the behaviors being exploited are precisely those expected.

7 Architecture

The recognition of generic types and behaviors in a domain provides a way in which the performance of a planner can be improved, both in terms of the time it takes to solve problems in that domain, and the quality of the solutions found. The decomposition of a domain around its generic type structure enables the exploitation of specialized technology for solution of the subproblems that tend to be associated with the different generic types. We have observed that route-planning subproblems tend to arise when mobiles occur in a domain, including in cases where they co-occur with portables and other types in the transportation clusters. When driven mobiles arise, the problem of driver allocation complicates the route-planning problem. We have observed more general resource-allocation subproblems arising where types in the MPS cluster (see Section 5) can be detected. These problems, while interdependent with the planning context in which they arise, can be subjected to specialized treatment in a way that informs the search behavior of the planner.

As described in Section 1, we have developed a hybrid architecture based on the integration of planning with a selection of specialized techniques for addressing commonly occurring subproblems. This architecture, which comprises STAN5, uses TIM to identify the generic types associated with transportation (the mobile and mobile-related types) and with a range of other generic behaviors (Fox and Long 2001b; Long and Fox 2001; Long et al. 2000). Recognition of these types triggers the selection of appropriate subsolving technology from a library of tools that can be integrated with the domain-independent planning component of STAN5.

Figure 1, in Section 1, shows the integrated architecture of STAN5. The details of this integration, in terms of the relationships between the components of the architecture and the operation of the constraint layer, are described in depth in (Fox and Long 2001b). This chapter does not address these issues, focusing instead on the techniques TIM employs to discover the presence of subproblems in a planning domain.

The key component of the integration is the TIM system, which analyzes a domain description to determine what generic types and behaviors are present. Having identified the presence of one or more generic structures, appropriate subsolvers are identified for the corresponding subproblems. These are then integrated with a domain-independent planner through a uniform interface, called a *contraint agenda*, allowing constraints to be passed between the planner and the subsolvers, and between the subsolvers themselves. This interface allows the subsolvers to influence the development of a plan while themselves being constrained by planned commitments. The way this integration is achieved in STAN4 is discussed in (Fox and Long 2001a)—its extension to STAN5 is discussed in (Fox and Long 2001b). The development of the interface between subsolvers and the generic planning engine, and the way it supports communication between the components of the integrated system, is an important current focus of our work.

In addition to exploitation of specialized subsolvers, we have also identified specific heuristics that can be applied to particular generic types to improve planning efficiency. In Section 5 we mentioned the fact that when a domain contains only *simple portables* it is possible to prune parts of the search space that will necessarily lead to long plans. Because this pruning heuristic is not safe to use in all transportation domains, it has to be recruited for use explicitly, as a consequence of the appropriate structures having been identified in the domain. Another heuristic is to eliminate ground action instances that refer to unreachable map locations. It is possible to observe a commonality between such heuristics and control rules of the sort exploited by other researchers (Bacchus and Kabanza 2000; Kautz and Selman 1998; Kvarnstrom and Doherty 2000; Nau et al. 1999) and we are exploring the possibility of automatic instantiation of general rules using the inferred structure of generic-type clusters.

An interesting feature of STAN5 is its fail-safe behavior. If a domain features none of the known clusters, so that no specialized techniques can be recruited, the planner can be invoked to try generic search in the usual way. STAN5 is therefore not limited to solving problems in domains that fit the generic-type fingerprints we have so far defined. Where these can be recognized, STAN5 can benefit from the opportunity to exploit specialized approaches. In other cases, its performance is broadly comparable with that of other uninformed domain-independent strategies.

8 Results

In order to demonstrate the utility of our approach, we present data generated using two transportation domains featuring different transportation clusters. These domains are

1. *The Logistics benchmark domain.* This domain features a simple transportation cluster and can be handled using the STAN4 system (see below). We present a subset of the AIPS-2000 competition[4] data sets compiled by Fahiem Bacchus.

---

[4] The 2nd International Planning Competition held in Breckenridge, Colorado, during the 5th International Conference on AI Planning and Scheduling.

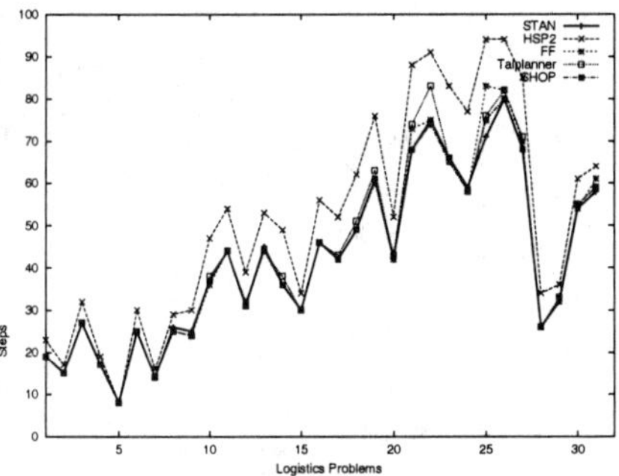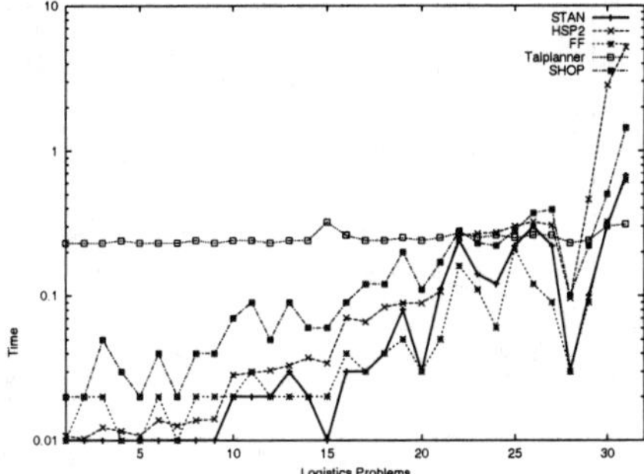

Figure 15   Quality of plans for, and time consumed to solve, Problems 0–30 in the first Logistics problem set. FF and STAN are fastest—TALplanner is slower than the fully automated planners on this problem set, and immune to variations in the problems. It overtakes the other planners at around Problem 30. Note that the thick line highlights STAN and that the graphs are log-scaled.

2. *The Bulldozer domain with multiple drivers.* The transportation cluster in this domain contains drivers and driven *commuting* mobiles. The use of this domain demonstrates the generality of the notion of mobility that TIM can identify, and that can be efficiently handled within STAN5, while completing the running example used in this chapter.

The data illustrates performance of STAN4 in the Logistics domain (because we present historical data, as mentioned above) and STAN5 in the Bulldozer domain. STAN4 (Fox and Long 2001a) is an early version of STAN5 able to cope with only the simplest transportation cluster containing mobiles, portables, and locations on simple maps containing no subparts or transit links. STAN5 extends STAN4 to handle more complex clusters. Nontrivial instances of the Bulldozer domain, which features an example of a more complex cluster, are beyond the capabilities of brute-force planning strategies. (We discuss this issue further in relation to Figure 17.) In the remainder of our experiments, we compare STAN5 with FF because FF is a planning system that is very similar to the general planning core of STAN5. The comparison therefore allows us to judge the extent to which the exploitation of the generic structure analysis presented in this chapter contributes to the power of the planner and the efficiency of the plans it generates. FF is one of the most successful of the current generation of domain-independent planners and, indeed, for the collection of bulldozer problems we consider, no Graphplan-based planning technology or SAT-planning-based technology is able to solve even the smallest of the problems.

The graphs in Figures 15 and 16 show how STAN4 performed in comparison with a diverse range of the best-performing planners in the AIPS-2000 competition, on problems from the Logistics data set. The planners used for comparison are FF (Hoffmann and Nebel 2000), HSP-2 (Bonet and Geffner 1997), TALplanner (Kvarnstrom and Doherty 2000), and SHOP (Nau et al. 1999). The Logistics domain was presented in two sets of problems. The problems increased in difficulty and the second set comprised larger (and hence harder) problems than the first.

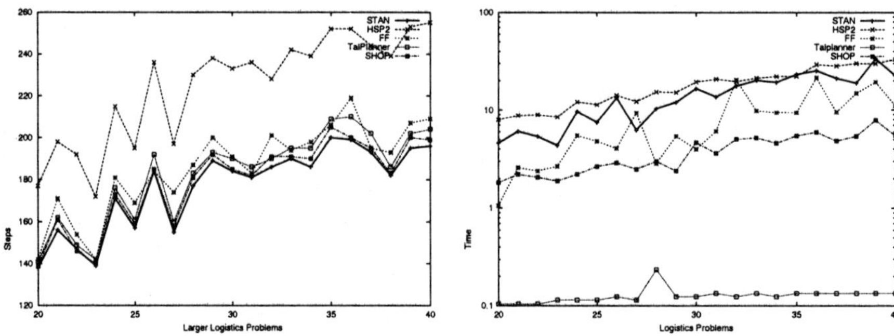

Figure 16 Quality of plans for, and time consumed to solve, Problems 20–40 in the second Logistics problem set. The data compares three fully automated planners, STAN4, HSP-2, and FF, with two hand-tailored planners. STAN4 is producing the best-quality plans because of its improved heuristic estimate.

The competition comprised a fully automated track and a hand-coded track in which planners were allowed to use hand-tailored domain knowledge. In the results presented here, STAN4, FF, and HSP-2 are all fully automated, while TALplanner and SHOP use hand-coded control knowledge. Despite the advantage of being supplied with hand-coded control knowledge, these planners did not consistently outperform the fully automated planners. For example, STAN4 and FF were both faster than TALplanner and SHOP on the first Logistics data set. More significantly, from the point of view of the exploitation of generic types, STAN4 produced the best-quality plans. The advantage STAN4 obtains in plan quality is particularly noticeable in the second Logistics data set (Figure 16), where plans are sufficiently complex for inefficiencies in the solution strategies to become clear. These results highlight the considerable benefits that can be gained by applying specialized technology to solving particular subproblems—including subproblems as apparently simple as the route planning in the Logistics domain—even compared with the exploitation of hand-coded control heuristics guiding general search procedures.

The second data collection (Figure 17) completes the running Bulldozer example, showing a data set for a randomly generated set of Bulldozer problems.[5] These problems include multiple bulldozers and drivers. One hundred problems were generated, with between 5 and 10 drivers, 10 to 40 bulldozers, and 10 to 50 locations. FF[6] failed to solve the 67 largest problems. On the 33 problems solved by both, the relative plan qualities are shown on the left in Figure 17, while on the right can be seen a plot showing how long it took each planner to produce plans of increasing length. As can be seen, STAN5 solved all the problems in the set in under 150 milliseconds, producing plans up to well over 1000 steps. IPP (Koehler et al. 1997), STAN in its Graphplan form, and Blackbox (version 3.9, using Chaff) (Kautz and Selman 1995) are all unable to solve even the smallest of these problems.

---

[5]Thanks to Jörg Hoffman for providing a generator for this collection.

[6]This data was generated using FF v1.0. We also tested version 2.2, which generally gives better quality plans (although still worse than STAN5 in all but one case), but solved only 17 problems, taking longer on each problem than version 1.0.

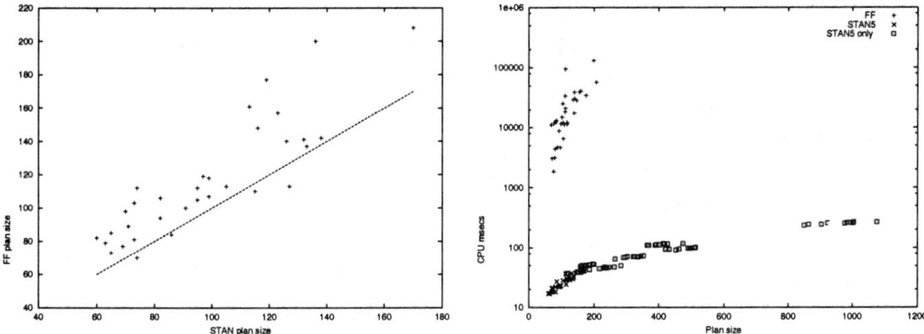

Figure 17 Relative plan quality and time performance of FF and STAN5 on Bulldozer problems. The line represents equal plan length in the first graph, with points above the line representing better STAN5 performance. On the right can be seen the time to produce plans comparing FF with STAN5 and also showing the problems that only STAN5 solved (marked by boxes).

The Bulldozer domain is interesting because, despite being a propositional domain with a simple structure, even moderately sized instances (5 drivers, 10 vehicles, and 20 to 30 locations) are beyond the scope of all other fully automated planning systems in the current literature. STAN5 can handle the domain because of its ability to decompose the route-planning components of the problem into a series of separate problems that can be solved without search. This decomposition is relatively simple in Bulldozer, because the route-planning aspects of the problem are not tightly integrated with its other features. STAN5 is capable of handling more sophisticated forms of integration as well, as discussed in (Fox and Long 2001b).

9   Conclusion

Planning domain descriptions represent the dynamics of specific problem domains in a way that facilitates the application of general problem-solving technology to the solution of problems in those domains. The advantage of exploiting general strategies is that they are reusable without extensive problem-solving effort on the part of the domain engineer. This has been an important argument in favor of knowledge-sparse, domain-independent planning since the inception of planning as a research field. However, because general problem-solving techniques are, by definition, uninformed about specific domain properties, they are impractical for solving all but the simplest planning instances. This clear disadvantage has led many researchers, motivated by application of planning to real problems, to adopt knowledge-rich approaches in which the domain description is engineered to constrain and direct the search behavior of the planner. This approach, while often effective in the domains to which they are tailored, places a heavy engineering burden on the domain designer and results in a planning system that cannot easily be generalized to apply to other domains.

The debate continues as to whether knowledge-sparse or knowledge-rich planning is the most fruitful direction for research in the planning field. A middle ground has been explored, with a number of researchers considering ways in which a knowledge-sparse planner can be informed by control rules, provided by a domain engineer, that can be used to prune undesirable regions from the search space. If the domain engineer fails to provide all relevant control rules, the planner can default to full search. One reason why this approach is interesting is that the control rules can, in principle, be generalized to apply to families of related domains, so there is scope for the reuse of the control knowledge invested in the modeling of a specific domain.

The idea of reuse is very powerful, with many implications for planning, because planning domains often share many structural features and subproblems. The work we have described in this chapter is motivated by the need to reuse specialized problem-solving technologies, where appropriate, rather than to tackle well-understood, often computationally hard, subproblems using brute-force search. An effective approach to reuse requires that the specific features of domains be abstracted so that common elements can be recognized and exploited. We have developed an abstraction process based on the notion of identifying, using automatic techniques, the occurrence of generic types, and behaviors in a domain description. When the generic structure of a domain is identified, appropriate specialized techniques can be recruited to assist a planner in the efficient solution of problems arising in that domain.

This chapter has focused on the description of how generic types and behaviors, and their associated subproblems, are identified in planning domains by the automatic techniques of the TIM system. We have given a brief description of the architecture of STAN5, an integrated system that exploits the results of the TIM analysis to configure a planner suited to tackling problems in a given domain. This architecture is described in detail in our papers (Fox and Long 2001a; Fox and Long 2001b). We have presented results to demonstrate the power of the integrated approach and have indicated the future directions of this research.

References

Bacchus, F., and F. Kabanza (1996). Using temporal logic to control search in a forward-chaining planner. In M. Ghallab and A. Milani (Eds.), *New Directions in Planning*. IOS Press.

Bacchus, F., and F. Kabanza (2000). Using temporal logic to express search control knowledge for planning. *Artificial Intelligence 116(1-2)*, 123–191.

Barret, A., D. Christianson, M. Friedman, K. Golden, J. Penberthy, Y. Sun, and D. Weld (1996). UCPOP v4.0 user's manual. Technical Report TR 93-09-06d, Dept. of Computer Science and Engineering, University of Washington, Seattle.

Bonet, B., and H. Geffner (1997). Planning as heuristic search: New results. In *Proceedings of Fourth European Conference on Planning (ECP)*, Springer-Verlag.

Bylander, T. (1992). Complexity results for serial decomposability. In *Proceedings of the 10th National Conference on AI*, Cambridge, MA: AAAI/MIT Press.

Clark, M. (2001). Construction domains: A generic type solved. In *Proceedings of the 20th U.K. Planning and Scheduling Workshop*, Edinburgh.

Currie, K., and A. Tate (1991). O-plan: The open planning architecture. *Artificial Intelligence 52(1)*, 49–86.

Fikes, R., and N. Nilsson (1971). STRIPS: A new approach to the application of theorem-proving to problem-solving. *Artificial Intelligence 2*(3), 189–208.

Fox, M., and D. Long (1998). The automatic inference of state invariants in TIM. *Journal of AI Research 9*, 367–421.

Fox, M., and D. Long (1999). The detection and exploitation of symmetry in planning problems. In *Proceedings of 16th Internation Joint Conference on AI*, San Francisco, pp. 956–961. Morgan Kaufmann Publishers.

Fox, M., and D. Long (2000). Utilizing automatically inferred invariants in graph construction and search. In *Proceedings of the Fifth Conference on Artificial Intelligence Planning Systems (AIPS)*, Breckenridge, CO. AAAI Press.

Fox, M., and D. Long (2001a). Hybrid STAN: Identifying and managing combinatorial sub-problems in planning. In *Proceedings of 17th International Joint Conference on AI*, San Francisco, pp. 445–452. Morgan Kaufmann Publishers.

Fox, M., and D. Long (2001b). Integrating a general planning strategy with sub-solvers for common problems. Technical report, University of Durham.

Gamma, E., R. Helm, R. Johnson, and J. Vlissides (1995). *Design Patterns: Elements of Reusable Software*. Boston: Addison Wesley.

Gerevini, A., and L. Schubert (1996a). Accelerating partial order planners: Some techniques for effective search control and pruning. *Journal of AI Research 5*, 95–137.

Gerevini, A., and L. Schubert (1996b). Computing parameter domains as an aid to planning. In *Proceedings of the Third Conference on AI Planning Systems*, pp. 94–101. AAAI Press.

Gerevini, A., and L. Schubert (1998). Inferring state constraints for domain-independent planning. In *Proceedings of the 16th National Conference on AI*, Cambridge, MA, pp. 905–912. AAAI/MIT Press.

Green, C. (1969). Theorem proving by resolution as a basis for question-answering systems. In B. Meltezer, D. Michie, and M. Swann (Eds.), *Machine Intelligence*, Volume 4. Edinburgh: Edinburgh University Press.

Hoffmann, J., and B. Nebel (2000). The FF planning system: Fast plan generation through heuristic search. *Journal of AI Research 14*, 253–302.

Jónsson, A., P. Morris, N. Muscettola, K. Rajan, and B. Smith (2000). Planning in interplanetary space: Theory and practice. In *Proceedings of the Fifth Conference on AI Planning Systems (AIPS)*, pp. 177–186. AAAI Press.

Kautz, H., and B. Selman (1995). Unifying SAT-based and graph-based planning. In *Proceedings of 14th Internation Joint Conference on AI*, San Francisco, pp. 318–325. Morgan Kaufmann Publishers.

Kautz, H. and B. Selman (1998). The role of domain-specific axioms in the planning as satisfiability framework. In *Proceedings of the Fourth Conference on AI Planning Systems*, Pittsburgh, PA, pp. 181–189. AAAI Press.

Kelleher, G., and A. Cohn (1992). Automatically synthesising domain constraints from operator descriptions. In *Proceedings of the 10th European Conference on AI*, pp. 653–655.

Koehler, J., B. Nebel, J. Hoffmann, and Y. Dimopoulos (1997). Extending planning graphs to an ADL subset. In *Proceedings of the Fourth European Conference on Planning*, Toulouse, pp. 273–285.

Kvarnstrom, J., and P. Doherty (2000). TALplanner: A temporal logic based forward chaining planner. *Annals of Mathematics and Artificial Intelligence 30(1-4)*, 119–169.

Long, D., and M. Fox (2000). Automatic synthesis and use of generic types in planning. In *Proceedings of the Fifth Conference on Artificial Intelligence Planning Systems (AIPS)*, Breckenridge, CO, pp. 196–205. AAAI Press.

Long, D., and M. Fox (2001). Multi-processor scheduling problems in planning. In *Proceedings of International Conference on AI (IC-AI)*, Las Vegas.

Long, D., M. Fox, L. Sebastia, and A. Coddington (2000). An examination of resources in planning. In *Proceedings of the 19th U.K. Planning and Scheduling Workshop*, Milton Keynes.

McCarthy, J. (1968). Programs with common sense. In M. Minsky (Ed.), *Semantic Information Processing*. Cambridge, MA: MIT Press.

McDermott, D. (1998). PDDL—the planning domain definition language. Technical report, Yale University. www.cs.yale.edu/users/mcdermott.html.

McDermott, D. (2000). The 1998 AI planning systems competition. *AI Magazine 21*(2), 35–56.

Morris, P., and R. Feldman (1989). Automatically derived heuristics for planning search. In *Proceedings of the Second Irish Conference on Artificial Intelligence and Cognitive Science*, School of Computer Applications, Dublin City University.

Muscettola, N. (1994). HSTS: Integrating planning and scheduling. In M. Zweben and M. Fox (Eds.), *Intelligent Scheduling*, pp. 169–212. San Mateo, CA: Morgan Kaufmann Publishers.

Nau, D., Y. Cao, A. Lotem, and H. Muñoz-Avila (1999). SHOP: Simple hierarchical ordered planner. In *Proceedings of the 16th International Joint Conference on AI*, San Francisco, pp. 968–975. Morgan Kaufmann Publishers.

Nau, D., S. Gupta, and W. Regli (1995). Artificial intelligence planning versus manufacturing-operation planning: a case study. In *Proceedings of the 14th International Joint Conference on AI*, San Francisco, pp. 1670–1676. Morgan Kaufmann Publishers.

Nebel, B., Y. Dimmopoulos, and J. Koehler (1997). Ignoring irrelevant facts and operators in plan generation. In *Proceedings of the Fourth European Conference on Planning*, Toulouse.

Newell, A., and H. Simon (1963). GPS, a program that simulates human thought. In E. Feigenbaum and J. Feldman (Eds.), *Computers and Thought*. New York: McGraw-Hill.

Pednault, E. (1989). ADL: Exploring the middle ground between STRIPS and the situation calculus. In *Proceedings of First International Conference on Principles of Knowledge Representation and Reasoning*, San Francisco, pp. 324–332. Morgan Kaufmann Publishers.

Wilkins, D., and M. desJardins (2000). A call for knowledge-based planning. In *Proceedings of the AI Planning and Scheduling (AIPS) Workshop on Analyzing and Exploiting Domain Knowledge for Efficient Planning*.

Bayesian Inference of Visual Motion Boundaries

David J. Fleet
Palo Alto Research Center
3333 Coyote Hill Road
Palo Alto, CA 94304
fleet@parc.com

Michael J. Black
Department of Computer Science
Brown University
Providence, RI
black@cs.brown.edu

Oscar Nestares
Instituto de Óptica (C.S.I.C.),
Serrano 121, 28006-Madrid, Spain
nestares@io.cfmac.csic.es

Abstract

This chapter addresses an open problem in visual motion analysis, the estimation of image motion in the vicinity of occlusion boundaries. With a Bayesian formulation, local image motion is explained in terms of multiple, competing, nonlinear models, including models for smooth (translational) motion and for motion boundaries. The generative model for motion boundaries explicitly encodes the orientation of the boundary, the velocities on either side, the motion of the occluding edge over time, and the appearance/disappearance of pixels at the boundary. We formulate the posterior probability distribution over the models and model parameters, conditioned on the image sequence. Approximate inference is achieved with a combination of tools: A Bayesian filter provides for online computation; factored sampling allows us to represent multimodal non-Gaussian distributions and to propagate beliefs with nonlinear dynamics from one time to the next; and mixture models are used to simplify the computation of joint prediction distributions in the Bayesian filter. To efficiently represent such a high-dimensional space, we also initialize samples using the responses of a low-level motion-discontinuity detector. The basic formulation and computational model provide a general probabilistic framework for motion estimation with multiple, nonlinear models.

1 Visual Motion Analysis

Motion is an intrinsic property of the world and an integral part of our visual experience. It provides a remarkably rich source of information that supports a wide variety of visual tasks. Examples include 3D model acquisition, event detection, object recognition, temporal prediction, and oculomotor control.

Visual motion has long been recognized as a key source of information for inferring the 3D structure of surfaces and the relative 3D motion between the observer and the scene (Gibson 1950; Longuet-Higgins and Prazdny 1980; Ullman 1979). In particular, the 2D patterns of image velocity that are produced by an observer moving through the world can be used to infer the observer's 3D movement (i.e., *egomotion*). Many animals are known to use visual motion to help control locomotion and their interaction with objects (Gibson 1950; Srinivasan et al. 2000; Sun and Frost 1998; Warren 1995).

It is also well known that visual motion provides information about the 3D structure of the observed scene, including the depth and orientation of surfaces. Given the 3D motion of the observer and the 2D image velocity at each pixel, one can infer a 3D depth map. In particular, it is straightforward to show that the 2D velocities caused by the translational component of an observer's 3D motion are inversely proportional to surface depth (Heeger and Jepson 1992; Longuet-Higgins and Prazdny 1980).

While much of the research on visual motion has focused on the estimation of 2D velocity and the inference of egomotion and 3D depth, it is also widely recognized that visual motion conveys information about object identity and behavior. Many objects exhibit characteristic patterns of motion. Examples include rigid and articulated motions, different types of biological motion, or trees blowing in the wind. From these different classes of motion we effortlessly detect and recognize objects, assess environmental conditions (e.g., wind, rain, and snow), and begin to infer and predict the object behavior. This facilitates a broad range of tasks such as the detection and avoidance of collisions, chasing (or fleeing) other animate objects, and the inference of the activities and intentions of other creatures.

Given the significance of visual motion, it is not surprising that it has become one of the most active areas of computer vision research. In just over two decades, the major foci of research on visual motion analysis include

- *Optical flow estimation.* This refers to the estimation of 2D image velocities from image sequences (Barron, Fleet, and Beauchemin 1994; Horn 1986; Otte and Nagel 1994). Although originally viewed as a precursor to the estimation of 3D scene properties, the techniques developed to estimate optical flow have also proven useful for other *registration* problems; examples are found in medical domains, in video compression, in forming image mosaics (panoramas), and in stop-frame animation.

- *Motion-based segmentation.* Although optical flow fields are clearly useful, they do not explicitly identify the coherently moving regions in an image. Nor do they separate foreground and background regions. For these tasks, layered motion models and the *expectation-maximization (EM)* algorithm have become popular (Jepson and Black 1993; Sawhney and Ayer 1996; Vasconcelos and Lippman 2001; Weiss and Adelson 1996), as have many other approaches, such as automated clustering based on spatial proximity and motion similarity.

- *Egomotion and structure-from-motion.* The estimation of self-motion and 3D depth from optical flow or tracked points over many frames has been one of the long-standing fundamental problems in visual motion analysis (Broida, Chandrashekhar, and Chellappa 1990; Heeger and Jepson 1992; Longuet-Higgins and Prazdny 1980; Tomasi and Kanade 1992). While typically limited to nearly stationary (rigid) environments, current methods for estimating egomotion can produce accurate results at close to video frame rates (Chiuso et al. 2000).

- *Visual tracking.* Improvements in flow estimation have enabled visual tracking of objects reliably over tens and often hundreds of frames. Often these methods are strongly model-based, requiring manual initialization and prior specification of image appearance and model dynamics (Irani, Rousso, and Peleg 1994; Shi and Tomasi 1994; Sidenbladh, Black, and Fleet 2000). One of the lessons learned from research on visual tracking is the importance of having suitable models of image appearance and temporal dynamics, whether learned prior to tracking (Black and Jepson 1998; Hager and Belhumeur 1998), or adaptively during tracking (Jepson, Fleet, and El-Maraghi 2001).

In this chapter, we focus on the problem of estimating 2D image velocity, especially in the neighborhoods of surface boundaries.

1.1 Optical Flow

The estimation of optical flow was first studied in detail over 20 years ago (Fennema and Thompson 1979; Horn and Schunk 1981). Since then, techniques for optical flow estimation have improved significantly. The use of benchmark data sets and publicly available code has helped to establish the quantitative accuracy of recent methods (Barron, Fleet, and Beauchemin 1994). Accordingly, it is now relatively well accepted that, for smooth textured surfaces, current methods provide accurate and relatively fast estimators for 2D image velocity.

Although many interesting variations exist, perhaps the simplest, most commonly used techniques are known as *area-based regression methods*. Broadly speaking, these techniques are derived from two main assumptions, namely, *brightness constancy* and *smoothness*. The brightness constancy assumption states that the light reflected from a surface toward the camera remains invariant through time. If we further assume that visible points at time $t - 1$ are also visible at time t, we can then express the image at time t as a deformation of the image at time $t - 1$:

$$I(\mathbf{x}, t) = I(\mathbf{x} + \mathbf{u}(\mathbf{x}), t - 1). \tag{1}$$

With (1), one can estimate the 2D optical flow, $\mathbf{u}(\mathbf{x}) = (u(\mathbf{x}), v(\mathbf{x}))^T$, at different spatial positions, $\mathbf{x} = ((x, y)^T$, by tracking points of constant brightness.

The second common assumption that underpins current methods is that the optical flow field is a smooth function of image position. This is often formulated by constraining the optical flow field $\mathbf{u}(\mathbf{x})$ to lie in a subspace spanned by a basis of smooth flow fields for a local neighborhood of image positions:

$$\mathbf{u}(\mathbf{x}; \mathbf{a}) = \sum_{j=1}^{n} a_j \, \mathbf{b}_j(\mathbf{x}) \tag{2}$$

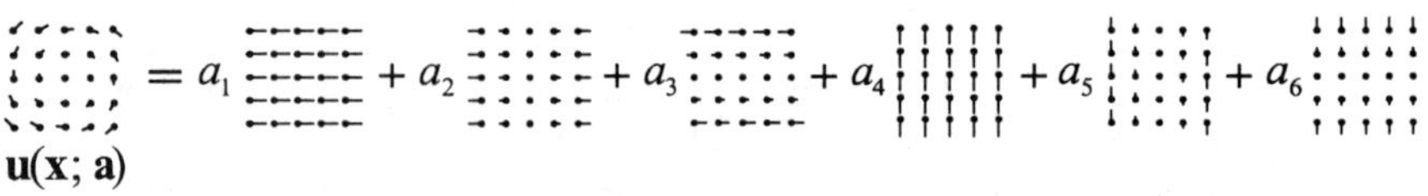

$$\mathbf{u}(\mathbf{x}; \mathbf{a}) = a_1 \, \cdots + a_2 \, \cdots + a_3 \, \cdots + a_4 \, \cdots + a_5 \, \cdots + a_6 \, \cdots$$

Figure 1 Affine flow fields can be expressed as a linear combination of the elements of a 6D basis set of flow fields, shown here for 5×5 local neighborhoods.

where $\{\mathbf{b}_j(\mathbf{x})\}_{j=1\ldots n}$ is the basis, and $\mathbf{a} = (a_1, \ldots, a_n)$ denotes the linear coefficients (Bergen et al. 1992; Fleet et al. 2000). For example, Figure 1 shows an affine basis that accounts for translation, scaling, rotation, and shear. Estimating the optical flow then amounts to estimating the coefficients $\mathbf{a}$ that produce the flow field that minimizes violations of brightness constancy (1) in the subspace spanned by $\{\mathbf{b}_j(\mathbf{x})\}_{j=1\ldots n}$. Alternatively, the smoothness constraint can be formulated as a regularization term that specifies how the motion at neighboring pixels may vary (Horn and Schunk 1981).

Several properties contribute to the effectiveness of such methods. First, the number of unknowns $\mathbf{a}$ is typically small compared to the number of pixels in the spatial neighborhood, each of which provides a brightness constancy constraint. Second, the solution can be found with straightforward numerical methods. If we linearize (1) and discard all but first-order terms, then we obtain a gradient constraint:

$$\nabla I(\mathbf{x}, t-1) \cdot \mathbf{u}(\mathbf{x}; \mathbf{a}) - \Delta I = 0 \tag{3}$$

where $\nabla I = (I_x, I_y)$ is the spatial image gradient, and $\Delta I = I(\mathbf{x}, t) - I(\mathbf{x}, t-1)$. Because (3) is linear in $\mathbf{u}(\mathbf{x}; \mathbf{a})$, and $\mathbf{u}(\mathbf{x}; \mathbf{a})$ is linear in $\mathbf{a}$, the collection of these constraints at each pixel in the spatial region yields a linear, least-squares system of equations.

1.2 Motion Boundaries

While current optical flow techniques produce reliable estimates for smooth textured surfaces, there are classes of motion for which they are not effective. There are many situations where brightness constancy does not hold and the motion is not smooth. Examples include motion discontinuities, the motion of bushes or trees in the wind, and the deformations and self-occlusions of clothing as people walk.

Optical flow at surface boundaries is often discontinuous because surfaces at different depths usually produce different image velocities. This violates the smoothness assumption. Furthermore, pixels that are visible at one time may not be visible at the next time as the foreground moves and thereby occludes a different portion of the background; this violates the brightness constancy assumption. As a consequence, most optical flow techniques produce poor estimates at occlusion boundaries.

Nevertheless, motion boundaries remain a rich source of scene information. First, they provide information about the position and orientation of surface boundaries. Second, analysis of the occlusion or disocclusion of pixels at motion boundaries can provide information about the relative depth ordering of the adjacent surfaces. In turn, information about surface boundaries and depth ordering may be useful for tasks as diverse as navigation, structure from motion, video compression, perceptual organization, and object recognition.

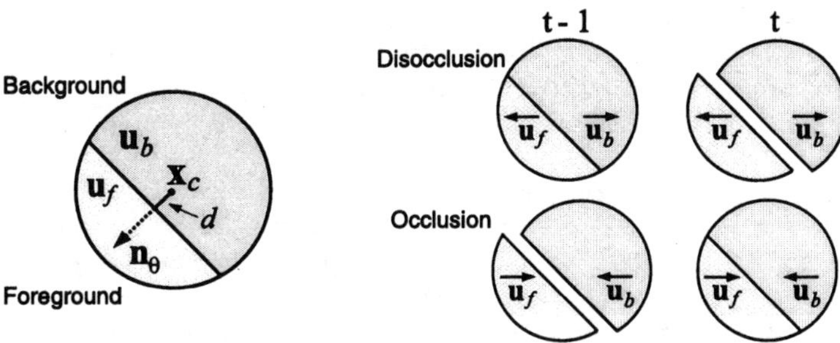

Figure 2 Our motion boundary model is parameterized by foreground and background velocities, $\mathbf{u}_f$ and $\mathbf{u}_b$, an orientation θ with normal $\mathbf{n}_\theta$, and a signed distance d from the neighborhood center $\mathbf{x}_c$. With this model, we can predict which pixels are visible between frames at times $t-1$ and t.

In this chapter we formulate a probabilistic, model-based approach to image motion analysis. The 2D motion in each local neighborhood of an image is estimated and represented using one of several possible models. This approach allows us to use different motion models that are suited to the diverse types of optical flow that occur with natural scenes. We consider two models, namely, *smooth motion* and *motion boundaries*. Regions of smooth motion may be modeled using conventional translational or affine models while the complex phenomena that occur at motion boundaries are accounted for by an explicit, nonlinear, boundary model.

The motion boundary model illustrated in Figure 2 encodes the boundary orientation, the image velocities of the pixels on each side of the boundary, the foreground/background assignment for the two sides, and the distance from the boundary to the region center. With this model, we can predict the visibility of occluded and disoccluded pixels so that these pixels may be excluded when estimating the probability of a particular motion. Moreover, the explicit offset parameter allows us to predict the location of the edge within the region of interest, and hence track its movement through the region. Tracking the motion of the edge allows foreground/background ambiguities to be resolved.

Generative models like this have not previously been used for detecting motion discontinuities due to the nonlinearity of the model and the consequent difficulty of estimating the model parameters. Furthermore, while the use of multiple models clearly complicates the resulting estimation problem, it provides us with a rich framework with which we can address the problem of model selection, to determine what type of motion model is most suited to the nature of the input, and to thereby estimate properties of the motion that provide useful information about the underlying 3D scene structure.

1.3 Previous Work on Motion Boundaries

The detection of motion boundaries has been a long-standing problem in optical flow estimation, primarily because most approaches to computing optical flow fail to be reliable in the vicinity of motion discontinuities (Barron, Fleet, and Beauchemin 1994; Fleet 1992; Otte and Nagel 1994). In addition, it has long been acknowledged that motion boundaries provide useful information about the position and orientation of surface boundaries.

Most previous methods cope with motion boundaries by treating them as a form of *noise*—that is, as the violation of a smoothness assumption. This occurs with regularization schemes where robust statistics, weak continuity, or line processes are used to locally disable smoothing across motion discontinuities (Cornelius and Kanade 1981; Harris et al. 1990; Heitz and Bouthemy 1993; Konrad and Dubois 1998; Murray and Buxton 1987; Nagel and Enkelmann 1986; Schunck 1989; Shulman and Hervé 1989; Thompson et al. 1985). Robust regression (Black and Anandan 1996; Sawhney and Ayer 1996) and mixture models (Jepson and Black 1993; Sawhney and Ayer 1996; Weiss and Adelson 1996) have been used to account for the multiple motions that occur at motion boundaries, but these methods fail to explicitly model the boundary and its spatiotemporal structure. They do not determine the boundary orientation, which pixels are occluded or disoccluded, or the depth ordering of the surfaces at the boundary.

Numerous methods have attempted to detect discontinuities in optical flow fields by analyzing local distributions of flow (Spoerri and Ullman 1987) or by performing edge detection on the flow field (Potter 1980; Schunck 1989; Thompson, Mutch, and Berzins 1985). It has often been noted that these methods are sensitive to the accuracy of the optical flow and that accurate optical flow is hard to estimate without prior knowledge of the occlusion boundaries. Other methods have focused on detecting occlusion from the structure of a correlation surface (Black and Anandan 1990), or of the spatiotemporal brightness pattern (Beauchemin and Barron 2000; Chou 1995; Fleet and Langley 1994; Niyogi 1995). Still others have used the presence of unmatched features to detect dynamic occlusions (Mutch and Thompson 1985; Thompson, Mutch, and Berzins 1985).

None of these methods explicitly capture the spatial structure of the image motion present in the immediate neighborhood of the boundary, and they have not proved sufficiently reliable in practice. One recent approach formulated an approximate model for motion boundaries using linear combinations of basis flow fields (Fleet et al. 2000). Estimating the image motion in this case reduces to a regression problem based on brightness constancy and parameterized models as in (2) and (3) above. Moreover, from the estimated linear coefficients, one can compute the orientation of the boundary and the velocities on either side, as shown Figure 5. While useful, the estimates of the motion and the boundary location produced by this approach are quite noisy. Moreover, they do not identify the foreground side, nor do they identify which image pixels are occluded or disoccluded between frames. Rather, pixels that are not visible in both frames are treated as noise. With the nonlinear model developed below, these pixels can be predicted and therefore taken into account in the likelihood computation (Belhumeur 1996).

Additionally, most of the methods above have no explicit temporal model. With our generative model (described below), we predict the motion of the occlusion boundary over time and hence integrate information over multiple frames. When the motion of the discontinuity is consistent with that of the foreground surface, we can explicitly determine the foreground/background relationships (local depth ordering) between the surfaces.

1.4 Bayesian Filtering and Approximate Inference

To cope with image noise, matching ambiguities, and model uncertainty, we adopt a Bayesian probabilistic framework that integrates information over time and represents multiple, competing model hypotheses. Our goal is to compute the posterior probability distribution over motion models and their parameters, conditioned on image measurements. The posterior is expressed in terms of a likelihood function and a prior (prediction) probability distribution. The likelihood is the probability of observing the current image given the correct model. The prior represents our belief about the motion at the current time based on previous observations. This *temporal* prior embodies our assumptions about the temporal dynamics of how the models and model parameters evolve over time.

Because we use multiple motion models, we need to cope with both discrete and continuous variables (i.e., a hybrid state space). The discrete state variable encodes the type of motion, smooth or discontinuous, and the continuous variables encode the corresponding motion parameters (we use two parameters for smooth motion, and six for the motion boundary model). As is well known, posterior distributions over hybrid state spaces, where continuous variables depend on discrete variables, are usually multimodal. To add further complexity, because our likelihood function and temporal dynamics are both nonlinear, we also expect the modes of the distribution to be non-Gaussian.

One form of approximate inference that has recently become very popular for such dynamical vision problems (e.g., motion and tracking) is the particle filter (Doucet, de Freitas, and Gordon 2001; Gordon, Salmond, and Smith 1993; Isard and Blake 1998a; Kitagawa 1987; Liu and Chen 1998; West 1992). Also known as *Condensation* and *Sequential Monte Carlo filtering,* the idea is to approximate the posterior with a weighted set of samples; particles (samples) are drawn randomly from a proposal distribution, often called a *temporal prior,* and then weighted by normalized likelihood values. With such *point-mass approximations* to probability distributions, particle filters are effective for nonlinear systems that produce non-Gaussian, multimodal distributions.

Additionally, we also want to estimate the motion in local image regions throughout the entire image. If we could assume that the motion in each region were independent of its neighbors, then we could estimate the motion in each separately. However, motion in one region is often a good predictor for motion of its neighbors, both at the current time and at successive times. Accordingly, the problem becomes Bayesian inference over a random field in which there is a relatively high-dimensional hybrid state space at each location in the field. The result, which is well known, is that computation of the exact posterior (i.e., Bayesian inference) is not tractable, requiring time-consuming approximate solutions. This is typical of many vision problems, and it leads us to search for methods that produce satisfactory approximations to the true posterior.

While the particle filter discussed above is suitable for hybrid state spaces with nonlinear dynamics and likelihood functions, it will not cope with a random field. As is well known, one problem with particle filters is the exponential increase in the required number of particles (i.e., computational cost) as a function of the dimensionality of the state space. Although effective for low-dimensional tracking, they do not scale well to high-dimensional problems (Choo and Fleet 2001; Deutscher, Blake, and Reid 2000; MacCormick and Isard 2000; Sminchisescu and Triggs 2001). This is particularly significant with random fields where the state dimension grows linearly with the number of random field locations and conventional iterative solutions (such as MCMC, see (Gilks, Richardson, and Spiegelhalter 1996)) can be prohibitively slow. The situation worsens when we consider an entire image sequence.

In this chapter, we explore two forms of approximate inference, drawing on research described in (Black and Fleet 2000; Nestares and Fleet 2001). In the first case, we approximate the posterior and the temporal dynamics by factoring each so that each local region of the image can be treated separately. This approach has problems since it prohibits us from encouraging boundary continuity and from allowing one region to predict when edges are going to move from one region to another.

The second model we describe combines Bayesian filtering with spatiotemporal predictions to detect and track motion boundaries. We continue to assume that the posterior can be approximated as the product of its marginal distributions for each region, but we introduce a dynamical model that explicitly represents interactions between neighboring regions. To do so we make use of several inference tools: in addition to approximating the joint posterior over multiple regions by its marginals (Murphy and Weiss 2001), we use Monte Carlo (sampled) approximations to these distributions to deal with nonlinear dynamics and non-Gaussian likelihoods, and we use mixture models to efficiently approximate the prediction distributions that arise from multiple neighborhoods.

While the method described here can be thought of simply as a motion boundary detector, the framework has wider application. The Bayesian formulation and computational model provide a general probabilistic framework for motion estimation with multiple, nonlinear models. This generalizes previous work on recovering optical flow using linear models (Bergen et al. 1992; Fleet et al. 2000). Moreover, the Bayesian formulation provides a principled way of choosing between multiple hypothesized models for explaining the image variation within a region. This work can also be viewed as an exploration of the suitability of different forms of approximate inference in the context of otherwise intractable inference problems in vision.

2 Generative Motion Models

Our Bayesian formulation rests on the specification of *generative* models for smooth motion and motion boundaries. These generative models define our probabilistic assumptions about the spatial structure of the motion within a region, how the parameters are expected to vary through time, and the probability distribution over the image measurements that one would expect to observe given the model.

Accordingly, we first describe our generative model for the motion in a single local image neighborhood. As suggested in Figure 2, we decompose an image into a grid of circular neighborhoods in which we estimate motion information. We assume that the motion in any region can be modeled by one of several motion models; here we consider only two models, namely, smooth (translational) motion and motion boundaries.

For the smooth-motion model, we express the optical flow within the circular region as image translation; more complex models can also be used. The translational model has two parameters, namely, the horizontal and vertical components of the velocity, denoted $\mathbf{u}_0 = (u_0, v_0)$. Exploiting the common assumption of brightness constancy, the generative model states that the image intensity, $I(\mathbf{x}', t)$, of a point $\mathbf{x}' = (x', y')$ at time t in a region R is equal to the intensity at some location $\mathbf{x}$ at time $t-1$ with the addition of noise ν_n :

$$I(\mathbf{x}', t) = I(\mathbf{x}, t-1) + \nu_n(\mathbf{x}, t), \tag{4}$$

where $\mathbf{x}' = \mathbf{x} + \mathbf{u}_0$. Here, we are assuming that the noise, $\nu_n(\mathbf{x}, t)$, is white and mean-zero Gaussian with a standard deviation of σ_n; that is, $\nu_n \sim \mathcal{N}(0, \sigma_n^2)$.

The motion boundary model is more complex and contains six parameters: the edge orientation, the velocities of the foreground ($\mathbf{u}_f$) and the background ($\mathbf{u}_b$), and the distance from the edge to the center of the region $\mathbf{x}_c$. In our parameterization, shown in Figure 2, the orientation, $\theta \in [-\pi, \pi)$, specifies the direction of a unit vector, $\mathbf{n} = (\cos(\theta), \sin(\theta))$, that is normal to the occluding edge. We represent the location of the edge by its signed perpendicular distance d from the center of the region (positive meaning in the direction of the normal). The edge is normal to $\mathbf{n}$ and passes through the point $\mathbf{x}_c + d\,\mathbf{n}$. Relative to the center of the region, we adopt a convention where the foreground side is that side to which the normal $\mathbf{n}$ points. Thus, a point $\mathbf{x}$ is on the foreground if $(\mathbf{x} - \mathbf{x}_c) \cdot \mathbf{n} > d$. Points on the background satisfy $(\mathbf{x} - \mathbf{x}_c) \cdot \mathbf{n} < d$.

At most motion boundaries, some pixels will be occluded or disoccluded. As a consequence, at boundaries one should not expect to find corresponding pixels in adjacent frames. Here, in order to resolve occlusions and disocclusions, we assume that the motion boundary edge moves with the same velocity as the pixels on the foreground side of the edge (i.e., the occluding side).[1] With this assumption, the occurrence of occlusion or disocclusion depends solely on the difference between the background and foreground velocities. Pixels become occluded from one frame to the next when the background moves faster than the foreground in the direction of the edge normal. More precisely, if $u_{fn} = \mathbf{u}_f \cdot \mathbf{n}$ and $u_{bn} = \mathbf{u}_b \cdot \mathbf{n}$ denote the two normal velocities, occlusion occurs when $u_{bn} - u_{fn} > 0$. Disocclusion occurs when $u_{bn} - u_{fn} < 0$. The width of the occluded/disoccluded region, measured normal to the occluding edge, is $|u_{bn} - u_{fn}|$.

With this model, parameterized by $(\theta, \mathbf{u}_f, \mathbf{u}_b, d)$, we can now specify how visible points move from one frame to the next. A pixel $\mathbf{x}$ at time $t - 1$, that remains visible at time t, moves to location $\mathbf{x}'$ at time t given by

$$
\mathbf{x}' = \begin{cases} \mathbf{x} + \mathbf{u}_f & \text{if } (\mathbf{x} - \mathbf{x}_c) \cdot \mathbf{n} > d \\ \mathbf{x} + \mathbf{u}_b & \text{if } (\mathbf{x} - \mathbf{x}_c) \cdot \mathbf{n} < d + w \end{cases} \tag{5}
$$

where $w = \max(u_{bn} - u_{fn}, 0)$ is the width of the occluded region. Finally, with $\mathbf{x}'$ defined by (5), along with the assumptions of brightness constancy and white Gaussian image noise, the image observations associated with a motion edge are also given by (4).

Referring to Figure 2(right), in the case of disocclusion, a circular neighborhood at time $t - 1$ maps to a pair of regions at time t, separated by the width of the disocclusion region $|u_{bn} - u_{fn}|$. Conversely, in the case of occlusion, a pair of neighborhoods at time $t - 1$, separated by $|u_{bn} - u_{fn}|$, map to a circular neighborhood at time t. Being able to look forward or backward in time in this way allows us to treat occlusion and disocclusion symmetrically.

So far we have focused on the spatial structure of the generative models. We must also specify the evolution of the model parameters through time since this will be necessary to disambiguate which side of the motion boundary is the foreground. From optical flow alone one cannot determine the motion of the occlusion boundary using only two frames. The boundary must be observed in at least two separate instances (e.g., using three

---

[1]Physical situations that violate this assumption include rotating objects, such as a baseball where the edge of the ball moves in one direction, but, due to the spin on the ball, the surface texture of the ball moves in another direction. Nevertheless, assuming that the edge moves with the foreground velocity, as we do in this chapter, allows one to handle most cases of interest.

consecutive frames) to discern its motion. The image pixels whose motion is consistent with that of the boundary are likely to belong to the occluding surface. Thus, to resolve the foreground/background ambiguity, we propose to accumulate evidence over time using Bayesian tracking.

Toward this end, we assume that the motion parameters of both motion models obey a first-order Markov process—that is, given the parameter values at the time $t-1$, the values at time t are conditionally independent of the values before time $t-1$. For the smooth-motion model we assume that, on average, the image translation remains constant from one time to the next. More precisely, we assume that the image translation at time t, $\mathbf{u}_{0,t}$, is given by

$$\mathbf{u}_{0,t} \;=\; \mathbf{u}_{0,t-1} + \nu_u \;, \qquad \nu_u \sim \mathcal{N}(0, \sigma_u^2 \mathbf{I}_2), \tag{6}$$

where $\mathbf{I}_2$ is the 2D identity matrix. Here, ν_u represents the modeling uncertainty (process noise) implicit in this simple first-order dynamical model.

For the motion boundary model, we assume that, on average, the velocities on either side of the boundary and the boundary orientation remain constant from one time to the next. Moreover, as discussed above, we assume that the expected location of the boundary translates with the foreground velocity. More formally, these assumed dynamics are then given by

$$\begin{aligned}
\mathbf{u}_{f,t} &= \mathbf{u}_{f,t-1} + \nu_{u,f} \;, & \nu_{u,f} &\sim \mathcal{N}(0, \sigma_u^2 \mathbf{I}_2) & (7) \\
\mathbf{u}_{b,t} &= \mathbf{u}_{b,t-1} + \nu_{u,b} \;, & \nu_{u,b} &\sim \mathcal{N}(0, \sigma_u^2 \mathbf{I}_2) & (8) \\
\theta_t &= [\theta_{t-1} + \nu_\theta] \bmod 2\pi \;, & \nu_\theta &\sim \mathcal{N}(0, \sigma_\theta^2) & (9) \\
d_t &= d_{t-1} + \mathbf{n}_{t-1} \cdot \mathbf{u}_{f,t-1} + \nu_d \;, & \nu_d &\sim \mathcal{N}(0, \sigma_d^2). & (10)
\end{aligned}$$

Here we use a wrapped-normal distribution over angles; therefore, orientation, θ_{t-1}, is propagated in time by adding Gaussian noise and then removing an integer multiple of 2π so that $\theta_t \in [-\pi, \pi)$. The location of the boundary moves with the velocity of the foreground, and therefore its expected location at time t is equal to that at time $t-1$ plus the component of the foreground velocity projected onto the direction of the boundary normal. As above, Gaussian noise is added to represent the modeling errors implicit in this simple dynamical model. Note that more sophisticated models of temporal dynamics (e.g., constant acceleration) could also be used.

3 Probabilistic Framework

Given the generative models described above, we are now ready to formulate our state description and the posterior probability distribution over the models and model parameters. Initially we will make the assumption that there are no probabilistic dependencies between each local image region and its neighboring regions. This allows us to consider each neighborhood independently of all other neighborhoods.

For each single neighborhood, let the *states* be denoted by $\mathbf{s} = (\mu, \mathbf{c})$, where μ is the model type (translation or motion boundary), and $\mathbf{c}$ is a parameter vector appropriate for the model type. For the translational model, the parameter vector is 2D, $\mathbf{c} = (\mathbf{u}_0)$. For the motion boundary model, it is 6D, $\mathbf{c} = (\theta, \mathbf{u}_f, \mathbf{u}_b, d)$. Our goal is to find the posterior probability distribution over states at time t given the image measurement history up to time t—that is, $p(\mathbf{s}_t \,|\, \vec{\mathbf{Z}}_t)$. Here, $\vec{\mathbf{Z}}_t = (\mathbf{z}_t, ..., \mathbf{z}_0)$ denotes the measurement history, where $\mathbf{z}_t$ simply denotes the image at time t, $\mathbf{z}_t \equiv I(\mathbf{x}, t)$.

From the Markov assumption in the generative models above, the conditional independence of the current state at time t and states before time $t - 1$ is written as

$$p(\mathbf{s}_t \,|\, \vec{\mathbf{S}}_{t-1}) \;=\; p(\mathbf{s}_t \,|\, \mathbf{s}_{t-1}),$$

where $\vec{\mathbf{S}}_t = (\mathbf{s}_t, ..., \mathbf{s}_0)$ denotes the state history. Similarly, the generative model assumes conditional independence of the observations and the dynamics—that is, given $\mathbf{s}_t$ and $\mathbf{z}_{t-1}$, the most recent image observation, $\mathbf{z}_t$, is independent of previous observations $\vec{\mathbf{Z}}_{t-2}$. With these assumptions, we can show that the posterior distribution $p(\mathbf{s}_t \,|\, \vec{\mathbf{Z}}_t)$ can be factored and reduced using Bayes' rule to obtain

$$p(\mathbf{s}_t \,|\, \vec{\mathbf{Z}}_t) \;=\; k\, p(\mathbf{z}_t \,|\, \mathbf{s}_t, \mathbf{z}_{t-1})\, p(\mathbf{s}_t \,|\, \vec{\mathbf{Z}}_{t-1}), \tag{11}$$

where k is a constant used to ensure that the distribution integrates to one. Here, $p(\mathbf{z}_t \,|\, \mathbf{s}_t, \mathbf{z}_{t-1})$ represents the likelihood of observing the current measurement given the current state, while $p(\mathbf{s}_t \,|\, \vec{\mathbf{Z}}_{t-1})$ is the prediction of the current state given all previous observations; it is referred to as a *temporal prior* or *prediction density*.

The specific form of the likelihood function $p(\mathbf{z}_t \,|\, \mathbf{s}_t, \mathbf{z}_{t-1})$ follows from the generative models. In particular, the state specifies the motion model and the mapping from visible pixels at time $t-1$ to those at time t. The observation equation, derived from the brightness constancy assumption (4), specifies that the intensity differences between corresponding pixels at times t and $t - 1$ should be white and Gaussian, with zero mean and standard deviation σ_n.

Using Bayes' rule and the conditional independence assumed above, it is straightforward to show that the temporal prior, also called the *prediction distribution,* can be written in terms of the posterior distribution at time $t-1$ and the temporal dynamics that propagate states from time $t - 1$ to time t. In particular,

$$p(\mathbf{s}_t \,|\, \vec{\mathbf{Z}}_{t-1}) \;=\; \int p(\mathbf{s}_t \,|\, \mathbf{s}_{t-1})\, p(\mathbf{s}_{t-1} \,|\, \vec{\mathbf{Z}}_{t-1})\, d\,\mathbf{s}_{t-1}, \tag{12}$$

where the conditional probability distribution $p(\mathbf{s}_t|\mathbf{s}_{t-1})$ embodies the temporal dynamics, and $p(\mathbf{s}_{t-1} \,|\, \vec{\mathbf{Z}}_{t-1})$ is the posterior distribution over the state space at time $t - 1$.

This completes our description of the state space, and the mathematical form of the posterior probability distribution over the possible interpretations of the motion within an image region.

4 Computational Model: Individual Neighborhood

We now describe the details of our computational embodiment of the probabilistic framework outlined above for a single neighborhood. First, we consider the representation of the posterior distribution and its propagation through time using a particle filter. We then address the computation of the likelihood function and discuss the nature of the prediction distribution that facilitates the state space search for the most probable models and model parameters.

4.1 Particle Filter

The first issue concerns the representation of the posterior distribution, $p(\mathbf{s}_t \,|\, \vec{\mathbf{Z}}_t)$. Because of the nonlinear nature of the motion boundary model, the existence of multiple models, and because we expect foreground/background and matching ambiguities, we should assume that $p(\mathbf{s}_t \,|\, \vec{\mathbf{Z}}_t)$ is non-Gaussian, and often multimodal. For this reason we approximate the posterior distribution nonparametrically, using factored sampling. We then use a particle filter to propagate the posterior through time (Gordon, Salmond, and Smith 1993; Isard and Blake 1998a; Liu and Chen 1998).

The posterior is approximated with a discrete, weighted set of N samples $\{(\mathbf{s}_t^{(i)}, w_t^{(i)})\}$ for $i = 1 \ldots N$. At each time step, fair samples are drawn from the prediction distribution. The likelihood function is then evaluated at each sample state. Finally, by normalizing the likelihood values so that they sum to one, we obtain the weights $w_t^{(i)}$:

$$w_t^{(i)} = \frac{p(\mathbf{z}_t \,|\, \mathbf{s}_t^{(i)}, \mathbf{z}_{t-1})}{\sum_{n=1}^{N} p(\mathbf{z}_t \,|\, \mathbf{s}_t^{(n)}, \mathbf{z}_{t-1})} \; .$$

These weights ensure that our sample set $\{(\mathbf{s}_t^{(i)}, w_t^{(i)})\}_{i=1,\ldots,N}$ contains properly weighted samples with respect to the desired posterior distribution $p(\mathbf{s}_t \,|\, \vec{\mathbf{Z}}_t)$ (Liu and Chen 1998). A sufficiently large number of independent samples then provides a reasonable approximation to the posterior.

4.2 Likelihood Function

We assume that the likelihood of observing the current image observations can be written as a product of two factors, namely, a motion likelihood that depends on the difference between frames at time t and $t - 1$, and an edge likelihood that depends solely on the band-pass properties of the image at time t:

$$p(\mathbf{z}_t \,|\, \mathbf{s}_t^{(i)}, \mathbf{z}_{t-1}) \;=\; p_m(\mathbf{z}_t \,|\, \mathbf{s}_t^{(i)}, \mathbf{z}_{t-1}) \, p_e(\{\psi_k, a_k\}_t \,|\, \mathbf{s}_t^{(i)}) \,. \tag{13}$$

These two likelihood factors are discussed in detail below.

4.2.1 Motion Likelihood

According to the generative model, the motion likelihood $p_m(\mathbf{z}_t \,|\, \mathbf{s}_t^{(i)}, \mathbf{z}_{t-1})$ is straightforward to compute. Given the state, $\mathbf{s}_t^{(i)}$, we can warp one image according to the motion and subtract it from the other. According to the generative model, these image differences at each visible pixel should be normally distributed and independent. The likelihood function, to within a constant κ, is therefore given by

$$p_m(\mathbf{z}_t \,|\, \mathbf{s}_t^{(i)}, \mathbf{z}_{t-1}) \;=\; \kappa \left(\exp\left[\frac{-1}{2\sigma_n^2} \sum_{\mathbf{x} \in \mathcal{R}} D(\mathbf{x}, t; \mathbf{s}_t^{(i)})^2 \right] \right)^{1/T} , \tag{14}$$

where $D(\mathbf{x}, t; \mathbf{s}_t^{(i)}) = I(\mathbf{x}', t) - I(\mathbf{x}, t-1)$, $T = |\mathcal{R}|$ is the number of pixels in the circular neighborhood, and $\mathbf{x}'$ denotes the warped image coordinates that depend on the motion encoded in $\mathbf{s}_t^{(i)}$. (The warping here is done simply with bilinear interpolation.)

Figure 3 An image is shown, with its dominant level phase contours at $\pm\pi/2$, from the output of filters tuned to vertical and horizontal orientations, and at two different scales.

We note that this likelihood function differs from the generative model in one important respect—that is, the introduction of the exponent $1/T$. This is computationally, rather than probabilistically, motivated. A large value of T has the effect of smoothing the posterior distribution, making the peaks broader. Within a sampling framework, this allows a more effective search of the parameter space, reducing the chances of missing a significant peak.

4.2.2 Edge Likelihood

Intensity edges in static images have many physical causes, including surface reflectance variations, lighting effects, and of course surface boundaries. As shown in Figure 3, not all image edges are motion boundaries. But because motion boundaries are generally caused by depth discontinuities, most motion boundaries do coincide with intensity edges. Edge information can therefore provide useful information about the position and orientation of motion boundaries. To take advantage of this, we combine the motion likelihood with the likelihood of observing an image edge, conditioned on the location and orientation of a motion boundary.

We chose the edge likelihood to be the observation density over the responses of an oriented band-pass filter tuned to the edge orientation. Filtering the image in this way removes all oriented image structure except that near the orientation of the edge in question. To do this efficiently for many edges, we first apply a steerable transform to the image (Simoncelli et al. 1992). From the steerable basis set, we can quickly compute responses of filters tuned to any orientation. Here, we use the (G_2, H_2) quadrature-pair filters defined in (Freeman and Adelson 1991). These are complex-valued filters, so we express their response at each (subsampled) spatial location in terms of amplitude and phase (Fleet and Jepson 1993). The edge likelihood is simply the observation density over phase and amplitude of the subsampled filters responses at points along the edge.

Modeling this observation density can, however, be difficult. The appearance of image edges at surface boundaries depends greatly on surface reflectance properties and on local surface illumination. Given the variability of natural surface textures, and the variability of local lighting, the local structure of images at surface boundaries differs greatly from image to image. Therefore, rather than attempting to design an edge likelihood that captures

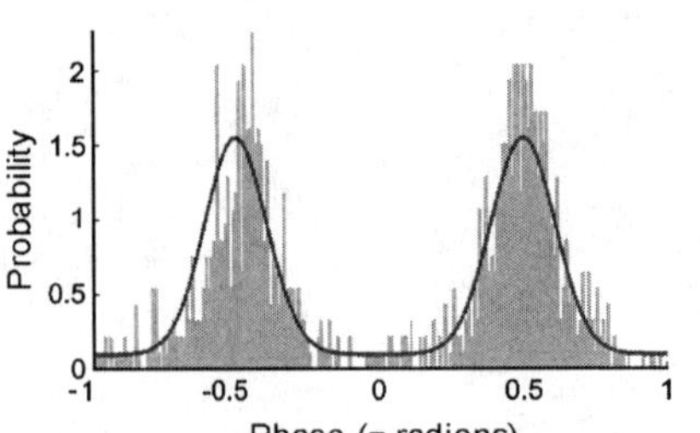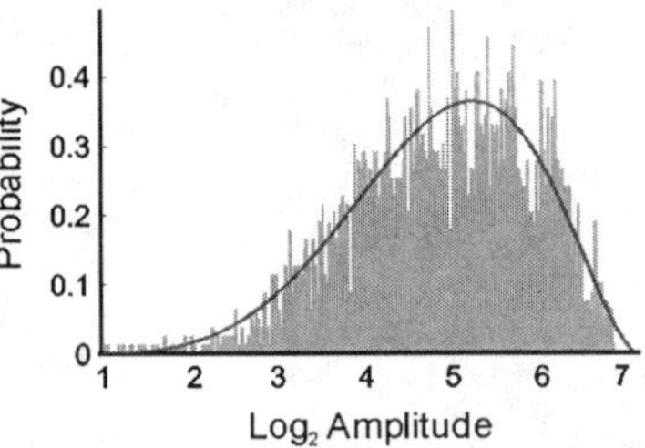

Figure 4 Histograms are shown of (left) phase conditioned on amplitude and the edge, $p_\phi(\phi \,|\, a, E)$, and of (right) log amplitude conditioned on the edge, $p_a(a \,|\, E)$.

the variability of edge appearance from first principles, we develop an empirical model for the observation density based on the statistics of natural images.

In short, we manually labeled 800 surface boundaries in 25 images. To each image we applied the steerable filters and extracted phase ϕ and log amplitude a of the responses along each edge at each scale. We sampled these responses with a sampling distance of one wavelength of the filters' tuning frequency. This sparse sampling reduces measurement correlations and allows us to make the simplifying assumption that the measurements at the different locations along the edge are conditionally independent.

The resulting ensemble of phase and amplitude measurements exhibits a striking regularity that suggests a factorization of the joint observation density:

$$p_e(\phi, a \,|\, \mathbf{s}) \;=\; p_\phi(\phi \,|\, a, \mathbf{s}) \; p_a(a \,|\, \mathbf{s}). \tag{15}$$

As shown in Figure 4(left), phase responses, ϕ, are typically close to $\pm\pi/2$, depending on the sign of the intensity gradient at the edge. These conditional phase distributions are very well described by a mixture of two Gaussian modes at $\pi/2$ and $-\pi/2$, and a uniform outlier density. A maximum likelihood fit of this model to the data with the EM algorithm is shown as the solid curve in Figure 4(left). Alternatively, collapsing the two modes by wrapping the phase about π yields the equivalent density for $\psi \equiv (\phi \bmod \pi)$:

$$p_\psi(\psi \,|\, a, \mathbf{s}) \;=\; m(a)\, G(\psi;\, \frac{\pi}{2}, \sigma^2) + (1 - m(a))p_0, \tag{16}$$

where $p_0 = 1/\pi$ is the phase outlier probability, and m is the Gaussian mixing probability.

With this mixture model (16), we find that the mixing probability m depends significantly on log amplitude. When amplitude is very small, phase is unreliable (Fleet and Jepson 1993), and when it is approximately 20% or more of its typical range in 8-bit images, then it is usually quite stable. The standard deviation of the Gaussian is also found to decrease slowly as a function of log amplitude. Using simple Bayesian model selection criteria (MacKay 1991), we find that a good model for the phase observation density is the mixture in (16) where the standard deviation of the Gaussian mode is held fixed at approximately $\pi/8$, and the mixing probability $m(a)$ is a linear function of log amplitude, given approximately by $m(a) = 0.1(1.5 + \log a)$ where $8 > \log a > 0$ on 8-bit images.

Amplitudes vary widely over the different edges that are encountered in natural scenes. In practice, we find that a simple Beta distribution fits the conditional distribution of amplitudes. An example of this is shown in Figure 4(right). The Beta distribution is natural in that it is defined on a finite interval, which is appropriate for images with a limited range of intensities, and it provides a reasonable approximation to the empirical distribution.

Our edge-based likelihood is given by the factorization in (15), along with the parametric models for the phase and amplitude densities. Given a set of K phase and amplitude measurements, conditioned on a motion boundary state, $\mathbf{s}_t^{(j)}$, the joint likelihood is

$$p_e(\{\psi_k, a_k\} \mid \mathbf{s}_t^{(j)}) = \left(\prod_k p_\psi(\psi_k \mid a_k, \mathbf{s}_t^{(j)}) \, p_a(a_k \mid \mathbf{s}_t^{(j)}) \right)^{1/2K}. \tag{17}$$

Finally, when the state is a smooth-motion model, the observation density for the phase is taken to be a uniform density.

4.3 Prediction Distribution

The prediction distribution serves to shepherd our samples to relevant portions of the parameter space. Because we are seeking solutions from a high-dimensional state space with continuous state variables, naive approaches for representing or searching it will be inefficient. Therefore, unlike a conventional particle filter for which the prediction is derived solely by propagating the posterior from the previous time instant, we also exploit an *initialization prior* that provides a form of bottom-up information to initialize new states. This is useful at time 0 when no posterior is available from the previous time instant. It is also useful to help avoid getting trapped at local maxima, thereby missing the occurrence of novel events that might not have been predicted from the posterior at the previous time. For example, it helps to detect sudden appearances of motion edges in regions where only translational state samples existed at the previous time instant. This is particularly important since information is not passed between adjacent regions in this formulation.

The actual prediction used here is a linear mixture of a temporal prior and an initialization prior. In the experiments that follow in Section 5, we use constant mixture proportions of 0.8 and 0.2 respectively—that is, 80% of the samples are drawn from the temporal prior. Importance sampling (Gordon, Salmond, and Smith 1993; Isard and Blake 1998b; Liu and Chen 1998) provides an alternative way of achieving similar results.

4.3.1 Temporal Prior

According to the temporal dynamics in generative model for the two motions, (6) through (10), our predictions about the current state, $\mathbf{s}_t$, given the previous state $\mathbf{s}_{t-1}$, are just Gaussian densities. For smooth motion, the temporal dynamics (6) yield

$$p(\mathbf{s}_t \mid \mathbf{s}_{t-1}) = \mathcal{N}(\Delta \mathbf{u}_0, \sigma_u^2), \tag{18}$$

where $\mathcal{N}(\Delta \mathbf{u}_0, \sigma_u^2)$ denotes a mean-zero Gaussian with covariance matrix $\sigma_u^2 \mathbf{I}_2$, evaluated at the temporal velocity difference $\Delta \mathbf{u}_0 = \mathbf{u}_{0,t} - \mathbf{u}_{0,t-1}$. Similarly, the generative model for the motion boundary ((7) – (10)) specifies that

$$p(\mathbf{s}_t \mid \mathbf{s}_{t-1}) = \mathcal{N}(\Delta \mathbf{u}_f, \sigma_u^2 \mathbf{I}) \, \mathcal{N}(\Delta \mathbf{u}_b, \sigma_u^2 \mathbf{I}) \, \mathcal{N}^w(\Delta \theta, \sigma_d^2) \, \mathcal{N}(\Delta d - \mathbf{n} \cdot \mathbf{u}_{f,t-1}, \sigma_\theta^2) \tag{19}$$

where $\mathcal{N}^w$ denotes a wrapped-normal (for circular distributions) and, as above, $\Delta\theta = \theta_t - \theta_{t-1}$ and $\Delta d = d_t - d_{t-1}$.

Because the posterior, $p(\mathbf{s}_{t-1}|\vec{\mathbf{Z}}_{t-1})$, at time $t-1$ is represented as a weighted sample set, and the dynamics in (18) and (19) are Gaussian, the temporal prior given by (12) can be viewed as a Gaussian mixture model (West 1992):

$$\sum_{j=1...N} w_{t-1}^{(j)}\, p(\mathbf{s}_t\,|\,\mathbf{s}_{t-1}^{(j)})\,. \tag{20}$$

To see this, note that the posterior is approximated by a weighted sum of delta functions (at the sample states). So (12) becomes a convolution of the Gaussian dynamics with the sum of delta functions. The result is a weighted sum of Gaussians, with one Gaussian for each sample $\mathbf{s}_{t-1}^{(j)}$ at time $t-1$. To draw a fair sample from a Gaussian mixture, one first draws a Gaussian component with probabilities equal to the weights. Then, one can draw a random sample from that Gaussian component. This amounts to first selecting a single state, $\mathbf{s}_{t-1}^{(j)}$, for propagation to time t, and then drawing a sample from the Gaussian dynamics, $p(\mathbf{s}_t|\mathbf{s}_{t-1}^{(j)})$. This is repeated for every sample drawn from the temporal prior. In practice, residual sampling and quasi–Monte Carlo sampling can be used to reduce random sampling variability (Liu and Chen 1998; Ormoneit, Lemieux, and Fleet 2001).

Thus far we have assumed that the motion class (i.e., smooth or boundary) remains constant as we propagate states from one time to the next. However, when a boundary passes through a region and out the other side, the motion type should switch from a motion boundary model to smooth motion. Accordingly, given a motion boundary state at time $t-1$, we let the probability of switching to a translational model at time t be given by the probability that the temporal dynamics will place the boundary outside the region of interest at time t. This can be computed as the integral of $p(\mathbf{s}_t|\mathbf{s}_{t-1})$ over boundary locations d that fall outside of the region. In practice, we accomplish this by sampling from the temporal prior as described above. Then, whenever we sample a motion boundary state $\mathbf{s}_t^{(j)}$ for which the edge is outside the circular neighborhood, we simply change model types, sampling instead from a translational model whose velocity is consistent with whatever side of the motion boundary would have remained in the region of interest.

4.3.2   Initialization Prior

Low-Level Motion Boundary Detection. To initialize new states and provide a distribution over their parameters from which to sample, we use the motion boundary detector in (Fleet et al. 2000). This approach uses a robust, gradient-based technique for estimating optical flow with a linear parameterized motion model. Motion edges are approximated with a linear basis (2), the coefficients of which are estimated using area-based regression. Fleet et al. then solve for the parameters of the motion edge that are most consistent (in a least-squares sense) with the linear coefficients.

Figure 5 shows the result of applying this method to two frames of an image sequence in which a camera moves to the right while viewing a Pepsi can sitting on a table. The resulting motions are all leftward as the camera moves to the right, with the can moving somewhat faster than the background. The method provides a mean velocity estimate at each pixel (i.e., the average of the velocities on each side of the motion edge). This is simply the translational velocity when no motion edge is present. A confidence measure,

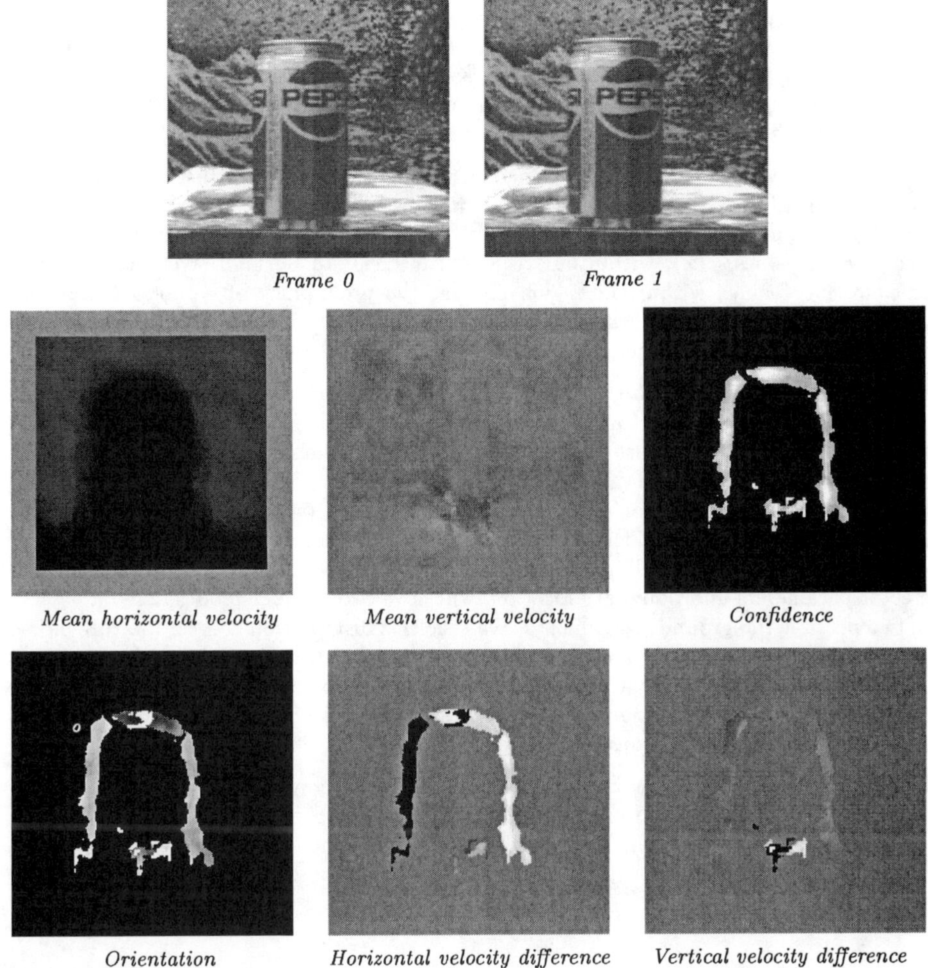

Figure 5 The top row shows two frames of the Pepsi sequence. The remaining two rows show responses from the low-level motion edge detector. The image velocities and velocity differences are nearly horizontal. In the orientation image, grey denotes vertical orientations, while white and dark grey denote near-horizontal orientations.

$c(\mathbf{x}) \in [0,1]$ is used in (Fleet et al. 2000) to detect the most likely edges (see Figure 5, "Confidence"). Figure 5(bottom) shows estimates for the edge orientation and for the horizontal and vertical velocity differences across the edge, at locations where $c(\mathbf{x}) > 0.5$.

While the method provides reasonable estimates of motion boundaries, it produces false positives and the parameter estimates are corrupted by noise. Localization of the boundary is particularly crude, and since the detector does not determine the foreground side, it does not predict the velocity of the occluding edge. Despite these weaknesses, it is a relatively straightforward, but sometimes error-prone, source of information about the presence of motion discontinuities. This information can be used to constrain the regions of the state space that we need to sample in the particle filter.

Formulating the Initialization Prior. When initializing a new state, we use the distribution of confidence values $c(\mathbf{x})$ within a region to first decide on the motion type (translation or motion boundary). If a motion boundary is present, then we expect some fraction of confidence values, $c(\mathbf{x})$, within our region of interest, to be high. We therefore rank the confidence values within the region and let the probability of a motion boundary state be the 95th percentile confidence value, denoted C_{95}. Accordingly, the probability of initializing a translation model is $1 - C_{95}$.

Given that we wish to initialize (sample) a motion boundary state, we assume that actual boundary locations are distributed according to the confidence values in the region— that is, the boundary is more likely to pass through pixel locations with large $c(\mathbf{x})$. Sampling from the confidence values gives potential boundary locations. Given a boundary position, the low-level detector parameters at that position provide estimates of the edge orientation and the image velocity on each side, but they do not specify which side is the foreground. Thus, the probability distribution over the state space, conditioned on the detector parameters and boundary location, will have two distinct modes, one for each of the two possible foreground assignments. We take this distribution to be a mixture of two Gaussians that are separable with covariance matrices $2.25\sigma_u^2 \mathbf{I}_2$ for the velocity axes, and variances $16\sigma_\theta^2$ for the orientation axis and $4\sigma_d^2$ for the position axis. The variances are larger than those used in the temporal dynamics described in Section 2 because we expect greater noise from these low-level estimates.

To produce a sample for the smooth (translation) model, we sample a spatial position according to the distribution of $1 - c(\mathbf{x})$. The distribution over translational velocities is then taken to be a Gaussian centered at the mean velocity estimate of the low-level detector at the sample position, with a covariance matrix of $2.25\sigma_u^2 \mathbf{I}_2$.

4.4 Algorithm Summary and Model Comparison

Initially, at time 0, a set of N samples is drawn from the initialization prior. Their likelihoods are then computed and normalized to give the weights $w_0^{(i)}$. At each subsequent time, as shown in Figure 6, the algorithm repeats the process of sampling from the combined prior, computing the likelihoods, and normalizing.

From the nonparametric, sampled approximation to the posterior distribution, $p(\mathbf{s}_t|\vec{\mathbf{Z}}_t)$, we can compute moments and marginalize over various parameters of interest. In particular,

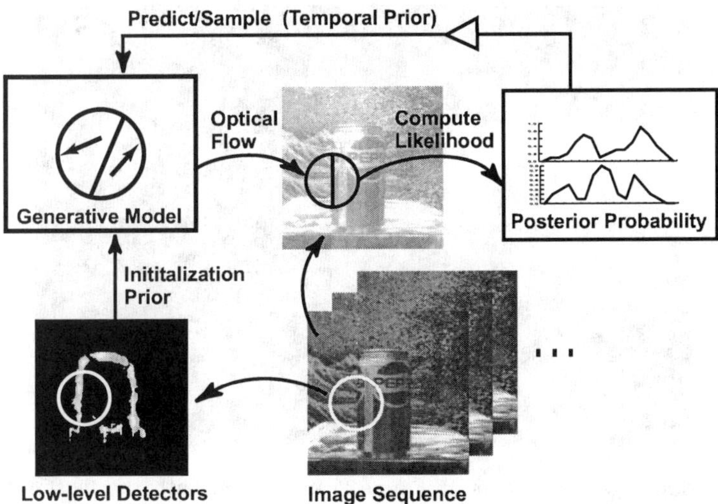

Figure 6 *Particle-filtering algorithm.* State samples are drawn from a mixture of the temporal prior and the initialization prior. The temporal prior combines information from the posterior probability distribution at the previous time instant with the temporal dynamics of the motion models. The initialization prior is derived from the responses of low-level motion boundary detectors within an image region. The parameters of a state determine the image motion within a neighborhood as specified by the generative models for each type of motion. These generative models assume brightness constancy and hence specify how to compute the likelihood of a particular state in terms of the pixel intensity differences between an image region at one time instant and a warped version of the image at the next time instant. Normalizing the likelihood values for N states gives an approximate, discretely sampled representation of the posterior probability distribution at the next time instant. In this way, the posterior distribution is predicted and updated over time, integrating new information within the Bayesian framework.

we can compute the expected value for some state parameter, $f(\mathbf{s}_t)$, as

$$E[f(\mathbf{s}_t) \,|\, \vec{\mathbf{Z}}_t] = \sum_{n=1\ldots N} f(\mathbf{s}_t^{(n)}) w_t^{(n)}.$$

However, in doing so, care needs to be taken because the posterior will often be multimodal, in which case the mean may not be a highly probable state. Thus, for model comparison and display purposes, we first isolate three distinct modes in the posterior: One mode is often associated with the best-fitting smooth-motion model. The other two modes are associated with the motion boundary model. These two boundary models typically differ in orientation by π, reflecting two opposite foreground assignments. For display purposes, a simple Bayesian model selection criterion is used to select the mode with the largest cumulative probability mass, and we display only the mean of that most likely mode.

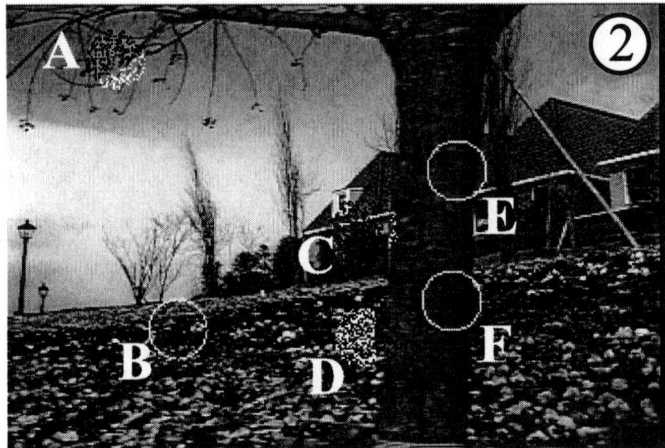

Figure 7 Flower garden results at Frame 2 are shown, with the most likely models overlaid on the image. Translational models are shown as empty circles (as in Region B). Motion boundaries are shown as filled disks (as in Region D). The white and black dots, respectively, lie on the foreground and background sides of the model. The position and orientation of the boundaries are depicted by the edges between the white and black sides.

5 Experimental Results: Individual Neighborhoods

We illustrate the method with experiments on 8-bit natural-image sequences. For these experiments, the standard deviation of the image noise was $\sigma_n = 7.0$. The standard deviations for the temporal dynamics were empirically determined and remained the same in all experiments. We used circular image regions with a 16-pixel radius and used 3500 state samples to represent the posterior probability distribution in each region. A few regions were chosen to illustrate the performance of the method and its failure modes.

As shown in Figure 7, in each of the selected regions we display the mean state of the most likely motion model. The smooth-motion (translation) models are shown as empty circles (e.g., Figure 7, Region B). For motion boundary models, we sample pixel locations from the generative model of the mean state; pixels that lie on the foreground are white, and background pixels are black. The position and orientation of the edge are depicted by the boundary between the white and black sides of the region. The occluded pixels are not color-coded (e.g., Figure 7, Region D).

5.1 Flower Garden Sequence

The flower garden image sequence (Figure 7) depicts a static scene while a camera translates to the right. Therefore the image velocities are leftward, with the tree moving quickly in front of a slowly moving background. The low-level detector responses for the initialization prior are shown in Figure 8. The detectors find the occluding and disoccluding sides of the tree and provide reasonable estimates of the edge orientation and the velocities on either side of the boundary. One can see from the confidence map in Figure 8, however, that the boundary localization is not precise.

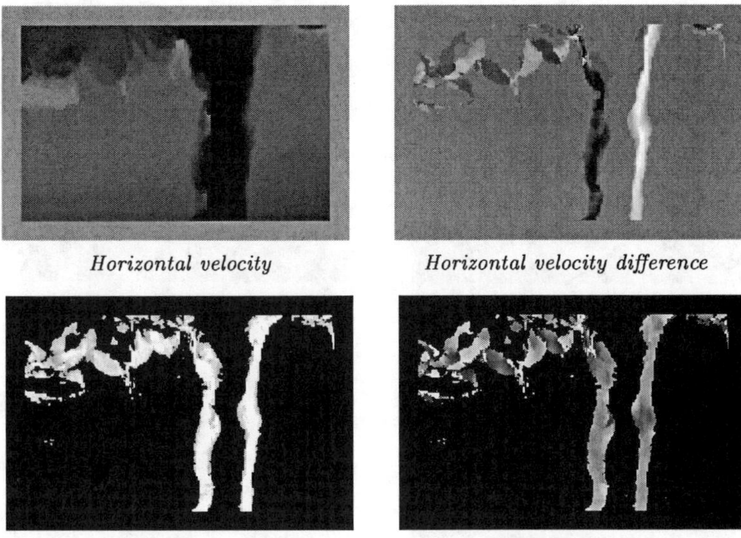

Figure 8 Typical low-level detector responses for the flower garden sequence are shown.

Results of the particle filter from Frames 2 through 7 are shown in Figure 9. Regions C, D, E, and F correctly model the tree boundary (both occlusion and disocclusion) and, after the first three frames, correctly assign the tree trunk as the foreground side. Initially, in Frame 2, Regions C and D detect a motion boundary, but Region D has incorrectly assigned the foreground to the flower garden rather than the tree. As discussed above, this is not surprising because we expect the correct foreground assignment to require more than two frames. By the third frame, the most likely mode of the posterior corresponds to the correct assignment of the foreground. Regions E and F are initially labeled with the smooth-motion model since the tree boundary is just touching the rightmost edge of the regions. These regions switch to boundary models in the next frame as the tree edge enters the regions. Motion boundary models then remain in all four regions along the tree-trunk boundary until the last frame, when the edge of the tree leaves the regions.

Beneath each of the images in Figure 9 are plots that show the marginal posterior distributions for the horizontal component of the foreground velocity for Region D. Initially, at Frame 2, there are two clear modes in the distribution. One mode corresponds to a fast speed, approximately equal to the image speed of the tree trunk, while the other mode corresponds to the slower speed of the flower garden. These two modes reflect the foreground ambiguity, where there is evidence for assigning the foreground to both sides. In Frame 2, it is the case that the probability of assigning the foreground to the flower garden is higher. However, with the accumulation of evidence through time, and because this foreground assignment is not consistent with the motion of the boundary, the probability of assigning the foreground to the flower garden decreases, while the probability of assigning the foreground to the tree trunk increases. In Frame 3, the probability of assigning the foreground to the tree trunk is slightly larger, and hence the foreground assignment in Region D switches between Frame 2 to Frame 3. As time continues, the

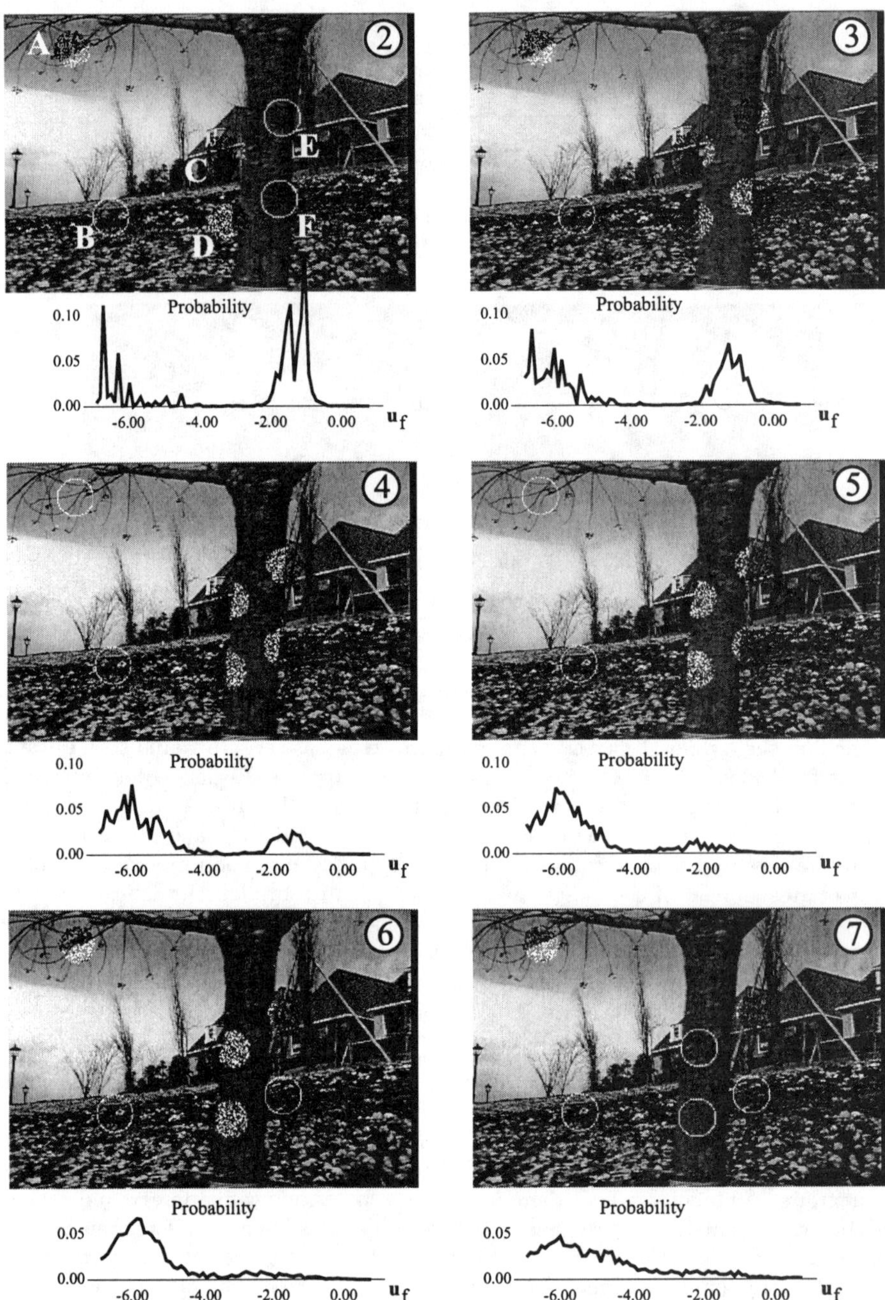

Figure 9 Flower garden Frames 2–7 are shown with the most probable motion models overlaid. Marginal distributions for the foreground velocity in Region D are also shown.

Figure 10   The most probable motion models in selected regions at Frames 1, 3, 5, 7, 9, and 10 of the Pepsi sequence are shown.

probability associated with this correct foreground assignment increases to become the dominant interpretation.

Region B corresponds to translation and is correctly modeled as such. While translation can be equally well accounted for by the motion boundary model, the low-level detectors do not respond in this region, and hence the distribution is initialized, with more samples corresponding to the translational model. Region A is more interesting; if the sky were completely uniform, this region would also be modeled as translation. Note, however, that there are significant low-level detector responses in this area (see Figure 8) due to the fact that the sky is not uniform. The probabilities of the translation and motion boundary models are roughly equal here, and the displayed model flips back and forth between them. For the motion boundary model, the orientation corresponds to the orientation of the tree branches in the region.

5.2   Pepsi Sequence

The Pepsi sequence, two frames of which are shown in Figure 3, depicts a translating camera that views a Pepsi can sitting on a table in front of a textured background. This is a relatively difficult sequence from which to detect motion boundaries, because the intensities of the foreground and the background are very similar, and because the can and the background are moving with similar speeds. The difference in the 2D-image speeds of the can and the background is less than one pixel per frame. Figure 10 shows the tracking behavior of the method. Figure 11 shows an enlarged, more detailed image of the

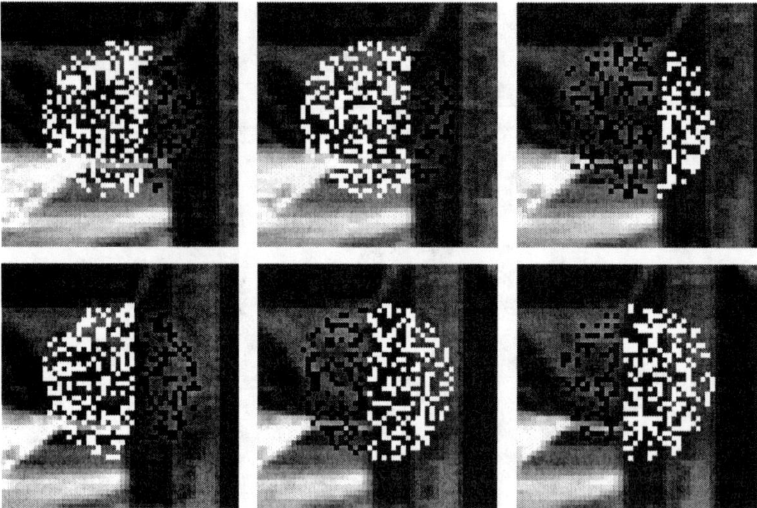

Figure 11 Enlargements of the neighborhood at the bottom left edge of the Pepsi can from the images in Figure 10.

bottom region on the left side of the can. Note that in most regions, the edge is tracked correctly and, in the detailed images, we see that the accuracy of the edge boundary location improves over time.

Note that, because the foreground and background velocities are very similar, the foreground/background ambiguity often remains for several frames. For example, consider the region that is enlarged in Figure 11. Here, in Frame 5 there is a switch from the incorrect foreground to the correct assignment and then back again in Frame 7. In this case, the posterior distribution has two modes of almost equal probability mass for these two interpretations. Finally, in Frame 9, the foreground assignment again switches to the correct interpretation. In general, propagation of information from neighboring regions would be needed to resolve such ambiguities.

Finally, it is important to note that the particle filter does not detect and track motion boundaries in all cases as desired. In the Pepsi sequence, the region at the top of those on the right side of the can is not tracking the boundary well. A motion boundary is detected in this region, but, in the first frame, the most likely mode does not place the edge in the correct location at the correct orientation. Over time the edge appears to move roughly with the can, but it never locks onto the can, nor is the foreground/background assignment correct. This behavior may be the result of low image contrast in this region and the similarity of the image velocities of the two surfaces.

6   Bayesian Filtering with Spatiotemporal Dynamics

Thus far we have only considered a Bayesian formulation for motion anaylsis in a single image region. By assuming that local regions are independent, we greatly simplified the mathematical development and the computational cost of the approach. However, by doing

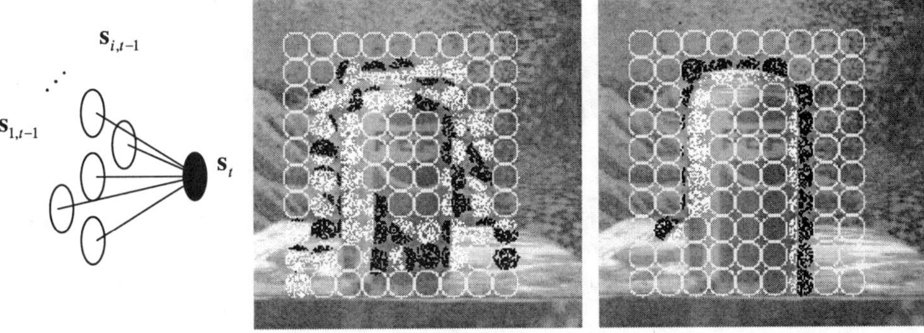

Figure 12   The assumed spatiotemporal dependency is shown on the left. The other two images show motion estimates at Frame 6 of the Pepsi sequence without (middle) and with (right) spatiotemporal dependencies.

so we also failed to exploit the information that one region could obtain from its neighbors; it is difficult to encourage boundary continuity and to make accurate predictions about boundary locations from one time to the next. For example, when we apply the algorithm described above to a dense array of small local regions with a separate Bayesian filter for each region, we typically find results very much like that shown in Figure 12(middle). By comparison, Figure 12(right) shows motion estimates produced when information is propagated between regions using the approach described below.

The main problem with introducing probabilistic dependencies between regions is that the estimation task then involves inference over the entire random field, the posterior and dynamics of which are no longer easily factored into products of the marginal distributions of individual regions. The research described in the remainder of this chapter is an attempt to consider a form of approximate inference that allows us to include some degree of spatiotemporal dependence. First, as illustrated in Figure 12(left), we assume a simple form of dependence where each region at time t, conditioned on nearby regions at time $t-1$, is independent of other regions at current and past times. In doing so, our goal is to pass information between regions from one time to the next, but not between adjacent regions at the same time. Second, we continue to approximate the joint posterior distribution over the motion in all image regions by the marginal distributions for each region. As shown in Figure 12, even with these crude approximations, the resulting inference often provides a vast improvement over the case in which regions are treated completely separately.

To accommodate spatiotemporal predictions, the main change required of the formulation in Section 3 concerns the prediction distribution in (12). Following the graphical model in Figure 12(left), let $\{\mathbf{s}_{i,t-1}\}_{i=1}^{M}$ denote the M neighbors at time $t-1$ that influence a specific region $\mathbf{s}_t$ at time t. We begin by writing the prediction distribution as a marginalization of the joint distribution for $\mathbf{s}_t$ and its neighbors $\{\mathbf{s}_{i,t-1}\}_{i=1}^{M}$:

$$p(\mathbf{s}_t \,|\, \vec{\mathbf{Z}}_{t-1}) \;=\; \int_{\{\mathbf{s}_{i,t-1}\}} p(\mathbf{s}_t, \{\mathbf{s}_{i,t-1}\}_{i=1}^{M} \,|\, \vec{\mathbf{Z}}_{t-1}) \;. \tag{21}$$

Factoring the integrand and exploiting assumed conditional independence yields

$$p(\mathbf{s}_t \mid \vec{\mathbf{Z}}_{t-1}) = \int_{\{\mathbf{s}_{i,t-1}\}} p(\mathbf{s}_t \mid \{\mathbf{s}_{i,t-1}\}) \, p(\{\mathbf{s}_{i,t-1}\} \mid \vec{\mathbf{Z}}_{t-1}) \,. \tag{22}$$

The dynamics, $p(\mathbf{s}_t \mid \{\mathbf{s}_{i,t-1}\})$, can be factored if we assume that the neighbors at time $t-1$ have uniform priors and are independent when conditioned on $\mathbf{s}_t$. The joint posterior over all neighbors cannot be factored in general. However, for computational efficiency, as above, we approximate the joint posterior as a product of its marginals (Murphy and Weiss 2001), to yield

$$p(\mathbf{s}_t \mid \vec{\mathbf{Z}}_{t-1}) \approx \kappa \prod_{i=1\ldots M} \int_{\mathbf{s}_{i,t-1}} p(\mathbf{s}_t \mid \mathbf{s}_{i,t-1}) \, p(\mathbf{s}_{i,t-1} \mid \vec{\mathbf{Z}}_{t-1}), \tag{23}$$

where κ is a constant to ensure that the distribution has unit probability mass. Note that this approximate prediction distribution is now the product of the predictions from each neighboring location, each of which has the form of (12).

6.1   Particles and Gaussian Mixtures

The simplified prediction distribution in (23) allows us to combine predictions from each of the neighbors at time $t-1$ in a straightforward manner. As with the particle filter above, we approximate each distribution $p(\mathbf{s}_{i,t-1} \mid \vec{\mathbf{Z}}_{t-1})$ with a weighted set of N samples $\{\mathbf{s}_{i,t-1}^{(j)}, w_{i,t-1}^{(j)}\}_{j=1}^{N}$. Accordingly, when this distribution is propagated through the dynamics, the approximate prediction distribution for $\mathbf{s}_t$, conditioned on the state of a single neighbor, $\mathbf{s}_{i,t-1}$, is just a mixture model:

$$\sum_{j=1\ldots N} w_{i,t-1}^{(j)} \, p(\mathbf{s}_t \mid \mathbf{s}_{i,t-1}^{(j)}) \,. \tag{24}$$

From this perspective, the multineighbor prediction distribution in (23) is just a product of mixture models. However, because we typically use thousands of particles (e.g., $N = 10^3$), and about $M = 5$ neighbors, the number of components in the product (i.e., N^M) quickly becomes unmanageable. We overcome this problem by fitting a mixture model to the individual prediction distributions prior to their multiplication in (23). We use mixture models with a small number of Gaussian components (often three to five) plus a uniform outlier process. As a result, the product in (23) reduces to fewer than 10^3 components. The mixture models are fit with a straightforward version of the EM algorithm (Dempster, Laird, and Rubin 1977).

Note that we first propagate individual samples from the neighboring posteriors at the previous time, and then we fit the mixture model. As with *assumed density filtering* and *unscented filtering*, this is done because it is relatively easy to propagate individual samples through nonlinear dynamics. The final prediction distribution in (23) is obtained by multiplying the individual mixture model predictions.

7 Computational Model: Spatiotemporal Predictions

Given weighted sample sets that approximate the posterior distribution in each local region at time $t - 1$, the steps toward the computation of the posterior distribution in a specific region at time t can be summarized as follows:

1. For each neighbor i at the previous time $t - 1$:
   - Draw N samples with replacement from the posterior at $t - 1$, $\{\mathbf{s}_{i,t-1}^{(j)}, w_{i,t-1}^{(j)}\}_{j=1}^{N}$.
   - Propagate the samples using the model dynamics (see Section 7.1), and then sample from the prediction density (24) to get a new sample set at time t.
   - Use EM to fit the robust mixture model to the new sample set.
2. Multiply the individual mixture models to form the joint prediction distribution (23).
3. Draw N samples with replacement from this prediction and compute their likelihoods.
4. Normalize the likelihoods to obtain the sample weights.

This yields a weighted sample set $\{\mathbf{s}_t^{(j)}, w_t^{(j)}\}$ that approximates the posterior for a region at time t, $p(\mathbf{s}_t \,|\, \vec{\mathbf{Z}}_t)$.

7.1 Temporal Dynamics

The final issue we must now consider is the form of temporal dynamics that is suitable for the spatiotemporal dependencies. Since the joint prediction in (23) is the product of the individual predictions, we need only specify the form of the dynamics between a state $\mathbf{s}_t$ and a single neighbor $\mathbf{s}_{i,t-1}$ at time $t - 1$. As this is somewhat more complicated than the case developed in Section 4, here we describe dynamics in more detail.

First, it is useful to expand the state $\mathbf{s}$ into its discrete and continuous components, μ and $\mathbf{c}$. This allows us to express the pairwise prediction distribution as

$$p(\mathbf{s}_t|\vec{\mathbf{Z}}_{t-1}) \;=\; \sum_{\mu_{t-1}} \int_{\mathbf{c}_{t-1}} [\, p(\mathbf{c}_t \,|\, \mu_t, \mu_{t-1}, \mathbf{c}_{t-1}) \, p(\mu_t \,|\, \mu_{t-1}, \mathbf{c}_{t-1}) \, p(\mu_{t-1}, \mathbf{c}_{t-1} \,|\, \vec{\mathbf{Z}}_{t-1}) \,], \quad (25)$$

where $p(\mu_t \,|\, \mu_{t-1}, \mathbf{c}_{t-1})$ and $p(\mathbf{c}_t \,|\, \mu_t, \mu_{t-1}, \mathbf{c}_{t-1})$ denote the discrete and continuous transition distributions. To avoid singularities (where probabilities go to zero) and to allow for modeling errors in the dynamics, we let both distributions be robust; that is, we define

$$p(\mu_t \,|\, \mu_{t-1}, \mathbf{c}_{t-1}) = \alpha \, p_\mu(\mu_t \,|\, \mu_{t-1}, \mathbf{c}_{t-1}) + (1-\alpha) \, p_{\mu,0}$$
$$p(\mathbf{c}_t \,|\, \mu_t, \mu_{t-1}, \mathbf{c}_{t-1}) = \beta \, p_\mathbf{c}(\mathbf{c}_t \,|\, \mu_t, \mu_{t-1}, \mathbf{c}_{t-1}) + (1-\beta) \, p_{\mathbf{c},0}$$

where $p_{\mu,0}$ and $p_{\mathbf{c},0}$ are uniform outlier distributions for discrete and continuous state variables, with mixing probabilities α and β. The inlier dynamics, $p_\mu(\mu_t \,|\, \mu_{t-1}, \mathbf{c}_{t-1})$ and $p_\mathbf{c}(\mathbf{c}_t \,|\, \mu_t, \mu_{t-1}, \mathbf{c}_{t-1})$, are summarized in Tables 1 and 2.

Referring to Table 1, where $\mu = 0$ denotes the smooth-motion model and $\mu = 1$ denotes the motion boundary model, we assume that smooth-motion states will encounter an edge and switch to a boundary model with probability $p_{0 \to 1}$. In the case of motion boundaries, as in Section 4, we assume dynamics such that edges move with the foreground velocity on average, and that there exists mean-zero Gaussian process noise in the velocities and the boundary orientation otherwise. Then, given a motion boundary state $\mathbf{s}_{i,t-1}$ in the

Neighbor \ Current	$\mu_t = 0$	$\mu_t = 1$
$\mu_{t-1} = 0$	$1 - p_{0 \to 1}$	$p_{0 \to 1}$
$\mu_{t-1} = 1$	$p_{1 \to 0}$	$1 - p_{1 \to 0}$

Table 1 Discrete transition probabilities $p_\mu(\mu_t | \mu_{t-1}, \mathbf{c}_{t-1})$ from a motion class at the neighbor (i.e., $\mathbf{s}_{i,t-1}$) to the motion class for $\mathbf{s}_t$, where $\mu = 0$ denotes the smooth-motion model and $\mu = 1$ denotes the motion boundary model.

region centered at $\mathbf{x}_{t-1}$, the distribution of motion boundary parameters at time t for the state $\mathbf{s}_t$ in a region centered at $\mathbf{x}_t$ is given by

$$f(\mathbf{c}_{e,t} | \mathbf{c}_{e,t-1}) = \mathcal{N}((\mathbf{u}_{f_{t-1}}, \mathbf{u}_{b_{t-1}}), \sigma_u^2 \mathbf{I}_4) \, \mathcal{N}^w(\theta_{t-1}, \sigma_\theta^2) \, \mathcal{N}(loc(\mathbf{c}_{e,t-1}), \sigma_d^2), \quad (26)$$

where $loc(\mathbf{c}_{e,t-1}) \equiv d_{t-1} + (\mathbf{u}_{f_{t-1}} + \mathbf{x}_{t-1} - \mathbf{x}_t) \cdot \hat{\mathbf{n}}_{t-1}$ is the mean-edge location at time t relative to the region center $\mathbf{x}_t$, and $\hat{\mathbf{n}}_{t-1} = (\sin(\theta_{t-1}), \cos(\theta_{t-1}))$. Given this distribution, we define the probability of changing from an edge state at $\mathbf{x}_{t-1}$ to a smooth-motion state at $\mathbf{x}_t$ as the probability of the edge not intersecting the region at $\mathbf{x}_t$ at time t: that is,

$$p_{1 \to 0} = \int_{|d_t| > R} \mathcal{N}_{d_t}(loc(\mathbf{c}_{e,t-1}), \sigma_d^2), \quad (27)$$

where $\mathcal{N}_{d_t}$ is the probability density for d_t and R is the region radius.

Table 2 defines the continuous prediction distributions conditioned on the discrete motion classes. For example, if the neighbor state at time $t - 1$ and the current state are both smooth motions, then the current velocity is normally distributed about the velocity of the previous state. If the previous state was a motion boundary and the current state is smooth, then the current velocity is normally distributed about the foreground or background velocity, depending on whether the current region is on the foreground or background side of the previous region. If the previous state was smooth and the current state is a boundary, then θ_t and d_t are uniformly distributed over values for which the edge does not intersect the previous region, and the velocity distributions depend on the previous velocity state. Finally, if previous and current states are motion boundaries, then the distribution over the current state is Gaussian, but only for parameters such that the edge intersects the current region.

This dynamical model is applied to individual particles. The nonlinear components of the dynamics include the model switching and the computation of the propagated edge distance, which depends on the normal to the edge direction $\hat{\mathbf{n}}_{t-1} = (\sin(\theta_{t-1}), \cos(\theta_{t-1}))$. Nonlinearities make it difficult to propagate distributions analytically, even if the neighbor posterior at the time $t - 1$ had been Gaussian.

8 Experimental Results: Spatiotemporal Predictions

We demonstrate some experimental results of this approach applied to the Pepsi sequence. We use small circular regions with radii of eight pixels, which overlap by two pixels. We use 5000 samples for particle approximations in each region. We draw 10% of the particles from the initialization prior, and the remaining 90% from the prediction density in (23). The parameters for the dynamics between a location at time t and a neighbor at time $t-1$

Neighbor \ Current	$\mu_t = 0$
$\mu_{t-1} = 0$	$p_{\mathbf{c}}(\mathbf{u}_t\|\mathbf{u}_{t-1}) = \mathcal{N}(\mathbf{u}_{t-1}, \sigma_u^2 \mathbf{I}_2)$
$\mu_{t-1} = 1$	if $\mathbf{x}_t$ is in neighbor's foreground $p_{\mathbf{c}}(\mathbf{u}_t\|\mathbf{c}_{e,t-1}) = \mathcal{N}(\mathbf{u}_{f_{t-1}}, \sigma_u^2 \mathbf{I}_2)$ else $p_{\mathbf{c}}(\mathbf{u}_t\|\mathbf{c}_{e,t-1}) = \mathcal{N}(\mathbf{u}_{b_{t-1}}, \sigma_u^2 \mathbf{I}_2)$

Neighbor \ Current	$\mu_t = 1$
$\mu_{t-1} = 0$	$p_{\mathbf{c}}(\mathbf{c}_{e,t}\|\mathbf{u}_{t-1}) = p(\theta_t, d_t)\, p(\mathbf{u}_{f_t}\|\mathbf{u}_{t-1})\, p(\mathbf{u}_{b_t}\|\mathbf{u}_{t-1})$ where $p(\theta_t, d_t) = \mathrm{Uniform}(\theta_t, d_t\|\text{edge outside neighbor})$ if $\mathbf{x}_{t-1}$ is in current foreground $\qquad p(\mathbf{u}_{f_t}\|\mathbf{u}_{i,t-1}) = \mathcal{N}(\mathbf{u}_{t-1}, \sigma_u^2 \mathbf{I}_2);$ $\qquad p(\mathbf{u}_{b_t}\|\mathbf{u}_{i,t-1}) = \mathcal{N}(\mathbf{0}, 50\mathbf{I}_2)$ (broad prior); else $\qquad p(\mathbf{u}_{f_t}\|\mathbf{u}_{i,t-1}) = \mathcal{N}(\mathbf{0}, 50\mathbf{I}_2)$ (broad prior); $\qquad p(\mathbf{u}_{b_t}\|\mathbf{u}_{i,t-1}) = \mathcal{N}(\mathbf{u}_{t-1}, \sigma_u^2 \mathbf{I}_2);$
$\mu_{t-1} = 1$	$p_{\mathbf{c}}(\mathbf{c}_{e,t}\|\mathbf{c}_{e,t-1}) = f(\mathbf{c}_{e,t}\|\mathbf{c}_{e,t-1})\,\mathbb{1}(\|d_t\| < R)\,/\,(1-p_{1\to0})$ where $\mathbb{1}(\|d_t\| < R) = 1$ when $\|d_t\| < R$, and 0 otherwise

Table 2 Model dynamics, $p_{\mathbf{c}}(\mathbf{c}_t \mid \mu_t, \mu_{t-1}, \mathbf{c}_{t-1})$, for the continuous parameters, conditioned on the discrete motion classes ($\mu = 0$ for smooth motion, and $\mu = 1$ for motion boundary). Here, $\mathbf{x}_t$ and $\mathbf{x}_{t-1}$ are the centers of the current and neighbor regions at times t and $t-1$. The variances, $\sigma_u^2, \sigma_\theta^2$, and σ_d^2, control the process noise in the dynamics; we let each of them increase as a function of the spatial distance between the region centers $\mathbf{x}_{t-1}$ and $\mathbf{x}_t$. We omitted the dependence on the neighbor (i) for notational simplicity.

depend on the spatial separation between the two locations. For the same spatial location at t and $t-1$, we use $\sigma_u = 0.75$ pixel/frame, $\sigma_\theta = 0.1$ radians, and $\sigma_d = 1$ pixel. For an adjacent region at $t-1$, we use $\sigma_u = 1.5$ pixels/frame, $\sigma_\theta = 0.2$ radians, and $\sigma_d = 1.5$. In both cases, $\alpha = 0.975$ and $\beta = 0.95$. Finally, the probability of a motion boundary, conditioned on the motion of a neighbor being smooth, is $p_{0\to1} = 0.4$; this value reflects the fact that edges occur in roughly 10% of the image regions and that such motion boundary predictions are relatively unconstrained, requiring a large number of samples to search the state space effectively.

Figure 13 shows results from Frames 2 through 10 of the Pepsi sequence. At Frame 1, the results look very much like those of the method above in which individual regions are treated separately (see Figure 12 [middle]). By Frame 2, the neighborhood interactions appear to introduce some coherence. By Frame 3, compared to the results obtained with individual regions, it is clear that the current method produces more coherent boundary estimates. Noteworthy in Figure 13 are the correct assignment of the foreground and the accurate localization of the motion boundaries. Also evident in Figure 13 is the importance of the neighborhood propagation that allows regions to anticipate the arrival of a boundary from a neighboring region. This is evident in Frames 7 to 9 on the left boundary and later

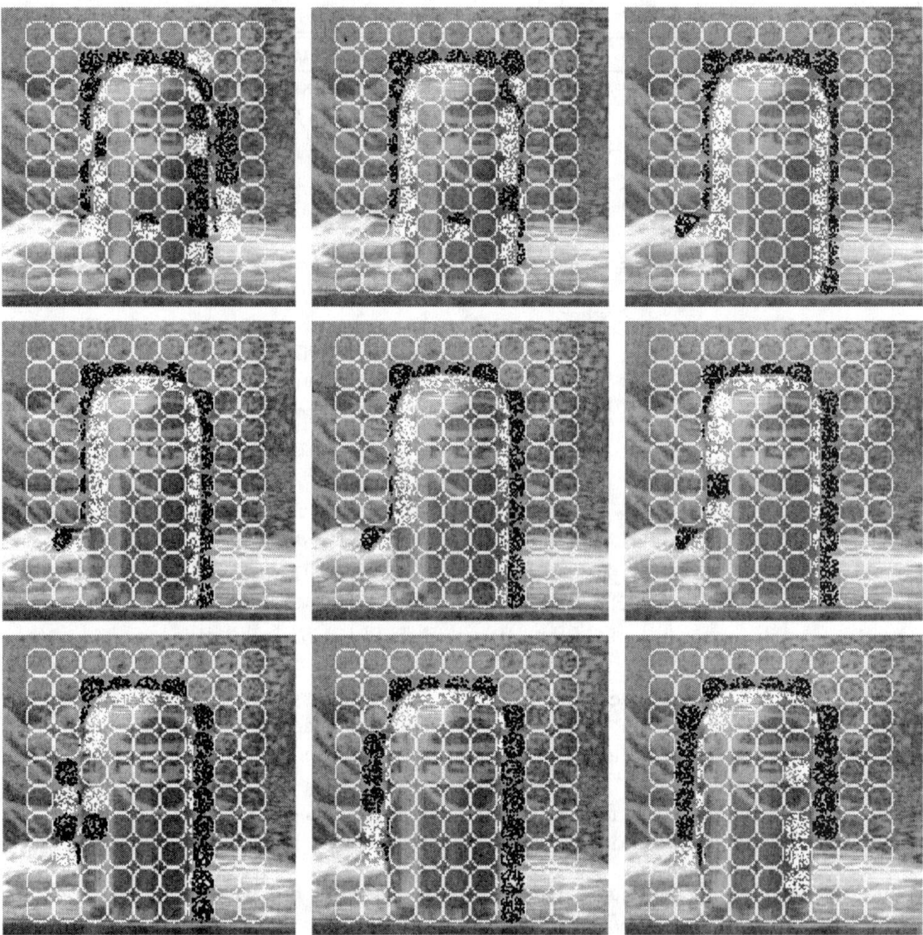

Figure 13 Pepsi results for Frames 2–10 (in lexicographic order and cropped slightly to improve the resolution of the display).

in Frames 9 to 10 on the right side. This propagation allows the correct assignment of the foreground to be inferred quickly.

9 Conclusion

Research on image motion estimation has typically exploited relatively weak models of the spatiotemporal structure of image motion. Our goal is to move toward a richer description of image motion using a vocabulary of motion primitives. Here we describe a step in that direction with the introduction of an explicit nonlinear model of motion boundaries and a Bayesian framework for representing a posterior probability distribution over models and model parameters. Unlike previous work that attempts to find a maximum-likelihood estimate of image motion, we represent the probability distribution over the parameter space using discrete samples. This facilitates the correct Bayesian propagation of information over time when ambiguities make the distribution non-Gaussian.

However, exact Bayesian inference for this problem, like many problems in vision, is not tractable. As a result, we explore different forms of approximate inference. Particle filters are effective for visual tracking, allowing for a Bayesian framework even with non-Gaussian distributions and nonlinear dynamics. Here we extend their use, in conjunction with other methods for approximate inference, to the detection and estimation of multiple motion models defined over a random field. In particular, we consider the detection and tracking of motion boundaries for which predictions of motion and of boundary locations/orientations are obtained from nearby image regions at the previous time. This helps to encourage boundary continuity and to direct samples to the appropriate regions of the state space as an edge leaves one region and enters another. It also improves the inference of surface depth ordering.

This work represents an early effort in what we hope will be a rich area of inquiry. In particular, we can now begin to think about the spatial interaction of these and other local-motion models. For example, we might formulate a more eleborate probabilistic spatial "grammar" of motion features and how they relate to their neighbors in space and time. This raises the questions of what is the right vocabulary for describing image motion and what role learning may play in formulating local models and in determining spatial interactions between them (Freeman and Pasztor 1999). In summary, the techniques described here (generative models, Bayesian propagation, and approximate inference with Monte Carlo methods) permit us to explore problems within motion estimation that were previously inaccessible.

Acknowledgments

We thank Allan Jepson for many discussions about motion discontinuities, generative models, sampling methods, probability theory, and, of course, GRITS. Also thanks to Ray Luo for helping to validate the edge likelihood model.

References

Barron, J. L., D. J. Fleet, and S. S. Beauchemin (1994). Performance of optical flow techniques. *International Journal of Computer Vision 12*(1), 43–77.

Beauchemin, S. S., and J. L. Barron (2000). The local frequency structure of 1d occluding image signals. *IEEE Trans. on Pattern Analysis and Machine Intelligence 22*(2), 200–206.

Belhumeur, P. (1996). A Bayesian-approach to binocular stereopsis. *International Journal of Computer Vision 19*(3), 237–260.

Bergen, J. R., P. Anandan, K. Hanna, and R. Hingorani (1992). Hierarchical model-based motion estimation. In *Proceedings of the European Conference on Computer Vision*, pp. 237–252. Springer-Verlag.

Black, M. J., and P. Anandan (1990). Constraints for the early detection of discontinuity from motion. In *Proceedings of the National Conference on Artificial Intelligence, AAAI-90*, Boston, pp. 1060–1066.

Black, M. J., and P. Anandan (1996). The robust estimation of multiple motions: Parametric and piecewise-smooth flow fields. *Computer Vision and Image Understanding 63*(1), 75–104.

Black, M. J., and D. J. Fleet (2000). Probabilistic detection and tracking of motion discontinuities. *International Journal of Computer Vision 38*(3), 229–243.

Black, M. J., and A. D. Jepson (1998). EigenTracking: Robust matching and tracking of articulated objects using a view-based representation. *International Journal of Computer Vision 26*(1), 63–84.

Broida, T. J., S. Chandrashekhar, and R. Chellappa (1990). Recursive 3-d motion estimation from a monocular image sequence. *IEEE Trans. Aerosp. Electron. Syst. 26*(4), 639–656.

Chiuso, A., P. Favarto, H. Jin, and S. Saotto (2000). 3D motion and structure from 2D motion causally integrated over time: Implementation. In D. Vernon (Ed.), *European Conference on Computer Vision*, Dublin, Part 2, pp. 734–750. Springer-Verlag.

Choo, K., and D. J. Fleet (2001). People tracking with hybrid Monte Carlo. In *Proceedings of the IEEE International Conference on Computer Vision*, Vancouver, Volume II, pp. 321–328.

Chou, G. T. (1995). A model of figure-ground segregation from kinetic occlusion. In *IEEE International Conference on Computer Vision*, Boston, pp. 1050–1057.

Cornelius, N., and T. Kanade (1981). Adapting optical flow to measure object motion in reflectance and X-ray image sequences. In *Proceedings of the ACM Workshop on Motion: Representation and Perception*, Toronto, pp. 50–58.

Dempster, A. P., N. M. Laird, and D. B. Rubin (1977). Maximum likelihood from incomplete data via the EM algorithm. *J. Royal Statistical Society B 39*, 1–38.

Deutscher, J., A. Blake, and I. Reid (2000). Articulated body motion capture by annealed particle filtering. In *Proceedings of the IEEE Conference on Computer Vision and Pattern Recognition*, Hilton Head, Volume II, pp. 126–133.

Doucet, A., N. de Freitas, and N. Gordon (2001). *Sequential Monte Carlo Methods in Practice*. Berlin: Springer-Verlag.

Fennema, C. L., and W. B. Thompson (1979). Velocity determination in scenes containing several moving objects. *Computer Vision, Graphics, and Image Processing 9*, 301–315.

Fleet, D. J. (1992). *Measurement of Image Velocity*. Boston: Kluwer.

Fleet, D. J., M. J. Black, Y. Yacoob, and A. D. Jepson (2000). Design and use of linear models for image motion analysis. *International Journal of Computer Vision 36*(3), 169–191.

Fleet, D. J., and A. D. Jepson (1993). Stability of phase information. *IEEE Trans. on Pattern Analysis and Machine Intelligence 15*, 1253–1268.

Fleet, D. J., and K. Langley (1994). Computational analysis of non-fourier motion. *Vision Research 22*, 3057–3079.

Freeman, W., and E. H. Adelson (1991). The design and use of steerable filters. *IEEE Trans. on Pattern Analysis and Machine Intelligence 13*, 891–906.

Freeman, W., and E. Pasztor (1999). Learning to estimate scenes from images. In *Adv. Neural Information Processing Systems*, Volume 11.

Gibson, J. (1950). *The Perception of the Visual World*. Boston: Houghton Mifflin.

Gilks, W. R., S. Richardson, and D. J. Spiegelhalter (1996). *Markov Chain Monte Carlo Methods in Practice*. London: Chapman & Hall.

Gordon, N. J., D. J. Salmond, and A. F. M. Smith (1993). Novel approach to nonlinear/non-Gaussian Bayesian state estimation. *IEEE Proceedings on Radar, Sonar and Navigation 140*(2), 107–113.

Hager, G. D., and P. N. Belhumeur (1998). Efficient region tracking with parametric models of geometry and illumination. *IEEE Trans. on Pattern Analysis and Machine Intelligence 27*(10), 1025–1039.

Harris, J. G., C. Koch, E. Staats, and J. Luo (1990). Analog hardware for detecting discontinuities in early vision. *International Journal of Computer Vision 4*(3), 211–223.

Heeger, D. J., and A. D. Jepson (1992). Subspace methods for recovering rigid motion I: Algorithms and implementation. *International Journal of Computer Vision 7*(2), 95–117.

Heitz, F., and P. Bouthemy (1993). Multimodal motion estimation of discontinuous optical flow using Markov random fields. *IEEE Trans. on Pattern Analysis and Machine Intelligence 15*(12), 1217–1232.

Horn, B. K. P. (1986). *Robot Vision.* Cambridge, Massachusetts: MIT Press.

Horn, B. K. P., and B. G. Schunk (1981). Determining optical flow. *Artificial Intelligence 17*, 185–203.

Irani, M., B. Rousso, and S. Peleg (1994). Computing occluding and transparent motions. *International Journal of Computer Vision 12*(1), 5–16.

Isard, M., and A. Blake (1998a). Condensation—conditional density propagation for visual tracking. *International Journal of Computer Vision 29*(1), 2–28.

Isard, M., and A. Blake (1998b). Icondensation: Unifying low-level and high-level tracking in a stochastic framework. In H. Burkhardt and B. Neumann (Eds.), *European Conference on Computer Vision, ECCV-98*, Freiburg, pp. 893–908. Springer-Verlag.

Jepson, A., and M. J. Black (1993). Mixture models for optical flow computation. In *Proceedings of the IEEE Conference on Computer Vision and Pattern Recognition*, New York, pp. 760–761.

Jepson, A. D., D. J. Fleet, and T. F. El-Maraghi (2001). Robust online appearance models for visual tracking. In *Proceedings of the IEEE Conference on Computer Vision and Pattern Recognition*, Kauai, Volume I, pp. 415–422.

Kitagawa, G. (1987). Non-gaussian state-space modelling of non-stationary time series. *Journal of the American Statistical Association 82*, 1032–1063.

Konrad, J., and E. Dubois (1998). Multigrid Bayesian estimation of image motion fields using stochastic relaxation. In *Proceedings of the IEEE International Conference on Computer Vision*, Tampa, FL, pp. 354–362.

Liu, J. S., and R. Chen (1998). Sequential Monte Carlo methods for dynamic systems. *Journal of the American Statistical Association 93*(443), 1032–1044.

Longuet-Higgins, H. C., and K. Prazdny (1980). The interpretation of a moving retinal image. *Proceedings of the Royal Society London B-208*, 385–397.

MacCormick, J., and M. Isard (2000). Partitioned sampling, articulated objects, and interface-quality hand tracking. In *Proceedings of the European Conference on Computer Vision*, Dublin, Volume II, pp. 134–149.

MacKay, D. J. C. (1991). Bayesian interpolation. *Neural Computation 4*, 415–447.

Murphy, K., and Y. Weiss (2001). The factored frontier algorithm for approximate inference in DBNs. In *Proceedings of the Uncertainty in Artificial Intelligence Conference*, Seattle, pp. 378–385.

Murray, D. W., and B. F. Buxton (1987). Scene segmentation from visual motion using global optimization. *IEEE Trans. on Pattern Analysis and Machine Intelligence 9*(2), 220–228.

Mutch, K., and W. Thompson (1985). Analysis of accretion and deletion at boundaries in dynamic scenes. *IEEE Trans. on Pattern Analysis and Machine Intelligence 7*(2), 133–138.

Nagel, H. H., and W. Enkelmann (1986). An investigation of smoothness constraints for the estimation of displacement vector fields from image sequences. *IEEE Trans. on Pattern Analysis and Machine Intelligence 8*(5), 565–593.

Nestares, O., and D. J. Fleet (2001). Probabilistic tracking of motion boundaries with spatiotemporal predictions. In *Proceedings of the IEEE Conference on Computer Vision and Pattern Recognition*, Kauai, Volume II, pp. 358–365.

Niyogi, S. A. (1995). Detecting kinetic occlusion. In *IEEE International Conference on Computer Vision*, Boston, pp. 1044–1049.

Ormoneit, D., C. Lemieux, and D. J. Fleet (2001). Lattice particle filters. In *Proceedings Uncertainty in Artificial Intelligence*, Seattle, pp. 395–402. San Francisco: Morgan Kaufmann Publishers.

Otte, M., and H. H. Nagel (1994). Optical flow estimation: Advances and comparisons. In J. Eklundh (Ed.), *European Conference on Computer Vision*, Stockholm, pp. 51–60. Springer-Verlag.

Potter, J. L. (1980). Scene segmentation using motion information. *IEEE Trans. on Systems, Man and Cybernetics 5*, 390–394.

Sawhney, H. S., and S. Ayer (1996). Compact representations of videos through dominant and multiple motion estimation. *IEEE Trans. on Pattern Analysis and Machine Intelligence 18*(8), 814–831.

Schunck, B. G. (1989). Image flow segmentation and estimation by constraint line clustering. *IEEE Trans. on Pattern Analysis and Machine Intelligence 11*(10), 1010–1027.

Shi, J., and C. Tomasi (1994). Good features to track. In *Proceedings of the IEEE Conference on Computer Vision and Pattern Recognition*, pp. 593–600.

Shulman, D., and J. Hervé (1989). Regularization of discontinuous flow fields. In *Proceedings of the IEEE Workshop on Visual Motion*, Irvine, CA, pp. 81–85.

Sidenbladh, H., M. J. Black, and D. J. Fleet (2000). Stochastic tracking of 3D human figures using 2d image motion. In *Proceedings of the European Conference on Computer Vision*, Dublin, Volume II, pp. 702–718. Springer-Verlag.

Simoncelli, E. P., W. T. Freeman, E. H. Adelson, and D. Heeger (1992). Shiftable multiscale transforms. *IEEE Trans. on Information Theory 38*(2), 587–607.

Sminchisescu, C., and B. Triggs (2001). Covariance scaled sampling for monocular 3d body tracking. In *Proceedings of the IEEE Conference on Computer Vision and Pattern Recognition*, Kauai, Volume I, pp. 447–454.

Spoerri, A., and S. Ullman (1987). The early detection of motion boundaries. In *IEEE International Conference on Computer Vision*, London, pp. 209–218.

Srinivasan, M., S. Zhang, M. Altwein, and J. Tautz (2000). Honeybee navigation: Nature and calibration of the odometer. *Science 287*(5454), 851–853.

Sun, H. J., and B. J. Frost (1998). Computation of different optical variables of looming objects in pigeon nucleus rotundus neurons. *Nature Neuroscience 1*, 296–303.

Thompson, W. B., K. M. Mutch, and V. A. Berzins (1985). Dynamic occlusion analysis in optical flow fields. *IEEE Trans. on Pattern Analysis and Machine Intelligence 7*, 374–383.

Tomasi, C., and T. Kanade (1992). Shape and motion from image streams under orthography: A factorization method. *International Journal of Computer Vision 9*(2), 137–154.

Ullman, S. (1979). The interpretation of structure from motion. *Proceedings of the Royal Society London B-203*, 405–426.

Vasconcelos, N., and A. Lippman (2001). Empirical Bayesian motion segmentation. *IEEE Trans. on Pattern Analysis and Machine Intelligence 23*(2), 217–221.

Warren, W. H. (1995). Self-motion: Visual perception and visual control. In *Handbook of Perception and Cognition*, Volume 5: *Perception of Space and Motion*. New York: Academic Press.

Weiss, Y., and E. H. Adelson (1996). A unified mixture framework for motion segmentation: Incorporating spatial coherence and estimating the number of models. In *Proceedings of the IEEE Conf. Computer Vision and Pattern Recognition*, San Francisco, pp. 321–326.

West, M. (1992). Mixture models, Monte Carlo, Bayesian updating and dynamic models. *Computer Science and Statistics 24*, 325–333.

Chapter 6

Knowledge Representation

Qualitative Spatiotemporal Representation and Reasoning: A Computational Perspective

Frank Wolter
Institut für Informatik
Universität Leipzig
Augustus-Platz 10-11, 04109 Leipzig,
Germany
wolter@informatik.uni-leipzig.de

Michael Zakharyaschev
Department of Computer Science
King's College
Strand, London WC2R 2LS,
United Kingdom
mz@dcs.kcl.ac.uk

> Although there has always been a temptation in KR to set the sights either too low (and provide only a data structuring facility with little or no inference) or too high (and provide a full theorem proving facility), this paper argues for the rich world of representation that lies between these two extremes.
>
> —Levesque and Brachman 1985—

1 Introduction

Time and space belong to those few fundamental concepts that have always puzzled scholars from almost all scientific disciplines, have given endless themes to science fiction writers, and are of vital concern to our everyday life and commonsense reasoning. So whatever approach to AI one takes (Russell and Norvig 1995), temporal and spatial representation and reasoning will always be among its most important ingredients (Hayes 1985).

Knowledge representation (KR) has been quite successful in dealing separately with both time and space. The spectrum of formalisms in use ranges from temporal and spatial databases, in which data is indexed by temporal and/or spatial parameters (see e.g., (Srefik 1995; Worboys 1995)), to numerical methods developed in computational geometry (Preparata and Shamos 1985) and various qualitative logical theories (Casati and Varzi 1999; Cohn and Hazarika 2001; Stock 1997). However, despite the modern view of space and time as *space-time* (not only in physics, but in AI as well[1]), apart from approaches based on classical quantitative models of kinematics (see e.g., (Hays 1989; Rajagopalan and Kuipers 1994)), surprisingly little has been done to design *qualitative* spatiotemporal representation formalisms (Galton 2000; Hornsby and Egenhofer 2000; Muller 1998; Vieu 1991; Wolter and Zakharyaschev 2000b), let alone implementations.

Although a deep ontological analysis of qualitative spatiotemporal entities seems still to be missing (Vieu 1997), there is a quite simple "naïve" approach to constructing such formalisms. Just take your favorite temporal logic T and your favorite spatial logic S, and merge them into a single spatiotemporal hybrid, allowing the desirable amount of interaction between space and time. The construction can be driven either by syntactical or by semantical considerations. In the former case, one joins the axioms of T and S together with some interacting principles (Muller 1998). The next step would be to supply the resulting system with an intended interpretation—to demonstrate which aspects of our intuitive views on space are captured by the theory—and show that they match (i.e., prove soundness and completeness). The example of the *region connection calculus (RCC)* (Randell, Cui, and Cohn 1992), as well as general results on multidimensional logics (Gabbay et al. 2002) shows, however, that this can be a hard mathematical problem (Gotts 1996a; Stell 2000).

By taking the semantic way—which will be done in this chapter—we first integrate the intended models of T and S into a multidimensional spatiotemporal structure (as seen in Figure 1), and then combine their languages into a "superlanguage" that is capable of speaking about these structures (Wolter and Zakharyaschev 2000b). It may be very difficult (if at all possible) to write down axioms for such a system, but for most KR purposes this should not be an obstacle, provided that the interpretation is transparent and convincing, and the system can be supplied with a reasoning procedure.

Our intended models of space are a variant of *mereotopological models*: the primitive entities—*regions*—are interpreted as regular closed sets of topological spaces (Gotts 1996b; Grzegorczyk 1960), so that any two regions can stand in precisely one of the eight relations depicted in Figure 2 (Egenhofer and Franzosa 1991; Randell, Cui, and Cohn 1992). As concerns time, we consider three fundamental paradigms: linear point-based time (discrete, dense, etc.), branching point-based time, and linear interval-based time (Allen 1983; Gabbay, Hodkinson, and Reynolds 1994; Gabbay, Reynolds, and Finger 2000; van Benthem 1996). The spatial dimension (topological space) is supposed to be always the same; however, regions can change their positions with time passing by (see Figure 1). Thus, our spatiotemporal interpretations can be regarded as the Cartesian products of spatial and temporal structures.

Having fixed the intended spatiotemporal structures, we still have a rich choice of spatial and temporal languages in which we can speak about these structures, and a variety of ways to combine the languages. Here we come to the main issue of this chapter: to investigate computational properties of spatiotemporal logics. Our concern is to find out

---

[1] "Events happen in time, but also in space—they have a where as well as a when. They are four-dimensional spatiotemporal entities" (Hayes 1985). "The spatial data models currently used as the foundation for geographical information systems (GISs) fall short of conveying the rich and complex ways in which phenomena change over space and time. One of the major limitations of today's systems, for example, is that they capture only a *snapshot* of reality, reliant as they are on databases that contain only current data" (Hornsby and Egenhofer 2000).

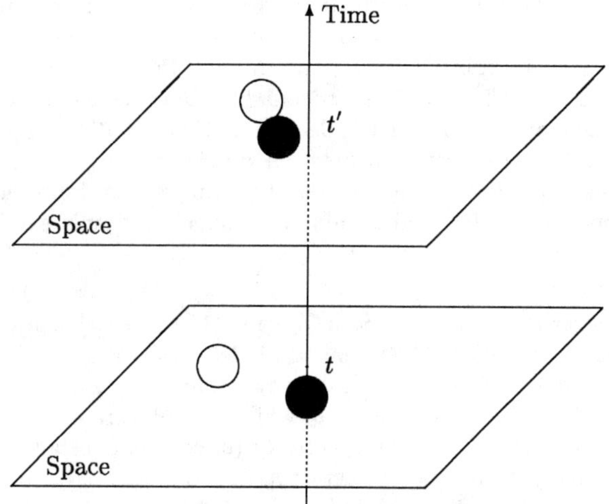

Figure 1 Spatial regions moving in time.

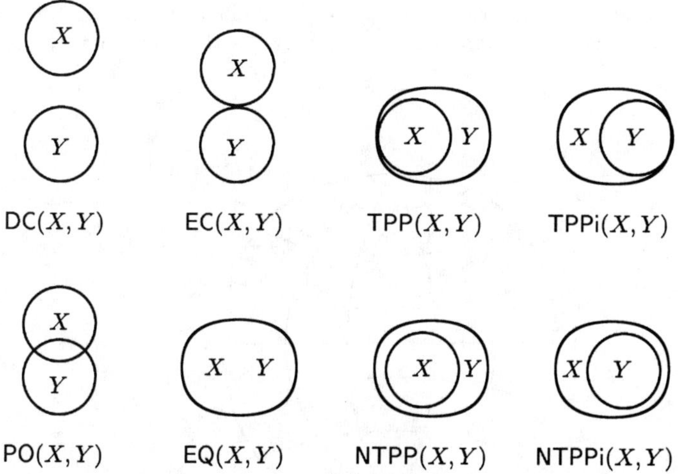

Figure 2 The eight relations between regions.

which constructors of the languages and which kinds of interaction between them cause a "bad computational behavior" and which result in "implementable" spatiotemporal formalisms.

A very important point here is that in this *multidimensional* case, the fundamental trade-off is not only between rich first- or higher-order theories on the one hand, and their less expressive (e.g., propositional) fragments on the other, say, between the full RCC (Randell, Cui, and Cohn 1992), which is undecidable (Dornheim 1998; Gotts 1996b), and its propositional fragment, RCC-8, which is decidable (Bennett 1994), in fact, NP-complete (Renz and Nebel 1999). An interaction between dimensions or, at the syntactical level, between connectives of the spatial and temporal languages can dramatically "spoil" nice computational properties of the components. The following simple example can serve as a good illustration.

Example 1. Consider the *compass logic* of Venema (1990), which can be viewed as a sort of *orientation logic* on the plane. The intended model is the map $\mathbb{N} \times \mathbb{N}$ with the standard orientation; see Figure 3 (in fact, we can take any infinite grid, say, $\mathbb{R} \times \mathbb{R}$). There are two compass operators, $\Diamond_N$ and $\Diamond_E$, on the map, which are interpreted as "somewhere to the north" and "somewhere to the east," respectively (of course, one can add their converses "somewhere to the south" and "somewhere to the west" as well), plus we can use the standard Boolean connectives. That Moscow is located to the northeast of London can be expressed in the compass logic by the formula

$$London \rightarrow \Diamond_N \Diamond_E Moscow,$$

where *London* and *Moscow* are treated as propositional variables that are either true or false at every point of the map.

This 2D logic can be regarded as a natural combination of two 1D compass logics interpreted on straight lines. The interaction between the dimensions is reflected by the

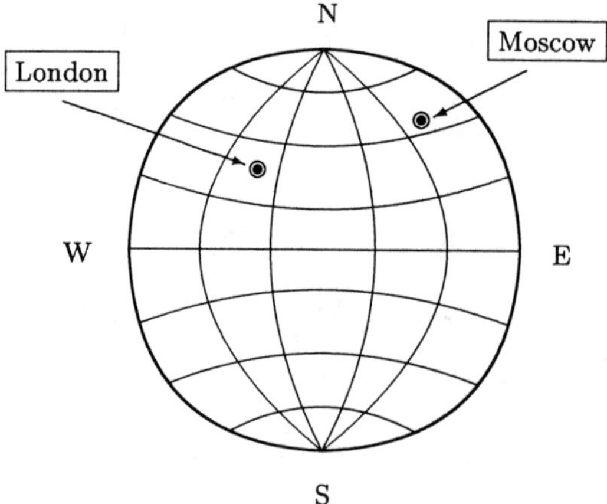

Figure 3 Compass relations.

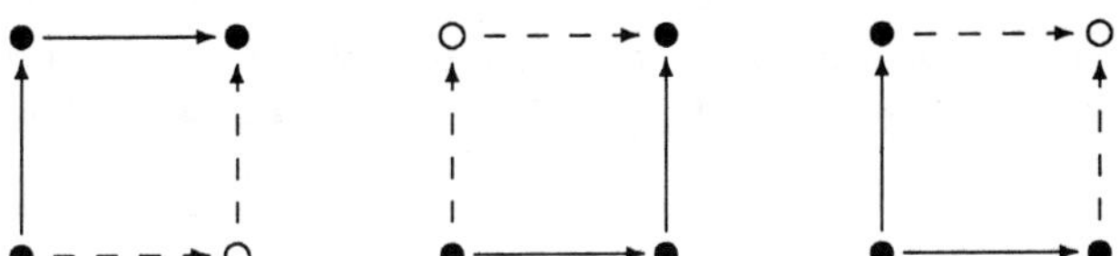

Figure 4 Commutativity and Church–Rosser properties.

formulas

$$\diamondsuit_N \diamondsuit_E \varphi \leftrightarrow \diamondsuit_E \diamondsuit_N \varphi, \qquad \diamondsuit_E \square_N \varphi \rightarrow \square_N \diamondsuit_E \varphi,$$

where $\square_N$ stands for "everywhere to the north." The meaning of these formulas is explained by the diagrams in Figure 4, which say: If there are two black arrows on the map, then there are two dashed arrows as well.

Now, the satisfiability problem for the 1D logics is known to be decidable in NP (Ono and Nakamura 1980; Sistla and Clarke 1985), while the satisfiability problem for the 2D compass logic on $\mathbb{N} \times \mathbb{N}$ or $\mathbb{R} \times \mathbb{R}$ is not even recursively enumerable (Marx and Reynolds 1999; Reynolds and Zakharyaschev 2001; Spaan 1993).

Where is the borderline between acceptable and unacceptable computational behavior of KR formalisms? Obviously, the compass logic above is not acceptable from the computational point of view: no algorithm is capable of even enumerating the formulas satisfiable on the map. On the other hand, its 1D fragments are often also regarded as intractable (Garey and Johnson 1979) in view of their NP-hardness. Yet there is the evidence of Horrocks (1998), who demonstrated that "some of the very expressive description logics for which tableaux algorithms are now available may also be usable in realistic applications." Here and in (Horrocks, Sattler, and Tobies 1999), "very expressive" means PSPACE-hard and EXPTIME-hard, respectively. Hustadt and Schmidt (2000) successfully used a full first-order prover for dealing with EXPTIME-complete modal logics. And MONA (Klarlund, Møller, and Schwartzbach 2000) is a good example of an implementation of decision procedures for theories with a nonelementary[2] worst-case complexity.[3] A possible explanation of this phenomenon is that "in all practically occurring situations the worst case never seems to happen. The reason is that definitions occurring in practice are somehow well-structured. ... and this does not only hold for knowledge representation systems based on description logic but also for object-oriented database systems" (Nebel 1996).

---

[2] We remind you that a problem "$x \in X$?" is called *elementary* if it is solvable by a deterministic algorithm in time $f(|x|)$, where f is an elementary recursive function of the size $|x|$ of x—that is, there is a natural number n such that

$$\forall x \; f(|x|) \leq \left. 2^{2^{\cdot^{\cdot^{\cdot 2^{|x|}}}}} \right\} n \; .$$

A problem is called *nonelementary* if it is not elementary.

[3] "Perhaps surprisingly, this complexity also contributes to successful applications, since it is provably linked to the succinctness of the logics" (Klarlund, Møller, and Schwartzbach 2000).

Of course, only experiments can show whether this or that KR formalism can be applied in practice. In this chapter, however, we regard a logic as having an acceptable computational behavior if it is

- decidable, and

- supported by a "practical" decision algorithm.

The organization of this chapter is very simple. In Sections 2 and 3, we introduce the spatial and temporal components of the spatiotemporal logics to be constructed in Section 4. We define both the syntax and the intended semantics of the logics, illustrate their expressive power by multiple examples, and focus attention on their computational behavior. It is to be noted from the very beginning that we are not putting forward a novel spatiotemporal paradigm. Nor are we designing *the* spatiotemporal KR formalism suitable for all potential applications in GISs, computer vision, robotics, image retrieval, and so on. Our aim is more modest: we combine (some of) the existing spatial and temporal logics and analyze the computational behavior of the resulting hierarchy of spatiotemporal hybrids. As the field of spatiotemporal representation and reasoning is still at the "embryo" stage, the chapter contains a considerable number of open problems.

Although all technical proofs are omitted, we nevertheless try to give you the underlying ideas in the hope of sharing our excitement about this interesting and promising field of KR based on multiple connections to geometry, algebra, topology, modal and temporal logics, and other disciplines.

2 Of Space

There are different approaches to qualitative spatial representation in AI (comprehensive surveys can be found in (Casati and Varzi 1999; Cohn and Hazarika 2001; Vieu 1997)). Here we consider only one, perhaps the most influential of them, which takes extended regions of space as the primitive spatial entity. Properties of regions are usually defined by first-order axiomatic theories (Clarke 1981; Pratt and Schoop 1997; Randell, Cui, and Cohn 1992), the (explicit or implicit) intended models of which are topological, in particular, Euclidean spaces.

2.1 Topological Spaces

Definition 1 (topological space). A *topological space* is a pair, $\mathfrak{T} = \langle U, \mathbb{I} \rangle$, in which U is a nonempty set, the *universe* of the space, and $\mathbb{I}$ is the *interior operator* on U satisfying the following *Kuratowski axioms*: for all $X, Y \subseteq U$,

$$\mathbb{I}(X \cap Y) = \mathbb{I}X \cap \mathbb{I}Y, \quad \mathbb{I}X \subseteq \mathbb{I}\mathbb{I}X, \quad \mathbb{I}X \subseteq X, \quad \mathbb{I}U = U.$$

The operator dual to $\mathbb{I}$ is called the *closure operator* and denoted by $\mathbb{C}$; thus, for every $X \subseteq U$, $\mathbb{C}X = U - \mathbb{I}(U - X)$ (or $\mathbb{C}X = -\mathbb{I} - X$, for short). A set $X \subseteq U$ is called *open* if $X = \mathbb{I}X$ ($\mathbb{I}X$ is known as the *interior* of X) and *closed* if $X = \mathbb{C}X$ ($\mathbb{C}X$ is the *closure* of X). The set $\mathbb{C}X - \mathbb{I}X$ is called the *boundary* of X.

In this chapter, we will need only two kinds of topological spaces, Euclidean and Kripkean. **Example 2 (Euclidean spaces).** Let X be a set of real numbers, that is, $X \subseteq \mathbb{R}$. A point $x \in \mathbb{R}$ is said to be *interior* in X if there is some $\epsilon > 0$ such that the whole open interval $(x - \epsilon, x + \epsilon)$ belongs to X. The interior $\mathbb{I}X$ of X is defined then as the set of all interior points in X. It is not hard to check that $\langle \mathbb{R}, \mathbb{I} \rangle$ is a topological space; it is called the *1D Euclidean space*. Open sets in $\langle \mathbb{R}, \mathbb{I} \rangle$ are (possibly infinite) unions of open intervals (a, b), where $a \leq b$. The closure of (a, b), for $a < b$, is the closed interval $[a, b]$, with the end points a and b being its boundary. In the same manner one can define *higher-dimensional Euclidean spaces* based on the universes $\mathbb{R}^n$ for $n > 1$ (in the definition of interior points x, one should take n-dimensional ϵ-neighborhoods of x).

There can be different views on what sets of a topological space $\mathfrak{T} = \langle U, \mathbb{I} \rangle$ can be taken as interpretations of spatial regions (Bennett 1997; Galton 2000; Gotts 1996a; Vieu 1997).[4] Following (Asher and Vieu 1995; Davis 1990; Gotts 1996a), we interpret regions only as *regular closed* sets, that is, sets X such that $X = \mathbb{C}\mathbb{I}X$ (an alternative would be to take *regular open* sets X for which $X = \mathbb{I}\mathbb{C}X$). For example, the circle

$$C(a, r) = \{(x_1, x_2) \in \mathbb{R}^2 : \sqrt{(x_1 - a_1)^2 + (x_2 - a_2)^2} \leq r\}$$

with center $a = (a_1, a_2)$ and of radius $r > 0$ on the Euclidean plane is a regular closed set, while the "balloon" obtained by attaching to $C(a, r)$ a "thread" (e.g., a segment of a straight line) is not regularly closed, because the interior of the thread in $\mathbb{R}^2$ is empty.

An important property of topological spaces is that any, even infinite, union (intersection) of open (closed) sets is open (respectively, closed). An infinite union (intersection) of closed (open) sets is not necessarily closed (open). For example, in $\mathbb{R}$ we have:

$$\bigcup_{n=1}^{\infty} [1/n, 1 - 1/n] = (0, 1), \qquad \bigcap_{n=1}^{\infty} [-1/n, 1/n] = \{0\}. \tag{1}$$

Example 3 (Kripke spaces). Recall that a *quasi-order* is a pair $\mathfrak{G} = \langle V, S \rangle$, where S is a reflexive and transitive binary relation on $V \neq \emptyset$. With every quasi-order $\mathfrak{G}$, one can associate a topological space $\mathfrak{T}_{\mathfrak{G}} = \langle V, \mathbb{I}_{\mathfrak{G}} \rangle$ by taking, for every $X \subseteq V$,

$$\mathbb{I}_{\mathfrak{G}}X = \{x \in X : \forall y \in V \, (xSy \to y \in X)\}. \tag{2}$$

We call $\mathfrak{T}_{\mathfrak{G}}$ the *Kripke space determined by* $\mathfrak{G}$ (the reason for this name will be explained in Section 2.2.4; these spaces are also known as *Alexandroff spaces*). The closure operator $\mathbb{C}_{\mathfrak{G}}$ on $\mathfrak{T}_{\mathfrak{G}}$ is defined then by

$$\mathbb{C}_{\mathfrak{G}}X = \{y \in V : \exists x \in X \, ySx\}. \tag{3}$$

It follows from (2) and (3) that arbitrary unions (intersections) of closed (open) sets of Kripke spaces are closed (respectively, open).

---

[4] Actually, the choice is determined by the way of characterizing a relation of connection between two regions. Our interpretation reflects the following definition: regions X and Y are connected iff $\mathbb{C}X \cap \mathbb{C}Y \neq \emptyset$. For a comparison of different definitions, consult (Cohn and Varzi 1998).

It is not hard to see that, for any two regions X and Y in a topological space $\mathcal{T} = \langle U, \mathbb{I} \rangle$, one and only one of the following eight relations can hold between X and Y (see Figure 2):

$$
\begin{array}{lll}
\mathsf{DC}(X,Y) & \text{iff} & \neg\exists x\ x \in X \cap Y, \\[4pt]
\mathsf{EQ}(X,Y) & \text{iff} & \forall x\ (x \in X \leftrightarrow x \in Y), \\[4pt]
\mathsf{PO}(X,Y) & \text{iff} & \exists x\ (x \in \mathbb{I}X \cap \mathbb{I}Y) \wedge \exists x\ (x \in \mathbb{I}X \cap -Y) \wedge \exists x\ (x \in -X \cap \mathbb{I}Y), \\[4pt]
\mathsf{EC}(X,Y) & \text{iff} & \exists x\ (x \in X \cap Y) \wedge \neg\exists x\ (x \in \mathbb{I}X \cap \mathbb{I}Y), \\[4pt]
\mathsf{TPP}(X,Y) & \text{iff} & \forall x\ (x \in -X \cup Y) \wedge \exists x\ (x \in X \cap -\mathbb{I}Y) \wedge \exists x\ (x \in -X \cap Y), \\[4pt]
\mathsf{TPPi}(X,Y) & \text{iff} & \mathsf{TPP}(Y,X), \\[4pt]
\mathsf{NTPP}(X,Y) & \text{iff} & \forall x\ (x \in -X \cup \mathbb{I}Y) \wedge \exists x\ (x \in -X \cap Y), \\[4pt]
\mathsf{NTPPi}(X,Y) & \text{iff} & \mathsf{NTPP}(Y,X).
\end{array}
$$

In English, these relations can be described as Disconnection, Equality, Partial Overlap, External Connection, Tangential Proper Part, Nontangential Proper Part, and the inverses of the last two.

In view of this property of being *jointly exhaustive and pairwise disjoint*, the eight relations above play a fundamental role in spatial representation and reasoning (the same as Allen's 13 relations between time intervals; see Section 3.4). We will call them the *basic relations*, or the RCC-8 *relations* (or *predicates*).

2.2   Spatial Logics

Languages of different expressive power can be used to talk about regions in topological spaces.

2.2.1   First-Order Logics

Often, logical formalisms for qualitative spatial representation are formulated as first-order theories (Casati and Varzi 1999; Clarke 1981; Randell, Cui, and Cohn 1992; Whitehead 1929). For instance, the language of RCC consists of individual variables $X, Y, \ldots$ (understood as variables over regions), the individual constant U (for the universal region), the binary predicate $\mathsf{C}(X,Y)$ (read as "X connects with Y"), a number of functions such as $\mathsf{sum}(X,Y)$, $\mathsf{compl}(X)$, $\mathsf{prod}(X,Y)$, the Boolean logical connectives, and the quantifiers $\forall$ and $\exists$. The eight basic predicates are defined via C as in Table 1 (where P stands for *part*, O for *overlaps*, and PP for *proper part*), and the axioms of RCC include, in particular,

$$
\begin{array}{l}
\forall X\ \mathsf{C}(X,X), \\[4pt]
\forall X, Y\ (\mathsf{C}(X,Y) \rightarrow \mathsf{C}(Y,X)), \\[4pt]
\forall X\ \mathsf{C}(X,\mathsf{U}), \\[4pt]
\forall X \exists Y\ \mathsf{NTPP}(Y,X), \\[4pt]
\forall X, Y, Z\ \big(\mathsf{C}(Z, \mathsf{sum}(X,Y)) \leftrightarrow \mathsf{C}(Z,X) \vee \mathsf{C}(Z,Y)\big).
\end{array}
$$

Unfortunately, from the computational point of view, full RCC turns out to be too expressive: as was shown in (Dornheim 1998; Gotts 1996b) (by applying the results

$$
\begin{aligned}
\mathsf{DC}(X,Y) &= \neg\mathsf{C}(X,Y) \\
\mathsf{P}(X,Y) &= \forall Z\ (\mathsf{C}(Z,X) \to \mathsf{C}(Z,Y)) \\
\mathsf{EQ}(X,Y) &= \mathsf{P}(X,Y) \wedge \mathsf{P}(Y,X) \\
\mathsf{O}(X,Y) &= \exists Z\ (\mathsf{P}(Z,X) \wedge \mathsf{P}(Z,Y)) \\
\mathsf{PO}(X,Y) &= \mathsf{O}(X,Y) \wedge \neg\mathsf{P}(X,Y) \wedge \neg\mathsf{P}(Y,X) \\
\mathsf{EC}(X,Y) &= \mathsf{C}(X,Y) \wedge \neg\mathsf{O}(X,Y) \\
\mathsf{PP}(X,Y) &= \mathsf{P}(X,Y) \wedge \neg\mathsf{P}(Y,X) \\
\mathsf{TPP}(X,Y) &= \mathsf{PP}(X,Y) \wedge \exists Z\ (\mathsf{EC}(Z,X) \wedge \mathsf{EC}(Z,Y)) \\
\mathsf{NTPP}(X,Y) &= \mathsf{PP}(X,Y) \wedge \neg\exists Z\ (\mathsf{EC}(Z,X) \wedge \mathsf{EC}(Z,Y))
\end{aligned}
$$

Table 1   Some relations between spatial regions, defined in terms of C.

of (Grzegorczyk 1951)), it is undecidable. Another problem with RCC is its semantic characterization. For example, it is an open question whether RCC is complete with respect to Euclidean spaces.

Of course, one can change direction and start from semantics. If we are satisfied with the mereotopological model for qualitative spatial representation, then we can use as a variant of spatial logic the set of all first-order formulas in a proper signature, say, containing the eight basic predicates in Figure 2, that hold in all topological models defined as follows (Dornheim 1998):

Definition 2 (topological model). A *topological model* is a structure of the form

$$
\mathfrak{S} = \left\langle \mathcal{R}(\mathfrak{T}); \mathsf{DC}^{\mathfrak{T}}, \mathsf{EQ}^{\mathfrak{T}}, \mathsf{PO}^{\mathfrak{T}}, \mathsf{EC}^{\mathfrak{T}}, \mathsf{TPP}^{\mathfrak{T}}, \mathsf{TPPi}^{\mathfrak{T}}, \mathsf{NTPP}^{\mathfrak{T}}, \mathsf{NTPPi}^{\mathfrak{T}} \right\rangle, \tag{4}
$$

where $\mathfrak{T}$ is a topological space, $\mathcal{R}(\mathfrak{T})$ the set of all regular closed subsets in $\mathfrak{T}$, and $\mathsf{DC}^{\mathfrak{T}}$, $\mathsf{EQ}^{\mathfrak{T}}$, $\mathsf{PO}^{\mathfrak{T}}$, $\mathsf{EC}^{\mathfrak{T}}$, $\mathsf{TPP}^{\mathfrak{T}}$, $\mathsf{TPPi}^{\mathfrak{T}}$, $\mathsf{NTPP}^{\mathfrak{T}}$, $\mathsf{NTPPi}^{\mathfrak{T}}$ are the basic predicates on $\mathcal{R}(\mathfrak{T})$ defined as above.

Let $\mathfrak{a}$ be an *assignment* in $\mathfrak{S}$ associating with every region variable X a set $\mathfrak{a}(X)$ in $\mathcal{R}(\mathfrak{T})$. A first-order formula $\varphi(X_1,\dots,X_n)$ in the signature of the RCC-8 predicates and with free variables $X_1,\dots,X_n$ is *satisfied* in $\mathfrak{S}$ under $\mathfrak{a}$ ($\mathfrak{S} \models^{\mathfrak{a}} \varphi$ in symbols) if $\mathfrak{S} \models \varphi[\mathfrak{a}(X_1),\dots,\mathfrak{a}(X_n)]$ in the standard model-theoretic sense.

Unfortunately, even this simplified approach turns out to be computationally unacceptable: as follows from Grzegorczyk (1951), this logic is undecidable as well.

2.2.2   RCC-8

As the eight basic region-relations play such an important role in spatial representation and reasoning (Egenhofer 1991; Egenhofer and Franzosa 1991; Smith and Park 1992), to obtain a computationally well-behaved spatial formalism, we can sacrifice quantification and consider the quantifier-free fragment of the logic of topological models defined above.

This fragment is known as RCC-8. Thus, RCC-8 *formulas* are simply Boolean combinations of the RCC-8 predicates.

Definition 3 (consequence). Say that an RCC-8 formula φ is a *consequence* of a set Σ of RCC-8 formulas if for every topological model $\mathfrak{S}$ and every assignment $\mathfrak{a}$ in it, we have $\mathfrak{S} \models^{\mathfrak{a}} \varphi$ whenever $\mathfrak{S} \models^{\mathfrak{a}} \Sigma$. In this case we write $\Sigma \models \varphi$.

For example, using the language of RCC-8, we can compose spatial knowledge bases like

$$EC(\textit{Catalunya, France}),$$
$$TPP(\textit{Catalunya, Spain}) \vee NTPP(\textit{Catalunya, Spain}),$$
$$DC(\textit{Spain, France}) \vee EC(\textit{Spain, France}),$$
$$NTPP(\textit{Paris, France}).$$

The formulas $EC(\textit{Spain, France})$, $TPP(\textit{Catalunya, Spain})$, and $DC(\textit{Spain, Paris})$ are then consequences of this knowledge base.

It should be clear that $\Sigma \models \varphi$ holds iff the formula $\neg\varphi \wedge \bigwedge \Sigma$ is not satisfiable in topological models. Thus, to understand the computational properties of RCC-8, we can confine ourselves to considering only the *satisfiability problem*.

That this problem is decidable was first observed by Bennett (1994), who encoded RCC-8 into propositional intuitionistic logic, which was known to be decidable. Later, Bennett (1996) used Gödel's (1933) embedding of propositional intuitionistic logic into the modal logic S4 to encode RCC-8 into a decidable propositional modal logic. Renz and Nebel (1999) showed that the satisfiability problem for RCC-8 formulas is NP-complete. (For more details see Section 2.2.4.)

2.2.3 BRCC-8

One apparent "deficit" of RCC-8 is that it operates only with *atomic* regions. We cannot form unions ($\sqcup$) or intersections ($\sqcap$) of regions to say, for instance, that

$$EQ(\textit{EU, Spain} \sqcup \textit{Italy} \sqcup \dots)$$

("the EU consists of Spain, Italy, etc."),

$$P(\textit{Alps, Italy} \sqcup \textit{France} \sqcup \dots)$$

("the Alps are located in Italy, France, etc."),

$$EC(\textit{Austria, Alps} \sqcap \textit{Italy})$$

("Austria is externally connected to the alpine part of Italy"), and deduce from these that if $EC(X, EU)$, for some country X, then $EC(X, Y)$ for some country Y in the EU, or that there is a country Z such that $TPP(Z, EU)$ (i.e., "Z is a tangential proper part of the EU"). Note, by the way, that the last formula is a correct conclusion only if we interpret our formulas in Euclidean (or, more generally, connected[5]) topological spaces (and if there

---

[5]A topological space is called *connected* if it cannot be represented as a union of two disjoint open sets.

are non-EU countries): in a discrete topological space (where all sets are open), the EU may be an open set with empty boundary. This simple observation and the result of Renz (1998), according to which every satisfiable RCC-8 formula is satisfiable in all Euclidean spaces $\mathbb{R}^n$, $n \geq 1$, show that the Boolean operations on region terms indeed increase the expressive power of RCC-8.

Definition 4 (Boolean region term). A *Boolean region term* is just a combination of region variables using the Boolean operators $\sqcup$, $\sqcap$, and $\neg$.

Denote by BRCC-8 the extension of RCC-8 that allows the use of Boolean region terms as arguments of the RCC-8 predicates. As the Boolean operators do not in general preserve the property of being regular closed, we have to adjust the interpretation of Boolean region terms in a topological model $\mathfrak{S}$ of the form (4) by taking, for region terms t and t',

$$
\begin{aligned}
\mathfrak{a}(t \sqcup t') &= \ \mathbb{CI}(\mathfrak{a}(t) \cup \mathfrak{a}(t')) = \mathfrak{a}(t) \cup \mathfrak{a}(t'), \\
\mathfrak{a}(t \sqcap t') &= \ \mathbb{CI}(\mathfrak{a}(t) \cap \mathfrak{a}(t')), \\
\mathfrak{a}(\neg t) &= \ \mathbb{CI}(U - \mathfrak{a}(t)).
\end{aligned}
$$

Thus, every region term is interpreted as a regular closed set of $\mathfrak{T}$. Note that $\mathfrak{a}(X \sqcap \neg X) = \emptyset$ and $\mathfrak{a}(X \sqcup \neg X) = U$ for any $\mathfrak{a}$ and $\mathfrak{T}$. We denote the region terms $X \sqcap \neg X$ and $X \sqcup \neg X$ by $\perp$ and $\top$, respectively. The constraint $\neg \mathsf{EQ}(X, \perp)$ asserts that X is a non-empty region.

The computational behavior of BCCR-8 in arbitrary topological models is precisely the same as that of RCC-8. However, if only Euclidean topological models are regarded as possible interpretations, the satisfiability problem for BCCR-8 formulas becomes PSPACE-complete (Wolter and Zakharyaschev 2000a).

2.2.4   Modal Logics as Spatial Logics

The proof of the decidability of RCC-8 in (Bennett 1994; Bennett 1996) brought in sight another kind of formalism, which can be used as a spatial logic. In fact, the logic was introduced independently by Orlov (1928), Lewis (Lewis and Langford 1932), and Gödel (1933) without any intention to reason about space. Lewis baptized the logic as S4 and understood it as a logic of necessity and possibility—that is, as a *modal logic*. Besides the Boolean connectives and propositional variables, its language contains two modal operators $\Box$ ("it is necessary"; Orlov and Gödel treated $\Box$ as "it is provable") and $\Diamond$ ("it is possible"). The axiom schemata of S4 are those of classical propositional calculus, three modal schemata,

$$
\Box(\varphi \to \psi) \to (\Box\varphi \to \Box\psi), \quad \Box\varphi \to \varphi, \quad \Box\varphi \to \Box\Box\varphi,
$$

and two inference rules, modus ponens and necessitation $\varphi / \Box\varphi$. The possibility operator is defined as dual to $\Box$—that is, $\Diamond\varphi = \neg\Box\neg\varphi$.

In the late 1930s and early 1940s, several logicians (McKinsey 1941; Stone 1937; Tarski 1938; Tsao-Chen 1938) noticed that S4 can be interpreted in topological spaces. Actually, there is a striking similarity between the axioms of S4 and Kuratowski's axioms for the interior operator. (The first schema and rule of necessitation can be replaced with $\Box(\varphi \wedge \psi) \leftrightarrow (\Box\varphi \wedge \Box\psi)$ and $\Box\top$, corresponding to the first and last topological axioms.)

Suppose that an assignment $\mathfrak{v}$ in a topological space $\mathfrak{T} = \langle U, \mathbb{I} \rangle$ is a map from the set of propositional variables in S4 to 2^U. We then inductively extend $\mathfrak{v}$ to all modal formulas by interpreting $\Box$ as $\mathbb{I}$, $\Diamond$ as $\mathbb{C}$, $\wedge$ as $\cap$, and $\neg$ as $-$. Now we say that a modal formula φ is *satisfied* in $\mathfrak{T}$ under $\mathfrak{v}$ if $\mathfrak{v}(\varphi) \neq \emptyset$; φ is *valid in* $\mathfrak{T}$ ($\mathfrak{T} \models \varphi$, in symbols) if $\mathfrak{v}(\varphi) = U$. It turns out that S4 is sound and complete with respect to this interpretation: a modal formula φ is derivable in S4 iff φ is valid in all topological spaces iff φ is valid in any n-dimensional Euclidean space ($n \geq 1$) (McKinsey 1941; McKinsey and Tarski 1944). A remarkable result due to Dummett and Lemmon (1959) and Kripke (1963) is that S4 is complete with respect to *finite* Kripke spaces (Kripke used quasi-orders to define his possible world semantics for S4).[6]

Thus, S4 can be regarded as a "logic of topological spaces." We can increase the expressive power of S4 by adding to it one more pair of modal operators, $\boxed{\forall}$ and $\langle\!\Diamond\!\rangle$, known as the *universal modalities*. The topological meaning of $\boxed{\forall}$ and $\langle\!\Diamond\!\rangle$ is "for all points in the space" and "for some point in the space," respectively. More precisely, for every formula φ in the extended language and every topological space $\mathfrak{T} = \langle U, \mathbb{I} \rangle$ with an assignment $\mathfrak{v}$, we have

$$\mathfrak{v}(\boxed{\forall}\,\varphi) = \begin{cases} U & \text{if } \mathfrak{v}(\varphi) = U, \\ \emptyset & \text{otherwise}; \end{cases} \qquad \mathfrak{v}(\langle\!\Diamond\!\rangle\varphi) = \begin{cases} U & \text{if } \mathfrak{v}(\varphi) \neq \emptyset, \\ \emptyset & \text{otherwise}. \end{cases}$$

The set of all formulas in this language that are valid in all topological spaces is denoted by $S4_u$; it can be axiomatized by adding to S4 the schemata

$$\boxed{\forall}\,(\varphi \rightarrow \psi) \rightarrow (\boxed{\forall}\,\varphi \rightarrow \boxed{\forall}\,\psi), \quad \boxed{\forall}\,\varphi \rightarrow \varphi, \quad \boxed{\forall}\,\varphi \rightarrow \boxed{\forall}\,\boxed{\forall}\,\varphi, \quad \langle\!\Diamond\!\rangle\varphi \rightarrow \boxed{\forall}\,\langle\!\Diamond\!\rangle\varphi, \quad \boxed{\forall}\,\varphi \rightarrow \Box\varphi,$$

and the rule $\varphi / \boxed{\forall}\,\varphi$. According to Goranko and Passy (1992), $S4_u$ is also complete with respect to finite Kripke spaces. Note, however, that in constrast to S4 itself, $S4_u$ is not complete with respect to Euclidean spaces. The set of formulas valid in all Euclidean spaces is strictly larger than $S4_u$. It was axiomatized in (Shehtman 1999) by adding to $S4_u$ the schemata $\boxed{\forall}\,(\Box\varphi \vee \Box\neg\varphi) \rightarrow \boxed{\forall}\,\varphi \vee \boxed{\forall}\,\neg\varphi$.

$S4_u$ is expressive enough to encode the topological meaning of the RCC-8 predicates and that of Boolean region terms.[7] Indeed, let us denote the box and the diamond of S4 by, respectively, I and C (to emphasize their topological interpretation as the interior and closure operators). For a Boolean region term t, define inductively a modal formula t^* by taking

$$X_i^* = CIp_i, \quad (X_i \text{ is a region variable, } p_i \text{ a propositional variable}),$$
$$(t_1 \sqcap t_2)^* = CI(t_1^* \wedge t_2^*),$$
$$(t_1 \sqcap t_2)^* = CI(t_1^* \vee t_2^*),$$
$$(\neg t)^* = CI\neg t^*.$$

---

[6]This story is really amazing. In 1908, Brouwer introduced intuitionistic logic, Int; later he also became famous in topology. Orlov and Gödel defined S4 in order to interpret intuitionistic logic in a classical one. Open sets in a topological space form a complete Heyting algebra, which is a model of Int and can be used as a model of RCC (Stell 2000; Stell and Worboys 1997).

[7]Recently, the expressive power of the language of $S4_u$ has been characterized in terms of bisimulations by Aiello and van Benthem (2000). The associated topo-games have been used in (Aiello 2001) to measure a difference between spatial regions.

Then, with every atomic BRCC-8 formula $P(s,t)$ we associate a modal formula $(P(s,t))^*$ defined by

$$(\mathsf{DC}(s,t))^* = \neg\lozenge\!\!\!\!\lozenge\,(s^* \wedge t^*),$$

$$(\mathsf{EQ}(s,t))^* = \boxdot(s^* \leftrightarrow t^*),$$

$$(\mathsf{PO}(s,t))^* = \lozenge\!\!\!\!\lozenge\,(\boldsymbol{I}s^* \wedge \boldsymbol{I}t^*) \wedge \lozenge\!\!\!\!\lozenge\,(\boldsymbol{I}s^* \wedge \neg t^*) \wedge \lozenge\!\!\!\!\lozenge\,(\neg s^* \wedge \boldsymbol{I}t^*),$$

$$(\mathsf{EC}(s,t))^* = \lozenge\!\!\!\!\lozenge\,(s^* \wedge t^*) \wedge \neg\lozenge\!\!\!\!\lozenge\,(\boldsymbol{I}s^* \wedge \boldsymbol{I}t^*),$$

$$(\mathsf{TPP}(s,t))^* = \boxdot(\neg s^* \vee t^*) \wedge \lozenge\!\!\!\!\lozenge\,(s^* \wedge \boldsymbol{C}\neg t^*) \wedge \lozenge\!\!\!\!\lozenge\,(\neg s^* \wedge t^*),$$

$$(\mathsf{NTPP}(s,t))^* = \boxdot(\neg s^* \vee \boldsymbol{I}t^*) \wedge \lozenge\!\!\!\!\lozenge\,(\neg s^* \wedge t^*).$$

Finally, given a BRCC-8 formula φ, denote by φ^* the result of replacing all occurrences of atomic formulas $P(s,t)$ in φ by $(P(s,t))^*$.

Since the definition of the translation $\cdot^*$ mimics the definition of the RCC-8 predicates and since the formula $\boldsymbol{CICI}\varphi \leftrightarrow \boldsymbol{CI}\varphi$ is provable in S4, we immediately obtain the following theorem, the original RCC-8 version of which is due to (Bennett 1994; Bennett 1996) (see also (Wolter and Zakharyaschev 2000a)):

Theorem 1. *For every* BRCC-8 *formula* φ, *the following conditions are equivalent:*

(i) φ *is satisfiable in a topological model.*

(ii) φ^* *is satisfiable in a topological space.*

(iii) φ^* *is satisfiable in a finite Kripke space.*

As a consequence we have

Corollary 1. *The satisfiability problem for* BRCC-8 *formulas is decidable.*

The modal translation φ^* of a BRCC-8 formula φ has a rather special form. Renz (1998) used this form to show that satisfiable RCC-8 formulas can be satisfied in very simple Kripke spaces, namely, in those determined by quasi-orders we call *quasisaws*.

A quasisaw is a partial order $\mathfrak{G} = \langle W, R \rangle$, every point in which has at most two successors, with these successors being R-incomparable. An example of a quasisaw is shown in Figure 5. It should be clear that if an $\mathsf{S4}_u$-formula is satisfied in a quasisaw, then it is satisfied in a disjoint union of forks (defined in Figure 5) as well. The following generalization of Renz's result was proved in (Wolter and Zakharyaschev 2000a).

Theorem 2. *A* BRCC-8 *formula* φ *is satisfiable iff* φ^* *is satisfiable in the Kripke space determined by a quasisaw containing* $\leq \ell(\varphi^*)$ *forks, where* $\ell(\varphi^*)$ *is the length of* φ^*.

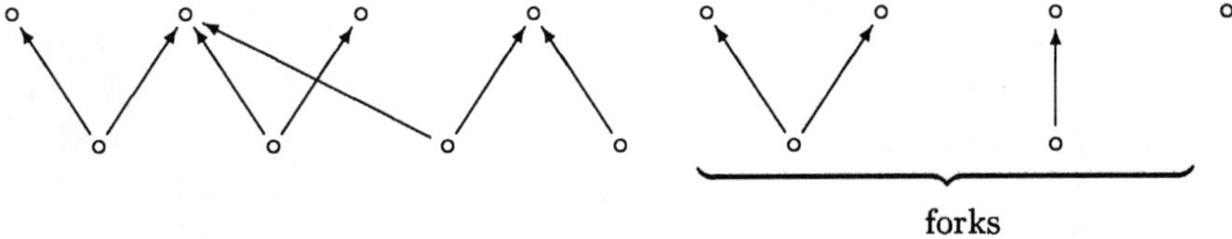

Figure 5 Quasisaw.

Thus, the satisfiability problem for BRCC-8 formulas φ in topological models reduces to the satisfiability problem for their modal translations φ^* in quasisaws that are disjoint unions of forks. We can make one step further by observing that the latter problem can be reduced to the satisfiability of first-order formulas with a *single* variable. The idea behind this reduction is to represent every subformula ψ of φ^* by means of three first-order formulas ψ^b, ψ^l, ψ^r, which encode the "behavior" of ψ at the three points of a fork. More precisely, we define inductively three translations $\cdot^b$, $\cdot^l$, and $\cdot^r$ by taking

$$p^i = P^i(x), \ p \text{ a propositional variable, for } i \in \{b, l, r\},$$

$$(\psi \circ \chi)^i = \psi^i \circ \chi^i, \text{ for } i \in \{b, l, r\} \text{ and } \circ \in \{\wedge, \vee\},$$

$$(\neg\psi)^i = \neg\psi^i, \text{ for } i \in \{b, l, r\},$$

$$(\boldsymbol{I}\psi)^b = \psi^b \wedge \psi^l \wedge \psi^r,$$

$$(\boldsymbol{I}\psi)^i = \psi^i, \text{ for } i \in \{l, r\},$$

$$(\boxdot\psi)^i = \forall x \ (\psi^b \wedge \psi^l \wedge \psi^r), \text{ for } i \in \{b, r, l\}.$$

Finally, we define the translation $\varphi^\dagger$ of a BRCC-8 formula φ into the *one-variable fragment* of first-order logic as $(\varphi^*)^b$. It should be clear that the length of $\varphi^\dagger$ is polynomial in the length of φ.

Theorem 3. *A* BRCC-8 *formula φ is satisfiable in a topological model iff $\varphi^\dagger$ is a satisfiable first-order formula.*

As is well known, the satisfiability problem for first-order formulas with one variable is NP-complete (the one-variable fragment of first-order logic is a notational variant of the propositional modal logic S5). As a consequence, we immediately obtain the following generalization of a result of Renz and Nebel (1999):

Theorem 4. *The satisfiability problem for* BRCC-8 *formulas in topological models is NP-complete.*

(Remember that satisfiability of BRCC-8 formulas in connected topological spaces is PSPACE-complete.)

3 Of Time

Let us now turn to semantic structures representing time and languages designed for speaking about these structures.

Definition 5 (flow of time). By a *flow of time* we mean any strict partial order $\mathfrak{F} = \langle W, < \rangle$, where W is a non-empty set of *time points* and $<$ a (transitive and irreflexive) *precedence relation* on W.

Depending on applications, we can distinguish between various kinds of flows of time. For example, a linear discrete flow like $\langle \mathbb{N}, < \rangle$ can represent ticks of the computer clock or years A.D. A linear dense flow like $\langle \mathbb{Q}, < \rangle$ or $\langle \mathbb{R}, < \rangle$ reflects the continuity of time. A branching flow, $\langle W, < \rangle$, where $<$ is a tree order on W (see Section 3.2) suggests that the future is nondeterministic, while the past is determined. For more discussions, consult (Gabbay, Hodkinson, and Reynolds 1994; Gabbay, Reynolds, and Finger 2000).

3.1 Linear Time

As in the case of space, we can choose between different languages to speak about flows of time.

3.1.1 First-Order Logic

First, we can take the first-order language $\mathcal{L}^<$ with one binary predicate $<$, interpreted by the precedence relation of a given flow of time $\mathfrak{F} = \langle W, < \rangle$, an infinite list $P_0, P_1, \ldots$ of unary predicates for expressing properties of the time points, and individual variables $x_0, x_1, \ldots$ ranging over these points. Formulas of $\mathcal{L}^<$ are built from atoms of the form $P_i(x_j)$ and $x_l < x_m$ by means of the Booleans $\wedge$ and $\neg$, and the first-order quantifiers $\forall x_i$ and $\exists x_i$.

The language $\mathcal{L}^<$ and its relation to automata has been thoroughly investigated (Büchi 1962; Burgess and Gurevich 1985; Gurevich 1964; Läuchli and Leonard 1966; Meyer 1975; Stockmeyer 1974). In particular, the following results have been obtained (consult the footnote above for the notion of non-elementary algorithmic problems):

Theorem 5. *The satisfiability problem for $\mathcal{L}^<$-formulas is decidable in the following classes of flows of time: all strict linear orders, $\{\langle \mathbb{R}, < \rangle\}$, $\{\langle \mathbb{Q}, < \rangle\}$, $\{\langle \mathbb{Z}, < \rangle\}$, $\{\langle \mathbb{N}, < \rangle\}$. However, in all these cases, the satisfiability problem is non-elementary.*

Thus, reasoning about time with first-order logic is "very expensive." On the other hand, in our everyday life we rarely use explicit quantification over time points, preferring expressions like "tomorrow," "always," "eventually," "since," and so on, which do not mention time points explicitly.

3.1.2 Propositional Temporal Logic

Temporal logic, as opposed to first-order logic, is an approach to reasoning about time (and computation) using such expressions as temporal connectives and not allowing for explicit quantification over time. Its most popular variant, the *propositional temporal logic* ($\mathcal{PTL}$), is successfully applied in program verification and specification (Manna and Pnueli 1992 and 1995). $\mathcal{PTL}$ formulas are constructed from propositional variables $p_0, p_1, \ldots$ using the Booleans and the binary *temporal operators* $\mathcal{S}$ ("since") and $\mathcal{U}$ ("until"), the intended meaning of which is as follows:

- $\chi_1 \mathcal{U} \chi_2$ stands for "χ_1 holds true until χ_2 holds";
- $\chi_1 \mathcal{S} \chi_2$ stands for "χ_1 has been true since χ_2 was true."

Other temporal connectives like $\Diamond_F$ ("sometime in the future"), $\Box_F$ ("always in the future"), their past counterparts, and $\bigcirc$ ("at the next moment") can be defined via $\mathcal{U}$ and $\mathcal{S}$. For instance, $\Diamond_F \varphi = \top \mathcal{U} \varphi$, $\bigcirc \varphi = \bot \mathcal{U} \varphi$.

To evaluate $\mathcal{PTL}$ formulas in a flow of time $\mathfrak{F} = \langle W, < \rangle$, we have to specify first at which time points the propositional variables hold. Thus, we start with a *valuation* $\mathfrak{V}$ associating with every variable p a subset $\mathfrak{V}(p)$ of W. The pair $\mathfrak{M} = \langle \mathfrak{F}, \mathfrak{V} \rangle$ is called a *model* based on the flow of time $\mathfrak{F}$. The *truth-relation* $(\mathfrak{M}, w) \models \varphi$, or simply $w \models \varphi$ if understood (which says that a $\mathcal{PTL}$ formula φ holds at moment w in $\mathfrak{M}$) is defined as follows: $w \models p_i$ iff

$w \in \mathfrak{V}(p_i)$, $w \models \varphi \wedge \psi$ iff $w \models \varphi$ and $w \models \psi$, $w \models \neg\varphi$ iff $w \not\models \varphi$, and

$$w \models \varphi \mathcal{S} \psi \text{ iff there is } v < w \text{ such that } v \models \psi \text{ and } u \models \varphi \text{ for all } u \in (v, w),$$
$$w \models \varphi \mathcal{U} \psi \text{ iff there is } v > w \text{ such that } v \models \psi \text{ and } u \models \varphi \text{ for all } u \in (w, v).$$

A formula φ is *satisfiable* in a class $\mathcal{C}$ of flows of time if there is a model based on a flow of time in $\mathcal{C}$ and a time point w in it such that $w \models \varphi$.

The following results are due to (Gabbay, Hodkinson, and Reynolds 1994; Reynolds 2001a; Reynolds 2001b; Sistla and Clarke 1985):

Theorem 6. *The satisfiability problem for $\mathcal{PTL}$ formulas is PSPACE-complete in any of the classes mentioned in Theorem 5.*

By comparing the complexity results in Theorems 6 and 5, one might conclude that the propositional temporal language is less expressive than the first-order language $\mathcal{L}^<$. Surprisingly enough, this is not the case: while $\mathcal{L}^<$ is considerably more succinct than $\mathcal{PTL}$, nevertheless the languages turn out to have the same expressive power over many flows of time. Obviously, every $\mathcal{PTL}$ formula φ is expressible as an $\mathcal{L}^<$ formula $ST(\varphi)$, called the *standard translation* of φ (van Benthem 1983). The following result is known as the (generalized) *Kamp theorem* (for proofs and more details, see (Gabbay, Hodkinson, and Reynolds 1994; Kamp 1968)).

Theorem 7. *The languages $\mathcal{PTL}$ and $\mathcal{L}^<$ have the same expressive power over the flows of time $\langle \mathbb{N}, < \rangle$, $\langle \mathbb{Z}, < \rangle$, or $\langle \mathbb{R}, < \rangle$. More precisely, for every $\mathcal{L}^<$ formula ψ with at most one free variable, there is a $\mathcal{PTL}$ formula φ such that ψ and $ST(\varphi)$ are equivalent in all models based on any Dedekind complete flow of time.*

3.2 Branching Time

The formalisms considered so far are not able to express the following statements (due to Aristotle):

- It is necessary that there will be a sea battle tomorrow.
- It is possible that there will be a sea battle tomorrow.

Our languages can only say

- $\bigcirc$*sea-battle*—that is, there will be a sea battle tomorrow.

They do not distinguish between possible, actual, or necessary future developments. A natural way to formalize assertions of this sort is to add the modal operators $\square$ and $\lozenge$ to the temporal language and understand them as quantifiers over *possible histories*. For example, by interpreting $\lozenge$ as "it is possible that" and $\square$ as "it is necessary that," we can express two of Aristotle's statements by the formulas $\square\bigcirc$*sea-battle* and $\lozenge\bigcirc$*sea-battle*, respectively.

Numerous extensions of $\mathcal{PTL}$ by means of such kind of modal operators have been introduced in different disciplines, say, computer science and AI (Clarke and Emerson 1981; Emerson and Halpern 1986; Lamport 1980) or philosophy (Prior 1968) (for more references and discussions, see (Gabbay, Reynolds, and Finger 2000; Thomason 1984)). Here we outline the essential ideas using the simple modal extension of $\mathcal{PTL}$ with $\square$ and $\lozenge$ (but without the temporal operator $\mathcal{S}$); it will be called $\mathcal{MPTL}$.

Having fixed the language, we need to choose time structures that could allow for nontrivial interpretations. Clearly, if the flow of time is linear, then at every moment the future is fixed, so $\Box\varphi$ is equivalent to φ. The flows of time we need should be able to represent different evolutions of history. Since, on the other hand, it is natural to assume that, in contrast to the future, the past is fixed, *trees* as defined below appear to be perfect structures for modeling different histories.

Definition 6 (branching time model). A *tree* is a flow of time $\mathfrak{F} = \langle W, < \rangle$ containing a point r, called the *root* of $\mathfrak{F}$, for which $W = \{v : r < v\} \cup \{r\}$, and such that for every $w \in W$, the set $\{w : v < w\}$ is finite and linearly ordered by $<$.[8] A *history* in $\mathfrak{F}$ is a maximal linearly $<$-ordered subset of W.

A *branching time model* is a structure $\mathfrak{B} = \langle \mathfrak{F}, \mathcal{H}, \mathfrak{V} \rangle$, where $\mathfrak{F} = \langle W, < \rangle$ is a tree, $\mathcal{H}$ a set of histories in $\mathfrak{F}$—the set of possible flows of time in the model—and $\mathfrak{V}$ is a *valuation* in $\mathfrak{F}$. Formulas are evaluated relative to pairs (h, w) consisting of an *actual history* $h \in \mathcal{H}$ and a time point $w \in h$. In such a pair (h, w), the temporal operators are interpreted along the actual history h as in the linear time framework, while the modal operators quantify over the set of all histories $\mathcal{H}(w) = \{h' \in \mathcal{H} : w \in h'\}$ coming through w. More precisely, the *truth-relation* $\models$ between pairs (h, w) and $\mathcal{MPTL}$ formulas φ is defined inductively in the following way (we omit the clauses for the Booleans):

- $(h, w) \models p$ iff $w \in \mathfrak{V}(p)$;
- $(h, w) \models \varphi\mathcal{U}\psi$ iff there is $v \in h$ such that $v > w$, $(h, v) \models \psi$ and $(h, u) \models \varphi$ for all $u \in (w, v)$;
- $(h, w) \models \Diamond\varphi$ iff there is $h' \in \mathcal{H}(w)$ such that $(h', w) \models \varphi$;
- $(h, w) \models \Box\varphi$ iff $(h', w) \models \varphi$ for all $h' \in \mathcal{H}(w)$.

Note that propositional variables are assumed to have no temporal aspect—their truth-values at (h, w) do not depend on the actual history h.

The branching time model defined above reflects the Ockhamist view of time. We refer the reader to (Burgess 1979; Gabbay, Reynolds, and Finger 2000; Reynolds 2002; Zanardo 1996) for more information about this and related approaches. Here we only note that our branching time logic is closely related to the computational tree logics CTL and CTL* that are widely used in program verification and specification (Clarke and Emerson 1981; Clarke, Grumberg, and Peled 2000; Emerson and Halpern 1986).

It might seem more natural to quantify with $\Diamond$ and $\Box$ over the set of *all* histories in the tree rather than its subset $\mathcal{H}$. But then we would be forced to accept possibly unintended histories in $\mathfrak{F}$ as possible flows of time. Here is an example of a formula satisfiable in a branching time model as defined above, but not in a branching time model in which $\mathcal{H}$ is the set of all histories. The formula is a conjunction of the following three $\mathcal{MPTL}$ formulas:

$$\mathsf{P}(Kosovo, Yugoslavia),$$
$$\Box\Diamond_F\Box_F\mathsf{EC}(Kosovo, Yugoslavia),$$
$$\Box\Box_F\big(\mathsf{P}(Kosovo, Yugoslavia) \to \Diamond\bigcirc\mathsf{P}(Kosovo, Yugoslavia)\big).$$

---

[8] Other definitions of trees can be more liberal, not requiring the finiteness of $\{w : v < w\}$. One can develop the whole formalism in this more general framework (Thomason 1984).

The first formula means that at present Kosovo is part of Yugoslavia. The second says that in all possible histories, there'll be a time starting from which Kosovo will be externally connected to Yugoslavia. And the last formula claims that in all possible histories, it is always the case that if Kosovo is part of Yugoslavia then it is still possible that it will remain in Yugoslavia at least one more day. (Since we do not have a combined spatiotemporal language yet, the RCC-8 predicates P($Kosovo, Yugoslavia$) and EC($Kosovo, Yugoslavia$) should be regarded as a propositional variable and its negation, respectively.)

The following result can be obtained using a reduction to satisfiability in CTL* (Hodkinson, Wolter, and Zakharyaschev 2001):

Theorem 8. *The satisfiability problem for $\mathcal{MPTL}$ formulas is decidable in 2EXPTIME.*

(It seems that the lower bound for the computational complexity of this problem is still unknown.)

3.3 First-Order Temporal Logic

So far, we have not endowed time points with any structures that could represent states of application domains (e.g., spatial knowledge bases) at these points. When doing this, we get into the realm of *first-order temporal logic* or its variants, say, *temporal description logic* (Wolter and Zakharyaschev 2000c).

Suppose that in order to represent our application domain we use a first-order language $\mathcal{FO}$ with predicates $P_0, P_1, \ldots$ of some fixed arity. Assume also that the intended flow of time $\mathfrak{F} = \langle W, < \rangle$ is linear. Then a *first-order temporal model based on* $\mathfrak{F}$ is a pair of the form $\mathfrak{M} = \langle \mathfrak{F}, \mathfrak{m} \rangle$, where, for each $w \in W$,

$$\mathfrak{m}(w) = \langle D, P_0^w, P_1^w \ldots \rangle \tag{5}$$

is an ordinary $\mathcal{FO}$ structure—that is, D is a non-empty set and the P_i^w are relations on D of the same arity as P_i. Note that the P_i^w depend on w, while the domain D of $\mathfrak{m}(w)$ is assumed to be constant. Models of this type are often called *models with constant domains*.

An appropriate language for speaking about such models is the combination of $\mathcal{FO}$ with $\mathcal{PTL}$ in which the temporal operators $\mathcal{S}$ and $\mathcal{U}$ can be applied to first-order formulas. It will be denoted by $\mathcal{FOTL}$. The temporal operators $\mathcal{S}$ and $\mathcal{U}$ take care of the temporal dimension, while the first-order part of the language allows us to speak about the domain dimension.

To define the *truth-relation* $\models$ between time points and formulas, we first fix an *assignment* $\mathfrak{a}$ associating elements in D to individual variables. Then $(\mathfrak{M}, w) \models^{\mathfrak{a}} \varphi$ is defined by taking

- $(\mathfrak{M}, w) \models^{\mathfrak{a}} P_i(x_1, \ldots, x_k)$ iff $\mathfrak{m}(w) \models P_i[\mathfrak{a}(x_1), \ldots, \mathfrak{a}(x_k)]$,
- $(\mathfrak{M}, w) \models^{\mathfrak{a}} \exists x \varphi$ iff there exists an assignment $\mathfrak{b}$ which may differ from $\mathfrak{a}$ only on x and such that $(\mathfrak{M}, w) \models^{\mathfrak{b}} \varphi$,

and the propositional clauses for the Booleans and temporal operators. Unfortunately, the resulting logics turn out to be highly undecidable for most important flows of time. In particular, we have the following result due to Scott and Lindström (unpublished); for a proof see, for example, (Gabbay, Hodkinson, and Reynolds 1994):

Theorem 9. *The satisfiability problem for $\mathcal{FOTL}$ formulas in models based on $\langle \mathbb{R}, < \rangle$, $\langle \mathbb{Z}, < \rangle$, or $\langle \mathbb{N}, < \rangle$ is not recursively enumerable.*

Moreover, even seemingly simple fragments, such as the two-variable fragment of $\mathcal{FOTL}$ (containing formulas with the variables x, y only) and the monadic fragment of $\mathcal{FOTL}$ (containing fomulas with unary predicates only), are undecidable in any natural class of flows of time (Hodkinson, Wolter, and Zakharyaschev 2000; Merz 1992). These "negative" results have been a serious obstacle for applying first-order temporal logic in computer science and AI.

A certain breakthrough has been recently achieved in (Hodkinson, Wolter, and Zakharyaschev 2000; Wolter and Zakharyaschev 2001), where a so-called *monodic fragment* of $\mathcal{FOTL}$ was shown to have a much better computational behavior. The monodic fragment consists of those $\mathcal{FOTL}$ formulas that do not contain a subformula starting with $\mathcal{S}$ or $\mathcal{U}$ and having more than one free variable. Unlike the full $\mathcal{FOTL}$, the set of monodic formulas valid in models based on $\langle \mathbb{N}, < \rangle$ turns out to be axiomatizable. Various decidable subfragments of the monodic fragment are described in (Hodkinson, Wolter, and Zakharyaschev 2000; Wolter and Zakharyaschev 2001). In particular, the following results will be used later in this chapter:

Theorem 10.
 (i) *Let C be one of the following classes of flows of time: the class of all strict linear orders, $\{\langle \mathbb{Q}, < \rangle\}$, $\{\langle \mathbb{Z}, < \rangle\}$, $\{\langle \mathbb{N}, < \rangle\}$. Then the satisfiability problem for the one-variable fragment of $\mathcal{FOTL}$ in models based on flows of time in C is decidable.*

(ii) *Let C^+ be one of the classes mentioned above or $\{\langle \mathbb{R}, < \rangle\}$. Then the satisfiability problem for the one-variable fragment of $\mathcal{FOTL}$ in models based on flows of time in C^+ and having finite first-order domains is decidable.*

(iii) *In both cases, the satisfiability problem in models based on $\langle \mathbb{N}, < \rangle$ or $\langle \mathbb{Z}, < \rangle$ is EXPSPACE-complete.*

(The complexity of satisfiability in the flows of time different from $\langle \mathbb{N}, < \rangle$ and $\langle \mathbb{Z}, < \rangle$ remains an open problem.)

Let us now turn to branching time. Given a tree $\mathfrak{F} = \langle W, < \rangle$, a set of histories $\mathcal{H}$ in $\mathfrak{F}$, and a function $\mathfrak{m}$ of the form (5), we can form the *first-order branching time model* $\mathfrak{M} = \langle \mathfrak{F}, \mathcal{H}, \mathfrak{m} \rangle$. Having fixed an assignment $\mathfrak{a}$ in D, we define the truth-relation $\models$ between pairs (h, w) and formulas φ of the *first-order branching temporal logic* ($\mathcal{FOBTL}$) by taking

- $(h, w) \models^{\mathfrak{a}} \Box\varphi$ iff $(h', w) \models^{\mathfrak{a}} \varphi$ for all $h' \in \mathcal{H}(w)$

and keeping the other inductive clauses similar to the linear case. The resulting logic is at least as complex as $\mathcal{FOTL}$ on $\langle \mathbb{N}, < \rangle$; hence, it is highly undecidable. Unfortunately, in the case of branching time even monodicity does not guarantee good computational behavior. The following theorem has been recently proved in (Hodkinson, Wolter, and Zakharyaschev 2001):

Theorem 11. *The satisfiability problem for the one-variable fragment of $\mathcal{FOBTL}$ is undecidable.*

Thus, to obtain decidable fragments, more conditions have to be imposed on the number of free variables in the scope of temporal and modal operators. So far we know of only one successful approach relevant to spatiotemporal reasoning.[9] Denote by $\mathcal{FOBTL}^1_\bigcirc$ the one-variable fragment of $\mathcal{FOBTL}$ in which only the temporal operator $\bigcirc$ can be applied to formulas with a free variable (the other temporal operators and the modal operators can be applied to sentences only). Then we have the following result of Hodkinson, Wolter, and Zakharyaschev (2001):

Theorem 12. *The satisfiability problem for $\mathcal{FOBTL}^1_\bigcirc$ is decidable.*

3.4 Interval Temporal Logic

Similar to RCC-8, instead of time points one can take extended time entities, that is, intervals, as primitives. This approach to temporal representation and reasoning reflects the fact that certain assertions can be evaluated only at periods of time (e.g., "John often drinks beer"). It was developed by Allen (1983 and 1984), who observed, in particular, that relative positions of any two intervals i and j of a strict linear order can be described by precisely 1 of the 13 basic interval relations: $\mathrm{before}(i,j)$, $\mathrm{meets}(i,j)$, $\mathrm{overlaps}(i,j)$, $\mathrm{during}(i,j)$, $\mathrm{starts}(i,j)$, $\mathrm{finishes}(i,j)$, their inverses (i.e., $\mathrm{before}(j,i)$, $\mathrm{meets}(j,i)$, etc.), and $\mathrm{equal}(i,j)$.[10] Let us denote by $\mathcal{All}$-13 the language whose alphabet contains the 13 binary predicate symbols as above, *interval variables* i, j, and so on and the Booleans. Formulas of $\mathcal{All}$-13 are just Boolean combinations of the basic predicates.

To provide a semantics for $\mathcal{All}$-13 formulas, suppose that the flow of time is a strict linear order $\mathfrak{F} = \langle W, < \rangle$. An *assignment* in $\mathfrak{F}$ is a function $\mathfrak{a}$ mapping the interval variables into *temporal intervals in* $\mathfrak{F}$. There may be different views on what the temporal intervals in $\mathfrak{F}$ should be. We take perhaps the most "liberal" version by defining them as arbitrary non-empty convex sets in $\mathfrak{F}$. In other words, a temporal interval $\mathfrak{a}(i)$ in $\mathfrak{F}$ is a non-empty subset of W such that

$$\forall x, y \in \mathfrak{a}(i)\ \forall z \in W\, (x < z < y \to z \in \mathfrak{a}(i)).$$

The truth-relation $\mathfrak{F} \models^{\mathfrak{a}} \varphi$ for atomic $\mathcal{All}$-13 formulas is defined in the natural way. For instance,

$$\mathfrak{F} \models^{\mathfrak{a}} \mathrm{meets}(i,j) \quad \text{iff} \quad \forall x, y\, (x \in \mathfrak{a}(i) \wedge y \in \mathfrak{a}(j) \to x < y \wedge \forall z (x < z < y$$
$$\to z \in \mathfrak{a}(i) \vee z \in \mathfrak{a}(j))),$$

$$\mathfrak{F} \models^{\mathfrak{a}} \mathrm{overlaps}(i,j) \quad \text{iff} \quad \mathfrak{a}(i) \cap \mathfrak{a}(j) \neq \emptyset \wedge \exists x, y\, (x < y$$
$$\wedge\, x \in \mathfrak{a}(j) \wedge x \notin \mathfrak{a}(i) \wedge y \in \mathfrak{a}(j) \wedge y \notin \mathfrak{a}(i)),$$

$$\mathfrak{F} \models^{\mathfrak{a}} \mathrm{starts}(i,j) \quad \text{iff} \quad \mathfrak{a}(i) \subseteq \mathfrak{a}(y) \wedge \mathfrak{a}(i) \neq \mathfrak{a}(j) \wedge \forall x, y\, (x < y$$
$$\wedge\, x \in \mathfrak{a}(j) \wedge y \in \mathfrak{a}(i) \cap \mathfrak{a}(j) \to x \in \mathfrak{a}(i)),$$

$$\mathfrak{F} \models^{\mathfrak{a}} \mathrm{during}(i,j) \quad \text{iff} \quad \exists x, y, z\, (x < y < z \wedge x \in \mathfrak{a}(j) \wedge x \notin \mathfrak{a}(i)$$
$$\wedge\, y \in \mathfrak{a}(i) \wedge z \in \mathfrak{a}(j) \wedge z \notin \mathfrak{a}(i)).$$

---

[9]Other successful approaches consider CTL-like conditions on the place of temporal operators in formulas (Hodkinson, Wolter, and Zakharyaschev 2001). However, they do not seem to be useful for spatiotemporal logics.

[10]In fact, Allen was not the first who considered those 13 relations. They are present already in (Nicod 1924).

We say that φ *is satisfiable in a class* C of flows of time if $\mathfrak{F} \models^{\mathfrak{a}} \varphi$ holds for some $\mathfrak{F} \in C$ and assignment $\mathfrak{a}$ in $\mathfrak{F}$.

Usually $\mathcal{A}\ell\ell$-13 serves as a basis for more complex languages, which, besides temporal constraints, use other predicates such as $\mathsf{HOLDS}(\phi, i)$ (property ϕ holds during interval i), $\mathsf{OCCUR}(e, i)$ (event e happens over interval i). Some examples will be provided in Section 4.3.

The following result was shown in (van Beek, Kautz, and Vilain 1986):

Theorem 13. *The satisfiability problem for $\mathcal{A}\ell\ell$-13 formulas in any class of linear flows of time is NP-complete.*

Note also that $\mathcal{A}\ell\ell$-13 can be easily embedded into point-based temporal logic; for details see (Blackburn 1992).

4 Of Space and Time

Following our semantic approach, we start designing logics of time *and* space by defining their intended models—spatiotemporal structures—as a combination of topological and temporal models. We consider first the linear point-based paradigm.

4.1 Spatiotemporal Logics: Linear Point-Based Time

Definition 7 (topological temporal model). A *topological temporal model* (or *tt-model*, for short) based on a topological model $\mathfrak{S}$ of the form (4) and a flow of time $\mathfrak{F} = \langle W, < \rangle$ is simply the pair $\mathfrak{M} = \langle \mathfrak{S}, \mathfrak{F} \rangle$. An *assignment* in $\mathfrak{M}$ is a function $\mathfrak{a}$ associating with each region variable X and each moment of time $w \in W$ a set $\mathfrak{a}(X, w) \in \mathcal{R}(\mathfrak{T})$, the *state of X at w*.

Thus, tt-models can be regarded as 2D structures. Having fixed a moment of time, we can move in the spatial dimension representing the states of regions at this moment. Having fixed a spatial region, we can move along the temporal dimension tracing the evolution of this region in time. (Note the difference from first-order temporal models in which the values of individual variables are constant over time, while the extensions of predicate symbols can vary.)

Let us turn now to the syntactical parameters of spatiotemporal hybrids.

4.1.1 Quantification Over Regions

Unfortunately, quantification over region variables in tt-models—even for extremely weak languages—results in undecidable or nonaxiomatizable logics. We show here only one example. Consider the first-order spatiotemporal language $\mathcal{FOST}$, based on the following alphabet:

- an infinite set of *local region variables* $X_0, X_1, \ldots$;
- an infinite set of *global region variables* $Y_0, Y_1, \ldots$;
- the binary temporal operator $\mathcal{U}$ ("until");
- the binary predicate $\mathsf{EQ}(Z_1, Z_2)$.

$\mathcal{FOST}$ *formulas* are defined as follows:

- EQ(Z_1, Z_2) is an atomic formula, where Z_1, Z_2 are region variables;

- if φ and ψ are formulas and Y is a *global* region variable, then $\neg\varphi$, $\varphi \wedge \psi$, $\varphi \mathcal{U} \psi$, and $\forall Y \varphi$ are formulas.

The difference between local and global region variables is that the former range over "mobile" regions, while the latter denote regions that are supposed to be immovable. Thus, an assignment $\mathfrak{a}$ in a tt-model $\mathfrak{M} = \langle \mathfrak{S}, \mathfrak{F} \rangle$ should be such that $\mathfrak{a}(Y_i, u) = \mathfrak{a}(Y_i, v)$ for any time points u and v in $\mathfrak{F}$ and any global variable Y_i. The definition of the truth-relation must be clear: we put

$$(\mathfrak{M}, w) \models^{\mathfrak{a}} \mathrm{EQ}(Z_1, Z_2) \quad \text{iff} \quad \mathfrak{a}(Z_1, w) = \mathfrak{a}(Z_2, w)$$

and define the Booleans, quantifiers, and the temporal operator in the standard way.

Thus, in this language, we can reason about the equality of regions over time, but nothing else. The language looks completely "harmless." And yet, the following is easily derived from results of Merz (1992):

Theorem 14. *The satisfiability problem for $\mathcal{FOST}$ formulas in tt-models based on infinite flows of time is undecidable; it is not even recursively enumerable for the flows $\langle \mathbb{N}, < \rangle$ and $\langle \mathbb{Z}, < \rangle$.*

The cause of such "bad" computational behavior is the *interaction* between the temporal operator and the quantifiers over region variables, which is similar to the interaction between the compass operators in Example 1. Again we are forced to omit quantification and take BRCC-8 as the spatial component of the spatiotemporal logics to be constructed.

4.1.2 Spatiotemporal Representation Based on BRCC-8

In this section, we construct three spatiotemporal logics based on BRCC-8. We denote them by $\mathcal{ST}_0$–$\mathcal{ST}_2$.

$\mathcal{ST}_0$. The simplest one allows applications of the temporal operators $\mathcal{S}$ and $\mathcal{U}$ only to BRCC-8 formulas. More precisely, the *spatiotemporal language* $\mathcal{ST}_0$ is defined as follows. Every formula of BRCC-8 is also an $\mathcal{ST}_0$ formula, and if φ and ψ are $\mathcal{ST}_0$ formulas, then so are $\varphi \mathcal{S} \psi$, $\varphi \mathcal{U} \psi$, $\varphi \wedge \psi$, and $\neg\varphi$. As usual, we use the abbreviations $\bigcirc\varphi = \bot \mathcal{U} \varphi$, $\diamond_F \varphi = \top \mathcal{U} \varphi$, $\square_F \varphi = \neg\diamond_F \neg\varphi$; a new one is $\varphi \mathcal{W} \psi = \square_F \varphi \vee (\varphi \mathcal{U} \psi)$, where $\mathcal{W}$ stands for "waiting for" (it is also known as "unless" (Manna and Pnueli 1992)).

For a tt-model $\mathfrak{M} = \langle \mathfrak{S}, \mathfrak{F} \rangle$, an assignment $\mathfrak{a}$ in it, an $\mathcal{ST}_0$ formula φ, and a time point w in $\mathfrak{F}$, define the truth-relation $(\mathfrak{M}, w) \models^{\mathfrak{a}} \varphi$ by induction on the construction of φ. Let $\mathfrak{a}_w$ be the assignment in $\mathfrak{S}$ defined by $\mathfrak{a}_w(X) = \mathfrak{a}(X, w)$, for every region variable X. Now,

- If φ contains no temporal operator, then $(\mathfrak{M}, w) \models^{\mathfrak{a}} \varphi$ iff $\mathfrak{S} \models^{\mathfrak{a}_w} \varphi$.

- $(\mathfrak{M}, w) \models^{\mathfrak{a}} \varphi \mathcal{U} \psi$ iff there is $v > w$ such that $(\mathfrak{M}, v) \models^{\mathfrak{a}} \psi$ and $(\mathfrak{M}, u) \models^{\mathfrak{a}} \varphi$ for every u in the interval $w < u < v$.

- $(\mathfrak{M}, w) \models^{\mathfrak{a}} \varphi \mathcal{S} \psi$ iff there is $v < w$ such that $(\mathfrak{M}, v) \models^{\mathfrak{a}} \psi$ and $(\mathfrak{M}, u) \models^{\mathfrak{a}} \varphi$ for every u in the interval $v < u < w$.

The interaction between time and space in $\mathcal{ST}_0$ is rather weak. In fact, satisfiability of $\mathcal{ST}_0$ formulas in a given infinite flow of time $\mathfrak{F}$ is easily, but exponentially, reducible to satisfiability of $\mathcal{PTL}$ formulas in $\mathfrak{F}$. Moreover, for $\langle \mathbb{N}, < \rangle$ a PSPACE satisfiability checking algorithm was constructed in (Wolter and Zakharyaschev 2000b). To sum up, using Theorem 6, we obtain:

Theorem 15. *Let $\mathcal{C}^+$ be one of the classes defined in Section 3.3. Then the satisfiability problem for $\mathcal{ST}_0$ formulas in tt-models based on flows of time in $\mathcal{C}^+$ is decidable in EXPSPACE. For $\langle \mathbb{N}, < \rangle$ it is PSPACE-complete.*

It is an open problem whether satisfiability of $\mathcal{ST}_0$ formulas in flows different from $\langle \mathbb{N}, < \rangle$ can be checked in PSPACE as well.

The language $\mathcal{ST}_0$ is expressive enough to capture some aspects of *continuity of changes* (Cohn 1997):

$$\mathsf{DC}(X,Y) \to \mathsf{DC}(X,Y)\,\mathcal{W}\,\mathsf{EC}(X,Y),$$
$$\mathsf{EC}(X,Y) \to \mathsf{EC}(X,Y)\,\mathcal{W}\,(\mathsf{DC}(X,Y) \vee \mathsf{PO}(X,Y)),$$
$$\mathsf{PO}(X,Y) \to \mathsf{PO}(X,Y)\,\mathcal{W}\,(\mathsf{EC}(X,Y)\ \vee$$
$$\mathsf{TPP}(X,Y) \vee \mathsf{EQ}(X,Y) \vee \mathsf{TPPi}(X,Y)),$$

etc.

The first of these formulas, for instance, says that if two regions are disconnected at some moment, then either they will remain disconnected forever or they are disconnected until they become externally connected. If the flow of time is discrete, then these conditions are equivalent to

$$\mathsf{DC}(X,Y) \to \bigcirc(\mathsf{DC}(X,Y) \vee \mathsf{EC}(X,Y)),$$
$$\mathsf{EC}(X,Y) \to \bigcirc(\mathsf{EC}(X,Y) \vee \mathsf{DC}(X,Y) \vee \mathsf{PO}(X,Y)),$$
$$\mathsf{PO}(X,Y) \to \bigcirc(\mathsf{PO}(X,Y) \vee \mathsf{EC}(X,Y)\ \vee$$
$$\mathsf{TPP}(X,Y) \vee \mathsf{EQ}(X,Y) \vee \mathsf{TPPi}(X,Y)),$$

etc.

However, the expressive power of $\mathcal{ST}_0$ is rather limited. In particular, we can compare regions only at one moment of time, but we are not able to connect a region as it is "today" with its state "tomorrow" to say, for example, that it is expanding or remains the same. In other words, we can express the dynamics of relations between regions, say,

$$\neg \Box_F \mathsf{P}(Kosovo, Yugoslavia)$$

("it is not true that Kosovo will always be part of Yugoslavia"), but not the dynamics of regions themselves, for instance, that

$$\Box_F \mathsf{P}(EU, \bigcirc EU),$$

where $\bigcirc EU$ at moment n intends to denote the space occupied by the EU at the next moment (so for the flow of time $\langle \mathbb{N}, < \rangle$, the last formula means "the EU will never contract"). This new constructor may also be important to refine the continuity assumption by requiring that

$$\Box_F(\mathrm{EQ}(X, \bigcirc X) \lor \mathrm{O}(X, \bigcirc X)),$$

that is, "regions X and $\bigcirc X$ either coincide or overlap."

$\mathcal{ST}_1$. To capture this dynamics, we extend $\mathcal{ST}_0$ by allowing applications of the next-time operator $\bigcirc$ not only to formulas but also to Boolean region terms. Thus, arguments of RCC-8 predicates can be now arbitrary $\bigcirc$-*terms* which are constructed from region variables using the Booleans and $\bigcirc$. For instance, $\bigcirc \bigcirc X$ represents region X as it will be "the day after tomorrow." Denote the resulting language by $\mathcal{ST}_1$, and let $\mathcal{ST}_1'$ be its sublanguage with only one temporal operator $\bigcirc$ ($\mathcal{S}$ and $\mathcal{U}$ are not allowed). Obviously, $\mathcal{ST}_1$ is more expressive than $\mathcal{ST}_0$ only for *discrete* flows of time; in dense flows like $\langle \mathbb{Q}, < \rangle$ or $\langle \mathbb{R}, < \rangle$ the "next-time" operator makes no sense. If $\mathfrak{M} = \langle \mathfrak{S}, \mathfrak{F} \rangle$ is a tt-model, $\mathfrak{a}$ an assignment in it, and t a $\bigcirc$-term, then we put

$$\mathfrak{a}(\bigcirc t, w) = \begin{cases} \mathfrak{a}(t, w') & \text{if } w' \text{ is an immediate successor of } w \text{ in } \mathfrak{F}, \\ \emptyset & \text{if } w \text{ has no immediate successor in } \mathfrak{F}. \end{cases}$$

Theorem 16.

(i) *The satisfiability problem for $\mathcal{ST}_1$ formulas in tt-models based on flows of time in $\mathcal{C}$ is decidable; for $\langle \mathbb{N}, < \rangle$ and $\langle \mathbb{Z}, < \rangle$ it is decidable in EXPSPACE.*

(ii) *The satisfiability problem for $\mathcal{ST}_1'$ formulas in tt-models based on $\langle \mathbb{N}, < \rangle$ is NP-complete.*

The EXPSPACE-upper bound and (ii) are proved in (Wolter and Zakharyaschev 2000b). A proof of (i) based on an embedding into first-order temporal logic is sketched below and given in detail in (Gabbay et al. 2002). (The lower bound is still unknown.)

Using $\mathcal{ST}_1$ we can express in $\langle \mathbb{N}, < \rangle$ that region X will always be the same—that is, X is global (or rigid):

$$\Box_F \mathrm{EQ}(X, \bigcirc X),$$

or that it has at most two distinct states, one on "even days," another on "odd ones":

$$\Box_F \mathrm{EQ}(X, \bigcirc \bigcirc X).$$

Note, by the way, that the $\mathcal{ST}_1$ formula

$$\Box_F \mathrm{NTPP}(X, \bigcirc X)$$

is satisfiable only in models based on infinite topological spaces—unlike BRCC-8 formulas, for which finite topological spaces are enough (see Theorem 2).

It may appear that $\mathcal{ST}_1$ is able to compare regions only within fixed time intervals. However, using an auxiliary global variable X, we can write, for instance,

$$\Box_F \mathrm{EQ}(X, \bigcirc X) \land \Diamond_F \mathrm{EQ}(X, EU) \land \mathrm{P}(\textit{Russia}, X).$$

This formula is satisfiable iff "some day in the future the *present* territory of Russia will be part of the EU." Note that the formula

$$\Diamond_F \mathsf{P}(Russia, EU)$$

means that there will be a day when Russia—its territory on that day (say, without Chechnya but with Byelorussia)—becomes part of the EU.

Imagine now that we want to express in our spatiotemporal language that all countries in Europe will pass through the Euro-zone, but only Germany (in its present territory) will use the euro forever. Unfortunately, we do not know which countries will be formed in Europe in the future, so we cannot simply write down all formulas of the form

$$\Diamond_F \mathsf{P}(X, Euro\text{-}zone).$$

What we actually need is the possibility of constructing regions $\Diamond_F X$ and $\Box_F X$, which contain all the points that will belong to region X in the future and only common points of all future states of X, respectively. Then we can write:

$$\mathsf{EQ}(Europe, \Diamond_F Euro\text{-}zone) \quad \text{and} \quad \mathsf{EQ}(Germany, \Box_F Euro\text{-}zone).$$

The formula $\mathsf{P}(Russia, \Diamond_F EU)$ says that all points of the present territory of Russia will belong to the EU in the future (but perhaps at different moments of time).

$\mathcal{ST}_2$. So let us extend $\mathcal{ST}_0$ by allowing the use of *temporal region terms*, constructed from region variables, the Booleans, and the temporal operators $\mathcal{U}$ and $\mathcal{S}$ with all their derivatives, as arguments of the RCC-8 predicates. The resulting language will be denoted by $\mathcal{ST}_2$. The intended semantics of temporal region terms is as follows. Suppose $\mathfrak{M} = \langle \mathfrak{S}, \mathfrak{F} \rangle$ is a tt-model and $\mathfrak{a}$ an assignment in it. Define inductively the *value* $\mathfrak{a}(t, w)$ of a temporal region term t under $\mathfrak{a}$ at w in $\mathfrak{M}$ by taking

$$\mathfrak{a}(\Diamond_F t, w) = \mathbb{CI} \bigcup_{v > w} \mathfrak{a}(t, v),$$

$$\mathfrak{a}(\Box_F t, w) = \mathbb{CI} \bigcap_{v > w} \mathfrak{a}(t, v),$$

$$\mathfrak{a}(t_1 \mathcal{U} t_2, w) = \mathbb{CI}\{x : \exists v > w \, (x \in \mathfrak{a}(t_2, v) \wedge \forall u \, (w < u < v \to x \in \mathfrak{a}(t_1, u)))\},$$

$$\mathfrak{a}(t_1 \mathcal{S} t_2, w) = \mathbb{CI}\{x : \exists v < w \, (x \in \mathfrak{a}(t_2, v) \wedge \forall u \, (w > u > v \to x \in \mathfrak{a}(t_1, u)))\},$$

and the corresponding clauses for $\Diamond_P$ and $\Box_P$. For example, the formula

$$\mathsf{DC}(Russia \, \mathcal{S} \, Russian\_Empire, Russia \, \mathcal{S} \, Germany)$$

can be used to say that the part of Russia that has been remaining Russian since 1917 is not connected to the part of Germany (Königsberg) that became Russian after the Second World War.

We remind the reader that we have to use the prefix $\mathbb{CI}$ in the right-hand parts of the definition above because infinite unions and intersections of regular closed sets are not necessarily regular closed (see (1); however, this is the case for models based on Kripke spaces), while all temporal region terms are supposed to be interpreted by "regions" of topological spaces.[11] Actually, as we shall see below, infinite operations bring various semantic complications. To avoid this problem, we can try to restrict assignments in models in such a way that infinite intersections and unions can be reduced to finite ones. There are different ways of doing this. One idea would be to accept the *Finite Change Assumption (FCA)*:

FCA *No region can change its spatial configuration infinitely often.*

This means that under **FCA**, we consider only those assignments $\mathfrak{a}$ in tt-models $\mathfrak{M} = \langle \mathfrak{S}, \mathfrak{F} \rangle$ that satisfy the following condition: for every temporal region term t there are pairwise disjoint convex sets $I_1, \ldots, I_n$ of points in $\mathfrak{F} = \langle W, < \rangle$ such that $W = I_1 \cup \cdots \cup I_n$ and the state of t remains constant on each I_j—that is, $\mathfrak{a}(t, u) = \mathfrak{a}(t, v)$ for every $u, v \in I_j$. Note that for the flow $\mathfrak{F} = \langle \mathbb{N}, < \rangle$, **FCA** can be captured by the $\mathcal{ST}_1$ formulas $\Diamond_F \Box_F \mathsf{EQ}(t, \bigcirc t)$.

Of course, **FCA** excludes some mathematically interesting cases. Yet it is absolutely adequate for many applications, for example, when we are planning a job which eventually must be completed (consider a robot painting a wall). Optimists would accept **FCA** to describe the geography of Europe in the examples above. In temporal databases, the time line is often assumed to be finite, though arbitrarily long, which corresponds to **FCA**. Another, more general, way of reducing infinite unions and intersections to finite ones is to adopt the *Finite State Assumption (FSA)*:[12]

FSA *Every region can have only finitely many possible states (although it may change its states infinitely often).*

Say that a tt-model $\mathfrak{M} = \langle \mathfrak{S}, \mathfrak{F} \rangle$ with an assignment $\mathfrak{a}$ satisfies **FSA**, or is an **FSA** *model*, if for every temporal region term t there are finitely many sets $A_1, \ldots, A_m \in \mathcal{R}(\mathfrak{T})$ such that $\{\mathfrak{a}(t, w) : w \in W\} = \{A_1, \ldots, A_m\}$. These models can be used, for instance, to capture periodic fluctuations due to season or climate changes, say, a daily tide.

Theorem 17.

(i) *The satisfiability problem for $\mathcal{ST}_2$ formulas in **FSA** models based on flows of time in $\mathcal{C}^+$ is decidable; for $\langle \mathbb{N}, < \rangle$ and $\langle \mathbb{Z}, < \rangle$ it is decidable in EXPSPACE.*

(ii) *An $\mathcal{ST}_2$ formula is satisfiable in an **FSA** model iff it is satisfiable in an **FSA** model based on a finite topological space.*

For the flow $\langle \mathbb{N}, < \rangle$, this result is proved in (Wolter and Zakharyaschev 2000b). A proof of the general result is provided in (Gabbay et al. 2002). It is based on an embedding into first-order temporal logic and sketched below. The complexity of the satisfiability problem in (i) is unknown.

It is worth noting that, instead of the propositional temporal language $\mathcal{PTL}$, we could have combined with BRCC-8 the first-order language $\mathcal{L}^<$. We would then obtain a *two-sorted* language with variables t of sort "time" ranging over time points and variables X of sort "region" ranging over regions in topological spaces. The new ingredient would

---

[11]It is also worth noting that the operators $\Diamond_F$ and $\Box_F$ on temporal region terms are dual in the sense that for every assignment $\mathfrak{a}$, every term t, and every moment w we have $\mathfrak{a}(\Diamond_F t, w) = \mathfrak{a}(\neg \Box_F \neg t, w)$.

[12]"What has been is what will be and what has been done is what will be done; there is nothing new under the sun" (Ecclesiastes).

be eight *ternary* predicates $DC(t, X, Y)$, $EC(t, X, Y)$, and so on, the intuitive meaning of which is "at moment t, region X is disconnected from region Y," and so on. Similarly to Kamp's theorem on the expressive equivalence of $\mathcal{L}^<$ and $\mathcal{PTL}$, one can show that certain two-sorted logics have the same expressive power as certain logics in the $\mathcal{ST}_i$ hierarchy.

4.1.3 Example

We illustrate possible applications of the language introduced in the previous section by showing a toy spatiotemporal knowledge base. Consider the following scenario of how the foot-and-mouth epidemic spreads across a country. Assume that the country consists of disjoint regions: farms, towns, forests, rivers, and so on. The map of the country can clearly be represented as a database of RCC-8 formulas. Besides, we require that all these regions are rigid—that is, $\Box_F^+ EQ(X, \bigcirc X)$ (as quantification over regions is not allowed, we have to write such formulas for all regions X on the map). Now, suppose that at moment 0 foot-and-mouth disease has been detected only at one farm, X_0:

$$EQ(F\&M, X_0) \wedge P(X_0, Farm).$$

The region $F\&M$, representing the current contaminated part of the country, is not rigid. Nor is the region *Stock* representing the farms with livestock. Let $X_0, \ldots, X_n$ be all the farms in the country. We then should clearly have, for all $i \le n$:

$$\Box_F^+ \big(O(X_i, Stock) \to P(X_i, Stock) \big).$$
$$\Box_F^+ P(Stock, X_0 \sqcup \cdots \sqcup X_n).$$
$$\Box_F^+ \big((O(X_i, F\&M) \to P(X_i, F\&M) \big).$$
$$\Box_F^+ P(F\&M, Stock).$$

Suppose also that if one farm suffers from foot-and-mouth disease, then at the next moment, the disease will spread to all neighboring farms with stock, but not further—that is, for all $i, j \le n$,

$$\Box_F^+ \big(P(X_i, F\&M) \wedge EC(X_i, X_j) \wedge P(X_j, Stock) \to \bigcirc P(X_j, F\&M) \big).$$
$$\Box_F^+ \big(\neg EC(X_i, F\&M) \to \bigcirc \neg P(X_i, F\&M) \big).$$

As the government takes proper measures against the disease, in a few moments (say, two for definiteness), a farm with foot-and-mouth disease will have no livestock. On the other hand, the government is going to help the farmers continue their business, so eventually new stock will be purchased (but nobody knows when):

$$\Box_F^+ \Big(P(X_i, F\&M) \to \bigcirc \bigcirc \big(\neg O(X_i, F\&M) \wedge \neg O(X_i, Stock) \big) \Big).$$
$$\Box_F^+ \big(P(X_i, Stock) \to \Diamond_F P(X_i, Stock) \big).$$

Denote the resulting knowledge base by Σ. We can use it to answer queries like "how much time the government needs to get rid of the disease" or "when it is safe to buy new animals," for instance, by checking whether formulas of the following form are logical consequences of Σ:

$$\bigcirc \cdots \bigcirc EQ(F\&M, \bot), \qquad \bigcirc \cdots \bigcirc \big(\neg \Diamond_F P(X_i, F\&M) \big)$$

It is worth noting that in this example we have a typical mixture of a "sort of" model checking and deduction: while the map of the country is simulated by taking all RCC-8 relations that hold true between farms, towns, forests, and so on, knowledge about fluents like $F\&M$ and $Stock$ is incomplete, since it depends on the future development. So to decide whether $\Sigma \models \varphi$ holds or not, *proper deduction* (or *theorem proving*) is required (Halpern and Vardi 1991).

4.1.4 Modal Formalisms for Spatiotemporal Reasoning

We saw in Section 2.2.4 that BRCC-8 can be embedded into the bimodal logic $S4_u$ (which yields decidability) and then into the one-variable fragment of classical first-order logic (which yields NP-completeness). Similarly, the constructed temporalizations of BRCC-8 can be translated into the language $\mathcal{PST}$, or *propositional spatiotemporal language*, that contains the temporal operators $\mathcal{S}$ and $\mathcal{U}$, and the "spatial" operators of $S4_u$ (i.e., $\boldsymbol{I}$, $\boxed{\forall}$ and their duals). The intended models of $\mathcal{PST}$, called *topological $\mathcal{PST}$ models*, are triples of the form $\mathfrak{N} = \langle \mathfrak{T}, \mathfrak{F}, \mathfrak{U} \rangle$, in which $\mathfrak{T} = \langle U, \mathbb{I} \rangle$ is a topological space, $\mathfrak{F} = \langle W, < \rangle$ a flow of time, and $\mathfrak{U}$ a *valuation* associating with every propositional variable p and every $w \in W$ a set $\mathfrak{U}(p, w) \subseteq U$. $\mathfrak{U}$ is then extended to arbitrary $\mathcal{PST}$ formulas in the following way:

- $\mathfrak{U}(\psi \wedge \chi, w) = \mathfrak{U}(\psi, w) \cap \mathfrak{U}(\chi, w)$;

- $\mathfrak{U}(\neg\psi, w) = U - \mathfrak{U}(\psi, w)$;

- $\mathfrak{U}(\boxed{\forall} \psi, w) = U$ if $\mathfrak{U}(\psi, w) = U$, and $\mathfrak{U}(\boxed{\forall} \psi, w) = \emptyset$ otherwise;

- $\mathfrak{U}(\boldsymbol{I}\psi, w) = \mathbb{I}\mathfrak{U}(\psi, w)$;

- $x \in \mathfrak{U}(\psi\mathcal{U}\chi, w)$ iff there is $v > w$ such that $x \in \mathfrak{U}(\chi, v)$ and $x \in \mathfrak{U}(\psi, u)$ for all $u \in (v, w)$;

- $x \in \mathfrak{U}(\psi\mathcal{S}\chi, w)$ iff there is $v < w$ such that $x \in \mathfrak{U}(\chi, v)$ and $x \in \mathfrak{U}(\psi, u)$ for all $u \in (v, w)$.

In particular,

- $\mathfrak{U}(\Diamond_F\psi, v) = \bigcup_{v > w} \mathfrak{U}(\psi, v), \quad \mathfrak{U}(\Box_F\psi, w) = \bigcap_{v > w} \mathfrak{U}(\psi, v)$.

A $\mathcal{PST}$ formula φ is *satisfied in* $\mathfrak{N}$ if $\mathfrak{U}(\varphi, w) \neq \emptyset$ for some $w \in W$.

Say that a topological $\mathcal{PST}$ model $\mathfrak{N} = \langle \mathfrak{T}, \mathfrak{F}, \mathfrak{U} \rangle$ *satisfies* **FSA** if, for every variable p, there are finitely many sets $U_1, \ldots, U_n \subseteq U$ such that

$$\{\mathfrak{U}(p, w) : w \in W\} = \{U_1, \ldots, U_n\}.$$

We can now extend the translation $\cdot^*$ from BRCC-8 into $S4_u$, defined in Section 2.2.4, to a translation from $\mathcal{ST}_2$ formulas into the language of $\mathcal{PST}$. For temporal region terms, we need two extra clauses:

$$(t_1 \,\mathcal{U}\, t_1)^* = \boldsymbol{CI}(t_1^* \,\mathcal{U}\, t_2^*), \qquad (t_1 \,\mathcal{S}\, t_1)^* = \boldsymbol{CI}(t_1^* \,\mathcal{S}\, t_2^*).$$

Note that we then also have:

$$(\bigcirc t)^* = \bigcirc t^*, \quad (\Diamond_F t)^* = \boldsymbol{CI}\Diamond_F t^*, \quad (\Box_F t)^* = \boldsymbol{CI}\Box_F t^*.$$

For atomic $\mathcal{ST}_2$ formulas $P(t_1, t_2)$, the translation $P(t_1, t_2)^*$ is defined in precisely the same way as in Section 2.2.4. Suppose now that φ is an arbitrary $\mathcal{ST}_2$ formula. Then φ^* denotes the result of replacing all occurrences of atoms $P(t_1, t_2)$ in φ with $(P(t_1, t_2))^*$. It should be clear from the definition that we have

Theorem 18. *An $\mathcal{ST}_2$ formula φ is satisfiable in a tt-model (with* **FSA**) *based on a flow of time $\mathfrak{F}$ iff φ^* is satisfiable in a topological $\mathcal{PST}$ model (with* **FSA**) *based on $\mathfrak{F}$.*

Unfortunately, we cannot conclude from this result that $\mathcal{ST}_2$ is decidable. It is a challenging open problem to find out whether satisfiability of $\mathcal{PST}$ formulas in arbitrary topological models, or even only in those based on Kripke spaces, is decidable.

Note that the $\mathcal{PST}$ formula $\diamond_F Cp \leftrightarrow C\diamond_F p$ is valid in all $\mathcal{PST}$ models based on Kripke spaces, but not on arbitrary topological spaces, simply because there is an infinite sequence of closed sets in $\mathbb{R}$, the union of which is not closed. However, the two types of models turn out to be equivalent with respect to the *modal translations* of (a) $\mathcal{ST}_1$ formulas, and (b) $\mathcal{ST}_2$ formulas provided that models satisfy the **FSA**. Moreover, in both cases we can again take advantage of the special form of these translations and show that $\mathcal{PST}$ models based on quasisaw Kripke spaces are enough to satisfy all satisfiable formulas (see (Gabbay et al. 2002) for a proof):

Theorem 19.

(i) *An $\mathcal{ST}_2$ formula φ is satisfied in a tt-model with* **FSA** *based on a flow of time $\mathfrak{F}$ iff φ^* is satisfied in a $\mathcal{PST}$ model with* **FSA** *based on $\mathfrak{F}$ and a quasisaw Kripke space.*

(ii) *An $\mathcal{ST}_1$ formula φ is satisfied in a tt-model based on a flow of time $\mathfrak{F}$ iff φ^* is satisfied in a $\mathcal{PST}$ model based on $\mathfrak{F}$ and a quasisaw Kripke space.*

We can now use this result to "lift" the translation $\cdot^\dagger$ of BRCC-8 formulas into the one-variable fragment of first-order logic to a translation of $\mathcal{ST}_2$ formulas into the one-variable fragment of first-order temporal logic. This can be done by adding to the definition of the translations $\cdot^b$, $\cdot^l$, and $\cdot^r$ in Section 2.2.4 two more clauses:

$$(\varphi\, \mathcal{U}\, \psi)^i = \varphi^i\, \mathcal{U}\, \psi^i, \quad \text{for } i = b, l, r,$$
$$(\varphi\, \mathcal{S}\, \psi)^i = \varphi^i\, \mathcal{S}\, \psi^i, \quad \text{for } i = b, l, r.$$

Given an $\mathcal{ST}_2$ formula φ, we put $\varphi^\dagger = (\varphi^*)^b$. Note that, as before, $\varphi^\dagger$ contains a single individual variable.

Theorem 20. *Suppose $\mathfrak{F}$ is a flow of time and φ an $\mathcal{ST}_2$ formula. Then the following conditions are equivalent:*

1. *φ^* is satisfiable in a $\mathcal{PST}$ model (with* **FSA***) based on $\mathfrak{F}$ and a quasisaw Kripke space.*

2. *$\varphi^\dagger$ is satisfiable in a first-order temporal model based on $\mathfrak{F}$ (and having a finite domain).*

Now a proof of Theorem 16(i) is obtained by combining Theorem 10(i) and 10(iii) with Theorem 19(ii) and Theorem 20. A proof of Theorem 17(i) follows from Theorem 10(ii) and 10(iii), and Theorems 19 and 20.

4.1.5 Temporal Models Based on Euclidean Spaces

As we observed in Section 2.2.2, there exist satisfiable BRCC-8 formulas that are not satisfiable in any connected (in particular, Euclidean) topological space. A simple example is the conjunction φ of the following predicates:

$$\mathrm{EQ}(X_1 \sqcup X_2, Y), \quad \mathrm{NTPP}(X_1, Y), \quad \mathrm{NTPP}(X_2, Y), \quad \mathrm{DC}(Y, Z).$$

Clearly, φ is satisfied in the discrete space with three points. Note now that if φ holds in some topological space, then $X_1 \sqcup X_2$ is closed and included in the interior of Y. On the other hand, it coincides with Y. Hence, Y is both closed and open. However, Y is not the whole space because it is disjoint with Z.

A similar effect can be achieved in the spatiotemporal case even without using the Boolean operations on region terms simply because unions of regions are implicitly available in $\mathcal{ST}_2$ in the form of $\Diamond_F$. Consider, for instance, the conjunction ψ of the predicates

$$\mathrm{EQ}(\Diamond_F X, Y), \quad \mathrm{NTPP}(\bigcirc X, Y), \quad \mathrm{NTPP}(\bigcirc\Diamond_F X, Y), \quad \mathrm{DC}(Y, Z).$$

One can readily check that ψ is satisfiable in some tt-model with **FSA**, but not in a model based on a connected topological space, in particular $\mathbb{R}^\varkappa$, for any $n \geq 1$.

It is an interesting open problem whether satisfiability of $\mathcal{ST}_2$ formulas (with or without the Booleans on region terms) in models (with **FSA**) based on Euclidean spaces is decidable (Renz 1998). We only know that the following holds (see (Wolter and Zakharyaschev 2000b) for a proof):

Theorem 21. *If a set of $\mathcal{ST}_1$ formulas without Boolean operations on region terms is satisfiable in a tt-model based on $\langle \mathbb{N}, < \rangle$, then it is also satisfiable in a model based on $\langle \mathbb{N}, < \rangle$ and $\mathbb{R}^n$, for any $n \geq 1$.*

4.2 Spatiotemporal Logics of Branching Time

In the framework of linear-time spatiotemporal logics, we can say, for instance, that the United Kingdom will join the Euro-zone: $\Diamond_F \mathrm{P}(UK, Euro\text{-}zone)$. We can also say that this will never happen. But we are not able to convey the reality, which is that both variants are possible:

$$\Diamond\Diamond_F \mathrm{P}(UK, Euro\text{-}zone) \wedge \Diamond\neg\Box_F \mathrm{P}(UK, Euro\text{-}zone).$$

Nor can we make the foot-and-mouth scenario above more realistic by saying that the disease *possibly* spreads to the neighboring farms. In this section, we show how the spatiotemporal formalisms developed so far can be extended to the branching time paradigm capable of making assertions about alternative histories.

At the syntactical level, we have two options: to allow applications of $\Box$ and $\Diamond$ only to $\mathcal{ST}_i$ formulas, or to both formulas and temporal region terms. The resulting languages will be denoted by $\mathcal{STB}_i$ (the former option) and $\mathcal{STB}_i^+$ (the latter one). In the latter case, we also have to update the notion of "temporal region term" by adding to its definition the clause: if t is a temporal region term, then so are $\Box t$ and $\Diamond t$. For example, the following $\mathcal{STB}_2^+$ formula

$$\Box\Box_F\big(\mathrm{EQ}(Europe, \bigcirc Europe) \wedge \mathrm{P}(EU, Europe)\big) \wedge$$

$$\mathrm{P}(Europe, \Diamond \bigcirc EU) \wedge \mathrm{P}(\Box \bigcirc EU, EU)$$

says that, whatever happens, the region occupied by Europe will always remain the same and the EU will be part of Europe; moreover, every part of Europe has a possibility to join the EU next year, while, on the other hand, what will certainly belong to the EU next year is only part of the EU as it is today.

The extension of tt-models to branching time topological models is straightforward:

Definition 8 (branching tt-models). A *branching time topological model* (a *btt-model*, for short) is a triple $\mathfrak{M} = \langle \mathfrak{S}, \mathfrak{F}, \mathcal{H} \rangle$, where $\mathfrak{S}$ is a topological model, $\mathfrak{F} = \langle W, < \rangle$ a tree, and $\mathcal{H}$ a set of histories in $\mathfrak{F}$. An *assignment* $\mathfrak{a}$ in $\mathfrak{M}$ associates with every region variable X and every $w \in W$ a set $\mathfrak{a}(X, w) \in \mathcal{R}(\mathfrak{T})$.

Given a region term t, a time point $w \in W$, and a history $h \in \mathcal{H}$, define the *value* $\mathfrak{a}(t, h, w)$ of t at w relative to h inductively by taking

$$\mathfrak{a}(X, h, w) = \mathfrak{a}(X, w), \ X \text{ a region variable;}$$

$$\mathfrak{a}(\Diamond t, h, w) = \mathbb{CI} \bigcup_{h' \in \mathcal{H}(w)} \mathfrak{a}(t, h', w);$$

$$\mathfrak{a}(\Box t, h, w) = \mathbb{CI} \bigcap_{h' \in \mathcal{H}(w)} \mathfrak{a}(t, h', w);$$

$$\mathfrak{a}(t \, \mathcal{U} \, s, h, w) = \mathbb{CI} \{ x \in U : \exists v > w \ (v \in h \wedge x \in \mathfrak{a}(t, h, v) \ \wedge$$
$$\forall u \in (w, v) \ x \in \mathfrak{a}(s, h, u)) \},$$

the standard clauses for the Booleans. Now, for a formula φ and a pair (h, w), the *truth* of φ at (h, w) in $\mathfrak{M}$ is defined inductively as follows:

- $(h, w) \models^{\mathfrak{a}} P(s, t)$ iff $\mathfrak{S} \models P[\mathfrak{a}(s, h, w), \mathfrak{a}(t, h, w)]$, for atomic $P(s, t)$;
- $(h, w) \models^{\mathfrak{a}} \psi \mathcal{U} \chi$ iff there is $v > w$ such that $v \in h$, $(h, v) \models^{\mathfrak{a}} \chi$, and $(h, u) \models^{\mathfrak{a}} \psi$ for all $u \in (w, v)$;
- $(h, w) \models^{\mathfrak{a}} \Diamond \varphi$ iff there is $h' \in \mathcal{H}(w)$ such that $(h', w) \models^{\mathfrak{a}} \varphi$;
- $(h, w) \models^{\mathfrak{a}} \Box \varphi$ iff $(h', w) \models^{\mathfrak{a}} \varphi$ for all $h' \in \mathcal{H}(w)$,

plus the standard clauses for the Booleans.

The computational behavior of spatiotemporal logics of branching time is less understood as compared with the linear case. First, we have the following positive result:

Theorem 22. *There is an algorithm which, given an $\mathcal{STB}_1$ formula φ, decides whether φ is satisfiable in a btt-model or not.*

This theorem can be proved by extending the embedding of $\mathcal{ST}_1$ into $\mathcal{FOTL}$ to an embedding of $\mathcal{STB}_1$ into $\mathcal{FOBTL}_\bigcirc^1$ and then applying Theorem 12. No significant result on the computational complexity of the satisfiability problem for $\mathcal{STB}_1$ formulas has been obtained yet.

As to satisfiability of $\mathcal{STB}_i^+$ formulas, we again face the problem of infinitary operations on temporal spatial terms. Now, besides the temporal operators, the spatial terms can also be affected by the modal operators $\Box$ and $\Diamond$. In fact, at least for discrete topological spaces (i.e., spaces $\mathfrak{T} = \langle U, \mathbb{I} \rangle$ in which $\mathbb{I}$ is the identity function), we have the following negative result:

Theorem 23. *The satisfiability problem for $\mathcal{STB}_2^+$ formulas in btt-models based on discrete topological spaces is undecidable.*

The proof is by embedding the undecidable one-variable fragment of $\mathcal{FOBTL}$ (see Theorem 11) into $\mathcal{STB}_2^+$. First, with every atom P_i and every formula of the form $\forall x \psi$, we associate region variables X_{P_i} and $X_{\forall x \psi}$, respectively, and define a translation $\cdot^*$ from the one-variable fragment of $\mathcal{FOTBL}$ into the set of region terms of $\mathcal{STB}_2^+$, which distributes over the Boolean, temporal, and modal operators, and

$$\chi^* = X_\chi$$

for any χ of the form $P_i(x)$ or $\forall x \psi$. Now, given a one-variable $\mathcal{FOBTL}$ formula φ, it is not hard to check that φ is satisfiable iff the $\mathcal{STB}_2^+$ formula

$$\neg(\varphi^* = \bot) \wedge \Box\Box_F \bigwedge_{\forall x \psi \in \Phi} \Big(\big((X_{\forall x \psi} = \top) \vee (X_{\forall x \psi} = \bot) \big) \wedge \big((X_{\forall x \psi} = \top) \leftrightarrow (\psi^* = \top) \big) \Big)$$

is satisfiable in a btt-model based on a discrete topological space. Here Φ is the set of all subformulas of φ of the form $\forall x \psi$; $X = \bot$ is an abbreviation for $\mathsf{EQ}(X, X_0 \sqcap \neg X_0)$; and $X = \top$ for $\mathsf{EQ}(X, X_0 \sqcup \neg X_0)$.

We conjecture that the satisfiability problem for $\mathcal{STB}_2^+$ formulas in btt-models based on arbitrary topological and Euclidean spaces is undecidable as well.

A natural way to search for useful decidable variants of the undecidable branching time logics discussed above is to restrict the class of btt-models to those satisfying the finite state assumption and having finite sets of histories. We conjecture that it is decidable whether an $\mathcal{STB}_2^+$ formula is satisfiable in a model with finitely many branches and satisfying **FSA**.

4.3 BRCC-8 + $\mathcal{All}$-13

Since the region-based approach to spatial reasoning was inspired by and closely mirrors the interval-based approach to temporal reasoning—they both take extended entities rather than points as primitives—it would seem far more natural to temporalize BRCC-8 by combining it with an interval-based temporal logic. In this section, we show a variant of such a combination.

Following Allen (1984), we write $\mathsf{HOLDS}(\varphi, i)$ to say that a formula φ holds during a time interval i. For example, $\mathsf{HOLDS}(\mathsf{PO}(X, Y), i)$ means that during interval i regions X and Y partially overlap. Let us call an $\mathcal{ARCC}$-8 *formula* any Boolean combination of atomic $\mathcal{All}$-13 formulas, and formulas of the form $\mathsf{HOLDS}(\varphi, i)$, where φ is a BRCC-8 formula.

$\mathcal{ARCC}$-8 formulas are interpreted in standard topological temporal models $\mathfrak{M} = \langle \mathfrak{S}, \mathfrak{F} \rangle$ based on linear flows of time. The only essential difference is that now an *assignment* $\mathfrak{a}$ in $\mathfrak{M}$ associates with every interval variable i a non-empty convex set $\mathfrak{a}(i)$ in $\mathfrak{F}$, and with every region variable X and every time point w, it associates a regular closed set $\mathfrak{a}(X, w)$ in $\mathfrak{S}$. The truth-relation for the $\mathcal{All}$-13 atomic formulas is defined as in Section 3.4, and $\mathsf{HOLDS}(\varphi, i)$ is true in $\mathfrak{M}$ iff for every point $w \in \mathfrak{a}(i)$, we have $\mathfrak{S} \models^{\mathfrak{a}w} \varphi$ (as defined in Sections 2.2.1 and 2.2.2).

Here is a simple example of a "knowledge base" Σ in this unsophisticated language:

$$\text{meets}(i, j) \wedge \text{during}(i, k) \wedge \text{during}(j, k).$$
$$\text{HOLDS}(\text{TPP}(Hong\_Kong,\ UK) \wedge \text{EC}(Hong\_Kong,\ China), i).$$
$$\text{HOLDS}(\text{DC}(Hong\_Kong,\ UK), j).$$
$$\text{HOLDS}(\text{EC}(UK,\ China) \vee \text{DC}(UK,\ China), k).$$

If Σ is true in a tt-model $\mathfrak{M}$ under an assignment $\mathfrak{a}$, then the formula φ

$$\text{HOLDS}(\text{EC}(UK,\ China), i)$$

also holds in $\mathfrak{M}$ under $\mathfrak{a}$—that is, φ is a logical consequence of Σ.

A straightforward combination of the satisfiability-checking algorithms for $\mathcal{All}$-13 and BRCC-8 yields a satisfiability-checking algorithm for $\mathcal{ARCC}$-8. More precisely, we have the following:

Theorem 24. *The satisfiability problem for $\mathcal{ARCC}$-8 formulas in tt-models is NP-complete.*

An interesting open problem is to find *tractable* fragments of $\mathcal{ARCC}$-8—for instance, by combining tractable fragments of RCC-8 and $\mathcal{All}$-13 (Nebel and Bürckert 1995; Renz 1999; Renz and Nebel 1999).

As was noted in Section 3.4, $\mathcal{All}$-13 can be embedded into propositional temporal logic. Together with the modal translation of BRCC-8, this yields an embedding of $\mathcal{ARCC}$-8 into the language $\mathcal{PST}$ interpreted in topological $\mathcal{PST}$ models based on linear flows of time, and then into the one-variable fragment of first-order temporal logic. (For details, see (Bennett et al. 2001; Gabbay et al. 2002).)

5 Conclusion

Now, as we have constructed a family of decidable spatiotemporal formalisms, a natural question is whether they are "implementable."

5.1 Implementable Algorithms

The satisfiability problems for all of our logics are polynomially reducible to the satisfiability problems for the one-variable fragments of first-order temporal logics. We have also seen that usually these fragments are decidable. So the question is whether they can be supported by "practical" decision procedures.

One idea would be take advantage of the fact that the one-variable (and other monodic) fragments of many temporal logics are embeddable into monadic second-order logic (in the cases of **FCA** or **FSA**, even weak monadic second-order logic may be enough) (Hodkinson, Wolter, and Zakharyaschev 2000) and use provers like MONA (Klarlund, Møller, and Schwartzbach 2000). Unfortunately, however, the translation from (Hodkinson, Wolter, and Zakharyaschev 2000) is exponential, which will make the prover's job much harder.

On the other hand, a tableau decision procedure for the one-variable fragment of first-order temporal logic based on $\langle \mathbb{N}, < \rangle$ has been developed in (Lutz et al. 2001) as a combination of Wolper's (1985) tableau for $\mathcal{PTL}$ and a standard tableau for (the one-variable fragment of) first-order logic. Currently, a similar tableau-based procedure is being implemented for temporal description logic (Günsel and Wittmann 2001), and we expect significant experimental results on the efficiency of the procedure shortly. Positive results would allow the construction of a practical system for the language $\mathcal{ST}_1$ (without $\mathcal{S}$) interpreted in tt-models based on $\langle \mathbb{N}, < \rangle$ and possibly infinite topological spaces. That would also open the door to an implementation of a decision procedure for $\mathcal{ST}_2$ in models based on $\langle \mathbb{N}, < \rangle$ and *finite* topological spaces. A resolution-type algorithm for the monodic fragment has been developed in (Degtyarev and Fisher 2001).

5.2 Further Extensions

The obtained results make only first steps in the study of effective spatiotemporal formalisms. Many interesting problems remain open for investigation. For instance, it would be interesting and practically important to extend the spatiotemporal logics with constructors allowing us to speak about orientation (say, "go West"; see (Ligozat 1998)),[13] change, and distances. On the other hand, we also need constructors to represent properties of regions different from purely spatial or temporal (e.g., "region X is a tourist attraction accessible only by plane"). A promising idea is to combine spatiotemporal logics with suitable description logics ((Haarslev, Lutz, and Möller 1998); combinations of description logics with logics of metric spaces and temporal logics have been proposed in (Kutz, Wolter, and Zakharyaschev 2001; Kutz, Wolter, and Zakharyaschev 2002).)

An interesting problem is to find and temporalize more expressive and still decidable fragments of RCC. For example, one can consider a Datalog-type language with built-in basic spatial predicates. We could then compose knowledge bases like the following:

$$P(Y, \textit{euro-zone}) \leftarrow \textit{country}(Y),\ PP(Y, \textit{europe}),\ EC(X, Y),\ P(X, \textit{euro-zone}).$$

$$P(\textit{germany}, \textit{euro-zone}).$$

$$EC(\textit{germany}, \textit{poland}).$$

$$PP(\textit{poland}, \textit{europe}).$$

$$EC(\textit{poland}, \textit{russia}).$$

$$O(\textit{russia}, \textit{asia}).$$

$$EC(\textit{europe}, \textit{asia}).$$

The answer to the query $?P(\textit{poland}, \textit{euro-zone})$ should be Yes, while the answer to $?P(\textit{russia}, \textit{euro-zone})$ should be No. The language can be extended with Boolean region terms.

Until now, we have not imposed any restrictions on the form of spatial regions. However, applications in GIS may require us to consider only the Euclidean space $\mathbb{R}^2$ and interpret regions in it as figures of some special form, say, as circles or polygons (Grigni, Papadias, and Papadimitriou 1995). But it is still an open problem whether the satisfiability problem for RCC-8 formulas under such interpretations is decidable. A similar question can be asked regarding BRCC-8 and the spatiotemporal logics constructed above.

---

[13]Some encouraging results in this direction have been recently obtained by Balbiani and Condotta (2002).

Halpern and Shoham (1991) introduced a modal logic of intervals whose modal operators are interpreted by the 13 relations of Allen's interval logic (see Section 3.4). One can construct a similar modal logic[14] of regions with eight modal operators of the form $\langle EC \rangle$, $\langle DC \rangle$, $\langle TPP \rangle$, and so on. The intended meaning of these modalities is as follows: Suppose we have a topological model $\mathfrak{S}$ of the form (4) and a region X in $\mathfrak{T}$. Then $\langle TPP \rangle \, \varphi$ holds at X in $\mathfrak{S}$ if there is a region Y in $\mathfrak{T}$ such that $TPP(X, Y)$ and φ holds at Y. An interesting research problem is to investigate the computational behavior of this logic for different classes of topological models. (The logic of Halpern and Shoham is undecidable if intervals are taken on an infinite time line.)

Acknowledgments

We would like to thank B. Bennett, A. Cohn, I. Hodkinson, A. Kurucz, A. Rabinovich, M. Reynolds, A. Voronkov, and A. Zanardo for comments and stimulating discussions. The work of Frank Wolter was partially supported by the DFG-grant Wo 583/3-1; the work of Michael Zakharyaschev was partially supported by U.K. EPSRC grants nos. GR/R45369/01 and GR/R42474/01, and by grant no. 99-01-00968 from the Russian Foundation for Basic Research.

References

Aiello, M. (2001). A spatial similarity measure based on games: Theory and practice. Unpublished.

Aiello, M., and J. van Benthem (2000). Logical patterns in space. In *Proceedings of the First CSLI Workshop on Visual Reasoning*. CSLI Publishers, Stanford.

Allen, J. (1983). Maintaining knowledge about temporal intervals. *Communications of the ACM 26*, 832–843.

Allen, J. (1984). Towards a general theory of action and time. *Artificial Intelligence 23*, 123–154.

Asher, N., and L. Vieu (1995). Toward a geometry of common sense: A semantics and a complete axiomatization of mereotopology. In *Proceedings of the International Joint Conference on Artificial Intelligence (IJCAI-95)*, Montreal.

Balbiani, P., and J-F. Condotta (2002). Computational complexity of propositional linear temporal logics based on qualitative spatial and temporal reasoning. In *Proceedings of Frontiers of Combining Systems*. Forthcoming.

Bennett, B. (1994). Spatial reasoning with propositional logic. In *Proceedings of the 4th International Conference on Knowledge Representation and Reasoning*, pp. 51–62. San Mateo, CA: Morgan Kaufmann Publishers.

Bennett, B. (1996). Modal logics for qualitative spatial reasoning. *Journal of the Interest Group on Pure and Applied Logic 4*, 23–45.

Bennett, B. (1997). *Logical Representations for Automated Reasoning about Spatial Relationships*. Ph. D. thesis, School of Computer Studies, University of Leeds. Available at *www.scs.leeds.ac.uk/brandon*.

Bennett, B., A. Cohn, F. Wolter, and M. Zakharyaschev (2001). Multi-dimensional modal logic as a framework for spatio-temporal reasoning. *Applied Intelligence*. Available at *www.dcs.kcl.ac.uk/staff/mz*.

---

[14]The idea is due to Cohn (1993) and Lutz (2000).

Blackburn, P. (1992). Fine grained theories of time. In M. Aurnague, A. Borillo, M. Borillo, and M. Bras (Eds.), *Semantics of Time, Space and Movement: Working Papers of the Fourth International Workshop TSM-92*, Château de Bonas, pp. 327–348.

Büchi, J. (1962). On a decision method in restricted second order arithmetic. In *Logic, Methodology, and Philosophy of Science, Proceedings of the International Congress*, pp. 1–11.

Burgess, J. (1979). Logic and time. *Journal of Symbolic Logic 44*, 566–582.

Burgess, J., and Y. Gurevich (1985). The decision problem for linear temporal logic. *Notre Dame Journal of Formal Logic 26*, 115–128.

Casati, R., and A. Varzi (1999). *Parts and Places. The Structures of Spatial Representations*. Cambridge, MA: MIT Press.

Clarke, B. (1981). A calculus of individuals based on "connection." *Notre Dame Journal of Formal Logic 23*, 204–218.

Clarke, E., and E. Emerson (1981). Design and synthesis of synchronisation skeletons using branching time temporal logic. In D. Kozen (Ed.), *Logic of Programs*, Volume 131 of *Lecture Notes in Computer Science*, pp. 52–71. Springer-Verlag.

Clarke, E., O. Grumberg, and D. Peled (2000). *Model Checking*. Cambridge, MA: MIT Press.

Cohn, A. (1993). Modal and non modal qualitative spatial logics. In F. Anger, H. Guesgen, and J. van Benthem (Eds.), *Proceedings of the Workshop on Spatial and Temporal Reasoning*, Chambéry. *IJCAI-93*.

Cohn, A. (1997). Qualitative spatial representation and reasoning techniques. In G. Brewka, C. Habel, and B. Nebel (Eds.), *KI-97: Advances in Artificial Intelligence*, Lecture Notes in Computer Science, pp. 1–30. Springer-Verlag.

Cohn, A., and S. Hazarika (2001). Qualitative spatial representation and reasoning: An overview. *Fundamenta Informaticae 43*, 2–32.

Cohn, A., and A. Varzi (1998). Connection relations in mereotopology. In H. Prade (Ed.), *Proceedings of the 13th European Conference on Artificial Intelligence (ECAI-98)*, pp. 150–154. Wiley & Sons.

Davis, E. (1990). *Representations of Commonsense Knowledge*. San Mateo, CA: Morgan Kaufmann Publishers.

Degtyarev A., and M. Fisher (2001). Towards first-order temporal resolution. In F. Baader, G. Brewka and T. Eiter (Eds.), *KI 2001: Advances in Artificial Intelligence*, Volume 2174 of *LNCS*, pp. 18–32. Springer-Verlag.

Dornheim, C. (1998). Undecidability of plane polygonal mereotopology. In A. Cohn, L. Schubert, and S. Shapiro (Eds.), *Principles of Knowledge Representation and Reasoning: Proceedings of the Sixth International Conference (KR'98)*, pp. 342–353. Morgan Kaufmann.

Dummett, M., and E. Lemmon (1959). Modal logics between *S4* and *S5*. *Zeitschrift für Mathematische Logik und Grundlagen der Mathematik 5*, 250–264.

Egenhofer, M. (1991). Reasoning about binary topological relations. In O. Gunther and H. Schek (Eds.), *Proceedings of the Second Symposium on Large Spatial Databases, SSD'91* (Zurich, Switzerland). Lecture Notes in Computer Science 525, pp. 143–160.

Egenhofer, M., and R. Franzosa (1991). Point-set topological spatial relations. *International Journal of Geographical Information Systems 5*, 161–174.

Emerson, E., and J. Halpern (1986). "Sometimes" and "not never" revisited: On branching versus linear time. *Journal of the ACM 33*, 151–178.

Gabbay, D., I. Hodkinson, and M. Reynolds (1994). *Temporal Logic: Mathematical Foundations and Computational Aspects*, Volume 1. Oxford: Oxford University Press.

Gabbay, D., A. Kurucz, F. Wolter, and M. Zakharyaschev (2002). *Many-Dimensional Modal Logics: Theory and Applications*. Studies in Logic. Elsevier. Available at *www.dcs.kcl.ac.uk/staff/mz*.

Gabbay, D., M. Reynolds, and M. Finger (2000). *Temporal Logic: Mathematical Foundations and Computational Aspects*, Volume 2. Oxford: Oxford University Press.

Galton, A. (2000). *Qualitative Spatial Change*. Oxford University Press.

Garey, M., and D. Johnson (1979). *Computers and Intractability. A Guide to the Theory of NP-Completeness*. Freemann, San Francisco.

Gödel, K. (1933). Eine Interpretation des intuitionistischen Aussagenkalküls. *Ergebnisse eines mathematischen Kolloquiums 4*, 39–40. In German.

Goranko, V., and S. Passy (1992). Using the universal modality: Gains and questions. *Journal of Logic and Computation 2*, 5–30.

Gotts, N. (1996a). An axiomatic approach to topology for spatial information systems. Technical Report 96.25, School of Computer Studies, University of Leeds.

Gotts, N. (1996b). Using the RCC formalism to describe the topology of spherical regions. Technical Report 96.24, School of Computer Studies, University of Leeds.

Grigni, M., D. Papadias, and C. Papadimitriou (1995). Topological inference. In *Proceedings of IJCAI'95*, pp. 901–907.

Grzegorczyk, A. (1951). Undecidability of some topological theories. *Fundamenta Mathematicae 38*, 137–152.

Grzegorczyk, A. (1960). Axiomatizability of geometry without points. *Synthese 12*, 228–235.

Günsel, C., and M. Wittmann (2001). Towards an implementation of the temporal description logic $\mathcal{TLALC}$. In *Proceedings of the 2001 International Description Logics Workshop (DL-2001)* Stanford, pp. 162–169.

Gurevich, Y. (1964). Elementary properties of ordered Abelian groups. *Algebra and Logic 3*, 5–39. In Russian.

Haarslev, V., C. Lutz, and R. Möller (1998). Foundations of spatioterminological reasoning with description logics. In A. Cohn, L. Schubert, and S. Shapiro (Eds.), *Principles of Knowledge Representation and Reasoning: Proceedings of the Sixth International Conference (KR'98)*, pp. 112–124. San Francisco: Morgan Kaufmann Publishers.

Halpern, J., and Y. Shoham (1991). A propositional modal logic of time intervals. *Journal of the ACM 38*, 935–962.

Halpern, J., and M. Vardi (1991). Model checking vs. theorem proving: A manifesto. In *Artificial Intelligence and Mathematical Theory of Computation (Papers in Honor of John McCarthy)*, pp. 151–176. San Diego: Academic Press.

Hayes, P. (1985). The second naive physics manifesto. In R. Brachman and H. Levesque (Eds.), *Readings in Knowledge Representation*, pp. 467–485. Los Altos, CA: Morgan Kaufmann Publishers.

Hays, E. (1989). On defining motion verbs and spatial prepositions. Technical report, Universität des Saarlandes.

Hodkinson, I., F. Wolter, and M. Zakharyaschev (2000). Decidable fragments of first-order temporal logics. *Annals of Pure and Applied Logic 106*, 85–134.

Hodkinson, I., F. Wolter, and M. Zakharyaschev (2001). Monodic fragments of first-order temporal logics: 2000-2001 A.D. In *Proceedings of the Eighth International Conference on Logic for Programming, Artificial Intelligence, and Reasoning (LPAR'2001)*, pp. 1–23.

Hornsby, K., and M. Egenhofer (2000). Identity-based change: A foundation for spatio-temporal knowledge representation. *International Journal of Geographical Information Science 14*, 207–224.

Horrocks, I. (1998). Using an expressive description logic: FACT or fiction? In A. Cohn, L. Schubert, and S. Shapiro (Eds.), *Proceedings of the Sixth International Conference on Principles of Knowledge Representation and Reasoning, KR'98*, Trento, Italy, pp. 636–647. San Francisico: Morgan Kaufmann Publishers.

Horrocks, I., U. Sattler, and S. Tobies (1999). Practical reasoning for expressive description logics. In *Proceedings of the Sixth International Conference on Logic for Programming and Automated Reasoning (LPAR'99)*, pp. 161–180.

Hustadt, U., and R. Schmidt (2000). MSPASS: Modal reasoning by translation and first-order resolution. In D. Dyckhoff (Ed.), *Proceedings of TABLEAUX 2000*, Volume 1847 of *LNAI*, pp. 67–71. Springer-Verlag.

Kamp, H. (1968). *Tense Logic and the Theory of Linear Order*. Ph. D. thesis, University of California, Los Angeles.

Klarlund, N., A. Møller, and M. Schwartzbach (2000). MONA implementation secrets. *International Journal of Foundations of Computer Science*.

Kripke, S. (1963). Semantical analysis of modal logic, Part I. *Zeitschrift für Mathematische Logik und Grundlagen der Mathematik 9*, 67–96.

Kutz, O., F. Wolter, and M. Zakharyaschev (2001). A note on concepts and distances. In *Proceedings of the 2001 International Description Logics Workshop (DL-2001)*, Stanford, pp. 113–121.

Kutz, O., F. Wolter, and M. Zakharyaschev (2002). Connecting abstract description systems. In *Proceedings of the Eighth International Conference on Principles of Knowledge Representation and Reasoning.* pp. 215–226. San Francisco: Morgan Kaufmann Publishers.

Lamport, L. (1980). "Sometimes" is sometimes "not never." In *Proceedings of the Seventh ACM Symposium on Principles of Programming Languages*, pp. 174–185.

Läuchli, H., and J. Leonard (1966). On the elementary theory of linear order. *Fundamenta Mathematicae 59*, 109–116.

Levesque, H., and R. Brachman (1985). A fundamental tradeoff in knowledge representation and reasoning (revised version). In R. Brachman and H. Levesque (Eds.), *Readings in Knowledge Representation*, pp. 41–70. Los Altos, CA: Morgan Kaufmann Publishers.

Lewis, C., and C. Langford (1932). *Symbolic Logic*. New York: Appleton-Century-Crofts.

Ligozat, G. (1998). Reasoning about cardinal directions. *Journal of Visual Languages and Computing 9*, 23–44.

Lutz, C. (2000). Personal communication.

Lutz, C., H. Sturm, W. Wolter, and M. Zakharyaschev (2001). Temporalizing tableaux. Unpublished.

Manna, Z., and A. Pnueli (1992). *The Temporal Logic of Reactive and Concurrent Systems: Specification.* Springer-Verlag.

Manna, Z., and A. Pnueli (1995). *Temporal Verification of Reactive Systems: Safety.* Springer-Verlag.

Marx, M., and M. Reynolds (1999). Undecidability of compass logic. *Journal of Logic and Computation 9*, 897–941.

McKinsey, J. (1941). A solution of the decision problem for the Lewis systems $S2$ and $S4$, with an application to topology. *Journal of Symbolic Logic 6*, 117–134.

McKinsey, J., and A. Tarski (1944). The algebra of topology. *Annals of Mathematics 45*, 141–191.

Merz, S. (1992). Decidability and incompleteness results for first-order temporal logics of linear time. *Journal of Applied Non-classical Logic 2.*

Meyer, A. (1975). Weak monadic second order theory of successor is not elementary-recursive. In *Proceedings of Boston University Logic Colloquium,* Boston 1972, Volume 453 of *Lecture Notes in Mathematics,* pp. 132–154. Springer-Verlag.

Muller, P. (1998). A qualitative theory of motion based on spatio-temporal primitives. In A. Cohn, L. Schubert, and S. Shapiro (Eds.), *Proceedings of the Sixth International Conference Principles of Knowledge Representation and Reasoning,* pp. 131–142. San Francisco: Morgan Kaufmann Publishers.

Nebel, B. (1996). Artificial intelligence: A computational perspective. In G. Brewka (Ed.), *Principles of Knowledge Representation,* pp. 237–260. Stanford, CA: CSLI Publications.

Nebel, B., and H.-J. Bürckert (1995). Reasoning about relations: A maximal tractable subclass of Allen's interval algebra. *Journal of the ACM 42,* 43–66.

Nicod, J. (1924). Geometry in the sensible world. English translation in *Geometry and Induction,* Routledge and Kegan Paul, 1969. Doctoral thesis, Sorbonne.

Ono, H., and A. Nakamura (1980). On the size of refutation Kripke models for some linear modal and tense logics. *Studia Logica 39,* 325–333.

Orlov, I. (1928). The calculus of compatibility of propositions. *Mathematics of the USSR, Sbornik 35,* 263–286. In Russian.

Pratt, I., and D. Schoop (1997). A complete axiom system for polygonal mereotopology of the plane. Technical Report UMCS-97-2-2, University of Manchester.

Preparata, F., and M. Shamos (1985). *Computational Geometry: An Introduction.* Berlin: Springer-Verlag.

Prior, A. (1968). Now. *Noûs 2,* 101–119.

Rajagopalan, R., and B. Kuipers (1994). Qualitative spatial reasoning about objects in motion: Application to physics problem solving. In N. Guarino (Ed.), *Proceedings of IEEE Conference on Artificial Intelligence for Applications (CAIA'94),* Volume 46. San Antonio.

Randell, D., Z. Cui, and A. Cohn (1992). A spatial logic based on regions and connection. In *Proceedings of the 3rd International Conference on Knowledge Representation and Reasoning,* pp. 165–176. San Mateo, CA: Morgan Kaufmann Publishers.

Renz, J. (1998). A canonical model of the region connection calculus. In *Proceedings of the Sixth International Conference on Knowledge Representation and Reasoning*, pp. 330–341. San Francisco: Morgan Kaufmann Publishers.

Renz, J. (1999). Maximal tractable fragments of the region connection calculus: A comparative analysis. In *Proceedings of the 16th International Joint Conference on Artificial Intelligence*, pp. 448–454. San Francisco: Morgan Kaufmann Publishers.

Renz, J., and B. Nebel (1999). On the complexity of qualitative spatial reasoning. *Artificial Intelligence 108*, 69–123.

Reynolds, M. (2001a). The complexity of temporal logic over the reals. Unpublished.

Reynolds, M. (2001b). The complexity of the temporal logic with until over general linear time. Unpublished.

Reynolds, M. (2002). Axioms for branching time. *Journal of Logic and Computation*. Forthcoming.

Reynolds, M., and M. Zakharyaschev (2001). On the products of linear modal logics. *Journal of Logic and Computation 11*, 1–24.

Russell, S., and P. Norvig (1995). *Artificial Intelligence: A Modern Approach*. Prentice Hall.

Shehtman, V. (1999). "Everywhere" and "here." *Journal of Applied Non-Classical Logics 9*, 369–379.

Sistla, A., and E. Clarke (1985). The complexity of propositional linear temporal logics. *Journal of the Association for Computing Machinery 32*, 733–749.

Smith, T., and K. Park (1992). An algebraic approach to spatial reasoning. *International Journal of Geographical Information Systems 6*, 177–192.

Spaan, E. (1993). *Complexity of Modal Logics*. Ph. D. thesis, Department of Mathematics and Computer Science, University of Amsterdam.

Srefik, M. (1995). *Introduction to Knowledge Systems*. San Francisco: Morgan Kaufmann Publishers.

Stell, J. (2000). Boolean connection algebras: A new approach to the region connection calculus. *Artificial Intelligence 122*, 111–136.

Stell, J., and M. Worboys (1997). The algebraic structure of sets of regions. In S. Hirtle and A. Frank (Eds.), *Spatial Information Theory: A Theoretical Basis for GIS, Proceedings of COSIT'97*, Volume 1329 of *LNCS*, Berlin, pp. 163–174. Springer-Verlag.

Stock, O. (Ed.) (1997). *Spatial and Temporal Reasoning*. Boston: Kluwer.

Stockmeyer, L. (1974). *The Complexity of Decision Problems in Automata Theory and Logic*. Ph. D. thesis, Department of Electrical Engineering, MIT.

Stone, M. (1937). Application of the theory of Boolean rings to general topology. *Transactions of the American Mathematical Society 41*, 321–364.

Tarski, A. (1938). Der Aussagenkalkül und die Topologie. *Fundamenta Mathematicae 31*, 103–134. In German.

Thomason, R. (1984). Combinations of tense and modality. In D. Gabbay and F. Guenthner (Eds.), *Handbook of Philosophical Logic*, Volume II, pp. 135–165. Reidel.

Tsao-Chen, T. (1938). Algebraic postulates and a geometric interpretation of the Lewis calculus of strict implication. *Bulletin of the American Mathematical Society 44*, 737–744.

van Beek, P., H. Kautz, and M. Vilain (1986). Constraint propagation algorithms for temporal reasoning: A revised report. In *Proceedings AAAI-86*, Philadelphia. Revised version in (Weld and De Kleer 1990).

van Benthem, J. (1983). *Modal Logic and Classical Logic*. Naples: Bibliopolis.

van Benthem, J. (1996). Temporal logic. In D. Gabbay, C. Hogger, and J. Robinson (Eds.), *Handbook of Logic in Artificial Intelligence and Logic Programming*, Volume 4, pp. 241–350. Oxford: Oxford Scientific Publishers.

Venema, Y. (1990). Expressiveness and completeness of an interval tense logic. *Notre Dame J. Formal Logic 31*, 529–547.

Vieu, L. (1991). *Sémantique des relations spatiales et inférences spatio-temporelles*. Ph. D. thesis, Université Paul Sabatier, Toulouse. In French.

Vieu, L. (1997). Spatial representation and reasoning in AI. In O. Stock (Ed.), *Spatial and Temporal Reasoning*, pp. 5–41. Boston: Kluwer.

Weld, D., and J. De Kleer (Eds.) (1990). *Readings in Qualitative Reasoning about Physical Systems*. San Mateo, CA: Morgan Kaufmann Publishers.

Whitehead, A. N. (1929). *Process and Reality*. New York: MacMillan Company. Corrected edition published in 1978 by Macmillan.

Wolper, P. (1985). The tableau method for temporal logic: An overview. *Logique ae Analyse 110–111*, 119–136.

Wolter, F., and M. Zakharyaschev (2000a). Spatial reasoning in RCC-8 with Boolean region terms. In W. Horn (Ed.), *Proceedings of the Fourteenth European Conference on Artificial Intelligence, ECAI 2000*, Berlin, Germany, pp. 244–248. IOS Press.

Wolter, F., and M. Zakharyaschev (2000b). Spatio-temporal representation and reasoning based on RCC-8. In *Proceedings of the Seventh Conference on Principles of Knowledge Representation and Reasoning, KR2000, Breckenridge, USA*, Montreal, Canada, pp. 3–14. San Francisco: Morgan Kaufmann Publishers.

Wolter, F., and M. Zakharyaschev (2000c). Temporalizing description logics. In D. Gabbay and M. de Rijke (Eds.), *Frontiers of Combining Systems II*, pp. 379–401. England: Research Studies Press.

Wolter, F., and M. Zakharyaschev (2001). Axiomatizing the monodic fragment of first-order temporal logic. *Annals of Pure and Applied Logic*. Available at *www.dcs.kcl.ac.uk/staff/mz*.

Worboys, M. (1995). *GIS: A Computing Perspective*. Taylor & Francis.

Zanardo, A. (1996). Branching-time logic with quantification over branches: The point of view of modal logic. *Journal of Symbolic Logic 61*, 1–39.

Chapter 7
AI and Education

Extending Virtual Humans to Support Team Training in Virtual Reality

Jeff Rickel and W. Lewis Johnson
Information Sciences Institute and Computer Science Department
University of Southern California
4676 Admiralty Way
Marina del Rey, CA 90292-6695
rickel@isi.edu, johnson@isi.edu
www.isi.edu/isd/carte

Abstract

This chapter describes the use of virtual humans and distributed virtual reality to support team training, where students must learn their individual role in the team as well as how to coordinate their actions with their teammates. Students, instructors, and virtual humans cohabit a 3D, interactive simulated mock-up of their work environment, where they can practice together in realistic situations. The virtual humans can serve as instructors for individual students, and they can substitute for missing team members, allowing students to practice team tasks when some or all human instructors and teammates are unavailable. The chapter describes our learning environment, the issues that arise in developing virtual humans for team training, and our design for the virtual humans, which is an extension of our Steve agent previously used for one-on-one tutoring.

1   INTRODUCTION

Complex tasks often require the coordinated actions of multiple team members. Team tasks are ubiquitous in today's society. For example, teamwork is critical in manufacturing, in an emergency room, and in rescue operations. To perform effectively on a team, each member must master their individual role *and* learn to coordinate their actions with their teammates. There is no substitute for hands-on experience under a wide range of situations, yet such experience is often difficult to acquire; required equipment may be unavailable for training, important training situations may be difficult to reproduce, and mistakes in the real world may be expensive or hazardous.

In such cases, distributed virtual reality (Durlach and Mavor 1995) provides a promising alternative to real-world training. Students, possibly at different locations, cohabit a 3D, interactive, simulated mock-up of their work environment, where they can practice together in realistic situations. Empirical results have demonstrated the effectiveness of virtual reality for training in areas as diverse as harbor navigation for submarine commanders (Hays et al. 1998), repair of the Hubble Space Telescope (Loftin and Kenney 1995), and therapy for fear of flying (Hodges et al. 1996). Nonetheless, the full potential of distributed virtual environments for education and training has only just begun to be explored.

The availability of a realistic virtual environment is not sufficient to ensure effective learning. Instructors are needed to demonstrate correct performance, guide students past impasses, and point out errors that students might miss. Yet requiring instructors to continually monitor student activities places a heavy burden on their time and may severely limit students' training time. In addition, team training requires the availability of all appropriate team members and may require adversaries as well. Thus, while virtual environments allow students to practice scenarios anywhere and anytime, the need for instructors and a full set of teammates and adversaries can provide a serious training bottleneck.

One solution to this problem is to complement the use of human instructors and teammates with intelligent agents that can take their place when they are unavailable. The agents cohabit the virtual world with human students and collaborate (or compete) with them in training scenarios. Intelligent agents have already proven valuable in this role as fighter pilots in large battlefield simulations (Hill et al. 1997; Jones et al. 1998), but such agents have a limited ability to interact with students. Our work focuses on a different sort of intelligent agent: a virtual human that interacts with students through face-to-face collaboration in the virtual world, either as an instructor or a teammate (Johnson et al. 2000). We call our agent *Steve (Soar Training Expert for Virtual Environments)*.

Our prior work focused on Steve's ability to provide one-on-one tutoring to students for individual tasks (Rickel and Johnson 1997; Rickel and Johnson 1999; Rickel and Johnson 2000). Steve has a variety of pedagogical capabilities one would expect of an intelligent tutoring system. For example, he can point out student errors and answer questions such as "What should I do next?" and "Why?" However, because he has an animated body and cohabits the virtual world with his student, he can provide more humanlike assistance than previous disembodied tutors can. For example, he can demonstrate actions, use his gaze and gestures to direct the student's attention, and guide the student around the virtual world. This makes Steve particularly valuable for teaching tasks that require interaction with the physical world. Johnson, Rickel, and Lester (2000) discuss these and other advantages of animated pedagogical agents.

This chapter describes our extensions to Steve to support team training. Steve agents can play two valuable roles: they can serve as a tutor for an individual human team member, and they can substitute for missing team members, allowing students to practice team tasks without requiring all their human teammates. Steve's prior skills provided a solid foundation for his roles in team training, but several new issues had to be addressed. Each agent must be able to track the actions of multiple other agents and people, understand the role of each team member as well as the interdependencies, and communicate with both human and agent teammates for task coordination. In the remaining sections, we describe our learning environment for team training, present our solutions to these new issues, and discuss related and future work.

2 RELATED WORK

Although several recent systems have applied intelligent tutoring methods to team training, none of them provide embodied virtual humans like Steve that can work with students in a 3D, simulated mock-up. The *PuppetMaster* (Marsella and Johnson 1998) serves as an automated assistant to a human instructor for large-scale simulation-based training. It monitors the activities of synthetic agents and human teams, providing high-level interpretation and assessment to guide the instructor's interventions. It models team tasks at a coarser level than Steve and is particularly suited to tracking large teams in very dynamic situations. The *advanced embedded training system (AETS)* (Zachary et al. 1998) monitors a team of human students as they run through a mission simulation using the actual tactical workstations aboard a ship, rather than a virtual mock-up. AETS employs detailed cognitive models of each team member (including eye movements, individual keystrokes, and speech) to track and remediate their performance. However, the system does not use these models to provide surrogate team members, and the automated tutor provides feedback to students only through a limited display window and by highlighting of console display elements. AVATAR (Connolly et al. 1998) provides simulation-based training for air traffic controllers. It monitors and remediates their verbal commands to simulated pilots and their console panel actions. However, the automated tutor and pilots have no planning capabilities, so scenarios must be more tightly scripted than in our approach. Perhaps the closest work to ours is the *Cardiac Tutor* (Eliot and Woolf 1995), which trains a medical student to lead cardiac resuscitation teams. The system includes a simulation of the patient, as well as simulated doctors, nurses, and technicians that play designated team roles. However, these teammates do not appear as virtual humans; they are heard but not seen. Medical protocols, expressed as linear sequences of actions, play the role of the task knowledge that guides our agents, and the system has some abilities to dynamically adapt protocols to the stochastic simulation and to errors by the student. However, the representation of task knowledge appears less general than ours, since it is tailored particularly to trauma care. Unlike our system, where any team member could be a student or agent, their system is limited to a single student playing the role of the team leader.

Our work is also closely related to other research on embodied conversational agents (Cassell et al. 2000) and, more specifically, animated pedagogical agents (Johnson et al. 2000). Cassell and her colleagues have built several sophisticated systems that support face-to-face conversations between a pair of virtual humans (Cassell et al. 1994) and between a human user and a virtual human (Cassell and Thórisson 1999; Cassell et al. 2000). However, their work does not allow multiple agents and people to collaborate on tasks in a 3D virtual world, and they do not address any pedagogical issues. Lester and his colleagues have built two animated agents that can tutor students through tasks (Lester et al. 1999a; Lester et al. 1999b). However, their agents do not support team training, and they only appear as 2D characters in a 2D virtual world. More recently, they built a 3D pedagogical agent that performs tasks in a 3D virtual world (Lester et al. 1999c). However, the agent does not collaborate with students on tasks; the student specifies high-level tasks via menus, and the agent carries them out. André et al. (2000) developed multiple animated agents that collaborate to present information to a user. The domain knowledge they give to agents is similar to our approach in representing roles and communication among agents playing different roles, but their agents do not collaborate with humans on tasks, and they do not address pedagogical issues. Bindiganavale et al. (2000) developed a training system that allows multiple virtual humans to collaborate on tasks in a virtual world. However, in their system, the student learns by giving natural language instructions (task knowledge) to the agents and viewing the consequences; the student can't participate in the scenario directly, and the virtual humans do not include any tutoring capabilities.

3   THE LEARNING ENVIRONMENT

Our learning environment is designed to mimic the approach used at the Great Lakes Naval Training Center, Illinois, where we observed team training exercises. The team to be trained is presented with a scenario, such as a loss of fuel oil pressure in one of the gas turbine engines that propels the ship. The team must work together, guided by standard procedures, to handle the casualty. At Great Lakes, the team trains on real, operational equipment. Because the equipment is in operation, the trainers have limited ability to simulate ship casualties. For example, they mark gauges with grease pencils to indicate hypothetical readings, and they use cardboard cutouts to indicate fires. In our learning environment, the team, consisting of any combination of Steve agents and human students, is immersed in a simulated mock-up of the ship; the simulator creates the scenario conditions. As at Great Lakes, an instructor (human or agent) accompanies each student to coach them on their role.

Each student gets a 3D view of the virtual world through a *head-mounted display (HMD)* and interacts with the world via data gloves, as shown in Figure 1. Lockheed Martin's Vista Viewer software (Stiles et al. 1995) uses data from a position and orientation sensor on the HMD to update the student's view as the student moves around. Additional sensors on the gloves keep track of the student's hands, and Vista sends out messages when the student touches virtual objects. These messages are received and handled by the simulator, which controls the behavior of the virtual world. Our current implementation uses VIVIDS (Munro et al. 1997; Munro and Surmon 1997), developed at the USC Behavioral Technology Laboratories (BTL), for simulation authoring and execution. Separate audio software broadcasts environmental noises through headphones on the HMD based on the student's proximity to the source in the virtual world. Our current training environment simulates the interior of a ship, complete with gas turbine engines, a variety of consoles, and their surrounding pipes, platforms, stairs, and walls. A course author can create a new environment by creating new graphical models, a simulation model, and the audio files for environmental sounds.

Our architecture for creating virtual worlds (Johnson et al. 1998), developed in collaboration with our colleagues from Lockheed Martin and BTL, allows any number of humans and agents to cohabit the virtual world. While a single simulator controls the behavior of the world, each person interacts with the world through their own copy of Vista and the

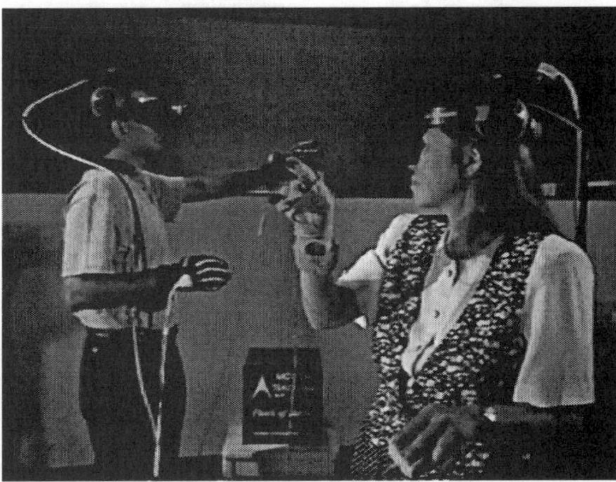

Figure 1 Two students interacting with a virtual ship via head-mounted displays and data gloves. Despite their physical proximity to one another, they are operating in completely different parts of the virtual ship.

audio software, and each agent runs as a separate process. The separate software components communicate by passing messages via a central message dispatcher; our current implementation uses Sun's ToolTalk as the message dispatcher.

This distributed architecture has several important advantages. First, since each software component runs as a separate process, the various processes can run on different machines, possibly at different locations. Second, this modular approach makes it easy to replace any of the software components with new alternatives that satisfy the same external interface. For example, VIVIDS and Vista could be replaced by a commercial product that supports the creation of interactive virtual mock-ups. Finally, the approach is extensible. Since components communicate via the message dispatcher rather than by sending messages to one another directly, one component need not know which other components are expecting its messages. This approach greatly facilitates team training, where arbitrary combinations of people and agents must cohabit the virtual world. Our extension to team training would have been more difficult had we originally designed a more monolithic system geared towards a single student and tutor.

Humans and agents communicate through spoken dialogue. An agent speaks to a person (teammate or student) by sending a message to the person's text-to-speech software, which broadcasts the utterance through the person's headphones. Our current implementation uses Entropic's TrueTalk for speech synthesis. When a person speaks, a microphone on his HMD sends his utterance to speech-recognition software, which broadcasts a semantic representation of the utterance to all the agents. The person activates speech recognition prior to each utterance by touching her two index fingers together; Vista detects the signal from the gloves and sends a message to activate that person's speech-recognition software. Our current implementation uses Entropic's GrapHvite for speech recognition. Currently, Vista provides no direct support for human-to-human conversation; if the humans are not located in the same room, they must use a telephone or radio to hear one another.

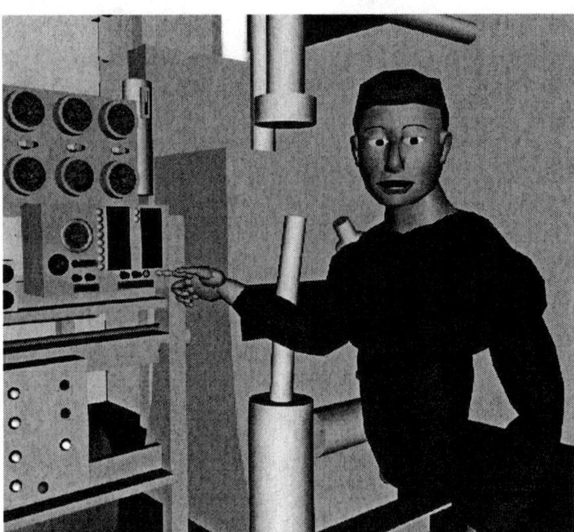

Figure 2 Steve describing an indicator light

For team training, teammates and instructors must be able to track each other's activities. Each person sees every other person in the virtual world as a head and two hands. The head is simply a graphical model, so each person can have a distinct appearance, possibly with their own face texture-mapped onto the graphical head. Each Vista tracks the position and orientation of its person's head and hands via the sensors, and broadcasts the information to agents and the other Vistas. Each agent appears as a human upper body, as shown in Figure 2. To distinguish different agents, each agent can be configured with its own shirt, hair, eye, and skin color. Its voice can be made distinct by setting its speech rate, baseline pitch, and vocal tract size; these parameters are supported by the TrueTalk software. The agents, of course, do not need audio or visual cues to distinguish other agents and humans; each Vista and speech recognizer indicates in its messages which person it is tracking, and agents send out similar messages about their activities.

4   EXAMPLE

To illustrate our learning environment and Steve's current capabilities, consider a training scenario in which two human students, Jack and Jill, are learning their roles in handling a loss of fuel oil pressure in one of the gas turbine engines aboard a ship. Jack is serving as the propulsion and auxiliary control console (PACC) operator, and Jill is in the engine room. Each student is assigned a Steve agent as their tutor. In addition, three other Steve agents serve as their teammates: one serves as the engineering officer of the watch (EOOW), one serves as the electrical plant control console (EPCC) operator, and one serves as the shaft control unit (SCU) operator.

Jack's tutor looks at him and introduces the scenario: "Let me show you how to handle a loss of fuel oil pressure. First, when you detect it, inform the EOOW." Looking over at the

EOOW, the tutor continues, "We have a loss of fuel oil pressure in engine room one." The EOOW nods in acknowledgment and passes the message on to the engine room. Jack's tutor leads him over to the normal stop button, points at it, and says, "First, press the normal stop button to stop the turbine." The tutor presses the button, and Jack watches its indicator light up and the engine's power lever angle go to idle. "I will now transfer thrust control to the central control station," the tutor informs Jack. Jack, believing that he remembers the procedure, says, "Let me finish." "Okay, you finish," replies the tutor, who shifts to monitoring Jack's performance of the task.

Jack steps forward to the console and presses the wrong button. "No," the tutor comments while shaking his head. Jack, suddenly less sure of himself, asks, "What should I do?" The tutor replies, "I suggest that you press the CCS button to initiate the transfer." Jack presses the button and his tutor nods approvingly. As a result of Jack's action, the central control station button blinks on both the PACC and the SCU. The SCU operator, in the engine room, presses the blinking CCS button on his console to complete the transfer, and the button stops blinking and remains illuminated on both consoles.

Jack looks over at the EOOW and says, "Thrust control is now at the central control station." The EOOW nods in acknowledgment and instructs the EPCC operator to switch to generator one. Jack watches as the agent operator pushes a series of buttons and informs the EOOW when the switch is complete. Now the EOOW commands the engine room to investigate the cause of the casualty.

Upon receiving the command, Jill's agent says, "Let me show you how to check for the cause of the loss of fuel oil pressure. First, check that all suction valves are wide open. A partially closed valve in the suction line can increase the suction lift above the pump's capabilities." The agent guides Jill around the engine room and shows her the location of the valves. They check each one, but all are already wide open.

Next, the agent leads Jill over to the relief valve. As she gets close, she can hear the sound of the oil passing through the valve. Her tutor continues, "Next, check the relief valve set pressure. As you can hear from the sound of the oil passing through the valve, the set pressure is too low, causing the loss of fuel oil pressure." The agent shows Jill how to reset the relief valve lifting pressure, then reports back to the EOOW, "The cause of the casualty has been determined and corrected."

Although this scenario does not illustrate all of the capabilities of our learning environment, it highlights some of the most important. Jack and Jill cohabit a virtual mock-up of their work environment, along with Steve agents that serve as their tutors and teammates. They can navigate around the environment to learn the location of relevant equipment, often under the guidance of their agent tutor. Agents and students can manipulate objects in the virtual world and see their visual and auditory effects. Finally, students can collaborate with each other, as well as their agent tutor and teammates, to practice realistic training scenarios.

5 AGENT DESIGN

5.1 ARCHITECTURE

To collaborate with students and other agents in a virtual world, Steve must be able to perceive the state of the world, choose appropriate actions, and execute those actions to change the state of the world. Thus, as shown in Figure 3, each Steve agent consists of three main modules: perception, cognition, and motor control (Rickel and Johnson 1999). The perception module monitors messages from other software components, identifies relevant events, and maintains a snapshot of the state of the world. It tracks the following information: the simulation state (in terms of objects and their attributes), actions taken by students and other agents, the location of each student and agent, and human and agent speech (separate messages indicate the beginning of speech, the end, and a semantic representation of its content). In addition, if the agent is tutoring a student, it keeps track of the student's field of view; messages from the student's Vista indicate when objects enter or leave the field of view. The cognition module, implemented in Soar (Laird et al. 1987; Newell 1990), interprets the input it receives from the perception module, chooses appropriate goals, constructs and executes plans to achieve those goals, and sends out motor commands to the motor control module. Steve's cognition module can typically react to new perceptual input in a fraction of a second, so it is very responsive (Rickel and Johnson 2000). The motor control module accepts the following types of commands: move to an object, point at an object, manipulate an object (about 10 types of manipulation are currently supported), look at someone or something, change facial expression, nod or shake the head, and speak. The motor control module decomposes these motor commands into a sequence of lower-level messages that are sent to the other software components (simulator, Vista Viewers, speech synthesizers, and other agents) to realize the desired effects. See Rickel and Johnson (1999) for more details on this architecture.

To allow Steve to operate in a variety of domains, his architecture has a clean separation between domain-independent capabilities and domain-specific knowledge. The code in the perception, cognition, and motor control modules provides a general set of capabilities that are independent of any particular domain. These capabilities include planning, replanning, and plan execution; mixed-initiative dialogue; assessment of student actions; question answering ("What should I do next?" and "Why?"); episodic memory; path planning; communication with teammates; and control of the agent's body (Rickel and Johnson 1999). To allow Steve to operate in a new domain, a course author simply specifies the appropriate domain knowledge in a declarative language. (Recent work has focused on acquiring the knowledge from an author's demonstrations and the agent's experimentation (Angros 2000; Angros et al. 2002).) The knowledge falls in two categories: *perceptual knowledge* (knowledge about objects in the virtual world, their relevant simulator attributes, and their spatial properties) and *task knowledge* (procedures for accomplishing domain tasks and text fragments for talking about them). For details about Steve's perceptual knowledge, see Rickel and Johnson (1999); the remainder of this chapter focuses on Steve's representation and use of task knowledge.

Low-level animation of Steve's body runs as software that is linked into the Vista Viewers rather than into Steve. Before each graphical frame is rendered (about 15 to 30 times per second), Vista calls the animation code to update Steve's body position. The animation code is controlled by messages it receives from Steve's motor control module. Because the

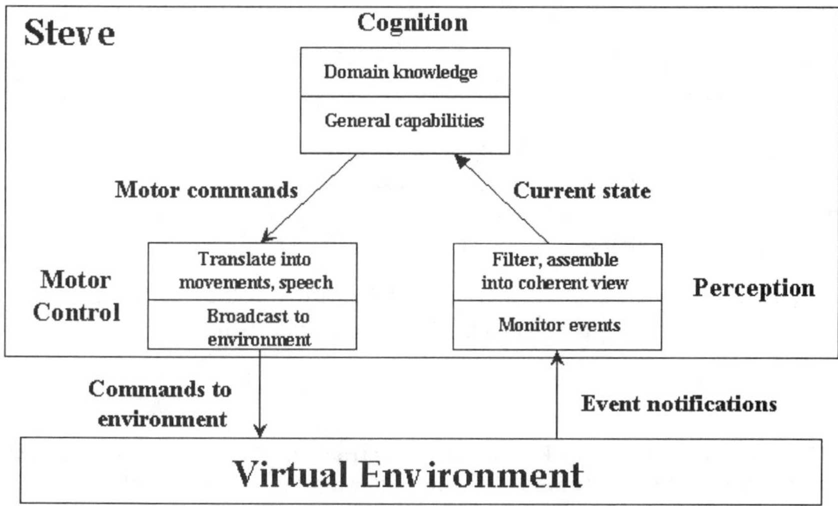

Figure 3   Steve's three main modules (perception, cognition, and motor control) and the types of information they send and receive.

animation code controls the dynamics of all body motions, the motor control module need only specify the type of motion it wants. The animation code generates all movements dynamically; there are no keyframes or canned animations. Movements involving different parts of the body can be performed simultaneously, and a new command to a body part interrupts any existing motion for that part. Steve's motor control module isolates the details of how to control the animation code, allowing the cognition module to send higher-level motor commands that do not depend on those details. This approach makes it easy to replace Steve's current body with a new one, such as a commercial product for human figure animation.

5.2   REPRESENTING TASK KNOWLEDGE

Most of Steve's abilities to collaborate with students on tasks, either as a teammate or tutor, stem from his understanding of those tasks. As the scenario unfolds, Steve must always know which steps are required, how they contribute to the task goals, and who is responsible for their execution. In order to handle dynamic environments containing other people and agents, he must understand the tasks well enough to adapt them to unexpected events; he cannot assume that the task will follow a prespecified sequence of steps. Moreover, our goal was to support a declarative representation that would allow course authors to easily specify task knowledge and update it when necessary (Rickel and Johnson 1997).

Our representation for individual tasks, used in our previous work for one-on-one tutoring, satisfies these design criteria. The course author describes each task using a standard plan representation (Russell and Norvig 1995). First, each task consists of a set of steps, each of which is either a primitive action (e.g., press a button) or a composite action (i.e., itself a

Task transfer-thrust-control-ccs
Steps press-pacc-ccs, press-scu-ccs
Causal links
    press-pacc-ccs achieves ccs-blinking for press-scu-ccs
    press-scu-ccs achieves thrust-at-ccs for end-task
Ordering press-pacc-ccs before press-scu-ccs
Roles pacc: press-pacc-ccs; scu: press-scu-ccs

Figure 4   Example of a team task description.

task). Composite actions give tasks a hierarchical structure. Second, there may be ordering constraints among the steps; these constraints define a partial order over the steps. Finally, the role of the steps in the task is represented by a set of causal links (McAllester and Rosenblitt 1991). Each causal link specifies that one step in the plan achieves a particular goal that is a precondition for another step in the plan or for termination of the task. For example, pulling out a dipstick achieves the goal of exposing the level indicator, which is a precondition for checking the oil level.

This task representation is suitable for structured tasks based on standard procedures. It would not be suitable for tasks that require creative problem solving, such as design tasks. Fortunately, many tasks in industry and the military have this type of structure, including operation and maintenance of equipment, trauma care (Eliot and Woolf 1995), and surgical procedures (Billinghurst and Savage 1996). Moreover, this representation need not be viewed as a fixed sequence of steps. Rather, it is a general causal network of steps and goals and can be used by a planning algorithm to dynamically order the steps even in the face of unexpected events, as described in Section 5.3.

To extend Steve to team training, we had to decide how to assign team members to task steps. Much of the research on multi-agent teams has addressed methods by which teammates dynamically negotiate responsibility for task steps. However, supporting such negotiation among a team of agents *and* people would require more sophisticated natural language dialogue capabilities than Steve currently has. Fortunately, many team tasks have well-defined roles that are maintained throughout task execution. We focus on this class of tasks.

Extending Steve to support such team tasks required one addition to each task description: a mapping of task steps to team roles. For example, Figure 4 shows a simplified task model for transferring thrust control to the central control station of a ship. Two roles must be filled: one operator is stationed at the propulsion and auxiliary control console (PACC) in the central control station (CCS), and another operator is stationed at the shaft control unit console (SCU) in the engine room. The PACC operator requests the transfer by pressing the CCS button on her console, which results in the CCS button blinking on both consoles. When the CCS button is blinking on the SCU, the SCU operator presses it to finalize the transfer. This last action achieves the end goal of the task, which is indicated in the task description by specifying its effect as a precondition of the dummy

Task loss-of-fuel-oil-pressure
Steps transfer-thrust-control-ccs, ...
Causal links ...
Ordering ...
Roles
  eoow: (transfer-thrust-control-ccs pacc), ... ;
  engrm: (transfer-thrust-control-ccs scu), ...

Figure 5 Specifying roles for a subtask.

step "end-task." This representation for end goals is standard in AI planners (Russell and Norvig 1995).

If a step in the task is itself a team task, it will have its own roles to be filled, and these may differ from the roles in the parent task. Therefore, the parent task specifies which of its roles plays each role in the subtask. For example, Figure 5 shows a partial description of a task for which the task in Figure 4 is a subtask. This task description calls for the engineering officer of the watch (EOOW) to play the role of the PACC operator and for the engine room officer (ENGRM) to play the role of the SCU operator for the transfer of thrust control.

Task descriptions (e.g., Figures 4 and 5) specify the structure of tasks, but they leave the goals (e.g., ccs-blinking) and primitive steps (e.g., press-pacc-ccs) undefined. The course author defines each primitive step as an instance of some action in Steve's extensible action library. For example, the step press-pacc-ccs would be defined as an instance of press-button in which the particular button to be pressed is pacc-ccs, the name of an object in the virtual world. The course author defines each goal by the conditions in the simulated world under which it is satisfied. For example, ccs-blinking is satisfied when the simulator attribute scu-ccs-state has the value "blinking." Thus, Steve is able to relate his task knowledge to objects and attributes in the virtual world.

5.3 USING TASK KNOWLEDGE

Any combination of human students, agent teammates, and human and agent instructors can participate in a training scenario. A request for a new scenario can come from a variety of sources, such as a human instructor or student (via a graphical user interface) or a curriculum-sequencing software component. Regardless of the source, the request is sent to each Steve agent as a message. The message specifies the name of the task to be performed (e.g., transfer-thrust-control-ccs or loss-of-fuel-oil-pressure) and assigns a student or agent to each role in that task. If an agent was previously assigned a student to tutor, and the agent or student is assigned a role in the team task, the agent coaches the student on that role. If an agent has not been assigned a student to tutor and is given a role in the task, the agent simply serves as the missing teammate. Currently, a single Steve agent cannot work with multiple students and cannot play one role while tutoring a student on another role. However, anyone (student or agent) can play multiple roles in a task; if an agent tutor or his student is assigned multiple roles, they work together on all those roles.

Given a request for a team task, each Steve agent involved in the task as a team member or instructor uses his task knowledge to construct a complete task model. Starting with the task description for the specified task, each agent recursively expands any composite step with his task description, until the agent has a fully decomposed, hierarchical task model. Role assignments in the request are propagated down to subtasks until the task model specifies which team member is responsible for each step. For example, if the task is loss-of-fuel-oil-pressure (see Figure 5), with Joe as the EOOW, then Joe will play the role of the PACC for the subtask transfer-thrust-control-ccs (see Figure 4), and hence he is responsible for the step press-pacc-ccs. Typically, all agents have the same task knowledge, so each agent will construct the same hierarchical task model with the same assignment of responsibilities. (Although our approach would permit different agents to have different knowledge.)

For simulation-based training, especially for team tasks, agents must be able to robustly handle unexpected events. Scripting an agent's behavior for all possible contingencies in a dynamic virtual world is difficult enough, but the problem is compounded when each agent must be scripted to handle unexpected actions by any human team member. One option is simply to prevent human students from deviating from standard procedures, but this robs the team of any ability to learn about the consequences of mistakes and how to recover from them. Instead, we have designed Steve to use his task knowledge to adapt task execution to the unfolding scenario.

To do this, each agent maintains a plan for how to complete the task from the current state of the world. The task model specifies all steps that might be required to complete the task; it can be viewed as a worst-case plan. Agents continually monitor the state of the virtual world, identify which goals in the task model are already satisfied, and use a partial-order planning algorithm to construct a plan for completing the task (Rickel and Johnson 1999). This plan is a subset of the task model, consisting of the steps relevant to completing the task, the ordering constraints among them, and the causal links that indicate the role of each step in achieving the end goals. In our prior work, this plan would specify how an agent intended to complete a task. For team training, the plan specifies how the agent intends for the team to collectively complete the task, with some causal links specifying the interdependencies among team members (i.e., how one team member's action depends on a precondition that must be achieved by a teammate). Thus, agents dynamically interleave construction, revision, and execution of plans to adapt to the unfolding scenario.

The evolving task context (task model and current plan for completing it) guides the behavior of the agents. If an agent is serving only as a missing team member, he simply performs his role in the task, waiting when appropriate for the actions of his teammates, and communicating with them when necessary. In contrast, an agent serving as an instructor for a human student interacts with that student in a manner similar to one-on-one tutoring. The agent can demonstrate the student's role in the task, explaining each action he takes, or he can monitor the student as the student performs the task, providing feedback on the student's actions and answering questions ("What next?" and "Why?") when the student needs help. Moreover, the agent instructor can easily shift between these two modes as the task proceeds; the student can always interrupt the agent's demonstration and ask to finish the task herself, and she can always ask the agent to demonstrate a step when she gets stuck. An agent instructor is responsible for handling student errors; currently, agent teammates do not provide any pedagogical feedback. The tutorial interactions between an agent instructor and a student arise from the agent's domain-independent capabilities for one-on-one instruction, detailed in our earlier papers (Rickel and Johnson 1999; Rickel and Johnson 2000), operating over the representation of the current team task context (described above) and the state of the dialogue between the agent and student (as described in the earlier papers). These tutorial capabilities only had to be extended to handle several new cases, such as students requesting help when they are not responsible for the next step.

5.4 TEAM COMMUNICATION

In team tasks, coordination among team members is critical. Although team members can sometimes coordinate their actions by simply observing the actions of their teammates, spoken communication is typically required. Team leaders need to issue commands. Team members often need to inform their teammates when a goal has been achieved, when they are starting an activity, and when they detect an abnormal condition. Because team communication is so important, it must be taught and practiced in team training.

To allow agents to communicate with their teammates and teach appropriate communication to their students, they must have a model of the appropriate communication. Agents must know what to communicate, when to say it, and how to say it. When a teammate says something, they must know how to interpret it and how it relates to the task. Addressing these issues required extensions to Steve's prior abilities.

We model team communication as explicit speech acts in the task descriptions. For the sort of structured tasks we have studied, this is natural; all the documented team procedures given to us specified when one team member should say something to another and how it should be said. To support this, we extended Steve's action library to include a new type of action: a speech act from one team member to another. Each speech act appears as a primitive action in the task description. This allows us to explicitly model its relationship to the task, including the role responsible for performing it, ordering constraints on when it should be said, and causal links that specify how its effect contributes to completing the task (i.e., which other steps depend on that result).

The definition of a particular speech act includes five components:

- *It specifies the name of the attribute being communicated.* For example, for a speech act informing the EOOW that thrust control has been transferred to the central control station, the attribute being communicated is thrust-location. The attribute may or may not be an actual simulator attribute.

- *It specifies the value being communicated for that attribute.* In the example above, the value is ccs (i.e., central control station).

- *It specifies the appropriate text string.* For the example above, the appropriate phrase might be "Thrust control is now at the central control station." Note that we do not want to leave this text string up to a natural language generator, because there is often a precise utterance that should be used.

- *It specifies the semantic representation that will be returned by a student's speech recognizer when she says the utterance or some acceptable variant of it.* Our speech recognition software currently maps each path through its grammar to a symbol that represents its content, but a more structured representation could also be used.

- *It specifies the name of the task role to which the speech act is directed (e.g., EOOW).* Recall that the task description containing the speech act specifies the role responsible for performing the speech act, so together these two pieces of information fully specify the appropriate speaker and hearer.

Given this representation for team communication, Steve agents can both generate and comprehend such utterances during task execution. When an agent's plan calls for him to execute one of these speech acts, he sends the text string to appropriate speech synthesizers for his human teammates to hear, and he broadcasts the semantic representation of the speech act for his agent teammates to "hear." When a human says the appropriate utterance, her speech recognizer identifies it as a path through its domain-specific grammar, maps it to an appropriate semantic representation, and broadcasts it to the agents. When an agent receives such a message from a person or another agent, he checks his plan to see if he expects such a speech act from that teammate at that time. If so, he updates the specified attribute in his mental state with the specified value and nods to the speaker in acknowledgment. If a speech recognizer fails to understand a student's utterance, or the utterance is not appropriate at the current time, the student's instructor agent is responsible for giving the student appropriate feedback.

There are several important points about this approach. First, it only applies to structured tasks for which the required team communications can be specified in the task description; it will not suffice for tasks that require more arbitrary communication. Fortunately, many well-structured team tasks, particularly in the military, include such a prescribed set of utterances. Second, since Steve does not include any natural language–understanding abilities, all valid variations of the utterances must be added to the grammar for the speech recognizer. Again, this is reasonable for tasks with prescribed utterances. Third, note the difference between our approach and communication messages in a purely multi-agent system; a speech recognizer cannot tell to whom an utterance is intended, so agents must use the task model to determine whether the speaker is addressing them. Finally, each agent must treat a human student and their instructor as jointly performing a role; if either of them generates the speech act, it must be treated as coming from that role.

Although spoken communication is typically required for team tasks, nonverbal communication is also important. Human students can observe the actions of their nearby agent and human teammates, which is often required for proper team coordination. Agents look at a teammate when expecting them to do something, which can cue a student that she is responsible for the next step. Agents look at the teammate to whom they are speaking (see Figure 6), allowing students to follow the flow of communication and recognize when they are being addressed. Finally, agents react to their teammates' actions; they look at objects being manipulated by teammates (see Figure 7), and they nod in acknowledgment when they understand something a teammate says to them. All of these nonverbal acts are generated from the agents' domain-independent capabilities (Rickel and Johnson 2000); they need not be included in task models. For tasks that require face-to-face collaboration among team members, such nonverbal communication is critical.

Figure 6 One Steve agent speaking to another.

6 DISCUSSION—STATUS

Steve has been tested on a variety of naval operating procedures. In our most complicated team scenario, five team members must work together to handle a loss of fuel oil pressure in one of the gas turbine engines. This task involves a number of subtasks, some of which are individual tasks while others involve subteams. Altogether, the task consists of about three dozen actions by the various team members. Steve agents can perform this task themselves as well as in concert with human team members. All of Steve's algorithms were designed for efficient real-time performance; there are no noticeable delays in the agents' behavior, even when running several agents on the same computer. However, the Vista Viewer software requires a high-end Silicon Graphics computer to achieve a reasonable frame rate given the complexity of the 3D ship model and the number of agents it must animate. We have not yet evaluated the training effectiveness of our system for team training, but we hope to perform a formal evaluation with actual naval personnel in the future.

7 FUTURE WORK

Some important limitations in our system could be alleviated by incorporating recent research results from related areas. To go beyond tasks with prescribed utterances, we could leverage ongoing research on robust spoken dialogue (Allen et al. 1996; Smith and Hipp 1994). To handle tasks with shifting roles and unstructured communication among teammates, we could incorporate a more general theory of teamwork (Jennings 1995; Levesque et al. 1990; Tambe 1997). To handle tasks that involve simultaneous physical collaboration (e.g., two people jointly lifting a heavy object), we will need a tighter coupling

Figure 7 One Steve agent watching another.

of Steve's perception and body control (Badler et al. 1993). Although research in these areas is still incomplete, many useful methods have been developed.

Steve agents serving as instructors should provide more information on team activities than they currently do. They should provide running commentary on relevant actions of teammates, which can be difficult because it requires the ability to synchronize verbal descriptions with real-time events in the virtual world (André et al. 2000). They should indicate perceptual cues that can help the student track teammates' actions. They should interleave their demonstrations of the student's role with descriptions of how and why the student's actions are needed by teammates and vice versa. Our representation of team tasks should support all these capabilities, but they have not yet been added to Steve's tutorial repertoire.

Another limitation in Steve agents is that they never make mistakes. This issue was raised by trainers at the Great Lakes Naval Training Center, who emphasized the importance of learning to recognize and recover from mistakes by teammates. Our approach of allowing students to make mistakes so that the team can learn their consequences and how to recover from them is consistent with this learning objective. However, students can currently only learn from their own mistakes and those of their human teammates. To better support this learning objective, we must incorporate an appropriate model of task errors into Steve agents. For example, we might generate errors automatically by degrading an agent's perception (e.g., it fails to notice something in the virtual world) or task knowledge.

There is a growing understanding of the principles behind effective team training (Blickensderfer et al. 1997; Burns et al. 1993; Smith-Jentsch et al. 1998; Swezey and Salas 1992). Empirical experiments are beginning to tease out the skills that make teams effective (e.g.,

Figure 8 An interactive peacekeeping scenario featuring (left to right) a sergeant, a mother, and a medic.

task skills vs. team skills), the basis for team cohesion (e.g., shared mental models), the best types of feedback (e.g., outcome vs. process), and the best sources of feedback (e.g., instructor vs. teammate). Because our approach allows us to model face-to-face interaction among human instructors and students and their agent counterparts, we are now in an excellent position to incorporate and experiment with a variety of these new ideas in team training.

We are currently addressing many of the issues discussed above in an ambitious new project (Rickel et al. 2001; Swartout et al. 2001). In contrast to our prior work, which focused on teaching well-defined tasks, our new project focuses on leadership training and decision-making in stressful situations. Figure 8 shows a screen shot from a prototype implementation of an example application, in which a young lieutenant (human user) is being trained for a peacekeeping mission. In the current implementation, there are three Steve agents that interact with the lieutenant: a medic (front right) that serves as his teammate, a Bosnian mother (front center) whose boy has been accidentally injured by one of the lieutenant's vehicles, and a sergeant (front left) who serves as both a teammate and mentor. All other characters (soldiers and an angry crowd of locals) are simple scripted agents.

This new type of team training exploits all of Steve's prior capabilities, but is pushing us in several new directions. First, we are aiming for more realism in the graphical bodies; in our latest implementation, shown in Figure 8, the bodies and animation algorithms for all the Steve agents and scripted characters were developed by Boston Dynamics. Second, since the human user must collaborate with agent teammates to formulate novel plans, rather than simply execute well-defined procedures, we are integrating state-of-the-art natural language–understanding and generation algorithms into Steve, as well as extending those algorithms to handle multiparty conversations in immersive virtual worlds (Traum and Rickel 2002). Third, to model the behavior of teammates in stressful situations, as well as to create virtual humans that can induce stress in the human user by reacting emotionally, we have integrated a computational model of emotions into Steve (Gratch and Marsella 2001). For example, the mother in our peacekeeping scenario becomes increasingly angry at the lieutenant if his decisions thwart her goal of getting assistance for her boy. Our challenge as we integrate these extensions into Steve is to maintain the efficient real-time performance and ease of authoring of the approach described in this chapter.

8 CONCLUSION

This chapter has described a new approach to team training based on virtual humans in distributed virtual reality. The approach builds on our learning environment and Steve agent developed for one-on-one tutoring of individual tasks. In our new learning environment, any combination of human students, agent teammates, and human and agent instructors can cohabit a 3D, interactive, simulated mock-up to practice team tasks. To support such training scenarios, Steve was extended in several ways. Rather than tracking the activities of a single student, Steve now tracks the actions of multiple other agents and people. Steve's representation for task knowledge was extended to include a representation for team roles, allowing each agent to understand the role of each team member as well as the interdependencies. Agents use their task knowledge to dynamically maintain a plan specifying how the team can collectively complete its task from the current situation. Because communication is essential for team coordination, we model such communication as explicit speech acts in the agents' task knowledge, allowing them to understand what to communicate, when and how to say it, and how the communication facilitates completion of their task. In addition, our use of embodied virtual humans supports the many types of nonverbal communication that are essential for face-to-face collaboration. Virtual humans and distributed virtual reality provide students the ability to practice team tasks in realistic scenarios anywhere and anytime, providing a training environment that is safer, cheaper, and more flexible than physical alternatives.

ACKNOWLEDGMENTS

This work was funded by the Office of Naval Research under grant N00014-95-C-0179 and AASERT grant N00014-97-1-0598. We are grateful to our collaborators who developed the other software components on which Steve relies. Randy Stiles and his colleagues at Lockheed Martin developed the visual interface software (Vista Viewer). Allen Munro and his colleagues at the Behavioral Technology Laboratories developed the simulator (VIVIDS). Ben Moore at ISI developed the speech-recognition and audio components. Finally, Marcus Thiébaux at ISI developed the 3D model of Steve's body and the code in the visual interface software that controls the animation. Our new work is funded by the Army Research Office through the USC Institute for Creative Technologies under contract DAAD19-99-C-0046.

References

Allen, J. F., B. W. Miller, E. K. Ringger, and T. Sikorski (1996). Robust understanding in a dialogue system. In *Proceedings of the 34th Annual Meeting of the Association for Computational Linguistics*, pp. 62–70. San Francisco: Morgan Kaufmann Publishers.

André, E., T. Rist, S. van Mulken, M. Klesen, and S. Baldes (2000). The automated design of believable dialogues for animated presentation teams. In J. Cassell, J. Sullivan, S. Prevost, and E. Churchill (Eds.), *Embodied Conversational Agents*. Cambridge, MA: MIT Press.

Angros, Jr., R. (2000). *Learning What to Instruct: Acquiring Knowledge from Demonstrations and Focussed Experimentation*. Ph. D. thesis, Department of Computer Science, University of Southern California, Los Angeles, CA.

Angros, Jr., R., W. L. Johnson, J. Rickel, and A. Scholer (2002). Learning domain knowledge for teaching procedural tasks. In *Proceedings of the First International Joint Conference on Autonomous Agents and Multi-Agent Systems*, New York: ACM Press. Forthcoming.

Badler, N. I., C. B. Phillips, and B. L. Webber (1993). *Simulating Humans*. New York: Oxford University Press.

Billinghurst, M., and J. Savage (1996). Adding intelligence to the interface. In *Proceedings of the IEEE Virtual Reality Annual International Symposium (VRAIS '96)*, Los Alamitos, CA, pp. 168–175. IEEE Computer Society Press.

Bindiganavale, R., W. Schuler, J. M. Allbeck, N. I. Badler, A. K. Joshi, and M. Palmer (2000). Dynamically altering agent behaviors using natural language instructions. In *Proceedings of the Fourth International Conference on Autonomous Agents*, New York, pp. 293–300. New York: ACM Press.

Blickensderfer, E., J. A. Cannon-Bowers, and E. Salas (1997). Theoretical bases for team self-correction: Fostering shared mental models. *Advances in Interdisciplinary Studies of Work Teams 4*, 249–279.

Burns, J. J., E. Salas, and J. A. Cannon-Bowers (1993). Team training, mental models, and the team model trainer. In *Proceedings of Advancement in Integrated Delivery Technologies*, Denver.

Cassell, J., T. Bickmore, L. Campbell, H. Vilhjálmsson, and H. Yan (2000). Conversation as a system framework: Designing embodied conversational agents. In J. Cassell, J. Sullivan, S. Prevost, and E. Churchill (Eds.), *Embodied Conversational Agents*. Cambridge, MA: MIT Press.

Cassell, J., C. Pelachaud, N. Badler, M. Steedman, B. Achorn, T. Becket, B. Douville, S. Prevost, and M. Stone (1994). Animated conversation: Rule-based generation of facial expression, gesture and spoken intonation for multiple conversational agents. In *Proceedings of ACM SIGGRAPH '94*, Reading, MA, pp. 413–420. Boston: Addison Wesley.

Cassell, J., J. Sullivan, S. Prevost, and E. Churchill (Eds.) (2000). *Embodied Conversational Agents*. Cambridge, MA: MIT Press.

Cassell, J., and K. R. Thórisson (1999). The power of a nod and a glance: Envelope vs. emotional feedback in animated conversational agents. *Applied Artificial Intelligence 13*, 519–538.

Connolly, C. A., J. Johnson, and C. Lexa (1998). AVATAR: An intelligent air traffic control simulator and trainer. In *Proceedings of the Fourth International Conference on Intelligent Tutoring Systems (ITS '98)*, Number 1452 in Lecture Notes in Computer Science, pp. 534–543. Berlin: Springer-Verlag.

Durlach, N. I., and A. S. Mavor (Eds.) (1995). *Virtual Reality: Scientific and Technological Challenges*. Washington, DC: National Academy Press.

Eliot, C., and B. P. Woolf (1995). An adaptive student centered curriculum for an intelligent training system. *User Modeling and User-Adapted Instruction 5*, 67–86.

Gratch, J., and S. Marsella (2001). Tears and fears: Modeling emotions and emotional behaviors in synthetic agents. In *Proceedings of the Fifth International Conference on Autonomous Agents*, New York, pp. 278–285. New York: ACM Press.

Hays, R. T., D. A. Vincenzi, A. G. Seamon, and S. K. Bradley (1998). Training effectiveness evaluation of the VESUB technology demonstration system. Technical Report 98-003, Naval Air Warfare Center Training Systems Division, Orlando, FL.

Hill, Jr., R. W., J. Chen, J. Gratch, P. Rosenbloom, and M. Tambe (1997). Intelligent agents for the synthetic battlefield: A company of rotary wing aircraft. In *Proceedings of the Ninth Conference on Innovative Applications of Artificial Intelligence (IAAI-97)*, Menlo Park, CA, pp. 1006–1012. AAAI Press.

Hodges, L. F., B. O. Rothbaum, B. Watson, G. D. Kessler, and D. Opdyke (1996). A virtual airplane for fear of flying therapy. In *Proceedings of the IEEE Virtual Reality Annual International Symposium (VRAIS '96)*, Los Alamitos, CA, pp. 86–93. IEEE Computer Society Press.

Jennings, N. (1995). Controlling cooperative problem solving in industrial multi-agent systems using joint intentions. *Artificial Intelligence 75*.

Johnson, W. L., J. Rickel, R. Stiles, and A. Munro (1998). Integrating pedagogical agents into virtual environments. *Presence: Teleoperators and Virtual Environments 7*(6), 523–546.

Johnson, W. L., J. W. Rickel, and J. C. Lester (2000). Animated pedagogical agents: Face-to-face interaction in interactive learning environments. *International Journal of Artificial Intelligence in Education 11*, 47–78.

Jones, R. M., J. E. Laird, and P. E. Nielsen (1998). Automated intelligent pilots for combat flight simulation. In *Proceedings of the 10th Conference on Innovative Applications of Artificial Intelligence (IAAI-98)*, Menlo Park, CA, pp. 1047–1054. AAAI Press.

Laird, J. E., A. Newell, and P. S. Rosenbloom (1987). Soar: An architecture for general intelligence. *Artificial Intelligence 33*(1), 1–64.

Lester, J. C., B. A. Stone, and G. D. Stelling (1999). Lifelike pedagogical agents for mixed-initiative problem solving in constructivist learning environments. *User Modeling and User-Adapted Interaction 9*, 1–44.

Lester, J. C., J. L. Voerman, S. G. Towns, and C. B. Callaway (1999). Deictic believability: Coordinating gesture, locomotion, and speech in lifelike pedagogical agents. *Applied Artificial Intelligence 13*, 383–414.

Lester, J. C., L. S. Zettlemoyer, J. Gregoire, and W. H. Bares (1999). Explanatory lifelike avatars: Performing user-designed tasks in 3d learning environments. In *Proceedings of the Third International Conference on Autonomous Agents*, New York: ACM Press.

Levesque, H. J., P. R. Cohen, and J. H. T. Nunes (1990). On acting together. In *Proceedings of the Eighth National Conference on Artificial Intelligence (AAAI-90)*, pp. 94–99. San Mateo, CA: Morgan Kaufmann Publishers.

Loftin, R., and P. Kenney (1995). Training the Hubble space telescope flight team. *IEEE Computer Graphics and Applications 15*(5), 31–37.

Marsella, S. C., and W. L. Johnson (1998). An instructor's assistant for team-training in dynamic multi-agent virtual worlds. In *Proceedings of the Fourth International*

Conference on Intelligent Tutoring Systems (ITS '98), Number 1452 in Lecture Notes in Computer Science, Berlin, pp. 464–473. Berlin: Springer-Verlag.

McAllester, D., and D. Rosenblitt (1991). Systematic nonlinear planning. In *Proceedings of the Ninth National Conference on Artificial Intelligence (AAAI-91)*, Menlo Park, CA, pp. 634–639. AAAI Press.

Munro, A., M. Johnson, Q. Pizzini, D. Surmon, and D. Towne (1997). Authoring simulation-centered tutors with RIDES. *International Journal of Artificial Intelligence in Education 8*, 284–316.

Munro, A., and D. Surmon (1997). Primitive simulation-centered tutor services. In *Proceedings of the AI-ED Workshop on Architectures for Intelligent Simulation-Based Learning Environments*, Kobe, Japan.

Newell, A. (1990). *Unified Theories of Cognition*. Cambridge, MA: Harvard University Press.

Rickel, J., J. Gratch, R. Hill, S. Marsella, and W. Swartout (2001). Steve goes to Bosnia: Towards a new generation of virtual humans for interactive experiences. In *AAAI Spring Symposium on Artificial Intelligence and Interactive Entertainment*.

Rickel, J., and W. L. Johnson (1997). Intelligent tutoring in virtual reality: A preliminary report. In *Proceedings of the Eighth World Conference on Artificial Intelligence in Education*, pp. 294–301. IOS Press.

Rickel, J., and W. L. Johnson (1999). Animated agents for procedural training in virtual reality: Perception, cognition, and motor control. *Applied Artificial Intelligence 13*, 343–382.

Rickel, J., and W. L. Johnson (2000). Task-oriented collaboration with embodied agents in virtual worlds. In J. Cassell, J. Sullivan, S. Prevost, and E. Churchill (Eds.), *Embodied Conversational Agents*. Cambridge, MA: MIT Press.

Russell, S., and P. Norvig (1995). *Artificial Intelligence: A Modern Approach*. Englewood Cliffs, NJ: Prentice Hall.

Smith, R. W., and D. R. Hipp (1994). *Spoken Natural Language Dialog Systems*. New York: Oxford University Press.

Smith-Jentsch, K. A., R. L. Zeisig, B. Acton, and J. A. McPherson (1998). Team dimensional training. In J. Cannon-Bowers and E. Salas (Eds.), *Making Decisions under Stress: Implications for Individual and Team Training*. American Psychological Association.

Stiles, R., L. McCarthy, and M. Pontecorvo (1995). Training studio interaction. In *Workshop on Simulation and Interaction in Virtual Environments (SIVE-95)*, Iowa City, IA, pp. 178–183. New York: ACM Press.

Swartout, W., R. Hill, J. Gratch, W. Johnson, C. Kyriakakis, C. LaBore, R. Lindheim, S. Marsella, D. Miraglia, B. Moore, J. Morie, J. Rickel, M. Thiébaux, L. Tuch, R. Whitney, and J. Douglas (2001). Toward the holodeck: Integrating graphics, sound, character and story. In *Proceedings of the Fifth International Conference on Autonomous Agents*, pp. 409–416. New York: ACM Press.

Swezey, R. W., and E. Salas (1992). Guidelines for use in team-training development. In R. W. Swezey and E. Salas (Eds.), *Teams: Their Training and Performance*, pp. 219–245. Norwood, NJ: Ablex.

Tambe, M. (1997). Towards flexible teamwork. *Journal of Artificial Intelligence Research 7*, 83–124.

Traum, D., and J. Rickel (2002). Embodied agents for multi-party dialogue in immersive virtual worlds. In *Proceedings of the First International Joint Conference on Autonomous Agents and Multi-Agent Systems*, New York: ACM Press. Forthcoming.

Zachary, W., J. Cannon-Bowers, J. Burns, P. Bilazarian, and D. Krecker (1998). An advanced embedded training system (AETS) for tactical team training. In *Proceedings of the Fourth International Conference on Intelligent Tutoring Systems (ITS '98)*, Number 1452 in Lecture Notes in Computer Science, Berlin, pp. 544–553. Berlin: Springer-Verlag.

Chapter 8
Reasoning under Uncertainty

Understanding Belief Propagation and Its Generalizations

Jonathan S. Yedidia
MERL
201 Broadway
Cambridge, MA 02139
yedidia@merl.com

William T. Freeman
MIT Artificial Intelligence Laboratory
200 Technology Square
Cambridge, MA 02139
wft@mit.edu

Yair Weiss
School of Computer Science and Engineering
The Hebrew University of Jerusalem
91904 Jerusalem, Israel
yweiss@cs.huji.ac.il

Abstract

"Inference" problems arise in statistical physics, computer vision, error-correcting coding theory, and AI. We explain the principles behind the *belief propagation* (*BP*) algorithm, which is an efficient way to solve inference problems based on passing local messages. We develop a unified approach, with examples, notation, and graphical models borrowed from the relevant disciplines.

We explain the close connection between the BP algorithm and the *Bethe approximation* of statistical physics. In particular, we show that BP can only converge to a fixed point that is also a stationary point of the Bethe approximation to the free energy. This result helps explaining the successes of the BP algorithm and enables connections to be made with variational approaches to approximate inference.

The connection of BP with the Bethe approximation also suggests a way to construct new message-passing algorithms based on improvements to Bethe's approximation introduced by Kikuchi and others. The new *generalized belief propagation* (*GBP*) algorithms are significantly more accurate than ordinary BP for some problems. We illustrate how to construct GBP algorithms with a detailed example.

1 INFERENCE AND GRAPHICAL MODELS

We will be describing and explaining an algorithm, called *belief propagation* (*BP*), which is supposed to solve "inference" problems, at least approximately. Inference problems come up in many different scientific fields, so it is not that surprising that a good algorithm to solve such problems has been repeatedly rediscovered. In fact, one can show that such apparently different methods as the forward-backward algorithm, the Viterbi algorithm, iterative decoding algorithms for Gallager codes and turbocodes, Pearl's belief propagation algorithm for Bayesian networks, the Kalman filter, and the transfer-matrix approach in physics are all special cases of the BP algorithm discovered in different scientific communities (Aji and McEliece 2000; Kschischang et al. 2001).

We will emphasize that a multidisciplinary approach yields important insights into the BP algorithm. We therefore begin with a small survey of "inference" problems from the AI, computer vision, statistical physics, and digital communications literatures, which will also give us a chance to introduce the different kinds of graphical models that are used to describe these problems. This first section is a basic review of well-known material, but we hope that it will be useful in elucidating the strong similarity between problems in these different fields. The reader interested in other reviews of this material may want to consult (Frey 1998) and (Kschischang et al. 2001).

1.1 BAYESIAN NETWORKS

In the AI literature, *Bayesian networks* are probably the most popular type of graphical model (Jensen 1996; Pearl 1988). They are used in expert systems involving problem domains such as medical diagnosis, map learning, language understanding, heuristic search, and so on. We will take as an example the medical diagnosis problem. Suppose that we want to construct a machine that will automatically give diagnoses for patients. For each patient, we will have some (possibly incomplete) information, such as symptoms and test results, and we would like to *infer* the probability that a given disease or set of diseases is causing the symptoms. We also assume that we know (presumably from expert advice) the statistical dependencies between different symptoms, test results, and diseases. For example, let us consider the fictional "Asia" example of Lauritzen and Spiegelhalter (1988), shown in Figure 1.

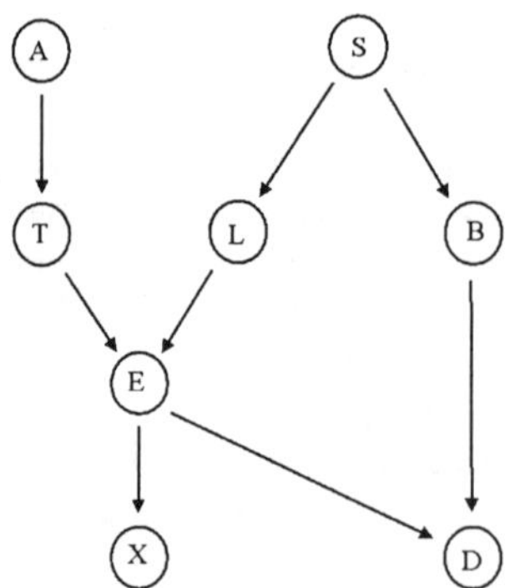

Figure 1　The fictional "Asia" Bayesian network, taken from (Lauritzen and Spiegelhalter 1988).

In words, the qualitative statistical dependencies shown in this small Bayesian network can be described as follows:

1. A recent trip to Asia (A) increases the chances of tuberculosis (T).

2. Smoking (S) is a risk factor for both lung cancer (L) and bronchitis (B).

3. The presence of either (E) tuberculosis or lung cancer can be detected by an X-ray result (X), but the X-ray alone cannot distinguish between them.

4. Dyspnea (D) (shortness of breath) may be caused by bronchitis (B), or either (E) tuberculosis or lung cancer.

Each node represents a variable that can be in a discrete number of possible states. We write x_i for the variable representing the different possible states of node i. In addition to the qualitative dependencies described by the Bayesian network graph, there are quantitative statistical relationships that we assign to each arrow in the graph. Associated with each arrow is a conditional probability: for example, we write $p(x_L|x_S)$ for the conditional probability of a patient having lung cancer given that the patient does or does not smoke. For this link, we say that the S node is the *parent* of the L node because x_L is conditionally dependent on x_S. Some nodes like the D node might have more than one parent, in which case we define their conditional probabilities in terms of all their parents; thus we write $p(x_D|x_E, x_B)$ for the conditional probability of having dyspnea.

Note that the Bayesian network defines an independency structure: the probability that a node is in one of its states depends directly only on the states of its parents. For nodes like A or S that do not have any parents, we introduce probabilities like $p(x_S)$ that are not conditioned on any other nodes. In general, a Bayesian network (and the other graphical models that we consider) is most useful if it is sparse, which means that most of the nodes do not have a direct statistical dependence.

In our example, the overall, or *joint probability*

$$p(\{x\}) \equiv p(x_A, x_S, x_T, x_L, x_B, x_E, x_X, x_D)$$

that the patient has some combination of symptoms, test results, and diseases, is just the product of all the probabilities of the parent nodes and all the conditional probabilities:

$$p(\{x\}) = p(x_A)p(x_S)p(x_T|x_A)p(x_L|x_S)p(x_B|x_S)p(x_E|x_L, x_T)p(x_D|x_B, x_E)p(x_X|x_E) \quad (1)$$

More generally, a Bayesian network is a directed acyclic graph of N random variables x_i that defines a joint probability function

$$p(x_1, x_2, ..., x_N) = \prod_{i=1}^{N} p(x_i|Par(x_i)) \quad (2)$$

where $Par(x_i)$ denotes the states of the parents of node i, and if node i has no parents, we take $p(x_i|Par(x_i)) = p(x_i)$. By *directed acyclic graph*, we mean that the arrows do not loop around in a cycle—it is still possible that the links form a loop when one ignores the arrows.

Our goal will be to compute certain *marginal* probabilities. For example, we might want to compute the probability that a patient has a certain disease. By *inference*, we simply mean the computation of these marginal probabilities. Mathematically, marginal probabilities are defined in terms of sums over all the possible states of all the other nodes in the system. For example, if we want the marginal probability of the last node $p(x_N)$, we in general need to compute

$$p(x_N) = \sum_{x_1} \sum_{x_2} \cdots \sum_{x_{N-1}} p(x_1, x_2, x_3, ..., x_N) \tag{3}$$

We will refer to marginal probabilities that we compute approximately as *beliefs*, and denote the belief at node i by $b(x_i)$.

If we have some information about some of the nodes (e.g., we know that the patient does not smoke in our "Asia" example), then we will be able to fix the corresponding variable and we will not have to sum over the unknown states of that node. We will call such a node an *observable node*, in contrast to the other nodes, which are *hidden nodes*. For all our graphical models, we will denote observable nodes by filled-in circles, and hidden nodes by empty circles.

For small Bayesian networks, we can easily do marginalization sums directly, but unfortunately, the number of terms in the sums will grow exponentially with the number of hidden nodes in the network. The virtue of the BP algorithm is that we can use it to compute marginal probabilities, at least approximately, in a time that grows only linearly with the number of nodes in the system. For that reason, BP can be used in practice as an *inference engine*, acting on the statistical data encoded in a large Bayesian network. Before we turn to BP, however, we will describe some other inference problems.

1.2   PAIRWISE MARKOV RANDOM FIELDS

BP has also recently begun to be used as an "engine" for low-level computer vision problems (Freeman et al. 2000). Humans often take for granted the solution of apparently simple computer vision problems like the segmentation and recognition of objects, or the detection and interpretation of motion. We solve these tasks so automatically that it can be surprising how difficult it is to teach a computer to solve the same tasks, given just a series of 2D arrays of pixel values. A key to progress in computer vision is to find theoretically solid models that are computationally tractable.

Pairwise *Markov random fields* (MRFs) provide attractive theoretical models for some computer vision problems (Geman 1984). In such problems, we normally want to infer a representation of whatever is "really out there" from the data that we are given, which is ultimately a 2D array of numbers representing pixel intensities. To take a concrete example, suppose that we want to infer the distance of the objects in a scene from the viewer. That is, imagine that we are given a 1000-by-1000 grey-scale image, and we pose our problem as trying to infer distance values d_i corresponding to intensity values I_i, where i ranges over the million possible pixel positions. Or, instead of distance, we might be inferring some other quantity about the scene—such as high-resolution details that are missing in the image, the optical flow in a series of images, and so on.

In general, we assume that we observe some quantities about the image y_i, and that we want to infer some other quantities about the underlying scene x_i. The indices i could represent single pixel positions, or they might represent the position of a small patch of pixels. We further assume that there is some statistical dependency between x_i and y_i at each position i, which we write as a joint compatability function $\phi_i(x_i, y_i)$. The function $\phi_i(x_i, y_i)$ is often called the *evidence* for x_i. Finally, for us to possibly be able to infer anything about the scene, there has to be some structure to the x_i. In general, if we do not assume such structure, computer vision problems are inherently hopelessly ill-posed. We encode the assumed structure of the scene by saying that the nodes i are arranged in a 2D grid, and scene variables x_i should, insofar as possible, be "compatible" with nearby scene

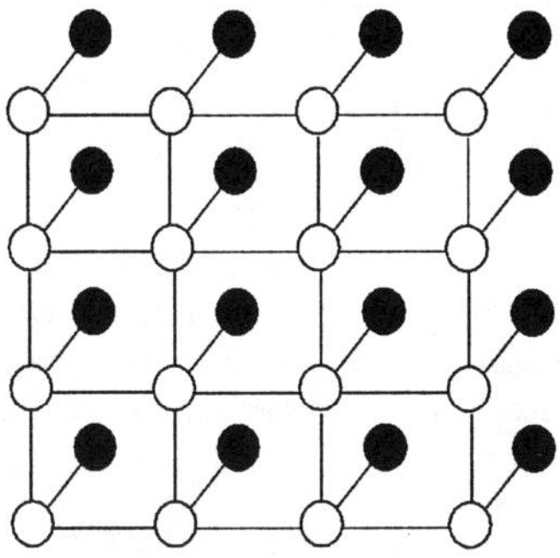

Figure 2   A square lattice, pairwise Markov random field.

variables x_j, as represented by a compatibility function $\psi_{ij}(x_i, x_j)$, where ψ_{ij} only connects nearby positions. We then take the overall joint probability of a scene x_i and an image y_i to be

$$p(\{x\}, \{y\}) = \frac{1}{Z} \prod_{(ij)} \psi_{ij}(x_i, x_j) \prod_i \phi_i(x_i, y_i) \tag{4}$$

where Z is a normalization constant and the product over (ij) is over, for example, nearest neighbors on the square lattice.

A graphical depiction of this model is shown in Figure 2. The filled-in circles represent the observed image nodes y_i, while the empty circles represent the hidden scene nodes x_i. The MRF is said to be *pairwise* because the compatibility functions only depend on pairs of sites i and j. In contrast to Bayesian networks, this graphical model is undirected. There is no notion, as is usually implicit in a Bayesian network, that the variable at one node x_i is a causal *parent* of its neighbor x_j, so we use undirected compatibility functions $\psi_{ij}(x_i, x_j)$ instead of conditional probability functions $p(x_i|x_j)$. Nevertheless, our agenda in doing inference will be very similar: we will want to compute the beliefs $b(x_i)$, for all positions i, so as to be able to infer something about the underlying unknown scene. Once again a direct computation of marginal probabilities would take exponential time (and the number of nodes is typically very large), so we need a faster algorithm like BP. We note in passing that for a restricted class of pairwise MRFs relevant to computer vision, fast algorithms based on *graph cuts* (Boykov et al. 2001) can also be used to estimate hidden states.

1.3 POTTS AND ISING MODELS

It is worth taking a small detour to show that the pairwise MRF described by Equation 4 can easily be brought into a form recognizable to physicists as the *Potts model* (Baxter 1982). Let us define the *interaction* $J_{ij}(x_i, x_j)$ between the variables at neighboring nodes by $J_{ij}(x_i, x_j) = \ln \psi_{ij}(x_i, x_j)$ and the *field* $h_i(x_i)$ at each node by $h_i(x_i) = \ln \phi(x_i, y_i)$. (Because we do inference for a given set of y_i, we can in fact consider the y_i as fixed variables and subsume them into our definition of $h_i(x_i)$.) If we now define the Potts model *energy* as

$$E(\{x\}) = -\sum_{(ij)} J_{ij}(x_i, x_j) - \sum_i h_i(x_i) \tag{5}$$

and appeal to Boltzmann's law from statistical mechanics

$$p(\{x\}) = \frac{1}{Z} e^{-E(\{x_i\})/T} \tag{6}$$

we see that our pairwise MRF corresponds exactly to a Potts model at a temperature T equal to one. The normalization constant Z is known in the physics literature as the *partition function*. If the number of states at each node is exactly two, the model is called the *Ising model*. In this case, physicists sometimes prefer to change variables from x_i to s_i, which can take on the values of 1 or -1, and to further restrict themselves to J_{ij} interactions, which have a symmetric form that can be written in terms of a *spin-glass* energy function (Mezard et al. 1987):

$$E(\{s\}) = -\sum_{(ij)} J_{ij} s_i s_j - \sum_i h_i s_i \tag{7}$$

In the context of the Ising model, the inference problem of computing beliefs $b(x_i)$ can be mapped onto the physics problem of computing local *magnetizations*:

$$m_i \equiv b(s_i = 1) - b(s_i = -1). \tag{8}$$

1.4 TANNER AND FACTOR GRAPHS

Another problem for which the BP algorithm has given excellent results is the iterative decoding of error-correcting codes (Frey and Mackay 1998; McEliece et al. 1998). BP is the decoding algorithm used to decode some of the best practical codes, including turbocodes (Berrou et al. 1993) and Gallager codes (Gallager 1963). Decoding error-correcting codes is in fact an elegant example of an *inference* problem—the receiver of the coded message that has been corrupted by a noisy channel is trying to *infer* the message that was initially transmitted. (For general background on error-correcting coding, see (Gallager 1968).)

Gallager codes and turbocodes can be formulated as *parity-check codes* (Mackay 1999). In a block parity-check code, we will typically try to send k information bits in a block of N bits. N will be greater than k so as to provide redundancy that can be used to recover from errors induced by the noisy channel. Let us give a small example: an $N = 6$, $k = 3$ binary code, shown by its *Tanner graph* in Figure 3. A Tanner graph (Tanner 1981) is a pictorial representation of the parity-check constraints on the codewords (legal configurations of bits) of an error-correcting code. Each square represents a parity check, and each circle connected to a square represents a bit that participates in that parity check. In our sample code, the first parity check forces the sum of Bits 1, 2, and 4 to be even, while the second parity check forces the sum of Bits 1, 3, and 5 to be even, and the third parity check forces the sum of Bits 2, 3, and 6 to be even. The only eight codewords that satisfy these three parity-check constraints are 000000, 001011, 010101, 011110, 100110, 101101, 110011, and 111000. Note that for this code, the first three bits are the *information* bits, so if you are transmitting messages, and you intend, for example, to transmit the 010 message, you will use those bits as the first three bits of your codeword, and then the remaining bits are uniquely determined (for that case, you would transmit the 010101 codeword).

The recipient of a coded message, after it has been corrupted by a noisy channel, may find that the received message is not a codeword after all. For example, let us suppose that the 010101 message was transmitted, but because of the noisy channel, one of the bits was flipped and the 011101 "word" was received. This word does not correspond to any codeword, and it is the job

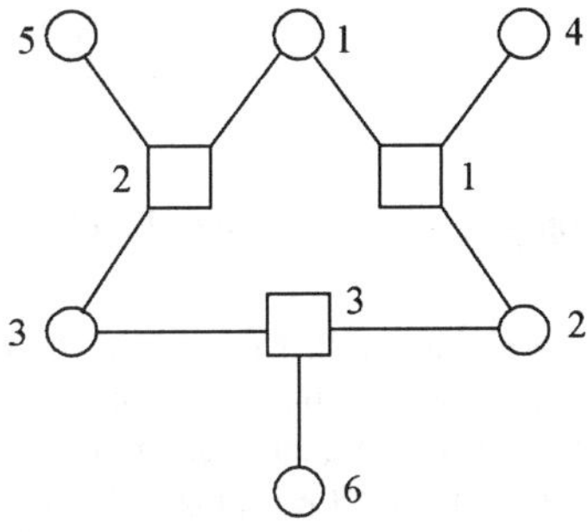

Figure 3   A Tanner graph for a small $N = 6$, $k = 3$ parity-check code.

of the decoding algorithm to infer which codeword was actually sent. For our code, we can readily see that the `010101` codeword is the only one that is only a single bit-flip away from the received word, so if the bit-flip probability is small, it is reasonable to decode to that codeword. Unfortunately, for many codes, N and k will be large, so that the number of codewords is exponentially huge and we cannot simply resort to examining all the codewords and finding the closest one. As is by now becoming a familiar refrain, we will be able to turn to the BP algorithm, because it will work in a time that only grows linearly with N.

The decoding problem can be given a probabilistic formulation. We assume that we have received a sequence of N bits y_i, and we are trying to find the N bits of the transmitted codeword x_i. Let us, for the purpose of simplicity, assume that the noisy channel is *memoryless*—that is, each bit i is flipped independently of every other bit. That means that we can associate a conditional probability $p(x_i|y_i)$ with each received bit. For example, if the first bit is received as a 0, and we know that the bits are flipped with a probability f, then the probability that the first bit was transmitted as a 0 is $1 - f$, while the probability that it was transmitted as a 1 is f. So $p(x_1 = 0|y_1 = 0) = (1 - f)$, while $p(x_1 = 1|y_1 = 0) = f$. The overall probability of each codeword is proportional to the product of these one-node probabilities: $\prod_{i=1}^{N} p(x_i|y_i)$. But to make sure that we only consider combinations of x_i that are codewords, we write a a joint probability function that combines these conditional probabilities with the parity-check constraints. For example, for our $N = 6$, $k = 3$ code given above, we write the overall joint probability distribution as

$$p(\{x\}, \{y\}) = \frac{1}{Z} \psi_{124}(x_1, x_2, x_4) \psi_{135}(x_1, x_3, x_5) \psi_{236}(x_2, x_3, x_6) \prod_{i=1}^{6} p(y_i|x_i) \qquad (9)$$

In the above equation, functions like $\psi_{124}(x_1, x_2, x_4)$ are parity-check functions. They have the value 1 if the sum of their arguments is even, and have the value 0 if the sum of their arguments is odd.

In general, for a parity-check code with transmitted bits x_i and received bits y_i, and $N - k$ parity checks, we can write the joint probability distribution as

$$p(\{x\}, \{y\}) = \frac{1}{Z} \prod_{a=1}^{N-k} \psi_a(\{x\}_a) \prod_{i=1}^{N} p(y_i|x_i) \tag{10}$$

where we have used the notation $\psi_a(\{x\}_a)$ to denote the ath parity-check function ψ_a and its arguments $\{x\}_a$.

A decoding algorithm for parity-check codes that minimizes the number of bits that are decoded incorrectly is to compute the marginal probabilities $p(x_i)$ for every bit i, and then to threshold each bit to its most probable value. Note that taking the most probable value of each bit independently is the strategy that is guaranteed to minimize the number of incorrectly decoded bits even though it may not yield a valid codeword (Gallager 1968). As usual, a direct computation of the marginal probabilities will take an exponentially huge time, so we resort to the efficient BP algorithm. The BP algorithm, while not exact for Gallager codes or turbocodes, is very effective in practice and has been used to achieve near–Shannon limit performance (Mackay 1999).

A *factor graph* (Kschischang et al. 2001) is a generalization of a Tanner graph, whose graph looks essentially identical, but now each square can represent *any* function of its variables (the nodes it is attached to). Each function can have varying numbers of variables, including just one. We take the joint probability distribution of a factor graph of N variables with M functions to be

$$p(\{x\}) = \frac{1}{Z} \prod_{a=1}^{M} \psi_a(\{x\}_a) \tag{11}$$

Note that we subsume any observable nodes y_i into functions that they generate of the hidden nodes x_i.

1.5 CONVERTING GRAPHICAL MODELS

It is very easy to convert arbitrary pairwise MRFs or Bayesian networks into equivalent factor graphs. Figure 4 shows a small pairwise MRF and the equivalent factor graph. Note that instead of using observable nodes, we introduce equivalent factor graph functions of a single variable. The factor graph functions $\psi_a(\{x\}_a)$ will be equivalent to either the two node functions $\psi_{ij}(x_i, x_j)$ if they link two hidden nodes, or the single node functions $\phi_i(x_i, y_i)$ if they are attached to a single hidden node.

In Figure 5, we have a small Bayesian network and the equivalent factor graph. Notice that there is always a factor graph function linking a node and all of its parents, because that is the form of the joint probability distribution in a Bayesian network. The factor graph functions $\psi_a(\{x\}_a)$ directly correspond to the Bayesian network probabilities $p(x_i|Par(x_i))$.

Finally, in Figure 6, we show the factor graph representation of the $N = 6$, $k = 3$ code discussed above. The received bits y_i are represented in terms of the functions that they induce on the corresponding bits x_i. There are also factor graph functions corresponding to the original parity-check functions.

Belief propagation algorithms specific to Bayesian networks, pairwise MRFs, and factor graphs have all been developed, and they are all mathematically equivalent; but it would certainly be confusing from the pedagogical point of view to present all these different versions. In fact, as we have just

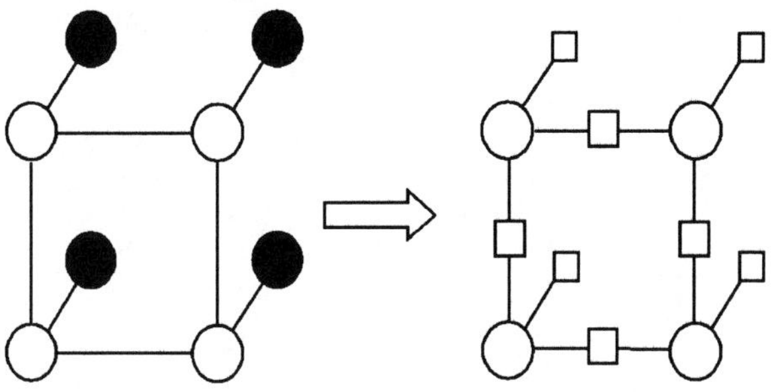

Figure 4 Converting a pairwise MRF into a factor graph.

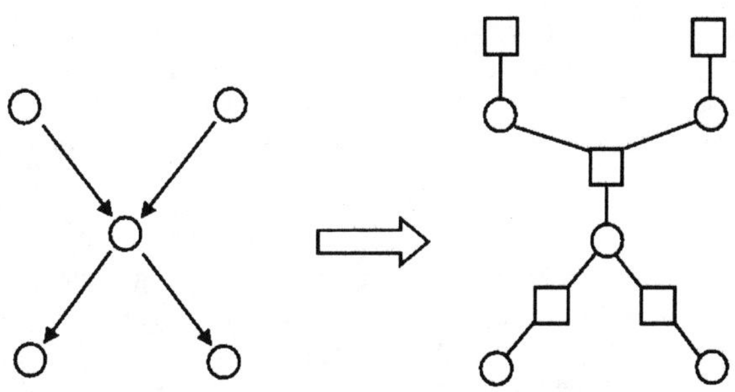

Figure 5 Converting a Bayesian network into a factor graph.

seen, arbitrary Bayesian networks and pairwise MRFs can be easily converted into equivalent factor graphs, and, as we shall see in a moment, we can also convert arbitrary factor graphs into equivalent Bayesian networks or pairwise MRFs. We can thus choose to work with Bayesian networks, pairwise MRFs, or factor graphs without losing any generality.

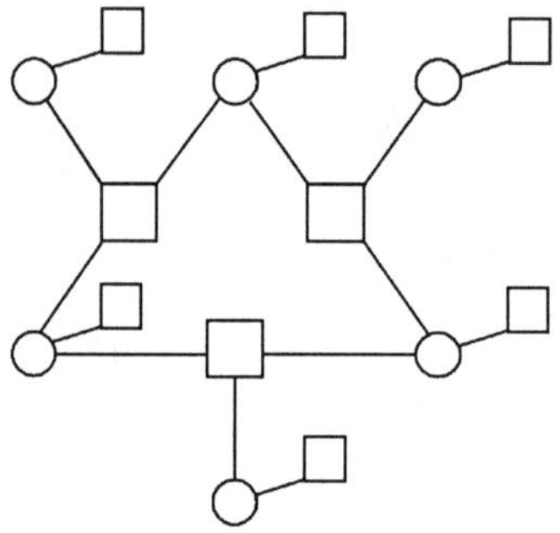

Figure 6   The factor graph representing the joint probability function of a small parity-check code.

We will choose to focus on pairwise MRFs. Our reason for this choice is purely pedagogical—although all the different BP algorithms are mathematically equivalent, the version of BP for pairwise MRFs is somewhat simpler in form because it has only one kind of message, while the BP algorithms for the other graphical models are normally described using two kinds of messages. The need for two kinds of messages arises either because of the arrows in Bayesian networks, or the two kinds of nodes in factor graphs. In any case, the BP algorithm that one derives by using the pairwise MRF formulation on a converted Bayesian network or factor graph is precisely mathematically equivalent at every iteration to the BP algorithm as it is normally described for the other graphical models, so we will actually lose nothing at all by using this description.

If you are impatient to learn about BP, you can skip ahead to the next section, but for the purposes of completeness, we will explain how to convert arbitrary factor graphs into equivalent Bayesian networks and pairwise MRFs. To convert a factor graph into an equivalent Bayesian network, convert every function node into an observable node that is observed to be in its first state. Then make the probability of the first state of that observable node, given its parents, equivalent to the factor graph function that was eliminated (see Figure 7).

We show the conversion of a factor graph into a pairwise MRF graphically in Figure 8. Each function in the factor graph is converted into a hidden node in a pairwise MRF with an observable node hanging off of it. For example, a function $\psi_a(x_i, x_j, x_k)$ of three nodes in a factor graph will be represented by a new hidden node x_a and a new observable node y_a. The node x_a can be in as many states as the product of all the variables of the corresponding function ψ_a. For example, if the factor graph function that we were converting was $\psi_a(x_i, x_j, x_k)$, and x_i, x_j, and x_k were each binary nodes taking on values 0 or 1, then the new node x_a could take on eight values ranging from 000 to 111. The "evidence" $\phi(x_a, y_a)$ is set to correspond to the factor graph function $\psi(\{x\})$. For example, if $\psi(\{x\})$ is a parity-check function, then $\phi(x_a, y_a)$ will just be equal to 1 if x_a corresponds to a state with an even number of ones and 0 otherwise. Finally, we need to introduce the notation $x_a(i)$ to denote the state that the ith node should be in to correspond with the a node being in state x_a. The compatibility functions $\psi_{ai}(x_a, x_i)$ between a new node x_a and an ordinary node x_i should be set to 1 if $x_a(i) = x_i$ and 0 otherwise.

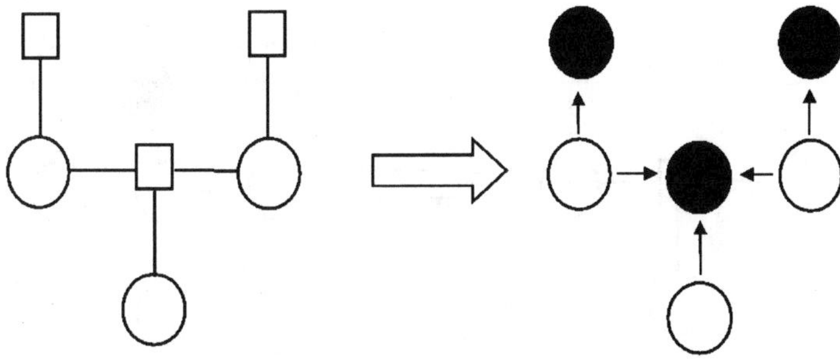

Figure 7 Converting a factor graph into a Bayesian network.

2 STANDARD BELIEF PROPAGATION

For the reasons given in the preceding section, we will focus on pairwise MRFs. We can consider the observable nodes y_i to be fixed, write $\phi_i(x_i)$ as a shorthand for $\phi_i(x_i, y_i)$, and focus on the joint probability distribution for the unknown variables x_i:

$$p(\{x\}) = \frac{1}{Z} \prod_{(ij)} \psi_{ij}(x_i, x_j) \prod_{i} \phi_i(x_i) \tag{12}$$

In the BP algorithm, we introduce variables such as $m_{ij}(x_j)$, which can intuitively be understood as a "message" from a hidden node i to the hidden node j about what state node j should be in (see Figure 9). The message $m_{ij}(x_j)$ will be a vector of the same dimensionality as x_j, with each component being proportional to how likely node i thinks it is that node j will be in the corresponding state. In the BP algorithm, the belief at a node i is proportional to the product of the local evidence at that node ($\phi_i(x_i)$), and all the messages coming into node i:

$$b_i(x_i) = k\phi_i(x_i) \prod_{j \in N(i)} m_{ji}(x_i) \tag{13}$$

where k is a normalization constant (the beliefs must sum to 1) and $N(i)$ denotes the nodes neighboring i (see Figure 10.) The messages are determined self-consistently by the message update rules:

$$m_{ij}(x_j) \leftarrow \sum_{x_i} \phi_i(x_i)\psi_{ij}(x_i, x_j) \prod_{k \in N(i) \setminus j} m_{ki}(x_i) \tag{14}$$

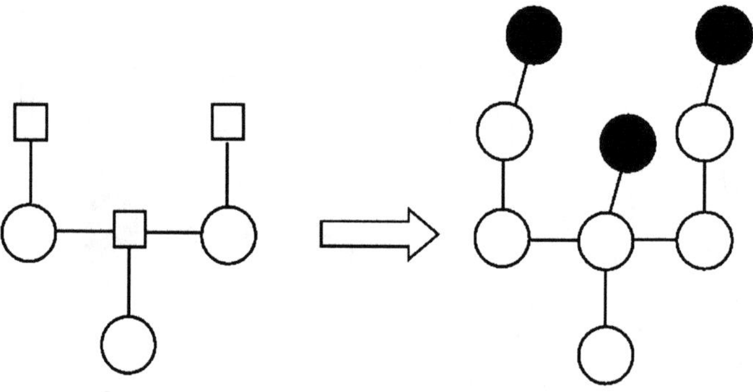

Figure 8 Converting a factor graph into a pairwise MRF.

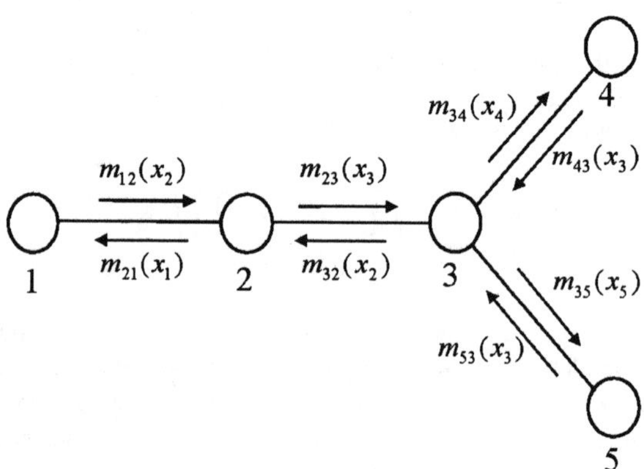

Figure 9 An illustration of the messages passed in BP.

Note that on the right side, we take the product over all messages going into node i except for the one coming from node j. The message-update rule is shown diagrammatically in Figure 11.

Where do these rules come from? It is not too hard to show that these rules give beliefs that are exact if the pairwise MRF is *singly connected*—that is, if there are no loops in the pairwise MRF. We will

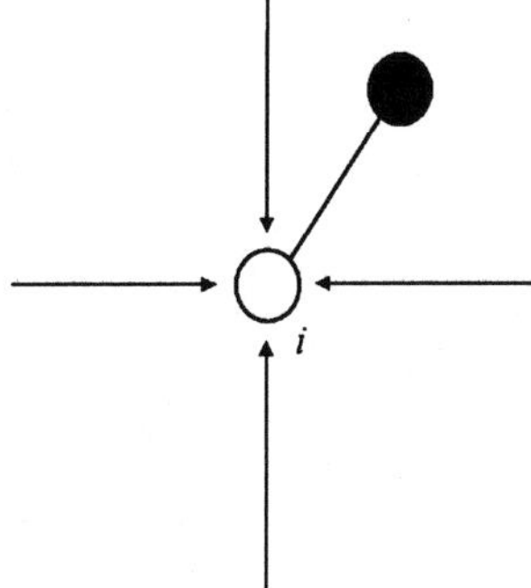

Figure 10 A diagrammatic representation of the BP belief equation $b_i(x_i) = k\phi_i(x_i)\prod_{j \in N(i)} m_{ji}(x_i)$.

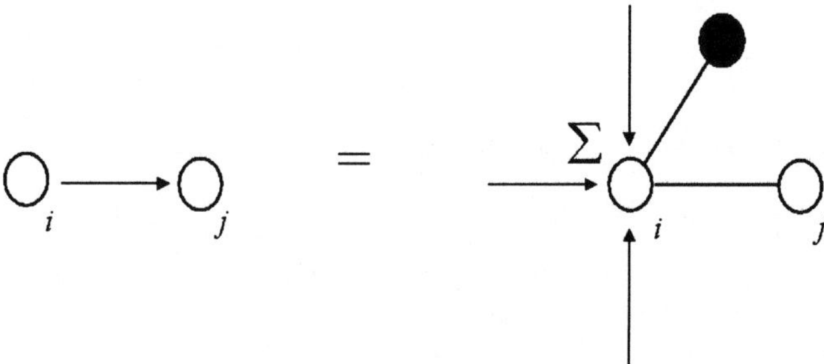

Figure 11 A diagrammatic representation of the BP message update rules $m_{ij}(x_j) \leftarrow \sum_{x_i} \phi_i(x_i)\psi_{ij}(x_i, x_j)\prod_{k \in N(i)\backslash j} m_{ki}(x_i)$. The summation symbol indicates that we are summing over all the states of node i.

not give a proof here, but just a small example that might help convince you. Consider the network with four hidden nodes shown in Figure 12. We will compute the belief at node 1 using the belief propagation rules. We have

$$b_1(x_1) = k\phi_1(x_1)m_{21}(x_1) \tag{15}$$

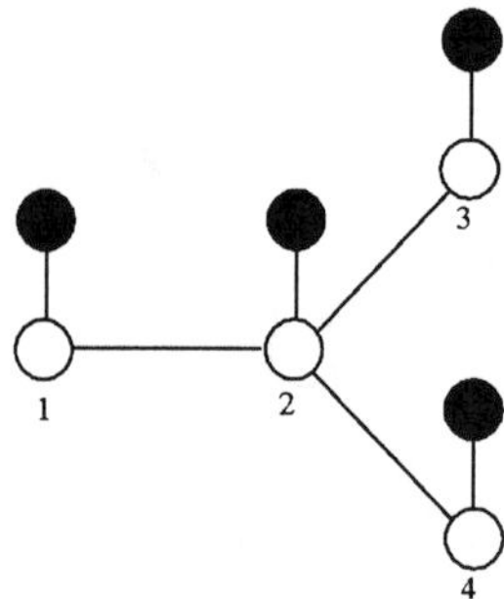

Figure 12   A pairwise MRF with four hidden nodes.

Using the message-update rules for $m_{21}(x_1)$, we find

$$b_1(x_1) = k\phi_1(x_1) \sum_{x_2} \psi_{12}(x_1, x_2)\phi_2(x_2)m_{32}(x_2)m_{42}(x_2) \tag{16}$$

Using the message-update rules for $m_{32}(x_2)$ and $m_{42}(x_2)$, we find

$$b_1(x_1) = k\phi_1(x_1) \sum_{x_2} \psi_{12}(x_1, x_2)\phi_2(x_2) \sum_{x_3} \phi_3(x_3)\psi_{23}(x_2, x_3) \sum_{x_4} \phi_4(x_4)\psi_{24}(x_2, x_4) \tag{17}$$

Finally, by reorganizing the sums, it is easy to see that the belief at node 1 is the same as the exact marginal probability at node 1:

$$b_1(x_1) = k \sum_{x_2, x_3, x_4} p(\{x\}) = p_1(x_1) \tag{18}$$

It is easy to convince oneself, and to prove, that BP in fact gives the exact marginal probabilities for all the nodes in any singly connected graph.

In a practical computation, one starts with the nodes at the edge of the graph, and only computes a message when one has available all the messages necessary. Thus, in our example, one would start with m_{32} and m_{42}, and then compute m_{21}, and then finally compute b_1. In general, it is easy to see that each message need only be computed once for singly connected graphs. That means that the whole computation takes a time proportional to the number of links in the graph, which is dramatically less than the exponentially large time that would be required to compute marginal probabilities naively.

The point of view illustrated by this example suggests that belief propagation is a way of organizing the "global" computation of marginal beliefs in terms of smaller local computations. The message flow is akin to the flow of a river, and each message summarizes all the computations that occurred further upstream along the branches that feed into that message. Thus, in our example, $m_{21}(x_1)$ is a summary of all the computations that occurred at nodes 2, 3, and 4. This is the classic point of view,

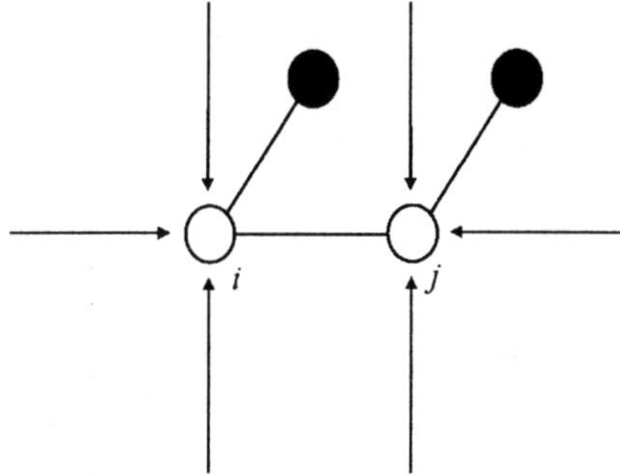

Figure 13 A diagrammatic representation of the BP two-node belief equation $b_{ij}(x_i, x_j) = k\psi_{ij}(x_i, x_j)\phi_i(x_i)\phi_j(x_j)\prod_{k\in N(i)\backslash j} m_{ki}(x_i)\prod_{l\in N(i)\backslash i} m_{lj}(x_j)$.

and it seems to suggest that it must be very important that there be no loops in the pairwise MRF, for otherwise the entire argument for the exactness of BP breaks down.

So for the time being, let us continue our discussion of singly connected (loop-free) pairwise MRFs. We will find it very convenient to introduce the two-node marginal probabilities $p_{ij}(x_i, x_j)$, for two neighboring sites i and j, which are obtained by marginalizing the joint probability function over every node except the two nodes i and j:

$$p_{ij}(x_i, x_j) \equiv \sum_{z: z_{ij}=(x_i, x_j)} p(\{z\}) \tag{19}$$

We write a belief equation for the two-node beliefs $b_{ij}(x_i, x_j)$ analogously to Equation 13 for the one-node beliefs:

$$b_{ij}(x_i, x_j) = k\psi_{ij}(x_i, x_j)\phi_i(x_i)\phi_j(x_j) \prod_{k\in N(i)\backslash j} m_{ki}(x_i) \prod_{l\in N(i)\backslash i} m_{lj}(x_j) \tag{20}$$

where $k \in N(i)\backslash j$ means that we consider all neighbors k of node i except for node j. We describe this equation diagrammatically in Figure 13. It can be justified on singly connected graphs by working out that for such graphs the two-node beliefs will correspond to the exact two-node marginal probabilities.

It is also worth noting that by combining Equations 13 and 20 with the marginalization condition

$$b_i(x_i) = \sum_{x_j} b_{ij}(x_i, x_j) \tag{21}$$

we consistently derive the message-update rules (14). (See Figure 14 for a diagrammatic version of this derivation.)

The BP algorithm, as defined in terms of the belief Equations 13 and 20, and the message-update rules (14), does not make reference to the topology of the graph that it is running on. Thus, there is

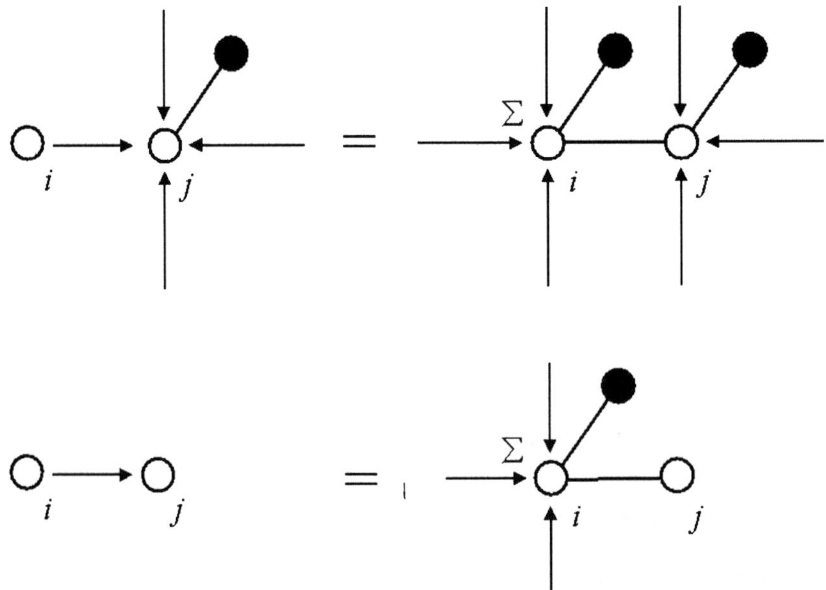

Figure 14   The top equation is a diagrammatic version of the equation $b_j(x_j) = \sum_{x_i} b_{ij}(x_i, x_j)$. By canceling the pieces that are common on both sides of the equation, we derive the message-update rules $m_{ij}(x_j) \leftarrow \sum_{x_i} \phi_i(x_i) \psi_{ij}(x_i, x_j) \prod_{k \in N(i) \backslash j} m_{ki}(x_i)$.

nothing to stop us from implementing it on a graph that has loops. One starts with some initial set of messages (one usually begins with completely unbiased messages), and simply iterates the message-update rules until they (possibly) converge, and then one can read off the approximate beliefs from the belief equations. But one would not necessarily expect the algorithm to work well. As Pearl (1988) warned, "If we ignore the existence of loops and permit the nodes to continue communicating with each other as if the network were singly connected, messages may circulate indefinitely around these loops, and the process may not converge to a stable equilibrium." One can indeed find examples of graphical models with loops, where, for certain parameter values, the BP algorithm fails to converge, or predicts beliefs that are inaccurate (Murphy et al. 1999). On the other hand, the BP algorithm has been successful as a decoding algorithm for error-correcting codes defined on Tanner graphs that have loops (Frey and Mackay 1998), and also for some computer vision problems where the underlying MRF if full of loops (Freeman et al. 2000). In the next section, we explain why this success might not be so surprising after all.

3 FREE ENERGIES

In this section, we introduce the Bethe approximation to the free energy and show that the fixed points of the BP algorithm correspond to the stationary points of the Bethe free energy. First we want to explain, to readers who might not have a physics background, the concept of a *free energy*. (See (Yedidia 2001) for more background.) All of our graphical models define a joint probability function $p(\{x\})$. If we have some other approximate joint probability function $b(\{x\})$, we can define a *distance* (known as the *Kullback-Leibler distance*) between $p(\{x\})$ and $b(\{x\})$ by

$$D\left(b(\{x\})||p(\{x\})\right) = \sum_{\{x\}} b(\{x\}) \ln \frac{b(\{x\})}{p(\{x\})} \tag{22}$$

The Kullback-Liebler distance does not have all the properties we normally associate with distances: it is not symmetric and does not satisfy the triangle inequality. Nevertheless, it is useful because it is always non-negative and it is zero if and only if the two probability functions $b(\{x\})$ and $p(\{x\})$ are equal (Cover and Thomas 1991).

Statistical physicists generally assume that Boltzmann's law $p(\{x\}) = \frac{1}{Z} e^{-E(\{x\})/T}$ is true. In our context, we can just consider it a tautology, defining the *energy* $E(\{x\})$. Furthermore, from our point of view, the *temperature* T is just a parameter that defines a scale of units for the energy, and for simplicity, we can choose our units so that $T = 1$. Substituting Boltzmann's law into our distance measure, and setting $T = 1$, we find that

$$D\left(b\{x\}||p(\{x\})\right) = \sum_{\{x\}} b(\{x\}) E(\{x\}) + \sum_{\{x\}} b(\{x\}) \ln b(\{x\}) + \ln Z \tag{23}$$

So we see that the Kullback-Leibler distance will be zero, and therefore the approximate probability function $b(\{x\})$ will equal to the exact probability function $p(\{x\})$, when the quantity

$$G\left(b(\{x\})\right) = \sum_{\{x\}} b(\{x\}) E(\{x\}) + \sum_{\{x\}} b(\{x\}) \ln b(\{x\}) = U(b\{x\}) - S(b\{x\}) \tag{24}$$

achieves its minimal value of $F \equiv -\ln Z$. F is called the *Helmholz free energy*, while the more important functional $G(b(\{x\}))$ unfortunately does not have a name that is universally agreed upon; we will use the name *Gibbs free energy*. The first term in the Gibbs free energy is called the *average energy* U, while the second is the negative of the *entropy* S.

3.1 MEAN-FIELD FREE ENERGY

Why is it useful to describe a system in terms of its Gibbs free energy G instead of directly in terms of its joint probability distribution? One reason is that it is often possible to make progress by constructing analytically tractable approximations to G (Yedidia 2001). For example, let us return to pairwise MRFs and restrict ourselves to consider approximate joint probability distributions $b(\{x\})$ that have a particularly simple form: they are factorized over the sites

$$b(\{x\}) = \prod_i b_i(x_i) \tag{25}$$

where the $b_i(x_i)$ are subject to the constraint $\sum_i b_i(x_i) = 1$. Note that within this *mean-field* approximation, the one-node beliefs are $b_i(x_i)$ and the two-node beliefs are just the products of the corresponding one-node beliefs: $b_{ij}(x_i, x_j) = b_i(x_i)b_j(x_j)$. Using this approximate joint probability function, it is easy to compute the approximate Gibbs free energy. The energy of a configuration of a pairwise MRF is

$$E(\{x\}) = -\sum_{(ij)} \ln \psi_{ij}(x_i, x_j) - \sum_i \ln \phi_i(x_i) \tag{26}$$

so the mean-field average energy is

$$U_{MF}(\{b_i\}) = -\sum_{(ij)} \sum_{x_i, x_j} b_i(x_i)b_j(x_j) \ln \psi_{ij}(x_i, x_j) - \sum_i \sum_{x_i} b_i(x_i) \ln \phi_i(x_i) \tag{27}$$

while the mean-field entropy is

$$S_{MF}(\{b_i\}) = -\sum_i \sum_{x_i} b_i(x_i) \ln b_i(x_i) \tag{28}$$

and mean-field Gibbs free energy is $G_{MF} = U_{MF} - S_{MF}$. Note that while the full Gibbs free energy is a function of the full joint probability distribution, the mean-field free energy is only a function of the one-node beliefs. Since we know the Gibbs free energy is bounded below by the Helmholz free energy, it is reasonable to search for that configuration of b_i's that minimizes G_{MF}. This is the standard variational justification for mean-field theory. (See (Jaakkola 2000) and (Jordan et al. 1998) for tutorial introductions to variational methods.)

3.2 BETHE FREE ENERGY

The justification for the Bethe free energy is different from that behind the mean-field theory, although there are some similarities. We would like to derive a Gibbs free energy that is a function of both the one-node beliefs $b_i(x_i)$ and the two-node beliefs $b_{ij}(x_i, x_j)$. The beliefs should obey the normalization conditions $\sum_{x_i} b_i(x_i) = \sum_{x_i, x_j} b_{ij}(x_i, x_j) = 1$ and the marginalization conditions $b_i(x_i) = \sum_{x_j} b_{ij}(x_i, x_j)$. Because of the pairwise property of pairwise MRFs, the one-node and two-node beliefs are actually sufficient to determine the average energy. In other words, for any pairwise MRF and for any approximate joint probability function such that the one-node marginal probabilities are $b_i(x_i)$ and the two-node marginal probabilities are $b_{ij}(x_i, x_j)$, the average energy will have the form

$$U = -\sum_{(ij)} b_{ij}(x_i, x_j) \ln \psi_{ij}(x_i, x_j) - \sum_i b_i(x_i) \ln \phi_i(x_i) \tag{29}$$

The average energy when computed with the exact marginal probabilities $p_i(x_i)$ and $p_{ij}(x_i, x_j)$ will also have this form, so if the one-node and two-node beliefs are exact, the average energy given by Equation 29 will be exact.

The entropy is not so easy to obtain, and we must normally settle for an approximation. We could compute the entropy exactly if we could explicitly express the joint distribution $b(\{x\})$ in terms of the one-node and two-node beliefs. If our graph were singly connected, we could in fact do that. In that case, we know that the correct joint probability distribution can be written in the form

$$b(\{x\}) = \frac{\prod_{(ij)} b_{ij}(x_i, x_j)}{\prod_i b_i(x_i)^{q_i - 1}} \tag{30}$$

where q_i is the number of nodes neighboring node i (Pearl 1988). Using this form, we obtain the Bethe approximation to the entropy:

$$S_{Bethe} = -\sum_{(ij)} \sum_{x_i, x_j} b_{ij}(x_i, x_j) \ln b_{ij}(x_i, x_j) + \sum_i (q_i - 1) \sum_{x_i} b_i(x_i) \ln b_i(x_i) \qquad (31)$$

For a singly connected graph then, the Bethe approximation of both the energy and the entropy will have the correct functional dependence on the beliefs, and the values of those beliefs that minimize the Bethe free energy $G_{Bethe} = U - S_{Bethe}$ will correspond to the exact marginal probabilities. For graphs with loops, the Bethe entropy and free energy will only be approximations, albeit ones that are usually quite good. In contrast to the mean-field free energy, the Bethe free energy is *not* generally an upper bound on the true free energy.

The average energy can be written in a form that is similar to that of the Bethe entropy if we introduce the local energies $E_i(x_i) = -\ln \phi_i(x_i)$ and $E_{ij}(x_i, x_j) = -\ln \psi_{ij}(x_i, x_j) - \ln \phi_i(x_i) - \ln \phi_j(x_j)$. Using the marginalization conditions on the beliefs, we obtain

$$U = \sum_{(ij)} \sum_{x_i, x_j} b_{ij}(x_i, x_j) E_{ij}(x_i, x_j) + \sum_i (q_i - 1) \sum_{x_i} b_i(x_i) E_i(x_i) \qquad (32)$$

which is exactly the same form as the Bethe approximation to the entropy except that we have replaced the $\ln b$ terms with local energy E terms.

3.3 EQUIVALENCE OF BP TO THE BETHE APPROXIMATION

In the previous section, we saw that the Bethe free energy

$$\begin{aligned} G_{Bethe}(b_i(x_i), b_{ij}(x_i, x_j)) \;=\; & \sum_{(ij)} \sum_{x_i, x_j} b_{ij}(x_i, x_j) \left(E_{ij}(x_i, x_j) + \ln b_{ij}(x_i, x_j) \right) \\ & - \sum_i (q_i - 1) \sum_{x_i} b_i(x_i) \left(E_i(x_i) + \ln b_i(x_i) \right) \end{aligned} \qquad (33)$$

is equal to the exact Gibbs free energy for pairwise MRFs when their graph has no loops, so that the Bethe free energy is minimal for the correct marginals. We also know that BP gives correct marginals when the graph has no loops (13) and (20). In other words, when there are no loops, the BP beliefs are the global minima of the Bethe free energy. It turns out that we can say more: *A set of beliefs gives a BP fixed point in any graph if and only if they are local stationary points of the Bethe free energy.*

To see this, we need to add Lagrange multipliers to G_{Bethe} in order to form a Lagrangian L: $\lambda_{ij}(x_j)$ is a multiplier that enforces the marginalization constraint $b_i(x_i) = \sum_j b_{ij}(x_i, x_j)$, while γ_{ij} and γ_i are multipliers that enforce the normalizations of b_{ij} and b_i. The equation $\frac{\partial L}{\partial b_{ij}(x_i, x_j)} = 0$ gives

$$\ln b_{ij}(x_i, x_j) = -E_{ij}(x_i, x_j) + \lambda_{ij}(x_j) + \lambda_{ji}(x_i) + \gamma_{ij} - 1 \qquad (34)$$

The equation $\frac{\partial L}{\partial b_i(x_i)} = 0$ gives

$$(q_i - 1)(\ln b_i(x_i) + 1) = (1 - q_i) E_i(x_i) + \sum_{j \in N(i)} \lambda_{ji}(x_i) + \gamma_i \qquad (35)$$

differentiating the Lagrangian with respect to the Lagrange multipliers gives the marginalization constraints.

Now, suppose that we have a set of messages and beliefs that are a fixed point of BP. We define $\lambda_{ij}(x_j)$ by

$$\lambda_{ij}(x_j) = \ln \prod_{k \in N(j)\setminus i} m_{kj}(x_j) \tag{36}$$

and using the BP Equations 13 and 20, it is easy to show that λ_{ij} and the beliefs satisfy the stationarity conditions (34) and (35). Similarly, given beliefs and Lagrange multipliers that satisfy the stationarity Equations 34 and 35, we use Equation 36 to define messages, and it is easy to show that these messages and beliefs must satisfy the BP fixed-point equations.

We can use the fact that Bayesian networks, error-correcting codes, and factor graphs can be converted into pairwise MRFs to define free energies for a wide range of different kinds of models. In every case, we have an identical story: the BP algorithm for each different model corresponds to the stationary point of a Bethe free energy for that model. The reader interested in more details should consult (Yedidia et al. 2001a).

The BP algorithm for graphical models with loops is not guaranteed to converge, but because the BP fixed points correspond to Bethe free energy minima, one can simply choose to minimize the Bethe free energy directly. Such free energy minimizations are slower than the BP algorithm, but they are at least guaranteed to converge (Welling and Teh 2001; Yuille 2001). On the other hand, empirical exploration of this idea indicates that when BP fails to converge, it is a clue that the results from minimizing the Bethe approximation will also be quite inaccurate (Welling and Teh 2001).

We refer the interested reader to the *tree-based reparameterization algorithm* developed in (Wainright et al. 2001), and the *expectation propagation algorithm* developed by Minka (2001). These algorithms provide new formulations and extensions of the BP algorithm that can also be connected to a free energy minimization framework.

4 KIKUCHI APPROXIMATIONS TO THE FREE ENERGY

Physicists, beginning with Kikuchi (1951, 1994), have developed a method, sometimes known as the *cluster variational method*, of deriving approximations that improve on and generalizes the Bethe approximation to the Gibbs free energy. Given the close relationship between the Bethe approximation and the BP algorithm, it is natural to ask whether there exist generalized BP algorithms whose fixed points correspond to the stationary points of these improved approximations. As we shall see in the next section, the answer is yes. In fact, just as ordinary BP can be defined without reference to the Bethe approximation, we shall be able to define generalized BP algorithms without referring directly to the *Kikuchi approximations* to which they correspond. Thus, if you are primarily interested in implementing improved BP algorithms, you could begin by reading the next section immediately, and only return to this section later to better understand the approximation made by the generalized BP algorithms.

In a general Kikuchi approximation, the free energy is approximated as a sum of the local free energies of a set of regions of nodes. The *cluster variational method* provides one way to choose that set of regions. One begins with a basic set of clusters of nodes that includes every interaction and node in the pairwise MRF, then subtracts the free energies of overcounted intersection regions, then adds back the free energies of the overcounted intersections of intersections, and so on.

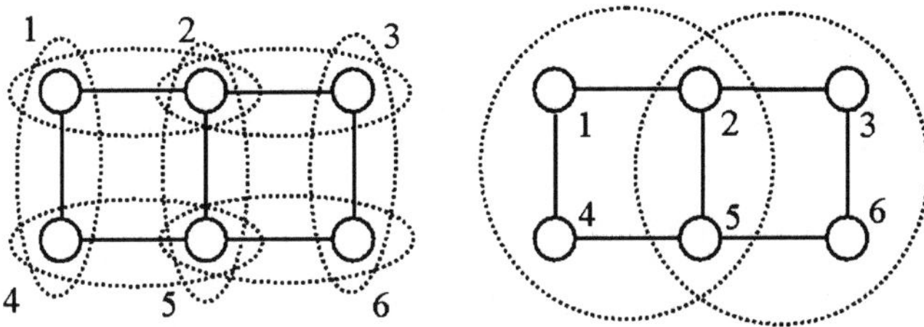

Figure 15   The basic clusters in the Bethe approximation (left) and a Kikuchi approximation (right) for a small, six-node pairwise MRF.

Figure 15 shows an example of the Bethe approximation and a Kikuchi approximation for a small pairwise MRF. In this figure we have omitted the observed nodes that are understood to be connected to each hidden node. The Bethe approximation can be considered as a particular Kikuchi approximation, where we choose the basic clusters of the cluster variational method to be the set of all pairs of hidden nodes. We define the local free energy involving a single node i by

$$G_i(b_i(x_i)) = \sum_{x_i} b_i(x_i)(\ln b_i(x_i) + E_i(x_i)) \tag{37}$$

and the local free energy involving two nodes by

$$G_{ij}(b_{ij}(x_i, x_j)) = \sum_{x_i, x_j} b_{ij}(x_i, x_j)(\ln b_{ij}(x_i, x_j) + E_{ij}(x_i, x_j)) \tag{38}$$

In the Bethe approximation for this sample pairwise MRF, the basic clusters are all the pairs of connected nodes, and the intersection regions are all the single nodes. Notice that when we start by summing over all local free energies of pairs of nodes, we overcount the local free energy of nodes 1, 3, 4, and 6 once, and the local free energies of nodes 2 and 5 twice. Taking node 2 as an example, we count it in the free energies of the pairs [12], [23], and [25], and we should have only counted it once, so we need to subtract $G_2(b_2(x_2))$ twice. Subtracting each of the single-node local free energies appropriately, we find that for this example,

$$\begin{aligned}
G_{Bethe} &= G_{12} + G_{23} + G_{45} + G_{56} + G_{14} + G_{25} + G_{36} \\
&\quad - G_1 - G_3 - G_4 - G_6 - 2G_2 - 2G_5
\end{aligned} \tag{39}$$

where we have suppressed the explicit dependence of each local free energy on its local beliefs. Notice that this equation is just a particular case of Equation 33.

Better Kikuchi approximations are derived by just extending this kind of logic. For example, if we consider the cluster of four nodes [1245] in Figure 15, we can define its local free energy to be

$$
\begin{aligned}
G_{1245}&(b_{1245}(x_1, x_2, x_4, x_5)) \\
&= \sum_{x_1, x_2, x_4, x_5} b_{1245}(x_1, x_2, x_4, x_5)(\ln b_{1245}(x_1, x_2, x_4, x_5) + E_{1245}(x_1, x_2, x_4, x_5) \quad (40)
\end{aligned}
$$

where the local energy $E_{1245}(x_1, x_2, x_4, x_5)$ is

$$
\begin{aligned}
E_{1245}(x_1, x_2, x_4, x_5) = \;&- \; \ln \psi_{12}(x_1, x_4) - \ln \psi_{14}(x_1, x_4) - \ln \psi_{25}(x_2, x_5) - \ln \psi_{45}(x_4, x_5) \\
&- \; \ln \phi_1(x_1) - \ln \phi_2(x_2) - \ln \phi_4(x_4) - \ln \phi_5(x_5) \quad (41)
\end{aligned}
$$

This definition of the local energy is a generalization of our previous notion: we just include all the compatibility matrices and evidence terms that influence only nodes in our cluster.

In our example of a Kikuchi approximation in Figure 15, we take our basic clusters to be the four-node clusters [1245] and [2356], and we subtract off the intersection region [25], which will be overcounted. The Kikuchi free energy in this case will be

$$
G_{Kikuchi} = G_{1245} + G_{2356} - G_{25} \quad (42)
$$

where we have again suppressed the explicit dependence of the local free energies on the local beliefs.

Figure 16 shows a more generic situation. (Again we omitted the observed nodes for clarity.) When we use the indicated quartets of nodes as our basic clusters in the cluster variational method, we find

$$
\begin{aligned}
G_{Kikuchi} = \;&G_{1245} + G_{2356} + G_{4578} + G_{5689} \\
&- G_{25} - G_{45} - G_{56} - G_{58} + G_5 \quad (43)
\end{aligned}
$$

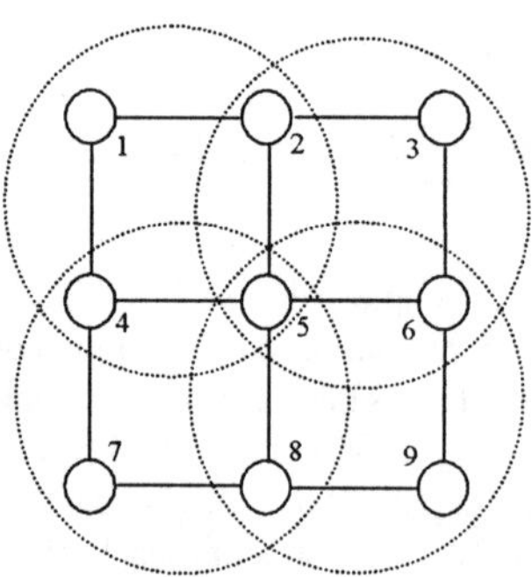

Figure 16 Four-node basic clusters in a a Kikuchi approximation for a small nine-node pairwise MRF.

Notice that the pairs of nodes [25], [45], [56], and [58] each appear in two basic clusters, so that we must subtract off their local free energies once. But once we do that, we see that node 5 appears in four basic clusters and then was subtracted in each of the intersection regions, so that its local free energy must be added again.

For a general pairwise MRF, we define a Kikuchi approximation by a set of regions R and a set of *counting numbers* c_r for each region $r \in R$. The counting numbers must satisfy the condition that each interaction and node is ultimately counted once when we include the contributions of every region. Formally, this means that we require that

$$\sum_{r \in R} c_r \left[i \in r \right] = \sum_{r \in R} c_r \left[i, j \in r \right] = 1 \tag{44}$$

for all nodes i and pairs of nodes i, j in the pairwise MRF. Here $[i \in r]$ is an indicator function equal to one if node i is in region r and equal to zero otherwise. In the cluster variational method, this condition can be guaranteed to be satisfied by defining

$$c_r = 1 - \sum_{s \in super(r)} c_s \tag{45}$$

where $super(r)$ is the set of all super-regions of r.

Let $\{x\}_r$ be a state of all the nodes in region r, and $b_r(\{x\}_r)$ be the belief in the state $\{x\}_r$. Define the energy of a region by

$$E_r(\{x\}_r) \equiv -\ln \prod_{(ij)} \psi_{ij}(x_i, x_j) - \ln \prod_i \phi_i(x_i) \tag{46}$$

where the products are over all nodes or pairs of nodes that are contained entirely in region r. Then the Kikuchi free energy is

$$G_K = \sum_{r \in R} c_r \left(\sum_{x_r} b_r(\{x\}_r) E_r(\{x\}_r) + \sum_{x_r} b_r(\{x\}_r) \ln b_r(\{x\}_r) \right) \tag{47}$$

Of course, the beliefs $b_r(\{x\}_r)$ in region r must sum to one and be consistent with the beliefs that intersect with r.

In general, increasing the size of the basic clusters improves the approximation obtained by minimizing the Kikuchi free energy. As we saw, the Bethe free energy for a pairwise MRF already has an average energy term that is exact, and this continues to be true of all improved Kikuchi approximations. The improvement arises in the treatment of the entropy, which becomes increasingly accurate as the basic clusters become larger. In the limit where a basic cluster covers all the nodes in the system, the Kikuchi approximation for the entropy becomes exact.

5 GENERALIZING BELIEF PROPAGATION

In ordinary BP, all messages are always from a single node to another single node. It is natural to expect that messages from groups of nodes to other groups of nodes could be more informative, and thus lead to better inference. That is the basic intuitive idea behind generalized belief propagation

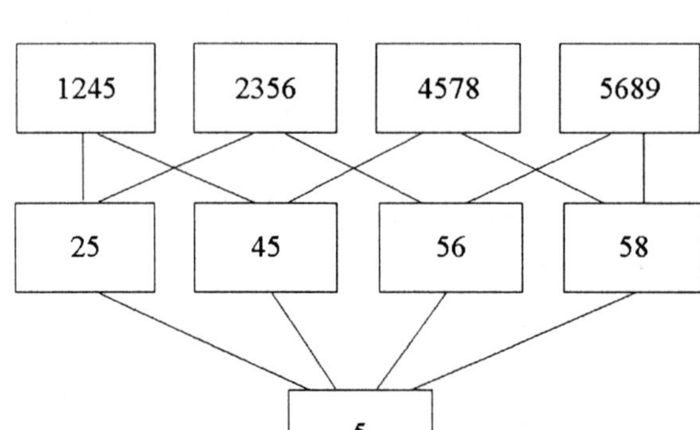

Figure 17 Region graph showing the hierarchy of regions in our nine-node example. Regions are connected to their direct subregions beneath them.

(GBP). The mathematical justification of GBP algorithms is that, if we define messages and message-update rules appropriately, we can show that the fixed points of a GBP algorithm are equivalent to the stationary points of a corresponding Kikuchi approximation to the free energy. In this chapter, we will not give the procedure to construct a GBP algorithm in the general case, or the proof of the equivalence to a Kikuchi approximation. We refer the interested reader to (Yedidia et al. 2001a). Instead, to illustrate the ideas involved, we will work step-by-step through the "canonical" method to construct a GBP algorithm for a pairwise MRF example.

Specifically, let us return to Figure 16 and try to construct a GBP algorithm that corresponds to the Kikuchi approximation described in the last section. The basic clusters had four nodes each: [1245], [2356], [4578], and [5689]. The first step in constructing a GBP algorithm is to find all the intersection regions of the basic clusters, and all their intersection regions, and so on. We find the intersection regions [25], [45], [56], and [58], and the single region that is an intersection of intersections: [5].

The next step in constructing a GBP algorithm is to organize all the regions into a *region graph*: a hierarchy of regions and their *direct subregions*. A direct subregion s of a region r is a subregion of R that is not also a subregion of another subregion of r. In Figure 17, we give the hierarchy of regions for our example. Note that region [5] is not a direct subregion of region [1245], because it is also a subregion of region [25].

The next step is to construct messages connecting all regions r to all their direct subregions s. In other words, we associate a message with each line in Figure 17. Consider, for example, the message connecting region [1245] to region [25]. We can consider this to be a message from nodes 1 and 4 to nodes 2 and 5. We will denote this message by $m_{14 \to 25}(x_2, x_5)$. In general, we can consider a

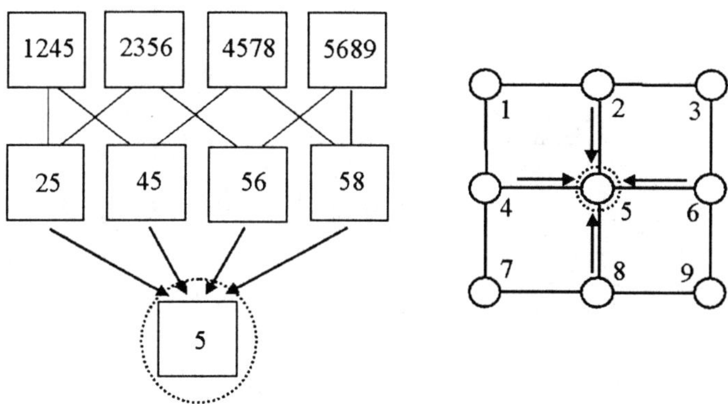

Figure 18   The belief equation $b_5 = k\,[\phi_5]\,[m_{2\to5}m_{4\to5}m_{6\to5}m_{8\to5}]$ for the region [5], illustrated both on the region graph (left) and on the original pairwise MRF (right).

message connecting a region r and a subregion s to be a message from those nodes in r that are not in s to the nodes in s.

The next step is very important. We construct belief equations for every region r, according to the rule that the belief $b_r(\{x\}_r)$ is proportional to the product of every compatibility matrix and evidence term contained completely in the region, and every message that goes into nodes in the region from nodes outside the region. For example, for the region consisting just of node 5, the belief equation is

$$b_5 = k\,[\phi_5]\,[m_{2\to5}m_{4\to5}m_{6\to5}m_{8\to5}] \tag{48}$$

where k is a normalization constant and we have suppressed all the obvious functional dependences on the states $\{x\}$. This equation is illustrated in Figure 18 on both the region graph and the original pairwise MRF. Taking the region [45] as an example of a two-node region, its belief equation is

$$b_{45} = k\,[\phi_4\phi_5\psi_{45}]\,[m_{12\to45}m_{78\to45}m_{2\to5}m_{6\to5}m_{8\to5}] \tag{49}$$

which we illustrate in Figure 19. Taking the region [1245] as an example of a four-node region, its belief equation is

$$b_{1245} = k\,[\phi_1\phi_2\phi_4\phi_5\psi_{12}\psi_{14}\psi_{25}\psi_{45}]\,[m_{36\to25}m_{78\to45}m_{6\to5}m_{8\to5}] \tag{50}$$

which is illustrated in Figure 20. The region belief equations are natural generalizations of the Bethe belief equations, but one might still wonder about their justification. Although we are omitting the proof here, the point is that this natural way to construct belief equations is precisely what you need for the GBP fixed points to be stationary points of the corresponding Kikuchi free energy.

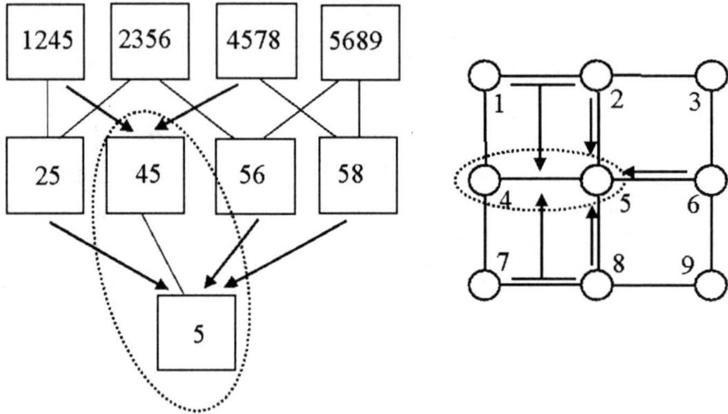

Figure 19   The belief equation $b_{45} = k\,[\phi_4\phi_5\psi_{45}]\,[m_{12\to45}m_{78\to45}m_{2\to5}m_{6\to5}m_{8\to5}]$, for the region [45], illustrated both on the region graph (left) and on the original pairwise MRF (right). Note that we include all messages that impinge upon the region [45] or its subregion [5].

The next, and final, step in constructing a GBP algorithm is to enforce the marginalization condition relating each pair of regions that are connected in the hierarchy shown in Figure 17. For example, the marginalization condition connecting the region [5] with the region [45] is $b_5(x_5) = \sum_{x_4} b_{45}(x_4, x_5)$. If we combine that with our previous belief Equations 48 and 49, we find, by canceling common terms, the message-update rule

$$m_{4\to5}(x_5) \leftarrow k \sum_{42} \phi_4(x_4)\psi_{45}(x_4, x_5)m_{12\to45}(x_4, x_5)m_{78\to25}(x_2, x_5) \tag{51}$$

The collection of all the belief equations and message-update rules defines our GBP algorithm. A GBP algorithm runs in the same way as the BP algorithm. One normally initializes all the messages to their unbiased states, and then iterates the message-update rules until they (hopefully) converge. Occasionally, it is helpful from the point of view of convergence to move only partway at each iteration toward the new values of the messages. When convergence of the messages is achieved, the desired beliefs can be read off from the belief equations.

How well do GBP algorithms work? For a longer answer with details, we refer you to (Yedidia et al. 2001b), where we describe experiments where GBP algorithms can significantly outperform ordinary BP on 2D pairwise MRFs, and for decoding error-correcting codes. The short answer is that GBP algorithms nearly always improve, at least slightly, over the performance of ordinary BP, and they can significantly outperform ordinary BP if the graphical model under consideration has short loops.

As for the complexity of GBP, the bad news is that it grows exponentially with the size of the basic clusters that are chosen. The good news is that if the basic clusters encompass the shortest loops in

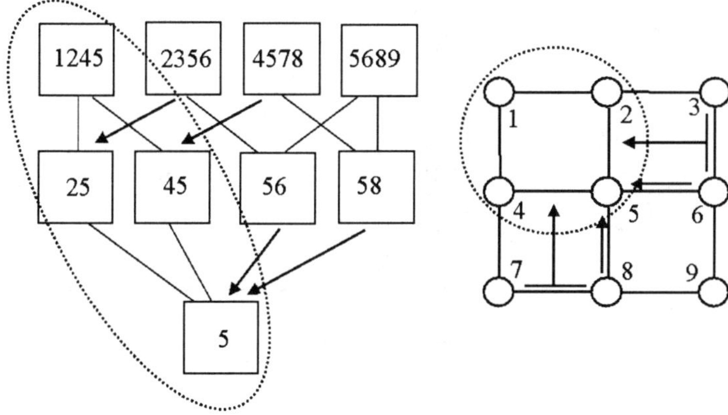

Figure 20

The belief equation $b_{1245} = k\,[\phi_1\phi_2\phi_4\phi_5\psi_{12}\psi_{14}\psi_{25}\psi_{45}]\,[m_{36\rightarrow25}m_{78\rightarrow45}m_{6\rightarrow5}m_{8\rightarrow5}]$, for the region [1245], illustrated both on the region graph (left) and on the original pairwise MRF (right).

the graphical model, one usually eliminates nearly all the error associated with the BP algorithm. For many graphical models (e.g., square lattice pairwise MRFs), using such basic clusters actually involves only minimally more computation than ordinary BP.

5.1 GBP, CLUSTERING, AND JUNCTION TREES

A standard algorithm for exact inference in graphical models is the *junction tree algorithm* (Cowell 1998), which we briefly illustrate in Figure 21(a)–(d). The graph is first *triangulated* (i.e., we add edges so that every cycle of length > 3 has a chord). In our example, this gives the graph in Figure 21(b). We then find the maximal cliques of the junction tree and connect these in a tree as in Figure 21(c). The potentials on the spanning tree are set so that the tree defines an equivalent MRF to the original problem. Once we have an equivalent tree, we can simply run BP on the junction tree to obtain marginals on the cliques (and an additional marginalization on each clique will give us marginals on individual nodes). However, since the nodes in the junction tree correspond to overlapping sets of variables in the original graph, one would like a BP algorithm that takes advantage of this fact to reduce the size of the messages. In the Shafer-Shenoy algorithm (Shafer and Shenoy 1990), messages between cliques are functions of the state of the *separators* or intersections between cliques. This algorithm is equivalent to running BP on a tree in which we have added extra nodes to denote the separators, as in Figure 21(d). This algorithm is known as the *generalized distributive law* in the information theory literature (Aji and McEliece 2000).

A related method is Pearl's method of clustering (Pearl 1988), illustrated in Figure 21(e). In this method we form clusters of nodes from the original graph and construct a new graph from the clusters

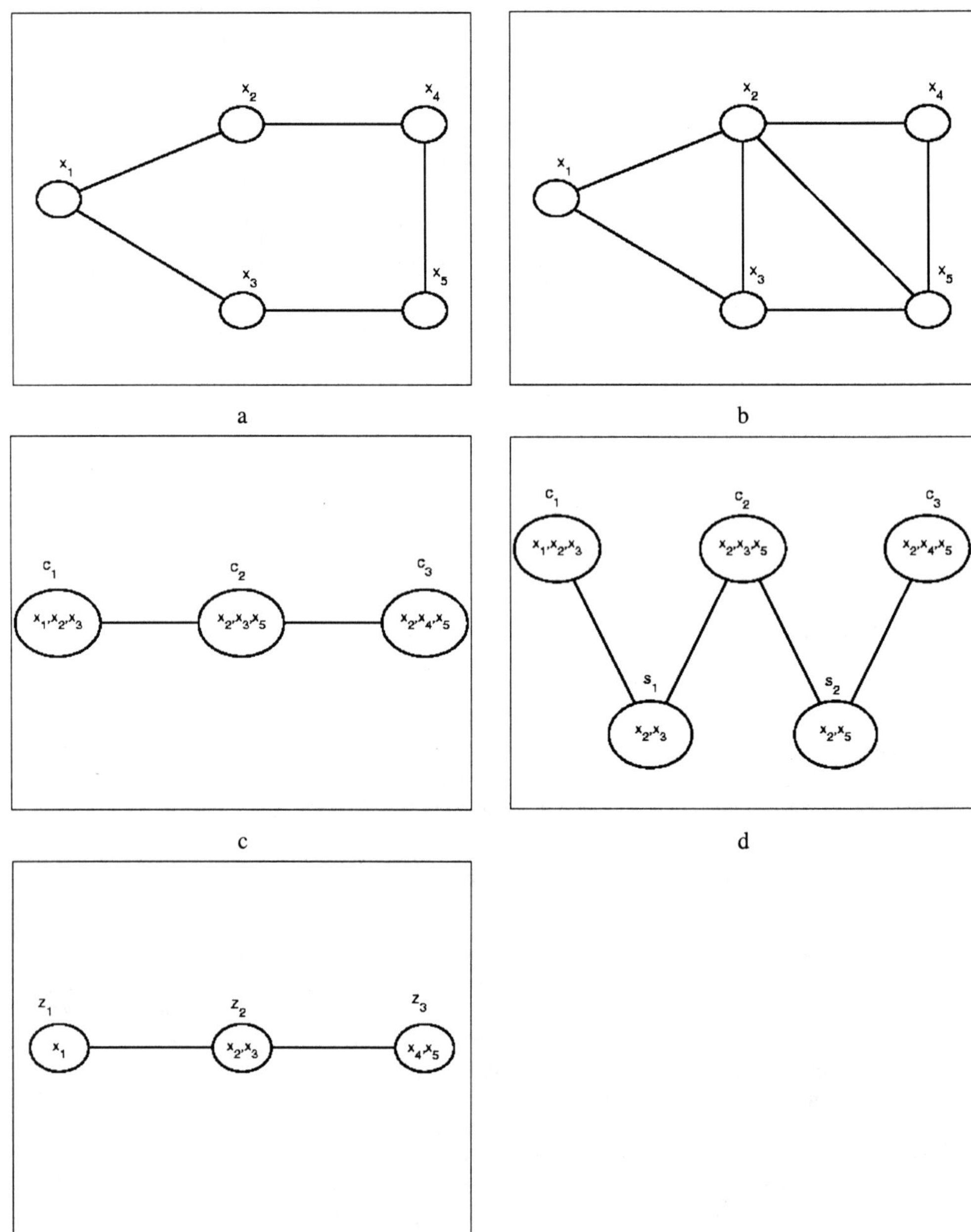

Figure 21 **a.** An undirected graph with loops. **b.** The same graph after triangulation: edges have been added so that every cycle of length > 3 has a chord **c.** The junction tree is a spanning tree of the maximal cliques of the triangulated graph. **d.** Inference in the junction tree can be performed by running BP on a graph that includes the cliques and the separators. **e.** An alternative way to convert the original graph into a tree is the method of clustering.

such that the new graph represents the same probability distribution. BP is then run on the cluster graph.

Both the junction tree and the clustering algorithms pass messages that are functions of clusters of nodes. How are these algorithms related to GBP? The short answer is that both the junction tree and the clustering algorithms are special cases of Kikuchi approximations. For example, the junction tree algorithm in Figure 21(d) approximates the Gibbs free energy using

$$G_{Kikuchi} = G_{123} + G_{235} + G_{245} - G_{23} - G_{25} \tag{52}$$

while the clustering method in Figure 21(e) approximates the Gibbs free energy using

$$G_{Kikuchi} = G_{123} + G_{2345} - G_{23} \tag{53}$$

Both (52) and (53) are cases where the Kikuchi approximation is no longer an approximation: it is an exact expression. It can be shown that whenever the region graph (e.g., Figure 17) contains only two levels (i.e., regions and their intersections) and the region graph has no cycles, the Kikuchi approximation is exact (Aji and McEliece 2001; Yedidia et al. 2001a).

While the junction tree and clustering methods can yield exact Kikuchi expansions, for many practical problems they require region sizes that are enormous. The goal of the general Kikuchi framework is to find expansions that are of reasonable accuracy but of far less complexity than the junction tree. In general, by choosing an appropriate Kikuchi approximation and corresponding generalized BP algorithm, one can adjust the trade-off between accuracy and complexity. As a practical matter, how to choose the "optimal" Kikuchi approximation is still more an art than a science. We only offer the advice that you should try to ensure that the shortest loops in the graph are entirely included in Kikuchi regions, so that they are handled exactly.

6 CONCLUSION

The success of BP and GBP algorithms is exciting, because it means that many different kinds of problems that seemed so difficult to handle, involving graphs with many nodes and loops, can actually be handled using efficient and systematically correctable algorithms. These algorithms are much faster than Monte Carlo approaches, and the approximations to the free energy that they are effectively implementing are more sophisticated and accurate than mean-field approximations. These algorithms give a principled framework for propagating, in parallel, information and uncertainty between nodes in a network. It would be exciting if they had relevance or modeling power for neural computational systems.

References

Aji, S. M., and McEliece, R. J. (2000). The generalized distributive law. In *IEEE Transactions on Information Theory 46*, 325–343.

Aji, S. M., and McEliece, R. J. (2001). The generalized distributive law and free energy minimization. *Proceedings of the 39th Annual Allerton Conference on Communication, Control, and Computing*. Forthcoming.

Baxter, R. J. (1982). *Exactly Solved Models in Statistical Mechanics*. New York: Academic Press.

Berrou, C., A. Glavieux, and P. Thitimajshima (1993). Near Shannon limit error-correcting coding and decoding: Turbo-codes. In *Proceedings of the IEEE International Conference on Communications*, Geneva, 1064–1070.

Boykov, Y., O. Veksler, and R. Zabih (2001). Fast approximate energy minimization via graph cuts. In *IEEE Transactions in Pattern Analysis and Machine Intelligence 23*(11), 1222–1239.

Cover, T. M., and J. A. Thomas (1991). *Elements of Information Theory*. New York: John Wiley & Sons.

Cowell, R. (1998). Introduction to inference for Bayesian networks. In *Learning in Graphical Models*, ed. M. Jordan. Cambridge, MA: MIT Press.

Freeman, W. T., E. C. Pasztor, and O. T. Carmichael (2000). Learning low-level vision. *International Journal of Computer Vision 40*(1), 25–47.

Frey, B. J. (1998). *Graphical Models for Machine Learning and Digital Communication*. Cambridge, MA: MIT Press.

Frey, B. J., and D. J. C. Mackay (1998). A revolution: Belief propagation in graphs with cycles. In *Advances in Neural Information Processing Systems*, Vol. 10, ed. M. Jordan, M. S. Kearns, and S. A. Solla. Cambridge, MA: MIT Press.

Gallager, R. G. (1963). *Low-Density Parity Check Codes*. Cambridge, MA: MIT Press.

Gallager, R. G. (1968). *Information Theory and Reliable Communication*. New York: John Wiley & Sons.

Geman, S., and D. Geman (1984). Stochastic Relaxation, Gibbs distributions, and the Bayesian restoration of images. *IEEE Transactions in Pattern Analysis and Machine Intelligence 6*(6), 721–741.

Jaakkola, T. (2000). Tutorial on variational approximation methods. Available online at *www.ai.mit.edu/people/tommi/papers.html*.

Jensen, F. (1996). *An Introduction to Bayesian Networks*. Berlin: Springer-Verlag.

Jordan, M. I., Z. Ghahramani, T. Jaakkola, and L. Saul (1998). An introduction to variational methods for graphical models. In *Learning in Graphical Models*, ed. M Jordan. Cambridge, MA: MIT Press.

Kikuchi, R. (1951). A theory of cooperative phenomena. *Phys. Rev. 81*, 988–1003.

Kikuchi, R. (1994). Special issue in honor of R. Kikuchi. *Progr. Theor. Phys. Suppl., 115*.

Kschischang, F. R., B. J. Frey, and H.-A. Loeliger (2001). Factor graphs and the sum-product algorithm. *IEEE Transactions on Information Theory 47*, 498–519.

Lauritzen, S. L., and D. J. Spiegelhalter (1988). Local computations with probabilities on graphical structures and their application to expert systems (with discussion). *Journal of the Royal Statistical Society, Series B 50*, 157–224.

Mackay, D. J. C. (1999). Good error-correcting codes based on very sparse matrices. *IEEE Transactions Information Theory 45*, 399–431.

McEliece, R. J., D. J. C. MacKay, and J. F. Cheng (1998). Turbo decoding as an instance of Pearl's "belief propagation" algorithm. In *IEEE Journal on Selected Areas in Communications 16*(2), 140–152.

Mezard, M., G. Parisi, and M. A. Virasoro (1987). *Spin Glass Theory and Beyond*. Singapore: World Scientific.

Minka, T.P. (2001). Expectation propagation for approximate Bayesian inference. In *Proceedings of the Annual Conference on Uncertainty in Artificial Intelligence*, Seattle, WA, 362–369.

Murphy, K., Y. Weiss, and M. Jordan (1999). Loopy belief propagation for approximate inference: An empirical study. In *Proceedings of the Annual Conference on Uncertainty in Artificial Intelligence*, Stockholm, 467–475.

Pearl, J. (1988). *Probabilistic Reasoning in Intelligent Systems: Networks of Plausible Inference*. San Francisco: Morgan Kaufmann Publishers.

Shafer G. R., and Shenoy P. P. (1990). Probability propagation. *Annals of Mathematics and Artifical Intelligence 2*, 327–352.

Tanner, R. M. (1981). A recursive approach to low complexity codes. In *IEEE Transaction on Information Theory IT-27*, 533–547.

Wainright, M. J., T. Jaakkola, and A. S. Willsky (2001). Tree-based reparameterization framework for approximate estimation in graphs with cycles. LIDS Technical Report P-2510. Available online at *ssg.mit.edu/group/mjwain/mjwain.shtml*.

Welling, M., and Y. W. Teh (2001). Belief optimization for binary networks: A stable alternative to loopy belief propagation. In *Proceedings of the Annual Conference on Uncertainty in Artificial Intelligence*, Seattle, WA, 554–561.

Yedidia, J. S. (2001). An idiosyncratic journey beyond mean field theory. In *Advance Mean Field Methods—Theory and Practice*, ed. D. Saad and M. Opper. Cambridge, MA: MIT Press.

Yedidia, J. S., W. T. Freeman, and Y. Weiss (2001a). Bethe free energies, Kikuchi approximations, and belief propagation algorithms. Available online at *www.merl.com/reports/TR2001-16/index.html*.

Yedidia, J. S., W. T. Freeman, and Y. Weiss (2001b). Characterizing belief propagation and its generalizations. Available online at *www.merl.com/reports/TR2001-15/index.html*.

Yuille, A. L. (2001). A double-loop algorithm to minimize the Bethe and Kikuchi free energies. Unpublished.

Chapter 9

Computational Learning Theory

Learning Theory and Language Modeling

David McAllester and **Robert E. Schapire**

AT&T Labs—Research

Shannon Laboratory

180 Park Avenue

Florham Park, NJ 07932

{dmac, schapire}@research.att.com

Abstract

We consider some of our recent work on Good-Turing estimators in the larger context of learning theory and language modeling. The Good-Turing estimators have played a significant role in natural language modeling for the past 20 years. We have recently shown that these particular leave-one-out estimators converge rapidly. We present these results and consider possible consequences for language modeling in general. In particular, other leave-one-out estimators, such as for the cross-entropy of various forms of language models, might also be shown to be rapidly converging using proof methods similar to those used for the Good-Turing estimators. This could have broad ramifications in the analysis and development of language modeling methods. We suggest that, in language modeling at least, leave-one-out estimation may be more significant than Occam's razor.

1 INTRODUCTION

How people manage to acquire language in the first few years of life is one of the great mysteries of human cognition. Computers cannot, at present, duplicate this ability. There has been considerable recent work in learning theory, and one would certainly expect a mathematical theory of learning to be relevant in the study of learning language. In this chapter we present some of our recent theoretical work motivated by the desire to better understand the learning of language. We take a statistical view of language, and our results are fundamentally statistical in nature. Ultimately we expect that a proper understanding of language learning will encompass syntax and semantics. However, it seems possible that language is statistical, at least to some extent, at all levels: sentences can be grammatically ambiguous, with some interpretations being more likely than others, and statements can have uncertain truth values, with some more likely to be true than others. It is hoped that the statistical results developed here, although not explicitly about syntax and semantics, will continue to prove their worth as our understanding of language learning evolves.

We are interested in what computational linguists call *language models*, attempts to capture regularities in language by statistically modeling the probabilistic distribution of words, phrases, and sentences as they occur in actual use.

The first section of this chapter consists of a formal definition of the notion of a language model in general and motivates a widely used formal measure of the "amount of regularity" uncovered by a given model.

The second section describes what is seemingly a very weak class of models—n-gram models. These are essentially simple Markov models of the language that do not capture any notions of grammar, meaning, and so on. In spite of the intuitive weakness of these models, they have proved very effective in supporting speech recognition, more effective than models that intuitively seem more sophisticated, and are today used in most if not all standard speech-recognition systems.

The third section considers n-gram models from the point of view of learning theory. Although we believe that ultimately n-gram models will be replaced in most applications by more sophisticated forms of language models, the fundamental learning-theory issues that arise in n-gram models seem likely to arise in more sophisticated models as well. A fundamental issue is the relation between n-gram models and the notion of Occam's razor as a foundation for learning theory. Informally, Occam's razor (Blumer et al. 1987) states that, for learning to occur—that is, for our model to give accurate predictions on data not seen during training—the model must be substantially "simpler" or "more compact" than the data itself. However, in general, n-gram models are not small—the model essentially memorizes the training data. So most standard theorems of learning theory that are based on Occam's razor become irrelevant; they do not provide meaningful performance guarantees for n-gram models even in the limit of infinite training data.

The fourth section introduces the Good-Turing leave-one-out estimators and discusses their relation to n-gram language models. The fundamental Good-Turing estimator is simply an estimate of the probability of seeing a word that has not been seen during training (or a word that has not been seen in a particular context). In other words, given a sample of English, Good-Turing estimators tell us how to estimate the probability of seeing a new English word in a new sample. Good-Turing estimators are relevant to n-gram models because they are used in setting certain key parameters called *interpolation coefficients* in the n-gram models. Empirically, setting these parameters according to Good-Turing performs better in practice than other methods, such as those inspired by so-called Bayesian methods (Goodman 2001). In this section, we present very recent theorems on the accuracy of the Good-Turing estimators.

A final section discusses leave-one-out error estimators in general. The leave-one-out error is computed by evaluating the expected error on a single, randomly chosen training example based on an estimate obtained using the remaining training examples. It seems likely to us that the proof methods developed for the Good-Turing estimators can be used to prove rapid convergence of other leave-one-out estimators for n-gram language models. This suggests a learning procedure in which one chooses the model whose generalization error, as measured by its leave-one-out estimate, is smallest. This approach seems fundamentally different from the more standard approach of minimizing training error over a large family of models.

2   LANGUAGE MODELS IN GENERAL

We would like a computer to read a large corpus of text, perhaps several years of issues of the *New York Times*, and find regularities in the text. For example, one might hope to discover that sentences tend to contain a noun phrase followed by a verb phrase. In this section, we describe a widely used mathematical notion of what it means to "find regularities."

Language can have various kinds of regularities. For example, one might find that, in the *New York Times* at least, grammatical sentences are much more common than ungrammatical ones. One might find that, among the grammatical sentences with objective truth values, true sentences are more common than false sentences—the *New York Times* is, to some extent, trustworthy. No unsupervised language-learning computer can currently find these syntactic and semantic regularities, although presumably these regularities do exist in the training corpus. Computers can currently find more obvious regularities, such as the statement that the word "of" tends to be followed by the word "the" or that the word "habit" is much more likely if the preceding word is "bad." Hopefully, computers will some day be able to find deeper regularities, either by using better learning methods or by seeding the search with sufficient initial regularities.

In spite of the current weakness of computers in finding regularities, it is possible to define a quantitative measure of the amount of regularity that has been found. We can then at least measure the progress of our learning systems. A common measure of the amount of regularity is based on data compression—any real regularity can, in principle, be exploited in compressing English text. For instance, simply knowing the frequency of each word allows us, using standard methods from information theory (Cover and Thomas 1991) to compress the text to a fraction of its original size (where that fraction turns out to be the entropy of the distribution of words). At the opposite extreme of sophistication, if objectively true statements are much more common in *The New York Times* than objectively false statements, then one could, in principle, exploit this fact for compression: if we represent each sentence by a bit string, then we can use smaller bit strings for the true sentences than for the false sentences. Of course, there is at present no computationally tractable method of modeling truth in a computer. Nonetheless, any regularity can in principle be exploited in compression.

Given a compression scheme, one can define the quantity of regularity implicit in that scheme to be the amount of compression achieved by the scheme. Consider a coding scheme c that compresses a sentence s into a bit string codeword $c(s)$. For a given probability distribution P on sentences, the average number of bits per sentence using coding scheme c, denoted $H(P||c)$, can be defined as follows where $|c(s)|$ denotes the number of bits in the codeword for s:

$$H(P||c) = \sum_s P(s)|c(s)| \tag{1}$$

Our objective is, essentially, to find a compression scheme c with a small quantity $H(P||c)$ of bits per sentence. (Actually, since sentence length varies from author to author, a more stable measure of regularity is $H(P||c)/\bar{n}$, where $\bar{n}$ is the average number of words per sentence. This is the number of bits per word in the compressed text.)

It turns out that any coding scheme for sentences corresponds to a probability distribution on sentences. We are interested in coding schemes that allow us to transmit a sequence of sentences as a sequence of codewords. It is important to know where one codeword ends and the next begins. This can be done if we assume that no codeword is a proper prefix of any other—such a code is called *prefix-free*. For a prefix-free code we can interpret $2^{-|c(s)|}$ as a probability of the sentence s—it is the probability that if we generate an infinite random bit string and then decode one sentence from the front of this string, we get sentence s.

Conversely, information theory gives a way of converting any probability distribution over sentences into a coding scheme. Let $\hat{P}$ be a model (such as a probabilistic grammar or an n-gram model) that defines a probability distribution over sentences where $\hat{P}(s)$ is the probability of sentence s under the model $\hat{P}$. If we use *block codes*—codewords for large blocks of sentences rather than for individual sentences—then in the limit of large block size, the average number of bits used to code sentence s in the code defined by $\hat{P}$ is exactly $\log_2(1/\hat{P}(s))$. So if the true probability of a sentence s is $P(s)$, then the average number of bits used to transmit a sentence under the code defined by $\hat{P}$ is given by

$$H(P||\hat{P}) = \sum_s P(s) \log \frac{1}{\hat{P}(s)} \tag{2}$$

Now suppose that $\hat{P}(s)$ is actually defined by a coding scheme c—that is, we have that $\hat{P}(s)$ is defined to be $2^{-|c(s)|}$. In that case we have that $\log(1/\hat{P}(s))$ equals $|c(s)|$ and so (1) and (2) agree. In general, coding schemes correspond to probability distributions and probability distributions correspond to (block) coding schemes. The quantity $H(P||\hat{P})$ is sometimes called the *cross-entropy* of P with respect to model (or coding scheme) $\hat{P}$.

If P is the true probability distribution over words, then one can show that P is its own best model—that is, the compression scheme implicit in the distribution P achieves the greatest possible compression. More formally, we have the following for any model $\hat{P}$:

$$H(P||P) \leq H(P||\hat{P})$$

The quantity $H(P||P)$ is usually written as $H(P)$ and is the entropy of the distribution P. A widely used quantity is the Kullback-Leibler divergence, written $D(P||\hat{P})$, which is defined as follows:

$$D(P||\hat{P}) \equiv H(P||\hat{P}) - H(P||P) = \sum_s P(s) \log \frac{P(s)}{\hat{P}(s)}$$

We can then write $H(P||\hat{P})$ as

$$H(P||\hat{P}) = H(P) + D(P||\hat{P})$$

In practice, however, the true entropy $H(P)$ of English is unknown and the only measurable quantity is $H(P||\hat{P})$ for particular models $\hat{P}$. Each model then provides an upper bound on the true entropy of English.

We are interested in finding a probability model (coding scheme) that minimizes the average compressed length of sentences. Again, the average number of bits per word, $H(P||\hat{P})/\overline{n}$, tends to be a more stable measure of the amount of identified regularity (it is not sensitive to variations in average sentence length). Most authors state the performance of language models by giving the perplexity, which is defined to be $2^{H(P||\hat{P})/\overline{n}}$. Here, however, we will use the cross-entropy per word $H(P||\hat{P})/\overline{n}$ rather than perplexity.

It has been shown that n-gram models of business news text achieve a cross-entropy of about 6.5 compressed bits per word as calculated by (2) (Chen and Goodman 1998). Models based on longer-distance syntactic regularities currently only reduce this by a small fraction of a bit per word (Chelba and Jelinek 1998). But it seems plausible that significantly greater reductions are possible.

3 n-GRAM MODELS

Among the simplest and most widely used language models are the n-gram models. Essentially, these models attempt to estimate the distribution of n-grams—that is, tuples of length n. This is roughly the same as estimating the distribution of words that will follow a sequence of $n - 1$ words. For instance, such a model might capture the fact that the word following the phrase "black and" is likely to be "white." Although n-gram models do not capture long-distance syntactic or semantic regularities, they have proved very useful in speech-recognition systems.

One of the remarkable characteristics of n-gram models is that they include parameters estimating conditional probabilities of the form $\hat{P}(\Phi|\Psi)$ where the conjunction $\Phi \wedge \Psi$ has only occurred a single time in the training data. For instance, in the example above, $\Phi \wedge \Psi$ is the event that the entire phrase "black and white" occurs. In a large corpus, such a phrase may occur repeatedly, but there are bound to be many others that occur only once.

We will call a model parameter derived from a single training sample a *one-count parameter*. By the nature of language, the number of one-count parameters in an n-gram language model is likely to be close to the number of samples in the training data—the n-gram model essentially memorizes the training data. It is well known that the one-count parameters of an n-gram model significantly improve the model—the one-count parameters significantly reduce cross-entropy of the model. More sophisticated language models, such as stochastic grammars used in open-domain parsing (Charniak 2000; Collins 1997), also involve a number of one-count parameters essentially equal to the size of the training data. The fundamental theoretical challenge is to explain why such "one-count models" do not overfit as is typical of overly complex models.

Bayesian explanations for the performance of one-count models can be given with an appropriate choice of the Bayesian model prior (Pereira and Singer 1999). The large one-count model is viewed as a posterior mixture of much smaller models. However, the validity of the Bayesian assumptions are questionable. Furthermore, the performance of Bayesian-inspired smoothing is inferior to the performance of Good-Turing-inspired smoothing (smoothing is described below). Here we are interested in non-Bayesian explanations that account for the performance of Good-Turing-inspired smoothing. The n-gram models provide a simple theoretical setting to explore this issue.

To simplify the discussion (and to allow provable bounds), we assume a finite fixed vocabulary of words. In speech-recognition applications one might simply restrict the vocabulary to the finite set of words known to the speech-recognition system—other words must be spelled out by the speaker.

An n-gram over vocabulary V is a tuple of n words. Intuitively, one can consider a probability distribution over n-grams defined by sampling a sequence of n words from a random position in a randomly selected sample of English text and replacing words not in V by an "unknown" token. Let S be a sample of m n-grams $\langle w_1^1 \cdots w_n^1 \rangle$, $\langle w_1^2 \cdots w_n^2 \rangle$, ..., $\langle w_1^m \cdots w_n^m \rangle$. In practice these n-grams would be adjacent so that $w_j^i = w_{j-1}^{i+1}$. However, considering independently sampled n-grams simplifies the theoretical analysis. For a given distribution on n-grams we can think of $w_1, \ldots, w_n$ as dependent random variables. We are interested in estimating $P(w_n|w_1, \ldots, w_{n-1})$. For a given sample S of m n-grams and $1 \leq j \leq k \leq n$, we define $C(\langle w_j \cdots w_k \rangle)$ to be the number of n-grams $\langle w_1^i \cdots w_n^i \rangle$ in the sample such that $w_h^i = w_h$ for $j \leq h \leq k$. For instance, $C(\langle w_{n-1} \rangle)$ is the number of n-grams whose second-to-last word is w_{n-1}, and $C(\langle w_{n-1} w_n \rangle)$ is the number of n-grams ending with the pair $w_n - 1, w_n$; thus, the ratio $C(\langle w_{n-1} w_n \rangle)/C(\langle w_{n-1} \rangle)$ is the empirical probability of w_n following w_{n-1}.

It may be very difficult to estimate the distribution of words following a phrase if that phrase was only seen a small number of times during training. To handle this very common case, an n-gram model is typically "mixed," or "smoothed," or "interpolated" with an $(n-1)$-gram model, and $(n-2)$-gram model, and so on. More specifically, for $0 \leq k \leq n$, we define the interpolated k-gram model $\hat{P}(w_n|w_{n-k} \ldots w_{m-1})$, derived from the sample as follows where $\lambda(\langle w_{n-k} \ldots w_{n-1} \rangle)$ is a real number in $[0,1]$ called the interpolation coefficient for the context $\langle w_{n-k} \ldots w_{n-1} \rangle$:

$$\hat{P}(w_n) \equiv \lambda(\langle \rangle)\frac{C(\langle w_n \rangle)}{m} + (1 - \lambda(\langle \rangle))\frac{1}{|V|}$$

$$\hat{P}(w_n|w_{n-1}) \equiv \lambda(\langle w_{n-1} \rangle)\frac{C(\langle w_{n-1}, w_n \rangle)}{C(\langle w_{n-1} \rangle)}$$
$$+ (1 - \lambda(\langle w_{n-1} \rangle))\hat{P}(w_n)$$

$$\vdots$$

$$\hat{P}(w_n|w_{n-k} \ldots w_{m-1}) \equiv \lambda(\langle w_{n-k} \ldots w_{n-1} \rangle)\frac{C(\langle w_{n-k} \ldots w_{n-1}, w_n \rangle)}{C(\langle w_{n-k} \ldots w_{n-1} \rangle)}$$
$$+ (1 - \lambda(\langle w_{n-k} \ldots w_{n-1} \rangle))\hat{P}(w_n|w_{n-k+1} \cdots w_{n-1})$$

The models $\hat{P}(w_n)$, $\hat{P}(w_n|w_{n-1})$, and $\hat{P}(w_n|w_{n-2}, w_{n-1})$ are called the *interpolated unigram*, *bigram*, and *trigram models*, respectively. The interpolated trigram model interpolates between trigram count ratios and the interpolated bigram model, which, in turn, interpolates between bigram count ratios and the interpolated unigram model, which, in turn, interpolates between empirical word frequencies and the uniform distribution. At all levels, a separate interpolation coefficient is used for each conditioning context—the trigram model has a separate interpolation coefficient for each bigram context, which, in turn, has a separate interpolation coefficient for each unigram context, which, in turn, has a single interpolation coefficient for its single empty context. If $C(\langle w_{n-k} \ldots w_{n-1} \rangle) = 0$, then we require that $\lambda(\langle w_{n-k} \ldots w_{n-1} \rangle) = 0$ so that we avoid division by zero in the count ratios. Interpolation is one form of "smoothing," where smoothing can be interpreted loosely as any method of mixing information from various empirical conditional probabilities (Chen and Goodman 1998).

Note that the empirical count ratios will typically assign zero probability to many words that in fact have non-zero probabilities. If a model assigns zero probability to an event that actually has non-zero probability, then the cross-entropy of that model is infinite. However, assuming all interpolation coefficients are less than one, each interpolated k-gram model assigns non-zero probability to all words for all contexts.

Intuitively, if a context has occurred a large number of times, then the count ratio should be somewhat reliable. Unfortunately, the count of the context turns out to be a poor predictor of the appropriate interpolation weight. A better analysis of the appropriate interpolation weight can be given in terms of leave-one-out estimators.

4 GOOD-TURING LEAVE-ONE-OUT ESTIMATORS

We will argue in Section 6 that the setting of the interpolation parameters in an interpolated n-gram model should be theoretically analyzed in terms of leave-one-out estimates of the cross-entropy of the model as a whole. Unfortunately, the theoretical analysis of leave-one-out estimators is mathematically challenging. In this section, we present a theoretical analysis of the Good-Turing leave-one-out estimators. The study of these estimators can be motivated in two ways: First, these estimators have played an important role in practical methods for setting interpolation coefficients in interpolated n-gram models. Second, they provide a case study in the analysis of leave-one-out estimation, a kind of warm-up exercise for the more challenging study of leave-one-out cross-entropy estimation for complete interpolated n-gram models.

Consider the problem of setting the interpolation coefficients in an interpolated n-gram model. In particular, consider the unigram model. This has one interpolation coefficient for mixing the unigram model with the uniform model. If the sample does not contain all words in V, then this interpolation coefficient should be strictly less than one. Intuitively we would like to set the interpolation coefficient to $(1 - M_0)$, where M_0 is the probability that, when we draw a fresh n-gram, the word w_n is one that did not occur in the training sample. More generally, we would intuitively like to set $\lambda(\langle w_{n-k} \ldots w_{n-1} \rangle)$ to $(1 - M_0(\langle w_{n-k} \ldots w_{n-1} \rangle))$, where $M_0(\langle w_{n-k} \ldots w_{n-1} \rangle)$ is the probability, given context $\langle w_{n-k} \ldots w_{n-1} \rangle$, that w_n has not occurred previously with this context in the sample. The fundamental Good-Turing estimator estimates this "missing mass."

Since the publication of the Good-Turing estimators in 1953 (Good 1953), these estimators have been used extensively in language-modeling applications (Chen and Goodman 1998; Church and Gale 1991; Katz 1987). According to Good (2000), the Good-Turing estimators were developed by Alan Turing during World War II while breaking Enigma codes. The Enigma was an encryption device used by the German navy. It used, as part of its encryption key, a three-letter sequence. These three-letter sequences were selected from a book containing all such sequences in a random order. However, a person opening the book and selecting an entry was likely to select a previously used entry, say, the entry on the top of a page where the binding of the book was creased. Given a sample of previously used entries, Turing wanted to estimate the likelihood that the current unknown entry was one that had been previously used, and further, to estimate the probability distribution over the previously used entries.

Although Good-Turing estimation can be motivated by n-gram models, the discussion of these estimators can be simplified by considering a process of drawing words from a single fixed distribution on words. In an n-gram model, the distribution will be the conditional distribution for some context of the model. But for the remainder of this section, we consider drawing words from an arbitrary fixed distribution on words. The analysis of Good-Turing estimators discussed here does not rely on the use of a finite vocabulary, so, for this section only, we allow the underlying vocabulary of words to be infinite. We simply assume an unknown probability distribution P on a countable set V and we denote the probability of word w by P_w. Although V can be any countable set, we will continue to call the elements of V "words." We consider a sample S of m words drawn independently from V, each according to distribution P. For a sample S of m words and for any word $w \in V$, we define the count of w, denoted $c(w)$, to be the number of times word w occurs in the sample S. For any integer $k \geq 0$, we define S_k to be the set of words $w \in V$ such that $c(w) = k$. Note that S_0 is the set of words in V not occurring in S. We define M_k to be the probability of drawing a word in the set S_k:

$$M_k \equiv \sum_{w \in S_k} P_w$$

Note that M_k depends on the sample—that is, it is a random variable. The quantity M_0 is the so-called *missing mass*—that is, the total probability mass of words not occurring in the sample.

The Good-Turing estimator of the missing mass M_0 is $G_0 \equiv |S_1|/m$—that is, the fraction of examples seen exactly once. More generally, the Good-Turing estimator G_k of M_k is defined to be

$$G_k \equiv \frac{k+1}{m}|S_{k+1}| \tag{3}$$

To understand these definitions, it is useful to view the Good-Turing estimators as leave-one-out estimators of the random variables M_k. We can define a general notion of a leave-one-out estimator by letting $\Phi[S, w]$ be any statement relating a sample S to a word w. Define $P(\Phi[S, w])$ to be the probability that when we draw a sample S and then a fresh word w we have that $\Phi[S, w]$ holds. Consider $P(w \in S_k)$. Note that $P(w \in S_k \mid S)$ equals the value of M_k for the sample S. So we have that the expected value of M_k is $\sum_S P(S)P(w \in S_k \mid S)$, which equals $P(w \in S_k)$. For any fixed sample S and element $w \in S$, we define $S \backslash w$ to be the sample with the element w removed (the count of w is reduced by one). The leave-one-out estimate of $P(\Phi[S, w])$ is defined to be $\frac{1}{m}|\{w \in S : \Phi[S \backslash w, w]\}|$. In general, we have that the expectation of the leave-one-out estimate of $P(\Phi[S, w])$ on a sample of size m equals $P(\Phi[S, w])$ on a sample of size $m - 1$. The leave-one-out estimate of $P(w \in S_k)$ turns out to be the fraction of the sample that occurs $k + 1$ times in the sample—that is, G_k as defined in (3).

It is not hard to show that the expectations of G_k and M_k are close to one another. Nevertheless, this does not tell us how good an estimate G_k will be of M_k. We are therefore interested in giving a confidence interval for M_k as a function of G_k, the sample size m and the confidence level δ. We do this by showing that, with high confidence, both G_k and M_k are near their respective expectations. In (McAllester and Schapire 2000), we prove the following where, for fixed constants, we have that (5) and (6) hold with probability at least $1 - \delta$:

$$|\mathrm{E}[G_k] - \mathrm{E}[M_k]| \;\leq\; O\left(\frac{k+1}{m}\right) \tag{4}$$

$$|G_k - \mathrm{E}[G_k]| \;\leq\; O\left((k+1)\sqrt{\frac{\ln\frac{2}{\delta}}{m}}\right) \tag{5}$$

$$|M_k - \mathrm{E}[M_k]| \;\leq\; O\left(\left(1 + k + \ln\frac{m}{\delta}\right)\sqrt{\frac{\ln\frac{2}{\delta}}{m}}\right) \tag{6}$$

Thus, together these bounds imply that as m gets large (with k fixed), the difference between G_k and M_k goes to zero; the bounds also tell us that this convergence to zero goes like $1/\sqrt{m}$. The constants in the bounds are modest but greater than one, and both (5) and (6) become vacuous for $k \geq \sqrt{m}$. Bound (5) is a simple corollary of McDiarmid's theorem (given below). Bound (6) is also proved using McDiarmid's theorem, but the proof is considerably more difficult and the term of $\ln(m/\delta)$ is probably an artifact of the proof method. In the next section we focus on the special case of M_0 and refer you to (McAllester and Schapire 2000) for the case of $k > 0$.

5 AN ANALYSIS OF G_0

Here we focus on the estimate G_0 of the missing mass. The accuracy of this estimator is covered by the theorem above for the case of $k = 0$. However, we were able to prove an upper bound M_0 that eliminates the term $\ln(m/\delta)$ in (6). More specifically, the following holds with high probability over the choice of the sample.

Theorem 1 *With probability at least $1 - \delta$ over the choice of the sample,*

$$M_0 \leq G_0 + (2\sqrt{2} + \sqrt{3})\sqrt{\frac{\ln(\frac{3}{\delta})}{m}}$$

Because Theorem 1 is potentially significant for language modeling, and because it provides a case study in the analysis of a nontrivial leave-one-out estimator, we now present some of the details of its proof.

It is shown in (McAllester and Schapire 2000) that $\mathrm{E}[M_0] \leq \mathrm{E}[G_0]$. This implies that

$$M_0 \leq G_0 + (\mathrm{E}[G_0] - G_0) + (M_0 - \mathrm{E}[M_0])$$

So it now suffices to give convergence rates of G_0 and M_0 to their respective means. To bound the difference between G_0 and its expectation, and the difference between M_0 and its expectation, we use McDiarmid's theorem. This beautiful and very useful theorem allows us to bound how fast *any* function of m independent random variables converges to its mean, provided that the function is not too sensitive to changes in individual variables.

Theorem 2 (McDiarmid 1989) *Let $X_1, \ldots, X_m$ be independent random variables taking values in a set V and let $f : V^m \to \mathbb{R}$ be such that*

$$\sup_{x_1,\ldots,x_m,x_i' \in V} |f(x_1,\ldots,x_m) - f(x_1,\ldots,x_{i-1},x_i',x_{i+1},\ldots,x_m)| \leq c_i$$

Then with probability at least $1 - \delta$

$$f(X_1,\ldots,X_m) - \mathrm{E}[f(X_1,\ldots,X_m)] \leq \sqrt{\frac{\ln(\frac{1}{\delta})\sum_{i=1}^m c_i^2}{2}}$$

and with probability at least $1 - \delta$

$$\mathrm{E}[f(X_1,\ldots,X_m)] - f(X_1,\ldots,X_m) \leq \sqrt{\frac{\ln(\frac{1}{\delta})\sum_{i=1}^m c_i^2}{2}}$$

A natural special case is $x_i \in [0,1]$ and $f(x_1, \ldots, x_n) = \frac{1}{m}\sum_{i=1}^m x_i$. In this case, $c_i = 1/m$ and McDiarmid's theorem reduce to the Hoeffding inequalities.

We first note that a single change in the sample can change G_0 by at most $2/m$. Thus, applying McDiarmid's theorem immediately gives a bound on the difference between G_0 and its mean. In the following, $\forall^\delta S\Phi[S, \delta]$ is an alternate notation for $P(\Phi[S, \delta]) \geq 1-\delta$, so we can read $\forall^\delta S\ \Phi[S, \delta]$ as "for all but a fraction δ of the samples S we have $\Phi[S, \delta]$."

Lemma 3

$$\forall\delta > 0\ \forall^\delta S\ \ \mathrm{E}[G_0] - G_0 \leq \sqrt{2}\sqrt{\frac{\ln\frac{1}{\delta}}{m}}$$

This leaves us with the more difficult problem of bounding $M_0 - \mathrm{E}[M_0]$. To bound this difference, we divide M_0 into a high-frequency component M_0^+ and a low-frequency component M_0^- as follows:

$$M_0^+ \equiv \sum_{w: P_w > 1/m,\ c(w)=0} P_w$$

$$M_0^- \equiv \sum_{w: P_w \leq 1/m,\ c(w)=0} P_w$$

We prove the following two lemmas separately:

Lemma 4

$$\forall\delta > 0\ \ \forall^\delta S\ \ \ M_0^+ \leq \mathrm{E}\left[M_0^+\right] + \sqrt{\frac{3\ln(\frac{1}{\delta})}{m}}$$

Lemma 5

$$\forall\delta > 0\ \ \forall^\delta S\ \ \ M_0^- \leq \mathrm{E}\left[M_0^-\right] + \sqrt{\frac{2\ln(\frac{1}{\delta})}{m}}$$

Lemma 5 follows from an application of McDiarmid's theorem and the observation that a single change in the sample can change M_0^- by at most $2/m$. Lemma 4 is more involved and is proved at the end of this section. Theorem 1 now follows by applying the union bound to Lemmas 3, 4, and 5. The union bound implies that if we have

$$\forall \delta > 0 \, \forall^\delta S \qquad \Phi_1[S, \delta]$$

$$\vdots$$

$$\forall \delta > 0 \, \forall^\delta S \qquad \Phi_k[S, \delta]$$

then we have

$$\forall \delta > 0 \, \forall^{k\delta} S \quad \Phi_1[S, \delta] \wedge \ldots \wedge \Phi_k[S, \delta]$$

since

$$\Pr\left[\bigvee_i \neg \Phi_i[S, \delta]\right] \leq \sum_i \Pr[\neg \Phi_i[S, \delta]]$$

It now remains only to prove Lemma 4. Let $B = \{w \in V : P_w > 1/m\}$. For each word $w \in B$, we introduce a random variable X_w, which is one if w does *not* occur in the sample and zero otherwise. We can then write M_0^+ as

$$M_0^+ = \sum_{w \in B} P_w X_w$$

The counts are *contravariant*, meaning that making one larger tends to make the others smaller and vice versa. Furthermore, any system of monotonic functions of the counts is also contravariant. This allows us to prove the following lemma, which generalizes an observation made in (Panconesi and Srinivasan 1997), and which will allow us to treat these dependent count variables as if they were independent.

Lemma 6 *For any finite subset B of the underlying vocabulary, and for any choice of a non-negative monotonically decreasing function f_w for each word $w \in B$, we have the following:*

$$\mathrm{E}\left[\Pi_{w \in B} \, f_w(c(w))\right] \leq \Pi_{w \in B} \mathrm{E}\left[f_w(c(w))\right]$$

Proof: See Appendix at end of chapter. $\qquad\qquad\square$

Lemma 6 also holds if all f_w are monotonically increasing, but we will only need the decreasing case here.

We now use Lemma 6 to prove the following.

Lemma 7 *For $\lambda > 0$ and $\epsilon > 0$ we have*

$$\Pr\left[M_0^+ \geq \mathrm{E}\left[M_0^+\right] + \epsilon\right] \leq e^{F(\lambda) - \lambda \epsilon}$$

where

$$F(\lambda) \equiv \sum_{w:\, P_w > 1/m} \left(\ln(Q_w e^{\lambda P_w} + (1 - Q_w)) - \lambda P_w Q_w\right)$$

and $Q_w = (1 - P_w)^m$ is the probability that word w does not occur in the sample.

Proof:

$$
\begin{aligned}
\Pr\left[M_0^+ \geq \mathrm{E}\left[M_0^+\right] + \epsilon\right] & \\
&= \Pr\left[\exp\left(\left(\lambda(M_0^+ - \mathrm{E}\left[M_0^+\right] - \epsilon)\right)\right) \geq 1\right] \\
&\leq \mathrm{E}\left[\exp\left(\lambda(M_0^+ - \mathrm{E}\left[M_0^+\right] - \epsilon)\right)\right] \\
&= e^{-\lambda(\mathrm{E}[M_0^+]+\epsilon)} \, \mathrm{E}\left[e^{\lambda M_0^+}\right] \\
&= e^{-\lambda(\mathrm{E}[M_0^+]+\epsilon)} \, \mathrm{E}\left[\Pi_{w \in B}\, e^{\lambda P_w X_w}\right] \\
&\leq e^{-\lambda(\mathrm{E}[M_0^+]+\epsilon)} \prod_{w \in B} \mathrm{E}\left[e^{\lambda P_w X_w}\right] \\
&= \exp\left(-\lambda\epsilon - \lambda\sum_{w \in B} P_w Q_w\right) \prod_{w \in B}\left(Q_w e^{\lambda P_w} + (1 - Q_w)e^0\right) \\
&= \exp\left(-\lambda\epsilon - \lambda\sum_{w \in B} P_w Q_w\right) \prod_{w \in B}\left(1 + \left(e^{\lambda P_w} - 1\right)Q_w\right) \\
&= \exp\left(-\lambda\epsilon - \lambda\sum_{w \in B} P_w Q_w\right) \exp\left(\sum_{w \in B} \ln\left(1 + \left(e^{\lambda P_w} - 1\right)Q_w\right)\right) \\
&= e^{F(\lambda) - \lambda\epsilon}
\end{aligned}
$$

The first inequality uses Markov's inequality ($\mathrm{E}[X] \geq a\Pr[X \geq a]$ for X non-negative).
Lemma 6 was used in the second inequality. $\qquad\square$

Next we prove the following bound on the function $F(\lambda)$:

Lemma 8 *For $\lambda \leq m/2$*

$$
F(\lambda) \leq \frac{\lambda^2}{(e-1)m}
$$

Proof: First, note that $F(0) = 0$. Now let $F'(\lambda)$ denote the first derivative of F—that is, $dF/d\lambda$ evaluated at λ. Then

$$
F'(\lambda) = \sum_{w:\, P_w > 1/m} \frac{Q_w P_w}{(1 - Q_w)e^{-\lambda P_w} + Q_w} - Q_w P_w
$$

Note that $F'(0) = 0$. Now, letting $F''(\lambda)$ denote the second derivative of F, we get that

$$
F''(\lambda) = \sum_{w:\, P_w > 1/m} \frac{Q_w P_w^2 (1 - Q_w)e^{-\lambda P_w}}{[(1 - Q_w)e^{-\lambda P_w} + Q_w]^2}
$$

$$
\leq \sum_{w:\, P_w > 1/m} \frac{Q_w P_w^2 (1 - Q_w) e^{-\lambda P_w}}{[(1 - Q_w) e^{-\lambda P_w}]^2}
$$

$$
= \sum_{w:\, P_w > 1/m} \frac{Q_w P_w^2}{(1 - Q_w) e^{-\lambda P_w}}
$$

$$
= \sum_{w:\, P_w > 1/m} P_w \frac{Q_w P_w e^{\lambda P_w}}{(1 - Q_w)}
$$

$$
\leq \sum_{w:\, P_w > 1/m} P_w \frac{P_w e^{(\lambda - m) P_w}}{(1 - Q_w)}
$$

$$
\leq \sum_{w:\, P_w > 1/m} P_w \frac{P_w e^{(\lambda - m) P_w}}{(1 - 1/e)}
$$

where the last two inequalities use the inequality $Q_w = (1 - P_w)^m \leq e^{-mP_w}$, which is at most $1/e$ for $P_w \geq 1/m$. For $\alpha > 0$ and $x \geq 0$, one can show, by maximizing over x, that

$$
xe^{-\alpha x} \leq \frac{1}{\alpha e}
$$

For $\lambda < m$, we can use this inequality with $\alpha = (m - \lambda)$ to get that

$$
F''(\lambda) \;\leq\; \sum_{w:\, P_w > 1/m} P_w \frac{1}{(e - 1)(m - \lambda)}
$$

$$
\leq \;\; \frac{1}{(e - 1)(m - \lambda)}
$$

Since $\lambda \leq m/2$ we then have that

$$
F''(\lambda) \leq \frac{2}{(e - 1)m}
$$

By Taylor's formula,

$$
F(\lambda) = F(0) + \lambda F'(0) + \frac{\lambda^2}{2} F''(\lambda')
$$

for some $\lambda' \in (0, \lambda)$. The lemma now follows from $F(0) = 0$, $F'(0) = 0$, and $F''(\lambda') \leq 2/((e - 1)m)$. $\qquad\square$

Proof of Lemma 4: Let $\lambda = m\epsilon/2$. Lemmas 7 and 8 together imply that

$$
\Pr\left[M_0^+ \geq \mathrm{E}\left[M_0^+\right] + \epsilon \right] \;\leq\; \exp\left(\frac{\lambda^2}{(e - 1)m} - \lambda\epsilon \right)
$$

$$
= \exp\left(\frac{m\epsilon^2}{4(e - 1)} - \frac{m\epsilon^2}{2} \right)
$$

$$
\leq \;\; e^{-m\epsilon^2/3}
$$

Lemma 4 now follows by setting this probability equal to δ and solving for ϵ. $\qquad\square$

6   CONCLUSION: LEAVE-ONE-OUT MINIMIZATION

We stated in Section 3 that one of the fundamental problems in the theory of language modeling is to explain why models that memorize the training data do not overfit. There are various approaches to this problem. Bayesian model averaging memorizes the training data and can be justified with Bayesian assumptions. *PAC-Bayesian model averaging* is similar to Bayesian model averaging in that it is based on a prior distribution on models, but, unlike Bayesian model averaging, PAC-Bayesian model averaging can be justified independent of Bayesian assumptions about the meaning of the prior (McAllester 1999). Unfortunately, neither the Bayesian approach nor the PAC-Bayesian approach justify the particular form of the smoothing methods in language modeling that work well in practice. So the real theoretical challenge is to explain the superiority of the methods that are in fact empirically best.

The Good-Turing estimate of the missing mass is fundamentally non-Bayesian: it is a direct measure of the quantity of missing mass and converges rapidly to the estimated quantity. The estimate of the missing mass is analogous to a statistical mean estimator, such as estimating the bias of a biased coin. The convergence rate guarantees that, for large samples, the estimate is accurate independent of Bayesian assumptions. It seems that a non-Bayesian justification—a justification not involving a prior on models—should be possible for modeling methods based on the Good-Turing estimators.

The Good-Turing estimators are leave-one-out estimators. The convergence results on the Good-Turing estimators show that, at least in some cases, leave-one-out estimators can be guaranteed to be accurate—one can give Chernoff-like confidence intervals for the true value of the estimated quantity. Recently, Bousquet and Elisseeff (2001) have defined a general notion of a stable learning algorithm and have used McDiarmid's theorem to show that for any algorithm that is stable in their sense, the leave-one-out estimate of the generalization loss has Chernoff-like convergence. Unfortunately, their definition of stability is fairly restrictive. They require, essentially, that changing a single instance in a sample of m instances does not change the model by more than $O(1/m)$ where the distance between models is taken to be the maximum difference between the loss of the two models over all possible instances. It is interesting that several well-known modeling algorithms can be shown to be stable in this very strong sense. But these stability requirements are too strong to make Bousquet and Elisseeff's results applicable to Good-Turing estimation or n-gram language models. A single change in a (very unlikely) sample can radically alter M_0^+. Our proof of a convergence rate for M_0^+ is not based on McDiarmid's theorem.

We will say that a learning algorithm is leave-one-out measurable if the leave-one-out estimate of the error of the algorithm has Chernoff-like convergence—with probability at least $1 - \delta$ the difference between the leave-one-out estimate of the generalization error and the true generalization error on a sample of size m is bounded by $O(\sqrt{\ln(1/\delta)/m})$. Bousquet and Elisseeff show that stable algorithms are leave-one-out measurable, but presumably many unstable algorithms are also leave-one-out measurable. It is known that many learning algorithms are not leave-one-out measurable—the algorithm that produces the model that either always guesses one or always guesses zero based on the number of ones and zeros in the sample is not leave-one-out measurable. However, we conjecture that n-gram language models under any of a variety of smoothing methods are leave-one-out measurable.

For any family of leave-one-out measurable algorithms we could select an algorithm by minimizing the leave-one-out error over the algorithms in the family. For example, we can define a family of n-gram learning algorithms where each algorithm uses a different (large) set of interpolation parameters. In general, one could combine the Chernoff-like convergence of the leave-one-out estimator with a union bound over a large class of learning algorithms to bound the generalization error of the algorithm minimizing the leave-one-out estimate. This leave-one-out minimization over a large class of algorithms seems fundamentally different from the usual empirical loss minimization over a class of models. We hope to investigate leave-one-out minimization in future work on language modeling.

APPENDIX

Proof of Lemma 6: To prove Lemma 6 we need some preliminary lemmas. For each word w fix a monotonically decreasing non-negative function f_w. For any sample S let S_B be the subset of the sample consisting of words in the set B. We start with the following lemma.

Lemma 9 *For any (possibly infinite) subset B of the vocabulary we have that*

$$\mathrm{E}\left[\Pi_{w \in B} \, f_w(c(w)) \mid |S_B| = k\right]$$

is a monotonically decreasing function of k.

Proof: For any sample S let $c(w, S)$ be the count of word w in sample S. For any pair of samples S and U we have $c(w, \, S_B \cup U_B) \geq c(w, \, S_B)$ and hence

$$\Pi_{w \in B} \, f_w(c(w, \, S_B \cup U_B)) \leq \Pi_{w \in B} \, f_w(c(w, \, S_B))$$

So for $k_1 \leq k_2$ we have

$$\sum_{|S_B|=k_1, \, |U_B|=k_2-k_1} P(S_B \mid |S_B| = k_1) P(U_B \mid |U_B| = k_2 - k_1) \Pi_{w \in B} \, f_w(c(w, \, S_B \cup U_B))$$

$$\leq \sum_{|S_B|=k_1, \, |U_B|=k_2-k_1} P(S_B \mid |S_B| = k_1) P(U_B \mid |U_B| = k_2 - k_1) \Pi_{w \in B} \, f_w(c(w, \, S_B))$$

The left hand side equals $\mathrm{E}\left[\Pi_{w \in B} \, f_w(c(w)) \mid |S_B| = k_2\right]$ and the right hand side equals $\mathrm{E}\left[\Pi_{w \in B} \, f_w(c(w)) \mid |S_B| = k_1\right]$. $\qquad\square$

Lemma 10 *For $w' \notin B$ we have that $\mathrm{E}\left[\Pi_{w \in B} \, f_w(c(w)) \mid c(w') = k\right]$ is a monotonically increasing function of k.*

Proof: Let $V \backslash w'$ be the set of all words other than w'. Let g_w be f_w for $w \in B$ and the constant function 1 otherwise. We then have $\Pi_{w \in B} f_w(c(w)) = \Pi_{w \in V \backslash w'} g_w(c(w))$, which gives the following:

$$\mathrm{E}\left[\Pi_{w \in B} \, f_w(c(w)) \mid c(w') = k\right] = \mathrm{E}\left[\Pi_{w \in V \backslash w'} \, g_w(c(w)) \mid \, |S_{V \backslash w'}| = m - k\right]$$

The result now follows from Lemma 9. $\qquad\square$

We now prove Lemma 6.

Proof: The proof is by induction on the number of words in B. The result is immediate if B contains only a single word. Now assume the result holds for sets smaller than B and consider $w \in B$. Let $B\backslash w$ be the word set B minus the word w. We now have

$$\mathrm{E}\left[\Pi_{w\in B}\, f_w(c(w))\right] = \sum_{k=0}^{m} P(c(w) = k) f_w(k) \mathrm{E}\left[\Pi_{w'\in B\backslash w}\, f_{w'}(c(w')) \mid c(w) = k\right].$$

We now use the fact that for any functions f and g from reals to reals, and any distribution P on the reals, we have that if f is monotonically decreasing and g is monotonically increasing, then $\mathrm{E}_{k\sim P}\left[f(k)g(k)\right] \le \mathrm{E}_{k\sim P}\left[f(x)\right]\mathrm{E}_{k\sim P}\left[g(x)\right]$. This gives

$$\mathrm{E}\left[\Pi_{w\in B}\, f_w(c(w))\right] \le \mathrm{E}\left[f_w(c(w)\right]\mathrm{E}\left[\Pi_{w'\in B\backslash w}\, f_{w'}(c(w'))\right]$$

Lemma 6 now follows from the induction hypothesis applied to the set $B\backslash w$. $\qquad\square$

References

Blumer, A., A. Ehrenfeucht, D. Haussler, and M. K. Warmuth (1987). Occam's razor. *Information Processing Letters 24*(6), 377–380.

Bousquet, O., and A. Elisseeff (2001). Algorithmic stability and generalization performance. *Advances in Neural Information Processing Systems 13*.

Charniak, E. (2000). A maximum-entropy-inspired parser. In *Proceedings of the First Meeting of the North American Chapter of the Association for Computational Linguistics*, 132–139.

Chelba, C., and F. Jelinek (1998). Exploiting syntactic structure for language modeling. In *Proceedings of the 36th Annual Meeting of the Association for Computational Linguistics and 17th International Conference on Computational Linguistics*.

Chen, S., and J. Goodman (1998). An empirical study of smoothing techniques for language modeling. Technical Report TR-10-98, Harvard University.

Church, K. W., and W. A. Gale (1991). A comparison of the enhanced Good-Turing and deleted estimation methods for estimating probabilities of English bigrams. *Computer Speech and Language 5*, 19–54.

Collins, M. (1997). Three generative, lexicalised models for statistical parsing. In *Proceedings of the 35th Annual Meeting of the ACL*.

Cover, T. M., and J. A. Thomas (1991). *Elements of Information Theory*. New York: John Wiley & Sons.

Good, I. J. (1953). The population frequencies of species and the estimation of population parameters. *Biometrika 40*(16), 237–264.

Good, I. J. (2000). Turing's anticipation of empirical Bayes in connection with the cryptanalysis of the Naval Enigma. *Journal of Statistical Computation and Simulation 66*(2), 101–112.

Goodman, J. (2001). A bit of progress in language modeling. *Computer Speech and Language*, 403–434.

Katz, S. M. (1987). Estimation of probabilities from sparse data for the language model component of a speech recognizer. *IEEE Transactions on Acoustics, Speech and Signal Processing ASSP-35*(3), 400–401.

McAllester, D. (1999). PAC-Bayesian model averaging. In *Proceedings of the 12th Annual Conference on Computational Learning Theory.*

McAllester, D., and R. Schapire (2000). On the convergence rate of Good-Turing estimators. In *Proceedings of the 13th Annual Conference on Computational Learning Theory.*

McDiarmid, C. (1989). On the method of bounded differences. In *Surveys in Combinatorics 1989*, pp. 148–188. Cambridge, UK: Cambridge University Press.

Panconesi, A., and A. Srinivasan (1997). Randomized distributed edge coloring via an extension of the Chernoff-Hoeffding bounds. *SIAM Journal of Computing 26*(2), 350–368.

Pereira, F. C., and Y. Singer (1999). An efficient extension to mixture techniques for prediction and decision trees. *Machine Learning 36.*

Chapter 10

Theorem Proving

A First-Order Logic
Davis-Putnam-Logemann-Loveland Procedure

Peter Baumgartner
Institut für Informatik
Universität Koblenz–Landau
Rheinau 1
D–56075 Koblenz, Germany
peter@uni-koblenz.de

Abstract

The *Davis-Putnam-Logemann-Loveland procedure (DPLL)* was introduced in the early 1960s as a proof procedure for first-order logic. Nowadays, only its propositional logic core component is widely used in efficient propositional logic provers and respective applications. This success has motivated lifting DPLL to the first-order logic level in a more contemporary way, by exploiting successful first-order techniques like *unification*. Following this idea, in this chapter, a first-order logic version of DPLL, *FDPLL*, is presented.

While propositional DPLL is based on a splitting rule for case analysis with respect to ground and complementary literals, FDPLL uses a lifted splitting rule—that is, the case analysis is made with respect to nonground and complementary literals now. To make this work, a new way of treating variables is employed. It comes together with a compact way of representing and reasoning with first-order logic interpretations, much like propositional DPLL reasons about propositional truth assignments. As a nice consequence, FDPLL naturally decides the class of Bernays-Schönfinkel formulas, which is notoriously difficult for most other calculi.

1 INTRODUCTION

Automated reasoning is among the most traditional disciplines in Artificial Intelligence. The beginnings date back about 40 years now, and many calculi popular today have their roots in the 1960s. Among the best-known ones from that time are the *Resolution calculus* (Robinson 1965a), the *Model Elimination calculus* (Loveland 1968), the *Analytic Tableau calculus* (Smullyan 1968), and the important *Davis-Putnam procedure* and its later but equally famous variant now called the *Davis-Putnam-Logemann-Loveland procedure* (*DPLL*) (Chinlund et al. 1964; Davis 1963; Davis and Putnam 1960; Davis et al. 1962). Of course, numerous other methods came up, and the "old" methods have been subject to further analysis, extension, and improvement. Nevertheless, at the heart of today's most successful first-order theorem provers (e.g., in terms of performance at annually held competitions) are in particular two "oldies," namely, Model Elimination and Resolution.

And what about DPLL? DPLL was introduced as a proof procedure for first-order logic and has an even longer history than Resolution and Model Elimination. So one might expect that DPLL procedures have been similarly evolving. But this is not the case. This observation may be explained by looking at the techniques behind DPLL and comparing them with the more contemporary ones: in essence, DPLL reduces first-order logic to propositional logic. Proof search is carried out by approximating a given first-order logic formula by step-by-step increased sets of propositional logic formulas. These sets are then checked for (un)satisfiability with a purely propositional technique.

A well-known milestone in the development of first-order logic calculi is the Resolution calculus (Robinson 1965a). For present purposes, there are two essential differences from DPLL that are worth emphasizing: first, Resolution employs *lifted data structures*. Instead of propositional formulas, clauses containing variables are the objects of computation now. Second, the Resolution inference rule employs at its core the *unification* operation to determine a new clause from two given clauses. As an advantage over the propositional methods, the search for a proof can be carried out at a much more general level. Resolution permits a finite representation of what would be infinitely many inferences at the propositional level. Also, powerful search-space pruning techniques like *subsumption* are now possible. In conclusion, it is the search space that is drastically pruned. Consequently, both features are present in almost all contemporary first-order calculi.

The two features—lifted data structures and the use of unification—are not as dependent on one another as one might expect. This can be explained by a brief look to the history of DPLL and to related work (see (Davis 1983) for a detailed account of the history of automated deduction, which also covers DPLL). This will also help to explain the contributions of the present chapter. In brief, unification has been integrated into DPLL-type calculi quite a number of times, but appropriately lifted data structures have apparently not been considered.

In the DPLL line of research, soon after its invention it was recognized that an uncontrolled generation of the propositional logic formulas may easily result in an unmanageable search space, even for small examples. This problem was put much more in the focus of interest than the design of the purely propositional part.[1] This problem was tackled in (Davis 1963) by the *linked conjunct* method. With it, a propositional logic formula (more precisely:

---

[1] For the propositional part, actually two different versions were considered: in (Davis and Putnam 1960), a (propositional) *resolution*-like inference rule is used, which is replaced in (Davis

a conjunction of propositional clauses) is passed to the propositional part only if for
each of its literals there is also at least one occurrence of the complementary literal in
a different clause. This eliminates clauses from the search space that cannot contribute
to a proof. The linked conjunct method is explained in more detail in (Chinlund et al.
1964). However, neither in (Davis 1963) nor in (Chinlund et al. 1964) is it spelled out
in full detail, but, according to (Davis 1983), the implementation anticipated *exactly* the
well-known unification algorithm of (Robinson 1965a)!

The linked conjunct method contains the first use of unification in a DPLL procedure. The
idea behind it was picked up and improved many years later—for instance, in the *partial
instantiation prover* (Chandru et al. 1998), and earlier, in the *Semantic Hyper Linking*
(*SHL*) calculus (Chu and Plaisted 1994). SHL contains additional ingredients to guide
the search that may drastically improve its performance. This calculus is the basis for
the further improved *Ordered Semantic Hyper Linking* (*OSHL*) calculus (Lee and Plaisted
1993; Plaisted and Zhu 2000). Both SHL and OSHL use the propositional DPLL part as a
core component. The SHL calculus is probably the first calculus in the family of modern
instance-based calculi. Other such calculi are described in (Baumgartner 1998; Billon 1996;
Hooker et al. 1996). In brief, the common idea is to derive propositional instances of the
given clauses in a clever way and to then analyze the set thus obtained for unsatisfiability.
These calculi will be discussed in more detail as the text proceeds.

In (Parkes 1999), a general method is proposed for lifting successful solvers for the
propositional satisfiability problem to the first-order logic level—that is, to adapt the
solvers to use quantified clauses instead of ground clauses. This is done by identifying
certain tasks that are central to the implementation of such solvers. These tasks involve
the extraction of information from the set of clauses and consume most of the running
time. In the case of DPLL, this means identifying the next propositional variable on which
to split (see Section 3) as the result of a computation at the first-order logic level. By means
of this device, exponential savings are possible.

All the approaches mentioned employ first-order techniques like unification in one way
or another, and most of them are based on the propositional part of DPLL. However,
it seems that a proper lifting of the propositional part of DPLL to the first-order logic
level, one where the *data structures* of DPLL are directly lifted, has not been investigated
before.[2] This, however, is the purpose of the FDPLL approach: FDPLL is conceived as a
"properly" lifted version of DPLL, where both the data structures *and* the inference rules
(by the use of unification) are at the first-order logic level. By way of analogy, FDPLL
relates to DPLL as, for example, the familiar Resolution calculus relates to the purely
propositional Resolution calculus. As with Resolution, the main advantage of FDPLL
over those variants of DPLL without lifted data structures is the possibility to represent

---

et al. 1962) by the *splitting* rule (cf. Section 3). Interestingly, the splitting rule was invented to
enable the use of external tape storage, as a solution to the problem of too much main memory
consumption in the resolution-like version (see (Davis et al. 1962) for more details). The mentioned
shift of focus went hand in hand with letting people refer to both propositional versions as the
Davis-Putnam procedure, because the differences were considered as purely pragmatic and not
fundamental (Davis 2001).

   [2] This should be taken with a grain of salt: already in the early book (Chang and Lee 1973), there
is a comparable method with directly lifted data structures. The difficulties with this approach
are discussed in Section 6.1.

infinitely many inferences in a finite way, which also enables powerful redundancy criteria that cannot be realized otherwise.

This provides a rather technical motivation. Given that a gap in the calculus landscape is (attempted to be) closed by FDPLL, one might well ask why it would be interesting to close this gap at all. The following attempts to answer this question from a more application-oriented point of view.

1.1 APPLICATIONS OF DPLL

The "old," purely propositional part of DPLL is still among the most efficient methods for propositional logic.[3] A lot of effort has been spent on its analysis and on implementations (see (Crawford and Auton 1996; Zhang 1997), and, in particular, (Moskewicz et al. 2001)), and the central ideas behind it have been grasped and developed further for application areas like *description logics* and *software verification*.

Description logics are a logical formalism for the structured representation of knowledge about individuals and classes of individuals. They are among the most-often investigated and applied formalisms for knowledge representation, and it may be expected that they will play an ever increasing role for such important application areas as the *Semantic Web*.

Technically, description logics can be understood as a syntactical variant of certain propositional modal logics (Schild 1991). Sophisticated implementations like the *FaCT* and *DLP* systems (Horrocks and Patel-Schneider 1998) are based on propositional modal logics Tableau calculi. Now, although propositional Tableau calculi may already be seen as special instances of the propositional DPLL procedure, it turns out that the explicit use of DPLL techniques considerably enhances the performance of respective systems (Horrocks and Patel-Schneider 1999). Another system, *KSat* (Giunchiglia and Sebastiani 2000) *directly* generalizes the propositional DPLL procedure toward propositional modal logic.[4]

Probably the most important trend in *verification* over the last 10 years is (symbolic) model checking (E. M. Clarke and Peled 1999).[5] Model checking is a technique for automatically proving the correctness of reactive systems, whose behavior over time is specified by temporal propositional logic. Notably, model checking is applied in the real world to solve significantly sized problems. Major basic techniques employed in respective systems are *ordered binary decision diagrams (OBDDs)*, the propositional part of DPLL, or the derivative, even patented and commercially exploited *Stalmarck's method*.

The reasoning in both these domains is heavily based on propositional logic. By a closer look, however, it soon becomes obvious that *predicate logic* might be a more appropriate basis. In model checking, for instance, the concretely given verification conditions typically employ first-order logic, and they have to be abstracted in order to be accessible to today's model-checking tools. This is a nontrivial step and is typically carried out by *interactive*

---

[3] Due to its popularity, it is even easily "forgotten" that DPLL was conceived as a *first-order logic* proof procedure.

[4] There seems to be no uniformly "best" approach, and there is dispute how to measure systems (Hustadt and Schmidt 1997).

[5] A look into recent proceedings of CAV, the Conference on Automated Verification, is recommended.

proof. Now, if the propositional reasoning in model-checking systems could be pushed more toward first-order logic, the gap to close by abstraction would possibly become smaller, and hence easier to close.

In conclusion, there are significant application areas where propositional logic and DPLL techniques play a major role. I speculate that these application areas would be helped a lot if the underlying propositional reasoning could be lifted to the first-order level. Can this be achieved? Which of the techniques developed over the years for propositional DPLL carry over to FDPLL? Or can the *techniques* in FDPLL be exploited in other contexts? For instance, FDPLL employs a new way of treating variables (wrt. the treatment of variables in Tableau or Resolution calculi). It comes together with a compact way of representing first-order logic models. Now, is it possible to port the technique of treating variables in FDPLL to the above-mentioned OBDDs? This might help with the space-explosion problem frequently encountered with OBDDs. Another speculative application within "planning" is sketched in Section 7. Currently, all of these questions remain open but serve as a major motivation for this work.

The rest of this introduction is concerned with less speculative motivations. In what follows, FDPLL is put into a somewhat more concrete perspective, by pointing at features not found in the more established calculi, and by indicating their relevance.

1.2 DECISION PROCEDURES AND MODEL COMPUTATION

The traditional theorem-proving task is to prove that a first-order logic sentence F is valid, or, equivalently, to prove that $\neg F$ is unsatisfiable. However, if a refutation of $\neg F$ does not exist, a theorem prover should ideally terminate and output a model for $\neg F$ (i.e., a countermodel for F). That would be useful in, for example, software-verification tasks, where unprovable "theorems" come up all the time due to faulty programs or errors in their specification. A model would then describe a counterexample to program correctness.

Generally speaking, a deduction system that can also compute models (or at least is guaranteed to terminate) for the class of formulas it is designed for, significantly extends the functionality of purely refutational systems. Such systems may be applied to problems from other, even nonclassic logics that can be mapped to decidable fragments of first-order logic. Such translation schemes have been proposed for a number of logics and reasoning schemes for knowledge-representation purposes, as for *description logics* (Nebel and Smolka 1989), *abduction* (Inoue et al. 1993; Konolige 1990), reasoning under *default negation (Prolog-like) principles* (Inoue et al. 1992), and certain classes of propositional modal logics (Ohlbach 1993). This way may indeed be feasible also from a performance point of view. For instance, in (Paramasivam and Plaisted 1998), a first-order logic prover is shown to be very competitive with dedicated systems for description logic reasoning. A competition among modal theorem provers showed that the MSPASS *Resolution* prover (Hustadt and Schmidt 2000) competes very well with dedicated systems.

But even model computation within classic first-order logic by itself has many important applications. For instance, Kautz and Selman (1996) propose a first-order logic formulation of *planning* problems that can be translated to a propositional-logic model computation problem. In natural language *discourse representation* (Blackburn et al. 1999), different models can be kept to represent different readings of discourses (Baumgartner and Kühn 2000); in *deductive databases*, models come up as materialized views or help to solve database updates (Aravindan and Baumgartner 2000; Bry 1990); in *model-based diagnosis* (Reiter 1987), a model points at possibly faulty components of a system; and so on.

In sum, model computation is among the most versatile services an automated deduction system can offer. A deduction system that supports model computation has a much higher application potential than a system that can "just" detect that *no* model exists. In order to turn a system of the latter kind into one supporting model computation, one "only" has to add a loop-detection mechanism. This loop-detection mechanism should guarantee the termination of the deduction system in as many cases as possible. Of course, the system should not only be a decision procedure for the satisfiability problem of some considered class or classes of formulas. Moreover, it should terminate with a description of a model in the satisfiable case.

Quite some work has been carried out along this line. There are approaches building on the Tableau calculus, such as (Peltier 1999). The very interesting calculus in (Bry and Torge 1998) can even compute a finite model whenever one exists. But, starting with (Joyner 1976), by far the most work has been carried out in the context of the Resolution calculus (see (Tammet 1991; Leitsch 1993) as anchors). This discussion is continued in the following section, which concentrates on a certain decidable subset of first-order logic.

1.3   THE BERNAYS-SCHÖNFINKEL CLASS

One of the most natural and useful decidable fragments of first-order logic is the *Bernays-Schönfinkel (BS) class*. A formula belongs to this class if and only if it is of the form $\exists x_1 \cdots \exists x_n \forall y_1 \cdots \forall y_m G$, where G is an arbitrary formula, which, however, contains only the mentioned variables, does not contain quantifiers, and does not contain function symbols. When expressed in clause logic, any formula in the BS class corresponds to a clause set without function symbols, except constants. But no other restrictions apply.

In the BS class one can encode, for instance,

- planning problems as formulated by Kautz and Selman (1996)
- many cases of modal logics and description logics (Hustadt and Schmidt 1997)
- the language Datalog commonly used in deductive database theory
- reasoning about feature structures as needed in various computational linguistic applications (Johnson 1994)

It is important to note, however, that such encodings may not be optimal, since typically those problems are in PSPACE, but the satisfiability problem of BS is NEXPTIME-complete.

In some cases, clauses containing function symbols are "harmless" and can be mapped to the BS class (see (Hustadt and Schmidt 1997) for such a mapping in the context of modal logics).

Figure 1 depicts a trivial example of a clause set corresponding to some BS formula. The BS class admits a trivial decision procedure: one simply has to replace in all clauses in all possible ways the variables by the constants. This gives a finite set of clauses, and a propositional prover can then be run (like propositional DPLL). Indeed, this seems to be the standard procedure nowadays—of course, like for DPLL more generally, there

(1)	$\mathrm{Tr}(x,y) \vee \mathrm{Fl}(x,y)$	%% Train from X to Y or flight from X to Y
(2)	$\neg \mathrm{Fl}(\mathrm{ko},x)$	%% No flight from Koblenz to anywhere
(3)	$\mathrm{Fl}(x,y) \leftarrow \mathrm{Fl}(y,x)$	%% Flight is a symmetric relation.
(4)	$\mathrm{Connect}(x,y) \leftarrow \mathrm{Fl}(x,y)$	%% A flight is a connection.
(5)	$\mathrm{Connect}(x,y) \leftarrow \mathrm{Tr}(x,y)$	%% A train is a connection.
(6)	$\mathrm{Connect}(x,z) \leftarrow \mathrm{Connect}(x,y) \wedge$ $\mathrm{Connect}(y,z)$	%% Connect is a transitive relation.

Figure 1 A clause set belonging to the Bernays-Schönfinkel class. Here and below, variables are denoted by x, y, or z, and constant and function symbols start with a different lowercase letter. Every clause is implicitly universally quantified. The first clause, for example, thus reads as $\forall x\, \forall y\, (\mathrm{Tr}(x,y) \vee \mathrm{Fl}(x,y))$.

are improvements that aim at a clever way of generating the ground instances (Gallo and Rago 1994). In a similar way proceeds the SATCHMO procedure (Manthey and Bry 1988), which opened the stage for a whole family of successor developments (Baumgartner et al. 1996; Loveland et al. 1995). The same holds for the "classic" Tableau calculus (Smullyan 1968).

One may well question if this is the best way to go. The set of clauses fed into the propositional prover may become too large, and many redundancies are not discovered. Even clever strategies such as those used, for example, in the S-models system (Niemelä and Simons 1996) occasionally reach their limits. Some systems, like SATCHMO and its successors, perform the reduction to propositional logic during proof search time, but the problems remain. For instance, suppose that the domain in Figure 1 were enhanced with thousands of constants, each one naming a city. The "train," "flight," and "connect" predicates would be computed *explicitly* then, for each constant, whereas the model representation computed by FDPLL would remain as stated.

Why are alternatives hardly explored? An answer might be that a nontrivial decision procedure for BS is not easy to find. Following are some considerations about established methods from the viewpoint of the BS class.

A class of calculi that has "model building" at its heart are Tableau calculi (Beckert and Hähnle 1998; Fitting 1990). As indicated above, *propositional* Tableau calculi are successfully applied to, for example, description logics, and there is considerable research activity on nonclassic and first-order logic variants.[6] Contemporary Tableau calculi (Beckert 2000; Giese 2001), the related *Connection calculi* (Bibel 1981; Baumgartner et al. 1999), and the special case of Model Elimination (Letz 1998; Loveland 1968) (which is among the best methods for *theorem proving*), do not terminate on the BS class (or are not known to terminate). Probably the most advanced Tableau calculus (Peltier 1999) decides the BS class, but faces a combinatorial explosion problem during its model-extraction phase. Only the Connection calculus variant in (Billon 1996) and a calculus in the SATCHMO tradition (Baumgartner 1998) decide the BS class.

---

[6] A look into the proceedings of the international conference *Analytic Tableaux and Related Methods* may confirm this.

A very interesting family of proof procedures for first-order logic was developed by David Plaisted and his co-workers. The final stage so far is the OSHL calculus (Lee and Plaisted 1993; Plaisted and Zhu 2000). OSHL is related to the DPLL procedure but does a much more clever reduction of first-order logic to propositional logic. Nethertheless, the mentioned reduction of first-order logic to propositional logic persists.

And what about Resolution? Surprisingly, there seems to be no refinement of the Resolution calculus that decides the BS class![7] For the special case of the Horn clause logic subset of BS, the *Hyper-Resolution calculus* (Robinson 1965b) can be used, but for the general case no solution seems to be known.[8] But even in special cases, when Hyper-Resolution terminates and detects satisfiability, nontrivial postprocessing is required to actually compute a model (Fermüller and Leitsch 1996).

Now, this I consider one of the strengths of FDPLL: FDPLL is a decision procedure for the BS class. Beyond this, in the satisfiable case, FDPLL does not only terminate but also reports a model. More specifically, a compact and natural *representation* of a model is computed[9] (this holds in all cases when FDPLL terminates without a refutation). Given the significance of the BS class, this feature of FDPLL could indeed be worth exploring further in practical applications.

1.4 THE IDEA BEHIND FDPLL

FDPLL can be described, at least superficially, quite easily by referring to the original DPLL procedure: the original DPLL procedure is based on the idea of analyzing a propositional formula for satisfiability by reasoning by cases. To do so, some propositional variable, say A, is randomly chosen, and a case analysis—"A is *true*" versus "A is *false*"— is carried out. Both cases give rise to simplifications of the formula based on the new information, thereby reducing the problem to two smaller subproblems (Section 3 contains a more detailed description of DPLL). Eventually, if all cases have been shown to lead to trivially unsatisfiable formulas, a refutation has been found. Otherwise, a model for the original formula can be extracted by tracing back the chosen case analysis.

Now, FDPLL follows exactly this idea, except that the splitting is lifted to the first-order level—that is, one splits with complementary literals now possibly containing variables, such as $\mathrm{Fl}(x, \mathrm{ko})$ and $\neg \mathrm{Fl}(x, \mathrm{ko})$. More precisely, the FDPLL calculus proceeds by maintaining sets of literals, a set of literals forks into two new sets when the splitting rule is applied, and the complementary literals are added respectively. Each set of literals represents an interpretation, and the splitting operation is guided by identifying a clause that is *false* in the "current" interpretation (unification is employed here).

If no such clause is found, FDPLL terminates with the current set of literals as a representation of a model for the clause set. Roughly speaking, in such a set, a literal specifies the truth values for all its ground instances, unless there is a more specific literal specifying opposite truth values. For instance, in the example in Figure 1, FDPLL

---

[7] The trivial way by reduction to propositional logic excluded.

[8] Interestingly, Hyper-Resolution does *not* terminate for the simple example in Figure 1. Ever longer clauses are derived.

[9] The tableau calculi in (Baumgartner 1998) and (Billon 1996) are conceptually different. Recently, it could be shown in (Letz and Stenz 2001) that the calculus in (Billon 1996) offers a similarly compact representation of models.

terminates with "satisfiable" and returns the following literals:[10]

$$\neg x$$
$$\text{Fl}(x, y)$$
$$\neg \text{Fl}(\text{ko}, y)$$
$$\neg \text{Fl}(y, \text{ko})$$
$$\text{Tr}(\text{ko}, y)$$
$$\text{Tr}(y, \text{ko})$$
$$\text{Connect}(x, y)$$

In order to determine the truth value of, for example, $\text{Fl}(\text{ko}, \text{fra})$, the literal $\text{Fl}(x, y)$ is a candidate to be assigned *true* to it. However, the presence of the more specific literal $\neg \text{Fl}(\text{ko}, x)$ with an opposite sign cancels this possibility, thus assigning *false* to $\text{Fl}(\text{ko}, \text{fra})$. Nevertheless, $\text{Connect}(\text{ko}, \text{fra})$ is *true* due to $\text{Connect}(x, y)$. The "literal" $\neg x$ acts as a catchall case that assigns *false* to otherwise unspecified atoms.

The rest of this chapter is structured as follows: Section 2 gathers the usual preliminaries in the theorem-proving area. This is necessary, as technicalities in the subsequent presentation are not completely avoidable. Section 3 recapitulates the traditional DPLL procedure in a semantic tree framework. This is the base for the subsequent development of FDPLL. This is done methodologically in a bottom-up way: Section 4 describes the model-representation technique, including elementary operations needed for the inference rules. The inference rules proper are introduced in Section 5. In Section 6, the calculus is proven as correct. It also contains a discussion on related work from a technical point of view. Finally, in Section 7, some conclusions are drawn, including ideas for further work.

2 PRELIMINARIES

In order to describe FDPLL in more detail, some technicalities are unavoidable. As the reader, you are assumed to have encountered propositional and first-order logic before; familiarity with theorem-proving concepts, however, should not be necessary. Nevertheless, although basic notions such as *clause logic* and *unifier* are recapitulated here, it might still be advantageous to further consult any standard textbook on theorem proving (Chang and Lee 1973; Fitting 1990) or on Artificial Intelligence.

2.1 SYNTAX OF PREDICATE LOGIC

A *signature* Σ consists of a finite set of *function symbols*, a finite set of *predicate symbols*, and a countably infinite set of *variables*, all mutually disjoint.

Predicate symbols start with a capital letter, as in P, Q, Fl; function symbols start with a lowercase letter, as in f, g, h, ko; and variables are usually written as x, y, or z. Sometimes, indices or primes are attached for convenient naming, as in P_1, x_{17}, or y'.

Predicate symbols and function symbols come with a nonnegative integer, the *arity* of the symbol. Function symbols of arity 0 are also called *constants*. A Σ-*term* is either a

---

[10] A derivation of this result by FDPLL is contained in Section 5 (Figure 8).

variable or an expression $f(t_1, \ldots, t_n)$, where f is an n-ary function symbol, and $t_1, \ldots, t_n$ are terms. The recursion stops in the case of a variable or in the case of a term with 0-ary function symbol. In the latter case, $a()$ is written as a (a constant).

A Σ-*atom* is an expression $P(t_1, \ldots, t_n)$, where P is an n-ary predicate symbol, and $t_1, \ldots, t_n$ are terms. A Σ-*literal* is either a Σ-atom or a negated Σ-atom, as $\neg P(a)$. The letters K and L are reserved to denote literals. The *complement* of a Σ-literal L is denoted as $\overline{L}$. More explicitly, for any atom A, one sets $\overline{A} = \neg A$ and $\overline{\neg A} = A$.

The *depth* of a term or an atom is the depth of its tree representation. For instance, the depth of the terms ko and $\mathrm{state}(x)$, and the atom $\mathrm{Fl}(\mathrm{ko}, \mathrm{state}(x))$, is 0, 1, and 2, respectively. The depth of a literal is the depth of its atom. Thus the depth of $\neg\mathrm{Fl}(\mathrm{ko}, \mathrm{state}(x))$ is the same as the depth of $\mathrm{Fl}(\mathrm{ko}, \mathrm{state}(x))$.

From a given signature Σ, the first-order Σ-formulas can be built in the usual way. However, as most first-order calculi for automated reasoning, FDPLL takes its input in clausal form. Clauses are a special case of first-order logic formulas. Many problems occurring in practice can be formulated naturally in clause logic. Since there are satisfiability-preserving translators from usual first-order logic syntax to a clause logic, this poses no real restriction.

A Σ-*clause* is a finite, possibly empty multiset $\{L_1, \ldots, L_n\}$ of Σ-literals, usually written as a disjunction $L_1 \vee \cdots \vee L_n$. Every clause thus is of the form $A_1 \vee \cdots \vee A_k \vee \neg A_{k+1} \vee \cdots \vee \neg A_n$ (where $0 \leq k \leq n$), which can be written equivalently as $A_1 \vee \cdots \vee A_k \leftarrow A_{k+1} \wedge \cdots \wedge A_n$. This notation is used in Figure 1.

The letters C and D are reserved to denote clauses. A Σ-*clause set* is a finite set of Σ-clauses. From now on the prefix "Σ-" is dropped if Σ is clear from the context or Σ is not important.

The clauses of a clause set are thought to be connected conjunctively, and the variables in clauses are implicitly governed by universal quantifiers. Together, thus, a clause set like

$$\{\neg\mathrm{Fl}(\mathrm{ko}, x),\ \mathrm{Connect}(x, y) \vee \neg\mathrm{Fl}(x, y)\}$$

is nothing but another notation for the formula

$$\forall x\, \forall y\, (\neg\mathrm{Fl}(\mathrm{ko}, x) \wedge (\mathrm{Connect}(x, y) \vee \neg\mathrm{Fl}(x, y)))$$

The clause set in Figure 1 serves as a running example for the rest of this text. For the purpose of describing FDPLL, the equivalent notation in Figure 2 is slightly more useful.

A *ground* term (atom, literal, clause, clause set) is a term (atom, literal, clause, clause set) that contains no variable. For instance, $\mathrm{Fl}(\mathrm{ko}, \mathrm{fra})$ is a ground atom, while $\mathrm{Fl}(\mathrm{ko}, x)$ is not. Any finite ground clause set is equivalent to some propositional logic formula. One only needs to consistently replace the atoms by propositional variables, using different propositional variables for different atoms. For instance, $\mathrm{Fl}(\mathrm{ko}, \mathrm{ko})$ might become A, $\mathrm{Fl}(\mathrm{ko}, \mathrm{fra})$ might become B, and so on. The term *propositional logic* can thus also be used to mean *predicate logic without variables*.

2.2 SEMANTICS OF PREDICATE LOGIC

The semantics of a predicate logic formula is based on the possible interpretations it can receive. An interpretation $\mathcal{I}$ consists of a domain of discourse (also called *universe*) $\mathcal{U}$ and

(1)	$\mathrm{Tr}(x,y) \vee \mathrm{Fl}(x,y)$	%% Train from X to Y or flight from X to Y
(2)	$\neg\mathrm{Fl}(\mathrm{ko},x)$	%% No flight from Koblenz to anywhere
(3)	$\mathrm{Fl}(x,y) \vee \neg\mathrm{Fl}(y,x)$	%% Flight is a symmetric relation.
(4)	$\mathrm{Connect}(x,y) \vee \neg\mathrm{Fl}(x,y)$	%% A flight is a connection.
(5)	$\mathrm{Connect}(x,y) \vee \neg\mathrm{Tr}(x,y)$	%% A train is a connection.
(6)	$\mathrm{Connect}(x,z) \vee \neg\mathrm{Connect}(x,y) \vee$ $\neg\mathrm{Connect}(y,z)$	%% Connect is a transitive relation.

Figure 2 The flight example from Figure 1 using a different notation for clauses.

two mappings. The one assigns to each n-ary function symbol f from the given signature Σ a (total) n-ary function $f_{\mathcal{I}} : \mathcal{U} \times \cdots \times \mathcal{U} \mapsto \mathcal{U}$, and the other assigns to each n-ary predicate symbol P from Σ an n-ary function $P_{\mathcal{I}} : \mathcal{U} \times \cdots \times \mathcal{U} \mapsto \{true, false\}$.

When dealing with the satisfiability problem of (in particular) clause logic, it is sufficient to restrict to *Herbrand interpretations*. There, the universe is fixed to consist of all the ground terms that can be built from the function symbols of Σ. To exclude trivial anomalies, it has to be assumed that Σ contains at least one constant symbol. If none is there, some constant a is added artificially.

The *only* degree of freedom when choosing a Herbrand interpretation concerns the interpretations $P_{\mathcal{I}}$ of the predicate symbols P. It is common to represent these in an equivalent way by the sets of ground atoms that are to be evaluated to *true*. For instance, if Σ consists of the predicate symbol Tr alone and the two constants ko and fra, then $\mathcal{I}_{\mathrm{Tr}} = \{\mathrm{Tr}(\mathrm{ko},\mathrm{fra}),\ \mathrm{Tr}(\mathrm{fra},\mathrm{ko})\}$ is a Σ-interpretation.

For the purposes of this chapter, however, it is slightly more convenient to use a symmetrical form: A *Herbrand Σ-interpretation* is defined to be a set of ground Σ-literals $\mathcal{I}$ such that either $A \in \mathcal{I}$ or $\neg A \in \mathcal{I}$ for every ground Σ-atom A. The example interpretation just mentioned thus reads as $\mathcal{I}_{\mathrm{Tr}} = \{\neg\mathrm{Tr}(\mathrm{ko},\mathrm{ko}),\ \mathrm{Tr}(\mathrm{ko},\mathrm{fra}),\ \mathrm{Tr}(\mathrm{fra},\mathrm{ko}),\ \neg\mathrm{Tr}(\mathrm{fra},\mathrm{fra})\}$. Any subset of a Herbrand Σ-interpretation is called a *partial Herbrand Σ-interpretation*.

The signature Σ is always given implicitly by the clause set under consideration, and hence the prefix "$\Sigma-$" is usually omitted. Also, since from now on only Herbrand interpretations are considered, the prefix "Herbrand" can be dropped.

A ground literal L and a ground clause C is evaluated wrt. an interpretation $\mathcal{I}$ as expected—that is, $\mathcal{I}(L) = true$ iff $L \in \mathcal{I}$ and $\mathcal{I}(C) = true$ iff $\mathcal{I}(L) = true$ for some $L \in C$. Furthermore, for a nonground clause C, define $\mathcal{I}(C) = true$ iff $\mathcal{I}(C') = true$ for every ground instance C' of C. As usual, $\mathcal{I} \models X$ means $\mathcal{I}(X) = true$ where X is a literal, clause, or clause set (interpreted conjunctively), and then $\mathcal{I}$ is called a *model for* X.

For instance, $\mathcal{I}_{\mathrm{Tr}} \not\models \mathrm{Tr}(x,x)$, because the ground instance $\mathrm{Tr}(\mathrm{ko},\mathrm{ko})$ is *false* in $\mathcal{I}_{\mathrm{Tr}}$.

2.3 SUBSTITUTIONS

A substitution is a total function σ from variables to terms, such that the domain of σ (i.e., the set $\{x \mid \sigma(x) \neq x\}$) is finite. A substitution σ is usually written as the finite set $\{x_1/t_1, \ldots, x_n/t_n\}$, where $\{x_1, \ldots, x_n\}$ is the domain of σ and $t_i = \sigma(x_i)$ are the terms that are to replace the variables (for $i = 1, \ldots, n$).

Substitutions are usually identified with their homomorphic extension to terms, and substitution application is written in postfix notation. Thus, for instance, if $\sigma = \{x/\text{ko}, y/\text{state}(x)\}$, then $\text{Fl}(x,y)\sigma = \text{Fl}(\text{ko}, \text{state}(x))$.

A *unifier* for a set Q of terms or literals is a substitution δ such that $Q\delta$ is a singleton. For instance, $\delta = \{x/\text{ko}, y/\text{ko}, z/\text{fra}\}$ is a unifier for $Q = \{\text{Fl}(x, \text{fra}),\ \text{Fl}(y, z)\}$, because $Q\delta = \{\text{Fl}(\text{ko}, \text{fra})\}$. For efficiency reasons, unifiers are usually computed at a most general level. A unifier σ is a *most general unifier* (MGU) for Q iff for every unifier δ for Q there is a substitution γ such that $\delta = \sigma \circ \gamma$. In the example, $\sigma = \{x/y,\ z/\text{fra}\}$ is an MGU for Q, and $\sigma \circ \{y/\text{ko}\} = \delta$. We assume as given a unification algorithm *unify*. The notation $\sigma = \text{unify}(Q)$ means that an MGU σ of Q exists and σ is computed by the function $\text{unify}(\cdot)$ applied to Q.

Quite frequently, a *simultaneous unifier for a set* $\{Q_1, \ldots, Q_n\}$ of unification problems is to be computed, which is a substitution δ that is a unifier for every $Q_1, \ldots, Q_n$. The notion of a *simultaneous most general unifier* can be defined analogously as above. A simultaneous most general unifier (simply called MGU as well) can be computed by iterative application of unify to $Q_1, \ldots, Q_n$. See (Eder 1985) for a thorough treatment. Thus, we may suppose as given a simultaneous unification algorithm s-unify and write $\sigma = \text{s-unify}(\{Q_1, \ldots, Q_n\})$ in analogy to $\sigma = \text{unify}(Q)$ above.

For literals K and L define $K \gtrsim L$, meaning that K *is more general than* L, iff there is a substitution σ_K such that $K\sigma_K = L$. For instance, by taking $\sigma_K = \{y/x\}$ one sees that $\text{Fl}(x, y) \gtrsim \text{Fl}(x, x)$. The literals K and L are *variants*, written as $K \sim L$, iff $K \gtrsim L$ and $L \gtrsim K$; equivalently, $K \sim L$ iff $K\sigma = L$ for some renaming substitution σ. For instance, $\text{Fl}(x, y) \sim \text{Fl}(y, x)$, but not $\text{Fl}(x, y) \sim \text{Fl}(x, x)$.

A literal K is *strictly more general* than a literal L, $K > L$, iff $K \gtrsim L$ and not $K \sim L$ (e.g., $\text{Fl}(x, y) > \text{Fl}(x, x)$). Then the literal L is said to be a *strict*, or *proper*, instance of K. If neither $K \gtrsim L$ nor $L \gtrsim K$, then K and L are *incomparable* (e.g., $\text{Fl}(x, x)$ and $\text{Fl}(\text{ko}, y)$ are incomparable).

Finally, define $L \in^{\sim} N$ iff $L \sim K$ for some $K \in N$, where N is a set of literals. This definition is motivated by the need to occasionally retrieve a literal L from a set N and unify it with some other literal L'. To make this work as intended, coincidental designation of variables in L and L' by the same name has to be avoided. For instance, when taking $N = \{\text{Tr}(x, \text{ko})\}$ and $L' = \text{Tr}(\text{fra}, x)$, then $\text{Tr}(x, \text{ko}) \in N$ and $\text{Tr}(\text{fra}, x)$ do not unify. However, the variant $\text{Tr}(x', \text{ko}) \in^{\sim} N$ and $\text{Tr}(\text{fra}, x)$ do unify, which is what is needed.

3 PROPOSITIONAL DPLL AS A SEMANTIC TREE METHOD

Originally, DPLL was formulated in a procedural notation. For the purpose of this chapter, however, a different, maybe more intuitive formulation based on *semantic trees* is better suited.

Semantic trees were introduced by Kowalski and Hayes (1969) as a tool to prove completeness of the Resolution calculus. Another application is the very elegant proof of compactness of first-order logic ((Chang and Lee 1973) contains both proofs). Since they serve as a base for the development of FDPLL, semantic trees shall now be briefly recapitulated. Building on that, it is then straightforward to describe DPLL.

Suppose the following propositional clause set S given

$$A \vee B$$
$$C \vee \neg A$$
$$D \vee \neg C \vee \neg A$$
$$\neg D \vee \neg B$$

The underlying signature Σ consists of the four propositional atoms $\{A, B, C, D\}$. Figure 3 depicts a semantic tree for Σ. A *semantic tree (for Σ)* is a labeled, unordered binary tree, such that (1) all nonroot nodes are labeled with Σ-literals, (2) sibling literals are labeled with complementary literals, and (3) along each branch no two distinct nodes are labeled with the same literal. The idea behind DPLL is to systematically investigate all possible interpretations for a given clause set by means of a semantic tree. The construction leads either to a model or otherwise to a proof of unsatisfiability of the clause set.

Each branch in a semantic tree stands for the interpretation that is obtained by extending the partial interpretation given by its labels with all negative literals $\neg A$, such that A is in Σ and neither A nor $\neg A$ are among the labels. That is, a branch uniquely assigns truth values as specified by the labels, and the other atoms are set to *false*.

For instance, in Figure 3, the branch labeled with the literals $(\neg A, B, \neg D)$ stands for the interpretation $\{\neg A, B, \neg C, \neg D\}$. The empty semantic tree stands for the interpretation that assigns *false* to all atoms.

Some of these interpretations of a semantic tree may be models of a specific clause set under consideration, while others may be not. In the example, the two interpretations depicted in Figure 3 are also models for the clause set S, while all other interpretations are not models of S. For instance, the extension of $\{A, C, \neg D\}$ (cf. the respective branch in Figure 3) is not a model for S, because $\{A, C, \neg D\}$ alone is sufficient to assign *false* to the clause $D \vee \neg C \vee \neg A$, and hence to S. In general, a branch p is *closed* (by a clause

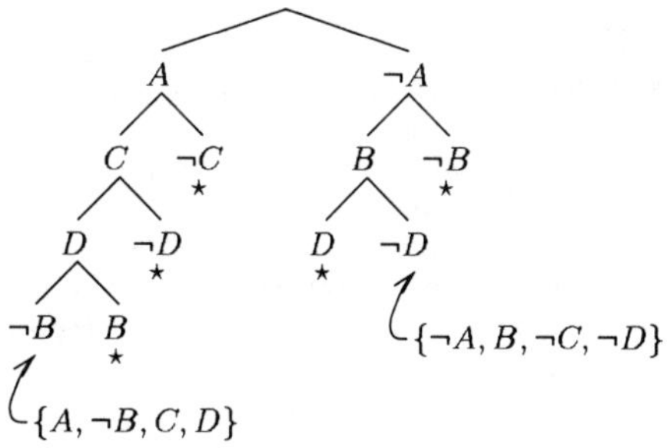

Figure 3   A sample semantic tree for S with associated interpretations for two of the branches.

C) iff there is a clause C each of whose literals is complementary to some literal in p. In Figure 3 the closed branches are marked with a "$\star$."

Now, DPLL in essence is a procedure to generate a semantic tree for a given clause set S in a left-to-right, depth-first manner. The extension of a branch p stops if (1) it is closed, or (2) the interpretation associated to it is a model for S. In the latter case, such a branch is called *open* (these are the branches not marked with a "$\star$" in Figure 3).

The detection of whether case (1) or case (2) holds (or neither) for a specific branch p is realized through an incremental construction: the splitting at an inner node, say into the cases A ("A is *true*") and $\neg A$ ("A is *false*"), gives rise to two respective simplification operations of the current clause set S. In the one case, S_A is obtained from S by deleting every clause containing the literal A, and then deleting from each remaining clause all occurrences of the literal $\neg A$. For instance, in the example we have $S_A = \{C, D \vee \neg C, \neg D \vee \neg B\}$.

In the other case, $S_{\neg A}$ is obtained by exchanging the roles of A and $\neg A$. The resulting clause sets S_A and $S_{\neg A}$ are the ones used in place of S when going down the respective branches.

Now, it is not too difficult to see that condition (1) holds for a branch p (i.e., p is closed) iff the clause set obtained by incremental simplification during construction of p, as just explained, contains the empty clause $\Box$. Further, condition (2) holds for p (i.e., the interpretation associated to p is a model for S) iff this clause set is empty. If neither (1) nor (2) holds, the information in p is not yet sufficient, and further case analysis is necessary.

Altogether, the main properties of DPLL can be summarized as follows.

Proposition 1 *Let S be a clause set. The DPLL procedure derives an open branch p iff S is satisfiable.*

The procedure may select any atom A for extending a branch p by case splitting, provided this split has not been carried out before.[11] Implementations may take advantage of this *confluence* property in order to try to keep the tree as small as possible. This, and other optimizations are realized, for example, in the *NTAB* system (Crawford and Auton 1996) and the *SATO* system (Zhang 1997).

3.1 DPLL AS A FIRST-ORDER PROCEDURE

The DPLL procedure was conceived as a proof procedure for *first-order* logic. In the first-order logic variant, which makes direct use of Herbrand's theorem, in an outer loop, successively increased sets of ground instances of first-order clauses are enumerated and fed into the propositional part of the procedure just described. The outer loop stops with success (i.e., a proof is found) if the propositional part reports "unsatisfiable." Otherwise, the procedure may loop forever.

---

[11] Note that a repeated splitting of an atom on a branch cannot happen anyway, if the atom is selected from the partially evaluated clause set associated with the branch.

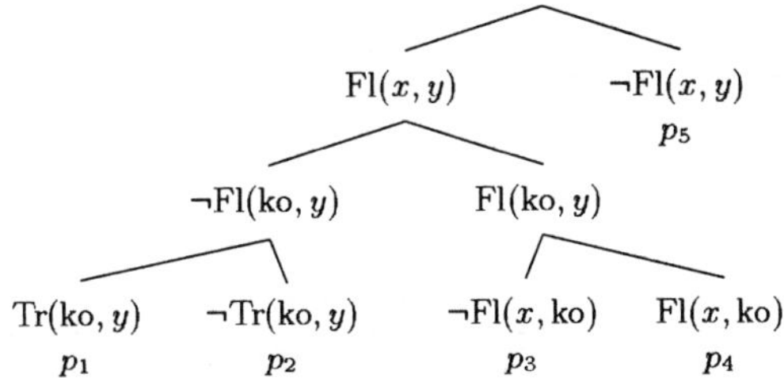

Figure 4 A first-order semantic tree. The labels p_1, p_2, p_3, p_4, and p_5 are added later to refer to the single branches.

An obvious disadvantage of this strategy is the danger of combinatorial explosion when enumerating the sets of ground instances. Consequently, the procedure is nowadays successfully applied almost exclusively to propositional problems.

4 FIRST-ORDER REPRESENTATION OF INTERPRETATIONS

4.1 MOTIVATION: FIRST-ORDER SEMANTIC TREES

The central idea of FDPLL is to compute with semantic trees built from first-order literals. That is, first-order semantic trees are just like the propositional semantic trees in Section 3, except that complementary literals (possibly containing variables) are used instead of complementary propositional variables. Figure 4 shows an example. In relation to the propositional semantic trees of Section 3, several questions may arise immediately: What is the meaning of a first-order semantic tree? More concretely, what interpretation is now associated to a branch? When is a branch closed? Do variants like $\mathrm{Fl}(x, y)$ and $\mathrm{Fl}(x', y')$ count as different? That is, is it allowed to carry out a split along one single branch with $\mathrm{Fl}(x, y)$ and $\mathrm{Fl}(x', y')$? And, how can one construct first-order semantic trees—that is, what are the calculus rules? All these questions will be addressed in the sequel. Before doing so, however, a preview of the central issue of the representation of interpretations might be useful.

Suppose that Σ contains just the constants ko and fra and the predicate symbols Fl and Tr. Now consider the branch p_1 in Figure 4. As is shown below, p_1 is derived by FDPLL in three steps. Initially, FDPLL starts with an empty branch. With respect to the represented interpretation, an empty branch stands for the interpretation that assigns *false* to all atoms; now, if the literal $\mathrm{Fl}(x, y)$ is added to the empty branch, $\mathrm{Fl}(x, y)$ stands *by default* for all its ground instances, which are $\mathrm{Fl}(\mathrm{ko}, \mathrm{ko})$, $\mathrm{Fl}(\mathrm{ko}, \mathrm{fra})$, $\mathrm{Fl}(\mathrm{fra}, \mathrm{ko})$, and $\mathrm{Fl}(\mathrm{fra}, \mathrm{fra})$ (recall that an interpretation is specified as a set of ground literals), and the represented interpretation is modified accordingly.

Now take additionally the second literal on p_1, which is $\neg\mathrm{Fl}(\mathrm{ko}, y)$. It has the opposite sign *and* is strictly more specific wrt. the instantiation order $\gtrsim$ than $\mathrm{Fl}(x, y)$ (the sign is neglected in the comparison). This circumstance raises an exception to the default:

Branch p	Interpretation $[\![p]\!]$
empty	$\{$ $\neg$Fl(ko, ko), $\neg$Fl(ko, fra), $\neg$Fl(fra, ko), $\neg$Fl(fra, fra), $\neg$Tr(ko, ko), $\neg$Tr(ko, fra), $\neg$Tr(fra, ko), $\neg$Tr(fra, fra) $\}$
Fl(x, y)	$\{$ Fl(ko, ko), Fl(ko, fra), Fl(fra, ko), Fl(fra, fra), $\neg$Tr(ko, ko), $\neg$Tr(ko, fra), $\neg$Tr(fra, ko), $\neg$Tr(fra, fra) $\}$
Fl(x, y), $\neg$Fl(ko, y)	$\{$ $\neg$Fl(ko, ko), $\neg$Fl(ko, fra), Fl(fra, ko), Fl(fra, fra), $\neg$Tr(ko, ko), $\neg$Tr(ko, fra), $\neg$Tr(fra, ko), $\neg$Tr(fra, fra) $\}$
Fl(x, y), $\neg$Fl(ko, y), Tr(ko, y)	$\{$ $\neg$Fl(ko, ko), $\neg$Fl(ko, fra), Fl(fra, ko), Fl(fra, fra), Tr(ko, ko), Tr(ko, fra), $\neg$Tr(fra, ko), $\neg$Tr(fra, fra) $\}$

Table 1 Development of interpretation for branch p_1 in Figure 4.

all instances of $\neg$Fl(ko, y) are now taken, thus overwriting their complements in the represented interpretation. So, the two literals Fl(x, y) and $\neg$Fl(ko, y) together stand for $\neg$Fl(ko, ko), $\neg$Fl(ko, fra), Fl(fra, ko), and Fl(fra, fra). This default-exception mechanism may recur: if additionally Fl(ko, fra) were present (this is not shown in Figure 4), this raises an exception to the default specified by $\neg$Fl(ko, y) and brings back Fl(ko, fra) to the interpretation.[12] In sum, the three literals Fl(x, y), $\neg$Fl(ko, y), and Fl(ko, fra) together stand for

$$\{\neg\text{Fl(ko, ko)}, \ \text{Fl(ko, fra)}, \ \text{Fl(fra, ko)}, \ \text{Fl(fra, fra)}\}$$

Table 1 summarizes the interpretations obtained as p_1 in Figure 4 is developed by FDPLL. In order to give an example of branch closure, consider the clause (1) from Figure 2 and its instance Tr(ko, y) $\vee$ Fl(ko, y). This clause closes the branch p_2 in Figure 4, because for every literal in the clause instance, there is a complementary variant in p_2. Likewise, the clause (2) closes p_3 and p_4.

4.2 LITERAL SETS

Next, the intuitions given so far shall be made more precise. It is sufficient to concentrate on *single* branches, because all operations on first-order semantic trees are branch-local. They do not interact with or depend on other branches. As a further preliminary remark, notice that the interpretation $[\![p]\!]$ is independent from the *order* of the literals in a branch p. This justifies the use of *sets* of literals instead of sequences of literals in the following. Such sets of literals are from now on denoted by the letter N, and it is allowed (and indeed needed for the proofs) in all the following definitions and results that N is an *infinite* set of literals.

---

[12] Assigning *true* to Fl(ko, fra) might not be too unrealistic, as Koblenz has a small airport for short-distance flights.

Definition 2 (most specific generalization) *A literal K is called a* most specific generalization (MSG) *of a literal L wrt. N iff $K \gtrsim L$ and there is no $K' \in N$ such that $K > K' \gtrsim L$.*

Notice that nothing is said regarding whether $K, L \in N$ or not.

Example 3 *Consider the literal set $p_4 = \{\mathrm{Fl}(x,y), \mathrm{Fl}(\mathrm{ko},y), \mathrm{Fl}(x,\mathrm{fra})\}$ (cf. Figure 4). Then both $\mathrm{Fl}(\mathrm{ko},y)$ and $\mathrm{Fl}(x,\mathrm{fra})$ are MSGs of $\mathrm{Fl}(\mathrm{ko},\mathrm{fra})$ wrt. p_4. This shows that MSGs need not be unique. The literal $\mathrm{Fl}(x,y)$ is not an MSG of $\mathrm{Fl}(\mathrm{ko},\mathrm{fra})$ wrt. p_4 because, for example, $\mathrm{Fl}(x,y) > \mathrm{Fl}(\mathrm{ko},y) \gtrsim \mathrm{Fl}(\mathrm{ko},\mathrm{fra})$.*

An MSG $K \in N$ of L wrt. N is a "potential reason" for L to be *true* in the interpretation associated to N, because $K \gtrsim L$ (as explained in Section 4.1). For efficiency reasons, it is desirable to have as few such "reasons" as possible. That is why *most specific* generalizations are used.

Next, we turn to the mentioned "exception" mechanism. It is covered implicitly by the following notion of *productivity* (note that there are several alternatives for defining productivity).

Definition 4 (productivity) *A literal K produces L wrt. N iff K is a MSG of L wrt. N and there is no $K' \in N$ such that $K > \overline{K'} \gtrsim L$.*

For a clause C, K produces C wrt. N iff K produces some literal $L \in C$ wrt. N.

The set N produces L (respectively C) iff some $K \in N$ produces L (respectively C) wrt. N.

Example 5 *Consider the literal set $\{\mathrm{Fl}(x,y), \neg\mathrm{Fl}(\mathrm{ko},y), \mathrm{Tr}(\mathrm{ko},y)\}$, which is p_1 in Figure 4. Then, $\mathrm{Fl}(x,y)$ produces the literal $\mathrm{Fl}(\mathrm{fra},\mathrm{fra})$ wrt. p_1. Therefore, since $\mathrm{Fl}(x,y) \in p_1$, p_1 produces $\mathrm{Fl}(\mathrm{fra},\mathrm{fra})$.*

However, $\mathrm{Fl}(x,y)$ does not produce $\mathrm{Fl}(\mathrm{ko},\mathrm{ko})$ wrt. p_1 (although $\underline{\mathrm{Fl}(x,y)}$ is a MSG of $\mathrm{Fl}(\mathrm{ko},\mathrm{ko})$ wrt. p_1), because $\neg\mathrm{Fl}(\mathrm{ko},y) \in p_1$ and $\mathrm{Fl}(x,y) > (\neg\mathrm{Fl}(\mathrm{ko},y) = \mathrm{Fl}(\mathrm{ko},y)) \gtrsim \mathrm{Fl}(\mathrm{ko},\mathrm{ko})$.

The set p_1 produces the clause instance $\mathrm{Tr}(\mathrm{ko},y) \vee \mathrm{Fl}(\mathrm{ko},y)$ of clause (1) in Figure 2, since p_1 produces $\mathrm{Tr}(\mathrm{ko},y)$. However, p_1 does not produce the clause instance $\mathrm{Fl}(\mathrm{ko},y) \vee \neg\mathrm{Fl}(y,\mathrm{ko})$ of clause (3) in Figure 2, since p_1 produces neither $\mathrm{Fl}(\mathrm{ko},y)$ nor $\neg\mathrm{Fl}(y,\mathrm{ko})$.

Productivity is the device to map literal sets to interpretations. The next definition approaches this.

Definition 6 (ground expansion) *Define the* ground expansion *of N as $[\![N]\!] = \{L \mid L$ is a ground literal and N produces $L\}$.*

Recall from Section 2 that an interpretation is a set of ground literals such that either $A \in \mathcal{I}$ or $\neg A \in \mathcal{I}$ for every ground atom A. There are two problems with Definition 6 when wanting $[\![N]\!]$ to be an interpretation:

Completeness: There is in general no reason for $[\![N]\!]$ to contain A or $\neg A$, for every ground atom A. For instance, building on the example so far, no branch in Figure 4 produces, say, $\mathrm{Tr}(\mathrm{ko},\mathrm{fra})$ or $\neg\mathrm{Tr}(\mathrm{ko},\mathrm{fra})$. Hence, no branch in Figure 4 is an interpretation then. As an extreme case, $N = \{\}$ does not produce a single literal.

Consistency: There is in general no reason for $[\![N]\!]$ not to contain both A and $\neg A$, for some ground atom A. For instance, the set p_3 in Figure 4 produces both $\mathrm{Fl}(\mathrm{ko},\mathrm{ko})$ and $\neg \mathrm{Fl}(\mathrm{ko},\mathrm{ko})$. Hence, $[\![p_3]\!]$ is not an interpretation.

The *completeness* problem can be solved quite easily, simply by adding to N an expression $\neg x$, where x is a variable; the "literal" $\neg x \in N$ then acts as a default case to assign *false* to positive literals. Thus, for instance, $[\![\{\neg x, \mathrm{Fl}(\mathrm{ko},\mathrm{ko})\}]\!]$ produces every negative literal except $\neg \mathrm{Fl}(\mathrm{ko},\mathrm{ko})$ and thus assigns *false* to every positive literal, except $\mathrm{Fl}(\mathrm{ko},\mathrm{ko})$.[13]

The *consistency* problem can be dealt with in (at least) two ways:

First, $[\![N]\!]$ could be *defined* as a consistent set by an asymmetrical construction. One could give preference to, say, positive literals and "override" inconsistencies with negative literals in N. For instance, the set $\{\mathrm{Fl}(\mathrm{ko},y),\ \neg \mathrm{Fl}(x,\mathrm{fra})\}$ would then produce $\mathrm{Fl}(\mathrm{ko},\mathrm{fra})$, but it would not produce $\neg \mathrm{Fl}(\mathrm{ko},\mathrm{fra})$. The reasons against this solution are (1) that it makes the definitions more complicated, and (2) it adds some computational overhead.

Second, and this is the chosen alternative, one can achieve consistency of $[\![N]\!]$ by a dedicated FDPLL inference rule, the Commit inference rule. The introduction of this rule is postponed until Section 5.2. For now, it suffices to remark that all inconsistencies in finite literal sets can be detected easily and at the first-order level (based on unification), and then repaired by applying the Commit rule finitely often.

We carry on by naming the problems in a more rigorous way.

Definition 7 (contradictory, consistent, complete) *A literal set N is called* contradictory *iff there are literals $L, K \in N$ such that $L \sim \overline{K}$. The term* noncontradictory *means "not contradictory."*

N is called consistent *with respect to a literal L iff N does not produce both L and $\overline{L}$; N is called* consistent *iff N is consistent wrt. every literal L.*

The term inconsistent *means "not consistent." N is called* complete *iff for every literal L, N produces L or $\overline{L}$. The term* incomplete *means "not complete."*

Note that any contradictory branch is inconsistent wrt. one of its literals.

Obviously, consistency and completeness are antagonistic concepts. Nevertheless, FDPLL generates literal sets having both properties.

Example 8 *For instance, $p_3 = \{\mathrm{Fl}(x,y), \mathrm{Fl}(\mathrm{ko},y), \neg \mathrm{Fl}(x,\mathrm{ko})\}$ from Figure 4 is noncontradictory and inconsistent wrt. $\mathrm{Fl}(\mathrm{ko},\mathrm{ko})$ (and hence wrt. $\neg \mathrm{Fl}(\mathrm{ko},\mathrm{ko})$ as well). Adding either $\mathrm{Fl}(\mathrm{ko},\mathrm{ko})$ or $\neg \mathrm{Fl}(\mathrm{ko},\mathrm{ko})$ renders the set consistent, and adding both renders the set contradictory and inconsistent wrt. $\mathrm{Fl}(\mathrm{ko},\mathrm{ko})$ again. Each of these sets is incomplete, and adding $\neg x$ achieves completeness.*

Rephrasing in current terminology what was demonstrated with the set p_4 in Example 3, we find that literals are not necessarily uniquely produced, not even by noncontradictory, consistent, and complete literal sets.

---

[13] Of course, instead of "$\neg x$," "x" could be taken as well, which would emphasize the use of negative clauses ("goals") in the calculus. Another alternative is to work with *partial* interpretations that assign by default *false* to atoms not receiving a truth value explicitly. This, however, would break the symmetry and lead to slightly more complex definitions.

Altogether, we arrive at the following facts about the representation of interpretations.

Proposition 9 (interpretation) *If $\neg x \in N$, then N is complete. If N is consistent and complete, then $[\![N]\!]$ is an interpretation.*

To summarize, one only has to add $\neg x$ to a literal set, and, by certain inference rule applications, establish consistency in order to ensure the interpretation property.

As another example, consider $N = \{\neg x,\ \mathrm{Fl}(x, y),\ \neg\mathrm{Fl}(ko, ko)\}$, and assume that Σ just consists of Fl and ko. One might have the impression that, since $\mathrm{Fl}(ko, ko)$ is the only instance of $\mathrm{Fl}(x, y)$, an inconsistency might be hidden. This, however, is not true: the set N is complete and consistent, and the interpretation is $[\![N]\!] = \{\}$—that is, $\mathrm{Fl}(ko, ko)$ is simply *false*. This example indicates that the model representation indeed complies with Herbrand interpretations as stated in Section 2.

Finally, it should be mentioned that "productivity" and "modelship" coincide for ground clauses, but are different on the nonground level. For instance, take

$$N = \{\neg x,\ \mathrm{Tr}(ko, ko),\ \mathrm{Tr}(fra, fra),\ \neg\mathrm{Tr}(fra, ko),\ \neg\mathrm{Tr}(ko, fra)\}$$

and $C = \mathrm{Tr}(x, x)$. Then $[\![N]\!] \models C$, but there is no $L \in N$ such that L produces C wrt. N. Conversely, N produces $\neg\mathrm{Tr}(x, x)$ but $[\![N]\!] \not\models \neg\mathrm{Tr}(x, x)$.

4.3   BRANCH UNIFIERS

In the propositional case, it is obvious when a branch p should be closed—that is, when its interpretation must be rejected as a candidate for a model for the given clause set, namely if there is a (ground) clause $L_1 \vee \cdots \vee L_n$ such that $\overline{L_1}, \ldots, \overline{L_n}$ are all in p. A generalization for the first-order case reads as follows:

Definition 10 (closed, open) *A literal set N is* closed by a clause C and a substitution δ iff $\overline{L} \in^{\sim} N$ for every $L \in C\delta$; N is closed by C iff N is closed by C and some substitution δ. Finally, N is closed by a clause set S iff N is closed by some clause $C \in S$.[14] The term open *means "not closed," and N is open wrt. S means "N is not closed by S."*

Example 11 *Consider again Figure 4. The branch p_2 there is closed by clause (1) from Figure 2, which is $C = \mathrm{Tr}(x, y) \vee \mathrm{Fl}(x, y)$, and $\delta = \{x/ko\}$, because for every literal in $C\delta = \mathrm{Tr}(ko, y) \vee \mathrm{Fl}(ko, y)$ there is a complementary variant in p_2. The branches p_3 and p_4 are closed by the clause (2), which is $\neg\mathrm{Fl}(ko, y)$, and $\delta = \{\}$. In fact, the split resulting in p_3 and p_4 is unnecessary and is not carried out by FDPLL.*

However, the question arises how to compute for a given branch p and clause C a substitution δ such that p is closed by C and δ (or detect that such a δ does not exist). The following definition realizes this, based on the computation of MGUs.

Definition 12 (branch unifier) *Let $C = L_1 \vee \cdots \vee L_n$ be a clause and N be a literal set. A substitution σ is called a* branch unifier *of C against N iff there are pairwise variable disjoint literals $K_1, \ldots, K_n \in^{\sim} N$, each variable disjoint from C, and such that the following holds:*

---

[14] There is a stronger notion of branch closure, one that allows us to close some branches earlier, which is not described here.

(i) $\sigma = \text{s-unify}(\{\{\overline{L_1}, K_1\}, \ldots, \{\overline{L_n}, K_n\}\})$ *and*

(ii) K_i *produces* $\overline{L_i\sigma}$ *wrt.* N, *for* $1 \leq i \leq n$

If N is closed by C and σ, then σ is called a closing branch unifier, *otherwise σ is called a* falsifying branch unifier, *and it is said that σ is falsifying C against N.*

The name *branch unifier* is actually a misnomer, because a *branch* is meant to be a *finite* literal set below, but the definition also applies to infinite literal sets. Nethertheless, the concept is mostly used in conjunction with branches, and therefore the name is chosen this way.

Item (i) in Definition 12 realizes that substitutions are computed at a most general level. Item (ii) acts as a further relevancy filter, by excluding those branch literals K_i that unify with $\overline{L_i}$ but do not produce $\overline{L_i\sigma}$.

Closing branch unifiers indicate an elementary contradiction between the interpretation $[\![N]\!]$ represented by the branch N and the considered clause C. As will be seen in Section 5, such branches are fully processed and need no further processing. Opposed to this, a *falsifying* branch unifier indicates that C is *false* in $[\![N]\!]$, but there is a chance to satisfy C by modifying N.

Example 13 *Consider again the branch p_1 in Figure 4, and clause (3), $C = L_1 \vee L_2 = \text{Fl}(x, y) \vee \neg\text{Fl}(y, x)$, from Figure 2. The following is a procedural description of how to compute a branch unifier σ of C against p_1 (Figure 5 is a graphic illustration).*

First, "candidate" literals according to item (i) in Definition 12 have to be picked. Here, take $K_1 = \neg\text{Fl}(\text{ko}, y')$ and $K_2 = \text{Fl}(x'', y'')$. Then, the simultaneous unification operation is carried out—that is,

$$\begin{aligned} \sigma &= \text{s-unify}(\{\{\neg\text{Fl}(x, y), \neg\text{Fl}(\text{ko}, y')\}, \{\text{Fl}(y, x), \text{Fl}(x'', y'')\}\}) \\ &= \{x/\text{ko},\ y'/y,\ x''/y,\ y''/x\} \end{aligned}$$

is computed. Thus, we obtain $C\sigma = \text{Fl}(\text{ko}, y) \vee \neg\text{Fl}(y, \text{ko})$. Next, it has to be checked if the chosen candidate literals K_1 and K_2 are "responsible" for falsifying L_1 and L_2 (respectively). Indeed, $K_1 = \neg\text{Fl}(\text{ko}, y')$ produces $\overline{L_1\sigma} = \neg\text{Fl}(\text{ko}, y)$ wrt. p_1, and $K_2 = \text{Fl}(x'', y'')$ produces $\overline{L_2\sigma} = \text{Fl}(y, \text{ko})$ wrt. p_1. Thus, σ is a (falsifying) branch unifier of C against p_1.

As a simple example for a closing branch unifier, take clause (1) from Figure 2, and observe that $\sigma = \{x/\text{ko}, \ldots\}$ is a closing branch unifier of this clause against p_2 (wrt. the clause variables, σ is the same as δ in Example 11 above).

Branch unifiers are a purely syntactical concept, and the existence of branch unifiers for *finite* literal sets N obviously is decidable. The following lemma then, read in the contrapositive direction, guarantees that N is a model for the given clause if no branch unifier exists.

Lemma 14 *Let N be consistent and complete, and C be a clause. If $[\![N]\!] \not\models C$, then there is a branch unifier σ of C against N.*

In the direction as stated, the lemma guarantees that if a clause C is not *true* in N, this fact can be detected by computing a branch unifier.

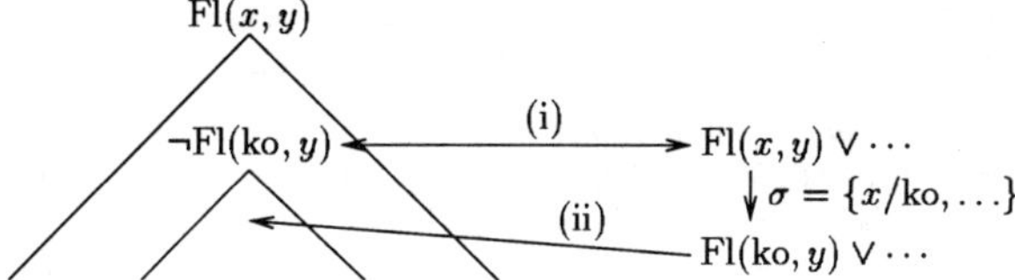

Figure 5 Computing branch unifiers. Depicted are the literals from the branch p_1 in Figure 4. A triangle symbolizes the set of all the ground instances of the literal at its top.

Unfortunately, the converse of Lemma 14 does not hold: At the very end of Section 4.2 it was observed that for the set N there, it holds $[\![N]\!] \models C$, where $C = \mathrm{Tr}(x, x)$. However, by taking $\neg x' \in^\sim N$ and $\sigma = \{x'/\mathrm{Tr}(x, x)\}$, we have a branch unifier of C against N. As a consequence, the calculus occasionally computes branch unifiers, although there is no need to.

In order to take advantage of the previous lemma, consistency has to be achieved (as previously stated, there is a respective inference rule in FDPLL). Fortunately, consistency is also a syntactical property and is decidable in the finite case as well. For the purposes here, the following lemma is sufficient (it can be strengthened, and a similar result for the converse direction holds as well):

Lemma 15 *Let N be a noncontradictory literal set. If N is inconsistent, then there is a pair of variable disjoint, noncomparable literals $K, L \in^\sim N$ with opposite sign (i.e., neither $K \gtrsim \overline{L}$ nor $\overline{L} \gtrsim K$) such that neither $K\sigma \in^\sim N$ nor $L\sigma \in^\sim N$, where $\sigma = \mathrm{unify}(\{K, \overline{L}\})$.*

For instance, the branch p_3 in Figure 4 is inconsistent, since it produces both $\mathrm{Fl}(\mathrm{ko}, \mathrm{ko})$ and $\neg\mathrm{Fl}(\mathrm{ko}, \mathrm{ko})$, and Lemma 15 is applicable to $\mathrm{Fl}(\mathrm{ko}, y) \in^\sim p_3$ and $\neg\mathrm{Fl}(x, \mathrm{ko}) \in^\sim p_3$.

Intuitively, if N is inconsistent, then two of its literals K and L intersect on the common (but complementary) instances, and this fact can be detected syntactically by unifying K and L and observing that neither $K\sigma \in^\sim N$ nor $L\sigma \in^\sim N$. In the contrapositive direction, if there are no candidate literals K and L as stated in the conclusion of the lemma, then we can be sure that N is consistent.

The converse of Lemma 15 is *not* true: In $\{P(x, a, u), \neg P(b, y, a), \neg P(b, a, u)\}$ take the first two literals, and observe that neither $P(b, a, a)$ nor $\neg P(b, a, a)$ is contained in the set. Nevertheless, this set is consistent.

5   THE FDPLL CALCULUS

In Section 3, DPLL is described as a procedure that searches the space of interpretations for a given clause set by means of (propositional) semantic trees, where each branch stands for one or more interpretations. The rather obvious representation of interpretations in DPLL is lifted in Section 4.2 toward the first-order case.

Now, the working of the FDPLL calculus can be described just as in the DPLL case, as a search through the space of interpretations in order to compute a model or prove that no model can exist. To this end, a *splitting rule* is present in FDPLL that performs a case analysis analogously as in DPLL. It is described in Section 5.1.

However, unlike as in DPLL, some care must be taken in FDPLL to make sure that a branch really represents an interpretation (recall Proposition 9, which indicates conditions under which this is the case). Therefore, FDPLL is equipped with an additional Commit *inference rule*, and the purpose of the Commit inference rule is to guarantee consistency of the branches. It is described in Section 5.2.

A calculus does not only comprise a set of inference rules. Furthermore, it has to be said how these inference rules are applied in a more global context (here: how semantic trees are constructed by means of the inference rules). This is formalized in *derivations*. Usually, one is not interested in all possible derivations. It is sufficient to restrict to those derivations that are guaranteed to lead to a refutation (for a given unsatisfiable clause set). This comes together with a notion of *fairness* (see Section 6).

Before turning to the inference rules, one more definition is needed. In the sequel, S always denotes a *finite* clause set.

Definition 16 (branch, branch set) *A* branch *is a possibly empty, finite set of literals p. A* branch set $\mathcal{P}$ *consists of a finite set of branches. The branch set $\mathcal{P}$ is* closed *by S iff every $p \in \mathcal{P}$ is closed by S (cf. Definition 10). The term* open *means "not closed."*

Notice that the empty branch set is closed wrt. every S, and that the branch set $\{\{\}\}$ is open wrt. S, unless S contains the empty clause. The same holds for $\{\{\neg x\}\}$, as no clause contains a "literal" x.

Note 17 *Branch sets serve as a formalization of the first-order semantic trees introduced informally in Section 4.1. In this regard, however, literal sets are defined too broadly: there are literal sets that do not correspond to first-order semantic trees, and uniqueness is an issue, too. This causes no real problem, as all the results hold within the literal set framework, and the literal sets are constructed by the FDPLL calculus in such a disciplined way that their representation as a first-order semantic tree is always possible. Therefore, the term* semantic tree *may also be used to refer to literal sets.*

5.1   THE SPLIT INFERENCE RULE

Suppose an open branch p in a semantic tree has been chosen for further processing. As has been said, one possibility is to split at its leaf with two complementary literals. The following definition formalizes this.

Definition 18 (Split inference rule) *We assume as given a literal selection function* $\mathrm{litsel}(C, p)$ *that maps a clause C and a branch p that is open wrt. C to some literal L such that $L \in C$ and neither $L \in^{\sim} p$ nor $\overline{L} \in^{\sim} p$. If no such literal $L \in C$ exists,* $\mathrm{litsel}(C, p)$ *may be undefined.*

The following inference rule Split *transforms a branch p, a clause C such that p is open wrt. C, and a substitution σ into two new branches:*

$$\text{Split}(p, C, \sigma) \quad \frac{p}{p \cup \{L\} \qquad p \cup \{\overline{L}\}} \quad \text{if} \begin{cases} \text{(i)} & \sigma \text{ is a branch-unifier of } C \text{ against } p, \\ & \text{and} \\ \text{(ii)} & \text{for some } L \in C\sigma, \text{ neither } L \in^{\sim} p \text{ nor} \\ & \overline{L} \in^{\sim} p, \text{ and} \\ \text{(iii)} & L = \text{litsel}(C\sigma, p) \end{cases}$$

If for given p, C, and σ the conditions (i) and (ii) hold, it is said that the Split *inference rule is applicable to p, C, and σ, and the result as the set $\{p \cup \{L\}, p \cup \{\overline{L}\}\}$ is denoted by* Split(p, C, σ). *The literal L in (iii) is called the literal* split on.

Whenever conditions (i) and (ii) hold, the Split rule is applicable to p, C, and σ. This means that there is at least one literal in $C\sigma$ that can be used for splitting (which, in turn, means that it will lead neither to a repetition of the same literal in form of a variant, nor to a contradictory branch). The choice of such a literal is the responsibility of the selection function litsel. Indeed, litsel$(C\sigma, p)$ is defined in such a situation, because the literal mentioned in condition (ii) is a candidate to be returned as litsel$(C\sigma, p)$. Observe that since litsel is a *function*, it can be seen to realize a don't-care nondeterminism.

The notion of "selection function" is also present in, for example, SLD-Resolution, the theoretical basis of Prolog. As will be explained in Section 5.3, there is a counterpart of this selection function in FDPLL. However, there is no corresponding *literal selection function* in SLD-Resolution, because in SLD-Resolution the inference steps have to be chosen in a *don't-know nondeterministic* way. Section 6 contains more on this topic in a more general setting.

Example 19 (Split application) *Consider again Figure 4 and the clauses in Figure 2. Let $p = \{\neg x,\ \text{Fl}(x, y),\ \neg\text{Fl}(ko, y)\}$ be the branch consisting of the first two literals of p_1 (and of p_2) together with $\neg x$, according to what was said in Section 4.2. Now, p_1 and p_2 are obtained from p by an application of the* Split *inference rule in the following way.*

First observe that p is open wrt. all clauses, hence in particular open wrt. clause (1), which is $C = \text{Tr}(x, y) \lor \text{Fl}(x, y)$. By taking $\neg x$ and $\neg\text{Fl}(ko, y)$ from p, one sees that there is branch unifier $\sigma = \{x/ko, \ldots\}$ of C against p, which yields $C\sigma = \text{Tr}(ko, y) \lor \text{Fl}(fra, y)$.

Since neither $\text{Tr}(ko, y) \in^{\sim} p$ nor $\neg\text{Tr}(ko, y) \in^{\sim} p$, litsel *can select $\text{Tr}(ko, y)$, and* Split *can be applied. It results in the two branches p_1 and p_2, as mentioned.*

As another example, consider the clause (3), the branch p_1, and the branch unifier σ of clause (3) against p_1 as mentioned in Example 13. Figure 6 depicts the respective application of the Split *inference rule.*

Observe that in general, due to condition (ii) in Definition 18, it is impossible to introduce by Split two (or more) variants or complements of variants of the same literal. In fact, this is the key argument that FDPLL is a decision procedure for the Bernays-Schönfinkel class of formulas.

The purpose of Split is to analyze a clause instance $C\sigma$ by trying to build a model that satisfies it, or by trying to work toward a contradiction with it. This analysis needs only be done if the clause C is violated by the current model candidate (cf. Lemma 14, which says that a branch unifier σ exists in this case).

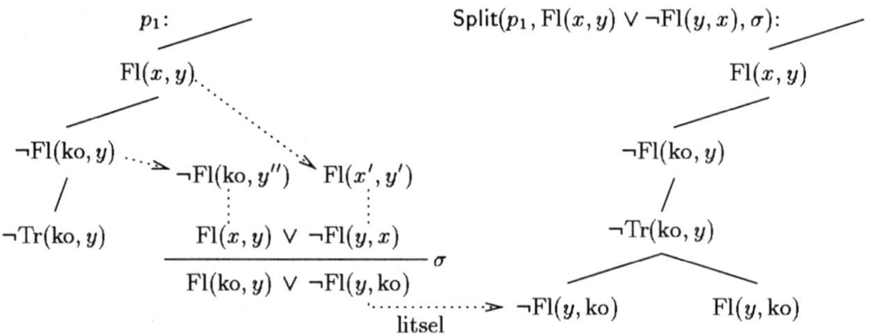

Figure 6 Sample application of Split according to Example 19.

More precisely, $C\sigma$ is produced in *one* of the two new branches, and in the other an elementary contradiction to a (one more) literal from $C\sigma$ comes up. Both cases mark some "progress." For instance, in Example 19, the left branch in the right semantic tree in Figure 6 produces the clause instance $C\sigma = \text{Fl}(\text{ko}, y) \vee \neg\text{Fl}(y, \text{ko})$, and the right branch is closed by $C\sigma$. A detailed argumentation is in the proof of the completeness theorem below (Theorem 27).

5.2   THE COMMIT INFERENCE RULE

FDPLL is based on the idea of model generation. To make this work, consistency of the branches is an issue. As the branch p_3 in Figure 4 shows, consistency does not hold automatically. The following inference rule helps to achieve consistency.

Definition 20 (Commit inference rule) *The following inference rule* Commit *transforms a branch p, a literal L from p and a substitution σ into two new branches:*

$$\text{Commit}(p, L, \sigma) \ \frac{p}{p \cup \{L\sigma\} \quad p \cup \{\overline{L\sigma}\}} \quad \text{if} \begin{cases} \text{(i)} & L \in p, \text{ and} \\ \text{(ii)} & \sigma = \text{unify}(\{L, \overline{K}\}) \text{ for some} \\ & K \in^{\sim} p, \text{ variable disjoint from} \\ & L, \text{ and} \\ \text{(iii)} & \text{neither } L\sigma \in^{\sim} p \text{ nor } \overline{L\sigma} \in^{\sim} p. \end{cases}$$

If for given p, L, and σ the conditions (i) – (iii) hold, it is said that the Commit *inference rule is applicable to p, L, and σ, and the result as the set $\{p \cup \{L\sigma\}, \{p \cup \{\overline{L\sigma}\}\}$ is denoted by* Commit(p, L, σ). *The literal $L\sigma$ is called the literal* split on.

Example 21 (Commit application) *Consider the branch p_3 in Figure 4. By taking $L = \text{Fl}(\text{ko}, y)$ and $K = \neg\text{Fl}(x, \text{ko})$, it is clear that* Commit *is applicable to p_3, $\text{Fl}(\text{ko}, y)$, and $\sigma = \{x/\text{ko}, y/\text{ko}\}$. The resulting branch set is depicted at the right of Figure 7.*

Lemma 15 states (almost directly) that Commit is applicable to p, for some L and σ, whenever p is inconsistent. Indeed, by repeated applicajust just just just just tion of Commit, one arrives at a consistent branch eventually. A detailed argumentation is in the proof of the completeness theorem below (Theorem 27).

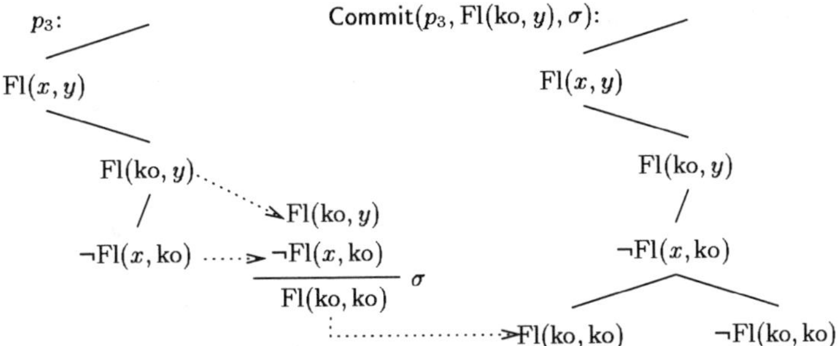

Figure 7   Sample application of Commit according to Example 21.

5.3   DERIVATIONS

A derivation is actually the step-by-step process of constructing a first-order semantic tree for a given clause set. In the branch set framework adopted here, this reads as follows:

Definition 22 (derivation) *Let S be a clause set. Assume as given a branch selection function sel, which maps any open branch set $\mathcal{P}$ wrt. S to one of its open branches. This branch is referred to as the selected branch in $\mathcal{P}$. On closed branch sets, sel may be undefined.*

A derivation $\mathcal{D}$ from S is a (possibly infinite) sequence of branch sets

$$\mathcal{D} \; = \; (\mathcal{P}_0 = \{\{\neg x\}\}), \mathcal{P}_1, \ldots, \mathcal{P}_n, \ldots$$

such that for $i \geq 0$,

(i) $\mathcal{P}_{i+1} = (\mathcal{P}_i \setminus \{p_i\}) \cup \mathsf{Split}(p_i, C, \sigma)$ for some clause $C \in S$ and substitution σ, or

(ii) $\mathcal{P}_{i+1} = (\mathcal{P}_i \setminus \{p_i\}) \cup \mathsf{Commit}(p_i, L, \sigma)$ for some literal L and substitution σ,

where in both cases $\mathcal{P}_i$ is open wrt. S and $p_i = \mathrm{sel}(\mathcal{P}_i)$ is the selected (hence open) branch in $\mathcal{P}_i$. A derivation is called a refutation (of S) iff some $\mathcal{P}_i$ is closed (by S). A derivation of $\mathcal{P}_n$ is a finite derivation that ends in $\mathcal{P}_n$.

That is, in each step in a derivation, a branch p_i is taken and replaced by the two branches resulting from an application of the Split or of the Commit inference rule. In a tree view, a derivation starts with a tree $\mathcal{P}_0$ that consists of a root node only, which is labeled with $\neg x$, and the successor tree $\mathcal{P}_{i+1}$ is obtained from $\mathcal{P}_i$ by means of a single application of one of the inference rules as indicated.

The purpose of the branch selection function is to pick one of the open branches for extension. This choice is completely don't-care nondeterministic, and it corresponds to the selection function used in SLD-Resolution for determing the next subgoal to be expanded (Lloyd 1987).

A good branch selection function is the one that selects the "'leftmost" open branch. Since closed branches can be deleted from memory, the resulting tree is degenerated into a linear list. This results in a space-efficient, one-branch-at-a-time strategy.

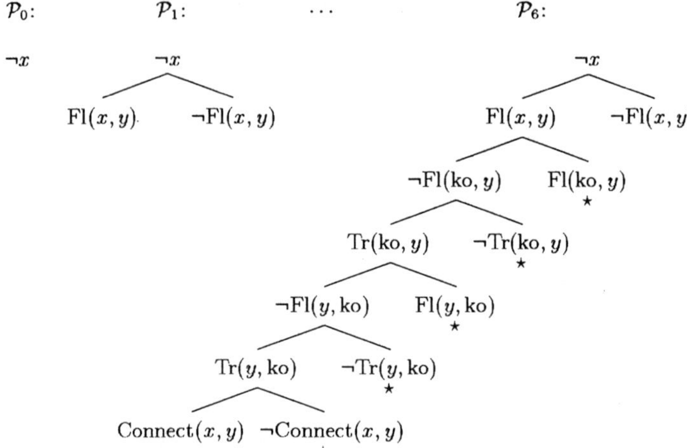

Figure 8 A derivation from the clause set in Figure 2. Closed branches are marked with a $\star$. The leftmost branch in $\mathcal{P}_6$ cannot be extended further, and thus encodes a model for the clause set. The branch with the leaf $\neg\mathrm{Fl}(x, y)$ can be extended further.

Both Split and Commit are applied to open branches only. Thus, if some branch set $\mathcal{P}_i$ is closed, then $\mathcal{P}_i$ contains no single open branch and the derivation necessarily stops as a refutation.

Example 23 (derivation) *The clauses in our running example (Figure 2) admit the derivation indicated in Figure 4. The computation of the (not depicted) branch sets $\mathcal{P}_3$ and $\mathcal{P}_4$ is explained in Example 19. The leftmost branch in $\mathcal{P}_6$ was already announced in the Introduction as the result of the FDPLL computation (see Figure 8).*

6 FAIRNESS, SOUNDNESS, AND COMPLETENESS

Consider the clause set $\{\mathrm{Fl}(\mathrm{ko}, y), \neg\mathrm{Fl}(x, y)\vee\mathrm{Fl}(\mathrm{state}(x), y), \neg\mathrm{Fl}(x, \mathrm{ko})\}$. It is unsatisfiable, and thus FDPLL should terminate with a refutation. However, there is an infinite derivation as well, and there is no particular reason why the obvious (or any other) refutation should be found. To obtain a complete calculus—that is, one that is guaranteed to derive a refutation for every unsatisfiable clause set, a notion of *fairness* is needed: no relevant inference rule application may be "forgotten" to be applied.[15]

Fairness may be achieved by applying all inference rules exhaustively in all possible ways.[16] Fairness thus is a property of *derivations*.

---

[15] This notion of completeness is occasionally called *strong completeness*.

[16] More precisely: Inference rules have to be applied exhaustively in all possible ways *up to redundancy*. If an inference rule is applicable at one stage in the derivation, there is no principal need to force its application eventually. What counts is that its *effect* is achieved eventually. The effect of applying the Split rule to a branch and a clause C is that a certain instance of C is

6.1 FAIRNESS IN FIRST-ORDER CALCULI

Before we turn to fairness as used in FDPLL, a more general discussion about issues around fairness in first-order calculi seems appropriate. This is done to motivate some design decisions of FDPLL, and to point out some differences to related, well-established calculi for first-order logic. Also, it leads to some recent issues in research on proof procedures for first-order Tableau and related calculi (FDPLL can also be seen as a member of the Tableau family).

A suitable definition of fairness depends strongly on the considered calculus. Fortunately, there are some abstract properties of calculi that allow one to lead the discussion at a general level, for classes of calculi. These abstract properties are *proof confluence*, *proof convergence*, and *destructiveness*.

The following discussion of these notions assumes as given a derivation of the form

$$\mathcal{D} \;=\; \mathcal{P}_0, \mathcal{P}_1, \ldots, \mathcal{P}_n, \ldots$$

Every calculus admits to write derivations in this way—only the objects $\mathcal{P}_i$ may differ: in typical Resolution calculi, for instance, the $\mathcal{P}_i$'s are sets of clauses, and in Tableau calculi the $\mathcal{P}_i$'s are tableau. Furthermore, suppose we are talking about derivations for unsatisfiable clause sets.

Now, *proof confluence* (Bibel 1987) means that any finite prefix of $\mathcal{D}$ *can* be continued to a refutation (recall that an unsatisfiable clause set is presupposed); there are no finite dead ends. Most Resolution and Tableau calculi, for instance, are proof confluent. Probably the best-known *non*proof confluent calculi are Model Elimination and SLD-Resolution.[17] Proof search in nonproof-confluent calculi works by enumerating *all* derivations up to a given length bound n, and, if no refutation is found, the length bound is set to $n + 1$, and so on.

In proof-confluent calculi, it is not necessary to withdraw a once-obtained derivation, because this derivation can be continued to the wanted refutation anyway. This is an attractive feature, as it avoids redundancies coming up in the sketched proof search scheme for nonproof-confluent calculi. For instance, situations easily come up where two derivations of length n derive actually the same object $\mathcal{P}_n$, but this circumstance will not be noticed.[18]

However, there is the possibility of infinite dead ends in derivations in proof-confluent calculi (cf. the example at the beginning of this section). This happens if the necessary inference rules that would lead to a refutation are not applied. Now, by *proof convergence* I just mean that any finite prefix of $\mathcal{D}$ is *guaranteed* to lead to a refutation.[19] This is the

---

produced (in the sense of Definition 4) by one of the two extensions of the branch. Certainly, any *other* inference rule application that achieves this effect will do as well. In fact, it might even be the case that Split is applicable at some time in the derivation to some branch, but no longer applicable later, when the branch has been extended.

[17] In fact, SLD-Resolution is an instance of Model Elimination, and Model Elimination can be seen as an instance of a certain Tableau calculus, the Connection Tableau calculus (Letz 1998).

[18] This disadvantage is compensated in, for example, Model Elimination by a drastically pruned local search space—that is, inference rules can be applied in a very restricted way only.

[19] This term seems not to be established in the literature, but the choice of this name is motivated by corresponding notions in the literature on term rewriting.

point where *fairness* comes in: by equipping a proof-confluent calculus with a suitable definition of fairness, infinite dead ends are made impossible. In brief:

$$\text{Proof convergence} = \text{proof confluence} + \text{fairness}$$

It may seem as a matter of course how to equip one's favorite proof-confluent calculus with a suitable definition of fairness, so that the above-mentioned relevance of proof confluence is taken advantage of. However, this is not the case! The difficulties can be explained by the property of *destructiveness*.

Roughly, a calculus is *nondestructive*, if an inference rule application does not shrink the information contained in the object derived so far. A typical example of a proof-confluent and destructive calculus is the Tableau calculus with "rigid" variables (Fitting 1990). For example, in this calculus, a branch $p = \{Fl(x, fra), Fl(fra, x)\}$ might come up, which stands for a currently unknown ground instantiation of its literals, like $\{Fl(ko, fra), Fl(fra, ko)\}$. In contrast to FDPLL, the two occurrences of x in the two literals each stand for the *same* term.

Now, p can be extended, for instance, with the clause $\neg Fl(ko, fra) \lor Q(a)$. Branch extension in Tableau calculi works by splitting with the literals from the clause and applying a substitution. In the example, the substitution $\{x/a\}$ is used and two branches result. The one branch $\{Fl(ko, fra), \neg Fl(ko, fra)\}$ is closed, and the other branch is $p' = \{Fl(ko, fra), Q(a)\}$. Observe that the substitution is applied to the whole Tableau. This justifies calling such a step *destructive*, because the possibility of representing a truth value for $Fl(fra, fra)$, for example, is lost afterward.

As a side remark, it is always possible to make a calculus nondestructive by modifying the definition of derivation and adapting the inference rules a little. In general, by putting more information into the data structure, the "less destructive" the calculus can be made. Nondestructiveness then can be achieved at the cost of having a bigger and more complex data structure (and usually longer derivations).

The rigid variable Tableau calculus, for instance, can be made nondestructive by considering not a sequence of tableau but a sequence of sets of tableau. When destructively modifying a tableau, a copy of the original tableau is kept in the set, thus preserving all the information derived so far. Of course, this is quite an artificial way to describe a tableau calculus, but it would indeed be nondestructive. Unfortunately, this modification is useless in practice, as the memory requirements are too high.

Now we can sum up and draw some conclusions from these considerations.

The notion of derivation in Definition 22 can be easily adapted to virtually every calculus for first-order reasoning. This holds in particular for proof-confluent calculi, which we concentrate on. For efficiency reasons, proof confluence should be taken advantage of. This is achieved by equipping the calculus with a suitable notion of fairness, which yields the stronger property of proof convergence. For nondestructive calculi, this typically causes no problem. However, for *destructive* calculi, the definition of fairness may be a real challenge. For many years, it was simply unknown how to do it. Consequently, the state of the art in proof procedures for proof-confluent Tableau and related calculi did not take advantage of proof confluence.[20] Proof search is done as for nonproof-confluent calculi as sketched above, thus showing avoidable redundancies. Only recently have solutions to this long standing problem come into sight (Baumgartner 1998; Baumgartner et al. 1999; Beckert 2000; Giese 2001; van Eijck 2001).

Another instance of this phenomenon is the first-order DPLL procedure described already in (Chang and Lee 1973). It uses the device of *pseudosemantic trees*, which, like FDPLL, realize splits at the nonground level. Nevertheless, the pseudosemantic tree method is very different: in contrast to FDPLL, a variable is treated rigidly there as in Tableau calculi—that is, as a placeholder for a (single) not-yet-known term. As a consequence, as in all rigid variable methods, only a very weak loop-check condition can be used. More concretely, it may be necessary to admit two variants of the same literal along one branch (e.g., $Fl(x, y)$ and $Fl(y, x)$). This is not admissible in FDPLL. Furthermore, proof confluence is not taken advantage of, which translates into a proof procedure that backtracks more than necessary.[21]

Now, FDPLL is an effort to *avoid* the difficulties that come with the rigid variables of destructive calculi. Expressed positively, the aim is to combine the desirable features *conceptual simplicity*, *proof convergence*, and reasonable *redundancy criteria*. The device to make this possible is the treatment of variables, which are not "rigid."

Also, FDPLL does not treat variables as "universally quantified" as Resolution calculi do. Resolution calculi are nondestructive and, in consequence, fairness criteria are generally easy to find. Like Resolution calculi, FDPLL is a nondestructive calculus. In fact, FDPLL was designed with nondestructiveness in mind, *because* fairness is then easy to find.

A problem in controlling Resolution calculi stems from the fact that in general no bound on the length of the derived clauses can be used. This is why Resolution calculi have difficulties in deciding the Bernays-Schönfinkel class. Unlike Resolution, FDPLL does not derive new clauses and thus is more analytical in this regard (and does not have these difficulties).

6.2 FAIRNESS IN FDPLL

It is advantageous to define fairness in an abstract way. This gives degrees of freedom for concretely implemented strategies. In concrete implementations, fairness is usually realized by employing some *resource bound* (e.g., a natural number), with the property, that all inference rule applications, when measured in some way, exhaust *finitely* within a given value of the resource bound. Starting with a low value for the resource bound and increasing it step-by-step, one exhausts within each level the inference rule applications until a proof is found (or never terminates).

There are many ways to define fairness and concrete resource bounds. For Resolution calculi, for example, one of the earliest strategies is *level saturation*, where, essentially, inferences to be carried out are put in a queue (see (Bachmair and Ganzinger 2001) for an overview of resolution-based theorem proving). Within the Tableau world, there are

---

[20] The trivial way of reducing first-order logic to propositional logic shall be excluded (cf. the discussion of the Bernays-Schönfinkel class in the Introduction).

[21] This is not to say that FDPLL does *not* backtrack. In a sense, FDPLL backtracks when switching in a derivation from a closed branch to some other open branch.

resource bounds that are based, for example, on the depth of tableau (Letz and Stenz 2000) or on the number of variants of admissible formulas (Beckert and Posegga 1995). In some cases, things may become quite subtle (Baumgartner et al. 1999; Beckert 2000).

In the sequel, fair derivations in FDPLL are defined in a rather concrete way. This is done in order to concentrate on the essentials.[22] Specifically, a resource bound based on a *maximal term depth* is used:

Definition 24 (depth bound, fair derivations) *A (maximal term) depth bound is a nonnegative integer d. A branch set with depth bound d is a branch set $\mathcal{P}$ such that the term depth of every literal in every branch in $\mathcal{P}$ is less than or equal to d. This is indicated by writing $\mathcal{P}^d$. A branch set $\mathcal{P}$ is exhausted on d iff (1) it is closed or else (2) in every possible* Commit *or* Split *rule application to the selected branch in $\mathcal{P}$, the term depth of the literal split on is strictly greater than d. Now, a derivation $\mathcal{D}$ from $\mathcal{S}$ is fair iff it is of the form*

$$(\mathcal{P}_0^1 = \{\{\neg x\}\}), \mathcal{P}_1^1, \ldots, \mathcal{P}_{n_1}^1,$$

$$\mathcal{P}_{n_1+1}^2, \ldots, \mathcal{P}_{n_1+n_2}^2,$$

$$\vdots$$

$$\mathcal{P}_{n_1+\cdots+n_{m-1}+1}^m, \ldots, \mathcal{P}_{n_1+\cdots+n_{m-1}+n_m}^m,$$

$$\vdots$$

and $\mathcal{P}_{n_1+\cdots+n_{d-1}+n_d}^d$ is exhausted on d, for $d \geq 1$ and some $n_d \geq 0$.

That is, in a fair derivation one increases, step-by-step, a current depth bound d, and for each value of d, the inference rules are applied *exactly* until the current branch set is exhausted on d. Notice that this may be true immediately when stepping from $d-1$ to d, thus skipping the level d (i.e., $n_d = 0$).

Note 25 (existence of fair derivations) *Fair FDPLL derivations are so far purely abstract mathematical objects, and it still has to be argued that fair derivations indeed exist (i.e., that Definition 24 is satisfiable). The only critical point is the finiteness of exhausting the inference rule applications within a depth bound value d (i.e., that no "..." have to be put at the end of the lines in the fairness definition). That this holds follows immediately from item (ii) in the definition of* Split *and item (iii) in the definition of* Commit. *Both achieve that a second variant of an already present literal is never added to the extended branch. But then, for a given term depth value of d, it is clear that only finitely many literals can be added to a branch and that have a term depth less or equal to d.[23]*

6.3 SOUNDNESS AND COMPLETENESS

There are two basic properties every calculus for classic first-order logic should enjoy: soundness and completeness.

---

[22] In a more technical paper (Baumgartner 2000), fair derivations are defined in an abstract way.

[23] It is possible to exclude the Commit rule applications from the depth bound control, because any sequence of Commit rule applications alone is finite anyway.

Theorem 26 (soundness of FDPLL) *Let S be a clause set and $\mathcal{D}$ be a refutation of S. Then S is unsatisfiable.*

Since FDPLL works in a refutational setting, this just means that any formula proven by FDPLL is indeed valid.

Proof: For the proof, one more concept is needed: let a be any constant from the signature under consideration (or a "new" constant if none is supplied). By p^a denote the branch obtained from p by replacing in every literal every occurrence of every variable by a. Similarly, for a clause C, let C^a denote the (ground) clause obtained from C by replacing in every literal every occurrence of every variable by a. A branch p is said to be ^{a}-*closed by* C iff for some substitution δ, for every literal $L \in C\delta^a$, it holds that $\overline{L} \in p^a$ (i.e., p^a is closed by $C\delta^a$ and ϵ). It is not too difficult to see that whenever p is closed by C, then p is ^{a}-closed by C as well.[24]

Now consider the last branch set $\mathcal{P}$ in the given refutation $\mathcal{D}$, every branch of which is closed, say by the clauses $C_1, \ldots, C_n$. Its ground instantiation $\mathcal{P}^a = \{p^a \mid p \in \mathcal{P}\}$ can be seen as a propositional semantic tree $\mathcal{T}$ (cf. Section 3) made up of splits with complementary ground literals. From the observation above we conclude that $\mathcal{P}^a$ is closed by the clauses $C_1^a, \ldots, C_n^a$. Now apply the soundness result for propositional semantic trees (Chang and Lee 1973). $\qquad\square$

Next we turn to completeness. Again, since FDPLL works in a refutational setting, this just means that the negation of any valid formula is refuted by FDPLL. However, the contrapositive direction of this statement is more useful, as it tells more about the model computation going on. To formulate it, the concept of a *path* is needed: suppose as given an infinite derivation $\mathcal{D}$ that is not a refutation. Then, at least one branch is extended infinitely often. That is, there is an infinite sequence of selected (hence open) branches in branch sets in $\mathcal{D}$ of the form

$$I \;=\; (p_0 = \{\neg x\}) \subset p_1 \subset \cdots \subset p_n \subset \cdots$$

and such that p_{i+1} is one of the branches obtained from p_i by an application of either the Split or the Commit inference rule. In tree notation, I corresponds to an *infinitely long* branch, which can be denoted by the chain limit $\sqcup I = \bigcup_{i \geq 0} p_i$.

As a special case, a (fair) derivation may stop with a branch set containing a selected (hence open) branch p_n that cannot be extended further. That is, neither Split nor Commit is applicable to p_n. In this case,

$$I \;=\; (p_0 = \{\neg x\}) \subset p_1 \subset \cdots \subset p_n$$

is taken instead, and the limit is set to $\sqcup I = \bigcup_{n \geq i \geq 0} p_i = p_n$.

In order to cover both cases by a single term, we call a *path (of $\mathcal{D}$)* any sequence I of the stated form that does *not* stop with a (selected) branch that can be extended further by a Commit or Split rule application.

---

[24] The converse, however, is not true: for instance, $\{\neg\mathrm{Fl}(x,y)\}$ is ^{a}-closed by $\mathrm{Fl}(x,y) \vee \mathrm{Fl}(x,x)$, but not closed by $\mathrm{Fl}(x,y) \vee \mathrm{Fl}(x,x)$ (because $\neg\mathrm{Fl}(x,x)$ cannot be instantiated to a variant of $\neg\mathrm{Fl}(x,y)$).

As an important property, $\cup I$ is open, because if $\cup I$ were closed, there would be a clause C closing $\cup I$. Since clauses are finite and $\cup I$ is the limit of a chain, some finite $p_j \subseteq \cup I$ would be closed by C. But if p_j were closed, it could not be selected (cf. Definition 22), thus contradicting the definition of I.

Now the main result can be stated:

Theorem 27 (completeness of FDPLL) *Let S be a clause set and $\mathcal{D}$ be a fair derivation from S. If $\mathcal{D}$ is not a refutation, then S is satisfiable. More specifically, for every path I of $\mathcal{D}$, $[\![\cup I]\!]$ is an interpretation and $[\![\cup I]\!] \models S$.*

Notice that in the contrapositive direction, the theorem is just a refutational completeness result. Unlike the supporting lemmas and propositions, this theorem is proven here, because the proof describes essentially how FDPLL works.

Proof: Occasionally we need the following *compactness property*: for any finite set of literals M, it holds that $M \subseteq \cup I$ iff $M \subseteq p$, for some *finite* $p \subseteq \cup I$. It follows immediately from the construction of $\cup I$ as the limit of a chain of ever-growing sets.

First of all, $\cup I$ must be noncontradictory (Definition 7), because otherwise there are $L, K \in \cup I$ such that $L \sim \overline{K}$. By the compactness property also $L, K \in p$, for some finite branch $p \subseteq \cup I$. This, however, is impossible by the design of the two inference rules (in case of **Split** by the definition of litsel, and in case of **Commit** by item (iii) in the definition). Hence, $\cup I$ is noncontradictory.

Beyond this, $\cup I$ is even consistent, by the following line of reasoning: suppose, to the contrary, that $\cup I$ is inconsistent. Let $K, L \in^{\sim} \cup I$ and σ as claimed by Lemma 15, and let d be the term depth of $K\sigma$. As a consequence of the compactness property, for some point in time k, $K, L \in^{\sim} p_k, p_{k+1}, \ldots$. Since neither $K\sigma \in^{\sim} \cup I$ nor $L\sigma \in^{\sim} \cup I$, trivially

$$K\sigma \notin^{\sim} p_k, p_{k+1}, \ldots \text{ and } L\sigma \notin^{\sim} p_k, p_{k+1}, \ldots \tag{1}$$

But then, the **Commit** inference rule is applicable to $p_k, p_{k+1}, \ldots$, L and σ. At some point in time $k_d \geq k$, the current depth bound in the derivation reaches d (or greater). By fairness (Definition 24), inference rules must be applied exhaustively within each value of the current depth bound. Therefore, in particular, the **Commit** rule must have been applied to some element in the sequence $p_{k_d}, p_{k_d+1}, \ldots$, L and σ, to the effect that $K\sigma$ or $L\sigma$ is added to one of these branches. This is a plain contradiction to (1) above. Therefore, $\cup I$ is consistent.

Since $\neg x \in \cup I$, and $\cup I$ is noncontradictory and consistent, by Proposition 9, the set $[\![\cup I]\!]$ is an interpretation. This finishes the first part of the proof.

Now we have to show that $[\![\cup I]\!] \models S$. Suppose, to the contrary, that $[\![\cup I]\!] \not\models C$, for some $C \in S$. That is, some ground instance of C is *false* in the interpretation $[\![\cup I]\!]$. By Lemma 14, there is a branch unifier σ of C against $[\![\cup I]\!]$. Let d be the maximum of the term depths of the literals in $C\sigma$. Consider

$$p = \{K \in \cup I \mid \text{the term depth of } K \text{ is less or equal to } d\}$$

The set p must be finite (in Note 25 above, it was observed that a second variant of an already present literal is never added to a branch).

Observe that $\cup I$ produces a literal K with term depth $\leq d$ iff p produces K. This is because each literal in $L \in \cup I \setminus p$ has a term depth $> d$, thus $|L| \not\preceq |K|$, and it is easy to see that adding such a literal L to any set cannot affect the property of producing (or not) K.

As a consequence, p is consistent wrt. every literal K with term depth $\leq d$, because, if not, there is such a literal K, and p produces both L and $\overline{L}$. By this conclusion, $\cup I$ would produce L and $\overline{L}$, contradicting the consistency of $\cup I$ proved in the first part.

By compactness, there is a branch $p_k \subseteq \cup I$ with $p \subseteq p_k$. The branch p_k contains only some additional literals with *greater* term depth, and this holds for the branches $p_{k+1}, p_{k+2}, \ldots$, too. Therefore, the just-proven properties hold for these branches, too: $\cup I$ produces a literal K with term depth $\leq d$ iff $p_k, p_{k+1}, \ldots$ produces K, and $p_k, p_{k+1}, \ldots$ is consistent wrt. every literal K with term depth $\leq d$.

Now we show that Split is applicable to $p_k, p_{k+1}, \ldots$, C, and σ. The goal is to conclude that (by fairness) Split must have been applied in this way, and eventually one of these branches is closed, which yields a contradiction.

In the following, p is any element in the sequence $p_k, p_{k+1}, \ldots$.

Concerning condition (i) in Definition 18: since σ is a branch unifier of C against $[\![\cup I]\!]$, σ is a branch unifier of C against p (because p contains all literals from $[\![\cup I]\!]$ with term depth $\leq d$, and branch literals with a term depth $> d$ cannot contribute in the computation of σ, because at least one literal in $C\sigma$ would then have a term depth $> d$).

Second, since p is open wrt. $\mathcal{S}$ (this is argued for immediately before the theorem statement), σ must be a *falsifying* branch unifier. More explicitly, p produces $\overline{L\sigma}$, for every $L \in C$ (by definition of branch unifier), and there is a literal $L \in C$ such that $\overline{L\sigma} \notin^{\sim} p$ (because otherwise p would be closed by C and σ). Furthermore, $L\sigma \notin^{\sim} p$, because otherwise p would produce $L\sigma$, and, since p produces $\overline{L\sigma}$, p would then be inconsistent (but above we concluded that p is consistent wrt. every literal with term depth $\leq d$). Therefore, condition (ii) holds as well. Together, thus, Split is applicable to $p_k, p_{k+1}, \ldots$, C, and σ.

At some point in time $k_d \geq k$, the current depth bound in the derivation reaches d (or greater). By fairness (Definition 24), inference rules must be applied exhaustively within each value of the current depth bound. Therefore, in particular, the Split rule must have been applied to some element in the sequence $p_{k_d}, p_{k_d+1}, \ldots$, C, and σ, to the effect that a selected literal $L\sigma$ or its complement $\overline{L\sigma}$ is added to one of these branches. It is impossible that $L\sigma$ is added, because, again, both $L\sigma$ and $\overline{L\sigma}$ would then be produced, being a contradiction to the consistency of $p_{k_d}, p_{k_d+1}, \ldots$ Therefore, $\overline{L\sigma}$ is added. This argument can be repeated for each literal in $C\sigma$ that can be selected in a Split rule application. At the end, thus (together with the compactness property), no literal can be selected anymore because $\overline{L\sigma} \in p_j$, for every $L \in C$, and some $j \geq k_d$. This just means that p_j is closed by C and σ, contradicting that $\cup I$ and therefore p_j is open. This finishes the proof of the second part, and thus the proof of the whole theorem. $\qquad\square$

7 CONCLUSION

7.1 SUMMARY

FDPLL is a first-order version of the Davis-Putnam-Logemann-Loveland procedure. While DPLL is based on a splitting rule for case analysis wrt. ground and complementary literals, FDPLL uses a lifted splitting rule—that is, the case analysis is now made wrt. nonground and complementary literals.

Propositional DPLL has certain desirable features: its conceptual simplicity, space efficiency ("one branch at a time"), few inference rules, efficient and adaptable implementations, and termination with a model if no refutation exists.

A goal of this work is to keep these features for the lifted version FDPLL, so that (hopefully) many applications for propositional DPLL and much of the technology developed for propositional DPLL carries over to FDPLL.

FDPLL has some proof-theoretic advantages when compared with other approaches that generalize the propositional DPLL procedure. First, it is a uniform procedure and hence avoids the weaknesses of all procedures that separate the process of ground instantiation from the refutation process like the original full DPLL method. Second, unification is integrated in a confluent and nondestructive manner. This is realized essentially by taking a novel view of the role of first-order variables. It also leads to the representation and computation with first-order interpretations, where a literal specifies truth values for all its ground instances, unless there is a more specific literal specifying opposite truth values. Based on this idea, the FDPLL calculus is developed and proven as sound and complete.

FDPLL is a decision procedure for the Bernays-Schönfinkel class, roughly, clause logic without function symbols except constants. This is a practically relevant, however nontrivial class, in the sense that most Resolution and Tableau systems cannot decide it, except in a trivial way by using the finite set of ground clauses (cf. the Introduction).

7.2 IMPROVEMENTS

This chapter concentrates on the core ideas behind FDPLL, which are the model representation by first-order semantic trees and the respective calculus. To get an efficient implementation, however, some improvements are mandatory. Important improvements include (1) a stronger notion of branch closure than the one in Definition 10 (one that allows closing some branches earlier), (2) the possibility to reason efficiently with unit clauses, which allows simulation of certain resolution strategies by FDPLL, and (3) taking advantage of a dependency-directed backtracking scheme, which allows forgeting about Split rule applications that are redundant to close a branch. These improvements are described in (Baumgartner 2000).

7.3 FDPLL AS A THEOREM PROVER

In this chapter, FDPLL is explained as a method that computes with interpretations. Conceptually, FDPLL searches for one such interpretation as a model of the clause set, and failure of this search indicates unsatisfiability of the given clause set. FDPLL implementations can therefore be used for (refutational) theorem-proving purposes. Following are some thoughts about FDPLL as a theorem prover.

In recent years, quite some effort has been spent on sophisticated implementations of first-order logic theorem provers. About 10 implementations participate in CASC (CADE Automated Systems Competition),[25] which is held annually at the International Conference on Automated Deduction (CADE). Basis for the measurements is the TPTP problem library (Thousands of Problems for Theorem Proving; see the CASC URL), which consists of more than 3000 unsatisfiable and satisfiable first-order logic problems from various domains.

There is a prototypical implementation of FDPLL in Prolog, which is available from *www.uni-koblenz.de/~peter/FDPLL/*. It is not trimmed toward performance. In particular, the central operation—the computation of branch unifiers—could be implemented much more efficiently. For instance, term-indexing techniques could be employed for faster literal retrieval from branches.

It is too early for a serious experimental comparison of FDPLL to other provers, in particular at CASC. Also, FDPLL lacks dedicated inference rules for equality, which are very important to score high at CASC. Nevertheless, some preliminary observations can be made. In general, different proof procedures for first-order logic show different search behavior (and thus may complement each other in proof search).[26] For instance, the Model Elimination calculus is designed as a top-down, goal-oriented calculus. Proof search in Model Eliminiation starts with the suspected theorem, and each inference step is connected in some way. Resolution calculi typically work in a bottom-up way. Quite different is the Ordered Semantic Hyper Linking calculus (Plaisted and Zhu 2000), which is controlled by supplying a model of the domain to guide the search. These properties may result in huge differences concerning performance. FDPLL makes no exception here. For instance, the FDPLL implementation has difficulties with a certain formalization of planning problems,[27] which are easy for Model Elimination systems, while FDPLL can solve some problems like the intermediate value theorem[28] very quickly, which is difficult for many other systems.

In 1999, FDPLL participated at CASC. The participating provers are evaluated on problems from various domains. The comparison of the FDPLL results to those of the other provers suggests that FDPLL is relatively strong on satisfiable or non-Horn problems without equality. Many of the problems in the former category stem from translating modal logic formulas to clause logic. They belong to the Bernays-Schönfinkel class, and the good performance of FDPLL did not come as too much of a surprise.

7.4 FUTURE WORK

Some of the more speculative thoughts on perspectives and future work are stated in the Introduction. Here, I will concentrate on more concrete issues.

There is always room for improvement. An obvious plan is to improve "loop checking," so that more classes of decidable fragments of first-order logic will be decidable by FDPLL. Also, dedicated inference rules for efficient treatment of equality should be conceived. A

---

[25] See *www.cs.miami.edu/~tptp/CASC/*.

[26] For a general analysis of some well-established theorem-proving methods, see the important paper by Plaisted (1994).

[27] The PLA category in the TPTP library.

[28] ANA002-4 in the TPTP library.

combination of FDPLL or techniques from FDPLL with other methods could be tried. For instance, it seems promising to combine the variable treatment in FDPLL with the semantic guidance feature in OSHL (Lee and Plaisted 1993; Plaisted and Zhu 2000).

A state-of-the-art implementation of FDPLL is needed. With it, problems of realistic size of the various application areas as mentioned in the Introduction could be tackled. Already the prototypical implementation is used, among other provers, as a component of the DORIS discourse representation system (Bos 1999).

In the discourse representation domain, as well as many other domains (e.g., planning), different constants like "tom" and "jerry" denote different individuals. Although not necessary from a theoretical point of view, this *unique name assumption* should be built in to FDPLL.

In some domains, *minimal* models are needed. A respective general reasoning scheme is *circumscription* (McCarthy 1985), which allows one to insist on minimality of certain interesting predicates. For instance, in diagnosis applications, one may insist on explanations of faulty behavior in terms of a minimum number of faulty components. It should be possible to extend FDPLL accordingly.

Other formalisms advocated for knowledge-representation purposes do (also) have non-monotonic logic inside. We have begun to exploit the model-representation technique of FDPLL in a modified reasoner for nonmonotonic (disjunctive) logic programming. This logic is used to formulate tasks in a document-management application. The task is to assemble a document, such as a mathematical textbook, from atomic components (definitions, theorems, examples, etc.) from various sources and according to the user's current interest.

The technique can perhaps also be used in an advantageous way in the formalization of planning tasks. For instance, consider the following rule taken from a hypothetical logic program (note the default negation "not" in the rule body):

$$\mathrm{Clear}(B, s(T)) \;\leftarrow\; \mathrm{Clear}(B, T) \;\wedge\; \mathrm{Holding}(A, T) \;\wedge\; \mathrm{not}\,\mathrm{PutOn}(A, B, T)$$

This rule says that a block B remains cleared at the successor time point $s(T)$ of T, if the currently held block A is not to be put on top of B.

Now, suppose that all blocks are clear initially, except block b_1. Further suppose that we are holding block a and that the action at time point 0 is to put a on b_2. This would be compactly represented by the interpretation

$$I_0 = \{\neg x,\; \mathrm{Clear}(B, 0),\; \neg\mathrm{Clear}(b_1, 0),\; \mathrm{Holding}(a, 0),\; \mathrm{PutOn}(a, b_2, 0)\}$$

Now, the rule is applicable to I_0 and the expected change in the world is represented by the interpretation $I_{s(0)}$ (only the Clear predicate is spelled out):

$$\begin{aligned}
I_{s(0)} = \{&\neg x,\; \mathrm{Clear}(B, 0),\; \neg\mathrm{Clear}(b_1, 0),\\
&\mathrm{Clear}(B, s(0)),\; \neg\mathrm{Clear}(b_1, s(0)),\; \neg\mathrm{Clear}(b_2, s(0)), \ldots\}
\end{aligned}$$

On the one side, the fact that all other, possibly many blocks remain clear after the transition to time point $s(0)$ does not need to be computed explicitly. This information is subsumed by the model representation. On the other side, the used rule is a frame axiom, and frame axioms are known to be computationally cumbersome. Optimally, the FDPLL model representation would turn out to help reasoning efficiently with frame axioms.

Nothing of this is worked out in detail. So, the conclusion is: A lot remains to be done!

ACKNOWLEDGMENTS

I am grateful to Antje Blohm, Martin Davis, Jan van Eijck, Alexander Fuchs, Uli Furbach, Ryuzo Hasegawa, Don Loveland, David Plaisted, Mark Stickel, and Cesare Tinelli for discussions about FDPLL or comments on this or earlier versions of this chapter. The reviewers gave valuable advice for improvement.

References

Aravindan, C., and P. Baumgartner (2000). Theorem proving techniques for view deletion in databases. *Journal of Symbolic Computation 29*(2), 119–147.

Bachmair, L., and H. Ganzinger (2001). Resolution theorem proving. In *Handbook of Automated Reasoning*, ed. A. Robinson and A. Voronkov. Amsterdam: North Holland.

Baumgartner, P. (1998). Hyper Tableaux—the Next Generation. See (de Swaart 1998), 60–76.

Baumgartner, P. (2000). FDPLL—a first-order Davis-Putnam-Logemann-Loveland procedure. In *CADE-17—the 17th International Conference on Automated Deduction*, ed. D. McAllester, Vol. 1831 of *Lecture Notes in Artificial Intelligence*, 200–219. Berlin: Springer-Verlag.

Baumgartner, P., N. Eisinger, and U. Furbach (1999). A confluent connection calculus. In *CADE-16—the 16th International Conference on Automated Deduction*, ed. H. Ganzinger, Vol. 1632 of *Lecture Notes in Artificial Intelligence*, Trento, Italy, 329–343. Berlin: Springer-Verlag.

Baumgartner, P., U. Furbach, and I. Niemelä (1996). Hyper tableaux. In *Proceedings of the European Workshop on Logics in AI (JELIA)*, Vol. 1126 of *Lecture Notes in Artificial Intelligence*. Berlin: Springer-Verlag.

Baumgartner, P., and M. Kühn (2000). Abducing coreference by model construction. *Journal of Language and Computation 1*(2), 175–190.

Beckert, B. (2000). Depth-first proof search without backtracking for free-variable clausal tableaux. In *FTP 2000—Third International Workshop on First-Order Theorem Proving*, ed. P. Baumgartner and H. Zhang. *Technical Report 5-2000*, 44–55. Universität Koblenz-Landau.

Beckert, B., and R. Hähnle (1998). Chapter 1: Analytic tableaux. See (Bibel and Schmitt 1998).

Beckert, B., and J. Posegga (1995). leanT^AP: Lean tableau-based deduction. *Journal of Automated Reasoning 15*(3), 339–358.

Bibel, W. (1981). On matrices with connections. *Journal of the Association for Computing Machinery 28*, 633–645.

Bibel, W. (1987). *Automated Theorem Proving*, 2nd ed. Wiesbaden: Vieweg.

Bibel, W., and P. H. Schmitt, ed. (1998). *Automated Deduction. A Basis for Applications*. Boston: Kluwer.

Billon, J.-P. (1996). The disconnection method. In *Theorem Proving with Analytic Tableaux and Related Methods*, ed. P. Miglioli, U. Moscato, D. Mundici, and M. Ornaghi, Vol. 1071 of *Lecture Notes in Artificial Intelligence*, 110–126. Berlin: Springer-Verlag.

Blackburn, P., J. Bos, M. Kohlhase, and H. de Nivelle (1999). Inference and computational semantics. In *Third International Workshop on Computational Semantics (IWCS-3)*, ed. H. Bunt and E. Thijsse, 5–21.

Bos, J. (1999). Available at *www.coli.uni-sb.de/bos/atp/doris.html*.

Bry, F. (1990). Intensional updates: Abduction via deduction. In *Proceedings of the 7th International Conference on Logic Programming, Jerusalem*, ed. D. H. Warren and P. Szeredi, 561–575. Cambridge, MA: MIT Press.

Bry, F., and S. Torge (1998). A deduction method complete for refutation and finite satisfiability. In *Proceedings of the European Workshop on Logics in AI (JELIA)*. Berlin: Springer-Verlag.

Bundy, A., ed. (1994). *CADE-12—the 12th International Conference on Automated Deduction*, LNAI 814, Nancy, France. Berlin: Springer-Verlag.

Chandru, V., J. N. Hooker, A. Shrivastava, and G. Rago (1998). A partial instantiation based first order theorem prover. In *Workshop First-Order Theorem Proving (FTP'98)*.

Chang, C., and R. Lee (1973). *Symbolic Logic and Mechanical Theorem Proving*. Academic Press.

Chinlund, T., M. Davis, P. Hinman, and M. McIlroy (1964). Theorem-proving by matching. Technical report, Bell Laboratories.

Chu, H., and D. Plaisted (1994). Semantically guided first-order theorem proving using hyper-linking. See (Bundy 1994), 192–206.

Clarke, E. M., O. Grumberg, and D. Peled (1999). *Model Checking*. Cambridge, MA: MIT Press.

Crawford, J., and L. Auton (1996). Experimental results on the crossover point in random 3SAT. *Artificial Intelligence 81*.

Davis, M. (1963). Eliminating the irrelevant from mechanical proofs. In *Proceedings of Symposia in Applied Mathematics—Experimental Arithmetic, High Speed Computing and Mathematics*, Vol. XV, 15–30. American Mathematical Society.

Davis, M. (1983). The prehistory and early history of automated deduction. In *Automation of Reasoning 1: Classical Papers on Computational Logic 1957-1966*, ed. J. Siekmann and G. Wrightson, 1–28. Berlin: Springer-Verlag.

Davis, M. (2001). Personal communication.

Davis, M., G. Logemann, and D. Loveland (1962). A machine program for theorem proving. *Communications of the ACM 5*(7).

Davis, M., and H. Putnam (1960). A computing procedure for quantification theory. *Journal of the ACM 7*, 201–215.

de Swaart, H., ed. (1998). *Automated Reasoning with Analytic Tableaux and Related Methods*, Vol. 1397 of *Lecture Notes in Artificial Intelligence*. Berlin: Springer-Verlag.

Eder, E. (1985). Properties of substitutions and unifications. *Journal of Symbolic Computation 1*(1).

Fermüller, C., and A. Leitsch (1996). Hyperresolution and automated model building. *Journal of Logic and Computation 6*(2), 173–230.

Fitting, M. (1990). *First Order Logic and Automated Theorem Proving*. Texts and Monographs in Computer Science. Berlin: Springer-Verlag.

Gallo, G., and G. Rago (1994). The satisfiability problem for the Schönfinkel Bernays fragment: Partial instantiation and hypergraph algorithms. Technical Report 4/94, Univ. di Pisa.

Giese, M. (2001). Incremental closure of free variable tableaux. In *CADE-18—the 18th International Conference on Automated Deduction*, ed. R. Goré, A. Leitsch, and T. Nipkov, *Lecture Notes in Artificial Intelligence*. Berlin: Springer-Verlag. Forthcoming.

Giunchiglia, F., and R. Sebastiani (2000). Building decision procedures for modal logics from propositional decision procedures—the case study of modal k(m). *Information and Computation 162*.

Hooker, J., G. Rago, V. Chandru, and A. Shrivastava (1996). Partial instantiation methods for inference in first order logic. Avalaible at *citeseer.nj.nec.com/hooker00partial.html*. Revised 2000.

Horrocks, I., and P. F. Patel-Schneider (1998). Optimising description logic subsumption. See (de Swaart 1998), 27–30.

Horrocks, I., and P. F. Patel-Schneider (1999). Optimising description logic subsumption. *Journal of Logic and Computation 9*(3), 267–293.

Hustadt, U., and R. A. Schmidt (1997). On evaluating decision procedures for modal logic. In *15th International Joint Conference on Artificial Intelligence (IJCAI 97)*, Nagoya, ed. M. E. Pollack, 202–207. San Francisco: Morgan Kaufmann Publishers.

Hustadt, U., and R. A. Schmidt (2000). MSPASS: Modal reasoning by translation and first-order resolution. In *Automated Reasoning with Analytic Tableaux and Related Methods, International Conference (TABLEAUX 2000)*, ed. R. Dyckhoff, Vol. 1847 of *Lecture Notes in Artificial Intelligence*, 67–71. Berlin: Springer-Verlag.

Inoue, K., M. Koshimura, and R. Hasegawa (1992). Embedding negation as failure into a model generation theorem prover. In *11th International Conference on Automated Deduction*, ed. D. Kapur, Vol. 607 of *Lecture Notes in Artificial Intelligence*, 400–415. Berlin: Springer-Verlag.

Inoue, K., Y. Ohta, and R. Hasegawa (1993). Bottom-up abduction by model generation. In *IJCAI-95—Proceedings of the 13th International Joint Conference on Artificial Intelligence*, 102–108.

Johnson, M. (1994). Computing with features as formulae. *Computational Linguistics 20*(1), 1–25.

Joyner, W. (1976). Resolution strategies as decision procedures. *Journal of the ACM 23*(3), 396–417.

Kautz, H., and B. Selman (1996). Pushing the envelope: Planning, propositional logic, and stochastic search. In *Proceedings of the 13th National Conference on Artificial Intelligence*, Portland, OR.

Konolige, K. (1990). Closure + minimization implies abduction. In *Proceedings of PRICAI-90*, Nagoya, Japan.

Kowalski, R., and P. Hayes (1969). Semantic trees in automatic theorem proving. In *Machine Intelligence 5*, ed. B. Meltzer and D. Mitchie. Edinburgh: Edinburgh University Press.

Lee, S.-J., and D. A. Plaisted (1993). Problem solving by searching for models with a theorem prover. *Artificial Intelligence 69*(1-2), 205–233.

Leitsch, A. (1993). Deciding clause classes by semantic clash resolution. *Fundamenta Informaticae 18*, 163–182.

Letz, R. (1998). Clausal tableaux. See (Bibel and Schmitt 1998).

Letz, R., and G. Stenz (2000). Model elimination and connection tableau procedures. In *Handbook of Automated Reasoning*, ed. J. A. Robinson and A. Voronkov, 2015–2114. Cambridge, MA: MIT Press.

Letz, R., and G. Stenz (2001). Proof and model generation with disconnection tableaux. In *Proceedings of LPAR*, ed. R. Nieuwenhuis and A. Voronkov, Vol. 2250 of *Lecture Notes in Computer Science*. Berlin: Springer-Verlag.

Lloyd, J. (1987). *Foundations of Logic Programming*, 2nd ed. Symbolic Computation. Berlin: Springer-Verlag.

Loveland, D. (1968). Mechanical theorem proving by model elimination. *JACM 15*(2).

Loveland, D., D. Reed, and D. Wilson (1995). SATCHMORE: SATCHMO with RElevance. *Journal of Automated Reasoning 14*, 325–351.

Manthey, R., and F. Bry (1988). SATCHMO: A theorem prover implemented in Prolog. In *Proceedings of the 9th Conference on Automated Deduction, Argonne, Illinois*, ed. E. Lusk and R. Overbeek, Vol. 310 of *Lecture Notes in Computer Science*, 415–434. Berlin: Springer-Verlag.

McCarthy, J. (1985). Circumscription—a form of non-monotonic reasoning. *Artificial Intelligence 13*, 27–39.

Moskewicz, M., C. Madigan, Y. Zhao, L. Zhang, and S. Malik (2001). CHAFF: Engineering an efficient SAT solver. In *39th Design Automation Conference*.

Nebel, B., and G. Smolka (1989). Representation and reasoning with attributive descriptions. In *Sorts and Types in Artificial Intelligence*, ed. K.-H. Bläsius, U. Hedtstück, and C. Rollinger, Vol. 418 of *Lecture Notes in Artificial Intelligence*, 112–139. Berlin: Springer-Verlag.

Niemelä, I., and P. Simons (1996). Efficient implementation of the well-founded and stable model semantics. In *Proceedings of the Joint International Conference and Symposium on Logic Programming*, Bonn, Germany. Cambridge, MA: MIT Press.

Ohlbach, H. J. (1993). Translation methods for non-classical logics—an overview. *Logic Journal of the IGPL 1*(1), 69–90.

Paramasivam, M., and D. A. Plaisted (1998). Automated deduction techniques for classification in description logic systems. *Journal of Automated Reasoning 20*(3), 337–364.

Parkes, A. J. (1999). *Lifted Search Engines for Satisfiability*. Ph. D. thesis, University of Oregon.

Peltier, N. (1999). Pruning the search space and extracting more models in tableaux. *Logic Journal of the IGPL 7*(2), 217–251.

Plaisted, D. (1994). The search efficiency of theorem proving strategies. See (Bundy 1994).

Plaisted, D. A., and Y. Zhu (2000). Ordered semantic hyper linking. *Journal of Automated Reasoning*.

Reiter, R. (1987). A theory of diagnosis from first principles. *Artificial Intelligence 32*(1), 57–95.

Robinson, J. (1965a). A machine-oriented logic based on the resolution principle. *JACM 12*(1), 23–41.

Robinson, J. A. (1965b). Automated deduction with hyper-resolution. *International Journal on Computer Mathematics 1*, 227–234.

Schild, K. (1991). A correspondence theory for terminological logics: Preliminary report. In *Proceedings of the 12th International Joint Conference on Artificial Intelligence*, pp. 466–471.

Smullyan, R. (1968). *First Order Logic*. Berlin: Springer-Verlag.

Tammet, T. (1991). Using resolution for deciding solvable classes and building finite models. In *Baltic Computer Science—Selected Papers*, ed. J. Barzdins and D. Bjoerner, Vol. 502 of *Lecture Notes in Computer Science*, 33–64. Berlin: Springer-Verlag.

van Eijck, J. (2001). Constrained hyper tableaux. In *Proceedings of the 15th International Workshop on Computer Science Logic*, ed. L. Fribourg, Vol. 2142 of *Lecture Notes in Computer Science*, 232–246. Berlin: Springer-Verlag.

Zhang, H. (1997, July). SATO: An efficient propositional theorem prover. In *Automated Deduction—CADE 14*, ed. W. McCune, Vol. 1249 of *Lecture Notes in Artificial Intelligence*, 272–275. Berlin: Springer-Verlag.

Chapter 11

Constraint Satisfaction

New Tractable Constraint Classes from Old

David Cohen
Department of Computer Science
Royal Holloway, University of London, U.K.
D.Cohen@rhul.ac.uk

Peter Jeavons and **Richard Gault**
Oxford University Computing Laboratory
Wolfson Building, Parks Road
Oxford, U.K.
R.Gault,P.Jeavons@comlab.ox.ac.uk

Abstract

Many applications in AI involve searching over a very large possibility space. Constraint satisfaction is a general problem-solving paradigm that expresses some of these search problems in a natural way.

The constraint-satisfaction paradigm consists of defining a problem in terms of variables that need to be assigned suitable values. Certain subsets of these variables are then constrained by restricting the simultaneous values they may be assigned.

In general, the constraint-satisfaction problem is NP-hard but there are well-known restrictions to the hypergraph of constraint interactions (structure) or to the allowable relations of constraint restrictions (language) that make the problem tractable (solvable in polynomial time). The trade-off here is expressiveness for tractability.

In this chapter, we introduce the constraint-satisfaction paradigm and briefly describe expressiveness and tractability. We then introduce an algebraic framework for describing language-based tractability and discuss some of the known results. Lastly, we derive a general technique for developing new, more expressive, tractable constraint languages from existing examples.

1 INTRODUCTION[1]

Many applications in AI involve searching over a very large possibility space. Constraint satisfaction is a general problem-solving paradigm that expresses some of these search problems in a natural way.

In the constraint paradigm , we define a *problem* as a set of variables that need to be assigned values in some consistent way. The variables can be seen as a set of interrelated questions that we need to answer in order to solve our problem. Consistency is maintained by constraining the allowed sets of values on certain subsets of the variables. In other words, we refuse to accept certain simultaneous assignments of values to these subsets. Such subsets of variables are called the *constraint scopes,* and the restrictions applied to their assigned values are called the *constraint relations.*

The *constraint satisfaction problem (CSP)* clearly generalizes both the *graph coloring problem* and the *satisfiability problem.* Hence it is known to be NP-hard in general (Mackworth 1977). This means that there are no general algorithms to solve the CSP in polynomial time (assuming that $P \neq NP$). However, it turns out that there are many subclasses of the general CSP that can be solved in polynomial time, and hence may be described as *tractable.*

In order to define these tractable subclasses, we define two different aspects of any CSP instance:

- The *constraint hypergraph* of a CSP instance is the hypergraph whose nodes are the variables and whose edges are the constraint scopes. This hypergraph describes the underlying *structure* of the constraints in the instance, in terms of how they are connected to each other. There are several well-known restrictions on the form of this hypergraph that serve to make the corresponding CSP instances tractable. A good survey of such structural restrictions is given by Gottlob et al (1999).

- The *constraint language* of a CSP instance is the set of all relations that appear as constraint relations. This language describes the *form* of the constraints in the instance, in terms of what combinations of values they allow and disallow. There are several well-known restrictions on the constraint language that serve to make the corresponding CSP instances tractable. These so-called tractable constraint languages have been well studied (Cooper et al. 1994; Feder and Vardi 1998; Jeavons and Cooper 1995; Jeavons et al. 1997; Kirousis 1993; Montanari 1974; Nebel and Bürckert 1995; van Beek and Dechter 1995). The most striking result obtained so far is the complete classification of tractable constraint languages over a two-valued domain (Schaefer 1978).

Most results concerning tractability in the CSP fall into one or other of these two camps: they either demand a restriction on the constraint hypergraph, or else on the constraint language. There are, however, a few hybrid results in the literature. For instance, there is a result obtained by Freuder for binary CSPs that guarantees tractability under certain restrictions on both tree width (a property of the constraint hypergraph) and level of

---

[1] The work presented in this chapter is derived from the paper presented by the same authors at the conference on the "Principles and Practice of Constraint Programming"—CP 2000 (Cohen et al. 2000). The work has been supported by an EPSRC grant, number GR/M12926.

consistency (a property of the constraint relations) (Freuder 1985). There is a result by Dechter that guarantees tractability under certain restrictions on the domain size (number of values available for each variable), the maximum constraint arity, and the level of consistency (Dechter 1992). This considerable body of research is at least partially motivated by the long-term goal of classifying *all* subproblems of the constraint satisfaction problem with respect to their tractability.

A novel approach to tractability that has so far received very little attention is that of *tractability by construction*. In this approach we combine two or more (tractable) classes of constraint problems with specified properties to give a new tractable class that is more expressive. It is this approach that we adopt here. It is clear that a taxonomy of tractable constraint classes can be more simply described if we have a base set of (simple) tractable classes and a (small) set of methods for generating all other tractable classes from them. This contrasts with the earlier descriptive approaches to classification, which specify membership tests that a subclass of the CSP problem has to pass in order to be tractable.

A first positive result for the constructive approach was obtained by Cohen et al. (2000). The method we describe here for combining tractable sets of relations, the *disjoint disjunctive union*, is a variation on the "or-cross" combining operator first described in this earlier paper. The principal difference is in how the operator is applied. In the earlier paper, the authors generally considered sets of relations over a single, fixed domain. In the present work on the other hand, we will restrict our attention to combining sets of relations over different—and disjoint—domains.

The results of this chapter are of key importance in the study of tractability of constraint satisfaction languages. We are able to guarantee the existence of new tractable languages. Even over finite domains, these novel languages are not explained by being closed under any particular polymorphism (see Section 4.1), unlike all previous known examples.

Ironically, this richness will make the classification of all tractable languages harder. Perhaps reasons for language *intractability* will be easier to identify.

1.1 ROAD MAP

In Section 2, we describe the constraint satisfaction problem and give some examples. In Section 2.3, we define what we mean by tractability of a subproblem of the general constraint satisfaction problem. This naturally motivates the introduction of a constraint language in Section 3. In Section 3.2, we define the expressiveness of a constraint language and show why this is an important question.

In Section 5, we describe our new construction for tractable languages. The algebraic techniques introduced in Section 4 are used in Sections 6 and 5.2 to show that the language we obtain is (often) genuinely novel and to describe its full expressiveness.

We round off the chapter with our conclusions, and suggest directions for future work.

2 BACKGROUND

2.1 THE CONSTRAINT SATISFACTION PROBLEM

Many applications in AI involve searching over a very large possibility space. Constraint satisfaction is a generic way to express some of these search problems. In this section we will demonstrate that the paradigm is natural and flexible.

Definition 1 (Ladkin and Maddux 1994; Mackworth 1977; Montanari 1974) *A constraint satisfaction problem instance P is a triple $< V, D, C >$ where*

- *V is a finite set of variables.*
- *D is any set (called the* domain *of P).*
- *C is a finite set of constraints $\{C_1, C_2, \ldots, C_q\}$. Each constraint C_i is a pair $\langle s_i, R_i \rangle$, where s_i is a tuple of variables of length m_i (called the* constraint scope*); and R_i is an m_i-ary relation over D (called the* constraint relation*).*

For each constraint, $\langle s_i, R_i \rangle$, the tuples of R_i indicate the allowed combinations of simultaneous value assignments for the variables in s_i. A *solution* to a CSP instance is a function from the variables to the domain such that the image of each constraint scope is an element of the corresponding constraint relation (and hence an allowed assignment).

To make this definition clear we will now present a few (toy) examples.

Example 2 (Scheduling) This is the problem of getting dressed in the morning! I have three questions:

- (Q1) When do I put on my trousers (American: pants)?
- (Q2) When do I put on my pants (American: underwear)?
- (Q3) When do I put on my shoes?

Each of these questions becomes a variable when I see this as a CSP. The domain of this constraint problem is the set of all possible answers to these questions—say the set of times between 6 a.m. and 11 a.m.

The answers to these questions are pairwise constrained. There is a constraint between any two variables. Each constraint is *before*. I must put on my pants *before* I put on my trousers. I must put on my trousers *before* I put on my shoes. I must put on my pants *before* I put on my shoes.

Any solution to this constraint problem answers these three questions with times that solve this simple scheduling task. □

Example 3 (SAT) This is a logical problem associated with travel. I have to get to work after getting dressed, and I can travel either by bus or by train. Again there are three questions that correspond to three constraint variables.

- (Q1) Do I travel by train?
- (Q2) Do I travel by bus?
- (Q2) Do I arrive on time?

Now of course the domain is just the set of truth values $\{T, F\}$.

In this case we describe the constraints as logical formulas that the (values of the) variables in their scopes must satisfy.

Again there are three binary constraints—one for each pair of variables. On variables Q1 and Q2 we have the constraint that says that exactly one of them has value T. If X represents the value of variable Q1 and Y the value of variable Q2, then we have the relation $X \otimes Y$.

Similarly the values of the variables Q2 and Q3 satisfy the proposition $X \Rightarrow (\neg Y)$.

Lastly, the constraint with scope $\langle Q1, Q3 \rangle$ has relation, $X \vee (\neg Y)$.

It is left as an exercise for you to determine both solutions to this CSP. $\qquad\square$

Example 4 (FAP) Here we are to assign frequencies to three mobile phone base stations. We have three base stations and so three variables that correspond to the questions:

- (Q1) What channel (frequency) should I use for transmitter A?
- (Q2) What channel (frequency) should I use for transmitter B?
- (Q3) What channel (frequency) should I use for transmitter C?

The domain of this problem is the set of channels that have been allocated to this service provider.

Transmitters B and C are quite close together, so we have to ensure that their frequencies are well separated. We can be less restrictive for the other two pairs of transmitters. The three constraints in this case are

$$\langle \langle Q1, Q2 \rangle, \{\langle x, y \rangle \ : \ |x - y| > 1\} \rangle$$
$$\langle \langle Q2, Q3 \rangle, \{\langle x, y \rangle \ : \ |x - y| > 2\} \rangle$$
$$\langle \langle Q1, Q3 \rangle, \{\langle x, y \rangle \ : \ |x - y| > 1\} \rangle$$

$\qquad\square$

2.2 COMPLEXITY OF THE GENERAL CONSTRAINT SATISFACTION PROBLEM

Deciding whether or not a given problem instance has a solution is NP-complete in general (Mackworth 1977). To see this, it is enough to observe that we can reduce the graph colorability problem or the satisfiability problem to the CSP (Garey and Johnson 1979), as the following examples indicate.

Example 5 Let G be a graph and D a set (of colors). We define the CSP P_G as follows:

- The variables of P_G are the nodes of G.
- The domain of P_G is just the set D.
- For each edge $\{a, b\}$ of G, we define a constraint with scope $\langle a, b \rangle$ and relation $\neq_D$, where $\neq_D$ is the binary "not equals" relation over D. (We may choose $\langle a, b \rangle$ or $\langle b, a \rangle$ arbitrarily.)

It is straightforward to check that any solution to P_G corresponds exactly to a D coloring of the graph G. Hence, we have reduced the graph colorability problem to the CSP. $\square$

Example 6 Let S be a set of propositional formulas. We define the CSP P_S as follows:

- The variables of P_S are the logical variables appearing in the formulas of S.

- The domain of P_S is just the set $\{T, F\}$.

- For each formula f is S we define a constraint in P_S. The scope of this constraint is an arbitrary listing of the set of logical variables appearing in f. The relation of this constraint is the set of tuples for these variables corresponding to satisfying assignments for f (where we make the domain value T correspond to logical truth and F correspond to falsity).

It is straightforward to check that a solution to P_S corresponds exactly to a satisfying assignment of the formulas of S. Hence, we have reduced the satisfiability problem to the CSP. $\square$

2.3   TRACTABLE SUBCLASSES OF THE GENERAL CSP

In order to write efficient solvers for constraint problems, it will be useful to know what restrictions to the general CSP make it tractable. In these cases we also want a way to decide which (polynomial) algorithm to use to solve instances of the tractable class.

There are two approaches that are most often used to define tractable classes: to restrict the possible hypergraph structure of the scopes of the constraints, or to restrict the allowable relations that can be used to define the constraints.

When we restrict the underlying hypergraph structure to obtain a tractable class, we call the class *structural*. There are several well-known tractable structural classes.

Alternatively, we can restrict the allowed relations. A set of possible relations that define a subclass of the general CSP is called a *constraint language*. We call a constraint language *tractable* if it gives rise to a tractable subclass of the general CSP. We will formalize constraint languages in Section 3.

Before concluding the background section, we will give two well-known examples of subclasses of the CSP that are tractable. The first of these is a structural class, while the second defines a tractable language.

Example 7 If we restrict the number of variables in any constraint scope to be at most two, and the underlying structure of the constraint problem to have no cycles, then we have a uniform polynomial algorithm for solving such problems.

To solve such a problem we proceed as follows:

We first make sure that every value for any variable is allowed (supported) by some value at every variable it constrains. If some value is not supported at a variable, then we can be sure it cannot occur in any solution. We mark such values "bad" and iterate the process. Naturally, in subsequent iterations we only allow values to be supported by "good" values at other variables.

We now consider the complexity of this procedure. Suppose that there are d values in the domain, and v variables, and e constraints. We only need perform the process of finding unsupported values at most vd times, since each iteration must mark some new value as bad. Also each iteration involves checking at most ed^2 pairs of values. So the whole iterative process is polynomial in the problem size.

If any variable ends up with only bad values, then we can be sure that there is no solution to the problem. Otherwise we have at least one good value left for every variable. We solve the problem by choosing an arbitrary variable and assigning it any good value, then by iteratively assigning (good) values to all of the (unassigned) neighbors. As the graph is acyclic, this will never cause us to backtrack. As every assigned value will be good, we can never fail.

This class is the best-known structural tractable subclass of the general CSP and was first described by Freuder (1982).

$\square$

Example 8 Consider CSP instances whose domain is the truth values $\{T, F\}$.

If we restrict the relations of these instances to be propositions concerning at most two logical variables, then we have restricted the class of CSPs to the familiar tractable class 2-SAT.

So the constraint language defined by logical formulas concerning at most two logical variables is tractable. $\square$

3   CONSTRAINT LANGUAGES

In the remainder of this chapter, we will not be considering structural restrictions, but only constraint languages.

We might have supposed that the constraint language over a domain with three elements consisting of all relations with arity at most two would be tractable. That this is not true was shown in Example 5 since this class generalizes three-colorability of graphs.

We might then have tried the constraint language over a domain with only two elements consisting of relations with arity to at most three. Unfortunately (using a similar construction to that of Example 6), this generalizes 3-SAT and so is still NP-hard.

At least we know from Example 8 that the language over a domain with two elements consisting of relations of arity at most two is tractable. This, however, does not complete the story. There is a dimension that we have not considered when only allowing restrictions to arity and domain size. This new dimension is the algebraic structure of the constraint language.

Before continuing, a few formal definitions will be useful.

Definition 9 *A constraint language Γ is any set of relations over some (given) domain. When the domain is clear from the context, or immaterial, we will omit it. We denote by $\delta(\Gamma)$ the domain of the constraint language Γ.*

For any constraint language Γ, $\mathbf{C}_\Gamma$ is the class of constraint satisfaction problems (with domain $\delta(\Gamma)$) in which all constraint relations are elements of Γ.

If there is some deterministic algorithm that solves every problem instance in $\mathbf{C}_\Gamma$ in polynomial time, then we shall say that Γ is *tractable*.

Example 10 Referring to Example 5, we see that if $\Gamma \stackrel{\text{def}}{=} \{\neq_D\}$, then $\mathbf{C}_\Gamma$ corresponds to the standard graph colorability problem with $|D|$ colors. Hence, in this case, the language Γ is tractable if and only if $|D| < 3$ (Garey and Johnson 1979). □

In order to motivate the search for tractable languages, we note that there are at least two very useful languages whose tractability is known by most AI researchers:

- *Horn clauses* define a tractable constraint language. Any problem with a Boolean domain, all of whose constraint relations are Horn clauses, is solvable using unit resolution. The usefulness of this tractable language should be clear!

- *The set of linear equations over a field* define a tractable language. The solution technique here is Gaussian elimination (for instance), and again the usefulness of the language is not in doubt.

The algebraic study of tractable languages has led to the simple description of a uniform property that all such languages over a finite domain must satisfy. This necessary condition was first described in Theorem 2 of a paper on the tractability of constraint languages by Jeavons et al. (1997). However, finding conditions both necessary and sufficient has proven more difficult.

An algebraic explanation of the tractability of Horn clauses is given in Example 21 and of linear equations is given in Example 22. The usefulness of the algebraic approach here is that it has allowed us to generalize both of these tractable classes in practically useful ways.

In this chapter we will describe a novel collection of tractable languages and so will move closer to an understanding of tractability.

3.1 A DIFFICULT LANGUAGE

Current algebraic techniques cannot determine the tractability of the following pair of relations:

Example 11 The relations R and R' defined by

$$
R \stackrel{\text{def}}{=} \{\langle 2,3,2,2,2\rangle, \quad \text{and} \quad R' \stackrel{\text{def}}{=} \{\langle 0,2,2\rangle,
$$

$$
\langle 0,1,2,0,0\rangle, \qquad\qquad\qquad \langle 1,3,2\rangle
$$

$$
\langle 0,0,2,0,1\rangle, \qquad\qquad\qquad \langle 0,3,3\rangle
$$

$$
\langle 1,0,2,0,0\rangle, \qquad\qquad\qquad \langle 2,0,2\rangle
$$

$$
\langle 2,2,2,3,3\rangle, \qquad\qquad\qquad \langle 3,1,2\rangle
$$

$$
\langle 1,1,2,0,1\rangle\}, \qquad\qquad\qquad \langle 2,1,3\rangle\}
$$

Nevertheless, they *are* tractable, as we will establish using the new techniques developed in this chapter. □

3.2 EXPRESSIBILITY OF CONSTRAINT LANGUAGES

We now have explained the paradigm of constraint satisfaction and introduced the notion of a constraint language as a tool for describing some useful subclasses of the general problem. This leads us to the question of exactly which kinds of real-world problems can be modeled in any particular (tractable or otherwise) constraint language.

In general, when modeling a problem using the constraint paradigm, we want to constrain some sets of variables with a given relation. If these relations are not in our constraint language, we may be able to build a *gadget* for them out of relations from our constraint language. These gadgets correspond to subroutines in other programming paradigms and extend the expressiveness of a constraint language.

To best explain how gadgets derive new relations, we will give an example.

Example 12 Suppose that we have a language over the domain of integers that contains only the relation $\rho \stackrel{\text{def}}{=} \{\langle a, b \rangle : a - b > 1\}$.

We are now required to model a problem in which the difference between two values must be at least two. This relation $\mu \stackrel{\text{def}}{=} \{\langle a, b \rangle : a - b > 2\}$ is not in our language.

We will define a gadget for this relation. A gadget is a constraint problem in our language with some list of variables labeled as construction variables.

In our gadget we will have three variables A, B, and C, and the construction variables will be the list $\langle A, C \rangle$.

The constraints of the gadget are $\langle \langle A, B \rangle, \rho \rangle$, and $\langle \langle B, C \rangle, \rho \rangle$.

We now look at all solutions to this problem but only concern ourselves with the values of the construction variables. In this case it is clear that the solutions allow the construction variables to have values that exactly form the relation μ.

Now when we model our real-world problem, whenever we find two variables that require the relation μ, we apply a copy of the gadget, renaming the variables, so that the construction variables become these two variables. The extra variable in the gadget takes the role of a local variable in a programming language. $\quad\square$

The previous example serves as the motivation for the following definition.

Definition 13 *Given a CSP P and any list of variables C of P, the derived relation for P on C is the set of tuples for the values of C that extend to solutions of P.*

Let Γ be any constraint language and μ be any relation over the domain of Γ. A gadget for μ in Γ is a pair $\langle P, C \rangle$ where P is a CSP over Γ, and C is a list of variables of P, such that P derives μ on C.

A language Γ expresses a relation μ if there is a gadget for μ in Γ.

We can add any finite set of expressible relations to a language without altering its complexity. This is a straightforward consequence of Theorem 18.

As constructors of constraint languages, we want a way to determine if a given relation is expressible in a language. We can then improve any claims for tractability by including such relations. As users (buyers) of constraint languages, we want to be able to determine (easily) whether, and how, a particular relation can be expressed in a given language. This reduces to the problem of finding a gadget for a relation in a language whenever one exists.

As the following example shows, this is a difficult problem. It is even hard to determine exactly what a particular gadget derives, let alone finding a gadget to derive a required relation.

Example 14 let Γ be the language only containing the binary "not equals" relation over a domain with three elements.

Consider the gadget $\langle P, C \rangle$ over Γ. The variables of P are $\{a, b, c, d\}$ and $C = \langle a, c \rangle$. The constraint relations are (of course) all "not equals" and the scopes are $\langle a, b \rangle$, $\langle b, c \rangle$, $\langle c, d \rangle$, $\langle d, a \rangle$, and $\langle b, d \rangle$.

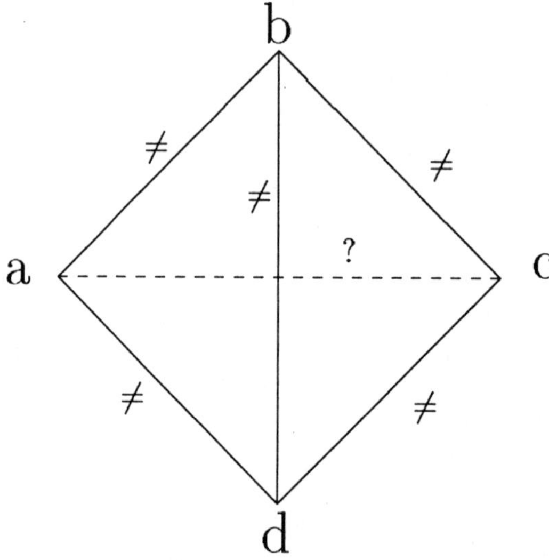

What is the relation expressed by this gadget?

□

Luckily, the same algebraic methods that determine the complexity of a constraint language also determine its expressiveness. It is the polymorphisms of a language that solve both problems.

A presentation of a solution to the expressiveness problem was given by Cohen et al. (1996). The general algebraic theory of polymorphisms applied to constraint languages was introduced by Jeavons et al. (1996, 1997). In this early work polymorphisms were called *closure properties*.

In Section 5.2, we will use the polymorphisms of our constructed language to determine its expressiveness. Also, by knowing the polymorphic descriptions of all previously discovered tractable classes, we will be able to show in Section 6 that the new class is indeed novel.

4 ALGEBRAIC BACKGROUND

Over the past few years, a good deal of fruitful research has been carried out on the connection between universal algebra and constraint satisfaction (Bulatov et al. 2000; Jeavons and Cohen 1995; Jeavons et al. 1997; Jeavons 1998; Jeavons et al. 1999). In particular, when constraint satisfaction is viewed as an application of universal algebra, a whole gamut of powerful algebraic tools immediately becomes available to us. In this section, we shall review some of the standard definitions and theorems that underpin this important connection. Most of the definitions are adapted from those in (Jeavons 1998).

A k-ary operation φ on a set D is just a function from D^k to D. We call k the *arity* of the operation. Except where stated otherwise, φ is permitted to be *partial*—that is, possibly undefined at one or more places.

Any operation defined on the domain of a relation can be extended pointwise to define an operation on tuples from that relation, as follows:

Definition 15 *Let R be an n-ary relation over a domain D, and let $\varphi : D^k \to D$ be a k-ary operation on D. For any n-tuples, $t_1, t_2, \ldots, t_k \in R$ (not necessarily all distinct) define the n-tuple, $\varphi(t_1, t_2, \ldots, t_k)$ as follows:*

$$\varphi(t_1, t_2, \ldots, t_k)[j] \stackrel{\text{def}}{=} \varphi(t_1[j], t_2[j], \ldots, t_k[j]), j = 1, \ldots, n$$

when each of $\varphi(t_1[j], t_2[j], \ldots, t_k[j]), j = 1, \ldots, n$ is defined.

Note that in this definition, and indeed throughout this chapter, we allow the possibility that $k = 0$—that is, that φ is a nullary operation. Such an operation takes no arguments and always returns the same (constant) domain element.

Definition 16 *Let R be a relation over a domain D, and let $\varphi : D^k \to D$ be a k-ary (possibly partial) operation on D. We say that R is closed under φ if, for all $t_1, t_2, \ldots, t_k \in R$ such that $\varphi(t_1, t_2, \ldots, t_k)$ is defined, it happens that $\varphi(t_1, t_2, \ldots, t_k) \in R$. A constraint language is said to be closed under φ if all its constituent relations are closed under φ.*

Lemma 17 *Let R be a relation over a domain D that is closed under some (possibly partial) operation φ. Let R' be a second relation over D that has been generated from R by permuting the order of elements in each tuple of R in the same way. Then R' is also closed under φ.*

Proof: Follows immediately from the definition of closure. □

For any constraint language Γ, the set of all *total* (i.e., not partial) operations on $\delta(\Gamma)$ under which Γ remains closed is called the set of *polymorphisms* of Γ, and is denoted by $Pol(\Gamma)$. Similarly, if Φ is a set of operations over D, then the maximal constraint language that is closed under every operation of Φ is called the set of *invariants* of Φ, and is denoted by $Inv(\Phi)$. Note that $Inv(\Phi)$ always contains the relations $\{\langle d, d \rangle : d \in D\}$ (denoted $=_D$) and $D \times D$ (denoted $\otimes_D$), since these are closed under all operations. Between them, the mappings $Pol()$ and $Inv()$ establish a *Galois connection* between constraint languages and sets of operations (Cohn 1965; McKenzie et al. 1987).

The following theorem was proved in (Jeavons 1998).

Theorem 18 *A finite constraint language Γ over a finite domain is tractable if, and only if, all finite subsets of $Inv(Pol(\Gamma))$ are tractable.*

Definition 19 *Any set of relations of the form $Inv(Pol(\Gamma))$, for some Γ, is known as a relational clone.*

This means that (in the finite domain case at least) we can restrict our attention to relational clones in our search for tractable languages. It also means that, given any constraint language over a finite domain, we can determine its complexity by studying its polymorphisms. Lastly it means that, given a tractable language over a finite domain, we can include finitely many expressible relations without affecting the tractability.

4.1   SOME KNOWN TRACTABLE CONSTRAINT LANGUAGES

At this stage it is appropriate to briefly review the current knowledge about tractable constraint languages.

Definition 20 *An operation φ is called* tractable *if any constraint language Γ for which $\varphi \in Pol(\Gamma)$ is tractable.*

A tractable constraint language Γ is maximal *if, for any $R \notin \Gamma$, $\Gamma \cup \{R\}$ is not tractable.*

A class Φ of operations is said to be defined by identities if it can be specified by giving one or more equations that must always be satisfied for any operation in that class.

Without the use of the disjoint disjunctive union of this chapter, all known maximal tractable constraint languages over finite domains are the invariant languages of individual tractable operations. That is, whenever Γ is a maximal tractable constraint language over a finite domain, there exists a tractable operation φ with $\Gamma = Inv(\varphi)$.

Furthermore, all previously known tractable sets of relations over finite domains can be defined by closure under some operation defined by identities.[2]

We end this section with a short description of some previously identified tractable constraint languages. The reader is referred to the original papers (Feder and Vardi 1998; Jeavons et al. 1997; Koubarakis 1997) for more detailed descriptions of these constraint languages. The first three languages are over finite domains and so are described in terms of a closure operation. The last is an example over an infinite domain.

Example 21 (**Semilattices**) A binary operation $f(x,y)$ is called a *semilattice operation*,[3] if it satisfies the following three identities:

- $f(x, f(y,z)) = f(f(x,y), z)$ (associativity)
- $f(x,y) = f(y,x)$ (commutativity)
- $f(x,x) = x$ (idempotency)

It was shown in (Jeavons et al. 1997) that semilattice operations are tractable.   □

---

[2] Occasionally, the operation must satisfy some additional side conditions as well, as is the case with relations that are closed under a commutative binary operation that also happens to be conservative (Bulatov and Jeavons 2000).

[3] In some earlier papers (Jeavons 1998; Jeavons et al. 1997; Pearson and Jeavons 1997), the term ACI operation is used for a semilattice operation.

It turns out that Horn clauses are closed under a semilattice operation. However, there are many other non-Boolean classes that are closed under semilattice operations. Indeed, specific examples have been used in practical applications (Lesaint et al. 1998; Purvis and Jeavons 1999).

Example 22 (Affine) Suppose that the domain has an Abelian finite group structure. The operation given by

$$m(x, y, z) = x + y - z$$

was shown by Feder and Vardi (1998) to be tractable. □

This example covers the well-known case of linear equations over a field. However, the same reason explains the tractability of other languages where the domain is simply a finite Abelian group.

Example 23 (Near-unanimity) An n-ary operation f is said to be a *near-unanimity operation* if $f(y, x, \ldots, x) = f(x, y, x, \ldots, x) = \cdots = f(x, \ldots, x, y) = x$ for any x, y in the domain.

It was shown in (Jeavons et al. 1997) that near-unanimity operators are tractable. □

The example above can be used to explain the tractability of any language where a specific level of consistency is a decision procedure. This discovery unified several known tractable languages and helped to construct many more.

Example 24 (Temporal) Over the domain $\mathbb{Z}$ it is reasonably easy to show that $\Gamma = \{\leq_{\mathbb{Z}}, \neq_{\mathbb{Z}}\}$ is tractable. Other properties of this language have been investigated (Koubarakis 1997) that highlight the differences between the analysis of finite and infinite domains. □

This last example has the property that 5-consistency implies global consistency. This property over a finite domain would guarantee that the language were closed under a near-unanimity operator. This infinite language is not closed under such an operator. We still have no fundamental understanding of tractable languages over infinite domains.

5   THE DISJOINT DISJUNCTIVE UNION

We now introduce our novel method for combining constraint languages.

Definition 25 *Let Γ_1 and Γ_2 be constraint languages over the non-empty disjoint domains D_1 and D_2, respectively. Then the disjoint disjunctive union (DDU) of Γ_1 and Γ_2, denoted $\Gamma_1 \, \overset{\times}{\cup} \, \Gamma_2$, is defined to be the following constraint language over $D_1 \cup D_2$:*

$$\Gamma_1 \, \overset{\times}{\cup} \, \Gamma_2 \overset{\text{def}}{=} \{R_1 \cup R_2 : R_1 \in \Gamma_1, R_2 \in \Gamma_2 \wedge arity(R_1) = arity(R_2)\}$$

Since this definition is so important, we have included a graphical presentation (Figure 1) of a relation in $\Gamma_1 \, \overset{\times}{\cup} \, \Gamma_2$. We draw binary relations in a natural way: a line indicates an allowed combination.

The following is a (toy) example of this rather technical construction.

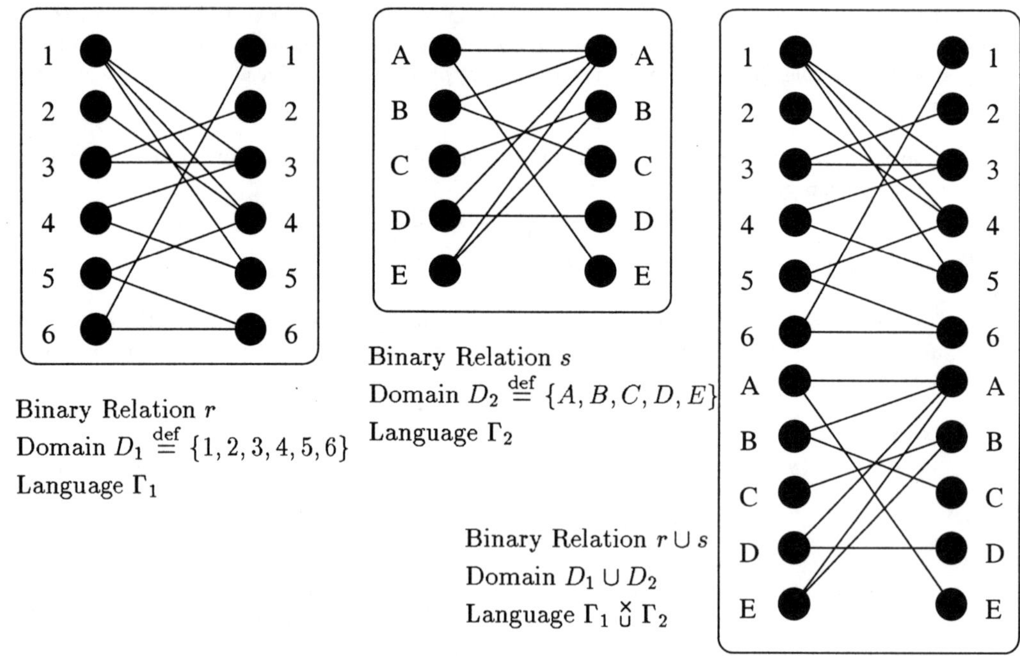

Binary Relation r
Domain $D_1 \stackrel{\text{def}}{=} \{1, 2, 3, 4, 5, 6\}$
Language Γ_1

Binary Relation s
Domain $D_2 \stackrel{\text{def}}{=} \{A, B, C, D, E\}$
Language Γ_2

Binary Relation $r \cup s$
Domain $D_1 \cup D_2$
Language $\Gamma_1 \mathbin{\check{\cup}} \Gamma_2$

Figure 1 Since the domains of Γ_1 and Γ_2 are non-empty and disjoint, we can form their disjoint disjunctive union. This diagram shows how two relations, r and s, with the same arity, one from Γ_1 and one from Γ_2, are combined to give a relation in the DDU.

Example 26 Consider a constraint language for bus journeys. The domain is the set of all possible bus journeys in the United Kingdom—a really large timetable.

Relations in this language will include unary relations such as

Stops in Birmingham.

Sometimes it will be possible to get off one bus and onto another. Such pairs of bus journeys will satisfy the binary relation

Is a connection.

We can specify a CSP in this language whose solutions are all bus journeys from Birmingham to Glasgow with at most one change. There are two variables B and G. The unary constraint "Stops in Birmingham" is applied to the variable B. The unary constraint "Stops in Glasgow" is applied to the variable G. The binary constraint "Is a connection" is applied to the pair $\langle B, G \rangle$.[4]

---

[4] To allow journeys without a change, we should include the *null* bus journey from Glasgow to Glasgow in our domain.

Now consider an analogous language that specifies train journeys. The relations will all have similar statements. Only the domain will have changed.

Furthermore, these two languages combine to give relations over both train and bus journeys. If we specify that bus journeys are never related to train journeys in our language, then we have the disjunctive union of the bus and train journey languages.

Over this disjunctive union we can specify a single CSP whose solutions are journeys that are either a set of connecting trains, or a set of connecting buses. $\square$

We shall show that the disjunctive union combines tractable languages to give new, more expressive tractable languages. We shall give some idea of applications of this result by applying it to the bus/train toy example. The following is the key theorem that justifies the construction.

Theorem 27 *Let Γ_1 and Γ_2 be two tractable languages over the disjoint domains D_1 and D_2, respectively. Then $\Gamma_1 \overset{\times}{\uplus} \Gamma_2$ is also a tractable language.*

Proof: Let $\mathcal{P}$ be an instance of $\mathbf{C}_{\Gamma_1 \overset{\times}{\uplus} \Gamma_2}$. We apply the following algorithm to each connected component H of the underlying hypergraph of P in turn.

Since D_1 and D_2 are disjoint, by connectedness of H, solutions can take values from D_1 or from D_2 but not from both.

First, by ignoring values from D_2, determine using the polynomial algorithm for Γ_1 if there is a solution taking values from D_1. If a solution is found, output it and move on to the next connected component.

Otherwise, try to find a solution taking values in D_2 using the polynomial algorithm for Γ_2. If one is found, output it and move on.

Otherwise fail and conclude that there is no solution. $\square$

The proof above relies on the assumption that it is tractable to decompose a relation $R \in \Gamma_1 \overset{\times}{\uplus} \Gamma_2$ into its two component parts. We shall assume that relations are specified in such a way that this is the case.

5.1 THE POLYMORPHISMS RESULTING FROM THE DDU

In this section, we will construct the polymorphisms of the constraint language obtained by using the DDU. There are two reasons to consider these:

- First, given Theorem 18, the whole of $Inv(Pol(\Gamma_1 \overset{\times}{\uplus} \Gamma_2))$ is tractable. To calculate this, it will be useful to determine $Pol(\Gamma_1 \overset{\times}{\uplus} \Gamma_2)$.

- Second, all known tractable constraint languages over finite domains have simple descriptions in terms of their polymorphisms. We will use this fact in Corollary 41 to demonstrate that by using the DDU we are indeed constructing novel tractable classes of the CSP.

The next result shows that the relationship between the sets $Pol(\Gamma_1 \overset{\times}{\uplus} \Gamma_2)$, $Pol(\Gamma_1)$, and $Pol(\Gamma_2)$ is not straightforward.

Proposition 28 *The set of polymorphisms of the DDU of two constraint languages is not in general determined by the polymorphisms of the constraint languages.*

Proof: We prove this result by giving a specific counterexample.

Let $D = \{0, 1\}$ and $E = \{2, 3\}$, and consider the following three binary relations over D, D, and E, respectively.

$$
\begin{aligned}
R_1 &= \{\langle 0, 0\rangle, \langle 0, 1\rangle\} \\
R_2 &= \{\langle 0, 0\rangle, \langle 1, 0\rangle\} \\
R_3 &= \{\langle 2, 3\rangle, \langle 3, 3\rangle\}
\end{aligned}
$$

Since, R_1 and R_2 are (column) permutations of each other, we have, by Lemma 17, $Pol(\{R_1\}) = Pol(\{R_2\})$.

Now consider $\varphi : (D \cup E)^2 \to (D \cup E)$, defined by the following table:

φ	0	1	2	3
0	0	1	3	3
1	0	1	0	3
2	0	1	2	3
3	0	1	2	3

So, for example, $\varphi(1, 2) = 0$.

We have that:

$$
\begin{aligned}
\{R_1\} \uplus \{R_3\} &= \{\{\langle 0, 0\rangle, \langle 0, 1\rangle, \langle 2, 3\rangle, \langle 3, 3\rangle\}\} \\
\{R_2\} \uplus \{R_3\} &= \{\{\langle 0, 0\rangle, \langle 1, 0\rangle, \langle 2, 3\rangle, \langle 3, 3\rangle\}\}
\end{aligned}
$$

It is straightforward (but tedious) to verify that $\varphi \in Pol(\{R_1\} \uplus \{R_3\})$.

However, $\varphi(\langle 1, 0\rangle, \langle 2, 3\rangle) = \langle 0, 3\rangle$, and $\langle 0, 3\rangle \notin Pol(\{R_2\} \uplus \{R_3\})$.

So $Pol(\{R_1\} \uplus \{R_3\}) \neq Pol(\{R_2\} \uplus \{R_3\})$ and we are done. $\square$

We will now construct all possible polymorphisms of a disjunctive union of two constraint languages over disjoint domains. We first show in Lemma 31 that any such polymorphism is an arbitrary composition of simpler functions, then we will describe these simpler components.

Definition 29 *Let D be a set, and fix $k \in \mathbb{N}$ (note that k may be 0). A k-ary pattern on D is just a k-tuple of subsets of D.*

Definition 30 *Let D be a set, and let p be a k-ary pattern on D. For any k-ary total operation φ on D, the restriction of φ to p, written $\varphi_{|p}$, is the partial operation defined so that*

$$
\varphi_{|p}(x_1, x_2, \ldots, x_k) \stackrel{\text{def}}{=}
\begin{cases}
\varphi(x_1, x_2, \ldots, x_k) & \text{whenever each } x_i \in p[i] \\
\text{undefined} & \text{otherwise}
\end{cases}
$$

Similarly, if Φ is a set of operations over D, then

$$\Phi|_p \overset{\text{def}}{=} \{\varphi|_p : \varphi \in \Phi \wedge \varphi \text{ has arity } k\}$$

We are now in a position to decompose a polymorphism of a disjoint disjunctive union of constraint languages.

Lemma 31 *Let Γ_1 and Γ_2 be constraint languages over disjoint domains D_1 and D_2, respectively. The following are equivalent:*

1. *$\varphi \in Pol(\Gamma_1 \overset{\times}{\cup} \Gamma_2)$*

2. *for every $p \in \{D_1, D_2\}^k$, $\Gamma_1 \overset{\times}{\cup} \Gamma_2$ is closed under $\varphi|_p$.*

Proof: We begin by assuming that statement 2 is true and prove statement 1.

If $\Gamma_1 \overset{\times}{\cup} \Gamma_2 = \emptyset$, then the result is trivially true. Otherwise, pick an arbitrary relation $R = (R_1 \cup R_2) \in \Gamma_1 \overset{\times}{\cup} \Gamma_2$, where $R_1 \in \Gamma_1$ and $R_2 \in \Gamma_2$. We shall show that R is closed under φ. Consider an arbitrary k-tuple $\langle t_1, t_2, \ldots, t_k \rangle$ of tuples from R. Define the pattern $p \in \{D_1, D_2\}^k$ by

$$p[i] \overset{\text{def}}{=} \begin{cases} D_1 & \text{if } t_i \in R_1; \\ D_2 & \text{if } t_i \in R_2. \end{cases}$$

By assumption, $\varphi|_p(t_1, t_2, \ldots, t_k)$ is defined and equal to some tuple $t \in R$. Thus $\varphi(t_1, t_2, \ldots, t_k) = t$, and we are done.

The proof of the converse is trivial: *any* set Γ of relations is closed under all partial versions of each of its polymorphisms. $\qquad\square$

Having given a decomposition of the polymorphisms into simpler functions, we now show that every such simpler function can occur as a component of a polymorphism.

Lemma 32 *Let Γ_1 and Γ_2 be constraint languages over disjoint domains D_1 and D_2, respectively.*

If $p \in \{D_1, D_2\}^k$, and φ is a partial k-ary closure operation on $\Gamma_1 \overset{\times}{\cup} \Gamma_2$ that is defined for all tuples of pattern p, then φ can be extended to a total closure operation on $D_1 \cup D_2$.

Proof: It is obvious that $Pol(\Gamma_1 \overset{\times}{\cup} \Gamma_2)$ contains the projection e_1 of arity k that picks out its first argument.

We use Lemma 31 to construct a polymorphism that extends φ. We simply set

$$\Phi(x) \overset{\text{def}}{=} \begin{cases} \varphi(x) & \text{whenever } x \text{ has pattern } p \\ e_1(x) & \text{otherwise} \end{cases}$$

$\qquad\square$

Our quest to determine the polymorphisms of the disjunctive union of two constraint languages over disjoint domains has now been reduced to determining the closure operations with domains restricted to particular patterns. The answer relies on the following definition.

Definition 33 *We say that a k-ary operation ψ masks an r-ary operation ψ', and write $\psi \leadsto \psi'$ if there exists some subset $\{u_1, \ldots, u_r\} \subseteq \{1, \ldots, k\}$ such that, whenever $\psi(x_1, \ldots, x_r)$ is defined:*

$$\psi(x_1, \ldots, x_k) = \psi'(x_{u_1}, \ldots, x_{u_r})$$

Clearly these are the same operation, except that ψ ignores some of its arguments (those not in $\{u_1, \ldots, u_r\}$).

Given two sets D_1 and D_2, and two sets of total operations Ψ_1, and Ψ_2, over D_1 and D_2, respectively, we say that an operation $\varphi : \{D_1 \cup D_2\}^k \to \{D_1 \cup D_2\}$ is synthesizable *from $\Psi = \Psi_1 \cup \Psi_2$ if every restriction of φ to a pattern in $\{D_1, D_2\}^k$ masks an operation from Ψ.*

$$\forall p \in \{D_1, D_2\}^k, \exists \psi \in \Psi, \varphi_{|_p} \leadsto \psi$$

The set of all operations that are synthesizable from Ψ will be denoted $Syn(\Psi)$.

Example 34 Define for each $j \leq r \leq k$ operations $\psi_{r,j}$ and $\overline{\psi}_{r,j}$ of arity r as follows:

$$\psi_{r,j} : \{0, 1\}^r \to \{0, 1\}, \quad \text{with} \quad \psi_{r,j}(x_1, x_2, \ldots, x_r) = x_j$$
$$\overline{\psi}_{r,j} : \{2, 3\}^r \to \{2, 3\}, \quad \text{with} \quad \overline{\psi}_{r,j}(x_1, x_2, \ldots, x_r) = 5 - x_j$$

Now let $\Psi_1 = \{\psi_{r,j} : j \leq r \leq k\}$, and $\Psi_2 = \{\overline{\psi}_{r,j} : j \leq r \leq k\}$, and $\Psi = \Psi_1 \cup \Psi_2$. We can describe a typical operation $\psi \in Syn(\Psi)$ as follows:

Let k be the arity of ψ. Then the restriction of ψ to any pattern $p \in \{\{0, 1\}, \{2, 3\}\}^k$ will ignore all but one of its arguments—say x_j—nd furthermore,

$$\psi_{|_p}(x_1, x_2, \ldots, x_k) = \begin{cases} x_j & \text{if } p[j] = \{0, 1\} \\ 5 - x_j & \text{if } p[j] = \{2, 3\}. \end{cases}$$

$\square$

The following proposition extends the set of polymorphisms of the disjoint disjunctive union guaranteed by Lemma 32.

Proposition 35 *Let Γ_1 and Γ_2 be constraint languages over the disjoint domains D_1 and D_2, respectively. Then*

$$Syn(Pol(\Gamma_1) \cup Pol(\Gamma_2)) \subseteq Pol(\Gamma_1 \uplus \Gamma_2)$$

Proof: Fix any $\varphi \in Syn(Pol(\Gamma_1) \cup Pol(\Gamma_2))$, of arity k, and let $p \in \{D_1, D_2\}^k$. By Lemma 31, it is enough to show that $\Gamma_1 \uplus \Gamma_2$ is closed under $\varphi_{|_p}$. Take any $R \in \Gamma_1 \uplus \Gamma_2$, where R is the union of some $R_1 \in \Gamma_1$ and $R_2 \in \Gamma_2$. By the definition of synthesis, we may assume without loss of generality that there exists some $\psi \in Pol(\Gamma_1)$ of arity r such that

$$\varphi_{|_p}(x_1, x_2, \ldots, x_k) = \psi(x_{u_1}, x_{u_2}, \ldots, x_{u_r})$$

where each $p[u_i] = D_1$.

Consider an arbitrary k-tuple $\langle t_1, t_2, \ldots, t_k \rangle$ of tuples from R with the property that for each i, t_i comes from relation R_1 if $p[i] = D_1$, and from R_2 otherwise. (By the definition of closure, these are the only tuples that we need to consider.) Then

$$\varphi_{|_p}(t_1, t_2, \ldots, t_k) = \psi(t_{u_1}, t_{u_2}, \ldots, t_{u_r}) = t$$

for some $t \in R_1$, since R_1 is closed under ψ. However, $R_1 \subseteq R$, so $t \in R$, and hence R is closed under $\varphi_{|_p}$. $\qquad\qquad\Box$

Example 36 To continue Example 34.

Choose any $\Gamma_1 \subseteq Inv(\Psi_1)$ and $\Gamma_2 \subseteq Inv(\Psi_2)$. Since the domains of Γ_1 ($\{0,1\}$) and of Γ_2 ($\{2,3\}$) are disjoint, all the operations described in the example are contained within $Pol(\Gamma_1 \overset{\times}{\cup} \Gamma_2)$. $\qquad\qquad\Box$

5.2 RESTRICTING THE POSSIBLE POLYMORPHISMS

Proposition 35 is a positive result: it tells us that no matter which sets Γ_1 and Γ_2 of relations we begin with, we can always guarantee the existence of certain operations in $Pol(\Gamma_1 \overset{\times}{\cup} \Gamma_2)$. We now turn our attention in the other direction and examine how placing restrictions on the allowable Γ_i restricts the polymorphisms of their disjunctive union. The motivation for doing this is provided by Example 28. That example shows that the containment demonstrated in Proposition 35 is not, in general, an equality. By restricting the Γ_i however, we will be able to give a sufficient condition to ensure that equality does hold in many important cases.

Proposition 37 *Let Γ_1 and Γ_2 be relational clones over disjoint domains D_1 and D_2, respectively. Then for every $\varphi_{|_p} \in Pol(\Gamma_1 \overset{\times}{\cup} \Gamma_2)_{|_p}$ of arity k (with $p \in \{D_1, D_2\}^k$) it is the case that either $range(\varphi_{|_p}) \subseteq D_1$ or $range(\varphi_{|_p}) \subseteq D_2$.*

Proof: Fix k, let $p \in \{D_1, D_2\}^k$ be a pattern, and choose any $\varphi_{|_p} \in Pol(\Gamma_1 \overset{\times}{\cup} \Gamma_2)$. Define $R = \otimes_{D_1} \cup \otimes_{D_2}$ (recall that $\otimes_D$ is defined to be $D \times D$). Since each Γ_i is a relational clone, $R \in \Gamma_1 \overset{\times}{\cup} \Gamma_2$, and is therefore closed under $\varphi_{|_p}$. Let t and t' be two k-tuples of pattern p. We shall show that $\varphi_{|_p}(t)$ and $\varphi_{|_p}(t')$ lie in the same domain.

Consider the sequence $s_1, s_2, \ldots, s_k$ of tuples from R defined for every i by $s_i = \langle t[i], t'[i] \rangle$. Then $\varphi_{|_p}(s_1, s_2, \ldots, s_k)$ is well defined (since t and t' are both of pattern p), and equal to some pair $r \in R$. Both elements of r lie in the same domain. But $r[1] = \varphi_{|_p}(t)$ and $r[2] = \varphi_{|_p}(t')$, so in particular, $\varphi_{|_p}(t)$ lies in the same domain as $\varphi_{|_p}(t')$. $\qquad\Box$

Lemma 38 *Let Γ_1 and Γ_2 be relational clones over disjoint domains D_1 and D_2, respectively, and let $p \in \{D_1, D_2\}^k$ be a pattern. For every $\varphi \in Pol(\Gamma_1 \overset{\times}{\cup} \Gamma_2)$, it is the case that $\varphi_{|_p}$ depends solely on those of its arguments that come from the same domain as does $range(\varphi_{|_p})$.*

Proof: In the light of Proposition 37, we may assume without loss of generality that $range(\varphi_{|_p}) \subseteq D_1$. Define $R \in \Gamma_1 \overset{\times}{\cup} \Gamma_2$ by $R \overset{\text{def}}{=} (\otimes_{D_2}) \cup (=_{D_1})$. By Lemma 31, R is closed under $\varphi_{|_p}$.

Let $t, t' \in (D_1 \cup D_2)^k$ be tuples of pattern p with the property that whenever $p[i] = D_1$, it is the case that $t[i] = t'[i]$. It is enough to show that $\varphi_{|_p}(t) = \varphi_{|_p}(t')$. So define the sequence

$s_1, s_2, \ldots, s_k$ of tuples from R by setting $s_i = \langle t[i], t'[i] \rangle$ for every i. Then $\varphi_{|_P}$ is well defined and, by assumption equal to some $r \in (=_{D_1})$. But then $\varphi_{|_p}(t) = r[1] = r[2] = \varphi_{|_p}(t')$. $\square$

Theorem 39 *Let Γ_1 and Γ_2 be relational clones over the disjoint domains D_1 and D_2, respectively. Then*

$$Pol(\Gamma_1 \mathbin{\breve{\cup}} \Gamma_2) = Syn(Pol(\Gamma_1) \cup Pol(\Gamma_2))$$

Proof: The inclusion $Syn(Pol(\Gamma_1) \cup Pol(\Gamma_2)) \subseteq Pol(\Gamma_1 \mathbin{\breve{\cup}} \Gamma_2)$ was proved in Proposition 35. Here, we prove the inclusion in the other direction.

Choose an arbitrary $\varphi \in Pol(\Gamma_1 \mathbin{\breve{\cup}} \Gamma_2)$ of arity k, and take some $p \in \{D_1, D_2\}^k$. Assume without loss of generality that $range(\varphi_{|_p}) \subseteq D_1$, and consider any r-ary operation φ' over D_1, which has been obtained from $\varphi_{|_p}$ by arbitrarily fixing those of its arguments that come from D_2. Since every relation in $\Gamma_1 \mathbin{\breve{\cup}} \Gamma_2$ is closed under $\varphi_{|_p}$, it is clear that every relation in Γ_1 is closed under φ'; that is, that $\varphi' \in Pol(\Gamma_1)$. By Lemma 38, $\varphi_{|_p}$ masks φ'. Since this argument holds for any pattern p, it follows that $\varphi \in Syn(Pol(\Gamma_1) \cup Pol(\Gamma_2))$.
$\square$

6 GENERATING NOVEL TRACTABLE CLASSES

We are now in a position to determine whether combining tractable relations using the DDU operator gives rise to tractable classes that are genuinely novel. We will do this using the characterization of all known tractable constraint languages over finite domains given in Section 4.1.

Proposition 40 *Suppose that Γ_1 and Γ_2 are relational clones over the disjoint domains D_1 and D_2, respectively. Let Φ be some class of operations that can be defined by identities, and suppose that there is no $\varphi \in Pol(\Gamma_1)$ that is in the class Φ. Then there is no nonconstant $\varphi \in Pol(\Gamma_1 \mathbin{\breve{\cup}} \Gamma_2)$ that is in the class Φ.*

Proof: Let $\varphi \in Pol(\Gamma_1 \mathbin{\breve{\cup}} \Gamma_2)$ be a nonconstant operation. By Theorem 39, $\varphi \in Syn(Pol(\Gamma_1) \cup Pol(\Gamma_2))$. Now, φ has a strictly positive arity, and so the restriction of φ to the domain D_1 is a member of $Pol(\Gamma_1)$, and thus fails to satisfy the identities defining property Φ. Consequently, φ itself fails to satisfy these identities, and so $\varphi \notin \Phi$. $\square$

Corollary 41 *The $\breve{\cup}$ operation is capable of generating genuinely new tractable sets of relations.*

Proof: This is because all previously known tractable constraint languages over finite domains are characterized by being closed under some polymorphism defined by identities.
$\square$

In fact, it is relatively easy to construct genuinely new tractable languages using the technique of DDU. Suppose that

Example 42

$$R_1 \;=\; \{\langle 0,0,1,0\rangle, \quad \text{and} \quad R_2 \;=\; \{\langle 3,2,2,3\rangle,$$
$$\langle 0,1,0,0\rangle, \qquad\qquad\qquad \langle 2,3,2,2\rangle\}.$$
$$\langle 1,0,0,0\rangle,$$
$$\langle 1,1,1,0\rangle\}$$

Let $\Gamma_1 = Inv(Pol(R_1))$ and $\Gamma_2 = Inv(Pol(R_2))$.

It is easy to check that R_1 is tractable. R_1 is closed under an affine operation that guarantees tractability, but not under any other operation known to yield tractability. Similarly, R_2 is closed under both near-unanimity and affine operations that guarantee tractability, but not under anything else significant.

We can verify by hand that $\Gamma_1 \mathbin{\breve{\cup}} \Gamma_2$ is not closed under any affine operations. By Proposition 40, therefore, $\Gamma_1 \mathbin{\breve{\cup}} \Gamma_2$ is a tractable set of relations that does not fall into any previously known tractable class. $\qquad\square$

Consider again the bus and train language of Example 26.

Example 43 If both the bus language and the train language are tractable (for any reason), or we restrict ourselves to tractable sublanguages, then the bus/train disjunctive union language is also tractable.

Determination of the polymorphisms of the disjunctive union has allowed us to investigate its novelty. We have shown in this section that the disjunctive union that allowed us to specify either bus journeys or train journeys in one problem could not (usually) have been constructed using any of the previously known reasons for tractability. $\qquad\square$

7 EXPRESSIVENESS OF THE DISJUNCTIVE UNION

We can also use our construction of the polymorphisms of the DDU to construct new relations whose inclusion will not affect tractability.

Theorem 18 says that in fact the whole of $Inv(Pol(\Gamma_1 \mathbin{\breve{\cup}} \Gamma_2))$ is tractable, so our question reduces to the following: Are there any relations that are present in $Inv(Pol(\Gamma_1 \mathbin{\breve{\cup}} \Gamma_2))$, but not present in $\Gamma_1 \mathbin{\breve{\cup}} \Gamma_2$?

Consider the Cartesian product operator, $\times$, defined on pairs of relations by

$$R_1 \times R_2 \stackrel{\text{def}}{=} \{r_1 r_2 : r_1 \in R_1 \wedge r_2 \in R_2\}$$

(where $r_1 r_2$ denotes the concatenation of the two tuples).

The following lemma comes essentially from (Jeavons 1998).

Lemma 44 *Let Γ_1 and Γ_2 be constraint languages over the disjoint domains D_1 and D_2, respectively, and let $R_1, R_2 \in Inv(Pol(\Gamma_1 \mathbin{\breve{\cup}} \Gamma_2))$ be any two relations (not necessarily over disjoint, or even different domains). Then $R_1 \times R_2 \in Inv(Pol(\Gamma_1 \mathbin{\breve{\cup}} \Gamma_2))$.*

Example 45 Let Γ_1 and Γ_2 be as defined in Example 42. Since these languages are over finite domains, we can appeal to Theorem 18. In this case, $Inv(Pol(\Gamma_1 \mathbin{\breve{\cup}} \Gamma_2))$ contains many additional relations whose tractability could not have been previously deduced. Among these, we not only have the relation

$$R_1 \times R_2 \;=\; \{\quad \langle 0, 0, 1, 0, 3, 2, 2, 3 \rangle,$$
$$\langle 0, 0, 1, 0, 2, 3, 2, 2 \rangle,$$
$$\langle 0, 1, 0, 0, 3, 2, 2, 3 \rangle,$$
$$\langle 0, 1, 0, 0, 2, 3, 2, 2 \rangle,$$
$$\langle 1, 0, 0, 0, 3, 2, 2, 3 \rangle,$$
$$\langle 1, 0, 0, 0, 2, 3, 2, 2 \rangle,$$
$$\langle 1, 1, 1, 0, 3, 2, 2, 3 \rangle,$$
$$\langle 1, 1, 1, 0, 2, 3, 2, 2 \rangle \;\},$$

itself, but also all of its permutations and projections. We also have the relation R of Example 11. For R is a permutation of $(R_1 \cup R_2) \times \{\langle 2 \rangle\}$, where $\{\langle 2 \rangle\}$, being a projection of R_2, is a member of $\Gamma_1 \overset{\times}{\cup} \Gamma_2$. $\qquad\qquad\Box$

This example demonstrates the power of the algebraic framework developed above and in (Jeavons 1998; Jeavons et al. 1997; Jeavons et al. 1999). For although the original algorithm given in Theorem 27 is a simple one, the algebraic results allow us to immediately extend it to a much larger class of constraint problems than is first apparent. These derived classes of problems appear to have little to do with disjoint domains.

To conclude this section, we return to our bus and train language of Example 26.

Example 46 Determination of the polymorphisms of the disjunctive union now allows us to investigate its expressiveness. We notice that we can include some relations involving both buses and trains. In fact, we can allow the constraints that change from bus to train journeys and vice versa. It follows that we can now specify CSPs that allow changes from bus to train and train to bus.

If both the bus language and the train language are tractable (for any reason), or we restrict ourselves to tractable sublanguages, then the bus/train language is also tractable.

The algebra has allowed us to discover this larger (more usable) tractable language. $\qquad\Box$

8 CONCLUSION

In this chapter, we have shown how combining tractable constraint languages can yield hitherto unknown, tractable languages. The algorithm (in the proof of Theorem 27) that establishes the tractability of these combinations is particularly simple, yet we have been able to exploit algebraic properties of the new constraint languages to show that even larger languages are tractable than those that can be directly solved by this algorithm. This result demonstrates once again the power of the algebraic approach to analyzing constraint satisfaction problems.

This work is related to that of (Cohen et al. 2000). In that paper, the authors considered the effect of combining tractable sets of relations on a *single* domain. One question that naturally arises is to ask what can be said about the disjunctive union when there are two domains that are partially disjoint, but that overlap in one or more places. This is a question we intend to address in the future.

The results presented in this chapter take us one step closer to the ultimate goal of classifying the complexity of all possible constraint languages over finite domains.

However, recall from the Introduction that limiting the constraint language is just one of the ways to ensure tractability of a subclass of the general CSP. Much successful work has been done both on constraint languages and on structural theorems. What seems to be missing is work that guarantees tractability based on some combination of structure and language.

To conclude, work on tractability in constraints has been very successful at identifying tractable classes, but as yet, little work has been done on related problems, such as the *recognition* problems for tractable classes: Given a general constraint problem, is it feasible to recognize whether it lies in one of the known tractable classes? Also, much of the work done in this field applies only to finite domains. It would be useful and interesting to extend the results to infinite domains.

References

Bulatov, A. A., and P. G. Jeavons (2000). *Tractable constraints closed under a binary operation.* Technical Report PRG-TR-12-00, Oxford University Computing Laboratory.

Bulatov, A. A., A. A. Krokhin, and P. G. Jeavons (2000). Constraint satisfaction problems and finite algebras. In *Proceedings of the 27th International Colloquium on Automata, Languages and Programming—ICALP'00*, Vol. 1853 of *Lecture Notes in Computer Science*, 272–282. Berlin: Springer-Verlag.

Cohen, D. A., M. Gyssens, and P. G. Jeavons (1996). Derivation of constraints and database relations. In *Proceedings of the 2nd International Conference on Constraint Programming—CP'96*, Boston, Vol. 1118 of *Lecture Notes in Computer Science*, 134–148. Berlin: Springer-Verlag.

Cohen, D. A., P. G. Jeavons, and R. L. Gault (2000). New tractable classes from old. In *Principles and Practice of Constraint Programming—CP 2000*, Vol. 1894 of *Lecture Notes in Computer Science*, 160–171. Berlin: Springer-Verlag.

Cohen, D. A., P. G. Jeavons, P. Jonsson, and M. Koubarakis (2000). Building tractable disjunctive constraints. *Journal of the ACM 47*, 826–853.

Cohn, P. M. (1965). *Universal Algebra.* New York: Harper & Row.

Cooper, M. C., D. A. Cohen, and P. G. Jeavons (1994). Characterising tractable constraints. *Artificial Intelligence 65*, 347–361.

Dechter, R. (1992). From local to global consistency. *Artificial Intelligence 55*(1), 87–107.

Feder, T., and M. Y. Vardi (1998). The computational structure of monotone monadic SNP and constraint satisfaction: A study through Datalog and group theory. *SIAM Journal of Computing 28*(1), 57–104.

Freuder, E. C. (1982). A sufficient condition for backtrack-free search. *Journal of the ACM 29*(1), 24–32.

Freuder, E. C. (1985). A sufficient condition for backtrack-bounded search. *Journal of the ACM 32*, 755–761.

Garey, M., and D. S. Johnson (1979). *Computers and Intractability: A Guide to the Theory of NP-Completeness.* San Francisco: Freeman.

Gottlob, G., N. Leone, and F. Scarcello (1999). A comparison of structural CSP decomposition methods. In *Proceedings of the 16th International Joint Conference on Artificial Intelligence (IJCAI)*, 394–399. San Francisco: Morgan Kaufmann Publishers.

Jeavons, P. G. (1998). On the algebraic structure of combinatorial problems. *Theoretical Computer Science 200*, 185–204.

Jeavons, P. G., and D. A. Cohen (1995). An algebraic characterization of tractable constraints. In *Computing and Combinatorics. First International Conference CO-COON'95*, Xi'an, China, Vol. 959 of *Lecture Notes in Computer Science*, 633–642. Berlin: Springer-Verlag.

Jeavons, P. G., D. A. Cohen, and M. Gyssens (1996). A test for tractability. In *Proceedings of the Second International Conference on Constraint Programming—CP'96*, Boston, Vol. 1118 of *Lecture Notes in Computer Science*, 267–281. Berlin: Springer-Verlag.

Jeavons, P. G., D. A. Cohen, and M. Gyssens (1997). Closure properties of constraints. *Journal of the ACM 44*, 527–548.

Jeavons, P. G., D. A. Cohen, and J. K. Pearson (1999). Constraints and universal algebra. *Annals of Mathematics and Artificial Intelligence 24*, 51–67.

Jeavons, P. G. and M. C. Cooper (1995). Tractable constraints on ordered domains. *Artificial Intelligence 79*(2), 327–339.

Kirousis, L. (1993). Fast parallel constraint satisfaction. *Artificial Intelligence 64*, 147–160.

Koubarakis, M. (1997). From local to global consistency in temporal constraint networks. *Theoretical Computer Science 173*(1), 89–112.

Ladkin, P. B., and R. D. Maddux (1994). On binary constraint problems. *Journal of the ACM 41*, 435–469.

Lesaint, D., N. Azarmi, R. Laithwaite, and P. Walker (1998). Engineering dynamic scheduler for work manager. *BT Technology Journal 16*, 16–29.

Mackworth, A. K. (1977). Consistency in networks of relations. *Artificial Intelligence 8*, 99–118.

McKenzie, R. N., G. F. McNulty, and W. F. Taylor (1987). *Algebras, Lattices and Varieties*, Volume I. Pacific Grove, CA: Wadsworth and Brooks.

Montanari, U. (1974). Networks of constraints: Fundamental properties and applications to picture processing. *Information Sciences 7*, 95–132.

Nebel, B., and H. Bürckert (1995). Reasoning about temporal relations: A maximal tractable subclass of Allen's interval algebra. *Journal of the ACM 42*(1), 43–66.

Pearson, J. K., and P. G. Jeavons (1997). A survey of tractable constraint satisfaction problems. Technical Report CSD-TR-97-15, Royal Holloway, University of London.

Purvis, L., and P. Jeavons (1999). Constraint tractability theory and its application to the product development process for a constraint-based scheduler. In *Proceedings of the First International Conference on the Practical Application of Constraint Technologies and Logic Programming—PACLP'99*, 63–79.

Schaefer, T. J. (1978). The complexity of satisfiability problems. In *Proceedings of the 10th ACM Symposium on Theory of Computing (STOC)*, 216–226.

van Beek, P., and R. Dechter (1995). On the minimality and global consistency of row-convex constraint networks. *Journal of the ACM 42*(3), 543–561.

User-Oriented Evaluation Methods for Information Retrieval: A Case Study Based on Conceptual Models for Query Expansion

Jaana Kekäläinen
Department of Information Studies
33014 University of Tampere
Finland
jaana.kekalainen@uta.fi

Kalervo Järvelin
Department of Information Studies
33014 University of Tampere
Finland
kalervo.jarvelin@uta.fi

Abstract

This chapter discusses evaluation methods based on the use of nondichotomous relevance judgments in *information retrieval* (*IR*) experiments. It is argued that evaluation methods should credit IR methods for their ability to retrieve highly relevant documents. This is desirable from the user's point of view in modern large IR environments. The proposed methods are (1) a novel application of P-R curves and average precision computations based on separate recall bases for documents of different degrees of relevance, and (2) two novel measures computing the cumulative gain the user obtains by examining the retrieval result up to a given ranked position. We then demonstrate the use of these evaluation methods in a case study on the effectiveness of query types, based on combinations of query structures and expansion, in retrieving documents of various degrees of relevance. Query expansion is based on concepts, which are selected from a conceptual model, and then expanded by semantic relationships given in the model. The test is run with a best-match retrieval system (InQuery)[1] in a text database consisting of newspaper articles. The case study indicates the usability of domain-dependent conceptual models in query expansion for IR. The results show that expanded queries with a strong query structure are most

---

[1] The InQuery software was provided by the Center for Intelligent Information Retrieval, University of Massachusetts Computer Science Department, Amherst, MA, USA.

effective in retrieving highly relevant documents. The differences between the query types are practically essential and statistically significant. More generally, the novel evaluation methods and the case demonstrate that nondichotomous relevance assessments are applicable in IR experiments and allow harder testing of IR methods. Proposed methods are user-oriented because users' benefits and efforts—highly relevant documents and number of documents to be examined—are taken into account.

1   INTRODUCTION

Information retrieval (IR for short) research develops concepts, methods, and systems through which all information—in different forms and places—is easily accessible in forms as convenient as possible for those who need it. IR is concerned with storage and retrieval of—mainly digital—documents. While natural language is the most common means in communication of information, the problems of textual retrieval have been a major issue in research. In this chapter we shall discuss text-based IR—that is, retrieval of text documents or text-based retrieval of multimedia documents.

The reasons why people seek information are called *information needs*. These needs are varied because persons looking for information have different background knowledge and situations, tasks, or activities from which information needs arise are varied. Information needs may be categorized into (1) *verificative*, (2) *conscious topical*, and (3)*muddled* or *ill-defined* needs. The first category refers to situations where documents with known properties are sought (e.g., by author name, titles of known authors, etc.). The second type implies that the topic is known and definable, but less exact than in the first category. The person looking for information has some level of understanding of it. In the third category are the cases in which a person wishes to find new knowledge and concepts he or she is not able to describe in detail (Ingwersen and Willett 1995).

Figure 1 illustrates the information storage and retrieval process. An IR system encompasses the belief that information can be organized and represented for retrieval, and the needed information can be described as a set of words. Because this study is about text retrieval, documents are assumed to have textual representations. In a database, documents are represented by their full text, some part of the text or a description in a documentation language, or by some combination of these. The representations—whatever they are—are saved as character strings, say, in an inverted file, which is a typical file structure used in text-based retrieval. A string representing a document is a *key*.

Information needs should be expressed in natural language to be communicable in text retrieval. This formulation is known as a *request* . If a decision is made to use an IR system, the request must be adapted to the conditions of the system—that is, it must be translated to correspond to the representation of documents. A request translated into a form acceptable for the retrieval mechanism is known as a *query* . Queries consist of *search keys*, which are usually words or phrases represented by character strings, and operators, which express the requirements for the occurrences of the keys. The query language of an IR system defines the operators and a syntax for queries. Queries are matched with the representations of documents. These representations consist of text keys, which are stored into the index of a database as character strings. *Matching* refers to matching of character

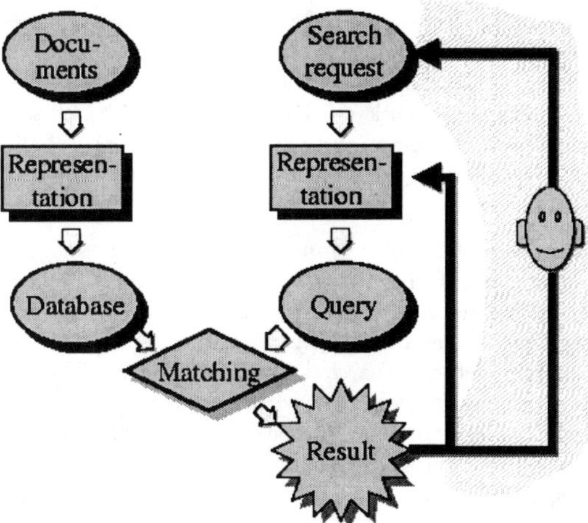

Figure 1 Information storage and retrieval process.

strings, hence, no meanings are involved and talking about matching of search words or terms is somewhat misleading.

Query formulation is not a trivial task, because the information need behind it may be ill-defined. In natural language one idea or subject may be expressed in countless ways. To retrieve all documents that contain potentially relevant[2] information for the information need, one should find all the expressions that have been used to represent that information. Thus, sticking to words obscures the many-to-many relationship between subjects and expressions, or concepts and words.

Nonprofessional searchers tend to formulate queries with only few search keys. This causes problems because of the variability of expressions in the natural language of documents. *Query expansion (QE)* is a method of adding new search keys to a query to obtain a better correspondence between the query and documents carrying potential information. Expansion keys are usually elicited from the search results of an original (unexpanded) query or some external source, such as vocabularies (Efthimiadis 1996; Xu and Croft 1996).

Text-retrieval methods may be divided into exact and partial (or best) match methods (Belkin and Croft 1987; Ingwersen and Willett 1995). The former is, in practice, Boolean retrieval; the latter consists of several methods, of which the most prevalent are perhaps probabilistic methods and methods based on the vector space model. In Boolean retrieval, a database is divided into two parts: documents that exactly match the query (the result set, presumed relevant documents), and documents that do not match (presumed nonrelevant

---

[2] Relevance is a central concept in IR research, and it is much debated. By relevant information, we mean information the searcher wants to retrieve for their information needs. In the evaluation of IR methods, relevant documents are those that match the topic of the information need (Cosijn and Ingwersen 2000; Saracevic 1996).

documents). The query expresses the retrieval conditions in Boolean logic. All documents in the result set are assumed to have equal relevance. In best-match retrieval, all documents of the database or documents containing at least one search key are ranked according to their presumed relevance. The scores of documents are calculated from weights given to text keys, and possibly also to search keys. The weighting of the keys is usually based on the frequency of the key in a document and the inverse frequency of the key in the whole database (known as *tf.idf* weighting[3]) (Hersh 1996; Ingwersen and Willett 1995; Salton 1989; Sparck Jones 1972).

The formulation of queries is different within the different retrieval methods. With *query structure*, we refer to the use of operators to express relations between search keys. In Boolean retrieval, operators based on Boolean logic are available to indicate conjunctions, disjunctions, and negations of search keys, as well as parentheses to mark the order of operations. In best-match methods search keys may appear without explicitly marked relations, or the relations may be expressed with operators, which guide the calculation of scores from the weights of the keys. The structure of queries may be described as weak (queries without differentiated relations between search keys) or strong (queries with several operators, differentiated relationships between search keys).

IR systems typically deliver documents containing the searched information rather than direct answers to questions. Yet the retrieved documents do not contain relevant information to the same degree. In modern large database environments, the number of topically relevant documents to a request may easily exceed the number of documents a user is willing to examine. It would therefore be desirable from the user's viewpoint to rank highly relevant documents highest in the retrieval results and to develop and evaluate IR methods accordingly. In the best-match methods, the scores given to documents do not reflect the degree of relevance but the probability of relevance (i.e., the probability that a document is either relevant or not) (Robertson and Belkin 1978).

For IR evaluation, documents are typically assessed for relevance and nonrelevance. IR methods or systems are then compared according to their ability to retrieve relevant documents and rank them high among retrieved documents. Documents can also be assessed according to the relevance levels. The effects of using multiple relevance levels may be evaluated through traditional IR evaluation methods such as *precision-recall* (*P-R*) *curves* (see Section 3). In this chapter we apply P-R curves in a new way, focusing on retrieval at each relevance level separately. Moreover, to emphasize the user's viewpoint, we develop new evaluation measures, which seek to estimate the cumulated relevance gain the user receives by examining the retrieval result up to a given rank. These measures facilitate evaluation where IR methods are credited more (or only) for highly relevant documents (Järvelin and Kekäläinen 2000). These novel measures are akin to some previous measures but offer several advantages by taking both the degree of relevance and the rank position (determined by the probability of relevance) of a document into account.

---

[3] The abbreviation *tf* means *term frequency*—that is, frequency of the key t in a document—and *idf* means *inverse document frequency*, which is often given as $\log(N/n)$, where N is the number of documents in the collection, and n is the number of documents containing the key t. NB. We use "key" rather than "term" because we reserve "term" to refer to certain units of documentation languages. A search key, by contrast, may be a natural language word, an abbreviation, a term, and so on.

The case demonstrating the effects of multiple-degree relevance assessments, and the application of traditional / novel evaluation measures explores query expansion and query structures in probabilistic IR. We have observed earlier (Kekäläinen 1999; Kekäläinen and Järvelin 1998) that the structure of queries influences retrieval performance when the number of search keys in queries is high—that is, when queries are expanded. We reported significant retrieval improvements with expanded, strongly structured queries. However, in our study the relevance assessments were dichotomous. We therefore do not know how different best-match query types (based on expansion and structure) are able to rank documents of varying relevance levels. In the case study we investigate their ability to do this.

The chapter is organized as follows: In Section 2 we shall discuss conceptual models and concept-based IR, which are needed in the case study; in Section 3 we shall present the evaluation methods and compare them to other, related measures in IR; and in Section 4 we present the case study. Discussion is in Section 5 and conclusions in Section 6.

2   CONCEPTUAL MODELS

Information science and related fields have employed conceptual models for data and information organization, representation, classification, and retrieval. A conceptual model explicitly describes a domain of interest by giving its concepts, relations between the concepts, and possibly the definitions of the concepts. Conceptual models are referred to by several names, such as thesauri, classifications, and ontologies (Soergel 1999). They differ in their formality, structure, and use. Less formal models use natural language or a restricted vocabulary for representing concepts and semantic relations, which may or may be not differentiated. Formal models are expressed in artificial languages (e.g., description logics), which allow meticulous definitions for concepts (Uschold and Gruninger 1996). As a consequence, semantic relations between concepts are differentiated and clear because the fuzziness of natural language is eliminated.

Conceptual models are used as unifying frameworks (or shared understanding) for communication between people with different viewpoints and needs, and for interoperability among systems with different paradigms, languages, and software tools (Guarino et al. 1998; Uschold and Gruninger 1996). Next we shall give some examples of the uses of different types of conceptual models.

- *Classification and categorization*[4] are the traditional methods for information organization. Information items are attached into the best-matching category in a predefined set of categories. Classification schemes are kind of conceptual models. They may use numeric notations like the *ACM Computing Classification System*[5] or terms like *Unified Medical Language System*.[6] Thesauri are the kind of classifications used for document content description. Classification may be intellectual or automatic; the latter does not necessarily require predefined classes, is less expensive but also

---

[4] Classification and categorization are not synonyms though they are often used as such (Jacob 1991). A rough distinction is that classes are mutually exclusive, but categories are necessarily not.

[5] CCS, see *www.acm.org/class/1998/*.

[6] UMLS, see *www.nlm.nih.gov/research/umls/UMLSDOC.HTML*.

less reliable and less understandable from a human point of view. Chen and Dumais (2000) report an example of automatic categorization of Web search results. The process involves a training phase and an operational phase. During the training phase, Web pages with known—and predefined—category labels are used to train the categorizer. During the operational phase, the learned system is used to categorize new Web pages on the fly.

- *Inference.* Conceptual models including conceptual relations have clear and explicit semantics that can be reasoned over. An obvious example is the use of hierarchical relations—if a document is about low-active waste, a conceptual model could state that then it also is about nuclear waste and radioactive waste. Ontologies typically have three major components that can be used in inference: a taxonomy (i.e., a generic classification with mutually exclusive classes), relations between concepts, and axioms for the relations (Bechhofer et al. 2001).

- *Personalization.* Because information needs and information-seeking situations vary from user to user, IR systems should support users in organizing (retrieved) information according to their personal needs (worldview). Chaffee and Gauch (2000) report on an IR system that allows users to build their own hierarchical concept trees, and maps a reference ontology to these personal models. The system classifies Web sites with concepts from the reference ontology and presents users the sites through their own model.

- *Concept-based IR* seeks to rise from the level of search keys to the level of concepts— that is, searchers should be able to express their information need in concepts rather than search keys. The IR system should support searchers in search key selection, query formulation, and expansion. Our aim is to equip the searcher with a conceptual model representing semantic relationships among concepts, and giving for each concept a set of search strings that may represent concepts in different search environments. The thesaural structure controlling hierarchies, associative relations, and synonymy is well suited for this kind of conceptual model. The model is managed by a tool that supports (1) searchers to automatically construct and expand effective queries without prior understanding about query structures and their interaction with expansion in various retrieval environments, and (2) QE experimentation with query structures, expansion, and other query construction parameters.

The conceptual model is based on a deductive data model and three abstraction levels (see Figure 2): the *conceptual level*, the *linguistic level*, and the *string level* (Järvelin et al. 2001; Järvelin et al. 1996). The conceptual level represents concepts and conceptual relationships (e.g., hierarchical generic and partitive relationship, association relationship). The linguistic level represents natural language expressions for the concepts and equivalence relations between them. Each concept may have several synonymous expressions with varied reliability. This is comparable to family resemblance or fuzzy membership: some expressions are more typical names for a concept, but others may be used as well. Each concept is denoted by a term (the principal name of the concept) and possibly a number of synonyms.[7] Concepts are identified through an identification code and the relations they have. One or more strings represent each expression—also of varied reliability—at

---

[7] Synonymy is understood rather loosely here (Miller 1995) Possible candidates are synonyms, quasisynonyms, corresponding verbs/nouns—a term is not necessarily a noun—and common names.

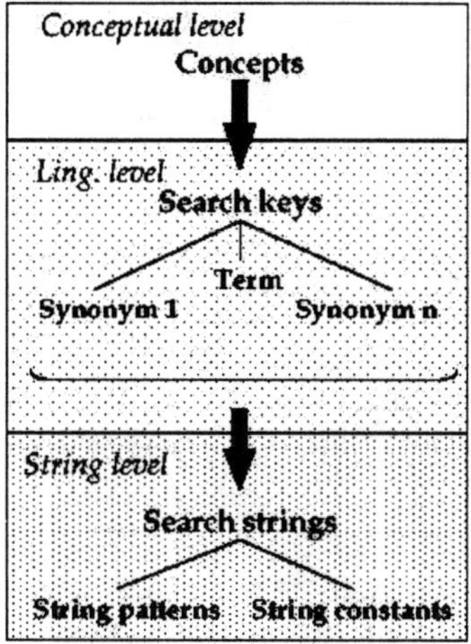

Figure 2 The abstraction levels of query formulation.

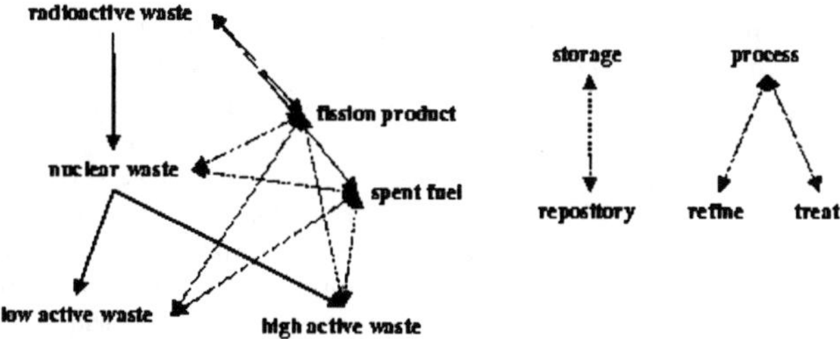

Figure 3 A sample of conceptual relations. Hierarchical relations are shown with solid arrows, associative relations with dashed arrows.

the string level. Each string is a matching pattern representing how the expression may be matched in database indices built in various ways (e.g., with or without compound words split into component words, and with or without *stemming*[8]). An example of the conceptual relations is given in Figure 3.

---

[8] Stemming means cutting off affixes in order to bring out the word stem (Alkula 2001).

3 EVALUATION METHODS EMPLOYING MULTIPLE-DEGREE RELEVANCE ASSESSMENTS

3.1 PRECISION AS A FUNCTION OF RECALL

Fundamental problems of IR experiments are linked to the assessment of relevance. In most laboratory tests, documents are judged relevant or irrelevant with regard to the request. However, binary relevance cannot reflect the possibility that documents may be relevant to a different degree; some documents contribute more information to the request, some less without being totally irrelevant. In some studies, relevance judgments are allowed to fall into more than two categories, but only a few tests actually take advantage of different relevance levels (Hersh and Hickam 1995). More often relevance is conflated into two categories at the analysis phase because of the calculation of precision and recall (Blair and Maron 1985; Saracevic et al. 1988).

Recall is defined as (Lancaster 1986)

$$Recall \;=\; \frac{number of relevant documents retrieved}{total number of relevant documents in the collection} \tag{1}$$

Precision is defined as (Lancaster 1986)

$$Precision \;=\; \frac{number of relevant documents retrieved}{total number of documents retrieved} \tag{2}$$

Retrieval evaluation results achieved by precision and recall are often presented as an average P-R curve which measures the precision at the same fixed levels of recall for all requests and averages the results. In the average P-R curve, precision and recall are used as a bivariate measure of retrieval effectiveness. Recall is defined as an independent variable and precision as a dependent variable, since precision is averaged at the fixed levels of recall. Because precision cannot be exactly defined at all fixed recall levels, interpolation is needed. Further, 100% recall is not reached by every algorithm or query, thus, a P-R curve is not faithful to actual data points. The assumptions attached to the P-R curve are that a particular level of recall must be attained by every request, and the best method is the one that reaches this level with the fewest number of nonrelevant documents. The P-R curve provides no information about the number of documents that have to be retrieved in order to reach a given recall level. Because requests have different numbers of relevant documents, a recall level of, say, 50% may mean a result set of 20 or 200 documents for different requests (Hull 1993; Keen 1992; Tague-Sutcliffe 1992).

The current practice of liberal binary assessment of topical relevance gives equal credit to a retrieval method for retrieving highly and fairly relevant documents. Therefore, differences between sloppy and excellent retrieval methods may not become apparent in evaluation. In order to see the difference in performance between retrieval methods, their performance should be evaluated separately at each relevance level. For example, in case of a four-point assessment (say, 0 to 3 points), separate recall bases[9] are needed for highly relevant documents (relevance level 3), fairly relevant documents (relevance level 2), and marginally

---

[9] In ideal IR experiments, the whole test collection is judged for relevance—that is, the relevance of each document in the collection in relation to every request is known. If the number of documents

relevant documents (relevance level 1). In this study, we compiled the recall bases for P-R curve computation in this way.

3.2   CUMULATED GAIN–BASED MEASUREMENTS

When examining the ranked result list of a query, it is obvious that

1. Highly relevant documents are more valuable than marginally relevant documents.

2. The greater the ranked position of a relevant document (of any relevance level), the less valuable it is for the user, because the less likely it is that the user will examine the document.

Point 1 leads to comparison of IR methods through test queries by their cumulated gain by document rank. In this evaluation, the relevance level of each document is somehow used as a gained-value measure for its ranked position in the result and the gain is summed progressively from position 1 to n. Thus the ranked document lists (of some determined length) are turned to gained-value lists by replacing document IDs with their relevance values. Assume that the relevance values 0 to 3 are used (3 denoting high value, 0 no value). Turning document lists up to rank 200 to corresponding value lists gives vectors of 200 components, each having the value 0, 1, 2, or 3. For example:

$$G' = \; <3,\, 2,\, 3,\, 0,\, 0,\, 1,\, 2,\, 2,\, 3,\, 0,\, \ldots>$$

The cumulated gain at ranked position i is computed by summing from position 1 to i when i ranges from 1 to 200. Formally, let us denote position i in the gain vector G by $G[i]$. Now the cumulated gain vector CG is defined recursively as the vector CG, where

$$CG[i] = \begin{cases} G[1] & \text{if } i = 1 \\ CG[i-1] + G[i] & \text{otherwise} \end{cases} \tag{3}$$

For example, from G' we obtain CG' = $<3, 5, 8, 8, 8, 9, 11, 13, 16, 16, \ldots>$. The cumulated gain at any rank may be read directly (e.g., at rank 7 it is 11).

Point 2 leads to comparison of IR methods through test queries by their cumulated gain based on document rank with a rank-based discount factor: the greater the rank, the smaller share of the document value is added to the cumulated gain. The greater the ranked position of a relevant document—of any relevance level—the less valuable it is for the user, because the less likely it is that the user will examine the document due to time, effort, and cumulated information from documents already seen. A discounting function is needed that progressively reduces the document value as its rank increases but not too steeply (e.g., as division by rank) to allow for user persistence in examining further documents. A simple way of discounting with this requirement is to divide the document value by the log of its rank. For example $^2\log 2 = 1$ and $^2\log 1024 = 10$; thus, a document at the position 1024 would still get one-tenth of it at face value. By selecting the base

---

in the collection is large, it may be impossible to judge the relevance of all documents. Then, recall should be estimated. For this, the number of relevant documents in the collection for each test request should be estimated. We refer to the estimation of the total number of relevant documents for all test requests as a *recall base*.

of the logarithm, sharper or smoother discounts can be computed to model varying user behavior. Formally, if b denotes the base of the logarithm, the cumulated gain vector with discount DCG is defined recursively as the vector DCG, where

$$DCG[i] = \begin{cases} G[1] & \text{if } i = 1 \\ DCG[i-1] + G[i]/^b log\ i & \text{otherwise} \end{cases} \tag{4}$$

Note that we must not apply the logarithm-based discount at rank 1 because $^b log\ 1 = 0$.

For example, let $b = 2$. From G' we obtain DCG' = $< 3, 5, 6.89, 6.89, 6.89, 7.28, 7.99,$ $8.66, 9.61, 9.61, \ldots >$.

The (lack of) ability of a query to rank highly relevant documents toward the top of the result list should show on both the *cumulated gain* by document rank *(CG)* and the *cumulated gain with discount* by document rank *(DCG)* vectors. By averaging over a set of test queries, the average performance of a particular IR method can be analyzed. Averaged vectors have the same length as the individual ones, and each component i gives the average of the ith component in the individual vectors. The averaged vectors can be directly visualized as gain-by-rank graphs (see Section 4.6).

The actual CG and DCG vectors by a particular IR method may also be compared to the theoretically best-possible vectors. The latter vectors are constructed as follows. Let there be k, l, and m relevant documents at the relevance levels 1, 2, and 3 (respectively) for a given request. First, fill the vector positions $1 \ldots m$ by the values 3, then the positions $m+1$ $\ldots m+l$ by the values 2, then the positions $m+l+1 \ldots m+l+k$ by the values 1, and finally the remaining positions by the values 0. Then compute CG and DCG as well as the average CG and DCG vectors and curves as above. Note that the curves turn horizontal when no more relevant documents (of any level) can be found. They do not unrealistically assume as a baseline that all retrieved documents could be maximally relevant. The vertical distance between an actual (average) (D)CG curve and the theoretically best-possible curve shows the effort wasted on less-than-perfect documents due to a particular IR method.

3.3   COMPARISON OF THE (D)CG TO RELATED MEASURES

The novel measures have several advantages when compared with several previous and related measures. The *average search length (ASL)* measure (Losee 1998) estimates the average position of a relevant document in the retrieved list. The *expected search length (ESL)* measure (Cooper 1968; Korfhage 1997) is the average number of documents that must be examined to retrieve a given number of relevant documents. Both are dichotomical—they do not take the degree of document relevance into account. The former also is heavily dependent on outliers (relevant documents found late in the ranked order).

The *normalized recall (NR)* measure (Rocchio 1966; Salton and McGill 1983), and the *satisfaction-frustration-total (SFT)* measure (Korfhage 1997; Myaeng and Korfhage 1990) all seek to take into account the order in which documents are presented to the user. The *NR measure* compares the actual performance of an IR technique to the ideal one (when all relevant documents are retrieved first). Basically it measures the area between the ideal and the actual curves. NR does not take the degree of document relevance into account and is highly sensitive to the last relevant document found late in the ranked order.

The *SFT measure* consists of three components: the *satisfaction measure* only considers the retrieved relevant documents, the *frustration measure* considers only the irrelevant documents, and the *total measure* is a weighted combination of the two. SFT assumes the same retrieved list of documents, which are obtained in different orders by the IR techniques to be compared. This is an unrealistic assumption for comparison since for any retrieved list size n, when $n << N$ (the database size), different IR techniques may retrieve quite different documents—that is the whole idea! A strong feature of SFT comes from its capability of punishing an IR technique for retrieving irrelevant documents while rewarding for the relevant ones. SFT does not have the discount feature of our DCG measure.

The relative relevance and ranked half-life measures (Borlund 2000; Borlund and Ingwersen 1998) were developed for interactive IR evaluation. The *relative relevance* (RR) measure is based on comparing the match between the system-dependent probability of relevance and the user-assessed degree of relevance, the latter by the real person in need or a panel of assessors. The match is computed by the cosine coefficient (Borlund 2000) when *the same* ranked IR technique output is considered as vectors of relevance weights as estimated by the technique, by the user, or by the panel. RR is (intended as) an association measure between types of relevance assessments and is not directly a performance measure. Of course, if the cosine between the IR technique scores and the user relevance assessments is low, the technique cannot perform well from the user point of view. The ranked order of documents is not taken into account.

The *ranked half-life* (RHL) measure gives the median point of accumulated relevance for a given query result. It thus improves on ASL by taking the degree of document relevance into account. Like ASL, RHL is dependent on outliers. The RHL may also be the same for quite differently performing queries. RHL does not have the discount feature of DCG.

The strengths of the proposed CG and DCG measures can now be summarized as follows:

- They combine the degree of relevance of documents and their rank (affected by their probability of relevance) in a coherent way.

- At any number of retrieved documents examined (rank), CG and DCG give an estimate of the cumulated gain as a single measure no matter what the recall base size.

- They are not heavily dependent on outliers (relevant documents found late in the ranked order) since they focus on the gain cumulated from the beginning of the result up to any point of interest.

- They are obvious to interpret; they are more direct than P-R curves and do not mask bad performance.

In addition, the DCG measure has the following further advantages:

- It realistically weights down the gain received through documents found later in the ranked results.

- It allows modeling user persistence in examining long ranked result lists by adjusting the discounting factor.

The measures considered above, both the old and the new ones, have weaknesses in two areas. First, none of them take into account order effects on relevance judgments, or document overlap (or redundancy). In the TREC interactive track (Over 1999), *instance recall* is employed to handle this. The user-system pairs are rewarded for retrieving distinct instances of answers rather than multiple overlapping documents. In principle, the (D)CG measures may be used for such evaluation. Second, the measures considered above all deal with relevance as a single dimension while it really is multidimensional (Schamber 1994; Vakkari and Hakala 2000). In principle, such multidimensionality may be accounted for in the construction of recall bases for search topics but leads to complexity in the recall bases and in the evaluation measures. Nevertheless, such added complexity may be worth pursuing because so much effort is invested in IR evaluation.

4 CASE STUDY: THE EFFECTIVENESS OF QE AND QUERY STRUCTURES AT DIFFERENT RELEVANCE LEVELS

We demonstrate the use of the proposed measures in a case study testing the co-effects of query expansion and structured queries in a database with nonbinary relevance judgments. Based on the results by Kekäläinen and Järvelin (1998), we already know that weak query structures are not able to benefit from query expansion, whereas the strong ones are. In the present study, we shall test whether the performance of differently structured queries varies with relation to the degree of relevance. We give the results as traditional P-R curves for each relevance level, and as CG and DCG curves that exploit the degrees of relevance. We hypothesize that expanded queries based on strong structures are better able to rank highly relevant documents high in the query results than unexpanded queries or queries based on other structures, whether expanded or not. Consequently, the performance differences between query types among marginally relevant documents should be marginal and among highly relevant documents essential. Expanded queries based on strong structures should cumulate higher CG and DCG values than unexpanded queries or queries based on other structures, whether expanded or not.

4.1 TEST ENVIRONMENT

The test environment was a text database containing newspaper articles operated under the InQuery retrieval system (version 3.1). The database contains 53,893 articles published in three different newspapers. The database index contains all keys in their morphological basic forms, and all compound words are split into their component words in their morphological basic forms. For the database there is a collection of requests, which are one to two sentences long, in the form of written information need statements. For these requests there is a recall base of 16,540 articles that fall into four relevance categories (see Section 4.2 regarding *relevance assessments*). The base was collected by pooling the result sets of hundreds of different queries formulated from the requests in different studies, using both exact and partial-match retrieval. We thus believe that our recall estimates are valid. For a set of tests concerning query structures, 30 requests were selected on the basis of their expandability—that is, they provided possibilities for studying the interaction of query structure and expansion (Kekäläinen 1999; Kekäläinen and Järvelin 2000; Sormunen 2000).

The InQuery system was chosen for the test, because it has a wide range of operators, including probabilistic interpretations of the Boolean operators, and it allows search key weighting. Moreover, InQuery has shown good performance in several tests (Allan et al. 1997; Harman 1995; Xu and Croft 1996)). InQuery is based on Bayesian inference networks (Allan et al. 1997; Turtle 1990). All keys are attached with a *belief value*, which is approximated by the following tf.idf modification:

$$0.4 + 0.6 \times \left(\frac{tf_{ij}}{tf_{ij} + 0.5 + 1.5 \times \left(\frac{dl_j}{adl} \right)} \right) \times \left(\frac{log\left(\frac{N+0.5}{df_i} \right)}{log(N + 1.0)} \right) \tag{5}$$

where tf_{ij} = the frequency of the key i in the document j; dl_j = the length of document j (as a number of keys); adl = average document length in the collection; N = collection size (as a number of documents); df_i = number of documents containing key i.

The InQuery query language provides a set of operators to specify relations between search keys. As with Boolean operators, it is possible to formulate structured queries and mark relationships between concepts. The probabilistic interpretations for the operators used in this study are given below:

$$P_{sum}(Q_1, Q_2, \ldots, Q_n) = (p_1 + p_2 + \ldots + p_n)/n$$
$$P_{wsum}(w_s, w_1 Q_1, w_2 Q_2, \ldots, w_n Q_n) = w_s(w_1 p_1 + w_2 p_2 + \ldots + w_n p_n)/(w_1 + w_2 + \ldots + w_n)$$

where P denotes probability, Q_i is either a key or an InQuery expression, $p_i, i = 1 \ldots n$, is the belief value of Q_i, $w_i, i = 1 \ldots n$, is the weight of Q_i, and w_s is a weight given for a clause (Rajashekar and Croft 1995; Turtle 1990).

The probability for operands connected by the SYN operator is calculated by modifying the tf.idf function as follows:

$$0.4 + 0.6 \times \left(\frac{\sum_{I \in S} tf_{ij}}{\sum_{I \in S} tf_{ij} + 0.5 + 1.5 \times \left(\frac{dl_j}{adl} \right)} \right) \times \left(\frac{log\left(\frac{N+0.5}{df_S} \right)}{log(N + 1.0)} \right) \tag{6}$$

where tf_{ij} = the frequency of the key i in the document j; S = a set of search keys within the SYN operator; dl_j = the length of document j (as a number of keys); adl = average document length in the collection; N = collection size (as a number of documents); df_S = number of documents containing at least one key of the set S.

4.2 RELEVANCE ASSESSMENTS

For the test requests and test collection of the present experiment, relevance was assessed by four persons: two experienced journalists and two information specialists. They were given written information need statements (requests), and were asked to judge the relevance on a four-level scale: (0) irrelevant, the document is not about the subject of the request; (1) marginally relevant, the topic of the request is mentioned, but only in passing; (2) fairly relevant, the topic of the request is discussed briefly; (3) highly relevant, the topic is the main theme of the article. The relevance of 20 requests (of 30) was assessed by two (one by three) people, the rest by one person. The assessors agreed in 73% of the parallel assessments; in 21% of the cases, the difference was one point; and in 6%, two or three points. If the difference was one point, the assessment was chosen from each judge in turn.

If the difference was two or three points, the article was checked by the researcher to find out if there was a logical reason for disagreement, and a more plausible alternative was selected (Kekäläinen 1999; Sormunen 2000).

The recall bases for the 30 requests of the present study include 366 highly relevant documents (relevance level 3), 700 fairly relevant documents (relevance level 2), and 857 marginally relevant documents (relevance level 1). The rest of the database, 51,970 documents, is considered irrelevant (relevance level 0).

4.3 QUERY STRUCTURES AND EXPANSION

In text retrieval, an information need is typically expressed as a set of search keys. In exact-match—or Boolean—retrieval, relations between search keys in a query are marked with the AND operator, the OR operator, or proximity operators, which, in fact, are stricter forms of the AND operator. Thus, the query has a structure based on conjunctions and disjunctions of search keys (Green 1995; Keen 1991). A query constructed with the Boolean block search strategy (a query in the conjunctive normal form) is an example of a *facet structure*. Within a facet, search keys representing one aspect of a request are connected with the OR operator, and facets are connected with the AND operator. A facet may consist of one or several concepts. In best-match retrieval, queries may either have a structure similar to Boolean queries, or queries may be "natural language queries" without differentiated relations between search keys.

Kekäläinen and Järvelin (1998) tested the co-effects of query structures and query expansion on retrieval performance, and ascertained that the structure of the queries became important when queries were expanded. The best performance overall was achieved with expanded, facet-structured queries. For the present study, we selected their best weak structure (SUM) and two of their best strong structures, one based on concepts (SSYN-C) and another based on facets (WSYN). SUM queries may be seen as typical "best-match" queries and therefore suitable as a baseline.

We formulated and expanded queries using a conceptual model with a thesaural structure. Since the test database includes newspaper articles, we needed a conceptual model for this domain to test QE based on semantic relationships. No such model was available; thus, we chose to construct a test model. The collection of concepts was started by identifying all concepts from the test requests. Then, for each of these concepts, all plausible hierarchically narrower and associatively related concepts were collected. Consideration was given to the completeness of hierarchies. In the organization of concept relations, concepts were treated independently of the context of the requests. However, the newspaper domain guided the selection of concepts and relations. For each concept, all plausible expressions were gathered, and these expressions were turned into search strings. The conceptual model was constructed by three people using dictionaries, handbooks, primary literature, and their own knowledge. The relations between concepts and between expressions are valid for the whole domain—that is, they are standard thesaurus or semantic relations. The test model was aimed at QE in a database of Finnish newspaper articles; thus, its language was Finnish (Kekäläinen 1999; Sormunen 2000).

The conceptual model includes 832 concepts, 1345 expressions for the concepts, and 1558 search strings for the expressions. Concepts have hierarchic (generic, partitive, and instance) and association relationships. Expressions representing concepts are each other's synonyms or quasisynonyms—that is, equivalence exists between expressions at the linguistic level. The most typical or obvious of the synonyms, in a linguistic sense, was chosen as a principal expression, *term*, of the concept. Several strings, which are spelling variants, may represent each expression. If these strings are phrases, they are formed with different proximity operators. There is no variation caused by word truncation because the words are in their basic forms in the database index. The conceptual model is a database managed with the ExpansionTool, which is a tool for concept-based query construction and expansion (Järvelin et al. 1996; Järvelin et al. 2001).

In query formulation, researchers identified search concepts from requests and elicited corresponding search keys from the conceptual model. In a practical setting, users would select the concepts of interest from the model by themselves, or their search keys would be mapped to the model. In QE, search keys that were semantically related (synonyms, hierarchies, associations) to the original search concepts in the test model were added to queries. This procedure gave unexpanded (*u*) and expanded (*e*) query versions, which were both formulated into different query structures.

The structures used to combine the search keys are exemplified in the following. Examples are based on a sample request, *The processing and storage of radioactive waste*. In the following samples, queries are expanded; the expressions of the unexpanded queries are in italics.

SUM (average of the weights of keys) queries represent weak structures. In these queries, search keys are single words—that is, no phrases are included.

> *SUM/e*
> #sum(*radioactive waste* nuclear waste high active waste low active waste
>   spent fuel fission product *storage* store stock repository *process* refine)

In a *SUM-of-synonym-groups query (SSYN-C)*, each search concept forms a clause with the SYN operator. SYN clauses were combined with the SUM operator. Phrases were used (marked with *#3*). All keys within the SYN operator are treated as instances of one key.

> *SSYN-C/e*
> #sum(#syn(#3(*radioactive waste*) #3(nuclear waste) #3(high active waste)
> #3(low active waste) #3(spent fuel) #3(fission product))
> #syn(*storage* store stock repository)
> #syn(*process* refine))

WSYN queries were similar to SSYN, but based on facets instead of concepts. Facets were divided into major and minor facets according to their importance for the request. In WSYN queries, the weight of major facets was 10 and of minor facets 7.

> *WSYN/e*
> #wsum(1 10 #syn(#3(*radioactive waste*) #3(nuclear waste)
> #3(high active waste) #3(low active waste) #3(spent fuel) #3(fission product))
> 7 #syn(*storage* store stock repository *process* refine)

4.4   TEST QUERIES AND THE APPLICATION OF THE EVALUATION MEASURES

In the queries for the 30 test requests, the average number of facets was 3.7. The average number of concepts in unexpanded queries was 4.9, and in expanded queries 26.8. The number of search keys of unexpanded queries when no phrases were marked (i.e., SUM structure) was 6.1 on average, and for expanded queries without phrases, on average, 62.3. The number of search keys with phrases (i.e., SSYN-C and WSYN structures) was 5.4 for unexpanded queries, and 52.4 for expanded queries, on average.

We present the analysis of the search results in two forms: First, we apply the conventional measures in the form of P-R curves. We also calculated precision after each retrieved relevant document and took an average over requests (*average noninterpolated precision, AvP* for short). We chose AvP rather than precision based on document cutoff values, because the sizes of recall bases vary at different relevance levels, and thus one cutoff value will not treat queries equally with relation to precision. The statistical significance of differences in the effectiveness of query types was established with the Friedman test (Conover 1980).

Second, we present the CG and DCG curves. For the cumulated gain evaluations, we tested the same query types in separate runs with the logarithm bases and the handling of relevance levels varied as parameters as follows: The logarithm bases 2, e, and 10 were tested for the DCG vectors. The base 2 models impatient users, base 10 persistent ones. For brevity, we show only the results obtained with the base 2 in Section 4.7.

We used document relevance levels 0 to 3 directly as gained value measures. This can be criticized, for example, by asking whether a highly relevant document is (only) three times as valuable as a marginally relevant document. Nevertheless, even this gives a clear difference for document quality to look at.

We first took all documents at relevance levels 1 to 3 into account; next, we nullified the values of documents at relevance level 1 (to reflect that they practically have no value); and finally, we nullified the values of documents at relevance levels 1 to 2 in order to focus on the highly relevant documents. The average actual CG and DCG vectors were compared to the theoretically best-possible average vectors.

4.5   P-R CURVES AND AVERAGE PRECISION

Figure 4 presents the P-R curves of the six query types at different relevance levels. At the relevance level 1, the curves are almost inseparable. At the relevance level 2, expanded WSYN and SSYN-C queries are more effective than the other query types. At the relevance level 3, the difference is even more accentuated. The higher the relevance level, the greater the differences between the best and the worst query types.

In Table 1, the average precision (AvP) figures are given. It can be seen that QE never enhances the average precision of SUM queries. In contrast, QE always improves the average precision of strongly structured queries. When queries are unexpanded, the differences in precision are negligible within each relevance level. The best effectiveness over all relevance levels is obtained with expanded WSYN queries. At best, the difference in average precision between unexpanded SUM and expanded WSYN queries is at the relevance level 3 (AvP: a change of 15.1 percentage units or an improvement of 58.3%). In

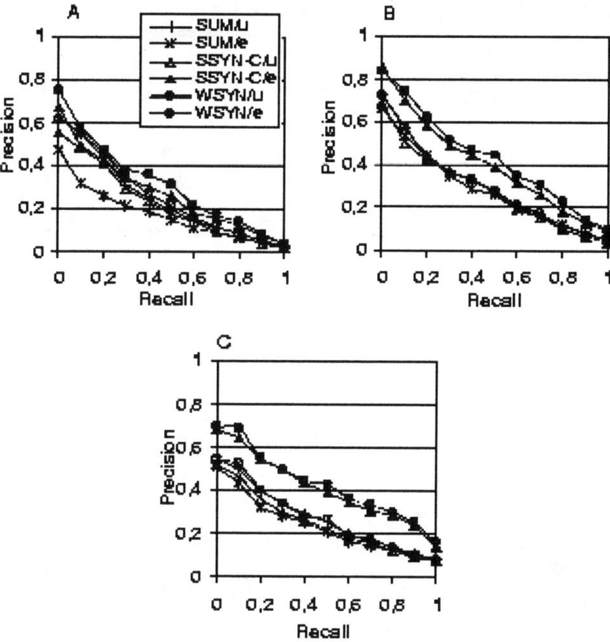

Figure 4 P-R curves of SUM, SSYN-C, and WSYN queries at relevance levels 1 (A), 2 (B), and 3 (C).

other words, expanded queries with strong structure are most effective in retrieving the most relevant documents.

The Friedman test corroborates that the differences in precision figures are more significant at relevance level 3 than at the other relevance levels. Expanded strong queries outperform most often expanded weak queries, but also unexpanded weak and unexpanded strong queries.

4.6   CUMULATED GAIN

Figure 5 presents the CG vector curves for ranks 1 to 100, the six query types studied above, and the theoretically best-possible (average) query. Figure 5(A) shows the curves when documents at both relevance levels 2 and 3 are taken into account (i.e., they earn 2 and 3 points, respectively). The best possible curve almost becomes a horizontal line at the rank 100, reflecting the fact that at rank 100 practically all relevant documents have been found. The two best (synonym-structured) query types hang below by 18 to 27 points

Rel.level	Expansion type	SUM	SSYN-C	WSYN
1	u	12.8	12.4	13.8
	e	10.1	13.3	14.3
2	u	22.4	21.5	22.9
	e	21.1	27.4	29.3
3	u	25.9	23.5	25.7
	e	22.2	39.1	41.0

Table 1   Average noninterpolated precision figures for different query types.

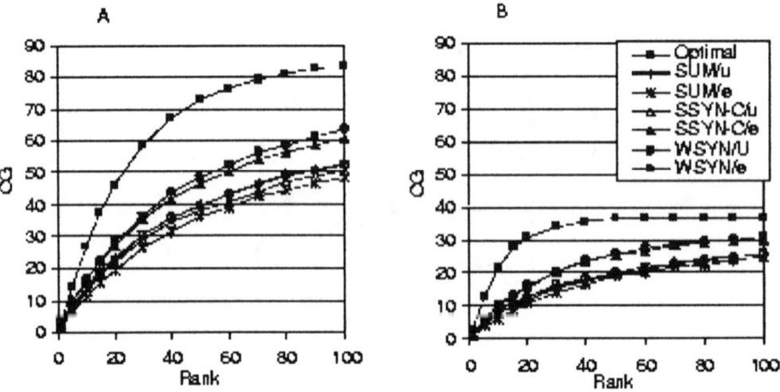

Figure 5   Cumulated gain curves at ranks 1 to 100, relevance levels 2 and 3 (A), and 3 (B).

(35% to 39%) from the rank 20 to 100. The difference is greatest in the middle range. The other four query types remain further below by 5 to 15 points (about 16% to 24%) from rank 20 to 100. The difference to the best-possible curve is 23 to 38 points (50%). Beyond the rank 100, the differences between the best-possible and all actual curves are all bound to diminish. Figure 5(B) shows the curves when documents only at the relevance level 3 are considered. The precise figures are different and the absolute differences smaller. However, the proportional differences are larger.

The curves can be interpreted also in another way: at the relevance level 3, one has to retrieve 34 documents by the best query types, and 62 by the other query types, in order to gain the benefit that could theoretically be gained by retrieving only 10 documents. In this respect, the best query types are nearly twice as effective as the others. At the relevance levels 2 and 3, the corresponding figures are 20 and 26 documents. At the greatest, the difference between the best and the remaining query types is 6 to 8 points (or two documents, relevance level 3) at ranks 40 to 60. At relevance levels 2 and 3, the greatest differences are 5 to 15 points (or 2 to 7 documents) at ranks 40 to 100.

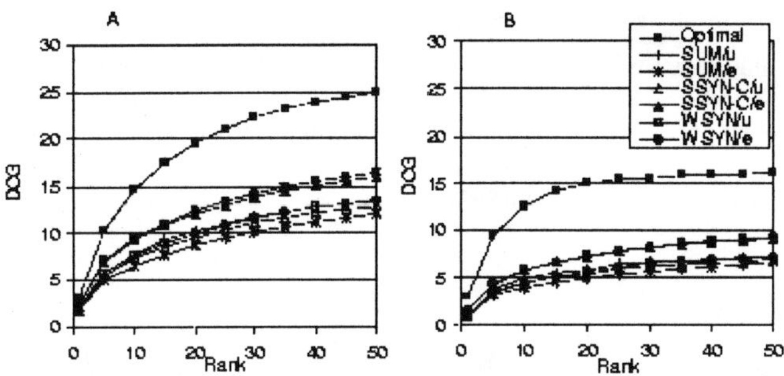

Figure 6 Discounted (^{2}log) cumulated gain curves ranks 1 to 50, relevance levels 2 and 3 (A), and 3 (B).

4.7 DISCOUNTED CUMULATED GAIN

Figure 6 shows the DCG vector curves for ranks 1 to 50, the six query types studied above, and the theoretically best possible (average) query. The ^{2}log of the document rank is used as the discounting factor. Figure 6(A) shows the curves when documents both at the relevance levels 2 and 3 are taken into account. The best-possible curve still grows at the rank 50 (it levels off at the rank 90). The two best (synonym-structured) query types hang below by 5 to 9 points (35% to 36%) from the rank 10 to 50. The difference is growing. The other four query types remain further below by 2 to 4 points (15% to 27%) from rank 10 to 50. The difference to the best-possible curve is 7 to 13 points (47% to 50%). Beyond the rank 50, the differences between the best-possible and all actual curves gradually become stable. Figure 6(B) shows the curves when documents only at the relevance level 3 are considered. The precise figures are different and the absolute differences smaller. However, the proportional differences are larger. At the greatest, the difference between the best and the remaining query types is 3 points (or one level 3 document) at the rank 40 and further. It is a consistent and statistically significant difference, but are the users able to notice it?

Also, these curves can be interpreted in another way: at the relevance levels 2 and 3 one has to expect the user to examine 35 documents by the best query types, and 70 by the other query types, in order to gain the (discounted) benefit that could theoretically be gained by retrieving only 10 documents. User persistence up to 35 documents is not unrealistic, whereas up to 70 it must be rare. The difference in query type effectiveness is essential. At the relevance level 3, the discounted gains of the best query types never reach the gain theoretically possible at the rank 10. The theoretically possible gain at the rank 5 is achieved at the rank 50 and only by the best query types.

One might argue that if users go down to 70 documents, they get the real value, not the discounted one and therefore the DCG data should not be used for effectiveness comparison. While this may hold for the user situation, the DCG-based comparison is valuable for the system designer. Users are less likely to scan that far, and thus documents placed there do not have their real relevance value; a retrieval system or method placing relevant documents later in the ranked results should not be credited as much as another system or method ranking them earlier.

The main findings are similar with the other logarithm bases we tested. However, the magnitude of the differences between the best and worst query types grows from 4 points for ^{2}log to 13 points for ^{10}log at the rank 50 (obviously). This means that for a persistent user, the best methods are 13 points (or 27%) better than the remaining ones. For an impatient one, they are only 4 points better.

5   DISCUSSION

We have argued that users should be allowed to start information retrieval from concepts rather than words. In the empirical case study we used a conceptual model for query formulation and expansion. This model is developed for the news domain and contains 832 concepts, 1345 expressions for the concepts, and 1558 search patterns for the expressions. It represents generally valid hierarchical, associative, and equivalence relationships for the news domain. The findings suggest that, when available, such conceptual models may be automatically used for query expansion and construction for varying retrieval environments. Thus, conceptual models or conceptual modeling can be used to support conceptual level interaction between the user and the collection, freeing the user from many details of search key selection and query formulation.

Our second argument is that, in modern large database environments, the development and evaluation of IR methods should be based on their ability to retrieve highly relevant documents. This is desirable from the user's viewpoint and presents a not-too-liberal test for IR methods. We developed two methods for IR method evaluation, which aim at taking the document relevance degrees into account. One is based on a novel application of the traditional P-R curves and separates recall bases for each relevance level of documents. The other is based on two novel evaluation measures, the CG and the DCG measures, which give the (discounted) cumulated gain up to any given document rank in the retrieval results.

In the case study, we demonstrated the use of these evaluation methods in the evaluation of the effectiveness of various query types, which were varied in structure and expansion. Our hypotheses were that

- The performance differences between query types among marginally relevant documents should be marginal and among highly relevant documents essential when measured by the P-R curves.

- Strongly structured expanded queries present better effectiveness than unexpanded queries or queries based on other structures, whether expanded or not.

- Expanded queries based on strong structures cumulate higher CG and DCG values than unexpanded queries or queries based on other structures, whether expanded or not.

These hypotheses were confirmed. The differences between the performance figures of the best and worst query types are consistent and statistically very significant. We valued the documents at different relevance levels rather equably; however, the user might value documents at relevance level 3 much higher than documents at other relevance levels. Thus, our analysis perhaps led to rather conservative, although significant results.

Sormunen et al. (2001) analyzed the contents of documents at different relevance levels. Their results suggest that highly relevant documents have the following characteristics: the topic of the request is discussed in them at length; they have more words pertaining to the topic; they deal with several aspects of the topic; the authors use multiple expressions to refer to the concepts they discuss in order to avoid tautology. In contrast, marginal documents may mention the topic briefly; contain just a few words pertaining to the topic; discuss the topic from a viewpoint not included in the request. The number of occurrences per document is about the same for an individual key word (expression) at all relevance levels. Queries that contain several alternative search keys for each search concept retrieve highly relevant documents in best-match systems because documents containing several search keys have "more evidence of being on the topic" than documents with few search keys. The structure is needed to balance the queries: strong structured queries with the SYN operator were the best alternatives, because treating all alternative search keys as instances of one search key is a proper way to interpret the idea of Boolean disjunction in best-match retrieval. Facet structuring with other operators[10] was not successful (Kekäläinen 1999).

The P-R curves demonstrate that the good performance of the expanded structured query types is due to, in particular, their ability to rank the highly relevant documents toward the top of retrieval results. The cumulated gain curves illustrate the value the user actually gets, but discounted cumulated gain curves can be used to forecast the system performance with regard to a user's patience in examining the result list. With a small log base, the value of a relevant document decreases quickly along the ranked list and a DCG curve turns horizontal. This assumes an impatient user for whom late-coming information is not useful because it will never be read. If the CG and DCG curves are analyzed horizontally, we may conclude that a system designer would have to expect the users to examine by 50% to 100% more documents by the worse query types to collect the same gain collected by the best query types. While it is possible that persistent users go way down the result list (e.g., from 30 to 60 documents), it often is unlikely to happen, and a system requiring such a behavior is, in practice, much worse than a system yielding the gain within 50% of the documents.

The novel CG and DCG measures complement the modified P-R measure. Precision over fixed recall levels hides the user's effort up to a given recall level. The DCV-based precision-recall curves are better but still do not make the value gained by ranked position explicit. The CG and DCG curves provide this directly. The distance to the theoretically best-possible curve shows the effort wasted on less-than-perfect or useless documents. The advantage of the P-R measure is that it treats requests with a different number of relevant documents equally, and from the system's point of view the precision at each recall level is comparable. In contrast, CG and DCG curves show the user's point of view as the number of documents needed to achieve a certain gain. Together with the theoretically best-possible curve they also provide a stopping rule—that is, when the best-possible curve turns horizontal, there is nothing to be gained by retrieving or examining further documents.

---

[10] For example, the OR operator in InQuery, which gives the product of argument probabilities, was not a suitable facet operator.

Generally, the evaluation methods and the case demonstrate that nondichotomous relevance assessments are applicable even in IR experiments, and may reveal interesting phenomena. The dichotomous relevance assessments generally applied may be too permissive, and, consequently, too easily give credit to IR system performance. We believe that, in modern large environments, the proposed modified P-R measure and the novel (D)CG measures should be used whenever possible, because they provide richer information for evaluation.

6 CONCLUSION

We tested the performance of different query types in regard to different relevance levels. Queries varied according to their structure and expansion. Queries had either a weak "bag of words" structure or a strong facet structure. Query expansion was based on a conceptual model that gives several alternative search keys for concepts. Our hypothesis was that the performance differences between query types among marginally relevant documents should be marginal; and among highly relevant documents, it should be essential. This was shown true by clear differences between P-R curves at different relevance levels. We also introduced a new method for illustrating the performance of ranked, nondichotomously assessed retrieval results from the user point of view. This was based on scoring the documents according to their relevance level and drawing a cumulated curve of scores of the result set. Our hypothesis was that expanded queries based on strong structures cumulate higher value for the user than unexpanded queries or queries based on other structures, whether expanded or not. This should show clearly also when the ranked position of each document is used to discount its worth in the cumulated value. These hypotheses were confirmed. The results also indicate the usability of domain-dependent conceptual models in query expansion for IR.

References

Alkula, R. (2001). From plain character strings to meaningful words: Producing better full text databases for inflectional and compounding languages with morphological analysis software. *Information Retrieval 4*(3/4), 195–208.

Allan, J., J. Callan, B. Croft, L. Ballesteros, J. Broglio, J. Xu, and H. Shu (1997). INQUERY at TREC 5. In *Information technology: The Fifth Text Retrieval Conference (TREC- 5)*, ed. E. M. Voorhees and D. K. Harman, 119–132. National Institute of Standards and Technology.

Bechhofer, S., L. Carr, C. Goble, and W. Hall (2001). Conceptual open hypermedia = the semantic web? Position paper. In *Proceedings of the Second International Workshop on the Semantic Web—SemWeb'01*.

Belkin, N. J., and W. B. Croft (1987). Retrieval techniques. In *Annual Review of Information Science and Technology*, Vol. 22, ed. M. E. Williams, 109–145. Amsterdam: Elsevier.

Blair, D. C., and M. E. Maron (1985). An evaluation of retrieval effectiveness for a full-text document-retrieval system. *Communications of the ACM 28*(3), 289–299.

Borlund, P. (2000). *Evaluation of interactive information retrieval systems.* Ph. D. thesis, Abo Akademi University.

Borlund, P., and P. Ingwersen (1998). Measures of relative relevance and ranked half-life: Performance indicators for interactive IR. In *Proceedings of the 21st Annual International ACM SIGIR Conference on Research and Development in Information Retrieval*, eds. W. Croft, A. Moffat, C. van Rijsbergen, R. Wilkinson, and J. Zobel, 324–331.

Chaffee, J., and S. Gauch (2000). Personal ontologies for web navigation. In *Proceedings of the Ninth International Conference on Information Knowledge Management—CIKM 2000*, 227–234.

Chen, H., and S. Dumais (2000). Bringing order to the web: Automatically categorizing search results. *CHI Letters 2*(1), 145–152.

Conover, W. J. (1980). *Practical Nonparametric Statistics*, 2nd ed. New York: John Wiley & Sons.

Cooper, W. S. (1968). Expected search length: A single measure of retrieval effectiveness based on weak ordering action of retrieval systems. *Journal of the American Society for Information Science 19*(1), 30–41.

Cosijn, E., and P. Ingwersen (2000). Dimensions of relevance. *Information Processing and Management 36*(4), 533–550.

Efthimiadis, E. N. (1996). Query expansion. In *Annual Review of Information Science and Technology*, Vol. 31, ed. M. E. Williams, 121–187.

Green, R. (1995). The expression of conceptual syntagmatic relationships: A comparative survey. *Journal of Documentation 51*(4), 315–338.

Guarino, N., C. Masolo, and G. Vetere (1998). Ontoseek: Using large linguistic ontologies for gathering information resources from the web. Technical Report 01/98, LADSEB-CNR.

Harman, D. K. (1995). *Overview of the fourth text retrieval conference (TREC-4)*. Available at *trec.nist.gov/pubs/trec4/papers/overview.ps*.

Hersh, W. R. (1996). *Information Retrieval: A Health Care Perspective*. Berlin: Springer-Verlag.

Hersh, W. R., and D. H. Hickam (1995). An evaluation of interactive Boolean and natural language searching with an online medical textbook. *Journal of the American Society for Information Science 46*(7), 478–489.

Hull, D. (1993). Using statistical testing in the evaluation of retrieval experiments. In *Proceedings of the 16th International Conference on Research and Development in Information Retrieval*, eds. R. Korfhage, E. M. Rasmussen, and P. Willett, 329–338.

Ingwersen, P., and P. Willett (1995). An introduction to algorithmic and cognitive approaches for information retrieval. *Libri 45*, 160–177.

Jacob, E. K. (1991). Classification and categorization: Drawing the line. In *Advances in Classification Research. Proceedings of the 2nd ASIS SIG/CR Classification Research Workshop*, Vol. 2, ed. B. H. Kwasnik and R. Fidel, 67–83.

Järvelin, K., and J. Kekäläinen (2000). IR evaluation methods for highly relevant documents. In *Proceedings of the 23rd Annual International ACM SIGIR Conference on Research and Development in Information Retrieval*, ed. N. J. Belkin, P. Ingwersen, and M.-K. Leong, 41–48.

Järvelin, K., J. Kekäläinen, and T. Niemi (2001). Expansiontool: Concept-based query expansion and construction. *Information Retrieval 4*(3/4), 231–255.

Järvelin, K., J. Kristensen, E. Sormunen, and H. Keskustalo (1996). A deductive data model for query expansion. In *Proceedings of the 19th Annual International ACM-SIGIR Conference on Research and Development in Information Retrieval*, ed. H.-P. Frei, D. Harman, P. Schäuble, and R. Wilkinson, 235–249.

Keen, E. M. (1991). The use of term position devices in ranked output experiments. *Journal of Documentation 47*(1), 1–22.

Keen, E. M. (1992). Presenting results of experimental retrieval comparisons. *Information Processing and Management 28*(4), 491–501.

Kekäläinen, J. (1999). *The effects of query complexity, expansion and structure on retrieval performance in probabilistic text retrieval.* Ph. D. thesis, University of Tampere. Available at *www.info.uta.fi/research/postscript_docs/JK1_99.pdf.*

Kekäläinen, J., and K. Järvelin (1998). The impact of query structure and query expansion on retrieval performance. In *Proceedings of the 21st Annual International ACM SIGIR Conference on Research and Development in Information Retrieval*, ed. W. B. Croft, A. Moffat, C. J. van Rijsbergen, R. Wilkinson, and J. Zobel, 130–137.

Kekäläinen, J., and K. Järvelin (2000). The co-effects of query structure and expansion on retrieval performance in probabilistic text retrieval. *Information Retrieval 1*(4), 329–344.

Korfhage, R. (1997). *Information Storage and Retrieval.* New York: John Wiley & Sons.

Lancaster, F. W. (1986). *Vocabulary Control for Information Retrieval*, 2nd ed. Arlington, VA: Information Resources Press.

Losee, R. M. (1998). *Text Retrieval and Filtering: Analytic Models of Performance.* Boston: Kluwer.

Miller, G. A. (1995). WordNet: A lexical database for English. *Communications of the ACM 38*(11), 39–41.

Myaeng, S. H., and R. R. Korfhage (1990). Integration of user profiles: Models and experiments in information retrieval. *Information Processing and Management 26*(6), 719–738.

Over, P. (1999). *TREC-7 interactive track report.* Available at *trec.nist.gov/pubs/trec7/papers/t7irep.pdf.gz.*

Rajashekar, T. B., and W. B. Croft (1995). Combining automatic and manual index representations in probabilistic retrieval. *Journal of the American Society for Information Science 46*(4), 272–283.

Robertson, S. E., and N. J. Belkin (1978). Ranking in principle. *Journal of Documentation 34*(2), 93–100.

Rocchio, Jr., J. J. (1966). *Document retrieval systems—Optimization and evaluation.* Ph. D. thesis, Harvard University.

Salton, G. (1989). *Automatic Text Processing: The Transformation, Analysis, and Retrieval of Information by Computer.* Boston: Addison-Wesley.

Salton, G., and M. J. McGill (1983). *Introduction to Modern Information Retrieval.* New York: McGraw-Hill.

Saracevic, T. (1996). Relevance reconsidered '96. In *Proceedings of the Second International Conference on Conceptions of Library and Information Science: Integration in Perspective*, ed. P. Ingwersen and N. O. Pors, 201–218. The Royal School of Librarianship.

Saracevic, T., P. Kantor, A. Chamis, and D. Trivison (1988). A study of information seeking and retrieving. I. Background and methodology. *Journal of the American Society for Information Science 39*(3), 161–176.

Schamber, L. (1994). Relevance and information behavior. In *Annual Review of Information Science and Technology*, Vol. 29, ed. M. E. Williams, 3–48.

Soergel, D. (1999). The rise of ontologies or the reinvention of classification. *Journal of the American Association for Information Science 50*(12), 1119–1120.

Sormunen, E. (2000). *A method for measuring wide range performance of Boolean queries in full-text database.* Ph. D. thesis, University of Tampere. Available at *acta.uta.fi/english/teos.phtml?3786*

Sormunen, E., J. Kekäläinen, J. Koivisto, and K. Järvelin (2001). Document text characteristics affect the ranking of the most relevant documents by expanded structured queries. *Journal of Documentation 57*(3), 358–376.

Sparck Jones, K. (1972). A statistical interpretation of term specificity and its application in retrieval. *Journal of Documentation 28*, 11–21.

Tague-Sutcliffe, J. (1992). The pragmatics of information retrieval experimentation, revisited. *Information Processing and Management 28*(4), 467–490.

Turtle, H. R. (1990). *Inference networks for document retrieval.* Ph. D. thesis, University of Massachusetts.

Uschold, M., and M. Gruninger (1996). Ontologies: Principles, methods and applications. *The Knowledge Engineering Review 11*(2), 93–136.

Vakkari, P., and N. Hakala (2000). Changes in relevance criteria and problem stages in task performance. *Journal of Documentation 56*, 540–562.

Xu, J., and W. B. Croft (1996). Query expansion using local and global document analysis. In *Proceedings of the 19th Annual International ACM-SIGIR Conference on Research and Development in Information Retrieval*, ed. H.-P. Frei, D. Harman, P. Schäuble, and R. Wilkinson, 4–11.

Data Mining for Manufacturing Control: An Application in Optimizing IC Tests

Tony Fountain
San Diego Supercomputing Center
9500 Gilman Drive
University of California, San Diego
La Jolla, CA 92093
fountain@sdsc.edu

Thomas Dietterich
Department of Computer Science
Oregon State University
102 Dearborn Hall
Corvallis, OR 97331
tgd@cs.orst.edu

Bill Sudyka
Hewlett-Packard Co.
1000 NE Circle Boulevard
Corvallis, OR 97330
bjs@hpcvibs.cv.hp.com

Abstract

We describe an application of machine learning and decision analysis to the problem of die-level functional tests in integrated circuit manufacturing. *Integrated circuits (ICs)* are fabricated on large wafers that can hold hundreds of individual chips (*die*). In current practice, large and expensive machines test each of these die to check that they are functioning properly (*die-level functional test* or *DLFT*), and then the wafers are cut up, and the good die are assembled into packages and connected to the package pins. Finally, the resulting packages are tested to ensure that the final product is functioning correctly. The purpose of the die-level functional test is to avoid the expense of packaging bad die and to provide rapid feedback to the fabrication process by detecting die failures. The challenge for a decision-theoretic approach is to reduce the amount of DLFT (and the associated costs) while still providing process feedback. We describe a decision-theoretic approach to DLFT in which historical test data is mined to create a probabilistic model of patterns of die failure. This model is combined with greedy value-of-information computations to decide in real time which die to test next and when to stop testing. We report the results of several experiments that demonstrate the ability of this procedure to make good testing decisions, to make good stopping decisions, and to detect anomalous die. Based on experiments with historical test data from Hewlett-Packard, the resulting system has the potential to improve profits on mature IC products.

Keywords: IC test, EM algorithm, machine learning, decision analysis, belief network, integrated circuit, manufacturing, VLSI

1   INTRODUCTION

Modern computer-integrated manufacturing lines provide many opportunities for applying data-mining techniques. These lines contain many sensors and computer-controlled devices, so the information needed for intelligent control is available and control decisions can be implemented easily. Furthermore, in most current computer-integrated manufacturing lines, the supply of available sensor data far outstrips the ability of the existing control systems to digest and apply it. Consequently, the combination of machine learning—to analyze data to build and update probabilistic models—and decision-theoretic control—to make decisions based on those models—can have a huge financial impact in reducing costs, increasing throughput, and raising profits.

In this chapter, we report our experiences with one such application. We developed a decision-theoretic controller for one phase of the VLSI integrated circuit manufacturing process. The controller manages the die-level functional test (DLFT) process with the goal of maximizing the expected utility of the overall manufacturing process. Our approach is based on combining concepts and methods from decision theory, decision analysis, and data mining.

Our methodology consists of three steps. First, we applied our expertise in VLSI testing to develop an influence diagram for the decision-making process. The influence diagram formalism—which was developed by the decision analysis and belief network research community—allows us to describe the process in terms of three parts: (1) a cost model of manufacturing operations, (2) a probability model of the way that defects are introduced during the manufacturing and testing process, and (3) a model of the points at which decisions must be made.

The second step involves assigning numerical values to the various parameters of the influence diagram. As a result of a related project at Hewlett-Packard, the costs of the manufacturing operations had already been determined, so we were able to plug these into the cost model. To acquire the probability model of IC defects, we applied machine learning algorithms to learn these automatically from historical data.

The third step involved implementing a decision-making algorithm that determines which decision would maximize the expected utility of the overall manufacturing process. We implemented a one-step greedy value-of-information algorithm that approximately maximizes the expected utility.

In simulation, our final system achieves substantial profit increases over the current control method. In addition to increasing profits, the system displays several desirable features. First, the system is modular, so that changes to the product under test, or changes to the manufacturing cost, can be integrated without reengineering the system. Second, the system is sensitive to product characteristics. Rather than a fixed testing policy, the system allocates testing resources to products that warrant more complex testing. Finally, the system is robust with respect to changes in the manufacturing costs. As manufacturing costs are updated, the system responds in a predictable, rational manner.

The remainder of this chapter is organized as follows: First, we describe the integrated circuit manufacturing process and the decision-making problem to be solved. Then we present our influence diagram and its probabilistic model of IC failures. The next sections describe the machine learning procedure and our experimental methods. The following section reports the results of several experiments to understand and evaluate the behavior of the system and its various components. We summarize our conclusions in the final section.

2   IC MANUFACTURING AND TEST

An integrated circuit (IC) is an electronic circuit in which a number of devices are fabricated and interconnected on a single chip of semiconductor material. According to current manufacturing practice, integrated circuits are produced en masse in the form of processed silicon wafers. While still in wafer form, the ICs are referred to as *dice;* an individual IC is called a *die*. The process of cutting the dice from wafers and embedding them into mountable containers is called *packaging*. Figure 1 is a simplified schematic of the major IC manufacturing steps.

Brief descriptions of the manufacturing steps are provided below.

A typical wafer is fabricated through a series of more than 100 process steps (Van Zant 1997; Zorich 1991). Virtually all of the processing is automated, but there are still many potential sources of failure that lead to defective wafers. An entire processing step may fail, in which case all of the die on a wafer will be bad. Many steps involve creating uniform thin layers on the wafer (e.g., by placing a drop of liquid material in the center and then spinning the wafer), and failures in this process can lead to radially symmetric patterns of failed die (e.g., in the center, in rings around the center, and most commonly, near the edges of the wafer). The wafers can also be scratched during automated handling, which creates linear failure patterns and edge defects. Finally, defects in the silicon substrate and in the applied materials, as well as dust particles, can create spatially uniform patterns of die failures.

Wafer parametric test: Parametric tests measure physical and electrical parameters of the wafer such as electrical conductivity and behavior of individual sample components (transistors, capacitors, resistors). Although Figure 1 depicts parametric testing as a distinct stage following wafer fabrication, in reality, parametric tests are performed throughout the fabrication process.

Die-level functional test (DLFT): Functional testing typically occurs once the wafers are completely fabricated and the dice are completely formed and functional. Functional tests measure the operational quality of the individual dice. A large and expensive

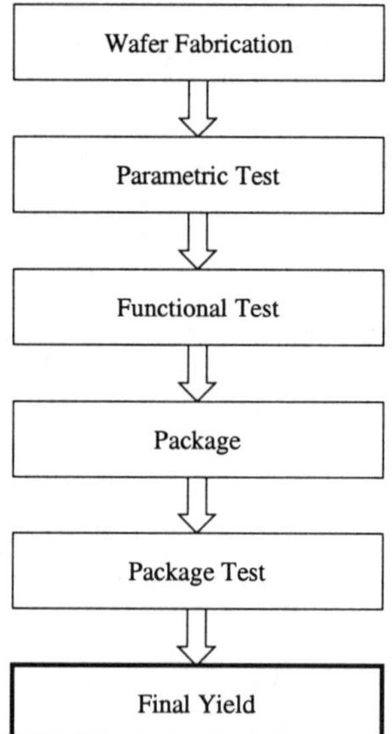

Figure 1   The major steps in IC manufacturing.

robotic machine presses electrical probes onto the die contacts, input signals are fed to the circuit, and output signals are measured. Functional testing simulates normal and abnormal operating conditions (e.g., high-, normal-, and low-voltage tests). The conventional approach to DLFT is exhaustive wafer tests—that is, all dice on all wafers undergo DLFT. If a die fails the functional test, an ink dot is placed on it, so that it will not be packaged later. The decision to place the ink dot is called the *inking decision*. After inking, the wafers are typically shipped to a separate location for packaging. Note that DLFT is expensive (machines, personnel) and potentially damaging (due to the physical act of probing).

Packaging: To convert the wafers into packaged ICs, the wafers are cut into individual dice by a high-precision diamond saw. All of the resulting (non-inked) chips are mounted into packages, electrical contacts are bonded in place, and then a protective covering is added.

Package test: Once the ICs are packaged, they are tested again to ensure that the packaging process was successful. Package tests usually repeat many of the functional tests that were performed during DLFT. The test results from package testing are used to decide which ICs to sell.

This brief summary shows that DLFT is not essential to the quality of the final product, because any failures will be detected during package tests. Hence, the main purpose of DLFT is to reduce costs by avoiding packaging defective dice. A secondary purpose of DLFT is to provide rapid feedback to the manufacturing process by detecting and diagnosing faulty manufacturing processes. The challenge for a decision-theoretic approach is to reduce the amount of DLFT (and hence reduce its cost) while not appreciably increasing the costs of packaging and manufacturing.

3   DECISION-THEORETIC WAFER TEST

The goal of our project was to replace the exhaustive test policy with a decision-theoretic policy that decides in real time which die to test and when to stop testing. Because the DLFT is performed by a robotic tester, it can be reprogrammed to test the die in any desired order based on the results of previous tests. The decision-theoretic policy seeks to maximize overall profit by combining a probabilistic model of the spatial distribution of die test results with a utility model of the costs of the IC manufacturing process.

A typical wafer test scenario under the decision-theoretic policy can be described as follows. The system begins with a learned probabilistic model of die test results and a utility model of processing costs. The system chooses the best die to test according to a value-of-information metric that measures the expected increase in profit for the whole wafer that would be obtained by testing each die and chooses the one die whose test result would be most valuable. This die is tested, and the results are incorporated into the system's probabilistic model of the wafer. The system then repeats this test-and-update cycle until the expected value of further testing is nonpositive. At that stage, the system makes an individual packaging decision for each of the dice on the wafer, marking those that are rejected. Die that were tested and found to be defective are marked with an ink dot. In addition, die that were not tested are marked based on the *predictions* of the (updated) probabilistic model. Once this is complete, the system determines whether the wafer should be shipped to the packaging facility or should be held for analysis (because it contains a large number of defective die or an unusual pattern of failed die). For each of the wafers shipped to packaging, the unmarked dice are packaged and sent to package testing. Those that pass package testing are sent to customers.

3.1   THE PROBABILISTIC MODEL

As this scenario indicates, the heart of the testing process is a probabilistic model of the spatial distribution of die failures on the wafer. Figure 2 shows our die failure model. This has the form of a standard Naive Bayes belief network of the kind that have already proven useful in diagnostic systems (Horvitz et al. 1991) and learning and discovery systems (Cheeseman et al. 1988; Dietterich 1997). Belief networks such as this provide a succinct representation for probabilistic models in the form of directed acyclic graphs (Charniak 1991; Jordan 1999; Pearl 1988). In this representation, nodes represent random variables and arcs between nodes correspond to relationships between variables (often causal relationships). Each node in the graph stores a probability distribution. Hence, the node labeled w stores the distribution $P(w)$, and the nodes labeled f_i store the conditional distribution $P(f_i|w)$. In our case, these distributions are stored as tables indexed by the discrete values of the random variables. Once these probability distributions are known, the belief network fully specifies the joint distribution of the random variables in the network.

Our probabilistic model assumes that the wafers produced during the fabrication process belong to four possible "classes." One class of wafers might be wafers where all of the die are working well (except, perhaps, for randomly distributed failures). A second class of

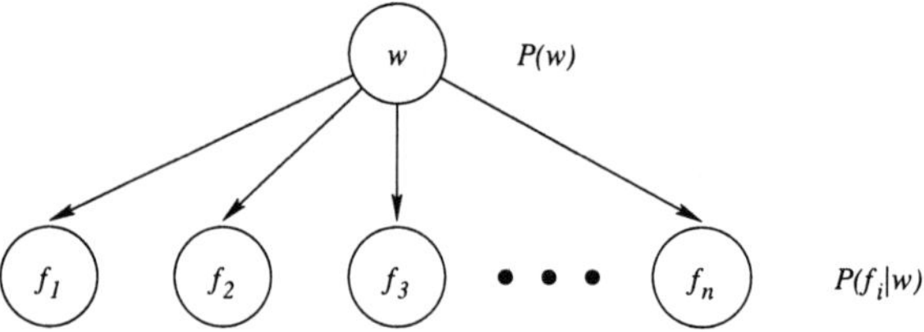

Figure 2   The wafer test belief net.

wafers might have virtually all die defective. A third class might have defective die in the center of the wafer, and good die everywhere else, and so on. As we will see below, the actual wafer classes are learned automatically, so these examples should just be considered suggestive. The key idea is that within each wafer class, the die at each given location has a fixed probability of being defective, and this probability may differ from one wafer class to another.

The class of a wafer is represented by a random variable w with four values. The Boolean random variable f_i indicates whether the die at location i is functioning correctly or not. The probabilistic model is represented by the probability distributions $P(w)$ and $P(f_i|w)$. The best way to understand this probabilistic model is to view it as a simulation of the process of manufacturing a wafer. According to this simulation, the fabrication process begins by "choosing" what class of wafer to generate. This is modeled as choosing the value of w at random according to a probability distribution $P(w)$. Then, once w is chosen, the fabrication process "decides" whether each die should be defective or not. This is modeled by choosing for each physical position i on the wafer, the value f_i at random according to $P(f_i|w)$.

Although we can view the model as a simulation of the fabrication process, the model will be used in a very different way. During testing, the system begins by not knowing the values of any of the random variables. Each time it performs a test (e.g., of die i), it learns the value of one of the variables f_i. Given the observed values of some of the f_i, probabilistic inference algorithms can compute the probability of the other random variables. Hence, given the result of testing dice 1, 5, 12, and 15, these algorithms can estimate the probability that die 23 is defective. They do this by first computing the probability that the wafer belongs to class $w = 1$, $w = 2$, and so on, and then multiplying this by the probability $P(f_{23}|w)$ that die 23 is defective.

This kind of probabilistic model is also known as a *mixture model*, because the probability that a particular die is defective is a weighted sum (i.e., a mixture) of the probability that it is defective in each of the wafer classes. Specifically, $P(f_i) = \sum_w P(w)P(f_i|w)$.

Note that this application of Naive Bayes is different from two other ways in which Naive Bayes networks have been applied previously. When Naive Bayes networks are employed in supervised learning, the true class w of each wafer would be known during training, and the goal during testing would be to determine the class w of the wafer. In our application, the true classes are never known. Indeed, the notion of a "wafer class" here is just a mathematical abstraction, and the wafer class variable w is a hidden variable. The learning algorithm has the freedom to adjust the probability distributions $P(w)$ and $P(f_i|w)$ to best fit the historical wafer testing data.

Another application of Naive Bayes networks is to find "clusters" in data (e.g., Autoclass; see (Cheeseman et al. 1988)). These clustering algorithms also fit a Naive Bayes network to the data, but the goal in those applications is to examine the resulting learned classes to gain insight into patterns that may exist in the data and to determine the "true" number of such classes. For our testing application, we simply view the mixture model as a convenient representation of the joint distribution $P(f_1, f_2, \ldots, f_n)$ of failures of the die on the wafers. The virtue of this representation is that it allows us to easily compute the probability of failure of all of the untested dice given the test results for the dice that have been tested so far. Nonetheless, we can visualize the learned wafer classes and attempt to relate these to aspects of the manufacturing process. This is an interesting and potentially promising application. However, it is not considered in this chapter.

3.2 LEARNING THE PROBABILISTIC MODEL VIA EXPECTATION MAXIMIZATION

In order to employ this probabilistic model to guide the testing of wafers, we must first learn the probability distributions $P(w)$ and $P(f_i|w)$. This is challenging, because the historical wafer test data only contains the values of the variables f_i—the wafer class variable is *latent* (i.e., unobserved). Fortunately, this is a well-understood learning problem that can be easily solved via the *expectation maximization (EM) algorithm* (Cheeseman et al. 1988; Dempster et al. 1977; McLachlan and Krishnan 1997). The EM algorithm is really an "algorithm schema" that can be instantiated in many ways. Rather than giving an abstract description of the algorithm, we will describe how it is instantiated in our wafer testing problem.

Consider the following: If we knew the value of w for each wafer in our historical data, then it would be trivial to estimate $P(w)$ and $P(f_i|w)$. In particular, $P(w = 1)$ can be estimated as the fraction of the wafers for which $w = 1$, and $P(f_{23}|w = 1)$ can be estimated as the fraction of wafers from class $w = 1$ in which die 23 was defective. Hence, if we could somehow *guess* the value of w for each wafer, then we could compute the probabilistic model. The basic idea of EM is to iteratively guess the value of w (based on the probabilistic model from the previous iteration or random guesses in the first iteration) and then update the probabilistic model based on these guesses. The process of guessing the w values is called the *E-step*, and the process of updating the probabilistic model based on those guesses is called the *M-step*. These two steps give the EM algorithm its name.

In EM, the E-step does not guess a *single value* for w. Instead, it hypothesizes a *probability distribution* over the possible values of w. Hence, for a particular wafer, EM might guess that $w = 1$ with probability 0.20, $w = 2$ with probability 0.60, $w = 3$ with probability 0.04, and $w = 4$ with probability 0.16. In the M-step, it then estimates the overall $P(w = 1)$ as the average value of the (hypothesized) probability that $w = 1$ for each wafer. Similarly, it estimates $P(f_i|w = 1)$ by identifying all wafers where f_i is true, adding up the hypothesized probability that $w = 1$ for each of these wafers, and dividing by the total hypothesized probability that $w = 1$.

Once $P(w)$ and $P(f_i|w)$ have been estimated in this fashion, the EM algorithm can compute new hypothesized distributions for the value of w for each wafer. These are computed by treating the wafer class w as unknown, and applying standard probabilistic inference algorithms (Jordan 1999; Pearl 1988) to propagate the evidence concerning each f_i to determine the probability distribution over w. Algebraically, this process involves computing for each wafer the normalized product of the current $P(W)$ with probability for each observed test result, $P(f_i = r|W)$ (where r is the test result for die i).

In each iteration, EM is guaranteed to improve its estimates of $P(w)$ and $P(f_i|w)$ until it reaches a local maximum in the likelihood of the training data. In our experiments, the algorithm typically converged in fewer than 50 iterations.

3.3   AN INFLUENCE DIAGRAM FOR WAFER TESTING

Once the probabilistic model is learned, it is incorporated into a much larger model of the decision-making process called an *influence diagram*. Figure 3 shows the influence diagram that we constructed for the DLFT problem. The probabilistic model described in the previous section is shown here using slightly heavier lines than the rest of the influence diagram.

This influence diagram includes several kinds of nodes that were not present in the simple probabilistic model of Figure 2. Specifically, it includes additional *random variables* (p_i), *decision nodes* $(F_i, I_i, \text{and } D)$, and *utility nodes* $(V_i \text{ and } V)$. We explain each of these in turn.

Additional random variables: The random variable p_i represents the result of the final package test for die i. Its probability distribution, $P(p_i|f_i)$, represents the probability that the die will fail package testing depending on the results of the functional test. Rather than learning this distribution from historical data, we acquired it from domain experts. If $f_i = 1$ (the die is defective), then $p_i = 1$ (the die fails final package testing) as well. But if $f_i = 0$ (the die passes functional testing), the die may still later fail the package test (with a low probability) because of problems introduced during the packaging process. The reason for relying on human estimates for the conditional package test probability values was that the actual data was unavailable for this study. In our application, packaging occurred at a remote facility, and although yield rates were reported, specific die-level package results were not available. However, in principle, these parameters could also be derived from historical data. It seems reasonable to assume that parameters derived from such historical data would yield more accurate predictions of die failure and thereby improve wafer test decisions.

Decision nodes: A decision node is a variable whose value can be chosen by the decision-making procedure. In Figure 3, the Boolean variable F_i represents the decision to test die i, and the Boolean variable I_i represents the decision to ink the die i. The Boolean variable D represents the wafer disposition decision: Should the wafer be sent to packaging or retained for analysis by the fabrication engineers? In the diagram, decision nodes are represented by rectangles.

Utility nodes: A utility node represents the cost or benefit of some combination of other nodes. Specifically, the node V_i represents the utility of various combinations of testing F_i, inking I_i, and final package test results p_i. For example, if $F_i = 0$, $I_i = 0$, and $p_i = 0$, this corresponds to a die that was not tested and was not packaged (and, therefore, we

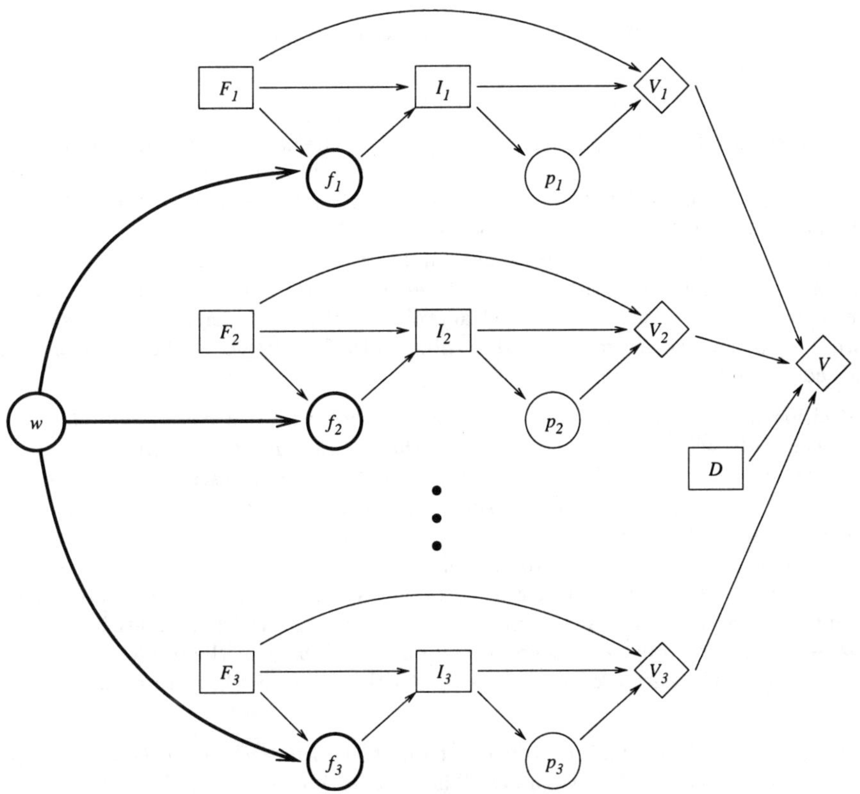

Figure 3   Influence diagram of the wafer test process.

$W_j \equiv \text{wafer}_j$	$c_k \equiv \text{cost of packaging a single die}$
$N_d(W_j) \equiv \#\text{ of dice on wafer}_j$	$c_h \equiv \text{single wafer handling cost}$
$N_f(W_j) \equiv \#\text{ of functional tests on wafer}_j$	$v_k \equiv \text{value of a single good package}$
$N_p(W_j) \equiv \#\text{ of package tests on wafer}_j$	$\text{value of package yield} \equiv V(Y(W_j)) = Y(W_j) \cdot v_k$
$N_k(W_j) \equiv \#\text{ of dice packaged from wafer}_j$	$\text{total cost of functional tests} \equiv C_f = N_f(W_j) \cdot c_f$
$Y(W_j) \equiv \text{package yield of wafer}_j$	$\text{total cost of package tests} \equiv C_p = N_p(W_j) \cdot c_p$
$c_f \equiv \text{cost of single functional test}$	$\text{total cost of packaging} \equiv C_k = (N_k(W_j) \cdot c_k) + c_h$
$c_p \equiv \text{cost of single package test}$	$\text{wafer profit} \equiv V(Y(W_j)) - C_f - C_p - C_k$

Table 1   The wafer test utility model.

consider it to have failed the package test, so $p_i = 0$). The utility of this die is zero, because we have not spent any money testing or packaging it, but, of course, we can't sell it for a profit either. On the other hand, if $F_i = 1$, $I_i = 1$, and $p_i = 1$, then the utility of this combination, $V_i(1, 1, 1) = v_k - c_f - c_p$, is the sales value of the die, v_k, less the cost of the die-level test, c_f, and the cost of packaging and testing, c_p. The utility node V represents the net profit obtained from the wafer, so it depends on the utilities of each individual die (represented by arcs from the V_i nodes) and also on the wafer disposition decision D. In Figure 3, utility nodes are represented by diamonds. The details of the utility model are described in Table 1.

If a decision node has an incoming arc from another node, this means that the value of that other node will be known at the time the decision must be made. Hence, before making the inking decision I_i, we will know whether die was tested (F_i) and the result of that test (f_i). To keep the diagram simple, however, it does not include all of the arcs connecting test results to decision variables. In particular, the diagram does not show that at the time that we are deciding to test die i (i.e., by choosing a value for F_i), we will know the values of f_j for any other die j that have already been tested. Similarly, the diagram does not show that at the time we are making the wafer disposition decision D, the values of all of the inking decisions I_i will be known (but not the results of the package tests, p_i). Although these arcs are omitted from the diagram, they are all present in the computational model.

If a utility node has incoming arcs from other variables, these show that the utility depends on the values of these other variables. The goal of inference algorithms for influence diagrams is to identify values of the decision variables that maximize the expected value of the value nodes. In our case, the goal is to choose values for the testing decisions F_i, inking decisions I_i, and wafer disposition decision D in order to maximize the expected utility of the entire wafer represented by V.

Our cost model does not capture three important costs. First, the cost (or benefit) of detecting fabrication problems is ignored. A reduction in die testing may reduce packaging costs but increase fabrication costs, because fabrication problems are not diagnosed as quickly. Second, the capital costs of purchasing and maintaining the die-testing machines are ignored. If die-level testing can be significantly reduced, then fewer machines are needed, and these capital costs can be saved. Third, for some IC products, the current exhaustive testing policy becomes a rate-limiting bottleneck. A decrease in the number of dice tested per wafer means that more wafers can be tested, and therefore, wafer starts, throughput, and profits per unit time can increase.

3.4 EVALUATING THE DECISION MODEL

Exact evaluation of the decision model to determine the decisions that maximize expected utility is infeasible, because it requires expanding a search tree consisting of all combinations of all testing decisions and test results. Hence, approximate methods must be employed.

One approximate method that has been employed previously in automated decision making is known as the *one-step value of information (VOI) heuristic*. According to this heuristic, we decide which die to test next by comparing two courses of action. One course of action is to stop testing immediately and make the inking and wafer disposition decisions. The other course of action is to test *one more die* and then proceed to the inking and wafer disposition decisions. The one-step VOI heuristic computes the expected value of these two courses of action and chooses the one with the larger expected value. Note that the heuristic does not consider testing two more die, three more die, and so on, and hence, it avoids the combinatorial explosion of possible testing policies.

In more detail, the VOI computation proceeds as follows. Initially, all of the functional test decision nodes F_i are set to 0 (no test). The die inking decisions, I_i, and the wafer disposition decision, D, are then made to maximize expected utility. The computed utility of this course of action is called the *termination utility*, U_{term}, because it is the utility of terminating functional testing and carrying out inking and packaging. The computation then computes the expected utility U_i of testing die i and then making the inking and wafer disposition decisions. If $\max_i U_i > U_{term}$, then test i is performed, f_i is observed, and the termination utility U_{term} is recomputed. Otherwise, testing terminates, and the inking and disposition decisions are made.

Because it is an approximate method, one-step greedy VOI does not in general yield the optimal policy for a sequential decision problem. However, we expect it to perform very well in this particular problem, because we are assuming that each testing action does not alter the wafer (e.g., by causing other die to fail). In addition, the inking decisions can be made independently, and the total utility is additive. Below, we will test experimentally how well greedy VOI works.

4 METHODS

Hewlett-Packard provided a data set for a mature IC product. The data consisted of the test results from 2400 wafers. We split this data into two separate data sets. Set 1 was used during model development and debugging. It consisted of 1200 wafers: 600 for training and 600 for testing. Set 2 was used for a final test of the system, and it also consisted of 1200 wafers: 600 for training and 600 for testing. The wafers are grouped into "lots" of 24 wafers, which are kept together (in a cassette) during the manufacturing process. Because there is a strong possibility that wafers within a lot share the same defects, we divided the wafers according to entire lots, so each training data consisted of 25 lots and each testing set of 25 lots. The lots were kept in chronological order.

Table 2 provides summary statistics for these two data sets. Each wafer contains 209 dice.

	Data Set 1	Data Set 2
Total number of good dice	102,288	101,516
Total number of dice	125,400	125,400
Yield	0.8157	0.8095

Table 2 Statistics summarizing the test set wafers in the two data sets. The yield is defined as the fraction of good dice out of the total number of dice.

We applied the EM algorithm to train the Naive Bayes probabilistic model. To determine the number of values of the latent variable w, we fit models with 1, 2, 4, 8, 12, 16, 20, and 24 values to the training data from Data Set 1 and measured the log likelihood of the wafers in the corresponding validation set. The log likelihood is a measure of how well the model predicts (or explains) the data. The best validation set log likelihood was achieved with a model containing 4 classes. For this model, the EM algorithm converged after no more than 50 iterations, which required less than three minutes of CPU time. To obtain our final probability model for the decision-theoretic tester, we trained a 4-class model on the training data from Data Set 2.

5 RESULTS

We performed four experiments to address the following questions:

- How well does the decision-theoretic approach perform compared to exhaustive testing, no testing, and optimal testing?

- How well does greedy value of information (VOI) perform in deciding when to stop testing?

- How does the system respond to abnormal wafers? Is the approach sensitive to process problems?

- How robust is the system with respect to changes in the utility parameters? Do changes in utility parameters result in rational responses from the system?

Each of these questions is addressed in turn.

5.1 PERFORMANCE

We compared the performance of the decision-theoretic testing policy ("DT") with three other policies: (1) the current exhaustive test approach ("Exhaustive"), (2) a policy that performed no tests and packaged all die ("Package All"), and (3) an optimal testing policy ("Oracle") that performs no testing but packages only those die that would have passed the functional test. The Oracle policy provides an upper bound on the best that any implementable policy could do.

The results from the model tests are presented in Tables 3 and 4 (for the test data in Data Set 1 and Data Set 2, respectively). Data Set 1 was employed in the original development and testing of the models. Data Set 2 was an independent data set that was used to get

	Total Profit	Number Tested	Number Packaged
Exhaustive	1,184,550	125,400	102,288
Package All	1,226,598	0	125,400
DT	1,229,531	8210	121,560
Oracle	1,278,600	0	102,288

Table 3 Comparison of the performance of four die-testing policies on Data Set 1. The "Exhaustive" policy tests all die and packages those found to be defective. The "Package All" policy tests no die and packages them all. The "DT" policy is our decision-theoretic VOI policy. The "Oracle" tests no die and only packages the good ones. The total profit is the total profit obtained by that policy on the 600 wafers in the test set of Data Set 1.

	Total Profit	Number Tested	Number Packaged
Exhaustive	1,174,900	125,400	101,516
Package All	1,215,211	0	125,400
DT	1,218,309	5194	122,292
Oracle	1,268,950	0	101,516

Table 4 Comparison of the performance of four test policies on Data Set 2. See Table 3 for an explanation of the policies.

some measure of how well the methods generalize. Both data sets were from the same wafer production and testing lines. The results show that the current Exhaustive testing policy is the worst, and the DT policy is the best, of the three implementable policies. Indeed, the DT policy achieves 96% of the profit that can be realized by the Oracle, and it gives a 3.8% improvement in profit over Exhaustive testing.

The Package All policy produces almost as much profit as the DT policy, so a reasonable question is what advantage the DT policy has over Package All. The answer is that on wafers with high yield there may be little benefit. The problem with Package All is that process problems will not be detected until package test results become available. This can be a problem, because often packaging is performed at a location (e.g., Asia) far from the wafer fabrication plant (e.g., United States). In these cases the delay in feedback and the costs of shipping and handling make the Package All policy risky. Furthermore, after packaging, the physical position of each die on the wafer is no longer known, so the spatial information provided by the die-level test is lost. This spatial information is valuable for diagnosing fabrication problems. One of the benefits of the DT policy is that for good wafers it can produce profits comparable to those produced with a Package All policy, but for bad wafers, it can detect process problems while the wafers are still at the fabrication plant.

	Total Profit	Number Tested	Number Packaged
Exhaustive	1,184,550	125,400	102,288
VOI	1,229,531	8210	121,560
Optimal stop	1,231,970	11,206	119,264

Table 5 An evaluation of how well the one-step VOI heuristic determines the optimal point to stop testing. "Exhaustive" tests all die; "Optimal Stop" tests die in the same sequential order as the VOI heuristic, but uses an oracle to determine the optimal stopping point.

5.2 EVALUATION OF THE GREEDY VOI STOPPING CRITERIA

The decision-theoretic policy relies on a greedy value of information (VOI) computation to decide when to terminate testing. To determine how well this heuristic works, experiments were performed in which greedy VOI stopping was compared to the optimal stopping point. To determine the optimal stopping point, the decision-theoretic policy was modified to continue testing past the point of nonpositive VOI until all dice were tested. Then the history of testing decisions was analyzed to find the moment at which the net profit would have been maximized had the system stopped then. Net profit includes the costs for functional tests up to that point and the sales obtained by making package decisions at that point.

Table 5 summarizes the results of this experiment on the test data from Data Set 1. The table shows that greedy VOI stopping tests less than Optimal Stopping (performing only about 73% as many tests) and packages more (about 2% more packages). So Optimal Stopping spends a bit more on functional testing in order to reduce the number of bad dice packaged. Despite this difference, greedy VOI stopping performs very well and realizes over 99% of the profit achieved by Optimal Stopping.

5.3 DETECTING PROCESS PROBLEMS

An interesting question for any testing policy is how it responds to abnormal wafers. Although the decision-theoretic approach was targeted toward a stable mature product, process problems are common, and abnormal wafer test results are often the first symptoms of such problems. An important question for a testing policy is: How well can it recognize abnormally bad wafers?

To explore this issue, we discuss six wafers from Data Set 1 in detail. The first two wafers are typical "good" wafers with yields over 80%. The next two wafers are "bad," with yields of less than 10%. The final two wafers are "mediocre," with yields of 66% and 65%. The test wafers are described in Table 6. The simulation results are presented in Table 7.

In Table 7, exhaustive test profit is the profit realized under the exhaustive test policy. VOI profit is the profit realized under the decision-theoretic policy.

To visualize the testing behavior, wafer test maps are presented in Figure 4. These maps show the good dice, the dice that were tested according to the selective test policy, and

Wafer ID Number	Number Good Die	Yield
1	178	0.85
2	180	0.86
3	17	0.08
4	2	0.01
5	138	0.66
6	118	0.56

Table 6 Statistics describing six wafers selected from the test set of Data Set 1. Wafers 1 and 2 have good yield, wafers 3 and 4 have poor yield, and wafers 5 and 6 have mediocre yield.

Wafer ID Number	Number Die Tested	Number Die Packaged	Exhaustive Test Profit	VOI Test Profit
1	8	205	2068.25	2158.25
2	8	206	2093.25	2185.50
3	201	25	55.75	43.75
4	201	10	−131.75	−143.75
5	57	182	1568.25	1583.25
6	12	202	1318.25	1277.00

Table 7 Summary of the behavior of the VOI heuristic on six selected wafers and a comparison of the profit obtained on each wafer by VOI to the profit obtained by exhaustive testing. Note that the number of die tested is directly related to the true yield of the wafer (see Table 6).

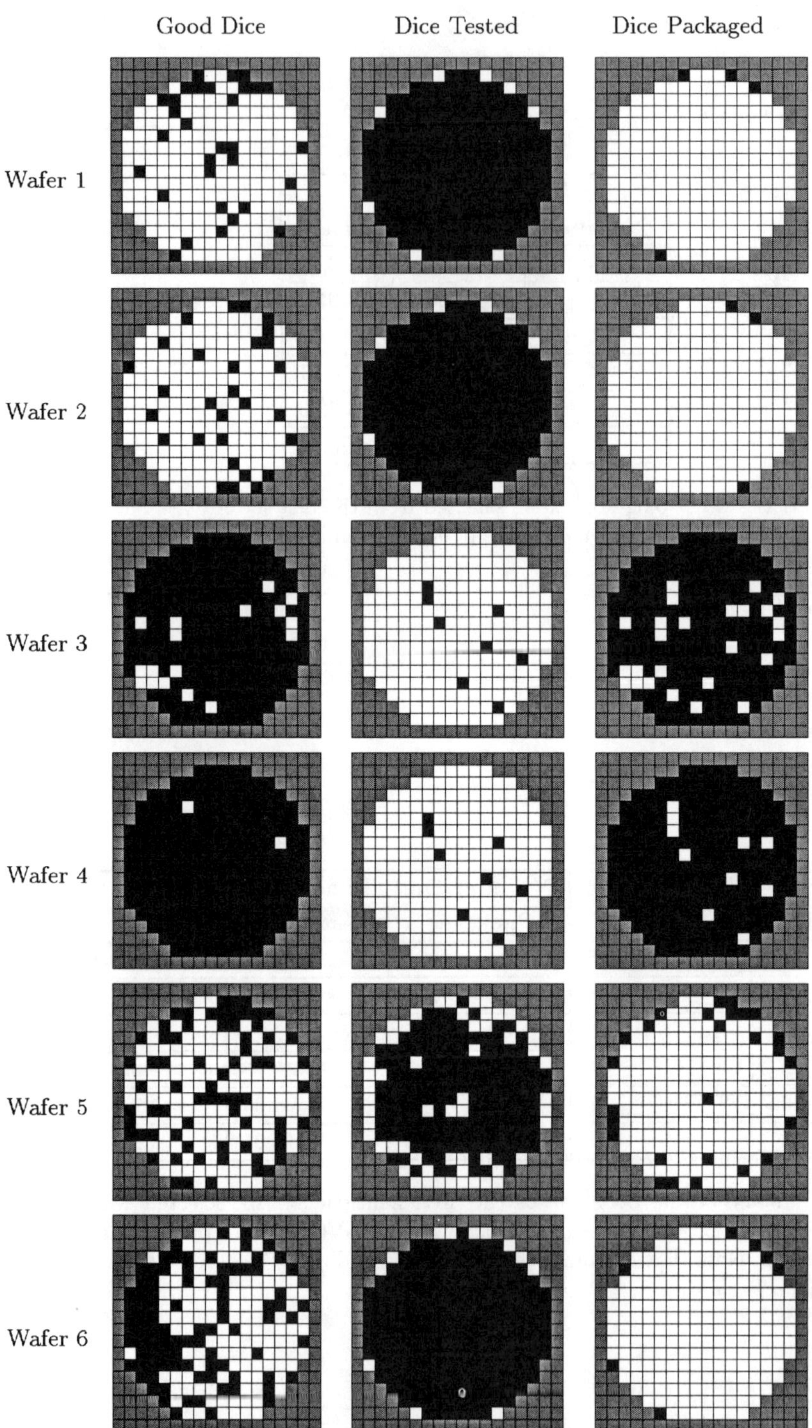

Figure 4   Detecting process problems.

the dice that were packaged according to this policy. In each map, white encodes true, so white represents good dice, tested dice, and packaged dice. Black represents bad dice, untested dice, and unpackaged dice. Wafers 1 and 2 are good wafers, wafers 3 and 4 are bad wafers, and wafers 5 and 6 are mediocre wafers.

The analysis of these six wafers shows that the decision-theoretic policy is responsive to abnormal wafers. There is a direct relationship between wafer yield and the number of functional tests performed. The higher the yield, the fewer tests. This means that, for a stable and mature product, the system tests only a small fraction of the total dice. However, the system is sensitive to abnormal yields, which indicate process problems. On such wafers, the system tests more thoroughly. For wafers with extremely low yield, the system responds by testing almost all dice. This means that a minimal amount of resources is expended on good wafers, yet bad wafers are detected.

The reasons for this highly desirable behavior are not entirely clear. One explanation is that because our IC product was a mature, high-yield product, the learned stochastic model is expecting to see good wafers. So when it encounters a bad wafer, its predictions concerning the untested dice become uncertain (near 0.5), and it must do more testing to make good inking decisions. If our product had been one where half of the wafers were good and the other half very bad, then a bad wafer would not have been surprising, and the decision-theoretic policy would only perform enough tests to be confident of which kind of wafer it had. Then it would proceed to the inking decisions.

This analysis suggests that the output from the decision-theoretic approach could be fed into *statistical process control (SPC)* methods that routinely monitor for process problems. A straightforward extension to the current SPC system would be to replace actual test measures with predicted measures. So, for example, rather than setting control limits around the actual functional test results, the control limits could be set around the predicted functional test results. Thus, the decision-theoretic approach provides dual benefits: First, it greatly reduces the requirement for testing resources. Second, it satisfies the requirement for prompt detection of process problems.

5.4   ROBUSTNESS TO CHANGES IN UTILITY PARAMETERS

One benefit of decision-theoretic methods is that changes in utility parameters should result in rational changes in performance without the need to manually reengineer the learned models or the control structures. To verify this, we experimented with changes to two of the utility parameters:

- Cost of performing a single functional test
- Cost of packaging a single die

For each of these parameters, a series of tests was performed in which the parameter of interest was swept through a range of values and performance on a testing scenario was measured. For these tests, we applied the stochastic model trained on the 600 training wafers from Data Set 1 to test 48 test-set wafers. Performance was measured by the number of functional tests performed, the number of dice packaged, the number of false positives (i.e., bad die packaged), and the number of true negatives (i.e., bad die not packaged).

	Number Die Tested	Number Die Packaged	Number False Positives	Number True Negatives
$0.5c_k$	240	9854	1658	178
c_k	796	9672	1386	360
$2c_k$	2484	9312	1026	720

Table 8 Robustness tests: changes to package cost.

	Number Die Tested	Number Die Packaged	Number False Positives	Number True Negatives
$0.1c_f$	10032	8286	0	1746
$0.67c_f$	1509	9485	1199	547
c_f	796	9672	1386	360
$1.33c_f$	321	9835	1549	197
$1.67c_f$	240	9854	1568	178
$2.0c_f$	169	9912	1626	120
$10c_f$	0	10032	1746	0

Table 9 Robustness tests: results of changes to functional test costs.

5.4.1 Changes to Package Cost

In the first set of tests, the cost to package a single die was manipulated. Let c_k represent the normal package cost. Then consider the effects of cutting the package cost in half $(0.5c_k)$ or doubling it $(2c_k)$. The results are summarized in Table 8.

The results show that when it is relatively inexpensive to package dice, the system packages more and tests less. As the package cost increases, false positives become more expensive, so more tests are performed to reduce this risk. Thus, with respect to changes in package cost, the system performs rationally by adjusting its testing and package decisions to maximize expected profits.

5.4.2 Changes to Functional Test Cost

A second set of tests was performed in which the functional test cost was manipulated. Let c_f represent the current cost of a single functional test. Then consider the effects of setting the functional test cost at $0.1c_f$, $0.67c_f$, c_f, $1.33c_f$, $1.67c_f$, $2c_f$, and $10c_f$. The results are summarized in Table 9.

This table shows that the system behaves rationally by adjusting its testing and packaging decisions to reflect changes in cost parameters. When the package cost is increased, the system tests more to avoid wasting resources by packaging bad dice. On the other hand, when the functional test cost is increased, the system tests less and packages more. If the test cost is set sufficiently low, then the system tests all dice. If the test cost is set sufficiently high, then the system tests none of the dice. In none of the test scenarios was it profitable to miss a good die, so the number of true positives was always equal to the total number of good dice, and the number of false negatives was always zero. This behavior is the result of two factors. First, given the quality of the wafers in the training set, all dice had a reasonable prior probability of being good. Second, the value of a good package was sufficient to justify packaging all dice based on these prior probabilities.

6 CONCLUSION

The experiments in this chapter have demonstrated that manufacturing data can be mined to produce effective decision-theoretic control methods. Furthermore, these methods can produce substantial improvements in the die-level functional testing stage of VLSI IC manufacturing. Specifically, the experiments have shown the following:

1. The decision-theoretic policy produced more net profit than either the exhaustive test policy or the policy of performing no die-level testing.

2. The greedy VOI stopping criterion produced near-optimal stopping behavior.

3. The decision-theoretic policy is able to detect abnormal wafers, and it responds by testing them more thoroughly. Hence, although the cost model does not reflect the value of die-level test for detecting fabrication problems, the decision-theoretic policy still detects these problems well. Existing process control statistics could be based on the predictions of the stochastic model.

4. The decision-theoretic policy is robust to changes in testing costs and packaging costs.

These experiments demonstrate that the decision-theoretic approach to die-level functional testing has the potential to reduce testing costs, increase wafer starts, and improve the bottom line. In addition, the method is easy to implement—the EM training was straightforward and efficient, and the cost model can easily be changed to reflect changes in market conditions. As market competition forces IC manufacturers to look for methods to reduce production costs, intelligent wafer testing is one promising area to explore. Although the current study performed simulations of historical test scenarios, we are optimistic that future work will lead to a production implementation of these methods. We believe that in this and many other computer-integrated manufacturing applications, data-mining and decision-theoretic methods have an important role to play.

ACKNOWLEDGMENTS

The authors thank Hewlett-Packard Company for providing the wafer test data for this project. T. Dietterich acknowledges the support of the National Science Foundation under grant number 9626584-IRI and the support of the Air Force Office of Scientific Research under contract F49620-98-1-0375.

References

Charniak, E. (1991). Bayesian networks without tears. *AI Magazine 12*(4), 50–63.

Cheeseman, P., M. Self, J. Kelly, W. Taylor, D. Freeman, and J. Stutz (1988). Bayesian classification. In *Proceedings of the Seventh National Conference on Artificial Intelligence*, 607–611. Cambridge, MA: AAAI Press/MIT Press.

Dempster, A. P., N. M. Laird, and D. B. Rubin (1977). Maximum-likelihood from incomplete data via the EM algorithm. *Journal of the Royal Statistical Society B39*, 1–38.

Dietterich, T. G. (1997). Machine learning research: Four current directions. *AI Magazine 18*(4), 97–136.

Horvitz, E., J. Breese, and M. Henrion (1991). Decision analysis and expert systems. *AI Magazine 12*(4), 64–91.

Jordan, M. L. (1999). *Learning in Graphical Models*. Cambridge, MA: MIT Press.

McLachlan, G., and T. Krishnan (1997). *The EM Algorithm and Extensions*. New York: John Wiley & Sons.

Pearl, J. (1988). *Probabilistic Reasoning in Intelligent Systems*. San Francisco: Morgan Kaufmann Publishers.

Van Zant, P. (1997). *Microchip Fabrication: A Practical Guide to Semiconductor Processing*, 3rd ed. New York: McGraw-Hill.

Zorich, R. (1991). *Handbook of Quality Integrated Circuit Manufacturing*. San Diego: Academic Press.

Key Word Index

A

B

C

D